Consciousness

CONSCIOUSNESS

An Introduction

SUSAN BLACKMORE

OXFORD
UNIVERSITY PRESS
2004

OXFORD
UNIVERSITY PRESS

Oxford New York
Auckland Bangkok Buenos Aires Cape Town Chennai
Dar es Salaam Delhi Hong Kong Istanbul Karachi Kolkata
Kuala Lumpur Madrid Melbourne Mexico City Mumbai
Nairobi São Paulo Shanghai Taipei Tokyo Toronto

Published by Oxford University Press, Inc.
198 Madison Avenue, New York, New York 10016
http://www.oup-usa.org

Oxford is a registered trademark of Oxford University Press

Library of Congress Cataloging-in-Publication Data
Blackmore, Susan J., 1951–
    Consciousness : an introduction / by Susan Blackmore.
        p. cm.
    Includes bibliographical references (p.) and index.
    ISBN 978-0-19-515342-2 (cloth) — ISBN 978-0-19-515343-9 (paper)
    1. Consciousness. I. Title.

BF311.B534 2003
153—dc22   2003056480

Printing number: 9 8 7 6 5 4

Printed in the United States of America
on acid-free paper

To all the students who took my consciousness course

Contents

Boxes and Sidebars

Chapter	Profile	Concept	Activity	Practice
1	Descartes	The hard problem	Definitions	Am I conscious now?
2	Chalmers	Zombie	Mary the color scientist	Being me now
3	Churchland	—	Does consciousness do anything?	Did I do this consciously?
4	James	Orwellian v Stalinesque	Cutaneous rabbit	Did I consciously attend?
5	Dennett	Seeing blue	Cartesian materialism	Where is this experience?
6	Ramachandran	—	Filling-in	How much am I seeing now?
7	Hume	Egos and bundles	Split brain twins	Who is conscious now?
8	Baars	Selves, clubs & universities	Teletransporter	Am I the same me now?
9	Wegner	—	1. Getting out of bed 2. Libet's activity	Am I doing this?
10	Dawkins	Evolution of Cons.	—	Function of awareness
11	Humphrey	Memes	Sentience line	Is this a meme?
12	M S Dawkins	—	Zoo choice	Is this animal conscious?
13	Turing	Brains v computers	Imitation game	Am I a machine?
14	Searle	Cog	7th Sally	Are you conscious?
15	Brooks	Kismet	—	What is conscious?
16	Crick	1. Scanning methods 2. Phantoms	Rubber hand	Where is this pain?
17	Eccles	Synesthesia	Are you a synesthete?	Is this a unity?
18	Damasio	Sensory substitution	Blind for one hour	Perception or memory?
19	Merikle	Flow	Incubation	Was this decision conscious?
20	Rhine	Ganzfeld	Telepathy tests	Living without psi
21	Siegel	Sleep paralysis	Discussing hypnagogia	Awake while falling asleep
22	Tart	1. Mapping SoCs 2. SSSc	Discussing ASCs	Is this my normal SoC?
23	Hilgard	1. Evolution of dreaming 2. Is hypnosis an ASC?	Inducing lucid dreams	Am I awake or dreaming?
24	Underhill	Features of the NDE	Survival debate	What survives?
25	Varela	New kind of science?	Positioning the theories	Is this really how it is?
26	Fenwick	Koans	Meditation	What is this?
27	Buddha	Four noble truths	Headless way	Mindfulness

Acknowledgments

I have loved writing this book. For many years, working as a lecturer, I never seemed to have enough time to read or think or do the work I really wanted to do. So in September 2000 I left my job and threw myself into the vast and ever-expanding literature of consciousness studies. Writing the book meant spending over two years mostly at home completely by myself, reading, thinking and writing, which was a real pleasure.

I could never have worked this way without three things. First, there are all the conferences at which I have met other scientists and philosophers and been able to share ideas and arguments. Second there is the Internet and email which makes it possible to keep in touch with colleagues all over the world instantly without moving from my own desk. Third, there is the WWW which has expanded beyond all recognition in the few years since I first thought of writing this book. I am constantly amazed at the generosity of so many people who give their time and effort to make their own work, and the work of others, freely available to us all.

I would like to thank the following people who have helped me with arguments and discussion, who advised me on how to set about writing a textbook, or who have read and commented on parts of the manuscript. The very thorough reviewing process of Oxford University Press meant that I was able to improve the text in many ways as it went along. My thanks go to David Chalmers, John Crook, Dan Dennett, Stan Franklin, David Goodworth, Nicky Hayes, Philip Merikle, Alva Noë, Susan Schneider and to my editor at Hodder, Emma Woolf, for her boundless enthusiasm.

Finally, I could never have enjoyed working at home so much were it not for my wonderful family: my partner Adam Hart-Davis, and my two children Emily and Jolyon Troscianko. Having Joly drawing the cartoons (see www.jolyont.co.uk) meant many happy battles over whether self is more like a candle, a raindrop or bladderwrack seaweed and what the Cartesian Theater would look like if it existed. My thanks go to them all.

The author and publishers would like to thank the following for their permission to reproduce images:

Profile picture of Susan Blackmore: Andreas Teichmann. Profile picture of Descartes: Bettmann/Corbis. Figure 2.1: Joe McDonald/Corbis. Figure 3.2: Duomo/Corbis. Profile picture of James: Bettmann/Corbis. Profile picture of Dennett: Steve Barney. Figure 5.4: Adam Hart-Davis. Figure 6.8: Jolyon Troscianko. Figure 7.1: Kurt Stier/Corbis. Figure 7.2: Bettmann/Corbis. Figure 7.7: from Gazzaniga and Le Doux, *The Integrated Mind* (1978) Kluwer Academic/Plenum Publishers. Figure 8.1: Law, S., *The Philosophy Files* (London: Orion, 2000). Figure 8.2: Jason Hawkes/Corbis. Figure 9.5: Mary Evans Picture Library. Figure 10.1: Adam Hart-Davis. Figure 10.3: Mary Evans Picture Library. Figure 11.6: Angelo Hornak/Corbis. Figure 12.1: Nature Picture Library. Figure 12.2: Behavioural Ecology Research Group, Department of Zoology, Oxford University. Figure 12.3: Jolyon Troscianko. Figure 12.5: Billy Weeks. Figure 12.6: David A. Northcott/Corbis. Figure 13.1: AKG London. Profile picture of Turing: Science Photo Library/Photo Researchers, Inc. Figure 13.4: Jolyon Troscianko. Figure 13.5: Science Photo Library/Photo Researchers Inc. Figure 13.6 (top): Archivo Iconografico, S.A./Corbis. Figure 13.6 (bottom): Laurence Kesterson/Corbis. Figure 15.1: Science Photo Library/Photo Researchers, Inc. Figure 15.2. Bruce Frisch/ Photo Researchers, Inc. Figure 15.4: Luc Steels. Figure 16.4: from Lumer "Binocular rivalry and human visual awareness" in T. Metzinger (ed.) *Neural Correlates of Consciousness* (2000) MIT Press. Profile picture of Eccles: Bettmann/Corbis. Profile picture of Damasio: Christian Steiner. Figures 18.1 and 18.2: Marshall and Halligan. Figure 18.7: David Chalmers. Figure 20.1: Bettmann/Corbis. Profile picture of Rhine: Mary Evans Picture Library. Figure 21.3: Werner Forman Archive. Figure 21.4: from Siegel "Hallucinations" in *Scientific American* 237, 132-40 (1977) Alan D. Iselin. Figure 21.7: David Howard. Figure 22.4: Adam Hart-Davis. Figure 22.6: Jolyon Troscianko. Figures 23.7 and 23.8: S. LaBerge. Figures 24.2 and 24.7: from S. Muldoon and H. Carrington, *The Projection of the Astral Body* (London: Rider & Co., 1929). Figure 26.1: Stephen Batchelor/Frances Lincoln Publishers. Figure 26.4: PA Photos. Figure 26.5: PA Photos. Profile picture of the Buddha: Craig Lovell/Corbis. Figure 27.2: Werner Forman Archive/Spink & Son, London. The following figures were drawn by Jolyon Troscianko: 1.1, 1.3, 1.5, 2.2, 2.3, 2.4, 4.1, 5.1, 6.1, 6.3, 6.6, 7.5, 7.8, 8.3, 8.4, 8.5, 9.2, 9.7, 10.4, 10.5, 11.1, 11.5, 12.4, 13.7, 14.1, 14.2, 15.3, 15.5, 16.3, 16.5, 17.1, 18.4, 18.5, 19.1, 19.2, 19.3, 19.5, 19.6, 19.7, 19.8, 21.1, 21.2, 21.8, 21.9, 22.1, 22.3, 22.5, 23.3, 23.4, 23.5, 23.6, 24.3, 24.4, 24.5, 25.1, 25.2, 25.7, 26.2, 26.3, 27.1, 27.3, 27.4, and 27.5.

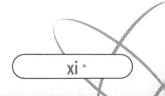

Consciousness

Introduction

WELCOME PERPLEXITY

If you think you have a solution to the problem of consciousness, you haven't understood the problem. Strictly, that is not true, of course. You may either be a genius and have found a real solution, or be sufficiently clear-sighted to understand why there was no problem in the first place. More likely, however, is that you are falling into a number of tempting traps that help you evade the real issues.

In 1986 the American philosopher Thomas Nagel wrote "Certain forms of perplexity—for example, about freedom, knowledge, and the meaning of life—seem to me to embody more insight than any of the supposed solutions to those problems" (Nagel, 1986: 4). This is equally true of the problem of consciousness. Indeed the perplexity can be part of the pleasure, as philosopher Colin McGinn points out, ". . . the more we struggle the more tightly we feel trapped in perplexity. I am grateful for all that thrashing and wriggling" (McGinn, 1999: xiii).

If you want to think about consciousness, perplexity is necessary—mind-boggling, brain-hurting, *I can't bear to think about this stupid problem any more* perplexity. For this reason a great deal of this book is aimed at increasing your perplexity rather than reducing it. So if you do not wish your brain to hurt (though of course strictly speaking brains cannot hurt because they do not have any pain receptors—and, come to think of it, if your toe, which does have pain receptors, hurts, is it really your toe that is hurting?), stop reading now or choose a more tractable problem to study.

My motivation for wishing to stir up perplexity is not cruelty or cussedness, nor the misplaced conviction that long words and difficult arguments are signs of cleverness or academic worth. Indeed I think the reverse: that the more difficult a problem is, the more important it becomes to use the simplest words and sentences possible. So I will try to keep my arguments as clear and simple

Susan Blackmore (b. 1951)

As a student in Oxford, reading physiology and psychology, Sue Blackmore had a dramatic out-of-body experience that convinced her that consciousness could leave the body, and made her determined, against much sound advice, to become a parapsychologist. By 1980, when she received one of the first PhDs in parapsychology in the UK, she had conducted many failed experiments on ESP (extrasensory perception) and PK (psychokinesis), and had become very skeptical. She turned to studying the unusual experiences that lead people to believe in the paranormal, including near-death experiences, sleep paralysis and dreams. She eventually gave up parapsychology altogether, concluding that it was a red herring in any attempt to understand consciousness. Meanwhile she learned meditation and has been practicing Zen since the early 1980s. She carried out one of the early experiments on change blindness, then in 1995 she became infected with the meme meme and wrote the controversial best seller, *The Meme Machine.* For ten years she was a lecturer in psychology at the University of the West of England, Bristol, and taught consciousness courses both there and at the University of Bristol, but she finally decided that the only way to learn more about consciousness was to give up her job and write this book.

as I can while tackling what is, intrinsically, a very tricky problem.

Part of the problem is that the word "consciousness" is common in everyday language, but is used in different ways. For example, "conscious" is often contrasted with "unconscious," and is taken as more or less equivalent to "responsive" or "awake." "Conscious" is used to mean the equivalent of knowing something, or attending to something, as in "She wasn't conscious of the crimes he'd committed" or "He wasn't conscious of the rat creeping up quietly under his desk." In addition, consciousness is used to mean the equivalent of "subjectivity" or personal experience, and this is the sense in which it is used throughout this book.

Another problem is that consciousness studies is a new and multidisciplinary subject. This can make life difficult because cognitive scientists, psychologists and philosophers sometimes use the very same words in completely different ways. Yet the interdisciplinary nature of the subject is also what makes it so exciting, and may, in time, prove to be its strength. In this book I have tried to cover all of the major approaches in consciousness studies, including psychology, philosophy, artificial intelligence, cognitive science, neuroscience, first-person methods and spiritual approaches. Even so, the emphasis is on a science of consciousness based on empirical findings and testable theories.

When people have tried to fit consciousness neatly into brain science, they find they cannot do it. This suggests that somewhere along the line we are making a fundamental mistake or relying on some false assumptions. Rooting out one's prior assumptions is never easy and can be painful. But that is probably what we have to do if we are to think clearly about consciousness.

THE ORGANIZATION OF THE BOOK

This book is divided into nine relatively independent sections containing three chapters each. Each section may be used as the topic for a lecture, or several lectures, or may be read independently as an overview of the area. However, all of them depend on the ideas outlined in Section One, so if you choose to read only parts of the book, I would recommend reading Section One, on the nature of the problem.

Each chapter contains not only a core text but profiles of selected authors, explanations of key concepts, exercises to do and questions to test your understanding. There are also suggestions for exercises and discussions that can be done in groups.

At the end of each chapter is a list of suggested readings. These texts are chosen to be short and readily accessible, while providing an original source of some important ideas in each chapter. Full references are provided throughout the text, but the suggested readings offer a quick way in to each topic. They should also be suitable as set reading between lectures for those whose courses are built around the book or as the basis for seminars.

Interesting quotations from a wide variety of authors appear in the margins. Some are repeated from the text, while others are just added to provide a different perspective. My advice is to learn those that appeal to you by heart. Rote learning seems hard if you are not in the habit, but it gets easier with practice. Having quotations at your mental fingertips looks most impressive in essays and exams, but, much more important, it provides a wonderful tool for thinking with. If you are walking along the road or lying in bed at night, wondering whether there really is a "hard problem" or not, your thinking will go much better if you can bring instantly to mind Chalmers' definition of the problem or the exact words of his major critics. At the risk of succumbing to a sound-bite mentality, often a short sentence is all you need.

PUTTING IN THE PRACTICE

Consciousness is a topic like no other. I imagine that right now, this very minute, you are convinced that you are conscious—that you have your own inner experience of the world—that you are personally aware of things going on around you and of your own inner states and thoughts—that you are inhabiting your own private world of awareness—that there is something it is like to be you. This is what is meant by being conscious. Consciousness is our first-person view on the world.

In most of our science and other studies, we are concerned with third-person views—with things that can be verified by others and agreed upon (or not) by everyone. But what makes consciousness so interesting is that it cannot be agreed upon in this way. It is private. I cannot know what it is like to be you. And you cannot know what it is like to be me.

So what is it like to be you? What are you conscious of now?

Well . . .? Take a look. Go on. I mean it. Take a look and try to answer the question, "What am I conscious of now?"

Is there an answer? If there is an answer, you should be able to look and see. You should be able to tell me, or at least see for yourself, what you are conscious of now, and now, and now—what is "in" your stream of consciousness. If there is no answer, then our confusion must be very deep indeed, for it certainly seems as though there must be an answer—that I really am conscious right now, and that I am conscious of some things and not others. If there is no answer, then at the very least we ought to be able to understand why it feels as though there is.

So take a look and first decide whether there is an answer or not. Can you do this? My guess is that you will probably decide that there is, that you really are conscious now and that you are conscious of some things and not others —only it is a bit tricky to see exactly what it is like because it keeps on changing. Every time you look things have moved on. The sound of the hammering outside that you were conscious of a moment ago is still going on but has changed. A bird has just flitted past the window casting a brief shadow across the window sill. Oh, but does that count? By the time you asked the question, "What am I conscious of now?" the bird and its shadow had gone and were only memories. But you were conscious of the memories, weren't you? So maybe this does count as "What I am conscious of now?" (or, rather, what I was conscious of then).

You will probably find that if you try to answer the first question, many more will pop up. You may find yourself asking, "How long is 'now'?" "Was I conscious before I asked the question?" "Who is asking the question?" Indeed you may have been asking such questions for much of your life. Teenagers commonly ask themselves difficult questions like these and don't find easy answers. Some go on to become scientists or philosophers or meditators and pursue the questions in their own ways. Many just give up because they receive no encouragement or because the task is too difficult. Nevertheless, these are precisely the kinds of questions that matter for studying consciousness.

I hope the practice tasks will help you. I have been asking these questions many times a day for about 20 years, often for hours at a stretch. I have also taught courses on the psychology of consciousness for more than 10 years, and encouraged my students to practice asking these questions. Over the years I have learned which ones work best, which are too difficult, in which order they can most easily be tackled, and how to help students who get into a muddle with them. I encourage you to work hard at your own inner practice, as well as study the science.

GETTING THE BALANCE RIGHT

Most of this book is about third-person views. We will learn about neuroscientific experiments, philosophical inquiries and psychological theories. We will learn to be critical of theories of consciousness and of the many ways of testing one against another. But underlying all of this is the first-person view, and we must strike a balance between studying one and studying the other.

That balance will be different for each of you. Some will enjoy the self-examination and find the science and philosophy hard. Others will lap up the science and find the personal inquiry troubling or trivial. I can only say this: both are needed, and you must find your own balance between them.

As you become acquainted with the growing literature of consciousness studies, and if you have managed to strike a balance between the inner and outer work, you will begin to recognize those writers who have not. At one extreme are theorists who say they are talking about consciousness when they are not. They may sound terribly clever, but once you have learned to see more clearly, you will immediately recognize that they have never looked into their own experience. What they say simply misses the point. At the other extreme are those who waffle about the meaning of inner worlds or the ineffable power of consciousness while falling into the most obvious of logical traps—traps that you will instantly recognize and be able to avoid. Once you can spot these two types, you will be able to save a lot of time by not struggling with their writings. There is so much to read on the topic of consciousness that finding the right things to struggle with is quite an art. I hope this book will help you to find the reading that is worthwhile for you, and to avoid the time-wasting junk.

WARNING

Studying consciousness will change your life. At least if you study it deeply and thoroughly, it will. As the American philosopher Daniel Dennett (see Profile, Chapter 5) says, "When we understand consciousness . . . consciousness will be different" (1991: 25). None of us can expect thoroughly to "understand consciousness." I am not even sure what that would mean. Nonetheless I do know that when people really struggle with the topic, they find that their own experience and their own sense of self change in the process.

These changes can be uncomfortable. For example, you may find that once-solid boundaries between the real and unreal, or the self and other, begin to look less solid. You may find that your own certainties—about the world out there, or ways of knowing about it—seem less certain. You may find yourself beginning to doubt your own existence. Perhaps it helps to know that many people have had these doubts and confusions before you, and have survived. Indeed, many would say that life is easier and happier once you get rid of some of the false assumptions we so easily tend to pick up along the way—but that is for you to decide for yourself. If you get into difficulties, I hope you will be able to find appropriate help and support, from peers, teachers or other professionals. If you are teaching a course using this book, you should be prepared to offer that support yourself, or be able to advise students on how to find it.

In some of my classes I have had a few students who held religious convictions or believed in God. They usually found that these beliefs were seriously challenged by the course. Some found this difficult—for example, because of the role of their beliefs in family ties and friendships, or because their beliefs, gave them comfort in the face of suffering and death. So if you do have such beliefs you should expect to find yourself questioning them. It is not possible to study the nature of self and consciousness, while labeling God, the soul, the spirit or life after death "off limits."

Every year I give this same warning to my students—both verbally and in writing. Every year, sooner or later, one of them comes to me saying, "You never told me that . . ." Happily most of the changes are, in the end, positive and the students are glad to have been through them. Even so, I can only repeat my warning and hope that you will take it seriously. **Studying consciousness will change your life.** Have fun.

"Warning – studying consciousness will change your life."

SECTION

ONE

The problem

What's the problem?

WHAT IS THE WORLD MADE OF?

The problem of consciousness is related to most of the oldest questions of philosophy: What is the world made of? How did it get here? Who or what am I? What is the point of it all? In particular it is related to the mind–body problem; that is, what is the relationship between the physical and the mental?

What makes the problem of consciousness somewhat different from other versions of the mind–body problem is the modern context. At the start of the twenty-first century many people used the term "consciousness" quite unproblematically in everyday language to refer to their own inner experience or awareness. It is not synonymous with "mind," which has many other meanings and uses, and seems to have lost some of its mystery. At the same time we are rapidly learning how the brain works. We know about the effects of brain damage and drugs, about neurotransmitters and neuromodulators, and about how changes in the firing of brain cells accompany changes in a person's experience. We might expect all this knowledge to have clarified the nature of conscious awareness, but it doesn't seem to have done so. Consciousness remains a mystery.

In many other areas of science increasing knowledge has made old philosophical questions obsolete. For example, no one now agonizes over the question "What is life?" The old theories of a "vital spirit," or *élan vital*, are

> " *Consciousness poses the most baffling problems in the science of the mind. There is nothing that we know more intimately than conscious experience, but there is nothing that is harder to explain.* "
>
> **Chalmers**, 1995a: 200

FIGURE 1.1

superfluous when you understand how biological processes make living things out of non-living matter. As the American philosopher Daniel Dennett puts it, "the recursive intricacies of the reproductive machinery of DNA make *élan vital* about as interesting as Superman's dread kryptonite" (Dennett, 1991: 25). The difference is not that we now know what *élan vital* is but that we don't need it any more. The same is true of the "caloric fluid," which was once needed to explain the nature of heat. Now that we think of heat as a form of energy, and know how various types of energy are transformed into each other, we no longer need "caloric fluid."

Might the same happen with consciousness? The American philosopher Patricia Churchland (see Profile, Chapter 3) thinks so, arguing that when our framework for understanding consciousness has evolved, consciousness "may have gone the way of 'caloric fluid' or 'vital spirit'" (1988: 301). Maybe it will. But so far it has not. Indeed, the more we learn about the brain and behavior, the more obviously difficult the problem of consciousness seems to be.

In essence it is this. Whichever way we try to wriggle out of it, in our everyday language or in our scientific and philosophical thinking, we seem to end up with some kind of impossible dualism. Whether it is spirit and matter, or mind and brain; whether it is inner and outer, or subjective and objective, we seem to end up talking about two incompatible kinds of stuff. You may disagree. You may, for example, say that you are a materialist—that you think there is only one kind of stuff in the world and that mind is simply the workings of that stuff—problem solved. I suggest that if you take this line, or many other popular ways of tackling the problem, you will only find that in thinking about consciousness, the dualism pops up somewhere else. Let's take an example.

Pick some simple object you have on hand and take a good look at it. You might choose a chair or table, the cat curled up on your desk, or a book. Anything will do. Let's take a pencil. You can pick it up, turn it around, play with it, write with it, put it down in front of you. Now ask yourself some basic questions. "What do you think it is made of?" "What will happen if you hold it two feet above the floor and let go?" "If you leave the room and come back, will it still be there?"

Now think about your experience of the pencil. You may have felt its sharp point and texture, smelled its distinctive smell when you sharpened it, seen its color and shape, and written with it. These experiences are yours alone. When you hold the pencil at arm's length, you see the pencil from your own unique perspective. No one else can have exactly the same pencil-watching experience as you are having now. And what about the color? How do you know that the way you see that yellow paint would be the same for someone else. You don't.

"Human consciousness is just about the last surviving mystery."

Dennett, 1991: 21

This is what we mean by consciousness. It is your private experience. No one else can know what it is like. No one else can get it from you. You can try to tell them, but words can never quite capture what it is like for you to be holding that pencil right now.

So where has this got us? It has forced us into thinking about the world in two completely different ways. On the one hand there is our private and intimately known experience of holding the pencil, and on the other there is the real pencil out there in the world. How can unsharable, private sensations be related to real existing objects in space? Does the activity in the visual cortex of your brain *cause* the private experience of pencil-watching? If so, how? What makes the smell like *this* for you?

Probably everyone has a different sticking point on this. For me it is this—I find that I have to believe both in subjective experiences (because I seem unquestionably to have them) and an objective world (because otherwise I cannot possibly explain why the pencil will drop when I let go, will still be here when I get back, or why you and I can agree that it is blunt and needs sharpening). Even with all my understanding of brain function, I cannot understand how subjective, private, ineffable suchness of experience arises from an objective world of actual pencils and living brain cells. These subjective and objective worlds seem to be too different from each other to be related at all. This is my own version of the problem of consciousness—my own sticking point. You should look hard at the pencil and find out where yours lies.

PHILOSOPHICAL THEORIES

Philosophers over the millennia have struggled with versions of this problem. Their solutions can be roughly divided into monist theories, which assert that there is only one kind of stuff in the world, and dualist theories, which have two kinds of stuff.

Among the monist theories, some emphasize the mental and others the physical. So, for example, you might doubt that real pencils actually exist out there and decide that only ideas or perceptions of pencils exist—so becoming a mentalist or an idealist. This does away with the division but makes it very hard to understand why physical objects seem to have enduring qualities that we can all agree upon—or indeed how science is possible at all. There have been many philosophical theories of this kind. The British empiricist George Berkeley (1685–1753), for example, replaced matter with sensations in minds.

At the other extreme are materialists who argue that there is only matter, and that the laws governing the interactions between matter and energy exhaust all the forces of the universe. These theories include identity theory, which makes mental states identical with physical states, and functionalism, which equates mental states with functional states. In these theories there is no mind, or mental force, apart from matter. Some people find materialism unattractive as a theory of consciousness because it seems to take away the very phenomenon, subjective

PRACTICE
AM I CONSCIOUS NOW?

For this first exercise I shall give you more detailed guidance than for future ones. All the rest build on the same foundation, so you should find that if you practice this one frequently, all the others will be easier.

The task is simply this.

As many times as you can, every day, ask yourself, **"Am I conscious now?"**

The idea is not to provide an answer—for example, "Yes"—20 or a hundred times a day, but to begin looking into your own consciousness. When do you answer "Yes" and when "No"? What does your answer mean?

You might like to ask the question and then just hold it for a little while, observing being conscious now. Since this whole book is about consciousness, this exercise is simply intended to get you to *look* at what consciousness is, as well as to think and argue about it intellectually.

This sounds easy but it is not. Try it and see. After a day of practicing, or—if you are working through the book, before you go on to the next chapter—make notes on the following.

- How many times did you do the practice?

- What happened?

- Did you find yourself asking other questions as well? If so, what were they?

- Was it difficult to remember to do it? If so, why do you think this is?

You may have found that you had intended to do the practice but then forgot. This might be just because you need reminding. There are many simple tricks for remembering. You might try the following.

- Ask the question whenever you hear or read the word "consciousness."

- Always ask the question when you go to the toilet.

- Write the question on stickers and place them around your home or office.

- Discuss the practice with a friend. You may help remind each other.

These may help. Even so you may still find that you forget. This is odd because there is no very good excuse. After all, this little practice does not take up valuable time when you could be doing something more useful. It is not like having to write another essay, read another paper or understand a difficult argument. You can ask the question in the middle of doing any of these things. You can ask it while walking along or waiting for the bus, while washing up or cooking, while cleaning your teeth or listening to music. It takes no time away from anything else you do. You just keep on doing it, pose the question and watch for a moment or two.

You must be interested in consciousness to be reading this book. So why is it so hard just to look at your own consciousness?

Are you conscious now?

why does it seem so real! alive alm

experience, that it was trying to explain. In particular, the powerful feeling we have that our conscious decisions *cause* our actions is reduced to purely physical causes. Another problem is the difficulty of understanding how thoughts and feelings and mental images can really *be* matter when they seem to be so different from matter. Materialism makes it hard to find any way of talking about consciousness that does justice to the way it *feels*.

The doctrine of "epiphenomenalism" is the idea that mental states are produced by physical events but have no causal role to play. In other words, physical events cause mental events, but mental events have no effect on physical events. Thomas Henry Huxley (1825–95), the English biologist and paleontologist who did so much to promote Darwin's theory of evolution by natural selection, was one of the best-known epiphenomenalists. He did not deny the existence of consciousness or of subjective experiences but denied them any causal influence. They were powerless to affect the machinery of the human brain and body, just as the steam-whistle of a locomotive engine is without influence on its machinery. He referred to animals, including humans, as "conscious automata." One problem with epiphenomenalism is this: if conscious experiences can have no effect on anything whatsoever, then we should never know about, or be able to speak about, consciousness since this would mean it had had an effect. Nevertheless, behaviorism is built on one version of this idea.

Trying to avoid either extreme are various kinds of "neutral monism." William James (see Profile, Chapter 4), for example, tried to understand the world as constructed out of various possible or actual sense-data, avoiding reducing mind to matter or doing away with matter altogether. Indeed, he saw psychology as integrating mind and brain: "A science of the relations of mind and brain must show how the elementary ingredients of the former correspond to the elementary functions of the latter" (James, 1890, i: 28). He did not, however, underestimate the difficulty of this task.

Another attractive way of avoiding the problem is panpsychism, the view that mind is fundamental in the universe, and that all matter has associated mental aspects or properties, however primitive. In some versions this means that everything in the universe is conscious, but in other versions everything is essentially mental but this can include both conscious and unconscious mind. Panpsychism raises difficult questions: Is a stone aware? Is every scrap of sand, or each molecule or atom within it? What would it mean for something as simple as an electron to have mental attributes? And why should there simultaneously be physical and mental properties to everything?

Given the difficulty of uniting the world it is not surprising that dualism is enduringly popular, and persists in much everyday thinking. The best-known version is that of René Descartes (see Profile, p. 12), the seventeenth-century French philosopher, and is therefore called Cartesian dualism. Descartes wanted to base his philosophy only on firm foundations that were beyond doubt. If he had been holding your pencil, he might have imagined that it did not exist and that his senses were deceiving him, or even that an evil demon was systematically

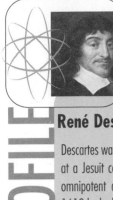

René Descartes (1596–1650)

Descartes was born near Tours in France, was educated at a Jesuit college and was a staunch believer in an omnipotent and benevolent God. On 11 November 1619 he had a series of dreams that inspired him with the idea of a completely new philosophical and scientific system based on mechanical principles. He was not only a great philosopher, now often called "the father of modern philosophy," but also a physicist, a physiologist and a mathematician. He was the first to draw graphs, and invented Cartesian coordinates, which remain a central concept in mathematics. He is best known for his saying "I think, therefore I am" (*je pense, donc je suis*), which he arrived at using his "method of doubt." He tried to reject everything that could be doubted and accept only that which was beyond doubt, which brought him to the fact that he, himself, was doubting. He described the human body entirely as a machine made of "extended substance" (*res extensa*), but concluded that the mind or soul must be a separate entity made of a non-spatial and indivisible "thinking substance" (*res cogitans*) that affected the brain through the pineal gland. This theory became known as Cartesian dualism. For the last 20 years of his life he lived mostly in Holland. He died of pneumonia in Sweden in 1650.

trying to fool him. But—he argued, in a famous passage in *The Meditations*—even the cleverest deceiver would have to deceive someone. And the fact that he, Descartes, was thinking about this was proof that he, the thinker, existed. In this way he came to his famous dictum "I think, therefore I am." Descartes concluded that this thinking self was not material, like the physical body that moves about mechanically and takes up space. In his view the world consists of two different kinds of stuff—the extended stuff of which physical bodies are made, and the unextended, thinking stuff of which minds are made.

Descartes' theory is a form of substance dualism, which can be contrasted with property dualism or dual aspect theory. According to property dualism, the same thing (e.g., a human being) can be described using mental terms or physical terms, but one description cannot be reduced to the other. So, for example, if you are in pain, this fact can be described in mental terms, such as how it feels to you, or in physical terms, such as which sorts of neurons are firing where in your nervous system.

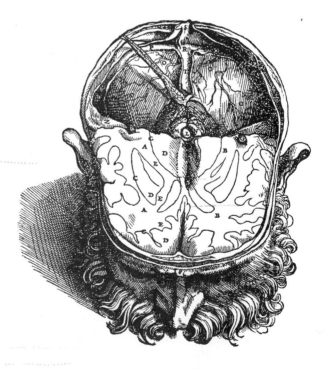

FIGURE 1.2 ● According to Descartes, the physical brain worked by the flow of animal spirits through its cavities. The immaterial soul was connected to the body and brain through the pineal gland which lies in the midline.

This theory avoids reducing the mental to the physical without the need for two different substances.

The insuperable problem for substance dualism is how the mind interacts with the body when the two are made of different substances. For the whole theory to work, the interaction has to be in both directions. Physical events in the world and the brain must somehow give rise to experiences of that world—to thoughts, images, decisions, longings and all the other contents of our mental life. In the other direction, thoughts and feelings must be able to influence the physical stuff. How could either of these work? Descartes supposed that the two interacted through the pineal gland in the center of the brain, but proposing a place where it happens does not solve the mystery. If thoughts can affect brain cells, then either they work by magic or they must be using some kind of energy or matter. In this case they are also physical stuff and not purely mental.

Dualism does not work. Almost all contemporary scientists and philosophers agree on this. In 1949 the British philosopher Gilbert Ryle derided dualism as "the dogma of the Ghost in the Machine"—a phrase that has entered into common use. He argued that when we talk of the mind as an entity that does things, we are making a category mistake—turning it into something it is not. Instead he saw mental activities as processes, or as the properties and dispositions of people.

This kind of view is apparent in many modern descriptions of mind: "Minds are simply what brains do" (Minsky, 1986: 287); "'Mind' is designer language for the functions that the brain carries out" (Claxton, 1994: 37); Mind is "the personalization of the physical brain" (Greenfield, 2000: 14). Such descriptions make it possible to talk about mental activities and mental abilities without supposing that there is a separate mind. This is probably how most psychologists and neuroscientists think of "mind" today, but there is much less agreement when it comes to consciousness.

There are very few dualists today. The most notable exceptions are the philosopher of science Sir Karl Popper and neurophysiologist Sir John Eccles (see Profile, Chapter 17), who proposed a modern theory of dualist interactionism (1977). They argued that the critical processes in the synapses of the brain are so finely poised that they can be influenced by a non-physical, thinking

FIGURE 1.3 • Gilbert Ryle dubbed the Cartesian view of mind "the dogma of the Ghost in the Machine."

and feeling self. Thus the self really does control its brain (Eccles, 1994). How it does so they do not explain, and admit that this remains mysterious. It seems that dualism, in its many forms, always arrives in the end at magic, or mystery, or something that science can never approach. As Dennett puts it *"accepting dualism is giving up"* (Dennett, 1991: 37). But avoiding it is not easy.

Given the lurking specter of dualism it is not surprising that psychology, as a discipline, has had trouble with the concept of consciousness.

ACTIVITY
What is consciousness?

There is no generally recognized definition of consciousness, which is why I have not given one here. See whether you can find your own.

First get into pairs. One person first proposes a definition of consciousness. Then the other finds something wrong with it. Don't be shy or think too long—just throw up a suggestion and wait for it to be knocked down. Then swap over. Do this as quickly as you reasonably can until each of you has had several turns.

Get back together into the group and find out what kinds of objections you all came up with.

Why is defining consciousness so hard when we all think we know what it is?

CONSCIOUSNESS IN PSYCHOLOGY

The term "psychology" first appeared in the eighteenth century to describe the philosophy of mental life, but it was toward the end of the nineteenth century that psychology first became a science. At that time several different approaches to the study of the mind were beginning. Some were more concerned with physiology and the idea of psychology as an objective science, and some were more concerned with the inner life, or studying subjective experience, but there was, as yet, no great split between the two.

William James's classic two-volume text *The Principles of Psychology* (1890)—perhaps the most famous book in the history of psychology—begins, "Psychology is the Science of Mental Life, both of its phenomena and their conditions." James includes among these phenomena, feelings, desires, cognitions, reasonings and volitions—in other words the stuff of consciousness. Another contemporary textbook defines psychology, or "Mental Science," as "the science that investigates and explains the phenomena of mind, or the inner world of our conscious experience. These phenomena include our feelings of joy and sorrow, love, etc., . . . our conscious impulses and volitions, our perceptions of external objects as *mental* acts, and so forth" (Sully, 1892 (i): 1).

James dismissed the dualist concepts of a soul or of "mind-stuff," and quickly pointed out that consciousness can be abolished by injury to the brain, or altered by taking alcohol, opium or hashish. So he assumed that a certain amount of brain-physiology must be included in psychology. Nevertheless, consciousness was at the heart of his psychology. He coined the phrase "the stream of consciousness" to describe the apparently ever-changing and flowing succession of thoughts, ideas, images and feelings. His psychology was therefore very much an integrated science of mental life. Consciousness was at its heart, but was not divorced either from the results of experiments on attention, memory and sensation nor from physiological study of the brain and nervous system.

James was able to build on a large body of research in anatomy, physiology and psychophysics. Psychophysics was the study of the relationship between physical stimuli and reportable sensations—or, you could say, between outer events and inner experience. Psychophysicists such as Ernst Weber (1795–1878) and Gustav Fechner (1801–87) studied the relationships between physical luminance and perceived brightness; weight and sensations of heaviness; or sound pressure and loudness. From this came the famous Weber–Fechner Law relating sensation to the intensity of a stimulus. Fechner also wanted to be able to relate sensations to excitations within the brain, but in his time this was simply not possible.

In 1850 Hermann von Helmholtz (1821–94) made the first measurement of the speed of conduction of nerve signals. This was popularly referred to as the "velocity of thought," although in fact he had measured peripheral processes and reaction times, and argued that conscious thought, and the interaction of physical and mental processes, goes on in the brain. He was especially interested in visual illusions and the tricks that our senses can play, and he proposed the new and shocking idea that perceptions are "unconscious inferences." This is close to the British psychologist Richard Gregory's notion (1966) of perceptions as hypotheses, or guesses about the world, and it fits well with much of modern neuroscience. James (1902) also talked about "unconscious cerebration."

This idea, that much of what goes on in the nervous system is unconscious and that our conscious experiences depend upon unconscious processing, seems quite natural to us today. Yet it was deeply disturbing to many Victorian scientists who assumed that inference and thinking, as well as ethics and morality, require consciousness. To them, the idea that thinking could go on without consciousness seemed to undermine the moral or spiritual superiority of 'Man.'

Note that this notion of the unconscious, derived from physiological studies, predated the more active psychodynamic notion of the unconscious developed by Sigmund Freud (1856–1939). In Freud's theory the unconscious consisted of the impulses of the 'id' including biological desires and needs, the defense mechanisms and neurotic processes of the 'ego,' and all the mass of unwanted or unacceptable material that had been repressed by the 'superego.' The effects of all these unconscious feelings, images or forbidden wishes might then appear in dreams or cause neurotic symptoms. Although Freud was trained as a neurologist, and frequently referred to his work and to psychology as a "new science," his theories were derived from studies of psychiatric patients and from his own self-analysis, not from scientific research.

Other notable developments in Europe included the emergence of existentialism and phenomenology. Phenomenology is both a philosophy and a psychology based on putting subjective experience first. The German philosopher Edmund Husserl (1859–1938) argued for going back to "the things themselves"

by a systematic inquiry into immediate conscious experience. This was to be done without preconceptions by suspending or "bracketing" any scientific and logical inferences about the world. This suspension of judgment he called the phenomenological reduction, or epoché (see Chapter 25).

Husserl's phenomenology built on the earlier work of Franz Brentano (1838–1917), whose theory of consciousness was based on the idea that every subjective experience is an act of reference. Conscious experiences are *about* objects or events, while physical objects are not about anything. For example, I might have a belief about horses, but a horse itself is not about anything. This "aboutness" he called "intentionality."

It is most important to realize that this awkward word gets used in many different senses. By and large philosophers use it in Brentano's sense, to mean meaning, reference or aboutness. In psychology (and in ordinary language when it is used at all) intentionality usually means "having intentions" or having plans or goals or aims. If you come across this word, remember these two meanings and ask yourself which is intended. This way you will avoid getting confused and will be able to spot some of the muddles created by people who mix them up.

A separate approach to studying subjective experience was that of introspectionism, initially developed by the German physiologist Wilhelm Wundt (1832–1920). Wundt had founded the first laboratory of experimental psychology in 1879, and for this he is often called the father of experimental psychology. While the physiology in which he was trained studied living systems from the outside, he wanted to build a psychology based on studying from the inside—in other words, introspection. This study had to be systematic and rigorous, and so he trained people to make precise and reliable observations of their own inner experience. Others, such as Wundt's student Edward Titchener (1867–1927), carried on these methods of introspectionism, primarily studying sensation and attention.

Wundt claimed to find that there were two kinds of "psychical elements": the objective elements, or sensations, such as tones, heat or light; and the subjective elements, or simple feelings. Every conscious experience depended on a union of these two types. Like many others around this time, he hoped to be able to build up a science of consciousness by understanding the units or atoms of experience that made it up (an approach to consciousness that William James utterly rejected). Although psychoanalysis, phenomenology and introspectionism all had the benefit of dealing directly with inner experience (or, at least, with what people said about their inner experience), they faced apparently insuperable problems in dealing with disagreements. When one person claims to observe some private experience quite different from another, how can you decide between them?

This was just one of the reasons why introspectionism fell out of favor and behaviorism became so successful. In 1913 the American psychologist John B. Watson argued that psychology did not need the methods of introspection and indeed could do without the concept of consciousness altogether. He proposed to abolish such nonsense and establish psychology as "a purely objective branch of natural science"; its theoretical goal being the prediction and control of behavior (Watson, 1913: 158). One advantage of this new approach was that behavior can be measured much more reliably than introspections can. Also human psychology could build on the considerable knowledge of the behavior of other animals. As Watson proclaimed, behaviorism "recognizes *no dividing line between man and brute*" (ibid.).

Although Watson is usually credited with—or blamed for—the expulsion of consciousness from psychology, similar views were already gaining ground long before. In 1890 James wrote, "I have heard a most intelligent biologist say: 'It is high time for scientific men to protest against the recognition of any such thing as consciousness in a scientific investigation.'" (James, 1890, i: 134).

Watson built many of his ideas on the work of Ivan Pavlov (1849–1936), the Russian physiologist famous for his work on reflexes and classical conditioning. Pavlov studied the way that repetition increased the probability of various behaviors and assumed that almost everything we do, including language and speech, is learned this way. Subsequently the emphasis in behaviorism shifted to the study of operant conditioning, with B.F. Skinner's studies of rats and pigeons that learned by being rewarded or punished for their actions. For Skinner human behavior was shaped by the history of reinforcements, and he believed that with the right reinforcement schedules a human utopia could be created (Skinner, 1948). As for consciousness, he believed it was just an epiphenomenon and its study should not be the task of psychology. In the

FIGURE 1.4 • When the rat presses the lever, it may receive a food pellet or a sip of water. Rats, pigeons and many other animals can easily learn to press a certain number of times, or only when a green light is on, or when a bell sounds. This is known as operant conditioning. Some behaviorists believed that studying animal learning was the best way to understand the human mind.

words of Watson's biographer David Cohen, "Behaviorism was a self-conscious revolution against consciousness" (Cohen, 1987: 72).

Behaviorism was enormously successful in explaining some kinds of behavior, particularly in the areas of learning and memory, but it more or less abolished the study of consciousness from psychology, and even the use of the word "consciousness" became unacceptable. Also, in sweeping away the worst excesses of introspectionism, behaviorism threw out the much more even-handed mind–body approach of William James's "science of mental life." This led to half a century of a very restricted kind of psychology indeed.

By the 1960s behaviourism was losing its power and influence, and cognitive psychology, with its emphasis on internal representations and information processing, was taking over, but "consciousness" was still something of a dirty word in psychology. In his widely read history *Psychology: The Science of Mental Life* (1962), George Miller warned:

> Consciousness is a word worn smooth by a million tongues.
> Depending upon the figure of speech chosen it is a state of being, a
> substance, a process, a place, an epiphenomenon, an emergent aspect
> of matter, or the only true reality. Maybe we should ban the word for
> a decade or two until we can develop more precise terms for the
> several uses which "consciousness" now obscures.
>
> (Miller, 1962: 40)

No one formally banned its use, but it was certainly more than a decade before even using the word "consciousness" became acceptable in psychology. In the 1970s the dirty word gradually began to creep in again with, for example, research on mental imagery (see Chapter 22), on altered states of consciousness such as sleep and drug-induced states (see Section Eight), and in the disputes over hypnosis (see Chapter 8), and with the beginnings of computer science (see Chapter 13). But it was nearly three decades before the sudden explosion of interest in the 1990s.

At the start of the twenty-first century we still cannot define consciousness, but at least we are allowed to talk about it.

THE MYSTERIOUS GAP

"Human consciousness is just about the last surviving mystery," says Dennett (1991: 21). He defines a mystery as a phenomenon that people don't know how to think about—yet. Once upon a time the origin of the universe, the nature of life, the source of design in the universe, and the nature of space and time were all mysteries. Now, although we do not have answers to all the questions about these phenomena, we do know how to think about them and where to look for answers. With consciousness, however, we are still in that delightful—or dreadful—state of mystification. Our understanding of consciousness is a muddle.

The cause of that mystification, as we have seen in our quick look at the history of consciousness, seems to be a gap. But what sort of a gap is it?

FIGURE 1.5

THE HARD PROBLEM

The hard problem is to explain how physical processes in the brain give rise to subjective experience. The term was coined in 1994 by David Chalmers, who distinguished it from the "easy problems" of consciousness. These include the ability to discriminate, categorize and react to stimuli; the integration of information by cognitive systems; the reportability of mental states; the focus of attention; deliberate control of behavior; and the difference between wakefulness and sleep. By contrast the hard problem concerns experience itself, that is, *subjectivity* or "what it is like to be . . ."

The hard problem can be seen as a modern version, or aspect, of the traditional mind–body problem. It is the problem of crossing the "fathomless abyss" or "chasm," or of bridging the "explanatory gap" between the objective material brain and the subjective world of experience.

Mysterians say that the hard problem can never be solved. Some argue that new physical principles are needed to solve it, while many neuroscientists believe that once we understand the easy problems, the hard problem will disappear (see Chapter 2).

"'A motion became a feeling!'—no phrase that our lips can frame is so devoid of apprehensible meaning." This is how William James describes what he calls the "'chasm' between the inner and the outer worlds" (James, 1890, i: 146). Before him, Tyndall had famously proclaimed, "The passage from the physics of the brain to the corresponding facts of consciousness is unthinkable" (James, ibid.: 147). Charles Mercier in his *The Nervous System and the Mind* (1888), referred to "the fathomless abyss" and advised the student of psychology to ponder the fact that a change of consciousness never takes place without a change in the brain, and a change in the brain never without a change in consciousness.

> Having firmly and tenaciously grasped these two notions, of the absolute separateness of mind and matter, and of the invariable concomitance of a mental change with a bodily change, the student will enter on the study of psychology with half his difficulties surmounted.
>
> (Mercier, 1888: 11)

"Half his difficulties ignored, I should prefer to say," remarks James, "For this 'concomitance' in the midst of 'absolute separateness' is an utterly irrational notion" (James, 1890, ibid.: 136). He quotes the British philosopher Herbert Spencer as saying

> Suppose it to have become quite clear that a shock in consciousness and a molecular motion are the subjective and objective faces of the

same thing; we continue utterly incapable of uniting the two, so as to conceive that reality of which they are the opposite faces.

(James, ibid.: 147)

To James it was inconceivable that consciousness should have nothing to do with events that it always accompanied. He urged his readers to reject both the automaton theory and the "mind-stuff" theory, and to ponder the how and why of the relationship between physiology and consciousness.

As we have seen, the automaton theory gained ground, and behaviorism, with its thorough-going rejection of consciousness, held sway over most of psychology for half a century or more. Behaviorists had no need to worry about the great gap because they simply avoided mentioning consciousness, subjective experience or inner worlds. It was only when this period was over that the problem became obvious again. In 1983 the American philosopher Joseph Levine coined the phrase "the explanatory gap," describing it as "a metaphysical gap between physical phenomena and conscious experience" (Levine, 2001: 78). Consciousness had been allowed back into science, and the mysterious gap had opened up once more.

Then, in 1994, a young Australian philosopher, David Chalmers (see Profile, Chapter 2), presented a paper at the first Tucson conference on consciousness. Before getting into the technicalities of his argument against reductionism he wanted to clarify what he thought was an obvious point—that the many problems of consciousness can be divided into the "easy" problems and the truly "hard problem." To his surprise, his term "the hard problem" stuck, provoking numerous debates and four special issues of the newly established *Journal of Consciousness Studies* (Shear, 1997).

> *"The hard problem . . . is the question of how physical processes in the brain give rise to subjective experience."*
>
> **Chalmers**, 1995b: 63

SELF-ASSESSMENT QUESTIONS

○ What is the mind–body problem? Name some traditional solutions to it.

○ What was Descartes' solution to the mind–body problem?

○ Why did behaviorism flourish and why did it ultimately fail?

○ What does the term "intentionality" mean?

○ Describe the "mysterious gap" in as many different ways as you can.

○ Who described the "hard problem" and what is it?

According to Chalmers, the easy problems are those that are susceptible to the standard methods of cognitive science, and might be solved, for example, by understanding the computational or neural mechanisms involved. They include the discrimination of stimuli, focusing of attention, accessing and reporting mental states, deliberate control of behavior, or differences between waking and sleep. All of these phenomena are in some way associated with the notion of consciousness, but they are not deeply mysterious. In principle (even though it may not really be "easy") we know how to set about answering them scientifically. The really hard problem, by contrast, is *experience*: what it is like to *be* an organism, or to *be in* a given mental state. "If any problem qualifies as *the* problem of consciousness," says Chalmers,

it is this one . . . even when we have explained the performance of all the cognitive and behavioral functions in the vicinity of experience—perceptual discrimination, categorization, internal access, verbal report—there may still remain a further unanswered question: *Why is the performance of these functions accompanied by experience? . . .* Why doesn't all this information-processing go on "in the dark," free of any inner feel?

(Chalmers, 1995a: 201–3)

Stated at its most succinct "The hard problem . . . is the question of how physical processes in the brain give rise to subjective experience" (Chalmers, 1995b: 63). This is the latest incarnation of the mysterious gap.

Chalmers, D.J. (1995) The puzzle of conscious experience. *Scientific American* (December), 62–8. This is the easiest version of Chalmers' "hard problem." For more detail read Chalmers (1995a; 1996).

Dennett, D.C. (1991) *Consciousness Explained.* Boston and London: Little, Brown and Co. Read Chapter 2 for the mystery of consciousness and the problems of dualism.

Gregory, R.L. (1987) *The Oxford Companion to the Mind.* Oxford: OUP. This contains short entries on most of the authors and ideas presented here. It is especially helpful for non-philosophers who want to look up philosophical concepts.

See also the following websites:

The Stanford Encyclopedia of Philosophy, http://plato.stanford.edu/index.html

The Internet Encyclopedia of Philosophy, http://www.utm.edu/research/iep/

READING

What's the problem? CHAPTER ONE

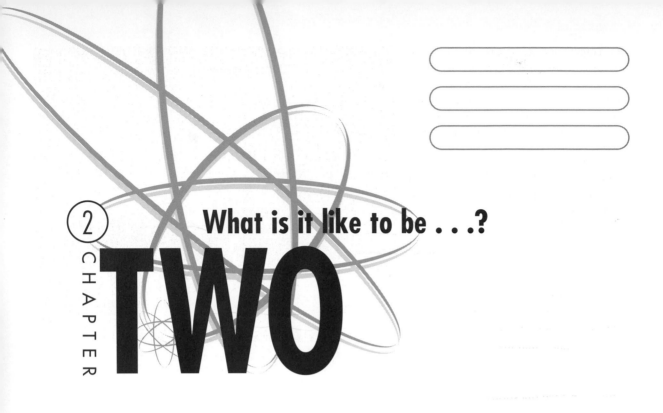

② **What is it like to be . . .?**

TWO

BEING A . . .

What is it like to be a bat? This is one of the most famous questions ever asked in the history of consciousness studies. First posed in 1950 it was made famous in a 1974 paper of that name by American philosopher Thomas Nagel. Nagel argued that understanding how mental states can *be* neurons firing inside the brain is a problem quite unlike understanding how water can be H_2O, or how genes can be DNA. "Consciousness is what makes the mind–body problem really intractable," he said (Nagel, 1974: 435; 1979: 165), and by consciousness he meant *subjectivity*. To make this clear he asked, "What is it like to be a bat?"

Do you think that your cat is conscious? Or the birds outside in the street? Perhaps you believe that horses are conscious but not worms, or living creatures but not stones. We shall return to these questions (Chapter 12), but here let's consider what it means to say that another creature is conscious. If you say that the stone is not conscious, you probably mean that it has no inner life and no point of view; that there is nothing it is like to *be* the stone. If you believe that the neighbor's vicious bloodhound, or the beggar you passed in the subway, is conscious, then you probably mean that they do have a point of view; there is something it is like to be them.

As Nagel put it, when we say that another organism is conscious, we mean that "there is something it is like to *be* that organism . . . something it is like *for* the organism" (1974: 436); "the essence of the belief that bats have experience is that there is something that it is like to be a bat" (ibid.: 438). This is probably the closest we can come to a definition of consciousness— that consciousness is subjectivity, or "what it is like to be . . ."

Here we must be careful with the phrase "what it is like . . ." Unfortunately there are at least two meanings in English. We might say "this ice cream tastes like rubber" or "lying on a beach in the sun is like heaven." In this case we are comparing things, making analogies, or saying what they resemble. This is *not* what Nagel meant. The other meaning is found in such questions as: What is it

FIGURE 2.1 ● The leaf-nosed bat uses sonar to navigate, sending out brief pulses of sound and analyzing the returning echoes so as to avoid obstacles, detect fruit and other food, and to find its mate. What is it like to be this bat?

like to work at McDonald's? What is it like to be able to improvise fugues at the keyboard? . . . to be someone inconceivably more intelligent than yourself? . . . to be a molecule, a microbe, a mosquito, an ant, or an ant colony? Hofstadter and Dennett (1981: 404–5) pose many more such provocative questions. In other words, what is it like from the inside?

Now, imagine being a bat. A bat's experience must be very different from that of a human. For a start the bat's sensory systems are quite different, which is why Nagel chose the bat for his famous question. Bats' brains, lives and senses are well understood (Akins, 1993; Dawkins, 1986). Most use either sound or ultrasound for echolocation. That is, they detect objects by emitting rapid high-pitched clicks that bounce off any objects in the vicinity and then measuring the time taken for the echo to return. Natural selection has found ingenious solutions to the many interesting problems posed by echolocation. Some bats cruise around emitting clicks quite slowly so as not to waste energy, but then when they are homing in on prey or approaching a potential danger, they speed up. Many have mechanisms that protect their ears from the loud blast of each click and then open them to receive the faint echo. Some use the Doppler shift to work out their speed relative to prey or other objects. Others sort out the mixed-up echoes from different objects by emitting downward-swooping sounds. The echoes from distant objects take longer to come back and therefore sound higher than the echoes from nearer objects. In this way we can imagine that a whole bat world is built up in which higher sounds mean distant objects and lower sounds mean nearer objects.

What would this be like? According to Oxford biologist Richard Dawkins (1986; see Profile, Chapter 10), it might be like seeing is for us. We humans do not know, or care, that color is related to wavelength or that motion detection is carried out in the visual cortex. We just see the objects out there in depth and color. Similarly the bat would just perceive the objects out there in depth, and perhaps even in some batty, sonar, version of color. Living in this constructed world would be what it is like to be the bat.

But can we ever know what it would *really* be like for the bat? As Nagel pointed out, the question is not answered by trying to imagine that *you* are a bat. This will not do. It is no good hanging upside down in a darkened room, making little clicks with your tongue and flapping your arms like wings. Perhaps if you could magically be transformed into a bat you would know. But even this won't do. For if *you* were a bat, the bat in question would not be an ordinary bat—what with having your memories and your interest in consciousness. But if you became an ordinary bat, then this bat would have no understanding of English, no ability to ask questions about consciousness, and could not tell us what it was like. So we cannot know what it is like to be a bat even if we believe that there *is* something it is like to be a bat.

Nagel's question clarifies the central meaning of the term "consciousness." It is what the American philosopher Ned Block (1995) calls "phenomenal consciousness" or phenomenality. He explains that "Phenomenal consciousness is experience; what makes a state phenomenally conscious is that there is something 'it is like' to be in that state." He distinguishes this from "access consciousness," which is "availability for use in reasoning and rationally guiding speech and action" (Block, 1995: 227). We will return to this distinction (Chapter 18), and consider issues to do with availability, but "phenomenal consciousness" is what this book is all about.

So what is it like to be you now? Everything I have said so far implies that there is, uncontroversially, something it is like to be you now—that the prob-

○ PRACTICE
WHAT IS IT LIKE BEING ME NOW?

As many times as you can, every day, ask yourself, **"What is it like being me now?"** If you worked through the "Practice" exercise in Chapter 1, "Am I conscious now?", you will have got used to remembering the task, and perhaps to opening your mind for a little while to watch your own awareness.

This question is important because so many arguments assume that we know, unproblematically, what our own experience is like; that we know our own qualia directly, and that of course we know what it is like to be ourselves, now. The only way to have an informed opinion on this important point is to look for yourself. What is it really like for you, now?

CONSCIOUSNESS

lems only begin when you start asking about what it is like to be someone or something else. But is this right? A thoroughly skeptical approach would mean questioning even this. I urge you to do this chapter's "Practice" and become a little more familiar with what it is like to be you.

SUBJECTIVITY AND QUALIA

Let us suppose that you are, right now, getting the unmistakable smell of fresh coffee drifting in from the kitchen. The smell may be caused by chemicals entering your nose and reacting with receptors there, but as far as you are concerned the experience is nothing to do with chemicals. It is a . . . well, what is it? You probably cannot describe it even to yourself. It just is how fresh coffee smells. The experience is private, ineffable and has a quality all its own. These private qualities are known, in philosophy, as qualia. The feel of the wind on your cheeks as you ride your bike is a quale (pronounced qua-lay). The sight of the browny pink of the skin on your hand is a quale. The ineffable chill of delight that you experience every time you hear that minor chord is a quale.

The concept of qualia has become mired in confusion, but the basic idea is clear enough. The term is used to emphasize quality, to get away from talking about physical properties or descriptions, and to point to phenomenology instead. A quale is what something is *like* (in the sense explained above). Our conscious experience consists of qualia. The problem of consciousness can be rephrased in terms of how qualia are related to the physical world, or how an *objective* physical brain can produce *subjective* qualia. The dualist believes that qualia are part of a separate mental world from physical objects like pots of coffee or brains. The epiphenomenalist believes that qualia exist but have no causal properties. The idealist believes that everything is ultimately qualia. The eliminative materialist denies that qualia exist, and so on.

You may think it unquestionable that qualia exist. After all, you are right now experiencing smells, sounds and sights, and these are your own private, ineffable qualia aren't they? Most theorists would agree with you, but some think you would be wrong. In "Quining qualia" Dennett sets out "to convince people that there are no such properties as qualia" (Dennett, 1988: 42). He does not deny the reality of conscious experience, or of the things we say and the judgments we make about our own experiences, but only of the special, ineffable, private, subjective "raw feels," or "the way things seem to us," that people call qualia.

Dennett provides many "intuition pumps" to undermine this very natural way of thinking. Here is a simple one. The experienced beer drinker says that beer is an acquired taste. When he first tried beer, he hated the taste, but now he has come to love it. But which taste does he now love? No one could love that first taste—it tasted horrible. So he must love the new taste, but what has changed? If you think that there are two separate things here, the actual quale (the way it *really* tastes to him) and his opinion about the taste, then you must be able to decide which has changed. But can you? We normally think in a

" 'To be conscious' . . . is roughly synonymous with 'to have qualia.' "

Chalmers, 1986: 6

" There simply are no qualia at all. "

Dennett, 1988: 74

mmm.... this taste, it's... well I can't explain!

FIGURE 2.2 • Is this an ineffable quale?

confused and incoherent way about how things seem to us, claims Dennett, and the concept of qualia just confuses the issue in this case, and many others. We should get rid of the notion of qualia altogether because "there simply are no qualia at all" (Dennett, 1988: 74).

How does one decide whether qualia exist or not? We cannot do experiments on qualia, at least not in the simple sense of first catching a quale and then manipulating it in some way. That is the whole point of qualia—they do not have physical properties that can be measured. We can, however, do thought experiments.

Thought experiments are, as the name implies, experiments done in the head. It is important to be clear about their purpose. In an ordinary experiment you manipulate something in order to get an answer about the world. If you do the experiment properly, you may get a reliable answer that is widely applicable and that helps decide between two rival theories. Thought experiments are not designed to provide reliable answers to anything. Rather, they help to clarify our thinking.

Einstein famously imagined riding on the back of a light wave, and from this idea came to some of his theories about relativity and the speed of light. Most thought experiments are, like that one, impossible to carry out, although some end up turning into real experiments as technology changes. Most philosophical thought experiments are of the impossible kind. They have not been done, cannot be done, will never be done, and do not need to be done. Their function is to make you think.

One of the best known of such thought experiments gets right to the heart of the problem of qualia. Are qualia something separate from the brain? Do qualia make any difference? Does a quale contain information above and beyond the neural information it depends on? Mary may help.

WHAT IS IT LIKE BEING ME NOW?

MARY THE COLOR SCIENTIST

Mary lives in the far future when neuroscience is complete and scientists know everything there is to know about the physical processes in the brain and how they produce behavior. Mary specializes in the neurophysiology of color vision. She knows everything there is to know about color perception, about the optics of the eye, the properties of colored objects in the world, and the processing of color information in the visual system. She knows exactly how certain wavelengths of light stimulate the retina and produce the contraction of the vocal chords and expulsion of air that results in someone saying "the sky is blue." But Mary has been brought up all her life in a black and white

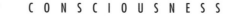

FIGURE 2.3 • What does Mary say when she finally emerges from her black and white room?

room, observing the world through a black and white television monitor. She has never seen any colors at all.

One day Mary is let out of her black and white room and sees colors for the first time. What happens? Will she gasp with amazement and say "Wow—I never realized red would look like *that*!" or will she just shrug and say "That's red, that's green, nothing new of course"? You may like to think about your own answer, or do the group activity before reading on.

The philosopher Frank Jackson devised the Mary thought experiment as an argument against physicalism (Jackson, 1982). He argued that when she comes out she obviously learns something fundamentally new—what red is *like*. Now she has color qualia as well as all the physical facts about color. As Chalmers puts it, no amount of knowledge about, or reasoning from, the physical facts could have prepared her for the raw *feel* of what it is like to see a blue sky or green grass. In other words the physical facts about the world are not all there is to know, and therefore materialism has to be false.

If you think Mary will be surprised, are you forced to reject materialism and adopt dualism? Chalmers does so, but there have been many objections to this conclusion and other ways of using the thought experiment. For example, some have argued that Mary comes to know an old fact in a new way or from a new viewpoint, or to connect up old facts in new ways, or that she learns a new skill rather than a new fact (see Chalmers, 1996, for a philosophical

ACTIVITY
Mary the color scientist

When Mary comes out of the black and white room, will she learn anything new? Will she be surprised at what colors are *like*? Or does she already know? Acting out Mary's story in class may help you decide.

Get two volunteers to act as Mary, and make a corner of the room as black and white as possible. You might give them a white tablecloth, a newspaper, a toy gray rat, a doll to do brain scans on, some black and white diagrams of brains, or dress them in white lab coats—whatever you have on hand. Ask the "Marys" to sink themselves into the role of futuristic color scientist while you explain to the rest of the group what is happening. The "Marys" know *everything* there is to know about the brain, the visual system and color. *Everything.*

Now let them out in turn to do their best possible impersonations. "Mary-amazed" acts completely surprised at what she sees, gasping at the delightful colors. "Mary-know-it-all" explains why she is not surprised at all—how she understood everything in advance. Mary-know-it-all is the far harder role, so it may be best to choose someone who is familiar with the arguments for this one. Everyone else can now ask questions of the "Marys," discuss their answers and make up their own minds.

Write down your own decision. You may be interested to find that it changes as you learn more about the nature of consciousness.

27 •

David Chalmers (b. 1966)

Born in Australia, David Chalmers originally intended to be a mathematician, but then he spent six months hitchhiking around Europe on his way to Oxford, and spent most of his time thinking about consciousness. This led him to Douglas Hofstadter's research group, and a PhD in philosophy and cognitive science. He is responsible for the distinction between the "easy problems" and the "hard problem" of consciousness, and he is one of that rare breed: a self-proclaimed dualist. His major aim now is to get a science of consciousness off the ground, but his other interests include artificial intelligence and computation, philosophical issues about meaning and possibility, and the foundations of cognitive science. He is Professor of Philosophy at the University of Arizona and Director of the Center for Consciousness Studies, where he organizes the conference "Toward a Science of Consciousness," held every two years in Tucson.

overview). This sort of argument allows you to think that Mary really does experience something surprising when she comes out—but not because there are irreducible *subjective* facts in the world.

An alternative is to deny that Mary will be surprised. Dennett, for example, argues that this story is not the good thought experiment it appears to be, but an intuition pump that lulls us into a vivid image and encourages us to misunderstand its premises. We simply fail to follow the instructions—we fail to allow Mary to know *everything* there is to know about color.

Dennett tells his own ending to the story. Mary's captors release her into the colorful world and, as a trick, present her with a blue banana. Mary is not fooled at all. "Hey," she says, "You tried to trick me! Bananas are yellow, but this one is blue!" (Dennett, 1991: 399). She goes on to explain that because she knew *everything* about color vision, she already knew exactly what impressions yellow and blue objects would make on her nervous system, and exactly what thoughts this would induce in her. This is what it means to know *all* the physical facts. When we readily assume that Mary will be surprised, it is because we have not really followed the instructions.

The imaginary Mary has led to many philosophical tangles, but she can be very helpful in making a tricky dichotomy easier to think about. If you believe that Mary will be surprised when she comes out, then you believe that consciousness, subjective experience, or qualia are something additional to knowledge of the physical world. If you think she will not be surprised, then you believe that knowing all the physical facts tells you everything there is to know—including *what it is like* to experience something.

THE PHILOSOPHER'S ZOMBIE

Imagine there is someone who looks like you, acts like you, speaks like you, and in every detectable way behaves exactly like you, but is not conscious. Perhaps this fake "you" has a silicon brain, has inherited a strange "no qualia" mutation, or has undergone a dangerous operation to remove all traces of consciousness. In any case, in spite of its normal behavior, there is *nothing it is like* to be this creature. There is no view from within. No consciousness. No qualia. This—not some grotesque and slimy half-dead Haitian corpse—is the philosopher's zombie.

The zombie has caused more trouble than Mary. As far as many thinkers are concerned, a zombie is easy to imagine and obviously possible, at least in principle. For example, the American philosopher John Searle (see Profile, Chapter 14) argues that there could be identical behavior in two systems, one of which is conscious and the other totally unconscious (Searle, 1992). It follows that one would be a zombie system.

Chalmers confesses that "the logical possibility of zombies seems . . . obvious to me. A zombie is just something physically identical to me, but which has no conscious experience—all is dark inside." He goes on, "I can detect no internal incoherence; I have a clear picture of what I am conceiving when I conceive of a zombie" (Chalmers, 1996: 96, 99). Chalmers' zombie twin, living on zombie earth, is quite conceivable, he argues.

He suggests we imagine a silicon version of Chalmers who is organized just like the real philosopher and behaves just like him but has silicon chips where the real one has neurons. Many people would expect such a creature to be unconscious (whether or not it would be in fact). Then, he suggests, just replace the chips with neurons in this conception, and you have his zombie twin—totally indistinguishable from the real philosopher, but all dark inside. This works, he argues, because there is nothing in either silicon or biochemistry that conceptually entails consciousness. The idea that zombies are possible, or that consciousness is a kind of optional extra, is "conscious inessentialism."

> **"** *A zombie is just something physically identical to me, but which has no conscious experience—all is dark inside.* **"**
>
> **Chalmers**, 1996: 96

FIGURE 2.4 • Which is which? Can you tell? Can they?

Zombie earth is a planet just like ours, peopled by creatures who behave exactly like us, but who are all zombies. There is nothing it is like to live on zombie earth. In "conversations with zombies," philosopher Todd Moody (1994) uses this thought experiment to reject conscious inessentialism. He imagines the whole zombie earth to be populated by people who use such terms as think, imagine, dream, believe or understand, but who cannot understand any of these terms in the way we do because they have no conscious experience. For example, they might be able to talk about sleep and dreaming because they have learned to use the words appropriately, but they would not have experiences of dreaming as we do. At best they might wake up to a sort of coming-to-seem-to-remember, which they learn to call a dream.

On such an earth, Moody argues, the zombies might get by using our language, but zombie philosophers would be mightily puzzled by some of the things we conscious creatures worry about. For them the problem of other minds, or the way we agonize about qualia and consciousness, would make no sense. They would never initiate such concepts as consciousness or dreams. So zombie philosophy would end up quite different from ours. From this he argues that although the zombies might be individually indistinguishable from conscious creatures, they would still show the mark of zombiehood at the level of culture. At this level, consciousness is not inessential—it makes a difference.

Moody's thought experiment inspired a flurry of objections and counter-arguments from philosophers, psychologists and computer scientists (Sutherland, 1995). One of the main objections is that Moody has broken the rules of the thought experiment. Zombies are defined as being behaviorally indistinguishable from conscious humans so they must be truly indistinguishable. If their philosophy, or the terms they invented, were different, then they would be distinguishable from us and hence not count as zombies. If you really follow the rules, there is nothing left of the difference between human and zombie.

Some philosophers think the whole debate is misguided. Patricia Churchland calls it "a demonstration of the feebleness of thought-experiments" (Churchland, 1996: 404). Dennett thinks it is based on bogus feats of imagination. As they point out, being able to say that you can imagine something counts for nothing. If you know no science, you might say you could imagine water that was not made of H_2O or a hot gas whose molecules were not moving fast. But this would tell us more about your ignorance than about the real world. To help us think clearly about zombies, Dennett introduces the concept of the zimbo.

Imagine there is a simple zombie, some sort of creature (biological or artificial) that can walk about and behave in simple ways appropriate to its needs. Now imagine a more complex kind of zombie. In addition, this complex zombie also

> . . . monitors its own activities, including even its own internal
> activities, in an indefinite upward spiral of reflexivity. I will call such
> a reflective entity a *zimbo*. A zimbo is a zombie that, as a result of

" I take this argument to be a demonstration of the feebleness of thought-experiments. "

Churchland, 1996: 404

CONSCIOUSNESS

self-monitoring, has internal (but unconscious) higher-order informational states that are about its other, lower-order informational states.

(Dennett, 1991: 310)

Imagine a conversation with such a zimbo. For example, we might ask the zimbo about its mental images, or about its dreams or feelings or beliefs. Because it can monitor its own activities, it could answer such questions—in ways that would seem quite natural to us, suggesting that it was conscious just like us. As Dennett concludes, "the zimbo would (unconsciously) believe that it was in various mental states—precisely the mental states it is in position to report about should we ask it questions. *It* would think it was conscious, even if it wasn't!" (ibid.: 311). This is how Dennett comes to make his famous claim that "We're all zombies. Nobody is conscious—not in the systematically mysterious way that supports such doctrines as epiphenomenalism!" (ibid.: 406). What he means is that we are complex self-monitoring zombies—zimboes—that can talk and think about mental images, dreams and feelings; that can marvel at the beauty of a sunset or the light rippling in the trees, but if we think that being conscious is something separable from all of this, we are mistaken.

At its simplest the zombie debate amounts to this. On the one hand, if you believe in the possibility of zombies, then you believe that consciousness is some kind of inessential optional extra to behavior. We might do everything we do either with or without it, and there would be no obvious difference. It is therefore a mystery why we have consciousness at all. On the other hand, if you believe that zombies are not possible, you must believe that anything that could perform all the behaviors we perform would necessarily be conscious. The mystery in this case is not why we have consciousness at all, but why or how consciousness necessarily comes about in creatures who behave like us. There are many different views in each of these camps, but this is the essential distinction.

IS THERE A HARD PROBLEM?

We can now return to Chalmers' hard problem with more mental tools at our disposal. There is no question that the problem of subjectivity is what makes

> *"A zimbo is a zombie that, as a result of self-monitoring, has internal (but unconscious) higher-order informational states that are about its other, lower-order informational states."*
>
> **Dennett**, 1991: 310

studying consciousness both difficult and interesting. Chalmers' distinction between the hard problem and the easy problems of consciousness relates directly to Nagel's question, "What is it like to be a bat?" and gets at the central issues of the two thought experiments just described: "Why aren't we all zombies?" and "What does Mary gain when she emerges from her black and white room?" The way people react to these thought experiments is intimately related to how they deal with the hard problem of subjectivity.

At the risk of oversimplifying I shall divide responses to the hard problem into four categories.

1. THE HARD PROBLEM IS INSOLUBLE

William James long ago wrote about believers in the soul and positivists who wish for a tinge of mystery. They can, he said, continue to believe "that nature in her unfathomable designs has mixed us of clay and flame, of brain and mind, that the two things hang indubitably together and determine each other's being, but how or why, no mortal may ever know" (James, 1890, i: 182).

More recently, Nagel argued that the problem of subjectivity is intractable or hopeless. Not only do we have no solution—we do not even have a conception of what a physical explanation of a mental phenomenon would be. The British philosopher Colin McGinn conceives the problem in terms of a "yawning conceptual divide" (1999: 51), an irreducible duality in the way we come to learn about mind and brain. As he puts it,

> You can look into your mind until you burst, and you will not discover neurons and synapses and all the rest; and you can stare at someone's brain from dawn till dusk and you will not perceive the consciousness that is so apparent to the person whose brain you are so rudely eye-balling.
>
> (McGinn, 1999: 47)

He argues that we are "cognitively closed" with respect to this problem—much as a dog is cognitively closed with respect to reading the newspaper or listening to poetry. However hard the dog tried, it would not be able to master mathematics because it does not have the right kind of brain. Similarly our human kind of intelligence is wrongly designed for understanding consciousness. In McGinn's view we can still study the neural correlates of conscious states (what Chalmers would call the easy problems), but we cannot understand how brains give rise to consciousness in the first place.

American evolutionary psychologist Steven Pinker thinks we can still get on with the job of understanding how the mind works even though our own awareness is "the ultimate tease . . . forever beyond our conceptual grasp" (Pinker, 1997: 565). Nagel, McGinn and Pinker have been called the "new mysterians."

2. SOLVE IT WITH DRASTIC MEASURES

Some people argue that the hard problem can be solved but only with some fundamental new understanding of the universe—what Churchland calls "a real humdinger of a solution" (1996: 40). Chalmers' own solution is in terms of a kind of dualism: a dual-aspect theory of information in which all information has two basic aspects—physical and experiential. So whenever there is conscious experience, it is one aspect of an information state, and the other aspect lies in the physical organization of the brain. In this view we can only understand consciousness when we have a new theory of information.

Others appeal to fundamental physics or to quantum theory for solutions. For example, British mathematician Chris Clarke treats mind as inherently non-local, like some phenomena in quantum physics (1995). In his view, mind is *the* key aspect of the universe and emerges prior to space and time: "mind and the quantum operator algebras are the enjoyed and contemplated aspects of the same thing" (i.e., the subjective and objective aspects) (ibid.: 240). Chalmers' and Clarke's are both dual-aspect theories and are close to panpsychism.

The British mathematician Roger Penrose (1989) argues that consciousness depends on non-algorithmic processes—that is, processes that cannot be carried out by a digital computer, or computed using describable procedures (Chapter 14). With American anesthesiologist Stuart Hameroff, Penrose has developed a theory that treats experience as a quality of space time and relates it to quantum coherence in the microtubules of nerve cells (Hameroff and Penrose, 1996). All these theories assume that the hard problem is soluble but only with a fundamental rethink of the nature of the universe.

3. TACKLE THE EASY PROBLEMS

There are many theories of consciousness that attempt to answer questions about attention, learning, memory or perception, but do not directly address the question of subjectivity. Chalmers gives as an example Crick and Koch's theory of visual binding. This theory uses synchronized oscillations to explain how the different attributes of a perceived object become bound together to make a perceptual whole (Chapter 17). "But why," asks Chalmers, "should synchronized oscillations give rise to a visual experience, no matter how much integration is taking place?" (1995b: 64). He concludes that Crick and Koch's is a theory of the easy problems.

If you are convinced, as Chalmers is, that the hard problem is quite distinct from the easy problems, then many theories of consciousness are like this, including theater metaphors of attention and processing capacity (Chapter 5), evolutionary theories based on the selective advantages of introspection (Chapter 11), and those that deal with the neural correlates of consciousness (Chapter 16). In all these cases one might still ask, "But what about subjectivity? How does this explain the actual phenomenology?"

> "*consciousness is indeed a deep mystery. . . . The reason for this mystery, I maintain, is that our intelligence is wrongly designed for understanding consciousness.*"
>
> **McGinn**, 1999: xi

Francis Crick (see Profile, Chapter 16) himself admits that he might be criticized for saying "almost nothing about qualia—the redness of red—except to brush it to one side and hope for the best" (1994: 256). However, he stresses that the study of consciousness is a scientific problem, and believes that we will get nearer to understanding it fully if we start with something reasonably tractable such as visual binding. To this extent he, and many others who work on the easy problems, come close to arguing that there is no separate hard problem.

4. THERE IS NO HARD PROBLEM

In "There is no hard problem of consciousness," O'Hara and Scutt (1996) give three reasons for ignoring the hard problem. First, we know how to address the easy problems and should start with them. Second, solutions to the easy problems will change our understanding of the hard problem, so trying to solve the hard problem now is premature. Third, a solution to the hard problem would only be of use if we could recognize it as such, and for the moment the problem is not well enough understood.

Churchland (1996) goes further. The hard problem is misconceived, she says. It's a "hornswoggle problem." First, we cannot, in advance, predict which problems will turn out to be easy and which hard. For example, biologists once argued that to understand the basis of heredity, we would have to solve the protein-folding problem first. In fact base-pairing in DNA provided the answer, and the protein-folding problem remains unsolved. So how do we know that explaining subjectivity is so much harder than the "easy" problems? Also, she questions whether the "hard" things—the qualia—are well enough defined to sustain the great division. For example, do eye movements have eye-movement qualia? Are thoughts qualia, or might they be more like auditory imagery or talking to oneself? Finally, the distinction depends on the false intuition that if perception, attention and so on were understood, there would necessarily be something else left out —the something that *we* have and a zombie does not.

Dennett likens the argument to that of a vitalist who insists that even if all the "easy problems" of reproduction, development, growth and metabolism were solved, there would still be the "really hard problem: life itself" (1996a: 4). Dividing the problem of consciousness into the "easy" and "hard" parts is, according to Dennett, "a major misdirector of attention, an illusion-generator" (1996a).

When asked, "But what about the *actual* phenomenology?" Dennett replies "There is no such thing" (1991: 365). This is not because he denies that we are conscious, but because he thinks we misconstrue consciousness. It only *seems* as if there is actual phenomenology—what we need to explain is not the phenomenology itself but how it comes to seem this way.

There is no doubt that the idea of subjectivity—what it's like to be—lies at the heart of the problem of consciousness. Beyond that there is plenty to doubt.

Churchland, P.S. (1996) The Hornswoggle problem. *Journal of Consciousness Studies* 3, 402–8 (reprinted in Shear, 1997: 37–44).

Dennett, D.C. (1991) *Consciousness Explained.* Boston and London: Little, Brown and Co. On Mary, see pages 398–401, and on zombies and zimboes pages 72–3, 280–2 and 310–11.

McGinn, C. (1999) *The Mysterious Flame: Conscious Minds in a Material World.* New York: Basic Books. See Chapter 1 on zombies and the mystery of consciousness.

Nagel, T. (1974) What is it like to be a bat? *Philosophical Review* 83, 435–50. Reprinted with commentary in Hofstadter, D.R. and Dennett, D.C. (1981) *The Mind's I: Fantasies and Reflections on Self and Soul.* London: Penguin, 391–414; and in Nagel, T. (1979) *Mortal Questions.* Cambridge: Cambridge University Press, 165–80.

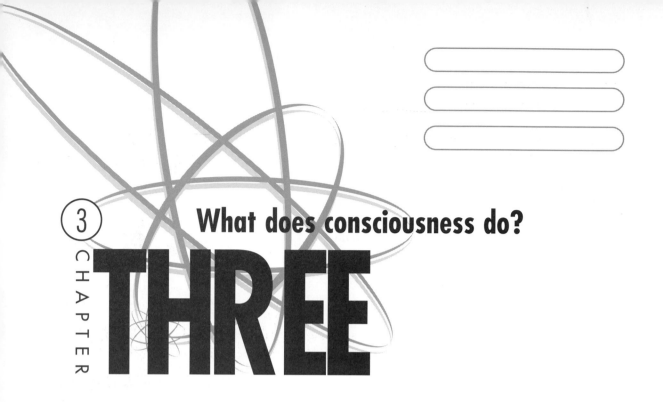

What does consciousness do?

THREE

Patricia Smith Churchland (b. 1943)

Pat Churchland is best known for her 1986 book *Neurophilosophy* and for her outspoken views on the philosophy of mind. Unlike many philosophers, she believes that to understand the mind philosophers must also understand the brain. She grew up on a poor but beautiful farm in British Columbia, where her parents were pioneers—in the genuine sense of the term. She is now Professor of Philosophy at the University of California, San Diego, and is married to the philosopher Paul Churchland. She thinks the hard problem is a "hornswoggle problem" that will go the way of phlogiston or caloric fluid, that zombies demonstrate the feebleness of thought experiments, and that quantum coherence in microtubules is about as good a theory as pixie dust in the synapses.

"The power of consciousness" is a common phrase in everyday use, implying that consciousness itself *does* things, that it has causal efficacy. If this is right, we need to know what consciousness does and how it does it. If not, such phrases are deeply misleading and we need to avoid falling into the traps they set. So what does consciousness do?

Imagine someone throws you a ball and you catch it—or to make things more realistic, crumple up a piece of paper into a ball right now, throw it up in the air and catch it yourself. Do this a few times and ask yourself what the role of consciousness was in this simple skilled action. You seemed conscious of doing the catching, and of the sight of the ball as your hands reached for it, but did the consciousness itself cause anything to happen? Without conscious vision could you have caught the ball?

In doing this simple task, it is easy to imagine that your conscious perception of the ball caused you to catch it. The causal sequence *seems* to be:

1 consciously perceive

2 act on basis of conscious experience.

When you think about it, this is a strange notion. It means two mysterious conversions; first the physical information in nerve firings in the visual system must somehow give rise to a conscious experience, and then the conscious experience must somehow cause more nerve firings to direct the appropriate action. But if consciousness is subjectivity (private experiences, non-physical qualia, or what it's like to be), how can it *cause* a physical action? How can non-physical experiences cause physical firings of nerve cells, or movements of muscles? And where and how does this consciousness bit happen in the brain? We are back to all the central problems of the mind–body debate and the hard problem.

In some ways, the better we understand brain function, the worse this problem becomes. Descartes faced it when he began to think about the human body as a mechanism, and realized that emotions and volition did not easily fit in. He took a dualist way out which, as we have seen, does not solve the problem. In the nineteenth century, as physiologists began to understand reflex arcs and nerve function, the problem loomed even larger. The British philosopher Shadworth Hodgson (1832–1912) declared that feelings, however intensely they may be felt, can

FIGURE 3.1 • Descartes tried to explain reflex responses, like removing your foot from a hot fire, in purely mechanical terms. He believed that the fire affected the skin, pulling a tiny thread which opened a pore in the brain's ventricle and caused animal spirits to flow. But what of conscious responses? It is tempting to think that a signal must come "into consciousness" before we can decide to act on it. But is this right?

have no causal efficacy whatever. He likened events in the nervous system to the stones of a mosaic, and feelings to the colors on the stones. All the work of holding the mosaic in place is done by the stones, not by the colors. In other words, sensations and feelings are epiphenomena. This was similar to Huxley's claim that we humans are "conscious automata" (see Chapter 1). James objected that "to urge the automaton-theory upon us . . . is an *unwarrantable impertinence in the present state of psychology*" (1890, i: 138).

More than a century later, and with far greater knowledge of the nervous system, we still face the same conundrum. The ordinary view is that our subjective feelings and conscious volitions cause our actions. Yet when we study the intricate workings of the brain, there seems to be no room for them to *do* anything. Information enters the nervous system through the senses, flows through numerous parallel pathways to various brain areas, and ultimately affects a person's speech and other actions. But where do the conscious sensations and volitions come in? How could they intervene—or why should they?—in such a continuous physical process.

British psychologist Max Velmans describes this as a causal paradox. "Viewed from a first-person perspective, consciousness appears to be necessary for most forms of complex or novel processing. But viewed from a third-person perspective, consciousness does not appear to be necessary for any form of processing" (2000a: 219). An adequate theory of consciousness, he says, must resolve this paradox without violating either our intuitions about our own experiences or the findings of science.

THE ROLE OF CONSCIOUSNESS IN SKILLED MOVEMENTS

The fastest serves cross the tennis court in a little over half a second, and the ball starts its flight at well over 100 miles per hour. Yet these superserves can be returned with stunning accuracy—at least some of the time. Does the receiver have time for the mysterious double conversion to consciousness and back? Is conscious perception even necessary for such skilled movements?

The answer, oddly enough, is no. Studies of skilled motor actions reveal a dissociation between fast visuomotor control and conscious perception. For example, in some experiments subjects are asked to point at a visual target; then just as they begin to move the target is displaced. If the displacement is made during a voluntary saccade, subjects do not notice the displacement even though they rapidly adjust their arm movement to point correctly at the final position (Bridgeman et al., 1979; Goodale et al., 1986). In other words their behavior is accurately guided by vision even though they do not consciously see the target move. Accurate movements can also be made to stimuli that are not consciously perceived at all. When small visual targets were masked by presenting a larger stimulus 50 milliseconds (ms) later, subjects still responded correctly to the target even though they claimed not to have seen it (Taylor and McCloskey, 1990).

In the case of the tennis serve, or catching your crumpled paper ball, the ball *is* consciously perceived—but when does this occur? Is it in time for the conscious perception to help in the action?

Paulignan et al. (1990) asked subjects to track by hand the displacements of a visual object. They

FIGURE 3.2 • Venus Williams serves at speeds of up to 125 miles per hour, yet opponents manage to respond. Is there time for a visual signal to "enter consciousness," be experienced and then cause a conscious response? Or is this natural way of thinking about our actions misguided?

were able to do this within about 100 ms, but when asked afterward to estimate at which point in the movement they had seen the displacement, they consistently reported that the object jumped just when they were about to touch it—that is, much later than either the actual displacement or their own corrective movement. This informal finding suggested that conscious awareness may come too late to play a causal role in the action.

Castiello et al. (1991) found out more by timing both motor responses and subjective awareness in the same experiment. It is worth considering this experiment in some detail because of the interesting questions it raises.

Subjects sat resting their right hand on a table with the tips of their thumb and index finger touching. At a distance of 35 cm from their hand—at 10°, 20° and 30° to the right of their midline—stood three translucent dowels, any of which could be lit up from below by computer-controlled LEDs. The task was to watch for a dowel lighting up and then to grasp and lift it. In addition subjects were asked to shout "Tah!" as soon as they saw a light. Infra-red emitting diodes were fixed to their arms to record their precise movements, a switch detected the start of their hand movements, and a microphone near their mouth detected their calls.

A

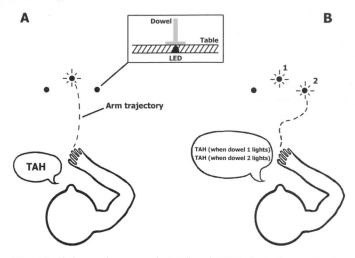

FIGURE 3.3 • The layout in the experiment by Castiello et al. (1991), showing the arm trajectories both when the lit dowel stays the same and when it changes.

B In the first session a single dowel was lit many times, and motor and vocal reaction times were measured. In a second session of 100 trials the central dowel was always lit first. In control trials it stayed lit, but in 20 percent of the trials, as soon as the hand started to move, the light was unexpectedly shifted to a different dowel. Subjects were asked to shout out when they first saw the central dowel light up and again if they saw the light shift. To deal with concerns that the two responses might interfere with each other, several control experiments were run. These confirmed that when the "Tah!" and the hand movements were produced in the same trial, they took the same length of time as they did when performed separately.

The results showed that in the perturbed trials the initial reaction time to move the hand was about 300 ms (as it was in control trials), but then a motor correction could be detected about 100–110 ms after the light moved. On these trials the subjects shouted twice; when the central dowel lit up, the vocal reaction time was 375 ms (the same as in control trials); when the light moved, it was, on average, 420 ms.

The authors interpreted their results as follows. In the simple case of reaching for the dowel, subjects' hands started to move about 325 ms after the dowel lit up. This time corresponds, at least in part, to the time needed to establish the motor program for accurate reaching. When the light shifted just as the movement began, only about 100–110 ms was needed to correct the direction of the movement. In these cases the vocal response came 420 ms after the light moved. That is, the vocal response occurred on average 315 ms after the movement correction began. They were convinced that this late vocal response was related to the subjects' conscious awareness of the change, partly because it fit with the fact that in this, as in the previous experiment by Paulignan et al. (1990), subjects reported that they only saw the dowel changing its position when they were already completing their corrected movement, not when they were initiating it. The authors conclude that "neural activity must be processed during a significant and quantifiable amount of time before it can give rise to conscious experience" (Castiello et al., 1991: 2639).

There are some potential problems with this conclusion. We know that fast reaction times can be obtained without awareness, so could the shout really have been initiated before the subject became consciously aware of seeing the light move? If so conscious awareness of the light might have come even later than estimated. Alternatively it might have come earlier and the full 420 ms would have been needed to produce the response. We cannot know because this method does not allow us to time precisely the "moment of awareness."

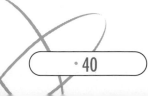

Perhaps we should be even more critical and question the very notion of there being a "moment of awareness" or a time at which the light comes "into consciousness." Problems with the idea of "arriving in consciousness" and with making such timings are discussed again in Chapter 5.

In spite of these doubts about timing, the results of these experiments suggest a dissociation between fast motor reactions and conscious perception. One explanation is that the two are based on entirely different systems in the brain.

Milner and Goodale (1995) suggest a functional dissociation between two vision systems: visual perception and visuomotor control. They map this onto the two neural streams in the visual system: the ventral and dorsal streams. These two streams have often been described as being concerned with object vision and spatial vision, respectively, or the "what" and "where" of vision (Ungerleider and Mishkin, 1982). Instead, Milner and Goodale argue for a distinction based on two fundamentally different tasks that the brain has to carry out—fast visuomotor control and less urgent visual perception.

Much of their evidence comes from patients with brain damage. For example, one patient, D.F., has visual form agnosia. She is unable to recognize the forms or shapes of objects by sight, even though her low-level vision and color vision appear to be intact. She cannot name simple line drawings or recognize letters and digits, nor can she copy them, even though she can produce letters correctly from dictation and can recognize objects by touch. She can, however, reach out and grasp everyday objects (objects that she cannot recognize) with remarkable accuracy.

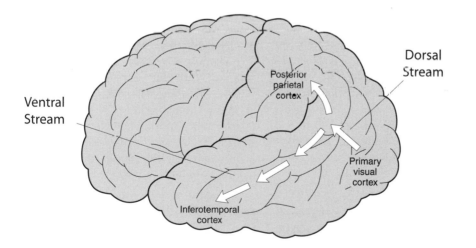

FIGURE 3.4 • The ventral and dorsal visual streams. Ungerleider and Mishkin called them the "what" and "where" streams. Milner and Goodale suggest that they carry out visual perception and visuomotor control, respectively.

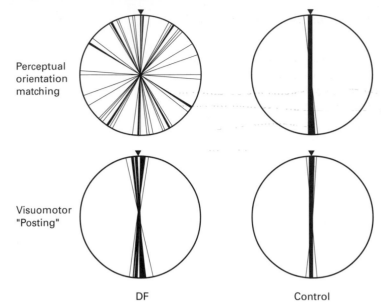

Perceptual orientation matching

Visuomotor "Posting"

DF

Control

FIGURE 3.5 • Polar plots illustrating the orientation of a hand-held card in two tasks of orientation discrimination, for D.F. and an age-matched control subject. On the perceptual matching task, subjects were required to match the orientation of the card with that of a slot placed in different orientations in front of them. In the posting task, they were required to reach out and insert the card into the slot. The correct orientation has been normalized to the vertical (after Milner and Goodale, 1995).

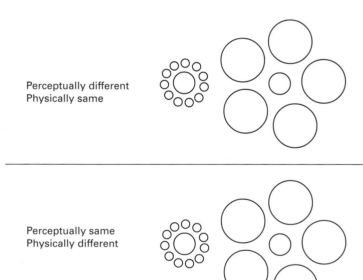

Perceptually different Physically same

Perceptually same Physically different

FIGURE 3.6 • Diagram showing the "Titchener circles" illusion. In the top figure the two central discs are the same actual size, but appear different; in the bottom figure, the disc surrounded by an annulus of large circles has been made somewhat larger in size in order to appear approximately equal in size to the other central disc (after Milner and Goodale, 1995).

One experiment with D.F. reveals this extraordinary split between motor performance and awareness. She was shown a vertically mounted disk in which a slot was randomly cut at 0°, 45°, 90° or 135°. When asked to draw the orientation of the slot, or to adjust a comparison slot to the same angle, she was quite unable to do so. However, when given a piece of card, she could quickly and accurately post it through the slot—a task requiring accurate alignment. How can this be? How can she be unaware of the angle of the slot and yet able to post the card into it? The answer, according to Milner and Goodale, is that she has lost much of the ventral stream that leads to visual perception but retains the dorsal stream needed for accurate visuomotor control.

The same dissociation between perception and motor control was claimed by Aglioti et al. (1995) using normal subjects tricked by a visual illusion. Thin discs were made to look different sizes by surrounding them with rings of larger or smaller circles, as in the Titchener illusion. Subjects had to pick up the left-hand disc if the two discs appeared equal in size and the right-hand disc if they appeared different, for many different sizes, and apparent sizes, of discs. The aperture of subjects' finger–thumb grip was measured as they did so, allowing motor performance and a perceptual decision to be measured in the same task. Subjects saw the usual size illusion (as shown by their choice of disc), but their grip fit the actual disc. Apparently the visuomotor system was not fooled, although the perceptual system was. It should be noted that subsequent experiments have challenged these findings (Franz et al., 2000), but according to Milner and Goodale, these experiments show that sometimes "what we think we 'see' is not what guides our actions" (1995: 177).

These studies underline the important difference between processing for perception and processing for motor control. This distinction makes sense in evolutionary terms because the constraints on the two systems are so different. Fast and accurate responses to changing visual stimuli are essential for catching prey, avoiding dangers, and even basic tasks like standing upright. The dorsal stream itself is probably modular, with different subsystems controlling these different kinds of skilled movement. By contrast, object identification can wait. Accuracy rather than speed may be more important when planning future actions and making strategic decisions. This may explain why we have two different visual systems for these different kinds of tasks. The result is that a great deal of what we do is done fast and accurately, and independently of what we consciously perceive.

Can we now conclude that one of the streams is conscious while the other is a zombie, as Ramachandran (see Profile, Chapter 6) and Blakeslee (1998) claim? Kanwisher suggests that "the neural correlates of the *contents* of visual awareness are represented in the ventral pathway, whereas the neural correlates of more general-purpose *content independent* processes . . . are found primarily in the dorsal pathway" (2001: 98). Note that this formulation makes several assumptions: that consciousness has contents, that the contents are representations, and that there is a difference between some areas or processes that are conscious and those that are not. We shall question every one of these assumptions in due course.

We can now return to that crumpled paper ball. These findings suggest that conscious perception of the ball depends on processing that is too slow to play a role in guiding the fast catch. So although the causal sequence *seems* to be:

1 consciously perceive

2 act on basis of conscious experience.

we now know that it cannot be. This conclusion should make us think twice before making assumptions about what consciousness does and does not do based on the way it feels. Nevertheless we do often make judgments about whether things were done consciously or not. It may be helpful to try to sort out what this means.

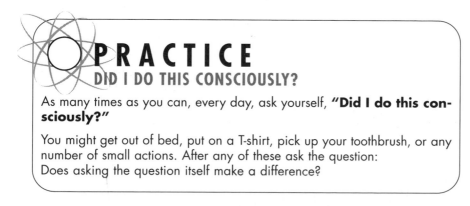

PRACTICE
DID I DO THIS CONSCIOUSLY?

As many times as you can, every day, ask yourself, **"Did I do this consciously?"**

You might get out of bed, put on a T-shirt, pick up your toothbrush, or any number of small actions. After any of these ask the question:
Does asking the question itself make a difference?

CONSCIOUS AND UNCONSCIOUS ACTIONS

There is no doubt that we seem to do some things consciously and others unconsciously. On this basis we can divide actions into five types: (a) are always unconscious; (b) can be made conscious; (c) start out being done consciously but with practice become unconscious; (d) can be done either way; (e) are always done consciously.

(a) Are always unconscious: so, for example, I can consciously wiggle my toes or sing a song, but I cannot consciously grow my hair or increase my blood sugar level. Spinal reflexes that depend on neural connections outside of the brain are always unconscious, and much of visuomotor control is carried out too quickly for consciousness to play a role. We shall encounter other examples in Chapter 19.

(b) Some actions that are normally carried out unconsciously can be brought under conscious control by giving feedback of their effects, or "biofeedback": for example, if a visual or auditory display is provided to indicate when your heart beats faster or slower, when your left hand is warmer than your right, or when your palms sweat more, you can learn to control these variables, even when obvious actions that might produce the changes, such as clenching your hands or jumping up and down, are prevented. The sensation is rather odd. You know you can do it, and feel in control, but you have no idea *how* you do it. This should remind us that the same is true of most of what we do. We may consciously open the door but have no idea how all the intricate muscular activity required to turn the handle is coordinated. The whole action seems to be done consciously, while the details remain unconscious.

(c) Many skilled actions are initially learned with much conscious effort: then, with practice, they come easily and smoothly. While biofeedback moves actions into conscious control, automatization does the reverse. You probably first learned to ride a bicycle with the utmost conscious concentration. Learning any motor skill is like this, whether it is skateboarding or skiing, using a mouse or keyboard, or learning the movements in yoga or t'ai chi. After complete automatization, paying conscious attention can even be counter-productive, and you fall off your bike or find you cannot even walk normally.

(d) Many such skilled actions, once well learned, can be done either way: sometimes I make a cup of tea with utmost mindfulness, but often I find I have put the kettle on, warmed the pot, found the milk, made the tea and carried it back to my study without, apparently, being conscious of any of those actions. The classic example is driving a car. Every driver must have had the experience of arriving at a familiar destination without apparently having been conscious of the journey (see Chapter 5). Here we have detailed, complex and potentially life-threatening decisions being made correctly without, apparently, any conscious awareness.

(e) Some actions seem always to be done consciously: for example, when I try to remember a forgotten name or phone number, I seem to struggle consciously, but dialing a familiar number comes automatically. When I have to

make a difficult moral decision, I seem to be far more conscious than when deciding what clothes to put on. It is tempting to say that these kinds of thinking or decision making *require* consciousness.

Here, then, is the rub. If the same action is carried out on one occasion consciously and on another occasion unconsciously, what makes the difference? Obviously there is a phenomenal difference—they *feel* different—but why?

We must avoid jumping to unwarranted conclusions. For example, we might start by observing that we made a difficult moral decision *consciously* while we made the tea *unconsciously*; jump from there to the conclusion that the former *requires* consciousness, while the latter does not; and finally jump to the conclusion that consciousness itself *does* the deciding. But this is not the only interpretation. Another possibility is that the processes involved in making difficult moral decisions also give rise to the impression of their being done consciously, while those involved in making tea do not. Whenever we compare actions done with and without consciousness, we must remember these two interpretations. This is relevant to perception (Chapter 4), the Cartesian theater (Chapter 5), the neural correlates of conscious and unconscious processes (Chapter 16), intuition and unconscious processing (Chapter 19), and the nature of free will (Chapter 9), but for now the question concerns the causal efficacy of consciousness.

The question is this—what is the difference between actions performed consciously and those done unconsciously? If you believe that consciousness has causal efficacy (i.e., *does* things), then you will probably answer that consciousness caused the former actions but not the latter. In this case you must have some explanation of how subjective experiences can cause physical events. If you do not think that consciousness can *do* anything, then you must explain the obvious difference some other way. Theories of consciousness differ considerably in their answers, as we can see from the following examples.

> *"to urge the automaton-theory upon us . . . is an unwarrantable impertinence in the present state of psychology"*
>
> **James**, 1890, Vol. 1: 138

DID I DO THIS CONSCIOUSLY?

THEORIES
CAUSAL AND NON-CAUSAL THEORIES

Some theories have a clear causal role for consciousness—they claim that it causes brain events. The most obvious (and honest) of these are dualist. Substance dualists maintain, as did Descartes, that consciousness is something separate from the physical body. Yet if consciousness is to have any effects (including being known about), there must be interaction between the two realms of mind and matter. As we have seen, Descartes located this interaction in the pineal gland.

Two centuries after Descartes, in his *Principles of Mental Physiology*, William Benjamin Carpenter (1813–85) described another form of interactionism. In one direction physiological activity excites sensational consciousness, while in the other direction sensations, emotions, ideas and volitions that attain sufficient intensity liberate the nerve-force with which the appropriate part of the brain is charged. He admitted, however, that we know nothing of how the physical change is translated into a psychical change.

The only modern theory of this kind is the dualist interactionism of Popper and Eccles. Their "self-conscious mind" is an independent entity that is "actively engaged in reading out from the multitude of active centres at the highest level of brain activity, namely the liaison areas of the dominant cerebral hemisphere" (1977: 362). The "liaison areas" are those "which have linguistic and ideational performance or which have polymodal inputs," such as areas 39 and 40 and the prefrontal lobes (ibid.: 363). There is a constant two-way interaction between the two worlds of mind and brain. In one direction, the scanning self-conscious mind reads out neural events in the brain and integrates them into a unified experience. In the other, the self-conscious mind acts on a large area of the brain, causing activity that eventually homes in on the motor pyramidal cells and brings about the action that it desired.

This theory provides a simple and unambiguous answer to the question raised here. The difference between the same action being carried out either consciously or unconsciously is that in the first case the self-conscious mind had a desire or intention and caused the brain to carry out that intention by interacting with it. In the second, the brain processes acted alone without interference from the self-conscious mind.

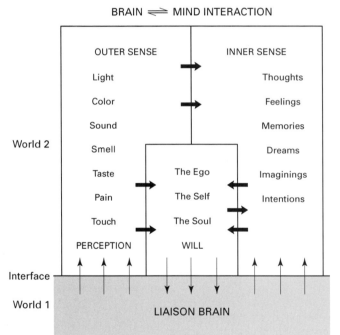

FIGURE 3.7 • How the brain interacts with the mind, according to Popper and Eccles. The area of the liaison brain is supposed to be enormous, with a hundred thousand or more open modules (after Popper and Eccles, 1977).

There are serious, and obvious, problems with this theory. Most important, it is all very well to hypothesize that the non-physical mind liaises with the physical brain in special liaison areas, but as in any dualist theory the sticking point is the nature of this interaction, and Popper and Eccles have no real answer. In later work Eccles (1994) proposes that all mental events and experiences are composed of "psychons," and that every psychon interacts with one dendron in the brain. Although the interaction is thus localized, the "chasm" remains. As far as any physical description is concerned, the influence of the self-conscious mind is magic. For this reason most scientists and philosophers reject this theory and all other dualist theories.

Some go to the other extreme and reject outright the idea that consciousness can *cause* events. The most extreme rejection is probably eliminative materialism, which denies the very existence of consciousness. Epiphenomenalism (see Chapter 1) accepts the existence of consciousness but denies that it has any effects. In its traditional form this is a somewhat strange idea, implying a causal chain of physical events leading from sensory input to behavior, with consciousness produced as a by-product that has no further effects at all. As we have seen, one problem here is that if consciousness had no effects, we could

• C O N S C I O U S N E S S

not even talk about it. Few people support epiphenomenalism in this sense, but many people use the word in rather looser ways, often to imply that they do not think that *subjectivity* itself is causally effective. This is compatible with some of the most popular theories of consciousness, although there is often confusion about exactly what people mean by consciousness when they say this.

REPRESENTATIONAL THEORIES

In the philosophy of mind there are two main representational theories: "higher-order perception" (HOP) theory and "higher-order thought" (HOT) theory. According to HOP theory, being conscious of a mental state means monitoring first-order mental states in a quasi-perceptual way—with something analogous to an "inner eye." According to HOT theories it means having a thought about the first-order state (Rosenthal, 1995), so a mental state is conscious if the person has a higher-order thought to the effect that they are conscious of being in that state. For example, my perception of a red flash is only conscious if accompanied by a HOT that I am seeing a red flash. HOT theory readily answers our questions. What is the difference between actions performed consciously and those done unconsciously? Answer: there are HOTs about them. No special place or kind of neuron is required, only that the brain must construct HOTs. There is no need to explain how consciousness *causes* things because although HOTs have effects, consciousness is not something separate from them. Indeed a HOT may take time to construct and so may happen *after* an action that is experienced as performed consciously, which fits with the evidence discussed above. However, such theories face difficulties, such as denying consciousness to creatures incapable of HOT and dealing with states, such as meditation (see Chapter 26), which do not seem to involve thought of any kind (Seager, 1999).

FUNCTIONALISM

Functionalism, like so many other words to do with consciousness, is used in many different and sometimes conflicting ways. Within the philosophy of mind it is the view that mental states are functional states. So, for example, if someone is in pain, the pain is understood in terms of the input from the damage done, the output of behaviors such as crying or rubbing the wound, and other mental states such as the desire for the pain to go away, which can also be specified functionally. This means that any system that executed exactly the same functions as a human being in pain would also be in pain.

The implications for consciousness are not obvious. Perhaps the most common view is that functionalism works well for explaining mental states, such as desires and beliefs, but cannot deal with phenomenal consciousness. In this view functionalism cannot answer questions about whether consciousness does anything or what difference there is between conscious and unconscious actions.

However, the term is also used, especially in discussions of artificial intelligence (see Chapter 13) to mean that any system that could carry out exactly the same functions as a conscious system would also, necessarily, be conscious. So, for example, suppose I am conscious when I chat with you on the phone and tell you how devastated I was when my boyfriend left me. A functionalist might say that any other system (robot, artificial life system, putative zombie) that was functionally organized so that it could chat in exactly the same way would also be conscious. In this view, the functions carried out by the system are what matters, and there is no consciousness separate from these abilities and performances. When we ask what is the difference between actions carried out consciously and those carried out unconsciously, the functionalist would answer in terms of the different functions involved. However, most theories of this kind do not explain how or why functions can *be* phenomenal consciousness or how to explain qualia.

We have already met a theory that deals in an unusual way with this issue: Dennett's zimbo. The zimbo is conscious because in order to do what it does (chat like us, move like us, etc.), it must have a "higher-order informational states that are about its other, lower-order informational states." To be conscious, in this view, is to have these informational states, and any creature that was organized this way would think it was conscious, and say it was conscious, just as we do. But it would have no qualia because qualia do not exist. In this view there is no fundamental difference between phenomenal and access consciousness (Dennett, 1995d).

GLOBAL WORKSPACE THEORY (GWT)

GWT was first explicated by American psychologist Bernard Baars (see Profile, Chapter 8) who proposes (1988) that the cognitive system is built on a global workspace or blackboard architecture, analogous to a stage in the theater of the mind (see Chapter 5). Unconscious processors compete for access to the bright spotlight of attention that shines on the stage, from where information is broadcast globally to the unconscious audience. It is this global broadcast that constitutes consciousness.

According to Baars consciousness is a supremely functional biological adaptation. It is a kind of gateway—"a facility for *accessing, disseminating, and exchanging information,* and for *exercising global coordination and control*" (1997a: 7). He lists nine functions for consciousness and describes it as "essential in integrating perception, thought, and action, in adapting to novel circumstances, and in providing information to a self-system" (ibid.: x). He firmly rejects the idea "that

SELF-ASSESSMENT QUESTIONS

○ What potential problems are there with the idea that consciousness causes our actions?

○ What kinds of evidence suggest a dissociation between visuomotor control and visual perception?

○ Does the experiment by Castiello et al. prove that consciousness comes too late to play a role in fast-reaching movements?

○ How do dualist theories explain the interaction between consciousness and the brain?

○ What is functionalism and can it explain phenomenal consciousness?

○ What are the two main kinds of representational theory of consciousness?

○ What functions does consciousness have according to Global Workspace Theory?

consciousness simply has no causal role to play in the nervous system" (ibid.: 165).

In this theory, actions that are performed consciously are shaped by conscious feedback, while unconscious actions are not. For example, you might unconsciously make a speech error, but when you consciously hear the mistake, you can put it right because consciousness creates global access to further unconscious resources.

Baars asks, "how would you use consciousness, as such, to survive, eventually to pass on your genes?" (1997a: 157). He gives the following example. Imagine that, as you are reading this book, you become aware of a strange, fetid, animal smell, the noise of heavy hooves, and hot breath down the back of your neck. Although reluctant to stop reading, you suddenly have the wild thought that there might be a large animal in the room. You turn your head, see the large angry ferocious bull, and leap from your chair. Consciousness, at least in our evolutionary past, would have saved us from danger. The problem with this interpretation lies in the timing. The results of all the experiments discussed above suggest that you would have leapt out of that chair long before you could have consciously thought of danger.

Baars claims that "the famous gap between mind and body is a bit of a myth" (1997a: x). Yet calling it a myth does not make it go away. His theory might be understood as a description of how integration and global control of actions is achieved in a complex brain, but then there is no need to bring in subjective experience as well. Once you do, the gap reappears, and with it an obvious question. Why is global availability equivalent to subjective experience, as Baars and others claim (Dehaene and Naccache, 2001)? We still do not know why there is *something it is like* to be a system with a global workspace or what it means to say that consciousness *causes* integration and global control.

We started with the simple idea that consciousness causes some of our actions, but the theories and experiments discussed reveal serious problems with this common-sense notion. They should make us wake up every time we read that consciousness directs attention or gives us the ability to introspect; that it drives our emotions and our higher feelings; or that it helps us assign priorities or retrieve long-term memories. Comments such as this are deeply embedded in our ordinary language about consciousness, and can easily be found in the writings of psychologists, cognitive scientists and others. It is not obvious which, if any, of them is true.

> *"from a third-person perspective, consciousness appears to be epiphenomenal . . . from a first-person perspective, it seems absurd to deny the role of consciousness in mental life"*
>
> **Velmans**, 2000: 218

READING

Castiello, U., Paulignan, Y. and Jeannerod, M. (1991) Temporal dissociation of motor responses and subjective awareness: a study in normal subjects. *Brain* 114, 2639–55.

Milner, A.D. and Goodale, M.A. (1995) *The Visual Brain in Action.* Oxford: Oxford University Press, 1–2, 122–33.

Velmans, M. (2000) *Understanding Consciousness.* London and Philadelphia: Routledge. For a brief explanation of the causal paradox see pages 217–19.

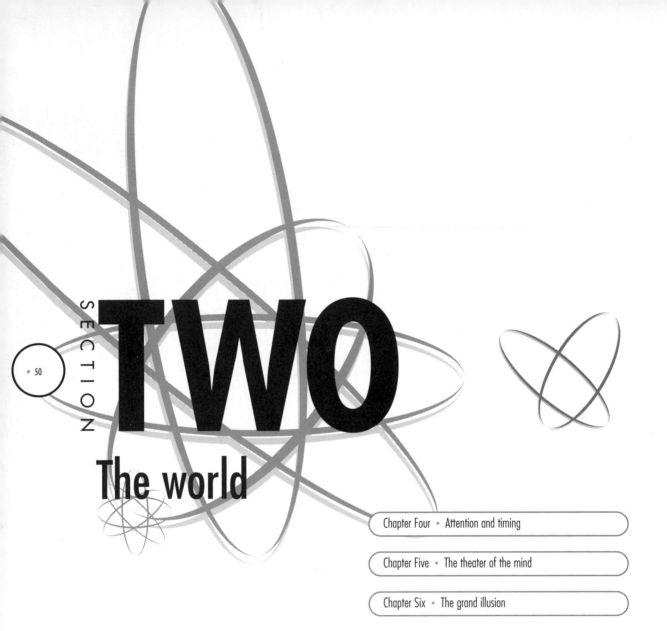

SECTION

TWO

The world

Attention and timing

Which comes first, your reaction to a noise or your awareness of it? Does consciousness *cause* attention to be directed, or is consciousness the *effect* of paying attention (or perhaps neither)? William James asked this question more than a century ago. Indeed he is responsible for what must be the most frequently quoted passage ever on attention.

> Every one knows what attention is. It is the taking possession by the mind, in clear and vivid form, of one out of what seem several simultaneously possible objects or trains of thought. Focalization, concentration, of consciousness are of its essence. It implies withdrawal from some things in order to deal effectively with others.
> (James, 1890, Vol. i: 403–4)

The very familiarity of the concept of attention can make it hard to think about clearly, but perhaps we should start with how it feels. The metaphor of the "spotlight of attention" comes easily to mind because paying attention does feel this way—as though there is a bright light pointed here and there, lighting up some parts of the world and leaving the rest in semi-darkness. Indeed this metaphor has found a place in many theories (Lindsay and Norman, 1977; Baars, 1988). Not only that, but it feels as though we can consciously direct our own spotlight to pay attention to what we choose. As James puts it, "*My experience is what I agree to attend to*. Only those items which I *notice*

William James (1842–1910)

William James was born in New York, the eldest of five children, one of whom was novelist Henry James. When the children were young, their wealthy father took the family traveling all over Europe, educating them inter-mittently along the way. James continued his trans-atlantic travels most of his life, speaking several languages fluently, and getting to know the foremost scholars and scientists of his day. At 18 he wanted to be a painter; then after long bouts of despair and depres-sion, studied medicine at Harvard, where he eventually taught physiology, psychology and philosophy. He married in 1878 and was a devoted family man.

His *Principles of Psychology* (1890) has been called "the best-known book in all psychology" (Gregory, 1987). It made him famous for such phrases as "the stream of consciousness" and "the specious present." His other books include *The Varieties of Religious Experience* (1902) and *Pragmatism* (1907). He was a firm believer in free will and a personal spiritual force.

FIGURE 4.1 • Attention feels like a searchlight in the attic, lighting up now the objects right in front of us, and then some long forgotten memory from the darkest corner of our mind.

shape my mind—without selective interest, experience is an utter chaos" (James, ibid.: 402).

Sometimes great effort is needed. As Crick points out "Everyone knows the common meaning of the phrase 'you're not paying attention'" (1994: 59). And James imagines "one whom we might suppose at a dinner-party resolutely to listen to a neighbor giving him insipid and unwelcome advice in a low voice, whilst all around the guests were loudly laughing and talking about exciting and interesting things" (James, ibid.: 420).

There have been thousands of experiments and numer-ous theories of attention. For example, in the nineteenth century, Helmholtz, Hering and Wundt were among the physiologists and psychologists who experimented with attention. In the 1950s many ingenious experiments with dichotic listening (two different streams of sound played to each ear) showed that normally only one stream can be tracked at once, but certain kinds of stimuli can break through from the non-attended ear, and others can have effects on behavior without being consciously heard. If the message being listened to moves from one ear to the other, people usually follow the meaning and don't even notice they have swapped ears.

At that time most theories treated attention as a bottleneck, with preconscious sensory filters needed to decide what should be let through to the deeper stages of processing (Broadbent, 1958). This makes some sense because clearly the brain does have a limited capacity for detailed processing, and also because the brain is a massively parallel system that produces serial outputs, such as speech and sequential actions. So somehow the many parallel processes have to be brought together, or selected, to ensure that a sensible serial output occurs.

The main problem with such theories was that to cope with the evidence, the proposed filters became more and more complicated, until the pre-attentive processing began to look as complex as the deeper processing it was supposed to provide access to. These models then gave way to those based on more subtle ways of allocating processing resources. The spotlight of attention was then seen as less like a narrow beam or single bottleneck and more like the outcome of many mechanisms by which the nervous system organizes its resources, giving more to some items (or features or senses) than others. But for some people the whole topic was becoming so unwieldy that perhaps the very concept of attention was at fault (Pashler, 1998).

Attention and memory are closely related and some theories of attention treat short-term memory, with its limited capacity, as the relevant resource to be competed for. In other words, being attended to is equivalent to getting into short-term memory. Other theories do not assume this equivalence, and there are numerous other ways in which attention and memory are connected. In fact theories of attention are relevant to almost every aspect of brain function, including the binding of separate features into whole objects (see Chapter 17), but here we must concentrate on the relationship between attention and consciousness.

ATTENTION AND CONSCIOUSNESS

Some authors equate consciousness with the results of paying attention, as James did when he said that "*My experience is what I agree to attend to*" (James, 1890, i: 402). This was also true of early theories of attention which tended, when they mentioned consciousness at all, to say that the filters and bottlenecks allowed information "into consciousness." A modern review of consciousness describes attention as "the sentry at the gate of consciousness" (Zeman, 2001: 1274). Another claims that "What is at the focus of our attention enters our consciousness. What is outside the focus of attention remains preconscious or unconscious" (Velmans, 2000a: 255). Others point out that even if attention controls access to consciousness, it is not the same as consciousness (Baars, 1997a); "attention is not sufficient for consciousness and is not the same as consciousness" (Damasio, 1999: 18).

Based on the phenomenon of "inattentional blindness" (Chapter 6), psychologist Arien Mack makes the strong claim that "there is no conscious perception without attention" (Mack and Rock, 1998: 10). Others are more cautious. For example, Crick says only that "Consciousness is closely associated with attention" (1994: 15). For all this variation, there are two main kinds of connection that are made between consciousness and attention. First is the idea that when something is attended to it is "in" consciousness. This may or may not be equated with being "in" short-term memory, or being available to verbal processing and therefore reportable. This question of what it means for something to be 'in' consciousness is discussed in more detail in Chapter 5.

Second, there is the idea that consciousness can direct attention, or even that directing attention is the major function of consciousness. This fits with the

"no one knows what attention is, and . . . there may even not be an 'it' there to be known about"

Pashler, 1998: 1

"Every one knows what attention is."

James, 1890, i: 403

common-sense notions that we can consciously choose what to attend to, that conscious decisions about priorities affect what we attend to, and that paying attention can be hard work. However, it is another of those ideas that gets more problematic the closer we look. So does, or can, consciousness direct attention? This has really been the central question about consciousness and attention for more than a century.

In 1890 James put the question this way: "Is voluntary attention a resultant or a force?" He imagined a single brain cell played upon from within either "by other brain-cells, or by some spiritual force" (ibid. i: 447). If brain cells alone were involved, then attention would be merely an *effect* of material events in the brain, rather than a *cause*. So he labeled the two theories the "effect theory" and the "cause theory." He was convinced that volition is nothing but the directing of attention and is central to what we mean by self. So, for him, the answer to this question was vital for thinking about the nature of self and of free will.

James presented the strongest case he could for the effect theory, even covering cases where we make an effort of will, which seem the most difficult to explain in purely mechanistic terms. Then, having surveyed all the evidence available, he came down on the side of cause theory. His reasons were not scientific; indeed he concluded that no amount of evidence could really help decide between the two, and therefore he made his decision on ethical grounds—his decision being to count himself among those who believe in a spiritual force. That force was the genuinely causal force of conscious, personal will.

More than a century later the evidence has changed dramatically, but the question has not. So I shall try to do the same job as James did in light of what we know now.

PRACTICE
DID *I* CONSCIOUSLY ATTEND TO THAT, OR DID *IT* GRAB MY ATTENTION?

As many times as you can, every day, ask yourself **"Did *I* consciously attend to that, or did *it* grab my attention?"**

You might begin by asking the question whenever you realize that you are attending to something and don't know why. With practice you may find that you can do it for much of the time. This way you can learn to watch the process and come to appreciate how and when your attention shifts. Make a note of the effect this has on your awareness.

DIRECTING ATTENTION

Imagine you are sitting in a lecture and the door opens. You notice the disturbance and turn around to see who it is. What has happened? If someone asked you, you might say, "I heard the door open and so I turned around to see who it was." The causal sequence seems to be:

1 consciously hear sound

2 turn around to look.

It *feels* as though our conscious perception of the noise *caused* us to pay attention. Is this right? Does conscious perception *cause* attention to be directed to a specific place? If it does not always do so, can it ever do so?

Attention is often directed involuntarily—for example, when we react quickly to something like a loud noise, or our name being called, and only realize afterward that we have done so. In fact the involuntary control of attention is a complex and important process that depends on many specialized systems in the brain.

An obvious example is the control of eye movements. In humans the fovea has much higher acuity than the rest of the retina, and therefore the eyes must be directed toward important objects or events. If a bright, salient or moving object is detected in the periphery, the eyes quickly turn to bring that part of the visual world onto the fovea. This must be done very fast to be useful to a moving, behaving animal. Not surprisingly, much of the control is coordinated by parts of the dorsal stream, in particular the posterior parietal cortex, and we are not consciously aware of it.

In addition the eyes do not stay still but make saccades several times a second. Saccades can be voluntary but need not be; we make them all the time whether aware of doing so or not. Saccadic eye movements are controlled largely by cells in the superior colliculus.

In "smooth pursuit" the eyes can track a moving object, keeping its image on roughly the same part of the fovea. Interestingly, this kind of eye movement cannot be made voluntarily. It needs an actual moving target. One study with a cortically blind man showed that although movement is necessary for accurate pursuit, awareness of the movement is not. This patient could not see movement at all, but was tested by being surrounded with a large moving stripe display. He denied having any visual experience of motion, yet his eyes behaved relatively normally in tracking the moving stripes, making slow pursuit movements followed by rapid flicks to catch up (Milner and Goodale, 1995: 84).

Moving the eyes is not the whole story because the head and body move as well, so there must be mechanisms for coordinating all these movements. Some systems use information about the motor output for body and eye movements to maintain a stable relationship to the world, even while the body, head and eyes are all moving. Some control systems appear to be based on retinocentric coordinates—keeping objects stable on the retina—while others use craniocentric coordinates—keeping the world stable with respect to the position of the head. Although we can voluntarily control body and head movements, and some kinds of eye movements, most of the time these complex control systems operate very fast and quite unconsciously. These are just some of the mechanisms that would be involved when you turned around to see who was coming in through the door.

Directing the eyes toward particular objects is not, however, equivalent to paying attention to that object. As Helmholtz (1821–94) long ago demonstrated, it is possible to look directly at one object or place, and pay attention somewhere else; a skill now called "covert attention scanning." Different systems are now thought to be involved in these two kinds of attention: probably the superior colliculus and frontal eye fields are associated with switches of gaze, while neurons in the posterior parietal cortex are implicated in shifts of attention occurring independently of gaze. Rizzolati and his colleagues (1994) have suggested a "premotor theory" of selective spatial attention. In this theory, attending to a particular position in space means the facilitation of subsets of neurons involved in preparing to make visually guided actions directed toward that part of space. So if you were looking at a person straight in front of you but attending to something happening off to your right, the neurons that would be activated would be the same ones that would be used if you were to swivel around to the right or reach out and grasp something there.

Another form of involuntary visual attention occurs in perceptual "pop-out." Imagine you are asked to search for a particular stimulus which is displayed among a lot of slightly different stimuli, say an upside-down L among a lot of Ls. For many such displays there is no alternative but a serial search, looking at each item in turn to identify it. In other cases the difference is so obvious to the visual system that the target just pops out—for example, when the target L is horizontal or is a different color. In these cases the search seems to be parallel and does not take longer if the total number of items increases. An obvious item like this can also act as a distractor, slowing down the search for other items—another example of how attention can be grabbed involuntarily.

These examples show that much of selective attention is controlled unconsciously. But this does not preclude the possibility that under other circumstances we really do consciously experience something first and then decide to pay closer attention to it. Returning to our example of the person coming into the room, could this be such a case? Might we actually experience the sight or sound of the disturbance first and then consciously decide to turn around and look? A crucial issue here is the time these processes take. In the previous chapter we met the idea that consciousness takes some time to build up. It would be helpful to know just what, if anything, this means.

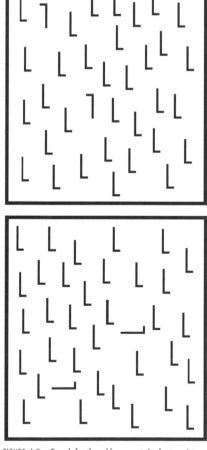

FIGURE 4.2 • Search for the odd ones out. In the top picture you will probably have to do a serial search, looking at each L in turn. In the bottom picture the horizontal Ls just pop out.

CONSCIOUSNESS

THE HALF-SECOND DELAY IN CONSCIOUSNESS

In the 1960s, American neuroscientist Benjamin Libet began a series of experiments which led to the conclusion that about half a second of continuous neuronal activity is required for consciousness. This became popularly known as Libet's half-second delay (McCrone, 1999; Nørretranders, 1998). The issues raised are fascinating, and there have been many arguments over the interpretation of the results, so it is worth considering these studies in some detail.

In these experiments, the sensory cortex of conscious, awake subjects was directly stimulated (Libet, 1982). The subjects had all had invasive neurosurgical procedures carried out for therapeutic purposes and had given their informed consent to take part in the experiments. Their somatosensory cortex was exposed, and electrodes were applied to stimulate it with trains of pulses that could be varied in their frequency, duration and intensity. The result, under certain conditions, was that the patients reported a definite conscious sensation. For example, it felt to them as though they were being touched on the skin, even though the only touch was a brief train of stimulation to the cortex.

The most interesting discovery from the earliest tests was the relationship between the intensity of the stimulation and the length of time for which it lasted (the train duration). Libet found that there is a minimum intensity below which no sensation is elicited no matter how long the stimulation continues. Conversely, a stimulus at this liminal intensity elicited no reportable experience unless the train of stimulation was continued for at least an

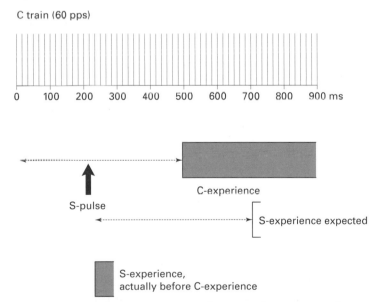

FIGURE 4.3 • Diagram of Libet's (1982) experiment on subjective time order. A continuous stimulus train at 60 pulses per second was applied to sensory cortex (C), and a single pulse at threshold to the skin of the arm 200 msec later (S). The conscious experience of C (C-experience) was reported to occur approximately 500 msec after stimulation began, and was not reported at all unless stimulation continued for 500 msec. On this basis one might expect S-experience to occur 200 ms after C-experience. In fact it was reported to occur at approximately the time of the skin pulse, before the C-experience. These findings led Libet to propose the "subjective referral of sensory experience backwards in time" (after Libet, 1982).

average of 0.5 seconds. At shorter train durations the required intensity to produce a reported experience rose very steeply. This length of time was roughly the same even when other stimulus variables, such as the frequency of the pulses, were varied. The same was found in some subcortical pathways, but not in the dorsal columns of the spinal cord, on peripheral nerves or on the skin.

Interestingly, a single pulse applied to the thalamus or medial lemniscus (which are parts of the specific pathway leading to somatosensory cortex) could induce a primary evoked potential that appeared just the same as the evoked potential induced by an actual sensory stimulus. But this single pulse never produced a conscious sensation, regardless of how intense it was or how large the evoked potential. Libet concluded that "neuronal adequacy" for conscious sensation is only achieved after half a second of continuous stimulation in somatosensory cortex. Indeed he suggested that "it is sufficient duration per se, of appropriate neuronal activities, that gives rise to the emergent phenomenon of subjective experience" (1982: 238). Obviously in ordinary life there is no direct stimulation of the cortex by electrodes, but the implication is that a sensory stimulus (such as a touch on the skin) sets up continuing activity in somatosensory cortex and this must continue for half a second if the touch is to be consciously perceived.

On the surface, this conclusion seems very strange. Does it mean that consciousness takes half a second to build up? And does this imply that our conscious perceptions lag half a second behind the events of the real world?

We should note that half a second is a very long time in terms of brain activity. Signals travel along neurons at about 100 m per second, and can take less than a millisecond to cross a synapse. Auditory stimuli take about 8–10 ms to get to the brain and visual stimuli 20–40 ms. So a great deal can happen in half a second. This is true of our behavior as well. The reaction time to a simple stimulus (say, pressing a button when a light comes on) can be as little as 200 ms, with times to recognize a stimulus being more like 3–400 ms. Drivers can usually stop in response to a sudden danger in less than a second, and if we touch something dangerously hot, our fingers will move out of the way in less than half a second. Could it really be that consciousness comes so much later?

Several further experiments clarified what was going on.

It was already known that a strong stimulus to somatosensory cortex could interfere with sensations coming from a touch on the skin. So if consciousness really takes half a second to build up, then it should be possible to touch someone on the skin—which would normally produce a conscious sensation—and then block that sensation by stimulating the cortex up to half a second later. This was exactly what Libet found. He stimulated the skin first and then stimulated the cortex. When the cortical stimulus came between 200 and 500 milliseconds after the skin stimulus, the skin stimulus was not consciously felt. In other words, a touch on the skin that the subjects would otherwise have reported feeling was retroactively masked up to half a second later. This cer-

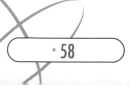

CONSCIOUSNESS

tainly seems to confirm the idea that neuronal adequacy for conscious perception is about half a second.

But how can this be? We do not experience things as happening half a second behind, and half a second is long enough that surely we would notice the delay. Libet checked this by asking subjects to report the subjective timing of two sensations. One was an ordinary stimulus to the skin, the other a cortically induced sensation (this feels a bit like a touch to the skin but is noticeably different). The interval between the two was systematically varied and subjects had to say which came first. They reliably reported that the skin stimulus came first, even when the skin stimulus came almost at the end of the train of pulses needed for neuronal adequacy in cortex. This is what might be expected from previous findings but is also very strange. If half a second of neuronal activity is required for conscious perception, why is the skin stimulus (which must also be followed by half a second of appropriate activity to produce a conscious sensation) felt first?

Libet's controversial suggestion was that sensory experiences are subjectively referred back in time once neuronal adequacy has been achieved. In other words what happens with any sensation is this. Information travels from, say, the skin, up to the relevant sensory area of cortex. If, and only if, activity continues there for the requisite half a second, the stimulus can be consciously perceived. At that point it is subjectively referred back to the actual time at which it happened. If neuronal adequacy is not achieved (either because the stimulus was not strong enough to produce it or because a devious experimenter interfered directly in the cortex), nothing is consciously experienced.

The question then concerns how subjective referral works. To what point in time is the experience referred and how? Libet surmised that the primary evoked potential might act as a timing signal to which the sensation is referred back—or "antedated." Evoked potentials occur very fast after peripheral stimulation—typically about 10–20 ms. If the sensation was referred back to this point, there would seem to be no delay in conscious perception even though half a second of activity is required for neuronal adequacy. To test this Libet and his colleagues (Libet et al., 1979) exploited two special features of what happens when the medial lemniscus (part of the cutaneous pathway to the cortex) is stimulated.

As with the cortex, long trains of pulses are required for neuronal adequacy, but unlike the cortex, a primary evoked potential is also produced, just as it is when the skin itself is stimulated. The backwards referral hypothesis makes a clear prediction—that stimulation to medial lemniscus should be referred back in time to the start of its train of impulses, in a way that stimulation to cortex is not. In this final experiment Libet again asked subjects about the relative subjective timing of different stimuli. As predicted he found that if a skin stimulus was delivered at the same time as the start of a train of stimuli to the medial lemniscus, the subjects felt the two as simultaneous—even though the second one was only felt at all if the stimulation went on long enough to achieve neuronal adequacy.

What should we make of these findings? In general, critics have not agreed over serious weaknesses in the methods or about the specific results. The ideal way to be sure is, of course, by replication, but experimenting on waking subjects with electrodes directly on the exposed brain is not something that can easily be replicated. Also, medical advances since these experiments were done mean that operations to expose the brain are less common than they were. So the experiments are unlikely ever to be repeated. It is probably best, then, that we assume the findings are valid. The real controversy surrounds how to interpret them.

INTERPRETING LIBET'S DELAY

In Libet's view consciousness can only occur when neural activity—wherever it is in the brain—continues long enough for neuronal adequacy. This provides an answer to the question we have already met, and will meet again, concerning the difference between conscious and unconscious processing. According to Libet, the difference is a question of whether neuronal adequacy is reached or not. So, to take one example, when Milner and Goodale (1995) suggest that processing for perception in the ventral stream leads to consciousness, while dorsal stream processing for action does not, Libet (1991) argues that the important difference for consciousness is not the brain areas where the processing occurs, nor what kind of activity it is, nor what it leads to, but only whether it continues for long enough.

Libet makes some much more controversial suggestions, though. In particular he claims that the evidence for backward referral raises problems for materialism and the theory of psychoneural identity (i.e., that consciousness and neural activity are the same thing). Similarly, Penrose (1994a) believes that the phenomena demand reference to non-locality and quantum theory. Popper and Eccles take up this theme, claiming that "This antedating procedure does not seem to be explicable by any neurophysiological process. Presumably it is a strategy that has been learnt by the self-conscious mind" (1977: 364). In other words they think that some kind of intervention by the non-physical mind is required to explain subjective antedating. On their view Libet's results provide evidence for dualism—a claim that Churchland (1981) and Dennett (1991) reject.

Libet himself points out that subjective referral in space has long been recognized and so we should not be surprised to find subjective referral in time as well. Although it may seem odd that we experience objects as "out there" when vision depends on our brain "in here," this kind of projection is not magical—and nor is subjective referral. Given

DID I CONSCIOUSLY ATTEND, OR DID SOMETHING GRAB MY ATTENTION?

SELF-ASSESSMENT QUESTIONS

○ Name three kinds of involuntary attention.

○ What did James mean by the "cause theory" and the "effect theory" of attention?

○ What is the evidence that half a second of neural activity is required for "neuronal adequacy"?

○ What is "subjective antedating"? How does it work?

○ Describe three examples that seem to show anomalies in time.

○ What is the difference between Orwellian and Stalinesque revisions?

the widely dispersed activity in the cortex, we should expect a mechanism that coordinates subjective timings. Subjective referral to the evoked potentials does just that.

We may now return to our question about the person coming into the room. If Libet is right, then conscious perception of the noise cannot occur unless there is at least half a second of continuous neural activity after the noise occurs. Since we often react far faster than that, this means that the causal sequence cannot be:

1 consciously hear sound

2 turn around to look.

In James's terms this is evidence for the effect theory not the causal theory of attention—at least for this sort of behavior. Note that we may still, like James, believe that consciousness can act as a cause in other circumstances (see Chapter 9).

The statement above was carefully worded. It said that conscious perception cannot occur unless there is at least half a second of continuous neural activity after the noise occurs, which is indeed suggested by Libet's results. What is not necessarily implied, though it is often assumed, is something like this: after the noise occurs there is a lot of unconscious processing; then, after half a second, the noise "becomes conscious" or comes "into consciousness"; at that point it is antedated so that it seems to have occurred earlier, at the right time. In this view consciousness really does trail along half a second behind the events of the real world, but we don't realize it. The difference between these two descriptions is important.

ACTIVITY
The cutaneous rabbit

The cutaneous rabbit is easy to demonstrate and a good talking point. To get it to work, you will need to choose the right tool. This can be a sharp pencil or a not-too-sharp knifepoint—something that has a tiny contact point but is not sharp enough to hurt. Practice the tapping in advance, and ensure that you can deliver the taps with equal force and at equal intervals.

Ideally, use a volunteer who has not read about the phenomenon. Ask the volunteer to hold out one bare arm horizontally and to look in the opposite direction. Take your pointed object, and as quickly as you conveniently can, tap five times at the wrist, three times near the elbow and twice on the upper arm, all at equal intervals. Now ask what it felt like.

If you got the tapping right, it will feel as though the taps ran quickly up the arm, like a little animal running. This suggests the following questions. Why does the illusion occur? How does the brain know where to put the second, third and fourth taps when the tap on the elbow has not yet occurred? *When was the volunteer conscious of the third tap?* Does Libet's evidence help us understand the illusion? What would Orwellian and Stalinesque interpretations be? Can you think of a way of avoiding both of them?

Most important is to recognize that experienced time and clock time are not the same thing. While events in the external world can be timed with clocks, as can events happening inside the brain (such as neurons firing), perceived time is not like this. We can only find out about it by asking a person to report in some way. Wilhelm Wundt (1832–1920) did relevant experiments in the late nineteenth century. He asked people to judge the relative timings of visual and auditory stimuli and found many examples of what he called "subjective time displacement" in which people made mistakes about which event occurred first. These, and many other experiments, make the obvious point that we don't always experience things in the order in which they happen. But we might still imagine something like this: there are two worlds—a physical

Is there a precise moment at which something "becomes conscious" or "comes into consciousness"? In *Consciousness Explained*, Dennett argues that this idea is both wrong and misleading. Take the simple example of backwards masking. A small solid disc is flashed first, followed quickly by a ring. If the timings and intensities are just right, the second stimulus masks the first and observers say they saw only the ring.

FIGURE 4.4 • If the disc is flashed briefly (e.g., 30 ms) and immediately followed by the ring, superimposed upon it, the subject reports seeing only the ring. One interpretation is that the ring prevents the experience of the disc from reaching consciousness, as though consciousness is delayed and then changed if necessary (Stalinesque). An alternative is that the disc is consciously experienced but memory for the experience is wiped out by the ring (Orwellian). How can we tell which is right? We cannot, says Dennett. This is a difference that makes no difference.

What is going on in consciousness? If you believe that there really is a time at which any visual experience "becomes conscious" or comes "into consciousness," then you have two alternative explanations to choose from. Dennett calls them Orwellian and Stalinesque revisions. The Orwellian explanation is named after George Orwell's novel *1984* in which the Ministry of Truth rewrote history to prevent people knowing what had really happened. According to the Orwellian explanation, the person really saw, and was conscious of, the disc, but then the ring came along and wiped out the memory of having seen it. So only the ring was reported. The Stalinesque alternative is named after Stalin's notorious show trials in which real

world in which events really happen in one order, and an inner experienced world of consciousness in which they happen in another order.

Libet's results do not necessarily imply this view of consciousness, and some further phenomena show just how problematic it is.

If two lights in different positions are flashed quickly one after the other, the observer seems to see one light that moves, rather than two lights. This is the well-known phi phenomenon. In "color phi" the lights are made, say, red and green. In this case something very odd happens. The person reports that the light not only moved but also changed from red to green as it did so. How can this be? The problem is that the light seems to start changing color before the second light is flashed.

A similar problem occurs with the "cutaneous rabbit" (Geldard and Sherrick, 1972; Dennett, 1991) (see Activity). If a person's arm is tapped, say five times at the wrist, three times near the elbow and then twice on the upper arm, they report not a series of separate taps coming in groups, but a continuous series moving upward—rather as though a little creature were running up their arm. Once again we might ask how taps two to four came to be experienced as moving up the arm when the next tap in the series had not yet happened. How did the brain know where the next tap was going to fall?

This certainly seems mysterious. So what is going on? We might, perhaps, think that it works like this: first the person consciously experienced a stationary red light; then when the green one came along, this experience was wiped out and replaced with the new experience of the light changing to green. Alternatively we might suppose that the person never did experience the stationary red light because the whole experience was delayed until later, when the experience of a changing light came "into consciousness."

Dennett investigates these and many other phenomena and asks how we might distinguish between these two views. Surely one must be right and the other wrong, mustn't it? Surely we must be able to say, at any point in time, what was actually in that person's stream of consciousness, mustn't we? No, says Dennett, because there is no way, in principle, of distinguishing these two interpretations. "This is a difference that makes no difference" (Dennett, 1991: 125) (see Concept).

How then can we understand these odd phenomena? When things seem mysterious, it is often because we are starting with false assumptions. Perhaps we need to look again at the very natural assumption that when we are conscious of something, there is a time at which that conscious experience happens.

It may seem odd to question this assumption, but the value of these oddities may lie precisely in forcing us to do so. The problem does not lie with timing neural events in the brain, which can, in principle, be done. It begins when we ask, "But when does the *experience itself* happen?" Is it when the light flashes? Obviously not, because the light hasn't even reached the eye yet. Is it when the activity reaches the lateral geniculate? Or the superior colliculus? Or V1, or V4? If so, which and why, and if not, then what? Is it when activity reaches a special consciousness center in the brain (or in the mind)? Or when it activates some particular cells? Or when a special consciousness-inducing process is carried out?

There are some theories that do give answers of this kind. For example, Libet says that consciousness happens when neuronal adequacy is achieved. Crick discusses how to "pin down the location of awareness in the brain" and how to find the "awareness neurons" (Crick, 1994: 174, 204). But any theory of this kind hits up against the hard problem: "How does subjective experience arise from this particular neuron, or this particular kind of neural activity?" There seems to be no answer.

Perhaps we need to drop the assumption that there must be a time at which consciousness happens. Indeed we may need to question the very idea that at any moment in time something either is, or is not, "in consciousness." In the next chapter we will do just that.

CONCEPT CONTINUED

people testified to things that never actually happened. On this explanation the experience of the disc is somehow delayed on its way up to consciousness so that before it gets there, the ring can come along and prevent the disc from ever reaching consciousness.

The difference hinges on the question, "Did the disc become conscious and get forgotten, or was it never conscious in the first place?" Do you think that there must be an answer to this question?

Dennett argues that there is no way, even in principle, that we could find out. So the question is meaningless. He analyzes the ways in which Orwellian and Stalinesque explanations have been used and shows that they always end in an impasse. The problem, he says, is a false assumption. We wrongly assume that there is not only a real time at which things happen in the brain but also a real time at which they happen "in consciousness"; a moment when they "enter consciousness" or "become conscious." If we drop this assumption (difficult as it is to do so), the problem disappears. His own alternative, the Multiple Drafts model, is considered in Chapter 5.

Libet, B. (1982) Brain stimulation in the study of neuronal functions for conscious sensory experiences. *Human Neurobiology* 1, 235–42.

Dennett, D.C. (1991) *Consciousness Explained.* Boston and London: Little, Brown and Co., 115–26, 153–62.

Popper, K.R. and Eccles, C. (1977) *The Self and its Brain.* New York, Springer, 256–9.

READING

The theater of the mind

"The mind is a kind of theatre, where several perceptions successively make their appearance; pass, repass, glide away and mingle in an infinite variety of postures and situations." This is how the Scottish philosopher David Hume (1711–76; see Profile, Chapter 7) described the mind, and certainly the idea of the mind as a theater has a natural appeal. In Plato's famous allegory of the cave, we humans do not directly see reality but are like prisoners in a dark cave who can watch only the shadows of people outside moving in front of a fire. Some 2000 years later many psychological theories make use of the same metaphor. Yet Hume urged caution: "The comparison of the theatre must not mislead us," he said. "They are the successive perceptions only, that constitute the mind; nor have we the most distant notion of the place where these scenes are represented, nor of the material of which it is composed" (Hume, 1739, Section IV). In this chapter we will consider the lure, and the dangers, of the theater metaphor.

INSIDE THE MENTAL THEATER

What does it feel like being you now? Many people say it feels something like this. I am somewhere inside my head, looking out through my eyes at the world. I can feel my hands on the book and the position of my body, and I can hear the sounds happening around me, which come into my consciousness whenever I attend to them. If I shut my eyes, I can imagine things in my mind, as though I am looking at mental images. Thoughts and feelings come into my consciousness and pass away again.

Does it feel like this?

If so, you may be conjuring up what Dennett (1991) calls the Cartesian theater. We seem to imagine that there is some place inside "my" mind or brain where "I" am. This place has something like a mental screen or stage on which images are presented for viewing by my mind's eye. In this special place everything that we are conscious of at a given moment comes together and consciousness happens. The ideas, images and feelings that are in this place are *in consciousness*, and all the rest are unconscious. The show in the Cartesian theater is the stream of consciousness, and the audience is me.

Certainly it may feel like this but, says Dennett, the Cartesian theater, and the audience inside it, do not exist.

Dennett, like most scientists and philosophers today, rejects all forms of Cartesian dualism. However, he claims that many materialists, who

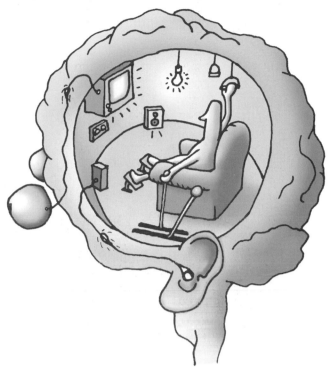

FIGURE 5.1 • Inside the Cartesian Theater

also claim to reject dualism, implicitly still believe in something like a central place or time where consciousness happens and someone to whom it happens. In other words there is still a kind of dualism lurking in their view of consciousness. He calls such a belief Cartesian materialism. There are probably few theorists who explicitly espouse Cartesian materialism, let alone call themselves Cartesian materialists. Indeed, "Cartesian materialist" has become something of a term of abuse. Nevertheless, says Dennett, this way of thinking is revealed in the way people write about consciousness.

Note that the terms "Cartesian theater" (CT) and "Cartesian materialism" (CM) are Dennett's and not Descartes'. The only connection with Descartes is that the concepts reflect a dualism of some kind. The terms are also open to various interpretations, and Dennett himself uses them in slightly different ways, which has led to much confusion (Dennett and Kinsbourne, 1992; Ross et al., 2000). Even so, the central idea is clear enough. You believe in the CT if you believe in some kind of metaphorical space or place or stage within which conscious experiences happen, and into which the "contents of consciousness" come and go. You are a Cartesian materialist if you also believe that consciousness is not separate from the brain and so there must be some brain basis for this theater of the mind where "'it all comes together' and consciousness happens" (Dennett, 1991: 39).

People may say they are not Cartesian materialists, but this clinging to the idea of a CT is found in such common phrases as "the information entered

Daniel C. Dennett (b. 1942)

Dan Dennett studied for his DPhil with Gilbert Ryle at Oxford, and since then has become one of the best known of contemporary philosophers. He is Director of the Center for Cognitive Studies at Tufts University in Massachusetts. Among his many books are *Elbow Room* (1984) about free will (see Chapter 6), *The Intentional Stance* (1987), *Consciousness Explained* (1991) and *Darwin's Dangerous Idea* (1996) (see Chapter 10). In the field of consciousness studies he is best known for his demolition of the Cartesian theater and its replacement with the theory of multiple drafts, for the method of heterophenomenology (see Chapter 25) and for his claim that we are all conscious robots (see Chapter 15). Unlike many philosophers he works closely with psychologists and computer engineers. He has long been fascinated by artificial intelligence, loves robots and works with the MIT team on "Cog" the "cognitive robot." Some critics accuse him of explaining consciousness away, but he insists that his really is a theory of consciousness. He spends the summers on his farm in Maine where he thinks about consciousness while mowing the hay and making his own cider.

consciousness," "the processing happened outside of consciousness," "the solution leapt into consciousness," "ideas come into consciousness." All these phrases imply that there is some criterion for what counts as "in" consciousness at any given time, and that things must be either in or out of consciousness, i.e., in or out of the metaphorical theater.

If the Cartesian theater really does not exist, then these commonly used phrases must be misleading, and the mistake they depend on may help us understand the confusion surrounding the whole idea of consciousness. If, in spite of Dennett's objections, some kind of theater does exist, we should be able to find out what or where it is. In this chapter we shall consider whether it does.

THE PLACE WHERE CONSCIOUSNESS HAPPENS

One version of CM implies that there must be a time and a place at which neural processing all comes together to produce a conscious experience. If this is so, we should be able to find that place. So where is it? Let's take a concrete example of a conscious experience to work with. Right now, please—consciously and deliberately—take a thumb, raise it to your face and press it against the end of your nose. Feel the thumb-on-nose sensations and then let go. It probably felt as though you were sitting in your Cartesian theater, deciding to do this simple action (or not) and then feeling the sensation. So where did the consciousness happen?

We can easily trace the kinds of neural processing that must have taken place. Reading the words that told you what to do would involve activity in much of the visual cortex, and in language areas, such as Wernicke's area, involved in understanding language. Motor cortex would be involved too, both in moving your eyes to read, and then in preparing and executing the skilled action of touching thumb to nose. So would frontal areas involved in planning and making the decision whether to bother or not. When thumb touched nose, the sensory cortex, especially the parts mapped for the hand and face, would be activated and connected with ongoing activity maintaining the body image. In principle we could examine this activity at any level of detail we wished. But where does the consciousness happen?

First, note the obvious point that there is no central place in the brain to which all this activity comes in, and from which the commands to act go out. As William James poetically put it, there is no "pontifical" neuron to which *our* consciousness is attached, "no cell or group of cells in the brain of such anatomical or functional pre-eminence as to appear to be the keystone or centre of gravity of the whole system" (James, 1890, i: 179–80). Even today it may be tempting to think that there must be a center or a top neuron. For example, Ornstein describes consciousness as "the center of the mind/brain system . . ." (1992: 147). But in terms of brain activity there is no center (Zeki, 2001).

To make this clear, we may try to ask which processing is happening on the way in, and which on the way out? Then we might find the middle—where input stops and output begins. This is a reasonable way to think when dealing with a whole organism. After all, light certainly goes into the eyes, and muscles move the arms and legs. So we can talk unproblematically about input and output. But now we are going right inside the system. Maybe it is just a bad habit of thought, derived from thinking about whole human beings, that leads us to believe we can go on looking for "the middle." In fact, as this simple example clearly shows, there can be no middle. For example, ask yourself whether the activity in Wernicke's area is on the way in or the way out? Or that in area V1 or V5, or in the temporal lobe? In fact there is not a single stream of neural activity coming into a middle and sending a new stream out; there is massive parallel processing. There are feedback loops, complex cell assemblies forming and dissolving, mutual interactions between distant areas and so on. There is plenty of integration but there is no middle.

Similarly there is no special *time* at which consciousness must happen. Certainly information comes in first and actions happen later, but between the two there are multiple parallel streams of processing, and no magic moment at which input turns into output or consciousness happens. Now here is the critical point: we naturally want to ask, "But what made me conscious of my thumb on my nose? Which bits of neural processing were the conscious

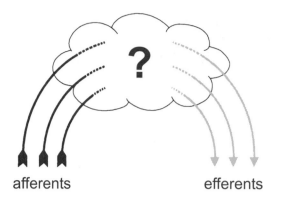

afferents   efferents

FIGURE 5.2 • Signals come in along afferent nerves, and go out along efferent nerves. So where is the middle, where I receive the impressions and send out the orders? Descartes thought it lay in the pineal gland. According to Dennett, the question betrays a commitment to the Cartesian Theater. There is no middle, and no "great mental divide" between input and output (Dennett, 1991, p. 109).

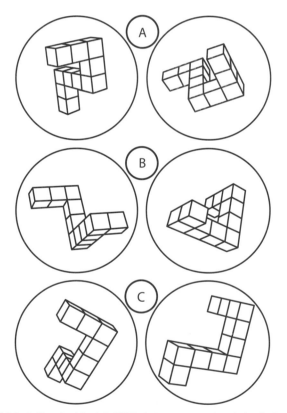

FIGURE 5.3 • In Shepard and Metzler's (1971) classic experiment, subjects had to decide whether the pairs of figures showed the same object rotated or two different objects. The time they took increased with the length of time it would take to rotate real three-dimensional objects (after Shepard and Metzler, 1971).

ones?" Dennett argues that even asking such questions betrays a commitment to the Cartesian theater. It sets us off looking for the special time or place where consciousness happens, and that place cannot be found.

This argument leads straight back to the hard problem. We assume that in some way all this brain activity is responsible for the powerful feeling I just had that I decided to move my thumb, the thumb did what I told it to, and then I consciously felt the sensation on my nose. So either we have to find an answer to the question, "How does subjective awareness arise from the objective actions of all these many brain and muscle cells?" or we have to work out what mistake has led us into posing such an impossible question in the first place. Certainly inventing a central place in which subjectivity happens is not a viable answer.

THE MENTAL SCREEN

In 1971 the American psychologist Roger Shepard published a classic experiment that changed forever how psychologists thought about mental imagery (Shepard and Metzler, 1971). Subjects were presented with pairs of diagrams, like those shown in Figure 5.3, and were asked to press a button to indicate whether the two were different shapes or different views of the same shape. If you try this, you will probably find that you seem to mentally rotate the objects in your mind's eye. Ask yourself *where* this mental rotation seems to be taking place.

Discussion of such private and unobservable experiences had been banished from psychology by behaviorism, but the importance of this experiment was that Shepard and Metzler made objective measurements. They found that the time taken to reach a decision correlated closely with the time it would actually take to rotate the objects in space. In other words, subjects responded more quickly if the object had only been rotated a few degrees, compared with a 180-degree rotation. Later experiments on imagery showed similar effects when people were asked to remember a map or drawing, concentrate on one area of it and then answer questions. The time taken to answer is related to the distance between the mental starting points and finishing points. In other words it appears that something is happening in the brain that takes time to traverse imagined distance. Many different interpretations of these findings have been proposed (Kosslyn, 1980), and the great "mental imagery debate" continues (Kosslyn, 1996; Tye, 1991).

These results *do* show that there is something measurable going on when people have private imaginings—imagery is not something mysterious and unamenable to scientific study. They *do not* show either that consciousness does the imagining, or that there must be a mental screen on which the images are projected.

First, such mental rotations can happen unconsciously, and indeed do so all the time. When we insert the front door key in the lock, reach out with an accurate grasp to pick up a cup by its handle or maneuver a car into a tight parking space, we deal with rotated imagined objects, but we are not necessarily aware of carrying out those rotations. Although imagery is often thought of as quintessentially conscious, the same processes must be going on in visual cortex whether the rotation is done consciously or not. When the experiments were first carried out, no one knew where, in the brain, the processing was taking place, although there were speculations that the same areas may be used for seeing an object as for imagining it. With the advent of MRI scans and other ways of measuring brain activity, it is now clear that this is correct. When we mentally scan a visual image, similar areas of the visual cortex are activated as when we look at a similar object (Kosslyn, 1988).

If you are tempted to think that there must be a mental screen on which the rotated image is projected, and that "you" either do or do not consciously look at the screen, then ask yourself where and what you and the screen could be. If you are a conscious entity looking at the screen, then the classic homunculus problem arises. The inner "you" must have inner eyes and brain, with another inner screen looked at by another inner you and so on—to an infinite regress. It does not help to propose that the self is really a different part of the brain looking at the vision parts because this still implies an unexplained kind of "looking." Perhaps all we can say is that there is distributed processing in various areas of the cortex, which somehow gives rise both to the solutions to rotation problems, and to the experience of watching a mental rotation and being able to describe it.

Another example may help. Look around until you find something blue to look at, perhaps a pen, a book or a coffee mug. Or close your eyes and imagine a blue cat. Now ask, what is this blueness and where is the blueness located? We know in some detail how color information is processed in the human brain, and that it must, in some sense, be responsible for the experience of seeing blue. But how?

This is, once again, a version of the hard problem—how does the subjective experience of blueness arise out of all these objective goings-on? An answer

SEEING BLUE

How do we see blue? The problem for consciousness lies in understanding just how an experience of seeing blue is related to neural activity in the brain. It may help to think about how color processing works.

There are three types of receptor in the retina (somewhat misleadingly called red, green and blue cones) that respond differentially to different wavelengths of light hitting them. Output from the red and green receptors is subtracted to produce one dimension of color and summed to produce a luminance signal (which then contributes to other kinds of visual processing). This sum is subtracted from the output from the blue cones to produce a second color dimension. These two color opponent signals are sent (as rates of neural firing) via the optic nerve to the thalamus and then to visual cortex. In visual cortex, some areas use only luminance information and construct edges, movement and other visual features, while some also use the color information and incorporate it into processing of visual scenes and perceived objects. Output from this processing is then used in further brain areas dealing with associations, memory and the coordination of behaviors. So, when you look at a blue mug, neurons throughout the visual system are firing at a different rate or in different patterns from how they would fire if the mug were orange.

But where does the *experience* of blue happen? Where are the qualia? Where or when, in all this processing, is the special bit that produces the *conscious experience* of blue? Theories of consciousness must either: (a) answer the question—for example, by proposing a brain area, a special kind of processing, or a feature of functional organization that is responsible for consciousness (such theories are versions of Cartesian materialism), or (b) explain why there is no answer.

that certainly does not work is that the incoming information is turned into a blue picture on a multicolored mental screen for us to look at. We know there is no single, central time and place where color happens; color information is distributed through the visual system and used in multiple parallel versions by different brain areas. Even if it were, what would make it blue? As Dennett points out, there is no need for blue *pigment* in the brain, but as soon as we think of mental screens, we think that something somehow has to be blue. So, he asks, could it be *figment*? Of course not. The central mystery is, what makes this experience of mine feel so undeniably blue? We cannot solve it by positing a mental screen covered with color figments and looked at by an inner self. So how can we solve it?

ALTERNATIVES TO A CARTESIAN THEATER

The problem that tempts us into imagining a Cartesian theater is the one we met in Chapter 3. That is, we seem to be aware of some of our actions but not others, conscious of some perceptions and not others; aware of some of our desires but not others. We know that all of them are related to neural activity somewhere in the brain. So we have to wonder—what makes the magic difference? In other words what makes some events *conscious* and others *unconscious*, some *in consciousness* and some *outside of consciousness*?

Let's take the most familiar example. You drive on a well-known route, say to work or to a friend's house. On one occasion you are acutely aware of all the passing trees, people, shops and traffic signals. Another day you are so engrossed in worrying about consciousness that you are completely unaware of the scenery and of your own actions. You only realize, on arriving at your destination, that you have driven all that way unaware of what you were doing. You have no recollection at all of having passed through all those places and made all those decisions. Yet you must, in some sense, have noticed the traffic signals because you did not drive through a red light, run over the old lady on the crossing, nor stray onto the wrong side of the road. You applied the brakes when necessary, maintained a reasonable driving distance from the car in front, and found your usual route. So, considering the red light, what makes the difference between its being *in consciousness* and *out of consciousness*?

This is where the Cartesian theater comes in. We can easily imagine that, in some sense, the *conscious* things were *in* the mental theater, and all the others were outside of it; the things "I" was aware of were those presented to my mind's eye, visible on my mental screen at the time, available to "me" to look at, consider or act upon. But, as we have seen, this metaphor, at least in its crudest form, has to be wrong. There is no literal place inside the brain that constitutes this theater. So what are the alternatives? Some theories keep the theater metaphor while trying to avoid the impossibilities of a Cartesian theater. Some throw out all

FIGURE 5.4 ● Experienced drivers may find that they arrive at their destination with no memory of having driven there at all. Were they really conscious all along but then forgot the experience (an Orwellian interpretation)? Was consciousness prevented by something else, such as paying attention to a conversation or music (a Stalinesque interpretation)? Were there two parallel consciousnesses, one driving and one talking? Or does the unconscious driving problem reveal the futility of asking questions about what is "in" consciousness at any time? Theories of consciousness account for this phenomenon in many different ways.

theater imagery and try to answer the question another way. Others are more radical and even throw out the idea that things are unequivocally *in* or *out* of the stream of conscious experience. Here are examples of each type, though almost any theory of consciousness can be categorized in terms of its answer to this central question.

GLOBAL WORKSPACE THEORY (GWT)

Baars' Global Workspace Theory (GWT) is explicitly based on the "Theater Hypothesis" (Baars, 1988; 1997a). Indeed, Baars describes conscious events as happening "in the theatre of consciousness" or on "the screen of consciousness" (1988: 31). He begins by pointing out the dramatic contrast between the very few items that are available in consciousness at any time and the vast number of unconscious neural processes going on. The best way to think about this, he argues, is in terms of a theater. In this theater, focal consciousness acts as a "bright spot" on the stage, which is directed to different actors by the spotlight of attention. This bright spot is surrounded by a fringe of events that are only vaguely conscious. The unconscious audience sitting in the dark receives information broadcast from the bright spot, while behind the scenes there are numerous unconscious contextual systems that shape the events happening in the bright spot.

What makes this theory more than just a loose metaphor is its grounding in psychology and neuroscience. The contents of consciousness are limited to the bright spot of attention, while the rest of the stage corresponds to immediate working memory (Baddeley, 2000). The interactions between the stage, backstage and audience are based on the idea of a global workspace architecture, first developed by cognitive modeling groups and common in computational approaches to human cognition. In this view the brain is structured in such a way that just a few items at a time are dealt with in a global workspace—similar to the 7±2 items conventionally held in short-term memory. The theater has numerous inputs from the senses and from the overall context and connections to unconscious resources such as language, autobiographical memory and learned skills. According to Baars, all this provides a real "working theatre," with consciousness acting as a gateway, providing global access to any part of the nervous system.

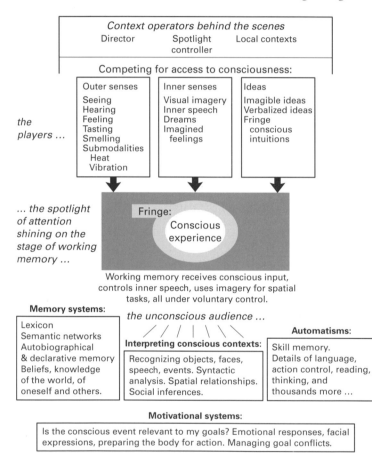

FIGURE 5.5 ● Baars' theater metaphor for conscious experience (after Baars, 1997, p. 300).

In this scheme consciousness has very definite effects and functions. It provides access to the mental lexicon, and to autobiographical memory and the self system. It recruits processors for ongoing tasks, facilitates executive decisions and enables voluntary control over automatic action routines. According to Baars, consciousness is not an epiphenomenon, nor is it anything mysterious. It is a working part of the whole cognitive system.

With this theory what makes an event conscious is that it is being processed within the global workspace and is made available, or is broadcast, to the rest of the (unconscious) system. So when you drive carefully and with full attention on the task, information pertaining to the red light is processed in the global workspace. When your workspace is filled with philosophical speculations and inner conversations, the red light is relegated to the fringe, or even to the darkness, and is no longer in the spotlight of consciousness.

Baars' preferred method of investigation is to treat consciousness as a variable, contrasting "more conscious" with "less conscious" events. He calls this "contrastive analysis." Experiments using scans or other methods can be designed to find out what processes in the brain are involved when the same thing is right in the spotlight of focal consciousness, in the less-conscious fringe, or outside consciousness altogether. An example is the fading of words into short-term memory. The same words might be at one time in conscious inner speech, then fade into unconscious short-term memory, and then become conscious again when retrieved. Any complete theory of consciousness has to explain the difference, says Baars. Rather than worrying about the hard problem we should get on with the task of finding out what makes events more or less conscious.

There are two main questions one might want to ask of this theory. "Does it entail a pernicious Cartesian theater?" and "Does it help with the problem of subjectivity?"

Baars (1997b) argues that "Working theatres are not just 'Cartesian' daydreams" and that fear of the Cartesian theater is misplaced; for no one believes in a single point at which everything comes together and this theory does not require it. Instead he suggests that there may be something like a convergence zone somewhere in the brain or particular areas involved in constructing the global workspace. Other aspects of the model could have testable physical correlates, such as a spotlight which might correspond to some kind of attention-directing mechanism, or self systems that construct inner speech and provide a running narrative on our lives. These are all empirical questions and, he claims, are usefully guided by the metaphor of a theater. Nevertheless, GWT does assume that at any given time some things are *in* consciousness, while others are not, the assumption which is, according to Dennett, at the heart of Cartesian materialism.

As for subjectivity, GWT posits that global availability, or being broadcast to the whole system, explains consciousness. In other words, accessibility is used to explain subjectivity. But the theory provides no explanation of how or why accessibility gives rise to, or is equivalent to, phenomenal consciousness.

THEORIES WITHOUT THEATERS

Many theories of consciousness avoid altogether the controversial imagery of stage and theater. One is Libet's theory of neuronal adequacy. In this theory events only become conscious when the neurons involved have been firing for a sufficient length of time (see Chapter 3). The majority of neural activity remains unconscious because it is too fleeting or too unstable for neuronal adequacy. In this view, the red traffic light would be consciously perceived only if the relevant neurons continuously fired for the requisite length of time.

Another example is Crick's "astonishing hypothesis": "that 'you,' your joys and your sorrows, your memories and your ambitions, your sense of personal identity and free will, are in fact no more than the behaviour of a vast assembly of nerve cells and their associated molecules" (1994: 3). This is perhaps the clearest statement of a thorough-going reductionist approach to consciousness. Conscious experience *is* the behavior of neurons, rather than being caused by it, or interacting with it.

How does this cope with the red traffic light? We have already seen how the visual system processes information about color, shape, movement and texture separately. In Crick's hypothesis these separate features are bound

"all of our unified models of mental functioning today are theater metaphors; it is essentially all we have"

Baars, 1997a: 7

"AM I CONSCIOUS NOW? WHERE IS THIS EXPERIENCE?"

together by coordinated firing of neurons, often with rhythms in the 40-hertz range (see Chapter 17). So we can only see the red light when this binding has been achieved. In addition, Crick suggests that consciousness is associated with certain neural activities and not others, possibly activity in the lower cortical layers (layers 5 and 6), which express the local results of computations taking place elsewhere. To reach consciousness, this special lower-layer activity needs to be sustained by some form of very short-term memory, possibly involving reverberatory circuits between the thalamus and cortex. So the traffic light will only be consciously perceived if its features are successfully bound together by coordinated firing and the right reverberatory circuit is set up and sustained.

We may ask the same two questions of this theory. Does it entail a Cartesian theater, and does it help with the problem of subjectivity? The theory involves no explicit theater imagery, yet Crick compares thalamic control of attention with a spotlight, giving a hint of the theatrical. Also, he talks about the brain activities that "reach consciousness" (1994: 71), claims that we all have "a vivid internal picture of the external world" (ibid.: 9), and uses phrases such as "the seat of visual awareness" (ibid.: 171) and "the location of awareness in the brain" (ibid.: 9, 71, 171, 174). So, arguably, Crick's theory is a form of Cartesian materialism. However, Crick is explicitly not a dualist. He claims that there is no separate "I" independent of neural firing. Indeed, his entire work can be seen as a sustained attempt to rid our thinking of the concept of a soul. As for subjectivity, Crick suggests that we are only groping our way toward a theory of consciousness and that the best way to proceed is through studying the neural correlates of consciousness (see Chapter 16).

MULTIPLE DRAFTS

The most radical way to avoid CM is to demolish the theater altogether. According to Dennett,

> When you discard Cartesian dualism, you really must discard the show that would have gone on in the Cartesian Theater, and the audience as well, for neither the show nor the audience is to be found in the brain, and the brain is the only real place there is to look for them.

> (Dennett, 1991: 134)

Dennett rejects all versions of Cartesian materialism and proposes instead his multiple drafts model. According to this model all kinds of mental activity, including perceptions, emotions and thoughts, are accomplished in the brain by parallel, multitrack processes of interpretation and elaboration of sensory inputs, and they are all under continuous revision. Like the many drafts of a book or article, perceptions and thoughts are constantly revised and altered, and at any point in time there are multiple drafts of narrative fragments at various stages of editing in various places in the brain.

You may then want to ask, "But which ones are conscious?" If you do so, you are imagining a Cartesian theater in which only some of these drafts are

---

"Cartesian materialism, the view that nobody espouses but almost everybody tends to think in terms of . . ."

Dennett, 1991: 144

represented for the audience to see—you would be falling for what Dennett calls the "myth of double transduction" (1998a)—the showing-again for the benefit of consciousness. This is precisely where Dennett's model differs from Cartesian materialism, for on the multiple drafts theory discriminations only have to be made once. There is no master discriminator, or self, who *has* some of the experiences. There is no "central meaner" who understands them. There are only multiple drafts all being edited at once. The sense that there is a narrative stream or sequence comes about when the parallel stream is probed in some way—for example, by asking a question or requiring some kind of response. For example, some of the drafts are used in controlling actions or producing speech, and some are laid down in memory while most just fade away.

To take a simple perceptual example, let's suppose that you just saw a bird fly past the window. Your conclusion or judgment that you consciously saw the bird is a result of probing the stream of multiple drafts at one of many possible points. There is a judgment all right, and the event may be laid down in memory, but there is not *in addition* the *actual experience* of seeing the bird fly past. According to Dennett contents arise, get revised, affect behavior and leave traces in memory, which then get overlaid by other traces, and so on. All this produces various narratives, which are single versions of a portion of the stream of consciousness, but "we must not make the mistake of supposing that there are facts—unrecoverable but actual facts—about just which contents were conscious and which were not at the time" (1991: 407). In other words, if you ask, "What was I actually experiencing at the time the bird flew past?", there is no right answer because there is no show and no theater.

What then of the audience? Dennett argues that when a portion of the world comes to compose a skein of narratives, that portion of the world is the observer. The observer is a "Center of Narrative Gravity" (ibid.: 410). As contents are fixed by probing the stream at various points, as we make judgments and as we speak about what

ACTIVITY
Cartesian materialism

Almost no one admits to being a Cartesian materialist, yet the literature about consciousness is full of theatrical metaphors and phrases implying that things are "in" or "out" of consciousness. It is worth trying to sort out what these mean before making up your own mind about the theater of consciousness. If you are doing this as a class exercise, ask each person to find examples in advance and bring them for discussion.

Theories: Take any theory of consciousness and ask, "Does this theory use theater imagery or metaphors? If so, is a Cartesian theater involved? Is this theory a form of Cartesian materialism?"

Tell-tale phrases: Look out for theater imagery or phrases that imply CM in any area of psychology. Here are a few possible examples for you to add to. In each case ask whether this imagery is helpful or a sign of problems with the theory concerned.

"There seems to be a presence-chamber in my mind where full consciousness holds court." (Galton, 1883: 203)

"ideas . . . pass in rapid succession through the mind" (James, 1890: 25–6)

"this may help to pin down the location of awareness in the brain" (Crick, 1994: 174)

"just for that particular moment, it all comes together as a glorious symphony of consciousness" (Greenfield, 1995: 32)

"percepts, memories, and thoughts are represented in awareness" (Atkinson et al., 1999: 188)

"The range and variety of conscious phenomenology . . . is everyman's private theater" (Edelman and Tononi, 2000a: 20)

"The phenomena of which we are conscious at any given moment are the *contents of consciousness*." (Velmans, 2000a: 225) we are doing or what we have experienced, so the benign illusion is created of there being an author. In this sense, the observer in the Cartesian theater, real and powerful as it feels, is a special kind of illusion (see Chapter 8).

How does this theory deal with our red traffic light? If you are a Cartesian materialist, you will insist that there is some fact of the matter about whether you were or were not conscious of the light at the time. According to the multiple drafts model there are no fixed facts about the stream of consciousness independent of particular probes, so it all depends on the way the parallel stream was probed. Had you been asked what was happening at any time during the drive, you would probably have remembered the most recent events and that you were conscious of them. But since there was no probe leading to speech or laying down in memory (only those leading to changing gears and pressing pedals), you conclude that you were unconscious of the red light at the time.

We can compare this theory with the others in terms of the two questions "Does it entail a pernicious Cartesian theater?" and "Does it help with the problem of subjectivity?" Obviously the first answer is "No." The multiple drafts theory is a radical way of completely replacing the idea of a theater and its audience. Similarly it deals with subjectivity by throwing out a lot of the assumptions that we usually make about it. If we think that at any time there is a truth about what "I" am subjectively experiencing now, then we are wrong. This is why Dennett is able to say, "But what about the *actual* phenomenology? There is no such thing" (1991: 365). This may be why critics complain that Dennett has not *explained* consciousness but *explained it away*. Yet, his theory does deal with subjectivity. He describes a vivid experience of sitting in his rocking chair, watching the sunlight on the trees and listening to music. This description, he says, is just one of the many possible ways the parallel stream could have been probed. If we ask, "What was he actually experiencing at the time?" there is no answer. If we sit now and ask, "What am I conscious of now?" the answer will also depend on how the stream is probed. As inner speech is produced, so content becomes fixed and we conclude that "I" was watching the white fluffy clouds go by. This is how the experience and the experiencer come to be created. This is what brains do. This is how experience can *be* electro-chemical happenings in a brain.

If you find Dennett's alternative difficult and worrisome, then you are probably beginning to understand it. It is difficult to understand because to do so means throwing out many of our usual habits of thought concerning our own consciousness. If

> *"there are no fixed facts about the stream of consciousness independent of particular probes"*
>
> **Dennett**, 1991: 138

SELF-ASSESSMENT QUESTIONS

- In what ways does being conscious feel like being in a theater?

- How do theories of attention use theater imagery?

- What is meant by Cartesian materialism (CM)?

- What is wrong with the idea of the Cartesian theater (CT)?

- How does Baars use the theater metaphor in his theory? Is it a CT?

- Name three theories that avoid theater imagery altogether.

- Explain, in your own words, Dennett's theory of multiple drafts.

you want to give this theory a fair hearing before deciding on its merits, then you really need to throw out all ideas of a Cartesian theater, which is not easy to do (but does get easier with practice). I have suggested various exercises as we have gone along—primarily asking yourself, "Am I conscious now?" as often as possible. Doing this will help you to assess whether Dennett's theory really does deal with subjectivity as he claims it does. What is it like for you now? If Dennett is right, this question itself acts as one of many possible probes and fixes the content. There is no answer beyond this.

READING

Baars, B.J. (1997a) *In the Theater of Consciousness: The Workspace of the Mind.* New York: Oxford University Press. The whole book is relevant, but his theory is outlined in Chapter 2, pages 39–61. Or read Baars (1988) *A Cognitive Theory of Consciousness.* Cambridge: Cambridge University Press, 31–44.

Baars, B.J. (1997b) In the theater of consciousness: Global Workspace Theory, a rigorous scientific theory of consciousness. *Journal of Consciousness Studies* 4, 292–309, with commentaries and reply 310–64. This provides more detailed debate about Baars' theory.

Dennett, D.C. (1991) *Consciousness Explained.* Boston and London: Little, Brown and Co. For Dennett's explanation of the CT and alternatives, read pages 101–15, 309–14 and 344–56.

Shepard, R.N. and Metzler, J. (1971) Mental rotation of three-dimensional objects. *Science* 171, 701–3.

6

The grand illusion

SIX

What does it mean to see? In particular, what does it mean to have a conscious visual experience, such as consciously seeing a yellow daffodil on a green lawn? You see it; you can reach out to it; you delight in the rich visual experience and the vivid translucent yellow of the petals.

Seeing comes so naturally that this may seem to be a silly question, but it is not. Indeed answering it is so difficult that some people have concluded that visual experience is all a grand illusion. The term "grand illusion" (Thompson et al., 2000; Noë, 2002) emerged from research on change blindness and inattentional blindness, which seemed to suggest that "the richness of our visual world is an illusion" (Blackmore et al., 1995). So could it be an illusion? And if so, what sort of illusion?

An illusion is not something that does not exist—like a fairy, a phantom or phlogiston. Rather, it is something that it is not what it appears to be—as in a visual illusion or a mirage. In Figure 6.1 the black lines and shapes really do exist, but the cube you see is an illusion. So when people argue that visual consciousness is an illusion, they do not mean that it does not exist. They mean that it is not what it seems to be.

The starting point, then, is how vision *seems*. How does it seem to you? It is important, before we go any further, to answer this question for yourself. This is partly because sometimes people propose novel solutions to difficult prob-

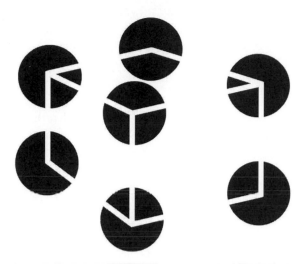

FIGURE 6.1 • Can you see a cube? If so, you are experiencing an illusion. An illusion is not something that does not exist, but something that is not what it appears to be.

lems only to find that others say, "Oh, I knew that all along," and partly because some of the debates over the grand illusion concern whether people really do experience vision as like a rich and detailed picture before their eyes (Noë, 2002). If they do not, then there is no need to talk about illusions. So how does it seem to you?

PRACTICE
HOW MUCH AM I SEEING NOW?

As many times as you can, every day, ask yourself, **"How much am I seeing now?"**

You may be looking at anything at all, from a busy city scene or a beautiful garden, to a piece of text or the back of your own hand. In each case you may at first get the impression that you can see everything at once, that there is an entire detailed scene in your awareness. Now look again, harder. What are you actually seeing right *now*?

If you do this a few hundred times, you may be in a better position to assess the various theories covered in this chapter. Eventually you may notice some profound changes. Can you describe what has happened?

Open your eyes and look around. It probably seems as though you see a rich, detailed and ever-changing picture of the world: a "stream of vision." You may also have some sort of theory about what is going on—something like this perhaps:

When we look around the world, unconscious processes in the brain build up a more and more detailed representation of what is out there. Each glance provides a bit more information to add to the picture. This rich mental representation is what we see at any time. As long as we are looking around, there is a continuous stream of such pictures. This is our visual experience.

There are at least two threads of theory here. The first is the idea that there is a rich stream of conscious visual impressions to be explained—something like James's stream of visual consciousness, or the "movie-in-the-brain" (Damasio, 1999), or "the vivid picture of the world we see in front of our eyes" (Crick, 1994: 159). The implication (as we saw in the previous chapter) is that at any time there are definite contents in the stream of vision. This is what Dennett (1991) rejects when he claims that there is no show in the Cartesian theater.

The second is the idea that seeing means having internal mental pictures, i.e., that the world is *represented* in our heads. This idea is at least several centuries old. Leonardo da Vinci was the first to describe the eye as a camera obscura—a dark chamber into which an image of the world is projected. Then in the early seventeenth century Kepler explained the optics of the eye but said he would leave to others the job of explaining how the image "is made to appear before the soul" (Lindberg, 1976). This is what Descartes tried to do.

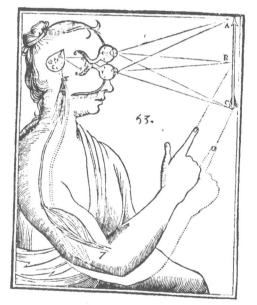

FIGURE 6.2 • Descartes believed that pictures were transmitted through the eyes to the pineal gland where they entered the mind. His theory has generally been rejected, but the idea of pictures in the head remains.

He studied actual images by scraping off the back of an ox's eye so that he could see them form on the retina and then showed, in his famous sketches, how he thought these images are transmitted to the non-material mind.

The details of Descartes' scheme were overthrown, but the idea of pictures in the mind remained. Two centuries later James, like his Victorian contemporaries, simply assumed that seeing involves creating mental representations, as did cognitive psychology in the twentieth century. Dennett calls the idea of pictures in the head "an almost irresistible model of the 'end product' of visual perception" and a "ubiquitous malady of the imagination" (1991: 52). If you disagree with either of these threads of theory, it may be useful to sort out in your own mind just how you think vision does work.

These assumptions may seem unremarkable if you agree with them, but they land us in difficulty as soon as we appreciate that much of vision is unconscious. This is the same problem that we considered in the previous chapter. In the case of vision we seem forced to distinguish between the mass of unconscious visual processes and the final conscious result, but if both are representations built by the activity of neurons, what is the magic difference between them? What makes some representations conscious and others not?

One way to approach this question is to stick with the idea of a stream of conscious visual representations and look for its neural correlates (see Chapter

CONSCIOUSNESS

16). The basic principle is simple. Take some examples of unconscious visual processing, take some examples of conscious visual processing and study what is happening in the brain until you discover the difference. This should reveal what is special or different about conscious, as opposed to unconscious, vision.

In this light Crick asks, "What is the 'neural correlate' of visual awareness? Where are these 'awareness neurons'—are they in a few places or all over the brain—and do they behave in any special way?" (Crick, 1994: 204). He adds that "so far we can locate no single region in which the neural activity corresponds exactly to the vivid picture of the world we see in front of our eyes" (ibid.: 159). He goes on to consider synchronised behavior in widely separated neurons (see Chapter 17), but note that he does not question the assumption that there is such a "vivid picture of the world we see in front of our eyes."

What if there is not? There are good reasons to question the natural idea that conscious vision consists of a stream of picture-like representations.

FILLING IN THE GAPS

The perceptive William James noticed something very odd, though obvious once someone points it out—that when we look around we do not, and cannot, take in everything at once, and yet we are unaware of having overlooked anything. "It is true," he wrote,

> that we may sometimes be tempted to exclaim, when once a lot of hitherto unnoticed details of the object lie before us, "How could we ever have been ignorant of these things and yet have felt the object, or drawn the conclusion, as if it were a *continuum*, a *plenum*? There would have been *gaps*—but we felt no gaps."
>
> (James, 1890, i: 488)

Why do we fail to notice the gaps? One answer might be that, in some sense, the brain fills in the missing bits. But if the brain already knows what needs to be filled in, who does it do the filling-in for, and why? Another possibility is that there is no need to fill in anything because the gaps are just a lack of information. And an absence of information is not the same as information about an absence.

Consider something that happens in vision all the time—we infer the presence of whole objects from the visible parts. A car parked behind a tree looks like a whole car, not two halves separated by a tree trunk; a cat sleeping behind a chair leg looks like a whole cat, not two odd-shaped furry lumps. This ability to see objects as whole is obviously adaptive, but what is going on? We don't literally "see" the hidden parts of the car, yet the car seems whole. This is sometimes referred to as amodal perception, or conceptual filling-in. The car is conceptually completed but not visually filled in.

A more controversial kind of filling-in arguably happens in the blind spot. Where the optic nerve leaves the back of the eye, there are no photoreceptors,

> *"There would have been gaps—but we felt no gaps."*
>
> **James**, 1890, Vol. i: 488

The grand illusion **CHAPTER SIX**

FIGURE 6.3 • **A: Do not turn the page yet.** On the next page you will see an illustration. Try to look at it for just three seconds. You might like to practice counting at the right speed first, or get a friend to time you. Then turn the page, look at the picture while you count to three, and then turn back.

What did you see? Try to describe the picture in words before you look again.

FIGURE 6.3 • **B:** Perhaps you clearly saw lots of identical portraits of Dan Dennett and just one with horns. But in three seconds you could not have looked directly at each one. Did you fill in the rest? Do you need to?

creating a blind spot on the retina that subtends about 6 degrees of visual angle, roughly 15 degrees away from the fovea. Most people are unaware of their own blind spots until shown a demonstration such as that in Figure 6.4.

Partly this is because we have two eyes, and the two blind spots cover different parts of the visual world, but even with one eye the blind spot is normally undetectable. Experiments can easily reveal it.

In classic demonstrations a small object can be made to disappear from sight by lining it up precisely on the blind spot. What is seen where the object should have been? Not a blank space or a gaping black hole, but a continuation of the background. If the background is boring gray, then boring gray fills the space where the object should have been. If the background is black and blue stripes, the stripes seem to cover the whole area. The obvious conclusion is that the brain has somehow filled in the gap with gray, or pink, or stripes, or checks (or more people in the crowd, or more pebbles on the beach?). But is this the right conclusion?

No, says Dennett, this kind of thinking "is a dead giveaway of vestigial Cartesian materialism" (1991: 344). He asks you to imagine walking into a room papered all over with identical portraits of Marilyn Monroe. You can see at a glance (or a few glances)

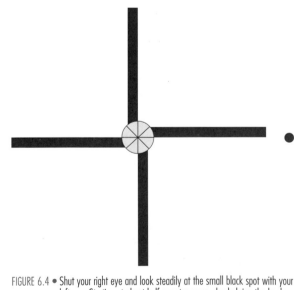

FIGURE 6.4 • Shut your right eye and look steadily at the small black spot with your left eye. Starting at about half a meter away, slowly bring the book toward you until the striped area disappears. It is then in your blind spot. You may need to try a few times to find it (remember to keep your eye on the black spot). What can you see there? Is the space filled in? Do the black lines join up? (after Ramachandran and Blakeslee, 1998).

that the portraits are all the same. If one had a moustache, or a silly hat, you would notice the difference straight away. It seems natural to conclude that you have seen the room in all its detail and now have a rich representation of it in your head.

This cannot be right. As Dennett points out, in order to identify one of the portraits, you would have to look straight at it so that the image fell on the fovea. While you did that, all the other portraits would just be face-shaped blobs. Now you turn to the next, foveate that one and again conclude that it is Marilyn and that it looks just the same as the first one. Now another . . . You can make at most four or five saccades a second. So you cannot possibly check every single one in the brief time it takes you to conclude—"all Marilyns." You never see just one clear portrait and a lot of bleary blobs; you see the whole complicated lot of them. How can this be?

Could the brain take one of its high-resolution foveal views of the portrait and reproduce it lots of times, as if by photocopying, over an inner mental wall? Of course not, says Dennett. Having identified one portrait, and having no information to suggest that the other blobs are not also Marilyns, the brain jumps to the conclusion that the rest are Marilyns too and labels the whole region "more Marilyns." This is more like paint-by-numbers than filling in pixel-by-pixel. The reason you would notice a moustache or a silly hat is that you have dedicated pop-out mechanisms to detect such anomalies (see Chapter 4). If none of these is activated, the conclusion "all the same" stands.

Of course, it does not seem that way to you. You are convinced that you are seeing hundreds of identical Marilyns. And in a sense you are, claims Dennett. There are hundreds of portraits out there in the world and that is what you are seeing. Yet it does not follow that there are hundreds of identical Marilyns represented in your brain. Your brain just represents *that* there are hundreds of portraits: "no matter how vivid your impression is that you see all that detail, the detail is in the world, not in your head" (Dennett, 1991: 355).

This does not apply only to the Marilyn room. When you walk along the street, you cannot possibly look at all the detail around you, yet you see no gaps in the places where you haven't looked. Does the brain fill in the spaces with plausible guesses about cars and trees and shop windows and children running to school? Does it need to?

We can see that there are two extreme views on filling-in: first, that the brain actually fills in all the details as though to complete a picture in the brain, second, that it has no need to fill in anything at all. The reality is a little more complicated.

Neuropsychologist V. S. Ramachandran (see Profile, p. 84) reports many experiments, both formal and informal (Ramachandran and Blakeslee, 1998). With normal subjects, if two vertical lines are shown, one above and one below the blind spot, the subject sees one continuous line. The lines can be offset slightly and still seem to get lined up to form a single straight line, but if the same is done with horizontal lines, they do not line up. Missing corners are not completed, but if the blind spot is positioned over the center of a radiating

> *"the detail is in the world, not in your head"*
> **Dennett**, 1991: 355

PROFILE

Vilayanur S. Ramachandran (b. 1951)

Usually known as Rama, V.S. Ramachandran is a flamboyant lecturer and an original thinker. He was originally trained as a doctor, did a PhD at Trinity College, Cambridge, and then worked on visual perception and neurology. He is Director of the Center for Brain and Cognition, and Professor of Neuroscience at the University of California, San Diego. Ramachandran is best known for his work on phantom limbs, his explorations of strange neurological diseases, and what has popularly come to be known as the brain's "God module." With a love of Indian painting and sculpture he lectures widely on art, synesthesia and the brain, and has appeared on many television and radio programs. He thinks that the blind spot is filled in with qualia, and that subjectivity resides mainly in the temporal lobes and the cingulate gyrus. *Newsweek* magazine included him in the "Century Club," one of the hundred people to watch out for in the twenty-first century.

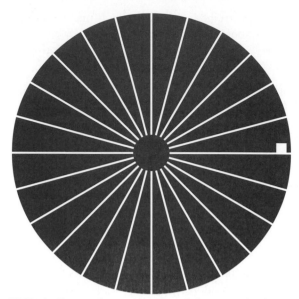

FIGURE 6.5 • Shut your right eye and fixate the small white square. Adjust the distance so that your blind spot falls on the center of the wheel. What do you see? Many people report that the spokes are completed and no gap is seen (after Ramachandran and Blakeslee, 1998).

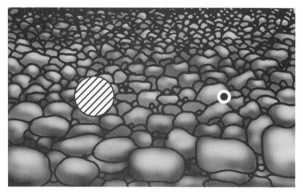

FIGURE 6.6 • What happens this time—is there a gap or is it filled in with pebbles? If it is, are they large or small pebbles, or a random mix, or what?

pattern—like a bicycle wheel with the center left out—the pattern is completed and the lines are seen to converge to a point.

In one demonstration Ramachandran uses a group of yellow doughnut shapes, with the central hole in one of them coinciding with the blind spot. A complete yellow circle appears and pops out from the surrounding doughnuts. From this Ramachandran concludes that filling-in cannot be just a question of ignoring the gaps, because in that case the circle would not pop out. It shows, he says, that "your brain 'filled-in' your blind spot with yellow qualia" (Ramachandran and Blakeslee, 1998: 237). But what exactly are yellow qualia? Are they a form of Dennett's "figment," painting in the blank space? If not, what is going on?

Other experiments used special subjects, such as Josh, whose right primary visual cortex was penetrated by a steel rod in an industrial accident. He has a large permanent scotoma (or blind area) to the left of his visual field. Like other people with similar brain damage, he manages perfectly well for most purposes and, although well aware that he has a large blind spot, does not see a black hole or a space with nothing in it. "When I look at you," he said to Ramachandran, "I don't see anything missing. No pieces are left out" (Ramachandran and Blakeslee, 1998: 98).

Ramachandran presented him with vertical lines above and below the large scotoma. At first Josh reported seeing a gap between the lines, but then the gap began to close and he saw the lines growing slowly together until they met in the middle. Offset lines took about five seconds to line up and grow together. In other experiments a column of large Xs was never completed across the scotoma, but a column of tiny Xs was. Ramachandran speculated that different levels of visual processing were involved: the former activating temporal lobe areas concerned with object recognition, the latter being treated as a texture and therefore completed. Oddly enough when a row of numbers was used, Josh reported that he could see numbers in the gap but could not read them, an odd effect that sometimes happens in dreams. Finally, when presented with a display of twinkling black dots on a red background, Josh reported that first the red color bled into his scotoma, then the dots appeared, and last of all the dots began to twinkle.

These results suggest not only a real effect but one that takes a measurable time to occur. The same was observed with "artificial scotomas" in normal subjects. Ramachandran and Gregory (1991) asked subjects to fixate the center of a display of flickering "snow" on a screen. Offset by 6° was a small gray square with no snow. At first the square was visible, but after about five seconds, it became filled with snow like the rest of the screen. When the whole screen was then made gray, a square of snow was seen and persisted for two to three

FIGURE 6.7 • A field of yellow doughnuts (shown in white here). Shut your right eye and look at the small white dot near the middle of the illustration with your left eye. When the page is about six to nine inches from your face, one of the doughnuts will fall exactly around your left eye's blind spot. Since the black hole in the center of the doughnut is slightly smaller than your blind spot, it should disappear and the blind spot then is "filled in" with yellow (white) qualia from the ring so that you see a yellow disc rather than a ring. Notice that the disc "pops out" conspicuously against the background of rings. Paradoxically, you have made a target more conspicuous by virtue of your blind spot. If the illusion doesn't work, try using an enlarged photocopy and shifting the white dot horizontally (caption from and figure after Ramachandran and Blakeslee, 1998).

seconds. Experiments with monkeys subsequently showed increasing activity of neurons in area V3 corresponding to this effect (De Weerd et al., 1995).

There is also evidence of separate mechanisms for filling in color, texture and movement (Ramachandran and Gregory, 1991). For example, in one experiment, the background was sparse, twinkling black dots on pink, and the square consisted of black spots moving horizontally on gray. In a few seconds the square faded, but it did so in two distinct stages. First the gray disappeared and was replaced by pink; then the moving dots faded and were replaced by twinkling ones. In another experiment the square was allowed to fade and was then replaced by an identical square shifted by about 0.4°. Oddly this second square seemed to *move* to its new location, rather than simply appearing there. As Ramachandran and Gregory note, this means that the first square, which was not consciously visible, could nevertheless provide input to apparent motion perception. They speculate that the fading of the square from consciousness occurs from area V4 and other form areas, but information about its motion is processed separately in area MT.

In other experiments, a background of English, Latin or nonsense text was used. The square was filled in all right, but like Josh with his numbers, the subjects could not read the text produced. This throws doubt on the idea that filling-in is literally a process of completing a picture dot by dot. For how would one create visible letters and numbers that could not be read? But what then is it?

CONSCIOUSNESS

What should one conclude from these results? Contrary to the extreme skeptical view, there is clearly a real effect to be explained. The brain does not just ignore a lack of information but responds by providing information of various kinds and at varying speeds. However, the findings do not support the opposite extreme either. We cannot make sense of them by assuming that somewhere inside the brain there is a picture-like representation which must be filled in all over or gaps will be noticed.

FIGURE 6.8 ● When these two pictures are alternated with brief flashes of gray in between or moved slightly when they are swapped, people rarely notice the change. This is one way to demonstrate change blindness.

CHANGE BLINDNESS

Look at the picture above on the left for a few moments. As you take it in, you have probably made many saccades and blinked numerous times but you hardly notice these interruptions. It feels as though you look over the picture, take it in, and now have a good idea of what is there. Now ask yourself this question. If the keyboard disappeared while you blinked, would you notice? Most people are sure they would.

Research showing they are wrong began with the advent of eye-trackers, which made it possible to detect a person's eye movements and then make a change to a display during a saccade. In experiments beginning in the 1980s (Grimes, 1996), subjects were asked to read text on a computer screen and then, during their saccades, parts of the surrounding text were changed. An observer watching the experiment would see a rapidly changing screen of text, but the subjects noticed nothing amiss. Later experiments used complex pictures, with an obvious feature being changed during saccades. The changes were so large and obvious that under normal circumstances they could hardly be missed, but when made during saccades, they went unnoticed.

This may seem very strange, but under normal circumstances motion detectors pick up transients and direct our attention to that location. A saccade causes a massive blur of activity that swamps out these mechanisms, leaving only memory to detect changes. The implication was that trans-saccadic memory is extremely poor. With every saccade most of what we see must be thrown away.

This research complements earlier research on trans-saccadic memory and on visual integration across blinks and saccades (see Irwin, 1991, for a review). For a long time it was assumed that the visual system must somehow integrate its successive pictures into one big detailed representation that would remain stable across body movements, head movements, eye movements and blinks. This would, of course, be a massive computational task, and although it was not clear how it could be achieved, most researchers assumed that somehow it must be—otherwise how could we have such a stable and detailed view of the world in consciousness? Change blindness implies that perhaps we do *not* have a stable and detailed view of the world in consciousness after all, in which case massive integration of successive views is not necessary.

In fact expensive eye-trackers are not needed. It was soon found that the same effect can be obtained by moving the whole picture slightly (thus forcing a saccade) while making the change (Blackmore et al., 1995). Change blindness has since been observed with brief gray flashes between pictures, with image flicker, during cuts in movies or during blinks (Simons, 2000). That the findings are genuinely surprising is confirmed in experiments in which people were asked to predict whether they or others would notice the changes. A large metacognitive error was found—that is, people grossly overestimated both their own and others' ability to detect change (Levin, 2002).

One of the simplest methods for demonstrating change blindness is the flicker method. Rensink, O'Regan and Clark (1997) showed an original image alternating with a modified image (each shown for 240 ms), with blank gray screens (shown for 80 ms) in between. Then they measured the number of presentations until the subject noticed the change. Typically subjects take many alternations before they detect the change. The changes are all large enough that if they are presented without the blanks in between, they are readily noticed in one or two alternations.

Rensink et al. used this method to investigate whether change blindness is specific to saccades or is an attentional effect. When changes were made in areas of central interest, an average of seven alternations were needed for subjects to notice the change, whereas changes in areas of marginal interest took an average of 17 alternations, with some subjects taking up to 80 alternations to notice a change that was obvious once seen. This suggests that changes are more likely to be detected if subjects are attending to the part of the image that changes. If they are not, they have to search serially until they find the part that changes. In another experiment verbal clues were provided before the display began, sometimes accurate and sometimes misleading. With the valid cues detection was greatly speeded up, and the difference between changes of central and marginal interest disappeared.

INATTENTIONAL BLINDNESS

Could it be that if you don't pay attention to something you simply do not see it? Or as psychologists Arien Mack and Irvin Rock put it, "there is no *conscious* perception without attention" (1998: 14) (see Chapter 4). They reached this conclusion from studying the odd phenomenon of inattentional blindness.

In a typical experiment subjects were asked to look at a screen and fixate a marker. When a cross briefly appeared, they had to decide whether the horizontal or vertical arm was longer. Then in a critical trial an unexpected stimulus appeared nearby, perhaps a black square or a colored shape. Afterward they were asked, "Did you see anything on the screen on this trial that had not been there on previous trials?" On average, 25 percent of subjects said "No." The effect was even stronger when the cross they were attending to was slightly to one side of their fixation point, in the parafovea, and the unexpected shape appeared on their fovea. Under these conditions, 65 to 95 percent said "No," suggesting that they had to actively inhibit attention at the fovea when trying to attend somewhere else.

Interestingly, if the unexpected stimulus was a smiley face icon or the person's own name, they were much more likely to notice it, suggesting that the unseen stimuli must still be processed to quite a high level.

Perhaps the most dramatic demonstration of inattentional blindness is the film *Gorillas in our Midst* (Simons and Chabris, 1999). Two teams of students are seen throwing balls to each other and observers are told to watch the white team very carefully and count the number of passes made. Afterward they are asked whether they saw anything unusual in the film. What most usually miss is that a woman dressed in a gorilla suit walks right into shot, turns to the camera and thumps her chest, and then walks off on the opposite side. If you are an observer, it is quite shocking to see the film again and realize what you missed. In experiments approximately 50 percent of observers failed to notice the gorilla; they were more likely to see it when the counting task was easier or when they were watching the black team (since the gorilla was black).

Returning to change blindness, attention may be necessary to detect change, but American psychologists Daniel Levin and Daniel Simons (1997) wondered whether it is sufficient. They created short movies in which various objects were changed during a cut, some in arbitrary locations and others in the center of attention. In one movie two women are seen chatting over a meal. When the camera cuts to a new position, a small change is made: one woman's

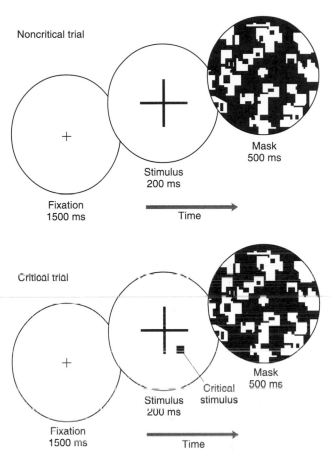

FIGURE 6.9 • Displays for the critical and non-critical trials in Mack and Rock's experiments. In this experiment the critical stimulus is in the parafovea. In other experiments the cross was in the parafovea and the critical stimulus was at the fixation point (after Mack and Rock, 1998).

scarf disappears or the pink plates are changed to white. Most observers failed to notice the changes. You might think that you are good at spotting the little mistakes made by TV producers and film directors, but these results suggest that only a very few people will notice such inconsistencies, those people who just happened to be attending to the detail in question. So is attention enough?

Levin and Simons' next film showed an actor sitting at a desk. The telephone rings and she gets up and moves toward the door. The camera then cuts to a new view in the hallway where a different actor walks to the telephone and answers it. When 40 subjects were asked to write a description of what they had seen, only 33 percent mentioned the change in actor, even though subsidiary experiments showed that the two actors were easily discriminable. From their descriptions it was clear that the subjects had attended to the main actor in the film, but this was not sufficient for them to detect the change. Levin and Simons concluded that even when we attend to an object, we may not form a rich representation that is preserved from one view to the next.

Oddly enough, these effects are not confined to films and artificial laboratory conditions. Simons and Levin (1998) arranged for an experimenter to approach a pedestrian on the campus of Cornell University and ask for directions. While they talked, two men rudely carried a door between them. The first experimenter grabbed the back of the door, and the person who had been carrying it let go and took over the conversation. Only half of the pedestrians noticed the substitution. Again, when people are asked whether they think they would detect such a change, they are convinced that they would—but they are wrong.

Change blindness could have serious consequences in ordinary life. For example, change blindness can be induced by using "mudsplashes" appearing at the time of the change (O'Regan et al., 1999). Comparable events happen all the time on the road and in the air, suggesting that dangerous mistakes might be made by drivers or pilots if a crucial event occurs just as some mud splats onto the windshield.

IMPLICATIONS FOR THEORIES OF VISION

What do these results mean? Certainly they challenge the "stream of vision" theory described at the start of the chapter and imply that vision is not a process of building up rich and detailed inner representations that can be used to compare details from one moment to the next. We do not

SELF-ASSESSMENT QUESTIONS

O Describe two alternative explanations for the apparent filling-in of the blind spot.

O List some kinds of display that are, and are not, filled in across a scotoma.

O Why did Dennett imagine a room papered all over with identical portraits of Marilyn Monroe?

O Describe two or three methods for demonstrating change blindness.

O What implications does change blindness have for theories of vision?

O How might change blindness affect us in daily life?

O What is inattentional blindness? Give some examples.

store nearly as much information as was previously thought: to this extent the richness of our visual world is an illusion (Blackmore et al., 1995). Yet obviously something is retained, otherwise there could be no sense of continuity and we would not even notice if the entire scene changed. Theorists vary in how much, and what sort of, information they claim is retained (Simons, 2000).

Perhaps the most straightforward interpretation is given by Simons and Levin (1997). During any single fixation we have a rich visual experience. From that we extract the meaning or gist of the scene. Then, when we move our eyes, we get a new visual experience, but if the gist remains the same, our perceptual system assumes the details are the same and so we do not notice changes. This, they argue, makes sense in the rapidly changing and complex world we live in. We get a phenomenal experience of continuity without too much confusion. In this view what is retained is the gist of the scene, some kind of meaningful analysis of what was seen.

Somewhat more radical is the view of Canadian psychologist Ronald Rensink (2000). He suggests that observers never form a complete representation of the world around them—not even during fixations—and there is no visual buffer that accumulates an internal picture of the scene. Instead, object representations are built one at a time, as needed. Focused attention takes a few proto-objects from low-level processing and binds them into a "coherence field," representing an individual object that persists for some time. When attention is released, the object loses its coherence and dissolves, or falls back into an unbound soup of separate features. To explain why we seem to experience so many objects at once, when so little is held in focused attention, Rensink argues that vision is based on "virtual representation." We get the impression of a rich visual world because a new representation can always be made "just in time" using information from the world itself.

French psychologist Kevin O'Regan (1992) builds on this idea that the visual system has no need to store large amounts of information because it can use the world as an external memory or as its own best model (see Chapter 13). Along with American philosopher Alva Noë, he rejects the idea that seeing something consists of building an internal representation of that thing. Instead they propose a sensorimotor theory of vision and visual consciousness—a fundamentally new way of thinking about vision (O'Regan and Noë, 2001). They argue that traditional theories do not explain how the existence of an internal representation gives rise to visual consciousness. In their theory this problem is avoided because vision is not about building internal representations, rather "seeing is a way of acting" (ibid.: 883).

More specifically, an organism has the experience of seeing when it masters the governing laws of sensorimotor contingencies—that is, when it develops routines for extracting information from the world, for interacting with the visual input and for exploiting the ways in which that input changes with eye movements, body movements, blinks and other actions. What remains between saccades is not a picture of the world, but the information needed for further exploration. A study by Karn and Hayhoe (2000) confirms that

spatial information required to control eye movements is retained across saccades. Could this be sufficient to give an illusion of continuity and stability?

This kind of theory is dramatically different from most existing theories of perception, but is similar to theories of embodied or enactive cognition (Chapter 13), the idea of perception as a kind of "reaching out" (Humphrey, 1992) and J.J. Gibson's (1979) ecological approach to perception. In this view, vision is not about building representations of the world: instead seeing, attending and acting all become the same thing. In this view what you see is those aspects of the scene that you are currently "visually manipulating." If you don't manipulate the world, you see nothing. When you stop manipulating some aspect of the world, it drops back into nothingness.

Could visual consciousness really be this way? If we were convinced that this theory was correct, would we begin to experience vision as a means of acting in the world, and would seeing cease to seem like a stream of pictures?

We began with the idea of a stream of vision and the assumption that it is a stream of internal pictures or representations. The results on filling-in, inattentional blindness and change blindness all call that idea into question (Blackmore, 2002). It is too early to say how these results are best interpreted, and how much of previous thinking has to be overthrown, but the most extreme position is that the stream of vision is all a grand illusion.

READING

Dennett, D.C. (1991) *Consciousness Explained.* London: Little, Brown & Co., 344–56.

Noë, A. (ed.) (2002) *Is the Visual World a Grand Illusion? Special issue of the Journal of Consciousness Studies* 9(5–6), and Thorverton, Devon: Imprint Academic. This contains several articles debating the grand illusion, useful for seminars and discussions.

Pessoa, L., Thompson, E. and Noë, A. (1998) Finding out about filling-in: a guide to perceptual completion for visual science and the philosophy of perception. *Behavioral and Brain Sciences* 21, 723–802, with commentaries and authors' responses. This debate takes the arguments on filling-in much further than in this chapter, including both neuroscience and philosophy.

Ramachandran, V.S. and Gregory, R.L. (1991) Perceptual filling-in of artificially induced scotomas in human vision. *Nature* 350, 699–702.

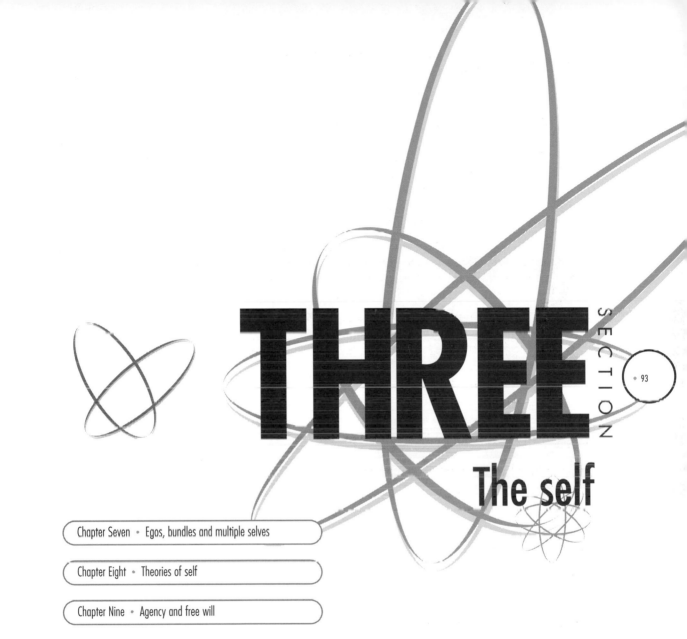

THREE

SECTION

The self

7

Egos, bundles and multiple selves

SEVEN

Who is reading this book? Who is conscious of the writing on the page, the attempt to understand and answer the question, or the sounds of revelry in the next room?

Questions about the nature of consciousness are intimately bound up with those about the nature of self because it *seems* as though there must be someone having the experience, that there cannot be experiences without an experiencer. Our experiencing self seems to be at the center of everything we are aware of at a given time and to be continuous from one moment to the next. In other words, it seems to have both unity and continuity. The problems start when you ask what kind of thing that experience might be.

In everyday language we talk unproblematically about our "self." "I" got up this morning, "I" like muesli for breakfast, "I" can hear the robin singing, "I" am an easy-going sort of person, "I" remember meeting you last week, "I" want to be an engine driver when I grow up. It seems that we not only think of this self as a single thing, but we accord it all sorts of attributes and capabilities. In ordinary usage, the self is the subject of our experiences, an inner agent who carries out actions and makes decisions, a unique personality, and the source of desires, opinions, hopes and fears. This self is "me"; it is the reason why anything matters in my life.

That this apparently natural way of thinking about ourselves is problematic has been recognized for millennia. In the sixth century BC the Buddha (Profile, Chapter 27) challenged contemporary thinking with his doctrine of annatta or no-self. He claimed that the self is just a name or a label given to something that does not really exist, a suggestion that seems as hard to understand and accept today as it was then. The Greek philosophers struggled with similar issues, including Plato (427–347 BC), who wanted to know whether the psyche (the soul or true essence of a person) is immortal. In his famous dialogues he argued both that the psyche is immortal and that it has parts— appetitive, emotional and rational parts— creating a serious problem since he also believed that only a unitary and indivisible thing could be immortal. Similar problems have plagued many thinkers since. In philosophy there are numerous theories of the nature of self (or what persons are), of personal identity (or what makes someone the same person over time) and of moral responsibility. In psychology research has

FIGURE 7.1 ● The Buddha taught the doctrine of annatta, or no self. Parfit calls him the first bundle theorist.

studied the construction of social selves, self-attribution, the factors affecting personal identity, dissociative states and various pathologies of selfhood. We cannot consider all of these here, so in this chapter and the next, we will concentrate on a few of those theories that are most relevant to consciousness.

The central question is why it seems as though I am a single, continuous self who has experiences. Possible answers can be divided into two major types. The first answers the question by claiming that it is true—there really is some kind of continuous self that is the subject of my experiences, that makes my decisions and so on. The second accepts that it *seems* this way but claims that this is misleading. Really there is no underlying continuous and unitary self. The illusion that there is has to be explained some other way. Oxford philosopher Derek Parfit (1987) has aptly described these two types as "ego theories" and "bundle theories."

The most popular ways of thinking about human beings are undoubtedly ego theories. Many religions, including Hinduism and Islam, entail notions of spirits or souls. In both Christianity and Islam the soul is a continuing entity that is central to a person's life and to their moral responsibility, as well as being able to survive the death of the physical body. Among major religions Buddhism alone denies the existence of such entities. Parfit (1984, 1987) calls the Buddha the first bundle theorist.

David Hume (1711–1776)

David Hume was born in Edinburgh and studied law at Edinburgh University, though he never graduated. He then tried his hand at commerce in Bristol, but nearly had a nervous breakdown. In 1734 he moved to France and there wrote his masterpiece *A Treatise of Human Nature*, in his mid-twenties. This long book was not a great success but the shortened version, *An Enquiry Concerning Human Understanding*, became a classic. He built on the empiricism founded by Locke and Berkeley, and wrote on causation, morals and the existence of God.

Hume distinguished between "ideas" and "impressions" according to the force and liveliness with which they make their way into consciousness. He reported that he could never catch himself without a perception, and never found anything but the perceptions, which is why he concluded that the self is not an entity but a "bundle of sensations."

"a Bundle Theorist denies the existence of persons. . . . Bundle Theory is hard to believe."

Parfit, 1987: 20, 23

Most forms of substance dualism are ego theories because they equate the separate mind, or non-physical substance, with the experiencing self. An example is Popper and Eccles' dualist interactionism (see Chapter 3) in which the self-conscious mind controls its brain and scans the brain's activity. But the distinction between ego and bundle theories should not be confused with the distinction between dualism and monism. As we shall see, many materialist scientists, while denying dualism, still assume a persisting self.

Bundle theories take their name from the philosophy of the Scottish empiricist David Hume (1711–76), who argued that the self is not an entity but is more like a "bundle of sensations." A person's life is a series of sensations, impressions and ideas that seem to be tied together not because they happen to one person but because of such relationships as those that hold between experiences and later memories of them. In *A Treatise of Human Nature* Hume wrote:

> For my part, when I enter most intimately into what I call *myself*, I always stumble on some particular perception or other, of heat or cold, light or shade, love or hatred, pain or pleasure. I never can catch *myself* at any time without a perception, and never can observe anything but the perception.
> (Dennett 1984, *Treatise*, I, VI, iv)

By staring deep into his own experience Hume, like the Buddha, seems to have discovered that there is no experiencer. Not surprisingly, Hume's ideas were unpopular, and his denial of self was countered by the commonsense approach of his fellow Scottish philosopher Thomas Reid (1710–96) who protested, "I am not thought, I am not action, I am not feeling: I am something which thinks and acts and feels." In other words, Reid appealed to ego theory.

These two views capture a fundamental split in the way people think about the nature of self. On the one hand, ego theorists believe in continuously existing selves who are subjects of experience and who think, act and feel. On the other hand, bundle theorists deny there is any such thing.

As Hume knew all too well, bundle theory is counter-intuitive—for the non-existence of my self is difficult even to contemplate. But there are many good reasons at least to try. We will begin with some extraordinary case histories challenging the natural assumption that each human being has one conscious self.

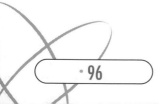

PRACTICE
WHO IS CONSCIOUS NOW?

As many times as you can, every day, ask yourself the familiar question, "Am I conscious now?" You will probably be sure that you are—for example, you may be conscious of the road you are walking along, the room around you or the music you are listening to. Now turn your attention to whoever or whatever is having this experience. This is presumably what Hume was doing when he made his famous realization about self. Can you see or feel or hear the *experiencer*, as opposed to the experienced world? At first you will probably be sure that there is an experiencer, but it may be difficult to see any further than that. Keep looking. Keep asking, **"Who is conscious now?"**

This is not an easy exercise, but it will repay practicing over many weeks or months. Try to see whether there is a separation between the experienced and the experiencer, and if so what the experiencer is like. This practice forms the basis of the next two exercises as well.

> *"I am not thought, I am not action, I am not feeling: I am something which thinks and acts and feels."*
> **Reid**, 1785

MULTIPLE PERSONALITY

On 17 January 1887, an itinerant preacher called Ansel Bourne walked into a bank in Providence, Rhode Island, withdrew $551, paid some bills and got into a horsecar bound for Pawtucket. He did not return home that day and nothing was heard of him for two months. The local papers reported him as missing and the police hunted for him in vain.

Meanwhile, two weeks after Bourne disappeared, a certain Mr. A.J. Brown rented a small shop in Norristown, Pennsylvania, stocked it with stationery, confectionery, fruit and small articles, and set up a quiet trade. He went to Philadelphia several times to replenish his stock, slept and cooked his meals in the back room, regularly attended church and, according to neighbors, was quiet, orderly and "in no way queer." Then at 5 am on 14 March Mr. Brown woke up in a terrible fright to the sound of an explosion and found himself in an unfamiliar bed, feeling very weak, as though he had been drugged. He called the people in the house to tell him where he was and said that his name was Ansel Bourne. He knew nothing of Norristown, was ignorant of shop-keeping, and the last thing he remembered was taking money out of a bank in Providence. He would not believe that two months had gone by. His neighbors thought him insane and so, at first, did the doctor they called to attend him. But, happily, they did as he asked and telegraphed his nephew in Providence saying, "Do you know Ansel Bourne? Please answer." The reply came back "He is my uncle" and soon the Rev. Ansel Bourne was taken home again.

Early in 1890 William James and Richard Hodgson conceived the idea that if Bourne could be hypnotized, they might be able to contact the dissociated

EGO AND BUNDLE THEORIES OF SELF

Ego theory

The reason each of us feels like a continuous, unified self is because we are. Underlying the ever-changing experiences of our lives there is an inner self who experiences all these different things. This self may (indeed must) change gradually as life goes on, but it is still essentially the same "me." In other words, according to any kind of ego theory, the self is a continuous entity that is the subject of a person's experiences and the author of their actions and decisions.

Ego theories include:

- Cartesian dualism
- immortal souls
- reincarnating spirits
- Gazzaniga's interpreter
- MacKay's self-supervisory system.

Add your own examples.

Bundle theory

The feeling that each of us is a continuous, unified self is an illusion. There is no such self but only a series of experiences linked loosely together in various ways. Bundle theory does not deny that each of us *seems* to be a unified conscious being. It denies that there is any separately existing entity that explains that appearance. There are experiences, but there is no one who has them. Actions and decisions happen but not because there is someone who acts and decides.

Bundle theories include:

- the Buddhist notion of annatta, or no self
- Hume's bundle of sensations
- self as a discursive production
- Dennett's no audience in the Cartesian theater.

Add your own examples.

personality and find out what had happened during those missing two weeks. James successfully put Bourne into a hypnotic trance, whereupon Mr. Brown reappeared and was able to describe his travels and the places he had stayed during the missing two weeks. In this state he seemed unaware of any connection with Ansel Bourne and could not remember Bourne's life. James and Hodgson tried in vain to reunite the two personalities, and Hodgson concluded that "Mr. Bourne's skull to-day still covers two distinct personal selves" (James, 1890, i: 392).

What does this extraordinary case of fugue tell us? At the time doctors, psychologists and psychical researchers argued over whether it could be explained by epilepsy, fraud, splitting of the personality, psychic phenomena or even spirit possession (James, 1890; Hodgson, 1891; Myers, 1903). There was good evidence of blackouts and seizures that might indicate epilepsy, but this does not, on its own, explain the extraordinary phenomena. Perhaps the most obvious thing to note is the connection between memory and selfhood. When the character of Brown reappeared, the memories of those missing two weeks came back and the rest of life seemed vague or non-existent. When Bourne reappeared, the memories of Mr. Brown and the whole of his short and simple life were gone. As far as we know, Mr. Brown never came back, and by 1887 this personality seemed to be gradually disintegrating.

At about that time, Robert Louis Stevenson's fantastic tale of *The Strange Case of Dr. Jekyll and Mr. Hyde* (1886) was published. By then many real-life cases of what became known as multiple personality had appeared. Hypnosis, or mesmerism, was very popular for treating such conditions as hysteria, and occasionally doctors or psychiatrists found that under hypnosis their patients, almost always women, seemed to manifest a completely different personality. By this they did not mean that their patients just behaved differently or showed different personality traits (the way we use the term "personality" today), but that there seemed to be two or more distinct and separate people inhabiting a single body (what we might call persons or selves).

FIGURE 7.2 • Dr. Jekyll and Mr. Hyde; good doctor and evil murderer sharing the same body, from Robert Louis Stevenson's classic novel.

Perhaps the most famous case was reported by Dr. Morton Prince (1854–1929) of Boston, Massachusetts (Prince, 1906). Early in 1898 he was consulted by Miss Christine Beauchamp, who had suffered a miserable and abusive childhood and was suffering from pain, fatigue, nervousness and other symptoms which he treated both with conventional treatments and with hypnosis. Under hypnosis a second, rather passive personality appeared (labeled BII), but one day Miss Beauchamp began speaking about herself as "she." An entirely new personality (BIII) had appeared and was soon named Sally. Sally was childish, selfish, playful and naughty, quite unlike Miss Beauchamp who was religious, upright, reserved and almost saintly in her self-control. During many years of treatment several more personalities appeared and seemed to vie for control of a single body. They all had different tastes and preferences, skills and even states of health. Miss Beauchamp was generally weak and nervous, while Sally was fit, fearless and strong. Indeed Sally used to delight in tricking Miss Beauchamp by taking a long walk in the dark and then "folding herself up," to leave poor Miss Beauchamp to walk home, terrified and ill.

Even worse dramas were played out between them, with Sally tearing up Miss Beauchamp's letters, shocking her friends or making her smoke cigarettes, which she hated. As Prince put it, she

> . . . at one moment says and does and plans and arranges something to which a short time before she most strongly objected, indulges tastes which a moment before would have been abhorrent to her

ideals, and undoes or destroys what she had just laboriously planned and arranged.

(Prince 1906: 2)

On several occasions Sally kept poor Miss Beauchamp awake at night by throwing off all the bedclothes and piling the furniture on the bed before folding up again. Imagine waking up to find yourself in such a situation, with no recall of the past few hours, but knowing that no one else could have entered your room.

Two of the personalities had no knowledge of each other, or of the third, and each life had blanks in memory corresponding to times when the others were active. Poor Miss Beauchamp had to invent excuses for her forgetfulness and explanations for not recognizing people Sally had befriended. Oddly enough, though, Sally knew of all the others and claimed to be able to remember events that happened when each was in control. She even claimed that she was still conscious, though "squeezed," when Miss Beauchamp was "out," and spoke as though she had her own thoughts, perceptions and will during these times. She claimed to be conscious of all Miss Beauchamp's dreams, although she herself neither slept nor dreamt. In other words, the case seemed not to be one of alternating consciousness (as we might interpret Ansel Bourne's case) but of simultaneous consciousness, or "co-consciousness." Thus when Prince speaks of a "subconscious self," or a "subconsciousness," he means a self that has its own stream of conscious experiences while another self is in control of the body.

Prince considered the possibility that there was no "real or normal self," but in the end he set about finding the "real Miss Beauchamp." Despite their protests, he concluded that most of the subpersonalities, including Sally, were "a dissociated group of conscious states" (1906: 234) and not real selves. So, they had to die. It was, he said, "psychical murder" (1906: 248). This extraordinary story had a happy ending, for eventually he succeeded in bringing all the personalities together into what he called (though others might disagree) "the real, original or normal self, the self that was born and which she was intended by nature to be" (Prince, 1906: 1).

This case proved to be one of the last of the classic cases of multiple personality, most of which were reported between 1840 and 1910. After that, there was a wave of reaction against the whole notion, due at least partly to the spread of psychoanalysis, but partly to the increasingly bizarre phenomena described. Critics pointed out that most of the discoverers were men hypnotizing young women who were eager to please, and suggested that many of them had been duped. Most psychiatrists became skeptical of the whole story.

But the phenomena did not entirely cease. In the 1950s, Chris Sizemore's three personalities, Eve White, Eve Black and Jane, were made famous in the film *The Three Faces of Eve* (Thigpen and Cleckley, 1954). While Eve White was

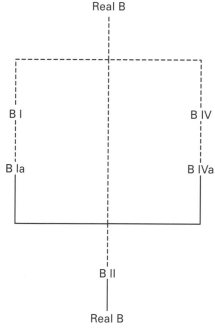

FIGURE 7.3 • According to Morton Prince, the real Miss Beauchamp disintegrated into BI and BIV. These two personalities could be hypnotized to give BIa and BIVa, who could be synthesized into BII. Alternatively Real B could be hypnotized immediately into BII who could be dissociated into BIa and BIVa.

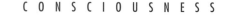

CONSCIOUSNESS

retiring and conventional, Eve Black was a childish daredevil with an eroti- cally mischievous glance, quite different from Eve White's careworn expres- sion. Eve White was generally caring and gentle, while Eve Black showed no sympathy for their real marital troubles. She even enjoyed getting drunk and then watching Eve White suffer a bewildered hangover the next day. Tests showed that Eve White's IQ was 110, but Eve Black's was 104, and Eve White scored much higher on a memory test. Eve Black's EEG was faster and bor- derline normal, while Eve White's and Jane's were both judged normal. As far as consciousness is concerned, Eve White became unconscious when Eve Black took over, but Eve Black claimed to preserve awareness while absent. By this time the concept of dissociation had been revived, especially in the form of the neo-dissociation theory proposed by Harvard psychologist, Ernest Hilgard (Hilgard, 1986; see Profile, Chapter 23).

WHO IS CONSCIOUS NOW?

In the 1970s the case of Sybil, "a woman possessed by sixteen separate per- sonalities," became famous thanks to a popular book (Schreiber, 1973) and then a film. Then in the early 1980s a veritable epidemic of cases began. By 1990 more than 20,000 cases had been diagnosed in the USA alone. Television appearances and notoriety doubtless tempted many into inventing or exag- gerating their symptoms, and accusations of compliance and collusion began again. People accused of serious crimes claimed that "it wasn't me," with serious implications for the legal system. Critics argued that the disease was iatrogenic in origin (i.e., created by the treatment or the therapist). Patients accused therapists of implanting false memories, and multiple personality became linked with satanic abuse, exorcism and even demonic possession.

Feminist writer Elaine Showalter (1997) describes such phenomena as alien abductions, chronic fatigue syndrome, Gulf War syndrome and multiple per- sonality as "hystories"—epidemics of hysteria spread through stories. These culturally created narratives are perpetuated through interactions between troubled patients and willing therapists, by novels, self-help books, articles, TV shows and films. Like viruses or infectious memes (see Chapter 11), they spread from person to person and country to country. Having started in the USA, and once thought to be culture-specific, the epidemic of multiple personality even- tually escaped, and in the 1990s reached Europe, New Zealand and elsewhere. In 1994, the American Psychiatric Association's *Diagnostic and Statistical Manual of Mental Disorders—IV* changed Multiple Personality Disorder (MPD) to Dissociative Identity Disorder (DID). With all the controversy that surrounds the "multiple personality movement," it is perhaps not surprising that the phenomenon is rarely mentioned in modern texts on psychology.

Should we therefore reject all the cases as being "hystories"? If so, multiple personality tells us more about culture than it does about the nature of self and consciousness. But this wholesale rejection of the phenomenon may be misguided. Some cases could not have been created by therapy, such as that of Ansel Bourne who, as far as we know, never had any therapy. In any case, if even a few of these fascinating cases really happened as described, then they should tell us something very interesting about the relationship between self, memory and consciousness. But what?

The distinction between ego and bundle theories may be helpful here. Prince was clearly an ego theorist, for he believed not only in the existence of the "real Miss Beauchamp" but in several other different selves who were distinct consciousnesses with separate wills. Hodgson and Myers thought so too, and, like many of their contemporaries, their ideas were rooted in spiritualist notions of mediumship, possession and the idea of human personality as an entity that might survive bodily death (remember that they used the term "personality" to describe a conscious entity, rather than a type of person). William James thought that cases like this, along with other hypnotic phenomena (see Chapter 22), provided proof of a secondary consciousness, or "under self," co-existing with the primary consciousness. Indeed he believed that "The same brain may subserve many conscious selves, either alternate or coexisting" (James, 1890, i: 401). But his ideas are also rather more subtle, as we shall see in the next chapter.

An example of bundle theory comes from discursive psychology—a field built on the principle "that the mind of any human being is constituted by the discourses that they are involved in" (Harré and Gillett, 1994: 104). Within this framework the sense of self is a product of the way the first person pronoun, "I," is used in discourse. The philosopher and pioneer of discursive psychology, Rom Harré, and philosopher and neurosurgeon Grant Gillett, use the case of Miss Beauchamp to illustrate "the difference between the old idea of the self as something inside a person and the new idea of the self as a continuous production" (Harré and Gillett, 1994: 110). They studied what went on in the many conversations between Dr. Prince and his patient, and argue that Prince made sense of Miss Beauchamp's utterances by organizing them in terms of three independent pronoun systems. While BI spoke of herself as "I" and Sally as "you" or "she," Sally referred to herself as "I," and so on. This produces three distinct selves in the sense that each "I" indexes the same body, but a different continuous sequence of events and a different morally responsible agent. Taking the "discursive turn," there is no more to the selves than that. As Harré and Gillett put it, "There are not three little egos inside Miss Beauchamp, each speaking up through her mouth. The speaking parts are all there is to it. They are the phenomenon, and these speaking parts are the selves" (Harré and Gillett, 1994: 110).

This kind of theory has the advantage of not having to rely on mysterious entities called selves, but runs the risk of failing completely to say anything about consciousness. If the words are all there is to it, why do we have this compelling sense of a continuous and unitary self who is the subject of experiences?

Miss Beauchamp	Chris/Sally	Miss X
I	You	–
You	I	She
She	You	I

FIGURE 7.4 • The power of pronouns to create selves. According to Harré and Gillett (1994), three distinct systems of pronouns were used in Miss Beauchamp's speech. This means that one body housed three distinct selves, not because Miss Beauchamp had three selves inside her, but because three selves were discursively produced.

SPLIT BRAINS, SPLIT CONSCIOUSNESS?

In cases of multiple personality the person's brain remains intact, and the dissociation is mental rather than physical. The reverse seems to occur in those rare cases when a person's brain is divided in two.

Epilepsy can be a debilitating disease, at its worst causing almost continuous seizures that make a worthwhile life impossible. For such serious cases a drastic operation was carried out many times in the 1960s. The two halves of the brain were separated from each other to prevent seizures spreading from one side to the other. In some patients only the corpus callosum, or part of the corpus callosum, was cut, in others the smaller anterior and hippocampal commissures were cut as well. Remarkably all these patients recovered well and seemed able to live a relatively normal life. Tests showed that their personality was little changed and their IQ, verbal and problem-solving abilities were hardly affected (Gazzaniga, 1992; Sperry, 1968), but in the early 1960s some carefully designed experiments tested the two hemispheres independently. The dramatic consequences of this disconnection, and the work that followed, earned a Nobel prize for pioneering psychobiologist Roger Sperry (1913–94).

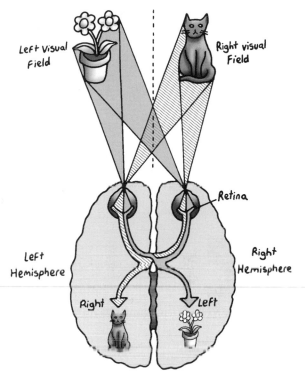

FIGURE 7.5 • The human visual system is organized as shown. Information from the left visual field of both eyes (in this case the flowers) goes to the right hemisphere, and information from the right visual field of both eyes (in this case the cat) goes to the left hemisphere. Note that by this partial crossing over of fibers in the optic chiasm, the effect is that the two sides of the brain deal with opposite sides of the world, not with opposite eyes.

Information from the left visual field goes to the right hemisphere (and vice versa), information from the right ear goes to the right hemisphere (and vice versa) and the left half of the body is controlled by the right hemisphere (and vice versa). Knowing this, it is possible to ensure that information goes only to one hemisphere, and a response is obtained from only one hemisphere. In 1961 neuroscientist Michael Gazzaniga first tested a split-brain patient, W.J., using such a procedure. At that time research on cats and monkeys had shown that the two hemispheres appeared to function almost entirely separately when disconnected, but no one expected this to be true of humans—after all, the patients appeared to act and speak and think like normal people. But the research showed that, as in the animals, each half-brain could behave independently.

In a typical experiment the patient sat in front of a screen, which was divided into two, and fixated the center. Words or pictures were then flashed to either visual field, thus sending information to only one hemisphere. The patient responded verbally or by using one hand or the other to indicate an answer. Suppose that a picture of an object was flashed to the right visual field. Since in most people verbal ability is restricted to the left hemisphere, the patient could then say exactly what it was. But if it was flashed to the left side, he could not. In other words the left hemisphere, with its ability to speak, knew the correct answer only when the picture appeared on the right. In a normal person the information would quickly flow across to the other side, but in these split-brain patients it could not. The interesting finding was that the right hemisphere could communicate in other ways. So if a pile of objects was given, out of sight, to the left hand, that hand could easily retrieve the object seen in the left visual field.

The tasks could even be done simultaneously. For example, asked to say what he had seen, the subject might answer "bottle," while his left hand was busy retrieving a hammer from a heap of objects—or even retrieving a nail as the closest association. When a dollar sign was flashed to the left and a question mark to the right, the patient drew the dollar sign, but when asked what he had drawn he replied "a question mark." As Sperry (1968) put it, one hemisphere does not know what the other has been doing. In addition, each hemisphere could remember what it had been shown, but these memories were inaccessible to the other. So the left hand could retrieve the same object an hour later, but the person (i.e., speaking left hemisphere) would still deny having any knowledge of it.

Sperry (1968) thought that these results revealed a doubling of conscious awareness, and even that his patients had two free wills in one cranial vault. "Each hemisphere seemed to have its own separate and private sensations," he said, and he concluded that "the minor hemisphere constitutes a second conscious entity that is characteristically human and runs along in parallel with the more dominant stream of consciousness in the major hemisphere" (ibid.: 723). In other words, for Sperry a split-brain patient was essentially two conscious people.

At first, Gazzaniga also believed that consciousness had been separated to give dual consciousness, or a "double conscious system" (ibid. 1992: 122). But later he began to doubt this conclusion with his discovery of what he called "the interpreter," located in the left hemisphere. In one test a picture of a chicken claw was flashed to the left hemisphere and a snow scene to the right. From an array of pictures, the subject, P.S., then chose a shovel with the left hand and a chicken with the right. When asked why, he replied, "Oh, that's simple. The chicken claw goes with the chicken, and you need a shovel to clean out the chicken shed" (ibid.: 124).

This kind of confabulation was common, especially in experiments with emotions. If an emotionally disturbing scene was shown to the right hemisphere, then the whole body reacted appropriately with, for example, blushing, anxiety and signs of fear. When asked why, the uninformed left hemisphere always made up some plausible excuse. Or when the right hemisphere was commanded, for example, to laugh or walk, the person would obey. When asked why, he replied that he found the experiments funny, or that he wanted to fetch a Coke. The patients never said things like "Because I have a split brain and you showed another picture to the other half." Gazzaniga argued

CONSCIOUSNESS

FIGURE 7.6 • The split brain patient P.S. was shown a snow scene to the right hemisphere and a chicken claw to the left, and asked to choose from an array of pictures. He chose the shovel with his left hand and the chicken with his right (after Gazzaniga and LeDoux, 1992).

FIGURE 7.7 • When the silent right hemisphere is given a command, it carries it out. At the same time the left doesn't really know why it does so, but it makes up a theory quickly. Reprinted from Gazzaniga and LeDoux, *The Integrated Mind* (New York: Plenum Press, 1978), fig 5.2, p. 149, with permission.

that only the left hemisphere interpreter uses language, organizes beliefs and ascribes actions and intentions to people. Only this hemisphere has what he calls "high-level consciousness."

Where does that leave the non-dominant hemisphere? Is it conscious? Does it have a sense of self? Sperry wondered whether it has "a true stream of conscious awareness" or is just an "automaton carried along in a reflex or trance-like state," what we would now call a zombie (1968: 731). Much research showed that the two hemispheres have very different abilities; for example, the left has far superior language skills and the right superior face recognition. The right hemisphere has often been described as having the linguistic ability of a three-year-old child or the reasoning capacity of a chimpanzee. Yet we often ascribe consciousness to children and animals. In those rare cases where a person's entire left hemisphere is destroyed or removed, we still consider them to be conscious. This might suggest that Sperry was right, and that there are two streams of consciousness involved.

SELF-ASSESSMENT QUESTIONS

○ In your own words, describe the difference between ego and bundle theories. Where did each get its name?

○ What role does memory play in cases of multiple personality?

○ What is the evidence that Sally Beauchamp's body was inhabited by more than one conscious self at a time?

○ What is the status of multiple personality disorder in psychiatry today?

○ Describe a typical experiment for testing the two hemispheres of a split-brain patient independently.

○ Give examples of confabulation in both multiple personality and split-brain cases.

○ How many selves are there in a split-brain patient: one, two or none? Describe at least one theory that gives each answer.

Scottish neuroscientist Donald MacKay (1922–1987) was determined to find out whether split-brain patients are really two persons or one, and he devised an ingenious test for the purpose (MacKay, 1987). He taught each hemisphere, separately, to play a "20 questions"–type guessing game with him. One person chooses a number from 0 to 9 and the other has to guess what it is. In response, the first person replies "up," "down" or "OK" until the correct answer is reached. Both halves of patient J.W. learned the game easily. Then they were asked to play each other with J.W.'s mouth (controlled by his left hemisphere) making the guesses and his left hand (controlled by his right hemisphere) pointing to cards saying "go up," "go down" or "OK." With this game it proved possible for the two half-brains to play against each other, and even to cooperate and pay each other winnings in tokens, but MacKay concluded that there was still no evidence of two separate persons or of true "duality of will."

How, he asked, could anything play a game of 20 questions without being conscious? He noted all the intelligent actions we can carry out unconsciously, and the artificial systems that can play games, and came to the following conclusion. To understand human behavior, we must distinguish between the executive and supervisory levels of brain function. The executive level can (unconsciously) control goal-directed activities and evaluate them in terms of current criteria and priorities, but only the self-supervisory system can determine and update those priorities. We are conscious only of those features of our world that engage this self-supervisory system.

With this theory MacKay provides his own answers to some of our recurring questions about consciousness. Question: what makes some things conscious and others not? Answer: whether they engage the self-supervisory system or not (though he admits that how the activity of this system gives rise to conscious experience remains totally mysterious). Question: what makes each of us a psychological unity? Answer: that we have only one self-supervisory system to determine our overall priorities. As for the split-brain patient, he has only one self-supervisory system and therefore is still only one conscious person.

So who was right? Are split-brain patients one conscious person or two?

At first sight it seems as though there must be a right answer to this simple question. But we have already encountered several ways of thinking about consciousness that might lead us to doubt this, including the problematic notion of zombies, the idea that vision is a grand illusion, and the non-existence of the Cartesian theater. Most helpful, though, is the distinction between ego and bundle theories of self.

Sperry, Gazzaniga and MacKay are all, in Parfit's terms, ego theorists. Each of them assumes that selves are countable things, that there must either be one or two of them inhabiting the split-brain body. I pointed out earlier that belief in ego theory is not the same as belief in dualism, and we can see this clearly here. Sperry (1980) believed in the causal efficacy of consciousness, but his theory was entirely monist, with consciousness being an emergent, self-regulatory property of neural networks. Gazzaniga rejected dualism, as did MacKay, who wrote about "duality without dualism." Nevertheless they all tried to answer the question, "How many selves in a split-brain patient?"

For Parfit (1987), this is a non-sensical question because ego theory is false. He asks us to imagine

(Activity continues on next page)

ACTIVITY
Split-brain twins

FIGURE 7.8 ● Experiment 1. RH puts his free left hand in the bag and feels the object. When you ask what he feels, only LH can speak.

Ask for two volunteers — one to play the role of a disconnected left hemisphere and the other the right. Ask them to sit close together on a bench or table. You might like to put a sticker on each, labeling them as LH and RH. To reduce confusion, for the purposes of this explanation we'll assume that LH is female and RH is male.

LH sits on her left hand; her right hand is free to move. RH sits on his right hand; his left hand is free to move. Their two free arms now approximate to those of a normal person. RH cannot speak (although we will assume that he can understand simple verbal instructions). You might like to tape his mouth over, but make sure the tape will not hurt him when removed.

Now you can try any of the split-brain experiments described in this chapter. Here are just two examples.

1 You will need a large carrier bag or a pillow case and several small objects (e.g., pen, shoe, book, bottle). Out of sight of the twins place one object in the bag. Now ask RH to put his left hand into the bag and feel the object. Ask "What can you feel?" Only LH can speak. Press her to answer (if RH tries to give her non-verbal clues, this only adds to the fun).

(Activity continued)

Now put all the objects into the bag, let RH put in his left hand and ask him to select the correct object. He should do this easily.

2 Re-create MacKay's experiment.
Ask RH to think of a number between 0 and 9 (or, if you want better control, prepare numbered cards and show one to RH out of sight of LH). LH now has to guess what the number is. For each guess RH points "up," or "down" or nods for the correct answer. You might like to try inventing a method for playing the game the other way around.

The "twins" should be able to play this game successfully. Does it show that there are two conscious selves involved? Does this game help us to understand what it is like to have a split brain?

READING

an experiment in which one hemisphere sees a red screen and the other sees blue. When asked how many colors there are, both hands write "Only one," but when asked to say which color, one writes "blue" and the other "red." Now, assuming that this thought experiment worked as Parfit said it would, are there two streams of consciousness? Are there two conscious selves? Parfit concludes that there are indeed two separate streams of consciousness—one stream seeing red and the other seeing blue—but there are not two conscious persons who do the seeing. Why? Because only an ego theorist can count the number of persons involved. For a bundle theorist, there is no such thing as a continuous self who experiences the stream. So whether we consider split brains or whole brains, "the number of persons involved is none" (Parfit, 1987: 20).

MacKay, D. (1987) Divided brains—divided minds? In C. Blakemore and S. Greenfield (eds) *Mindwaves*. Oxford: Blackwell, 5–16.

Parfit, D. (1987) Divided minds and the nature of persons. In C. Blakemore and S. Greenfield (eds) *Mindwaves*. Oxford: Blackwell, 19–26.

Sperry, R.W. (1968) Hemisphere deconnection and unity in conscious awareness. *American Psychologist* 23, 723–33 (also reprinted in R.D. Gross (ed.) (1990) *Key Studies in Psychology*. London: Hodder & Stoughton, 197–207).

Thigpen, C.H. and Cleckley, H. (1954) A case of multiple personality. *Journal of Abnormal and Social Psychology* 49, 135–51 (also reprinted in R.D. Gross (ed.) (1990) *Key Studies in Psychology*. London: Hodder & Stoughton, 374–83).

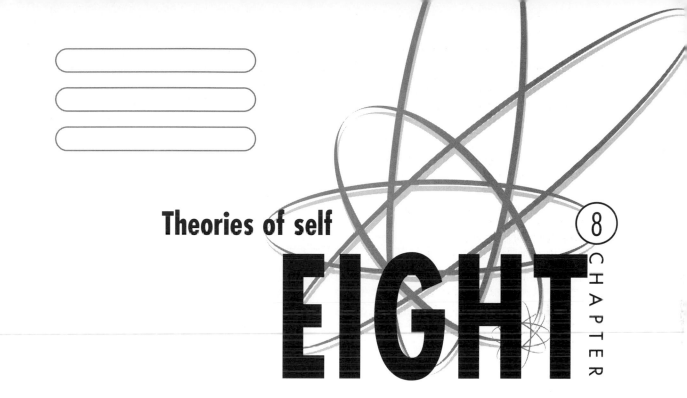

Theories of self

So far we have divided theories of self crudely into two categories: ego theories, which entail some kind of continuing entity, and bundle theories, which do not. When taken in their most extreme versions, neither deals adequately with the strange cases of split brains and multiple personality, nor explains ordinary self-awareness. On the one hand, extreme ego theories entail mysterious, untestable entities. On the other hand, extreme bundle theories do not explain why we *feel* as though we are a continuing entity. In this chapter we consider some theories that try to avoid these problems.

First we must be as clear as possible about the fundamental difference between the two types of theory. It might seem obvious that reductionist scientists should agree with Parfit, accept Hume's denial, and be bundle theorists. After all, if the brain consists of millions of inter-connected neurons whose activity gives rise to behaviors, memories and perceptions, then there is no need for an experiencing self as well. Yet, as we have seen, some scientists still try to count the number of selves in a split-brain patient or ask whether multiple personalities are really separate selves, implying at least some components of ego theory.

The situation may be rather like that with the Cartesian theater. While it is easy, intellectually, to deny the existence of a persisting experiencing self, it is another matter to accept all the consequences of such a view. Some of these consequences are brought to life by some classic philosophers' thought experiments.

THOUGHT EXPERIMENTS WITH THE SELF

Imagine that in the middle of the night, without leaving any traces or doing any harm, a mad Martian scientist comes into your room, removes your brain and swaps it with your friend John's brain (impossible, of course, but this is a thought experiment). In the morning you stir, your dreams recede, and you wake into full consciousness. But who has woken up? Have you woken up in John's body? Will you scream and protest, and hope that you are only dreaming that you are in the wrong room and have hairy legs and a beard?

FIGURE 8.1

If you think that each of you will wake up in the "wrong" body, then presumably you think that the conscious self depends on the brain and not the rest of the body. So in another popular kind of thought experiment the Martians only scan the brains and then swap the patterns of neural information. This time all your memories and personality traits are swapped over but the brains stay in place. Now who is it that experiences the feel of the hairy legs and the beard? You or John? Is the experiencing self tied to the body, the brain, the memories or what?

Ego and bundle theorists differ fundamentally in their responses to such questions. The ego theorist might say "of course it will be me" (or "of course it will be John") because the experiencing self must be associated with something, whether it is the body, the brain, personal memories, personality traits and preferences or some combination of these or other things. In other words, for the ego theorist there has to be an answer. Ego theorists may try to find that answer by investigating the relationships between the conscious self and memory, personality, attention or other brain functions.

For the bundle theorist this is all a waste of time. According to bundle theory there is no continuous experiencing self so there is no problem with any of these strange imaginary tales. Yes, the person in the bed might scream and shout and be very unhappy and confused, but if you ask "Is it really me?" then you reveal your own confusion. There can be no answer to this question because there is no such thing as the "real me."

Are you an ego theorist or a bundle theorist? If you are not sure, this next thought experiment is a good way to find out.

Imagine that you are offered a free trip, anywhere you want to go, in a teletransporter. You are invited to step inside a cubicle in which there is a special button. When you press it, every cell of your body is scanned and the information is stored (though your body is destroyed in the process). All the information is then sent, at the speed of light, to your chosen destination and used to reconstruct a replica of you, exactly as you were before. Note that this is only meant to be a thought experiment, but some people believe that this, or similar processes, may soon be a reality (Kurzweil, 1999).

Since your replica has a brain in exactly the same state as yours was when it was scanned, he or she will seem to remember living your life up to the moment when you pressed the button. This replica will behave just like you, have your personality and foibles, and will in every other way be just like you. The only difference is that this psychological continuity will not have its normal cause, the continued existence of your brain, but will depend on the information having been transmitted through space.

The question is—would you go?

Many people would be happy to go. They reason that if their brain is completely replicated, they won't notice the difference—they will feel just the same as before, and indeed will be just the same as before. Others would refuse to go. Their reasons may not be as rational but may be even more forcefully felt. "This journey is not traveling but dying," they may say. "The person who appears on Mars is just a replica, not the real me. I don't want to die." It may be some consolation that the replica will be able to take over their life, see their friends, be part of their family, finish their projects and so on, but still it will not really be "me." These people cannot accept, as the bundle theorist must, that it is an empty question whether you are about to live or die (Parfit, 1987).

ACTIVITY
The teletransporter

Imagine you want to go to the beautiful city of Cape Town for a holiday. You are offered a simple, free, almost instantaneous, and 100 percent safe way of getting there and back. All you have to do is step inside the box, press the button and . . .

The box is, of course, Parfit's teletransporter. In making the journey every cell of your body and brain will be scanned and destroyed, and then replicated exactly as they were before, but in Cape Town. Would you press the button?

As a class exercise get everyone to answer "Yes" or "No." Do not allow any "Don't knows" (If people do not want to answer publicly, then get them to write down "Yes" or "No"). Do not allow quibbles over safety or any other details. This is, after all, a thought experiment, so we are not constrained by reality. The box is 100 percent safe and reliable. If you won't go in, this has to be for some other reason than that it might go wrong.

Now ask for a volunteer who said "Yes" and ask him or her to explain why. Other members of the group can then ask further questions to work out, for example, why this person is not worried about having their body completely destroyed. Next ask for a "No" volunteer and let others ask why she or he will not go. Bear in mind that people's reasons for not going may involve their deepest beliefs about their soul, spirit, God or life after death. It is helpful to respect these beliefs even while pushing people hard to explain what they mean.

After the discussion, find out how many people have changed their minds. In a course on consciousness it is instructive to ask this same question again after a few weeks or months of study, and for this purpose it is helpful for people to keep a record of their answers. They may change.

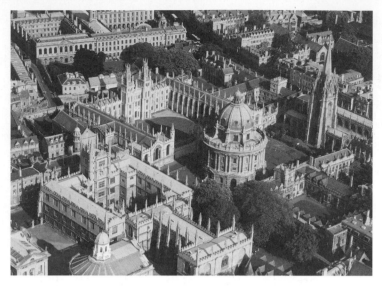

FIGURE 8.2 • Where's the University?

To delve deeper into these objections, consider some further thought experiments. Imagine now that only a few cells are replaced, or any proportion of them you like. Is there now some critical percentage beyond which *you* die and a replica is created in your place? If 50 percent are replaced, what would you conclude? Would the person who wakes up be half you and half replica? This conclusion seems ludicrous, but still you may be tempted to say that there must be an answer—the resulting person must really either be you or someone else. If that is how you think, then you are an ego theorist.

With this in mind we may now explore a few of the very many theories of self. The examples given here in no way cover all possible approaches to the nature of self, but I have chosen those that seem to bear especially on the relationship between self and consciousness. In each case we can consider, first, whether the theory is an ego or bundle theory; second, how it accounts for the experience of *seeming* to be a unified and continuous self; and, third, whether it helps us to understand the nature of consciousness.

WILLIAM JAMES

William James is the obvious starting point, for he wrote extensively about both self and consciousness, and his ideas are still widely respected today. James built his theory first and foremost on the way it *seems*. Central to the concept of personal identity, he said, is the feeling of unity and continuity of oneself. He stressed that this is a matter of *feeling*, that one's own thoughts have a warmth and intimacy about them that distinguishes them from others'.

> The universal conscious fact is not "feelings and thoughts exist," but "I think" and "I feel." No psychology, at any rate, can question the *existence* of personal selves. The worst a psychology can do is so to interpret the nature of these selves as to rob them of their worth.
>
> (James, 1890, i: 226)

He begins by dividing the self into two ever-present elements: the empirical self, or objective person, which he calls the "me," and the subjective knowing thought, or pure ego, which he calls "I." The empirical self is easier to deal with and includes three aspects. The material self is a person's body, his clothes and possessions, his family and friends—indeed all those things he is likely to call "mine"—together with personal vanity or modesty, love of wealth and fear of poverty. Then there is his "social self," which includes his reputation and how he is seen by others. As James points out, we each have as many social selves as there are people who recognize us and carry an image of us in their mind, but in practice these divide into groups and we may behave differently with these different groups and feel ourselves to be a different person in different company. Finally there is what he calls the "spiritual self" (though this may seem an odd name to us today), by which he means mental dispositions and abilities, and intellectual, moral and religious aspirations, together with moral principles, conscience and guilt.

In this last part of the empirical self he includes subjective experience. Within the stream of consciousness, says James, it seems as though there is a special portion that welcomes or rejects the rest— that which can disown everything else but cannot be disowned itself. This "active element" in consciousness seems to receive the sensations and perceptions of the stream of consciousness, it seems to be the source of effort and attention and the place from which the will emanates. It is something like a sort of junction at which sensory ideas terminate and from which motor ideas proceed. He could hardly have described the Cartesian theater better.

Yet the deepest problem lies with the "I": that self that I care about, that *felt* central nucleus of my experience. This is "the most puzzling puzzle with which psychology has to deal" (James, 1890, i: 330). He describes the two main ways of dealing with it in a way that should seem thoroughly familiar to us:

> Some would say that it is a simple active substance, the soul, of which they are thus conscious; others, that it is nothing but a fiction, the imaginary being denoted by the pronoun I; and between these extremes of opinion all sorts of intermediaries would be found.
>
> (James, 1890, i: 298)

James criticizes both extremes. Those who side with the spiritualists and opt for a substantial soul can give no positive account of what that soul may be. So he rejects the "soul theory," including the substantialist view of Plato and

SELVES, CLUBS AND UNIVERSITIES

The theory that the self is just a bundle of sensations, or a stream of words, or a collection of events happening to no one is not easy either to understand or to accept. To make the task easier, we can think about clubs or universities.

Suppose that the Bristol gardening club thrives for many years and then, for lack of interest, folds. The few remaining members put away the books, tools and other club possessions and move on to something else. A few years later a new gardening enthusiast starts the club up again. She retrieves the books but redesigns the stationery. She attracts a few of the old members and lots of new ones too. Now, is this the same club or a different one? If you think there must be a right answer, then you do not understand the nature of clubs. According to bundle theories, the self is a bit like this.

Have you heard the old joke about Oxford University? An American visitor asks a student to show him the famous and ancient University of Oxford. The student takes him all around the city. He shows him the Bodleian Library and the Sheldonian Theatre, Brasenose College and Christ Church, St. Edmund Hall and Lady Margaret Hall, the Department of Experimental Psychology and the grand Examination Schools, Magdalen bridge and students punting on the Cherwell. At the end of his extensive tour the visitor says, "But where's the university?" (Ryle, 1949).

Do clubs exist? Of course. Do collegiate universities exist? Of course. But neither is something more than, or additional to, the events, people, actions, buildings or objects that make it up. Neither is an entity that can be found. According to bundle theory, the self is a bit like this.

Aristotle, as well as Descartes' beliefs and later variations. The idea of a soul, he says, explains nothing and guarantees nothing. He also rejects Locke's associationist theory and Kant's transcendentalist theory. The transcendental ego is just a "cheap and nasty" edition of the soul, he says, and inventing an ego does not explain the unity of consciousness: "the Egoists themselves, let them say what they will, believe in the bundle, and in their own system merely *tie it up*, with their special transcendental string, invented for that use alone" (James, 1890, i: 370).

On the other hand, those who side with the Humeans in saying that the stream of thought is all there is, run against the entire common sense of mankind. According to common sense the unity of our many selves is not a mere appearance of similarity and continuity, ascertained after the fact, but implies a real "owner," a pure spiritual entity of some kind. Common sense cannot accept that our unity is only potential, like that of a herd of animals or a center of gravity in physics, but insists there must be a real proprietor to hold the selves together in personal consciousness. This "holding together," then, is what needs explaining.

So how does James escape from inventing a real proprietor or a special string of his own? His well-known adage is that "*thought is itself the thinker*, and psychology need not look beyond" (1890, i: 401). "The phenomena are enough, the passing Thought itself is the only *verifiable* thinker, and its empirical connection with the brain-process is the ultimate known law" (1890, Vol. 1: 346). What he means is this. At any moment, there is a passing thought (he calls this special thought "the Thought") that incessantly remembers previous thoughts and appropriates some of them to itself. In this way, what holds the thoughts together is not a separate spirit or ego, but only another thought of a special kind. This judging Thought identifies and owns some parts of the stream of consciousness while disowning others. It pulls together those thoughts that it finds "warm" and calls them "mine." The next moment, another Thought takes up the expiring Thought and appropriates it. It binds the individual past facts with each other and with itself. In this way the passing Thought seems to be the thinker. The unity we experience is not something

The thought itself is the thinker.

James, 1890

PRACTICE
AM I THE SAME "ME" AS A MOMENT AGO?

As many times as you can, every day, ask yourself the familiar question "Am I conscious now?" and then keep watching. As "now" slips away, and things change around you, try to keep steadily watching, and wondering who is watching. Is there some kind of continuity of self as you remain aware? Can you see what that continuity is like? Or is there none?

The question is, **"Am I the same 'me' as a moment ago?"** What is really required is not asking (or answering) the question in words, but looking directly into how it seems.

CONSCIOUSNESS

separate from the Thoughts. Indeed it does not exist until the Thought is there.

He uses, again, the metaphor of a herd and herdsman. Common sense rules that there has to be a herdsman who owns the cattle and holds the herd together. But, for James, there is no permanent herdsman, only a passing series of owners, each of which inherits not only the cattle but the title to their ownership. Each Thought is born an owner and dies owned, transmitting whatever it realized as its self to the next owner. In this way is the apparent unity created.

Is James then a bundle theorist? He rejects any substantial ego, so we might assume so. And presumably he ought to step happily into the teletransporter because when the replica stepped out at the other side, a new Thought would immediately appropriate the memories and warm thoughts sustained by the replicated brain and so induce just the same sense of unity and continuity as before. Yet James placed his own theory somewhere between the extremes and criticized Hume for allowing no thread of resemblance or core of sameness to tie together the diversity of the stream of consciousness. For James the task was to explain both the diversity and unity of experience, and he felt he had accomplished this with his "remembering and appropriating Thought incessantly renewed" (1890, i: 363).

Does his theory account for the experience of *seeming* to be a unified and continuous self? Yes. He starts from how it *feels* and builds his entire theory around that. Finally, does it help us to understand the nature of consciousness? Up to a point—and James himself tells us where that point lies. In the end he cannot explain the law by which the stream of thought accompanies a stream of cerebral activity, nor why; as he puts it, "such finite human streams of thought are called into existence in such functional dependence upon brains" (1890, i: 401). In other words, the great chasm still yawns.

NEUROSCIENTIFIC MODELS OF SELF

Many neuroscientists deliberately avoid talking about the self or about self consciousness (e.g., Crick, 1994). Others discuss self-awareness as a subcategory of awareness in general, and some consider how the self concept develops and how it can go wrong (see Chapter 18). Only a few attempt to explain why the self seems to be a continuous agent and a subject of experience. Their most common strategy is to equate the self with one particular brain process or functional area of the brain.

Ramachandran suggests that his experiments on filling-in (see Chapter 6) mean, "we can begin to approach the greatest scientific and philosophical riddle of all—the nature of the self" (Ramachandran and Blakeslee, 1998: 255). Part of the motivation for these experiments was Dennett's argument that filling-in would have to be done for *someone*, some viewer or homunculus, and since homunculi cannot exist, filling-in does not occur. As we saw, some kinds of filling-in do occur. But the argument is not entirely false, says

"The worst a psychology can do is so to interpret . . . selves as to rob them of their worth."

James, 1890, Vol. i: 226

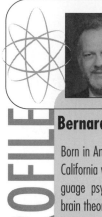

Bernard Baars (b. 1946)

Born in Amsterdam, the Netherlands, Baars moved to California with his family in 1958. He trained as a language psychologist and then moved into cognitive brain theory. He says that living with cats makes it difficult not to think of them as conscious, which has ethical implications for the way we deal with animals, babies, fetuses and each other. His view of consciousness was shaped by artificial intelligence architectures in which expert systems communicate through a common blackboard or global workspace. From this he developed the well-known Global Workspace Theory. He describes conscious events as happening "in the theatre of consciousness" where they appear in the bright spotlight of attention and are broadcast to the rest of the nervous system. He believes that the most exciting developments are in brain imaging, and the most revealing method for investigating consciousness is contrastive analysis: comparing closely matched conscious and unconscious events. He is Senior Fellow in Theoretical Neurobiology at the Neurosciences Institute in San Diego, California, where Gerald Edelman is Director. He is co-editor of the journal *Consciousness and Cognition* and founding editor of the web newsletter *Science and Consciousness Review*. He thinks that as far as consciousness is concerned, we are at last beginning to see the light.

Ramachandran. Filling-in occurs for *something* rather than *someone*, and that something is another brain process, an executive process (Ramachandran and Hirstein, 1997).

He considers MacKay's executive process, and control processes located in frontal or prefrontal areas, but argues instead for the limbic system. The processes that best match what the self is traditionally supposed to do are those involved in connecting motivation and emotion with the choice of actions to perform, based on a certain definite incoming set of qualia. Filling-in can then be seen as a way of preparing qualia for interaction with limbic executive structures. So our conscious experiences are the input to this executive system.

Ramachandran concludes not only that a single unified self "inhabiting" the brain is an illusion, but that "It is not difficult to see how such processes could give rise to the mythology of a self as an active presence in the brain—a 'ghost in the machine'" (ibid.: 455). However, he does not explain how this happens, nor how qualia can be inputs, nor how inputs can *be* experiences.

Portuguese neurologist Antonio Damasio (see Profile, Chapter 18) distinguishes between the proto-self, the core-self, and the autobiographical self, based on his studies of brain damage and psychopathology (see Chapter 18). The sense of self, he argues, has a preconscious biological precedent in the simplest organisms. This *proto-self* is a set of neural patterns that map the state of an organism moment by moment. The basic kind of consciousness is core consciousness. This is not exclusively human, is not dependent upon memory, reasoning or language, and provides the organism with a sense of self in the here and now. Associated with this is the core self: "a transient entity, ceaselessly re-created for each and every object with which the brain interacts" (Damasio, 1999: 17).

Extended consciousness entails more complex levels of organization and develops over an organism's lifetime. Possibly present in other species, it is only fully developed in humans and depends upon working memory and autobiographical memory. This gives rise to the *autobiographical self*, which depends on personal memories. Damasio is clear that this self is not any kind of separate entity but is the you that is born as the story of your life is told. As he puts it, "You are the music while the music lasts," "the owner of the movie-in-the-brain emerges within the movie" (ibid.: 191, 313). For Damasio, consciousness *is* a feeling, and feelings *are* neural patterns. His theory entails not only a movie-in-the-brain (see Chapter 6) but the idea that neural patterns "are displayed in the appropriate areas of the brain stem, thalamus, and cerebral cortex" to generate the feelings (ibid.: 73). Damasio is clear that there is no need for a homunculus to watch the display. It is watched by other brain processes. But, as with the broadcast in Global Workspace Theory (GWT), there is no explanation of how the display or the global availability accounts for subjectivity (see Chapter 5).

According to Baars' GWT, the self-system is part of the context hierarchy that influences what gets into the spotlight, or onto the stage, of the theater of consciousness. Indeed it is the dominant and unifying context of experience and action—the "deep context." Baars uses James's distinction between the "me" and the "I" to distinguish the self-concept (including values and beliefs about oneself) from the more fundamental self-system (including self as observer and self as agent). This self-system is fundamental because "Consciousness inherently needs to interact with a self-system, at least if its information is to be reportable and usable" (Baars, 1988: 344). In this way self and consciousness are intimately related. They are not the same thing, but stand in the relationship of context to content.

Applying his method of contrastive analysis, Baars considers experiences in which the sense of the self is disrupted or abnormal, including fugue and multiple personality, as well as depersonalization (a fairly common syndrome in which people feel themselves to be unreal or mechanical or not themselves, and experience distortions of their body image). All of these self-alien phenomena, Baars notes, are precipitated by events that disrupt the stable dominant context, as his model predicts, and they are associated with loss of autobiographical memory. Also the disruption may happen quickly, but recovery is slow because it means rebuilding the whole context.

In dissociative conditions such as fugue and multiple personality, different selves alternate because different context hierarchies vie for access to the global workspace. This access means access to the senses and to autobiographical memory and is required for any reportable conscious experience. This seems to preclude the possibility (accepted by James, Prince and others) of simultaneous consciousnesses.

Is this an ego or bundle theory? In GWT the self is not an illusion; it *is* the higher levels of the dominant context hierarchy. As with MacKay's executive and Gazzaniga's interpreter, the self-system is physically instantiated and presumably one could, as with ego theories, count how many there were in a given brain. However, I imagine that all these theorists would happily step into the teletransporter because the physical systems ought to be completely reconstructed by the machine.

The continuity of self is also real in this theory. Selves persist because self-systems do. But the unstated problem here is how a mass of neurons with changing interconnections and ephemeral activity can *be* a continuous experiencing self. So this theory faces all the problems that remained for James and the additional problem of explaining how physical continuity translates into experience. Perhaps we should conclude with Baars' own words, "*You* are the perceiver, the actor and narrator of your experience, although precisely what that means is an ongoing question" (Baars, 1997a: 143).

SESMETS AND PEARLS ON A STRING

Oxford philosopher Galen Strawson provoked a lengthy debate on the nature of self with his idea of the SESMET (Gallagher and Shear, 1999). Like James, he began with how it *seems*. The ordinary human sense of the self is the sense of being "a mental presence; a mental someone; a single mental thing that is a conscious subject of experience, that has a certain character or personality, and that is in some sense distinct from . . . all other things" (Strawson, 1997: 407). In addition, the self seems to have unity both at one moment and over longer periods of time and to be an agent. How much of this, he wonders, is really true of the self—if there is a self. The conclusion he comes to is one that he thinks will not satisfy most people who want there to be a self. He calls it "the Pearl view, because it suggests that many mental selves exist, one at a time and one after another, like pearls on a string" (ibid.: 424).

FIGURE 8.3 ● According to the pearl view of self, "many mental selves exist, one at a time and one after another, like pearls on a string."

According to the "Pearl view," selves are genuine subjects of experience and are distinct things, as we imagine them to be, but they are not separately existing entities as in Parfit's egos. Rather they are particular patterns of neural activity, or states of activation, that come and go. The distinctive features of Strawson's view are, first, what he retains of the ordinary view—that selves really are "Subjects of Experience that are Single MEntal Things," or SESMETS (Strawson, 1999)—and, second, what he throws out. He suggests that neither agency nor personality is necessary and, most controversially, nor is long-term continuity over time. Each self may last a few seconds, or a much longer time, but then it disappears and a new one appears.

His reasons for rejecting the persistence of self come mainly from introspection, though he suggests that much of the evidence reviewed by Dennett (1991) supports it too. So, looking into his own experience, he describes James's concept of the flowing stream of consciousness as inept and prefers Hume's descriptions of it as fluctuating, uncertain and fleeting. James described "the wonderful stream of our consciousness" as "Like a bird's life, it seems to be made of an alternation of flights and perchings" (James, 1890, i: 243). But for Strawson even this does not capture the radically disjunctive nature of experience. There are gaps and fadings, disappearances and restartings. He describes his own experience when alone and thinking as "one of

● CONSCIOUSNESS

repeated returns into consciousness from a state of complete, if momentary, unconsciousness" (Strawson, 1997: 422). It is as though consciousness is continually restarting.

A common tendency, when introspecting, is to accept that consciousness is "gappy" but still assume an underlying continuity, or a return to the same conscious self after a break. Or you might acknowledge that our thoughts switch and flip from one topic to another, but still imagine that the same consciousness, *your* consciousness, is thinking them. But Strawson rejects these common ways of thinking about continuity over time. In the Pearl view there is no such underlying continuity at all. The Buddhists are right to deny the existence of a *persisting* mental self, says Strawson, even though most people who want there to be a self want it to be a persisting self.

The Pearl view is interestingly different from all the other theories we have considered here. First, it is certainly not an ego theory because of its radical rejection of any long-term continuity. Nevertheless the pearl-self has unity at any given moment and in that sense is more than just an untied bundle of sensations and perceptions.

FIGURE 8.4 ● Perhaps there is no string that ties selves together and no requirement for only one to exist at a time. Selves may be more like raindrops, forming and disappearing again, sometimes lots at a time, sometimes only one. Being any one raindrop, you would not know about the rest.

Does it account for the experienced unity and continuity of self? The pearl-self is somewhat similar to James's idea that each moment entails a new Thought, but it has no equivalent of the continuous appropriation, or passing on of "ownership," from one Thought to the next. So it does not explain how or why we come to believe so strongly in the long-term continuity of the same self over a lifetime. Nor does Strawson explain why his pearls, or SESMETs, really *are* subjects of experience. The closest he comes is to outline "mental-and-non-mental" materialism—the view that every experiential phenomenon also has a non-mental character. Why this is so he does not explain.

NO AUDIENCE IN THE CARTESIAN THEATER

According to Dennett there is no Cartesian theater, no show in the Cartesian theater and no audience to watch the non-existent show. So how come we feel as though there is? Explaining how we come to believe things about consciousness that are untrue is Dennett's forte. We have already met this with zimbos, qualia and vision. Now we can see how it applies to the self.

Do selves exist? Of course they do—and of course they don't, says Dennett! There is obviously something to be explained, but it is not going to be explained by invoking Ryle's "ghost in the machine," James's "pontifical neuron" or any mysterious entity controlling our bodies. So what kind of existence is it? Using the same metaphor as James, Dennett likens the self to a center of gravity—invisible but real. But in Dennett's theory the self is a "center of narrative gravity."

One problem in thinking about selves, claims Dennett, is the tendency to think in terms of all or none, existence or non-existence, the same mistake that is often made in thinking about species, or the origin of life. Is that cabbage really the same species as that Brussels sprout? What was the first *truly* living creature? But just as we can be comfortable with fuzzy boundaries between species, or between living and non-living things, so we should be with selves and non-selves.

Selves are biological products just as spiders' webs or bowerbirds' bowers are. They appeared gradually during evolution, and they are built gradually in each of our lives. Every individual *Homo sapiens* makes its own *self*, spinning a web out of words and deeds to build a protective string of narrative. Like spiders and bowerbirds, it doesn't have to know what it's doing; it just does it. The result is a web of discourses, without which an individual human being is as incomplete as a bird without feathers or a turtle without its shell.

But perhaps it is wrong to say that "we" build the narrative. We humans are embedded in a world of words, a world of memes that tend to take over, creating us as they go (Chapter 11). As Dennett puts it, "Our tales are spun, but for the most part we don't spin them; they spin us. Our human consciousness, and our narrative selfhood, is their product, not their source" (Dennett, 1991: 418).

AM I THE SAME "ME" AS A
MOMENT AGO?

SELF-ASSESSMENT QUESTIONS

○ What is the point of the teletransporter thought experiment?

○ What does James mean when he says that the thoughts themselves are the thinkers?

○ Describe some neuroscientific approaches to the nature of self.

○ In Strawson's theory which aspects of the sense of self are said to be real and which illusory?

○ In your own words explain Dennett's theory of the self.

○ If there is a continuum between bundle and ego theories, where along it would you place the theories covered in this chapter?

This is where the "center of narrative gravity" comes in. When we speak, we speak *as if* the words come from a single source. Yes, they may be spoken by a single mouth, or written by a single hand, but there is no single center in the brain (or in the mind, or anywhere else) from which the edicts come. Yet we end up speaking as though there is. "Who owns your car? You do. Who owns your clothes? You do. Who owns your body? You do." When we say, "This is my body," we do not mean the same as "This body owns itself." In these, and many other ways, our language leads us into speaking and thinking *as though* there is someone inside: the witness in the Cartesian theater, the "central meaner," the "owner of record," the inner agent. This self is an abstraction but, like the physicists' center of gravity, it is a wonderfully useful and simplifying abstraction. This is why we have it.

In this view the phenomena of multiple personality only seemed so strange because of the false idea that selves are all-or-none things and there has to be one whole self to a body. Abandoning the idea of the audience in the Cartesian theater allows us to accept fragmentary selves, narratives that cover only part of a given body's life story, and multiple

FIGURE 8.5 • Maybe a self can be snuffed out like a candle flame and rekindled later. Maybe this is happening all the time even though we do not realize it (see Chapter 27).

selves that are just as much real selves as the more common one-to-a-body type (Humphrey and Dennett, 1989). There might even be fewer selves than one to a body, and Dennett describes the case of the Chaplin twins, Greta and Freda, who seem to act as one, speak together or in alternation and are insep arable.

Bad habits of thinking also beset us in the case of split brains. Like Parfit, Dennett rejects the idea that there must either be one, or two or some other countable number of selves in a split-brain patient, but he goes further. "So *what is it like* to be the right hemisphere self in a split-brain patient?" This, he says, is the most natural question in the world and conjures up a terrifying image of a self, desperate to get out, but trapped without its phone lines to the speech center in the other hemisphere. This is as much a fantasy as Peter Rabbit, says Dennett, not because it could not be true, but because the oper- ation doesn't leave an organization robust enough to support a separate self— a separate center of narrative gravity. The most it leaves is the capacity, under special laboratory conditions, to give split responses to particular predica- ments, temporarily creating a second center of narrative gravity. That this self could have gaps should come as no surprise. Both self and consciousness appear to be continuous but are in fact gappy. They can lapse "into nothing- ness as easily as a candle flame is snuffed, only to be rekindled at some later time" (Dennett, 1991: 423).

You may have noticed that Dennett's views on self sound like those of the dis- cursive psychologists and deconstructionists, which seems odd if you think of realist theories grounded in neuroscience as being the opposite from relativist, post-modern theories that deal only with texts. Yet the similarities are real enough, and Dennett finds his own view parodied in David Lodge's novel *Nice*

> " *Our tales are spun, but for the most part we don't spin them; they spin us.* "
>
> **Dennett**, 1991: 418

Work, in which the heroine, Robyn Penrose, claims there is no such thing as a "Self" but only a subject position in an infinite web of discourses. The important difference is this. While Robyn is content to stick with studying the discourses themselves, Dennett tries to show how such discourses are constructed by physical, evolved brains and how they generate the illusion of a continuous self who is the subject of our experiences.

Dennett's is a bundle theory in which the string is a web of narratives. He explains how and why the sense of unity and continuity is an illusion; it is an abstraction from real words and deeds to the false idea of a single source. And does this help us to understand the nature of consciousness? By denying that there is anything it is like to be an experiencing self, Dennett changes the problem completely. This is how he manages to explain consciousness—or alternatively, as some critics prefer to say, he explains it away.

READING

Baars, B.J. (1997) *In the Theatre of Consciousness: The Workspace of the Mind.* New York: Oxford University Press. See Chapter 7 (pages 142–53).

Dennett, D.C. (1991) *Consciousness Explained.* Boston and London: Little, Brown & Co. See Chapter 13 (pages 412–30).

James, W. (1890) *The Principles of Psychology.* London: Macmillan. James's chapter on the self, in Volume 1, is over 100 pages long, but it is worth reading even a little of it to get a sense of his ideas. I especially recommend pages 298–301 and 329–42 and his own summary on pages 400–1.

Strawson, G. (1997) The self. *Journal of Consciousness Studies* 4, 405–28 (also reprinted in Gallagher, S. and Shear, J. (eds) (1999) *Models of the Self.* Thorverton, Devon: Imprint Academic).

CONSCIOUSNESS

Agency and free will

"We know what it is to get out of bed on a freezing morning in a room without a fire, and how the very vital principle within us protests against the ordeal," said William James, describing the agonizing, the self-recrimination and the lure of comfort against the cold. "Now how do we *ever* get up under such circumstances?" he asked. "If I may generalize from my own experience, we more often than not get up without any struggle or decision at all. We suddenly find that we *have* got up" (James, 1890, Vol. 2: 524). When the inhibitory thoughts briefly cease, he said, the idea of getting up produces its appropriate motor effects, by "ideo-motor action," and we are up. What, then, is the role of free will?

The problem of free will is reputed to be the most discussed philosophical problem of all time. Since the Greek philosophers 2000 years ago, the main problem has seemed to lie with determinism. If this universe runs by deterministic laws, then everything that happens must be inevitable, so the argument goes, and if everything is inevitable, there is no room for free will, no point in my "doing" anything, no sense in which I "could have done otherwise"—with obvious implications for morality and the law.

Among modern philosophers, non-compatibilists argue that if the universe is deterministic, then free will must be an illusion, while compatibilists find many and varied ways in which determinism can be true and yet free will remain.

PRACTICE
AM I DOING THIS?

When you find yourself asking "Am I conscious now?" observe what you are doing and ask yourself, **"Am I doing this?"** You might be walking, drinking a cup of coffee or picking up the phone to ring a friend. Whatever it is, ask yourself what caused the action. Did you consciously think about it first? Did your own conscious thoughts cause it to happen? Did it just happen by itself?

You might like to take a short time—say 10 minutes—and try to observe the origins of all your actions during that time. In each case ask, **"Did I do that?"**

There are many arguments here, and little agreement, except perhaps for a widespread rejection of free will as a magical or God-like force that comes out of nowhere. If free will is not illusory, it is certainly not magic. The question is, what other possibilities are there? If we add chance or randomness, as modern physics does, we get back to the Greek philosopher Democritus, who said that "everything in the universe is the fruit of chance and necessity." And it is not chance or randomness that we seek, but some way in which our own efforts really make a difference.

This is where the connection with self comes in, for we feel as though "I" am the one who acts, "I" am the one who has free will. "I" decided to spring out of bed this morning, and did so. When the chosen action then happens, it *seems* as though my conscious thought was responsible. Indeed it seems that without the conscious thought I would not have done what I did, and that *I* consciously caused the action by deciding to do it. The question is, does consciousness really play a role in decision making and choice? Is this sense of conscious agency real or an illusion?

As ever, William James got to the heart of the matter when he said

> . . . the whole feeling of reality, the whole sting and excitement of our voluntary life, depends on our sense that in it things are *really being decided* from one moment to another, and that it is not the dull rattling off of a chain that was forged innumerable ages ago. This appearance, which makes life and history tingle with such a tragic zest, *may* not be an illusion.

(James, 1890, i: 453)

As we have seen (Chapters 2 and 3), James rejected the idea of a persisting self but still believed in a spiritual force. The sense of effort in both attention and volition is, in his view, not an illusion but the genuinely causal force of conscious, personal will.

As with all talk of illusions, remember that an illusion is not something that does not exist, but something that is not what it seems. So, once again, it is important to be clear about the way it *seems* for you. Does it *seem* as though you have conscious free will? If so, then ask yourself whether this could be an illusion, and if it is an illusion, how you can possibly live with that idea (Chapter 27). If it does *not* seem to you that you have conscious free will, then you may read all this with an air of amused detachment.

Note that we are concerned here with *consciousness*. The question is not whether human beings are agents. We may safely assume that they are. Humans are living biological creatures that survive, like all other creatures, by having boundaries between themselves and the outside world and by taking control over certain aspects of their environment. They respond to events, make plans and act accordingly, at least when they are not restrained or coerced. We humans are very complicated agents with intricate plans and many available options.

Neither need we doubt that thought, deliberation and emotions play a part in decisions. Weighing possible actions and comparing their likely outcomes is the sort of thing that intelligent animals are good at, from a cat deciding when to pounce, to a chimpanzee weighing the likely consequences of challenging a dominant ally. We can look to see which parts of the brain are active in such decision making and, in principle at least, trace how their activation results in motor activity.

The tricky question concerns where consciousness comes into all of this.

THE ANATOMY OF VOLITION

When we carry out any voluntary act, many areas of the brain, especially the frontal lobes, are involved (Spence and Frith, 1999). In outline, prefrontal regions are thought to initiate motor acts. These send connections to premotor regions, which program the actions, and they in turn project to the primary motor cortices and hence to motor output. Broca's area produces the motor output for speech and, in most right-handed people, is in the left inferior frontal gyrus. Medially, near the midline, are the supplementary motor area, which is involved in the sequencing and programming of motor acts to fit a "motor plan," and the anterior cingulate, which is a complex area involved in attention to, and selection of, the information needed for action, as well as emotion and pain.

> " *All theory is against the freedom of the will; all experience is for it.* "
>
> **Samuel Johnson**, 1791

ACTIVITY
Getting out of bed on a cold morning

Try William James's famous meditation (as he called it) and watch what happens when you get out of bed on a cold morning. If you don't live somewhere cold enough, just choose a morning when you really *don't* want to get up. Alternatively try getting out of a bath when the water is going cold and you've been in there too long.

Watch what happens. What thoughts go through your mind as you struggle to get out? What emotions do you feel? Do you speak to yourself or try to persuade yourself? If so, who or what is struggling against whom or what? What happens in the end? You might like to write a short description, as James did (see James, 1890, ii: 524–5). What does this tell you about free will?

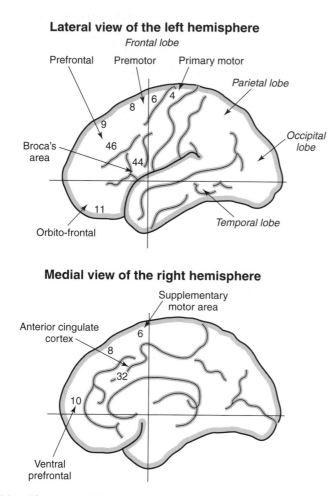

Lateral view of the left hemisphere

Frontal lobe

Prefrontal   Premotor   Primary motor

Parietal lobe

8   6   4

9

Broca's
area

46

44

*Occipital
lobe*

11

Orbito-frontal

Temporal lobe

Medial view of the right hemisphere

Supplementary
motor area

Anterior cingulate
cortex

6

8

32

10

Ventral
prefrontal

FIGURE 9.1 • Schematic view of the human brain showing the four lobes and the major subdivisions of the frontal cortex. The numbers refer to the regions delineated by Korbinian Brodmann on the basis of a detailed study of neural architecture. Only a subset of these regions are shown. The dorsolateral prefrontal cortex consists of the regions labeled 9 and 46 (after Spence and Frith, 1999).

Some of this is known from the effects of brain damage. For example, there is the famous case of railroad worker Phineas Gage. In 1848 a tamping iron was blown straight through his frontal cortex, leaving him a changed personality and no longer able to behave responsibly (Damasio, 1994). Damage to dorsolateral prefrontal cortex can lead to a lack of spontaneous activity and to repetitive, stereotypic actions. Lesions of the prefrontal region and corpus callosum can produce the extraordinary complaint of "alien hand," in which patients say that their hand is out of their control and has a will of its own. Damage to only the corpus callosum can produce "anarchic hand" syndrome in which the patient's two hands struggle to produce opposite effects—for example, one trying to undo a button while the other tries to do it up.

Experiments with single cell recording in monkeys also provide information about the neuronal mechanisms of voluntary control of behavior (Schultz, 1999), and new methods of brain imaging have recently allowed detailed study in humans. For example, Frith et al. (1991) used PET (positron emission tomography; see Chapter 16) to investigate the functional anatomy of volition. In one condition subjects repeated words read by the experimenter at the rate of one every three seconds. In the other condition they heard only one letter and had to say a word of their choice beginning with that letter. Subtracting the activations seen in one condition from those in the other revealed a difference in the left dorsolateral prefrontal cortex (DLPFC) and anterior cingulate. Other similar studies showed an increase in activity in DLPFC when actions were being selected and initiated. From a review of such studies Spence and Frith (1999) conclude that even the simplest motor procedures require complex and distributed neuronal activity, but the DLPFC seems to be uniquely associated with the subjective experience of deciding when and how to act.

The problem for our purposes here is that it doesn't feel like neurons firing, whether in the DLPFC or anywhere else. It feels as though there is something else—my consciousness—that makes me free to act the way I want. In Chapter 3 we dealt with theories that do, and do not, give a causal role to consciousness. Here we will consider how this relates to the sense of personal conscious agency.

THE ROLE OF CONSCIOUS WILL IN VOLUNTARY ACTION

Hold out your hand in front of you. Now, whenever you feel like it, consciously, deliberately, and of your own free will, flex your wrist. Keep doing this for some time—until your arm gets too tired. Just flex your wrist whenever you want, and try to observe what goes through your mind as you do so. If you don't want to do it at all that's fine—that is your conscious decision. If you want to do it frequently, that is fine too. Now ask yourself what started the movement, or prevented it, each time. What caused your action?

This simple task formed the basis of one of the best-known experiments in the history of consciousness studies: Libet's study of "Unconscious cerebral initiative and the role of conscious will in voluntary action" (1985). Since the 1960s it had been known that voluntary motor actions are preceded by a "readiness potential" (RP): a slow negative shift in electrical potential that can be recorded from electrodes on the scalp up to a second or more before the action takes place. This long time interval (on average 800 ms) prompted Libet to wonder "whether the conscious awareness of the voluntary urge to act likewise appears so far in advance" (ibid.: 529).

He reasoned that if a conscious intention or decision initiates the action, then the subjective experience of intending should come first, or at the latest together with the start of the cerebral processes. This was what his experiment investigated. He needed to time three events: the start of the action itself, the start of the RP, and the

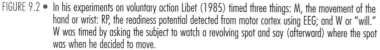

FIGURE 9.2 • In his experiments on voluntary action Libet (1985) timed three things: M, the movement of the hand or wrist: RP, the readiness potential detected from motor cortex using EEG; and W or "will." W was timed by asking the subject to watch a revolving spot and say (afterward) where the spot was when he decided to move.

moment of the conscious decision to act.

Timing the action itself was easily done with electrodes on the appropriate muscle. Timing the RP was also relatively straightforward. The change in potential that marks the beginning of the RP can only be clearly seen when averaged over many repetitions, so Libet had his subjects carry out the flexion 40 times in each series of trials. Using the time of the action as a reference, these 40 trials could then be mathematically averaged even though the subject freely chose when to move (Libet et al., 1983). The source of this RP was thought to be the supplementary motor area.

The real problem is how to measure the moment when the subject becomes conscious of the urge, or will, to move—Libet called this moment "W" for "will." If you ask subjects to say "Now" when they feel like moving, the action of speaking may not only interfere with the wrist movement but may also involve its own RP and another delay. So Libet used the following method. A spot of light revolved once every 2.56 seconds, in a clock circle on a screen. Subjects were asked to watch the spot carefully and then, after they had flexed their wrist, to report where the spot was at the moment they felt the urge to move. So on each trial they would flex their wrist and then say "15" or "35," meaning that this was the position of the spot at the moment they decided to act. A control series, in which subjects reported the time of a skin stimulus by using the clock method, showed that their estimates were generally accurate and slightly in advance of the actual stimulus. In another control, subjects were asked to time their awareness of actually moving (M). They had no trouble following these instructions nor in discriminating M from W, W being, on average, 120 ms before M. Using these controls, Libet was convinced that the timing of W was sufficiently accurate. He could now answer his question: which comes first, the readiness potential or the conscious decision to act?

The answer was clear. The RP came first. On average the RP started 550 ms (±150 ms) before the action and W only 200 ms before. In some trials the subjects said they had been thinking about the action some time in advance, or preplanning it. On these trials the RP began over a second before the action, but for series in which all 40 acts were reported as fully spontaneous and unplanned, the RP began 535 ms before the action, and W just 190 ms before the action. Further analysis showed that this held for different ways of measuring both RP and W. In conclusion, the conscious decision to act occurred approximately 350 ms *after* the RP.

What should we make of this finding? With Libet we may wonder, "If the brain can initiate a voluntary act before the appearance of conscious intention . . . is there any role for the conscious function?" (Libet, 1985: 536). That is the crux. These results seem to show (as did Libet's previous work; see Chapter 3) that consciousness comes too late to be the cause of the action.

For those who accept the validity of the method, there are two main ways of responding to Libet's results. The first is to say, "Well, that's obvious! If consciousness came first, it would be magic." Presumably this ought to be the standard reaction of anyone who denies dualism. Indeed, the result should have been completely unsurprising. Instead, even though most psychologists and philosophers deny believing in magic, these results caused a great stir. Not only was there a wide-ranging debate in *Behavioral and Brain Sciences*, but the experiment was still frequently cited, and hotly argued over, nearly 20 years after it was carried out (Libet, 1999).

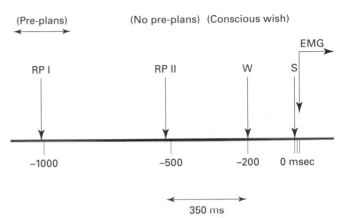

Self-initiated act: sequence

FIGURE 9.3 • According to Libet the sequence of events in a self-initiated voluntary act is as shown. Preplanning (RPI) occurs as much as a second before the movement. For spontaneous actions without preplanning, activity (RPII) begins about half a second before the movement. Subjective awareness of the will to move appears about 200 ms before the movement. Subjective timings of a randomly delivered skin stimulus (S) averaged about −50 ms from actual time (after Libet, 1999).

The second response is to seek some remaining causal role for consciousness in voluntary action. Libet took this route and argued as follows. It is possible to believe, he said, that conscious intervention does not exist and the subjective experience of conscious control is an illusion, but such a belief is "less attractive than a theory that accepts or accommodates the phenomenal fact" (Libet, 1999: 56) and is not required even by monist materialists. For example, Sperry's emergent consciousness (see Chapter 7) is a monist theory in which consciousness has real effects. Alternatively the results are compatible with dualist interactionism (Popper and Eccles, 1977). Libet therefore proposed "that conscious control can be exerted before the final motor outflow to select or control volitional outcome. The volitional process, initiated unconsciously, can either be consciously permitted to proceed to consummation in the motor act or be consciously 'vetoed'" (Libet, 1985: 536–7).

> " *We don't have free will, but we do have free won't.* "
>
> **Gregory**, 1990

The idea, then, is that unconscious brain events start the process of a voluntary act, but then just before it is actually carried out, consciousness may say either "Yes" or "No"; the action either goes ahead or not. This would happen in the last 150 to 200 ms before the action. Libet provides two kinds of evidence for this conscious veto. First, subjects sometimes reported that they had had an urge to act but then it seemed to be aborted or suppressed before the action happened. Unfortunately the neural correlates of aborted self-timed actions cannot be measured because averaging over many trials is required. Second, in additional experiments, subjects were asked to move at pre-arranged times and then abort some of the actions, allowing the averaging to be done. These showed ramplike pre-event potentials that then flattened or reversed about

VOLITION AND TIMING

Why don't you laugh when you tickle yourself? In experiments using a robot tickling arm, fMRI showed activity in secondary somatosensory cortex, anterior cingulate and cerebellum that was reduced when subjects tickled themselves instead of being tickled. Timing proved critical to the experience. When the sensations were made less predictable by introducing a delay in the robot arm, a delay of more than 200 ms made the sensation ticklish again (Blakemore, Wolpert and Frith, 2000).

Does the time at which an event seems to happen depend on its cause? Although this may seem peculiar, there is evidence to suggest that "when we perceive our actions to cause an event, it seems to occur earlier than if we did not cause it." (Eagleman and Holcombe, 2002).

In experiments on voluntary action and conscious awareness, Patrick Haggard and his colleagues at University College, London, asked subjects to watch a clock face and judge the timing of onset of four single events: a volun-

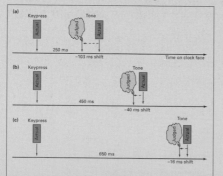

FIGURE 9.4 • Haggard et al. report that the judged time of a tone changes as a function of the delay between the tone and a previously executed voluntary act. As the delay is lengthened (a–c), the time misestimation is reduced. Mean judged time is represented by thought bubbles. In the experiment, time judgments are always retrospective, which is why they can appear to precede the actual times of occurrence on the timelines.

tary key press, a muscle twitch produced by stimulating their motor cortex with TMS, a click made by sham TMS and a tone. Next the events were connected so that in a

150–250 ms before the preset time. This suggested to Libet that the conscious veto interfered with the final development of the RP.

In this way Libet was able to retain a causal role for consciousness in voluntary action. He concluded that his results are not antagonistic to free will, but rather they illuminate how free will operates. When it comes to morality and matters of conscience, we can still be expected to behave well. Although we cannot consciously control having an impulse to carry out an unacceptable action (say, rape or murder or stealing sweets in the supermarket), we can be held responsible for consciously allowing its consummation—or not. As Richard Gregory characteristically put it, "We don't have free will, but we do have free won't" (1990).

THE LIBET DEBATE

The debate following publication of these results raised both philosophical and methodological problems (*references in this section without dates refer to commentaries following Libet, 1985*). While Eccles used the data to support his dualist-interactionist theory, others criticised Libet for his unstated dualist assumptions (Wood), and even for "double dualism" (Nelson) and "metaphysical hysteria" (Danto). These criticisms revolve around the way that Libet compares physical with mental events and tries to defend what seems to be a magical "conscious control function" in his proposed veto.

The main methodological criticisms concerned the nature of the task and the method of timing W. Although Libet's subjects reported being aware of intending to move on each trial, several commentators argued that the task was not a good model of volition in general. This was partly because the action was so trivial, and partly because the subjects were only free to choose the timing of their action, not the act itself, so any conscious willing would have happened before their decision about *when* to act. The results should not, therefore, be generalized to other, more complex willed actions, let alone to questions of moral responsibility (Breitmeyer, Bridgeman, Danto, Näätänen, Ringo).

Latto raises the question of backward referral (see Chapter 3). If perception of the position of the spot, *and* W, are both subjectively referred backward in time, then the two will be in synchrony, but if W is not referred back, then the timing procedure is invalidated. In response Libet points out that backward referral is not expected for the spot because the time at which the subject became aware of the spot was not the issue, only the position of the spot when he felt the urge to act. If this still seems obscure, we might imagine that the subject had the experience of deciding to move exactly as the spot reached 30. It would not matter how long this perception of simultaneity took to become conscious because he could report this spot position at his leisure.

The whole method of timing W was also criticized, as was the adequacy of using a skin stimulus as a control to test the accuracy of the timing and the failure to allow for delays involved in each, or in switching attention between the spot and W (Breitmeyer, Rollman, Underwood, Niemi). Some of these criticisms are undermined by subsequent replications. For example, Haggard and his colleagues not only replicated the basic findings, but showed that awareness of one's own actions is associated with a premotor event after the initial intention and preparation, but before the motor command is sent out (Haggard, Newman and Magno, 1999). Comparing trials with early and late awareness, they found that the time of awareness co-varied with the lateralized RP, concluding that "the processes underlying the LRP may cause our awareness of movement initiation" (Haggard and Eimer, 1999: 128).

But what is "time of awareness"? The most radical critique is given by Dennett, who asks us to join him in the following "all-too-natural vision" of Libet's task (1991: 165).

Unconscious intentions start out somewhere deep in the brain and then, gradually becoming more definite and powerful, make their way up to where "I" am. At this point they "enter consciousness" and "I" have the experience of deciding to act. Meanwhile spot-representations have been streaming up from the retina, gradually becoming more definite in brightness and location, until they too reach consciousness and "I" can watch them parading past. So at the very moment when the intention appears in consciousness, "I" can say where the spot was.

As Dennett points out, this is so easy to visualize. Isn't that how it has to be when two things happen together in consciousness? No it is not. Indeed it

voluntary condition, subjects had to press a key which caused a tone to sound 250 ms later. In the TMS condition their finger was made to twitch involuntarily and the tone followed, and in a control condition sham TMS was used. In each case subjects reported the time of the first event and when they heard the tone.

In these second conditions, large perceptual shifts were found as compared with the single event case. When the key was pressed voluntarily, the time of the press and the time of the tone were reported as being closer together. When involuntary twitches were caused by TMS, the shifts were in the opposite direction and the two events seemed further apart. There was no effect for sham TMS. In further experiments the time interval between the key press and tone was varied, showing that the effect is greatest with shorter time intervals.

What does this imply for consciousness? The experimenters themselves claimed that "the perceived time of intentional actions and of their sensory consequences ... were attracted together in conscious awareness, so that subjects perceived voluntary movements as occurring later and their sensory consequences as occurring earlier than they actually did" (Haggard et al., 2002, p. 382).

Note that this interpretation is a form of Cartesian materialism; it implies that events are perceived when they "enter consciousness," and can be attracted together "in conscious awareness." A more skeptical interpretation is that the brain's judgments about the timing and causation of events are linked, perhaps in the important process of discriminating between self-caused and external events. These judgments are revealed in behavior, but there is no sense in which any of them are either "in" or "out" of consciousness.

cannot be. There is no place or system in the brain where all the things currently "in consciousness" meet together, there is no time at which things "enter consciousness," and there is no self watching the display in that non-existent place. To try to escape this impossible vision, some theories hold that consciousness is not a matter of arriving at a place, but of exceeding a threshold of activation in a distributed system or network. So things can "enter consciousness" while staying put. This changes the imagery, but not the basic mistake, says Dennett. In this version, there has to be some moment at which physical activity achieves the special state and some way in which it acquires the special quality of *subjectivity*, so becoming "my conscious decision." This moment is what is timed in Libet's experiment.

These two visions sound rather different, but they both entail a Cartesian theater; a "central headquarters"—whether located or distributed—in which different things "come together" in consciousness, and from which consciousness does its controlling. Only with such a vision can you imagine, as Libet does, that "the conscious function" can trigger some actions and veto others. In this way, says Dennett, both Libet and most of his critics remain trapped in the Cartesian theater.

One way out is to abandon the notion that there is an answer to the question, "What is in my consciousness now?" You can retain the idea that the brain makes judgements of simultaneity—and often very accurate ones—but only because there are brain mechanisms that time events and produce behaviors or statements based on those timings. There is no additional "you" with a privileged view of the contents of your consciousness and the conscious power to act.

So does Dennett believe that free will is an illusion? He does not, but his reasons may cause some confusion because his view neatly fits the definition of "illusion" used here. He explains that if you believe that free will springs from an immaterial soul shooting arrows of decision into your brain, then there is no free will at all, but if you believe that free will might be morally important without being supernatural, then "free will is indeed real, but just not quite what you probably thought it was" (Dennett, 2003: 223). Human freedom is not magic but an evolved capacity for weighing options and dealing with multiple choices.

Where does this leave us? If personal conscious will is a real force acting on the brain, as James, Libet, Eccles and others would have it, then there is no mystery about why we *feel* as though we have conscious free will. We do. On the other hand, if free will is an illusion, then we have a new mystery. Why do we *feel* as though our conscious decisions cause our actions when they do not? To find out, we must ask about the origins of the experience of will.

THE EXPERIENCE OF WILL

In 1853 the new craze of spiritualism was spreading rapidly from the United States to Europe (see Chapter 20). Mediums claimed that spirits of the dead, acting through them, could convey messages and move tables. Appreciating

> "*Those of us with common sense are amazed at the resistance put up by psychologists, physiologists, and philosophers to the obvious reality of free will.*"
>
> **Hobson**, 1999: 245

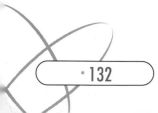

FIGURE 9.5 • A spiritualist séance from 1853. In table turning, or table tipping, the sitters believed that spirits moved the table and that their own hands just followed. Faraday proved that the movements were due to unconscious muscular action.

DID MY THOUGHTS CAUSE THIS ACTION?

the challenge to science, and infuriated by the public hysteria, the famous physicist and chemist Michael Faraday investigated what was going on (Faraday, 1853).

In a typical table-turning séance, several sitters sat around a table with their hands resting on the top. Although the sitters claimed only ever to press down, and not sideways, the table would move about and spell out answers to questions. The sitters all genuinely believed that the table moved their hands and not that their hands moved the table. Faraday set about showing that they were wrong. In an ingenious experiment he stuck pieces of card between the sitters' hands and the tabletop, using a specially prepared cement that would allow the cards to move a little. Afterward he could see whether the card had lagged behind the table—showing that the table had moved first as the sitters claimed—or whether it had moved ahead of the table. The answer was clear. The card moved ahead. So the force came from the sitters' hands. In further experiments Faraday fixed up a pointer that revealed any movements of the hands. When the sitters watched the pointer, "all effects of table-turning cease, even though the parties persevere, earnestly desiring motion, till they become weary and worn out" (ibid.: 802). He concluded that unconscious muscular action was the only force involved.

Daniel Wegner (b. 1948)

Once a physics student, Daniel Wegner changed to psychology as an anti-war statement in 1969 and became fascinated with questions of self-control, agency and free will. He has done numerous experiments on how the illusion of free will is created and on the effects of trying *not* to think about something. "Try not to think about a white bear," he suggests.

From the age of 14 Wegner helped his piano teacher mother run her music studio and taught piano twice a week after school. He not only plays the piano but has four synthesizers and composes techno music. He is Professor of Psychology at Harvard University, where he starts his classes with music. A colleague called him "one of the funniest human beings on two legs." He believes that conscious will is an illusion.

Another example in which it is possible to cause something without feeling responsible is the "precognitive carousel" (Dennett, 1991). In 1963 the British neurosurgeon William Grey Walter tested patients who had electrodes implanted in their motor cortex as part of their treatment. They sat in front of a slide projector and could press a button, whenever they liked, to see the next slide (a slightly more interesting task than flexing the wrist). Unbeknownst to the subjects, what advanced the slide was not the button but amplified activity from their own motor cortex. The patients were startled. They said that just as they were about to press the button, the slide changed all by itself. Perhaps with a longer delay they would have noticed nothing amiss but, sadly, Grey Walter did not experiment with variable delays. Nevertheless, this demonstrates that under certain conditions we can be in control of actions without *feeling* that we are.

A similar mismatch occurs as a symptom of schizophrenia. Many schizophrenics believe that their actions are controlled by aliens, by unspecified creatures or even by people they know. Others feel that their own thoughts are controlled by evil forces or inserted into their minds. This disconnection between voluntary action and the *feeling* of volition is deeply disturbing.

Can it happen the other way around? Can we have the sense of willing an action for which we are *not* responsible? Magicians have long exploited tricks to make the observer believe he has freely chosen a card or a number, when in fact the magician forced it. Recent experiments by psychologist Daniel Wegner (see Profile) have examined the mechanisms that produce the *experience* of conscious will.

Imagine that you are standing in front of a mirror with screens arranged so that what looks like your arms are actually someone else's. In your ears you hear various instructions to act, and just afterward the hands carry out those same actions. The experiments showed that, in such a situation, people felt as though they had willed the movements themselves.

Wegner likens experiences of conscious will to other judgments of causality. He proposes that "The experience of willing an act arises from interpreting one's thought as the cause of the act" (Wegner and Wheatley, 1999: 480). Wegner (2002) proposes that free will is an illusion created in three steps. First, our brain sets about planning actions and carrying them out. Second, although we are ignorant of the underlying mechanisms, we become aware of thinking about the action and call this an intention. Finally, the action occurs after the intention, and so we leap—erroneously—to the conclusion that our intention caused the action.

This is similar to James's theory of deliberate actions, proposed over a century earlier. First, various reinforcing or inhibiting ideas compete with each other to prompt a physical action—or not. Once one or the other finally wins, we say we have decided. "The reinforcing and inhibiting ideas meanwhile are termed the *reasons* or *motives* by which the decision is brought about" (James, 1890, ii: 528). Note that both these theories explain how the powerful *feeling* that we willed an action might come about, whether or not we have free will. Interestingly James and Wegner come to opposite opinions on this central question.

Wegner suggests that there are three requirements for the experience of willing to come about: the thought must occur before the action, must be consistent with it and must not be accompanied by other causes. To test these proposals, Wegner and Wheatley (1999) carried out an experiment inspired by the traditional ouija board which, like Faraday's turning tables, depends on unconscious muscular action. The ouija board (the name comes from the French and German for "yes") is used to try to contact spirits. Several people place their fingers on an upturned glass in the middle of a ring of letters and the glass then moves, spelling out words. The participants are usually convinced that they did not push the glass. In Wegner's version the glass was replaced by a 20 cm square board mounted on a computer mouse. Movements

> *"Our sense of being a conscious agent who does things comes at a cost of being technically wrong all the time."*
>
> **Wegner**, 2002: 342

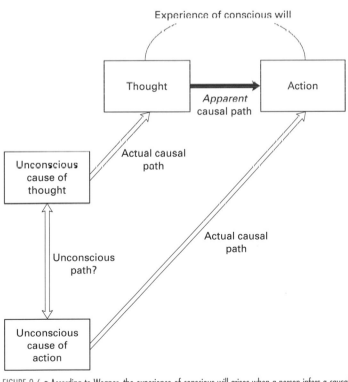

FIGURE 9.6 • According to Wegner, the experience of conscious will arises when a person infers a causal path from thought to action. Both thought and action are caused by unconscious mental events, which also may be linked to each other. The path from thought to action is apparent, not real (after Wegner, 2002).

of the mouse moved a cursor over a screen showing a picture of about 50 small objects. The experiment involved two participants: a subject and a confederate. To make the explanation easier, we can call them Dan and Jane.

Dan and Jane arrived at about the same time and were seated facing each other across a small table. Dan, of course, had no idea that Jane was a confederate. They were asked to place their fingers on the little board and to circle the cursor over the objects. They were asked to stop every 30 seconds or so and then rate how strongly they had intended to make that particular stop. Each trial consisted of 30 seconds of movement, during which they might hear words through headphones, and 10 seconds of music, during which they were to make a stop. Dan was led to believe that Jane was receiving different words from his, but actually she heard instructions to make particular movements.

On four trials she was told to stop on a particular object (e.g., swan) in the middle of Dan's music. Meanwhile Dan heard the word "swan" 30 seconds before, 5 seconds before, 1 second before or 1 second after Jane stopped on the swan. In all other trials the stops were not forced and Dan heard various words 2 seconds into the music; 51 undergraduates were tested.

The results confirmed what Wegner calls the "priority principle": that effects are experienced as willed when the relevant thoughts occur just before them. On forced trials, subjects gave the highest rating for "I intended to make the stop" when the word came 1 or 5 seconds before the stop, and the lowest when it occurred 30 seconds before or 1 second after. Wegner and Wheatley conclude that "Believing that our conscious thoughts cause our actions is an error based on the illusory experience of will—much like believing that a rabbit has indeed popped out of an empty hat" (Wegner and Wheatley, 1999: 490). The illusion of will really is like magic and arises for the same reason. Yet once again we must remember that to say something is an illusion is not to say that it does not exist. Illusions can have powerful effects. Wegner concludes

The fact is, it seems to each of us that we have conscious will. It seems we have selves. It seems we have minds. It seems we are agents. It seems we cause what we do. Although it is sobering and ultimately accurate to call all this an illusion, it is a mistake to conclude that the illusory is trivial.
(Wegner, 2002: 342)

A similar conclusion is reached by British psychologist Guy Claxton, though from the perspective of spiritual practice (Chapters 26 and 27). He argues that much of the trouble in our lives is caused by the false idea of self, and he explores some of the bizarre ways in which we try to defend the theory that our decisions cause our actions: "I meant to keep my cool but I just couldn't. . . . I'd decided on an early night but somehow here we are in Piccadilly Circus at four a.m. with silly hats and a bottle of wine." Then if all else fails we can even re-interpret our failure as a success: 'I changed my mind,' we say, temporarily withdrawing our identification from the 'mind' that has been 'made up,' and aligning ourselves instead with some higher decision-maker and controller who can 'choose' to override this mind" (Claxton, 1986a: 59–60). But there is no self who really has this control, says Claxton. It makes better sense to see the relationship between thought and action as a hit-and-miss attempt at *prediction* rather than control.

So, is free will an illusion? Whether it is or not, we may draw one firm conclusion. The fact that we *feel* as though we have free will is not convincing evidence either way.

FIGURE 9.7 • Remember that an illusion is not something that does not exist but something that is not what it seems. In this visual illusion the upper person seems far bigger and more frightening than the lower one. In fact they are identical. Is consciousness what it seems to be? Is free will?

Libet, B. (1985) Unconscious cerebral initiative and the role of conscious will in voluntary action. *The Behavioral and Brain Sciences* 8, 529–39.

Commentaries following Libet's article. *The Behavioral and Brain Sciences* 8, 539–66, and *The Behavioral and Brain Sciences* 10, 318–21. If each student reads one or two commentaries, a good discussion can follow. Otherwise try the commentaries by Breitmeyer, Latto and Nelson.

Wegner, D.M. and Wheatley, T. (1999) Apparent mental causation: sources of the experience of will. *American Psychologist* 54, 480–92.

READING

Agency and free will
CHAPTER NINE

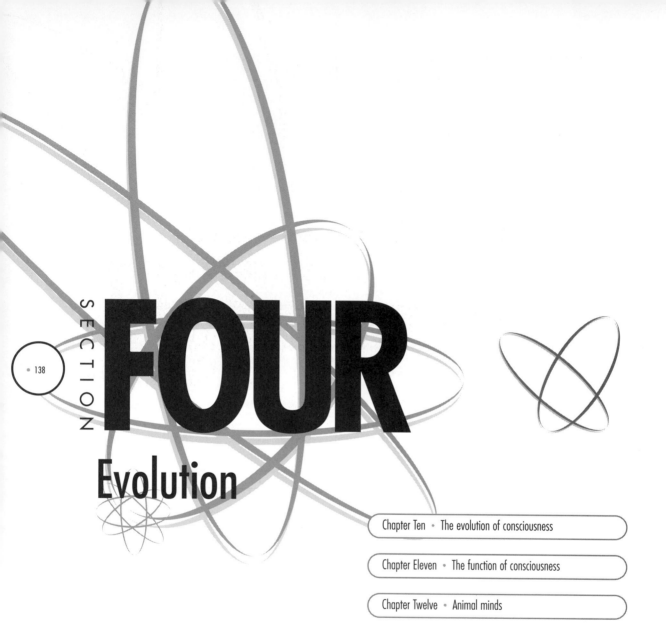

SECTION

FOUR

Evolution

TEN

CHAPTER ⑩

MINDLESS DESIGN

Suppose you are walking along a deserted sandy beach on a tropical island when you come across a magnificent pile of sand. At each corner is a square tower, decorated with rows of shells, and all around is a moat with a flat stone for a bridge, neatly attached to threads of seaweed for pulling it up. What will you conclude? It's a sand castle of course. And somebody must have built it.

When we see obvious signs of design, we readily infer a designer. This, in essence, is the "argument from design," made famous in 1802 by the Reverend William Paley. He supposed that, crossing a heath, he found either a stone or a watch. For the stone, he might as well conclude that it had always been there, but for the watch he *must* conclude that it had a maker. All the parts are so ingeniously linked, he said, that together they serve the purpose for which it was constructed—telling the time. If any pieces were missing or in the wrong place or made of the wrong material, the watch would not work. These many complex pieces could not possibly have come together by accident, nor by the effects of natural forces. Paley concluded

> that the watch must have had a maker: that there must have existed, at some time, and at some place or other, an artificer or artificers who formed it for the purpose which we find it actually to answer: who comprehended its construction, and designed its use.
>
> (Paley, 1802: 3)

> *"There cannot be design without a designer"*
>
> **Paley**, 1802: 3

FIGURE 10.1 • These are some of the finches that Darwin collected in the Galapagos Islands in 1835. Each species has a different shape of beak, essentially a tool designed for a specific job, from picking tiny seeds out of crevices to crushing nuts or shells. At the time it seemed obvious that God must have designed each one. In 1859 Darwin explained how beaks, finches and the entire natural world could have been designed without a designer — by natural selection.

He thought it self-evident that "There cannot be design without a designer; contrivance, without a contriver; order, without choice." The arrangements of the parts to serve their many functions in the watch "imply the presence of intelligence and mind" (Paley, 1802: 13).

So it is, he said, with the wonders of nature, the intricate design of the eye for seeing, the ways in which animals attract their mates, the design of valves to aid the circulation of the blood—all these show complex design for a purpose and hence they must have had a designer. In this way the argument from design becomes evidence for the existence of God.

We now know that Paley was wrong. As Oxford biologist Richard Dawkins puts it, "Paley's argument is made with passionate sincerity and is informed by the best biological scholarship of his day, but it is wrong, gloriously and utterly wrong" (1986: 5). Yet no one could have understood why it was wrong until there was an alternative theory available, a theory that could explain how design for function can appear without a designer. That alternative was Darwin's theory of evolution by natural selection.

"Evolution" means gradual change, and the idea that living things might, in this general sense, evolve was already current in Darwin's time. His own grandfather, Erasmus Darwin, had questioned the prevailing assumption that species were fixed; and Sir Charles Lyell's theory that geological forces could carve landscapes, shape rivers and throw up mountains already threatened the idea that God had designed the earth just as we find it today. The fossil record suggested gradual change in living things and this demanded explanation. What was missing was any mechanism to explain how evolution worked. This is what Darwin provided, in his 1859 book *The Origin of Species*. Its full title is *On the Origin of Species by Means of Natural Selection or the Preservation of Favoured Races in the Struggle for Life*.

His idea was this. If, over a long period of time, creatures vary (as he showed they did), and if there is sometimes a severe struggle for life (which could not be disputed—he had read Malthus's famous *Essay on Population*), then occasionally some variation in structure or habits must occur that is advantageous

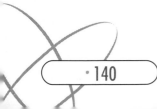

CONSCIOUSNESS

to a creature. When this happens, individuals with that characteristic have the best chance of being preserved in the struggle for life and they will produce offspring similarly characterized. This "principle of preservation, or the survival of the fittest" he called "natural selection." It leads to the improvement of each creature in relation to its conditions of life.

In more modern language we might put it this way. If you have lots of slightly different creatures in a given environment, and there is not enough food, space, water or other necessities for all of them to survive, then the survivors will be those who are best fitted to that environment. If those survivors then pass on whatever it was that helped them survive, their offspring must be better adapted to the environment than their parents were. If this process keeps on repeating then, over the course of billions of years, extraordinary adaptations can appear, including fur, legs, wings and eyes. Paley was especially concerned with eyes, with their intricate and delicate design, but the principle is just the same for eyes as for anything else. In a population of creatures with single photosensitive cells, those with more cells might have an advantage; in a population with eye pits, those with deeper pits might do better; and so on until eyes with corneas, lenses and foveas are forced into existence. It is now thought that eyes have evolved independently more than 40 times on planet earth. Such is the effectiveness of design by natural selection.

Darwin's simple idea has such extraordinary explanatory power that evolutionary biologist Theodosius Dobzhansky (1900–75) memorably proclaimed that "nothing in biology makes sense except in the light of evolution." It is "one of the most powerful ideas in all science" (Ridley, 1996: 3); "the single best idea anyone has ever had" (Dennett, 1995a: 4); "'Darwin's Dangerous Idea' is like a universal acid that eats through everything in its path, revolutionising our world view as it goes" (Dennett, 1995a). This "dangerous idea" has become the foundation for all the biological sciences.

As several authors have pointed out, the process that Darwin described as "descent with modification" *must* produce evolutionary change. For this reason Dennett calls it the "evolutionary algorithm"; if you have variation, heredity and selection, then you *must* get evolution. It is "a scheme for creating Design out of Chaos without the aid of Mind" (ibid.: 50). American psychologist Donald Campbell described the process as "blind variation and selective retention" (1960). However you describe it, this inevitable process requires no designer and no plan. It has no foresight and no intentions. It does not happen for any purpose or toward any end. It is what Dawkins (1986) calls "The Blind Watchmaker." Paley's eyes and ears, valves and mating calls were designed all right, but no God was required.

" . . . nothing in biology makes sense except in the light of evolution. "

Dobzhansky

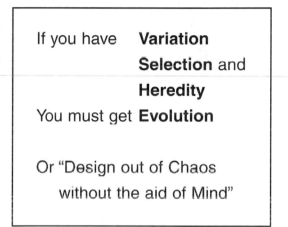

If you have **Variation**

 Selection and

 Heredity

You must get **Evolution**

Or "Design out of Chaos

 without the aid of Mind"

FIGURE 10.2 • The evolutionary algorithm

THE PROBLEM WITH LAMARCK

The major competitor to Darwin's theory of evolution was that of Jean-Baptiste Lamarck (1744–1829). Lamarck agreed with Darwin that species might change, over time, into other species, but his mechanism was quite different. First, he proposed an internal force that produced progress in one direction, and second, he proposed the inheritance of acquired characteristics (the theory he is best known for and which is now often referred to as Lamarckian inheritance or Lamarckism). Lamarck believed that if an animal wished or willed to change itself, the effect would be passed on to its offspring. So the giraffe that spent its life stretching to reach the highest branches would give birth to baby giraffes with slightly longer necks; the blacksmith who developed huge muscles in his own lifetime would pass on the effects of this hard work to his children.

As well as different mechanisms, these two theories give very different visions of how evolution operates and where it is going. On Lamarck's scheme, evolution is directional and progressive, with species gradually, but inevitably, improving over time. On Darwin's scheme, progress is not guaranteed and evolution produces something more like a vast tree or straggly bush. Branches appear all over the place and species become extinct whenever conditions can no longer support them. There is no built-in direction in which progress occurs; rather, change starts from whatever is available and is driven by whatever conditions prevail at the time. Darwin's scheme has no special place for humans, who must be seen as one of the many chance products of a long and complex process, rather than its inevitable consequence or highest creation.

Not surprisingly Lamarck's vision proved more popular than Darwin's. Darwin himself faced massive resistance from religion and was frequently met with ridicule and contempt. At a famous debate in Oxford in 1860, the Bishop of Oxford, Samuel Wilberforce, asked Thomas Henry Huxley, Darwin's main protagonist, whether he was descended from the apes on his grandmother's side or his grandfather's; such was the general understanding of Darwin's ideas.

Perhaps understandably, people preferred the idea of a "Great Chain of Being" with simple creatures at one end and glorious human beings at the other, or the image of a ladder with lowly creatures at the bottom, humans striving to become angels in between and God at the top. Such schemes lend themselves to the idea that variation is *directed*. In Lamarck's scheme the conscious striving of the creatures directs the path of their future evolution, and in religious schemes God

FIGURE 10.3 • Victorians were scandalized by Darwin's suggestion that civilized human beings might be related to the apes. He was mocked and lampooned, as in this cartoon from the London Sketch Book of 1874.

CONSCIOUSNESS

can direct evolution to produce human beings "in His image." Even today there is religious opposition to Darwinism in some countries, most notably in the United States of America.

Theories of directed evolution have often reappeared, many giving a central role to consciousness. For example, the Jesuit priest, Pierre Teilhard de Chardin (1881–1955) proposed that all life is striving toward higher consciousness, toward the "Omega Point" (Teilhard de Chardin, 1959). Julian Huxley believed that evolution has become truly purposeful and that evolution "is pulled on consciously from in front as well as being impelled blindly from behind" (Pickering and Skinner, 1990: 83). One popular theory of the evolution of consciousness is explicitly based on the Great Chain of Being and on the idea of inevitable progress from insentient matter to superconsciousness or transcendence (Wilber, 1997). And at the start of the twenty-first century, futurist Barbara Marx Hubbard (1997) urges us all to realize the potential of our higher consciousness and take control of our own future in "conscious evolution."

FIGURE 10.4 ● In the popular idea of a "Great Chain of Being," evolution proceeds through a line of ever-improving creatures to culminate in the most perfect and intelligent of them all — man. The reality is more like a branching tree, or a great bush, in which humans are on one twig of the primate branch. In this view, all the creatures alive today are successfully adapted to their niche, and none is necessarily "more evolved" than the rest.

Lamarckism is false. The reason why was first made clear by August Weismann (1833–1914) who emphasized the distinction, in sexual species at least, between the germ line (the sex cells) and the soma (the body). The sex cells are passed on from generation to generation, whereas the cells of the rest of the body die when the body dies. What happens to the body affects the *chances* that it will pass on its sex cells, but cannot influence those cells themselves. So, for example, if you spend your life slimming, you may make yourself more (or less) attractive, or even infertile, but you will not produce slimmer children. The eggs your children develop from are not affected by your behavior. That is, the information in the genotype is not affected by changes to the phenotype (the individual body).

There is good reason for evolution to work this way. Most things that happen to phenotypes are harmful, such as failures in development, damage of various kinds, and aging. If all these changes were passed on, useful developments in design would be lost, and evolution would be less effective, not more so. Another way of putting it is that schemes that copy the instructions for making

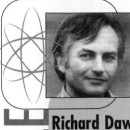
Richard Dawkins (b. 1941)

Born in Nairobi, Dawkins came to England with his family in 1949. He studied at Oxford University, where he subsequently became Lecturer in Zoology, Fellow of New College and then Charles Simonyi Professor of the Public Understanding of Science. His first book, *The Selfish Gene* (1976), established what came to be called "selfish gene theory" and was a best seller for many decades. He is one of the best-known evolutionary biologists in the world and one of the main protagonists in the "Darwin Wars," battling against Stephen Jay Gould over the importance of natural selection and adaptation in evolution (Brown, 1999; Sterelny, 2001). He describes human beings as mere "survival machines," the "lumbering robots" designed to carry our genes around. In promoting "Universal Darwinism" he invented the concept of the meme as a cultural replicator, and refers to religions as viruses of the mind. As for consciousness, he thinks it is "the most profound mystery facing modern biology."

a product (such as making organisms from instructions in the DNA) have higher fidelity than schemes that copy the product itself (Blackmore, 1999).

Darwin's theory ultimately triumphed over Lamarck's, and over other kinds of directed evolution, but not until a major problem was solved. Darwin's theory needed a mechanism of heredity and Darwin did not have one. In fact he believed in the inheritance of acquired characteristics as a mechanism alongside natural selection but could not see how it could produce adaptation. By the early twentieth century Darwinism was in the doldrums, and many biologists even assumed it was false.

By this time, research by Gregor Mendel (1822–84) on inheritance in peas had been rediscovered, and Mendelian inheritance was enthusiastically accepted. It provided an explanation of how variation was produced and passed on during sexual reproduction, but many saw it as opposed to Darwin. It was not until about 1930 that natural selection and Mendelian genetics were successfully brought together in what became known as "the modern synthesis," leading to neo-Darwinism. With this synthesis it became clear that no further processes such as Lamarckian inheritance or directed evolution were needed. Adaptive design could be entirely explained in terms of natural selection working on the variation introduced by the recombination and mutation of genes. Other processes such as genetic drift, historical accidents and other random forces are undoubtedly involved in evolution, and even today there are fierce arguments over their relative contributions (see Dawkins, 1986; Dennett, 1995a; Gould and Lewontin, 1979), but there is no doubt that natural selection, that simple and brilliant idea, can explain the origin of design in the natural world. There is no need for a designer nor for guidance by mind or consciousness.

SELFISH REPLICATORS

Who or what is evolution for? Who or what is the ultimate beneficiary of all those adaptations such as eyes, wings and digestive systems? This proves to be a most interesting question, and the answer is crucial to understanding modern evolutionary theory and its implications for consciousness.

Darwinism is frequently misunderstood as a mechanism that creates adaptations "for the good of the species." A simple example will show why it is not.

Imagine there is a population of rats successfully living off human rubbish in a huge modern city—let's say it is New York. Outside every food store and restaurant are plenty of trash cans that contain plenty of nice rat food. Every night

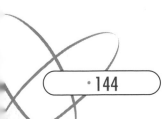

when the workers leave, there is a chance that the trash cans will not be properly sealed or food will be left on the ground. As long as the rats wait quietly until the humans have left, they will have it all to themselves. The best strategy "for the good of the species" is for every rat to wait, but will they? Of course not. If just one rat has genes that incline him to jump in first, causing the lid to clatter to the ground and the humans come running to close it, that rat will still be better off than the rest, running off with some nice rotting meat or a discarded sandwich. That rat will get fatter, take more food home and produce more offspring who will also tend to inherit the "jump first" tendency. The patient rats lose out. Note that this general point is not a recipe for unadulterated selfishness. There are many reasons why cooperative and altruistic behaviors can thrive alongside selfish ones (see Ridley, 1996; Wright, 1994). It is, however, an argument against evolution proceeding "for the good of the species." We must not, therefore, fall into the error of thinking that consciousness could have evolved because it was good for our species, or indeed for any other species.

So is the individual the ultimate beneficiary? Not necessarily. In his classic 1966 book *Adaptation and Natural Selection*, the American biologist George Williams argued that we should recognize adaptations at the level necessitated by the facts and no higher. Although selection may occasionally operate at the level of groups or species, the appropriate level to consider is mostly that of the hereditary information: the gene. Our New York rats would have genes for numerous traits, both physical and behavioral, and natural selection works on these traits. Although it is the individual rats who live or die, the net result is changes in the frequency of different genes in the gene pool. This lies at the heart of what has become known as "selfish gene theory" after Dawkins' 1976 book *The Selfish Gene*. The ultimate beneficiary of natural selection is neither the species nor the group, nor even the individual, but the gene.

Another way of putting it is to say that the gene is the "replicator"; it is the information that is copied, either accurately and frequently, or not. This explains how genes can be "selfish." They are *not* selfish in the sense of having their own desires or intentions (they couldn't; they are just information coded on strands of DNA); they are *not* selfish in the sense that they produce selfish behavior in their carriers (they produce altruistic behaviors too); they *are* selfish in the sense that they will get copied if they can—regardless of their effect on other genes, on their own organisms or on the species as a whole.

From this perspective, human beings (like all other animals) are the "lumbering robots" that have been designed by natural selection to carry the genes around and protect them (Dawkins, 1976). Any physical or behavioral traits those robots have that help them to survive and pass on their genes (i.e., traits that increase their fitness) can be seen as adaptations and are likely to persist. Traits that reduce their fitness are likely to die out. We can therefore understand why plants and animals are the way they are by considering which adaptations would have helped their ancestors to survive and reproduce.

There is a danger of seeing every trait as necessarily adaptive (a tendency derided as "panadaptationism" by paleontologist Stephen Jay Gould (Gould and Lewontin, 1979). In fact many features of organisms are not adaptations, or are far from optimal if they are. Some are strongly influenced by physical constraints and random forces, and none is optimally designed because evolution always has to start from what is available and work from there. Some useless traits survive because they are by-products of other traits that have been selected. Others survive because they were once adaptive and there has not been sufficient selection pressure against them to weed them out. All these may be possibilities when we ask why consciousness has evolved.

HUMAN EVOLUTION

Naturally the principles of evolution apply as much to human beings as to slugs and beetroot plants, although resistance to this idea has always been strong. At the end of *The Origin of Species*, Darwin cautiously suggested that psychology might be more securely based and that "Much light will be thrown on the origin of man and his history." But it was many years before he discussed how in *The Descent of Man* (1871). According to Williams (1966), "It is difficult for many people to imagine that an individual's role in evolution is entirely contained in its contribution to vital statistics . . . that the blind play of the genes could produce man" (ibid.: 4).

This opposition reached its height with the publication, in 1975, of *Sociobiology: The New Synthesis*, in which biologist Edward O. Wilson explored the evolution of social behavior, including that of human beings. For this he was abused and heckled, and even had water thrown over him when he lectured on the subject. Perhaps it is for such political reasons that the term "sociobiology" is rarely used today, but many of its principles survive in the new field of evolutionary psychology.

These two fields have much in common. For example, both have explored how human sexual behavior and sexual preferences have evolved, why there are sex differences in ability and aptitudes, and the evolutionary roots of aggression and altruism. The main difference between them is that whereas sociobiologists tended to treat most human traits as adaptations, evolutionary psychologists emphasize two reasons why they may not be. First, most of human evolution took place when our ancestors lived on the African savannah as hunters and gatherers. So we need to understand which traits would have been adaptive then, not which would be adaptive now (Barkow et al., 1992; Buss, 1999). So, for example, a taste for sugar and fatty foods was adaptive for a hunter-gatherer even though it leads to obesity and heart disease today; sickness and food cravings in pregnancy may have protected a fetus from poisons then, although well-fed women do not need this protection now; and superior spatial ability in males may have been adaptive when males were predominantly hunters and females were gatherers, even though we all have to read maps and get around cities today.

Second, evolutionary psychology emphasizes the difference between the replication strategies of genes and human strategies for gaining pleasure or success. As Pinker puts it,

. . . almost everyone misunderstands the theory. Contrary to popular belief, the gene-centered theory of evolution does *not* imply that the point of all human striving is to spread our genes . . . People don't selfishly spread their genes; genes selfishly spread themselves. They do it by the way they build our brains. By making us enjoy life, health, sex, friends, and children, the genes buy a lottery ticket for representation in the next generation, with odds that were favorable in the environment in which we evolved.

(Pinker, 1997: 43–4)

In other words, we like good food and crave sex because people with those desires would, in the past, have been more successful at passing on their genes.

Evolutionary psychology treats the human mind as a collection of specialized modules, or information processing machines, that evolved to solve particular problems, a view often caricatured as the "Swiss army knife" view of the mind. Although we all share the same collection of evolved modules, each of us behaves in our own unique ways, depending on the genes we were born with and the environment in which we find ourselves. Sadly few evolutionary psychologists have concerned themselves with consciousness, but Pinker lists some of the troubling questions already considered here and comes to what may be the most appropriate conclusion: "Beats the heck out of me!" (Pinker, 1997: 146).

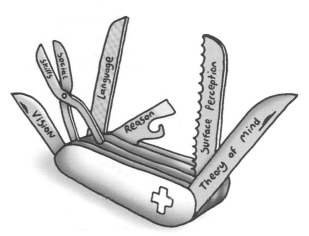

FIGURE 10.5 ● In the "Swiss army knife" of the mind there is a special tool for every essential task. But how many modules are there? How much do they interact, and how specialized do they have to be? Is consciousness just one more blade on the knife?

PRACTICE
AM I CONSCIOUS NOW? DOES THIS AWARENESS HAVE ANY FUNCTION?

As many times as you can every day, ask yourself, "Am I conscious now?"

If you have been practicing, you will know that asking this question seems to make you *more* conscious for a little while. Take this time to watch and wonder. **Does my awareness have any function?** Would my behavior be any different without consciousness? If so, is this the kind of difference that natural selection could work on?

CONSCIOUSNESS IN EVOLUTION
WHY ARE WE CONSCIOUS?

Evolutionary theory is especially good at answering "why" questions. Why are leaves flat and green? So they can photosynthesize efficiently. Why do cats

have fur? To keep them warm. Why do birds have wings? So they can fly. Why are we conscious? So we can . . .

It is therefore easy to think that since humans are conscious, consciousness itself must have a function and be adaptive. As British biologist, Nicholas Humphrey (see Profile, Chapter 11) put it, "either we throw away the idea that consciousness evolved by natural selection, or else we have to find a function for it" (Humphrey, 1987: 378).

Of course there are people who deny that consciousness evolved. For example, some Christians and Muslims believe that each of us has a soul created by God, and that consciousness is a property of that soul. So they do not believe that consciousness evolved. Some people believe that consciousness is the ultimate power in the universe and that consciousness is driving evolution along, rather than being an evolved product itself. Yet few scientists, even those who believe in God, would want to "throw away the idea that consciousness evolved by natural selection." So let us accept the idea that consciousness evolved. Does this mean that it must have a function? At first sight Humphrey's statement seems unexceptionable, and even looks like a useful prescription for finding out why we are conscious. First we find out what consciousness does. Then we find out whether that would have been useful for our ancestors' survival and reproduction. Then—hey presto!—we have found out why consciousness evolved. But things are not so simple. Lurking within this apparently obvious statement are two, closely related, problems.

The first is this. When we considered the question "What does consciousness do?" (see Chapter 3), we found no easy answer. Indeed a good case can be made for the idea that consciousness does nothing. If consciousness does nothing, how can it have a function? (We shall meet this problem again in Chapter 11.)

The second problem is related to the first. When we think about the evolution of consciousness, it seems easy to imagine that we might *not* have been conscious. The logic goes something like this. "I can see why intelligence has evolved because it is obviously useful. I can see why memory, imagination, problem solving and thinking have evolved because they are all useful. So why didn't we evolve all these abilities 'in the dark'? There must have been some extra reason why we got consciousness *as well*."

American philosopher, Owen Flanagan, uses this argument when he says, "Consciousness did not have to evolve. It is conceivable that evolutionary processes could have worked to build creatures as efficient and intelligent as we are, even more efficient and intelligent, without those creatures being subjects of experience" (Flanagan, 1992: 129). He calls this version of epiphenomenalism "conscious inessentialism," and claims that it is both true and important.

Scottish psychologist Euan Macphail applies the same thinking to the *painfulness* of pain:

> there does not in fact seem to be any need for the experience of either pleasure or pain. . . . What *additional* function does the pain serve

"either we throw away the idea that consciousness evolved by natural selection, or else we have to find a function for it"

Humphrey, 1987: 378

CONSCIOUSNESS

that could not be served more simply by a direct link between signals from the classificatory system and the action systems?

(Macphail, 1998: 14)

You will probably have noticed something familiar about this argument. Yes, it is the zombie all over again (see Chapter 2). If you believe in conscious inessentialism, then it follows that "We might have been zombies. We are not. But it is notoriously difficult to explain why we are not" (Flanagan and Polger, 1995: 321) or, to put it another way, "it is hard to explain why evolution produced us instead of zombies" (Moody, 1995: 369). This idea is so intuitively appealing that we must take it slowly and work out whether it really makes sense or not. In Chapter 2 we met some powerful reasons to reject the possibility of zombies, but for the sake of argument let us assume that zombies are (in principle, if not in fact) possible. This allows us to tell the imaginary tale of zombie evolution.

ZOMBIE EVOLUTION

As evolution proceeds, animals compete with each other to survive and reproduce, and traits like accurate perception, intelligence and memory spread. One creature becomes especially intelligent. There is, however, nothing it is like to be this or any of these creatures. They are all zombies.

One day a strange mutation appears by chance in one of these creatures: the "consciousness mutation." Instead of being a zombie, this creature is conscious. We can call it a "conscie." Unlike all the other creatures, there is something it is like to be this first conscie. It suffers, it feels pain and joy, it experiences the qualia of color and light, sound and taste. Its appearance is like Mary the color scientist (see Chapter 2) coming out of her black and white room for the first time.

Now what? Will this chance mutation prove adaptive and the gene for consciousness spread rapidly through the population? Will the conscies outperform the zombies and wipe them out? Or will the two continue to co-exist in an evolutionarily stable mixture? Might planet earth even be like this

THREE WAYS OF THINKING ABOUT THE EVOLUTION OF CONSCIOUSNESS

Each of these three ways has to answer a different question.

1. Conscious inessentialism (epiphenomenalism)

Zombies are possible. In principle there could be creatures that look and act exactly like us but are not conscious. Consciousness is separable from adaptive traits such as intelligence, language, memory and problem solving, but it makes no detectable difference (this is the definition of a zombie). For this approach the important (and mysterious) question is, "Why did evolution produce conscious creatures like us instead of zombies?"

2. Consciousness has a function (it is adaptive)

Zombies are not possible. Consciousness is separable from evolved adaptive traits such as intelligence, language, memory and problem solving. It adds something new, and this approach must say what that is. The important question is, "What is the function of consciousness?" This is related to the question, "What does consciousness do?" (Chapter 3).

3. Functionalism

Zombies are not possible. Consciousness is not separable from evolved adaptive traits such as intelligence, language, memory and problem solving. For this approach the important question is, "Why does consciousness necessarily come about in creatures that have evolved intelligence, language, memory and problem solving abilities like ours?"

(Note that the term "functionalism" can seem confusing. In this context functionalism denies that consciousness has its own separate function; it claims that mental states are functional states, so explaining the functions performed also explains consciousness.)

AM I CONSCIOUS NOW? DOES THIS AWARENESS HAVE ANY FUNCTION?

SELF-ASSESSMENT QUESTIONS

○ What was the "argument from design" supposed to prove? Why is it false?

○ In your own words, explain how natural selection works. List three or more phrases that describe the process.

○ Describe two or more theories in which consciousness directs evolution. What is wrong with them?

○ What is a selfish replicator?

○ Describe some differences between sociobiology and evolutionary psychology.

○ If you believe in the possibility of zombies, what is the function of consciousness?

○ How does a functionalist set about explaining the evolution of consciousness?

today, with some of us being zombies and some of us being conscies? Indeed, might some famous philosophers be zombies while others are real-live-properly-conscious people (Lanier, 1995)?

These questions *seem* to make sense. But we must remember to stick to the correct definition of the zombie. A zombie is a creature that is behaviorally indistinguishable from a conscious human being. The *only* difference is that there is nothing it is like to be the zombie. So what happens?

Absolutely nothing happens. Natural selection cannot detect any difference between the zombies and the conscies. As Chalmers points out, "The process of natural selection cannot distinguish between me and my zombie twin" (Chalmers, 1996: 120). They look the same and they act the same. They both do exactly the same thing in the same circumstances – *by definition* (if you argue that they don't you are cheating). If such a mutation were possible, then it would be entirely, and necessarily, neutral, and would make no difference at all to the way these creatures evolve.

This line of thought leads to an impasse. If we believe in the possibility of zombies, we find it natural to ask why evolution did not make us zombies. But then we find we cannot answer the question because (*on the definition of a zombie*) natural selection cannot distinguish between conscies and zombies.

This whole horrible problem is caused by the mis-imagination of zombies, says Dennett. Zombies are preposterous, but by persistently underestimating their powers, and hence breaking the rules of the definition, philosophers make them seem possible (Dennett, 1995b). If you imagine complex organisms evolving to avoid danger without experiencing pain, or intelligent self-monitoring zombies (i.e., zimboes, Chapter 2) evolving without being conscious like us, you are like someone who is ignorant of chemistry saying he can imagine water that is not actually H_2O.

"To see the fallacy," says Dennett, "consider the parallel question about what the adaptive advantage of *health* is. Consider 'health inessentialism'"(Dennett, 1995b: 324). For any activity that normally requires health to perform it, such as swimming the English Channel or climbing Mount Everest, suppose that it could in principle be done by someone who wasn't healthy at all. "So what is health *for*? Such a mystery!" (Dennett, 1995b: 325). But this mystery only arises for someone who thinks that you can remove health while leaving all the bodily powers and functions intact. In the case of health we can see the fallacy right away. Yet people keep making the mistake with consciousness. They imagine that it is possible to remove consciousness while leaving all the cognitive systems intact. "Health isn't that sort of thing, and neither is consciousness," says Dennett (Dennett, 1995b: 325). His conclusion is that when you have given an evolutionary account of the talents of zimboes, you have answered all the real questions there are about consciousness. There is not something else *in addition*. This is a version of functionalism (Chapter 3). On this view, any creatures that could carry out all the functions we do would necessarily be conscious like us.

We can now see that Humphrey was wrong. It is not true that "either we throw away the idea that consciousness evolved by natural selection, or else we have to find a function for it." There is an alternative. The alternative is to accept that consciousness is more like health than an optional-extra-awareness-module. If we do that, the mystery changes and so does the task of understanding the evolution of consciousness. The mystery becomes why consciousness is like health when it does not seem to be. The task is to explain how evolution produced humans with all their particular skills and abilities and why creatures like that must be conscious as we are.

With this in mind we can now see that there are three ways of approaching the evolution of consciousness (see Concept). If you believe in zombies, then it is forever a mystery why consciousness evolved and you might as well give up. If you reject the possibility of zombies, you have two choices. Either consciousness must be something separable from all the other skills and abilities we have evolved, in which case the task is to explain the function of consciousness and how and why it evolved. Alternatively, consciousness necessarily comes about when those skills and abilities evolve and the task is to explain why.

We can now consider a selection from the many theories of the evolution of consciousness. We will be able to see which mystery they claim to be tackling and how well they succeed.

Dawkins, R. (1986) *The Blind Watchmaker*. New York, Norton. See Chapter 1, pages 1–18.

Dennett, D.C. (1995) *Darwin's Dangerous Idea*. New York, Simon & Schuster. See pages 48–52, 61–80, 324–30 and 521.

Pinker, S. (1997) *How the Mind Works*. New York, Norton. See pages 131–48.

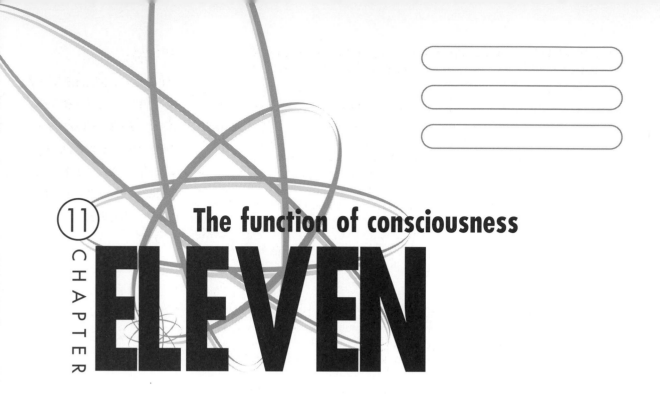

When in evolution did consciousness appear? It seems reasonable to suppose that a few billion years ago there was no consciousness on this planet and now there is, but how could consciousness (or awareness or subjectivity) evolve out of unconscious matter? A pioneer of evolutionary psychology, William James explained the central problem.

> The point which as evolutionists we are bound to hold fast to is that all the new forms of being that make their appearance are really nothing more than results of the redistribution of the original and unchanging materials. The self-same atoms which, chaotically dispersed, made the nebula, now, jammed and temporarily caught in peculiar positions, form our brains; and the "evolution" of the brains, if understood, would be simply the account of how the atoms came to be so caught and jammed . . . But with the dawn of consciousness an entirely new nature seems to slip in.
>
> (James, 1890, i: 146)

"with the dawn of consciousness an entirely new nature seems to slip in"

James, 1890, Vol. 1: 146

James set himself the task of trying to understand how consciousness could "slip in" without recourse to a mind-stuff, mind-dust or soul. This is essentially the task we face today. But before we tackle it, note that there are two other questions with which it should not be confused. The first is, "When does consciousness arise during human development?" For example, "is an egg or a human fetus conscious? and if not, when does a baby or a child become conscious?" The second is, "Which creatures alive today are conscious?" (Chapter 12).

There is much disagreement over how and when consciousness first appeared. Some believe that its appearance was gradual. British pharmacologist Susan Greenfield, for example, claims that "consciousness is not all-or-none but comes in degrees" increasing, like a dimmer switch, with increasing brain size or with the increase in size of the underlying neural assembly (2000: 176). Others think quite the reverse. "One thing of which we can be sure is that wherever and whenever in the animal kingdom consciousness has in fact emerged, it will not have been a gradual process" (Humphrey, 2002: 195).

Some place its arrival very early. For example, panpsychists believe that everything is conscious, although the consciousness of stones and streams is much simpler than that of slugs and sea lions. In this view consciousness itself came long before biological evolution began, but the kind and complexity of consciousness might still have evolved. Some believe that life and consciousness are inseparable, so that as soon as living things appeared on earth, approximately four billion years ago, there would have been consciousness. Some people equate consciousness with sensation, in which case it would have appeared with the first sense organs. The problems here concern defining sensation. For example, does the sunflower's ability to turn toward a source of light count as sensation and hence consciousness? Is the bacterium following a chemical gradient aware of the concentration it responds to? And so on.

Others think that consciousness requires a brain and that it must have evolved along with the evolution of more complex brains (Greenfield, 2000). Finally, there are those who believe that consciousness is a much more recent phenomenon, dating from the appearance of specialized social skills in our recent ancestors. Those skills include social perception, imitation, deception, theory of mind and the evolution of language. We will consider some of these abilities in more detail here and in the next chapter.

NATURE'S PSYCHOLOGISTS

Once upon a time there were animals ancestral to man who were not conscious. That is not to say that these animals lacked brains. They were no doubt percipient, intelligent, complexly motivated creatures, whose internal control mechanisms were in many respects the equals of our own. But it is to say that they had no way of looking in upon the mechanism. They had clever brains, but blank minds.

These animals' brains processed information from their sense organs without their having any conscious sensations, and their bodies acted to avoid fear and hunger without their minds being conscious of any accompanying emotion. And so they "went about their lives, deeply ignorant of an inner explanation for their own behaviour." So begins Humphrey's "Just-So Story" of the evolution of consciousness (Humphrey, 1983: 48), a story to explain how and why we humans became conscious.

> "This consciousness that is myself of selves, that is everything, and yet is nothing at all – what is it? And where did it come from? And why?"
>
> **Jaynes**, 1976

ACTIVITY
The sentience line

Is a stone conscious? Is a rose bush? Is a tadpole or a sheep? Is a baby? Are you? Where do you draw the line?

Gather together a collection of objects that you think span the range from definitely unconscious to definitely conscious. If you are doing this at home, you may have a pet to represent the animals and house plants or a bunch of flowers for the plant kingdom. Indeed you may be able to see enough examples just sitting in your own kitchen. Lay them out in front of you from the least to the most conscious and take a good look.

If you are doing this in class, you will need to be more inventive, but it is worth having actual objects to look at to bring the arguments to life. You might ask members of the class to bring in suitable objects or even animals. You might try the following items:

1 a stone or pebble

2 a weed pulled up from the garden, a house plant, or a piece of fruit

3 a fly, spider or wood louse (put them back where you found them afterward)

4 tadpoles or pet fish

5 an electronic calculator

6 a human volunteer.

Ask everyone to draw their own sentience line across the continuum you have created. Select the two people with the most extreme lines and ask them to defend their decisions against questions from the rest of the class. Does anyone move their line after the discussion?

FIGURE 11.1 • The sentience line. Which of these do you think is conscious? Where do you draw the line?

Humphrey describes his own surprise and pleasure at coming across Wittgenstein and behaviorism, and discovering the "naughty idea" that human consciousness might be useless. "But it is a naughty idea which has, I think, had a good run, and now should be dismissed" (Humphrey, 1987: 378). Consciousness must make a difference, he concludes, or else it would not have evolved.

Consciousness, he suggests, is an "emergent property." Emergent properties are those, like wetness or hardness, that are properties of a combination of things, but not of those things alone. So, for example, the wetness of water is not a property of either hydrogen or oxygen but emerges when the two form molecules of H_2O. Humphrey also describes it as a "surface feature," on which natural selection can act. For example, the fur on an animal's body is a surface feature, visible to natural selection, and has evolved for obvious reasons. So why did consciousness evolve?

Humphrey's answer is that the function of consciousness is social. Like our close relatives the chimpanzees, we humans live in highly complex social groups. Indeed, this sociability may be the most notable feature of the human species. So Humphrey imagined that his ancestral creatures were adapted to a largely social environment. Like modern chimpanzees they made friends and enemies, formed alliances and broke them again, had to work out who was dependable and who was not, and make many other crucial decisions about the behavior of others in their group. They needed the skills of understanding, predicting and manipulating the behavior of others. In other words they became what Humphrey calls "natural psychologists."

These skills of "natural psychology" might have been obtained by watching others and noting the consequences, as a behaviorist does it. But there is a better way. Imagine one of these ancestral creatures who, instead of just watching others, can watch itself. Imagine that early hominid Suzy notices that ferocious Mick has a large piece of food and that her friend Sally is close by, obviously hoping to get some. Should Suzy join in and help Sally snatch it? Should she distract Mick by grooming him so that Sally can get it? If she does will Sally share the food with her afterwards? By asking, "What would I do in the circumstances?" Suzy can make a better decision. She becomes a natural psychologist.

This is precisely what we humans do, argues Humphrey, quoting from Descartes' contemporary Thomas Hobbes who said

> Whosoever looketh into himself and considereth what he doth when he does think, opine, reason, hope, fear &c. and upon what grounds, he shall thereby read and know what are the thoughts and passions of all other men upon the like occasions.
>
> (Hobbes, 1648, in Humphrey, 1987: 381)

So Humphrey proposes that natural selection favored those of our ancestors who developed self-reflexive insight. "Now imagine that a new form of sense organ evolves, an 'inner eye,' whose field of view is not the outside world *but the brain itself*" (1987: 379; 2002: 75). Like other sense organs, this inner eye provides a partial and selective view, but instead of providing a view of the outside world, it gives a picture of the subject's own brain activity (Humphrey, 1986).

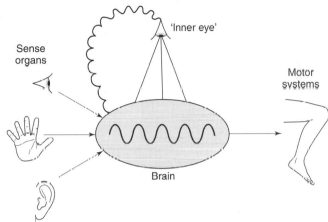

FIGURE 11.2 • According to Humphrey, consciousness arose when a new form of sense organ evolved, an "inner eye," whose field of view was not the outside world but the brain itself (after Humphrey, 1986)

In a similar vein, Dawkins speculates that "Perhaps consciousness arises when the brain's simulation of the world becomes so complete that it must include a model of itself" (1976: 59). But there is a problem here because what we experience is not a model of glial cells and neurons and synapses. Indeed most people on the planet know nothing of what their brain would look like if they could see it. Humphrey describes the picture as a user-friendly description, designed to tell the subject as much as he needs to know in a way he can understand. It allows him to see his own brain states *as* conscious states of mind. This, claims Humphrey, is what consciousness amounts to. It is a self-reflexive loop whose function is to give human beings an effective tool for doing natural psychology.

An interesting implication of this theory (and others that build on it) is that only intelligent and highly social creatures are conscious. These might include the other great apes, and possibly elephants, wolves and dolphins. But if these theories are true, most creatures throughout evolutionary history, and most alive today, would not be conscious at all.

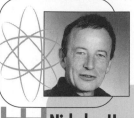
Nicholas Humphrey (b. 1943)

As a student Humphrey began studying physics and maths but soon switched to physiology and psychology. He got involved early on in consciousness research when, as a PhD student at Cambridge in 1967, he discovered that monkeys can still see after the visual cortex has been removed (the phenomenon that later became known as blindsight). For 10 years he worked in neuropsychology and animal behavior, including a spell of fieldwork with mountain gorillas. By the late 1970s he had turned to evolutionary psychology and developed his theory of the social function of intellect, and of human beings as "natural psychologists" with an "inner eye" capable of observing their own brain states. He dismissed the "naughty idea" that consciousness might be useless. In the 1980s Humphrey left academia to make television programs about the human mind and to devote himself to the cause of nuclear disarmament. Returning to Cambridge after three years working with Dan Dennett, his views about consciousness shifted from reflexive consciousness to the nature of sensation and qualia. He believes that to solve the "hard problem," we need "dual currency concepts," such as action, that can apply equally well to mental states and bodily states. In 2001 he became School Professor at the London School of Economics.

ASSESSING THE SOCIAL THEORIES

How well does this theory fare? One might object that it is dualist, that the inner eye is a kind of ghost in the machine. Humphrey makes clear that this is not, in spite of the diagram, what he means. Rather, the human brain is a kind of machine, and the inner eye is an aspect of the way it functions. But how can a brain describe itself? Who is the observer inside the brain, and doesn't this lead to an infinite regress of ever more observers? Humphrey says not. Consciousness is not, he says, a feature of the whole brain but only of the added self-reflexive loop, whose output is part of its own input. No regress is implied. Yet he does admit there is a problem. "Why this particular arrangement should have what we might call the 'transcendent,' 'other-worldly' qualities of consciousness I do not know" (2002: 75).

Another objection concerns the validity of introspection. British physiologist Horace Barlow (1987) argues that introspection does not give an accurate picture of the causes and motivations of behavior, whether of others or oneself. He gives three instructive examples. First there is pain. From introspection we might think that pain was a bad thing and we would be better off without it, when in fact it keeps us from harm. Those few unfortunate individuals who can feel no pain are constantly damaging themselves and, when injured, lack the automatic reactions that rest and protect them during recovery. Our introspections about pain are therefore wrong.

Then there is falling in love. Songs, poems and countless love stories reveal the delights and sorrows of romantic love and praise the beauty of the loved one, rather than dwelling on the number of children the lovers might produce. Though evolutionary psychologists might argue that this is not the point, because the feelings we have still serve the interests of the genes.

Third, there is that old chestnut—the raw redness of red—the qualia. This we get completely wrong, says Barlow. When we say, "This apple is red," we may, from introspection, think that the raw sensation of red comes first, followed by complicated processes leading to the utterance. But in fact a long sequence of computations is entailed in constructing the sensation, and our ability to see red the way we do depends on our whole history of seeing red objects and talking about them. He argues that "the sensation of redness is merely preparing you to communicate the fact that something is red; this is another case where introspection is misleading, for redness is a carefully cooked product and is never as raw as it seems" (1987: 372). This is reminiscent of James's claim that "No one ever had a simple sensation by itself" (1890, i: 224). Barlow concludes that introspection is simply not accurate enough to explain the evolution of consciousness. He suggests instead that consciousness is a social product derived from communication with others.

Several other theories of the evolution of consciousness build directly on Humphrey's original suggestion. For example, British archaeologist Steven Mithen (1996) agrees that consciousness has a biological function in social animals, and that chimpanzees probably have conscious awareness of their own minds. But he argues that if Humphrey is right, this conscious awareness should extend only to thoughts about social interaction. Yet we humans seem to be conscious of all sorts of other things. It is this broadening of awareness that he sees as critical in the creation of the modern human mind.

EXPERIENCE	INTROSPECTIVE MESSAGE	SURVIVAL VALUE
Pain	Unpleasant and to be avoided	Minimizes injuries
Love	Desire for lifelong attachment, feelings of unbounded admiration, etc.	Propagation of the human species
Redness	Attribute of a physical object	Ability to communicate about this attribute

Introspection on our experiences does not directly tell us their survival value

FIGURE 11.3 • According to Barlow, introspection on our experiences does not accurately reflect their survival value (after Barlow, 1987).

Mithen likens our minds to a vast cathedral with many smaller chapels. Early in hominid evolution many separate abilities evolved, largely cut off from each other. They were separate modules, as in the Swiss army knife analogy. In *Homo habilis*, and even in the later Neanderthals, social intelligence was isolated from that needed for making tools or interacting with the natural world. In these creatures "consciousness was firmly trapped within the thick and heavy chapel walls of social intelligence—it could not be 'heard' in the rest of the cathedral except in a heavily muffled form" (Mithen, 1996: 147). They had, he supposes, a fleeting ephemeral kind of consciousness with no introspection about their toolmaking or foraging activities. With increasing cognitive fluidity, the doors between the chapels began to open, and the truly modern human mind evolved.

According to Mithen, this opening-up coincided with the cultural explosion of 60,000–30,000 years ago. By then our ancestors had already evolved big brains and language and were physically very similar to us. Mithen adopts the theory that language evolved as a substitute for grooming as the size of hominid social groups increased (Dunbar, 1996). In this theory language was originally used only for talking about social matters, and even today the major topics of conversation between both men and women can be classified as "gossip"; that is, people talk about who said what to whom, who likes whom, and the status and relationships of themselves and other people (ibid.). But once language had evolved, it could be used for other purposes, providing selection pressure to extend its use to talk about other important matters such as hunting, foraging and the physical world. This, argues Mithen, opened up the chapels of the mind.

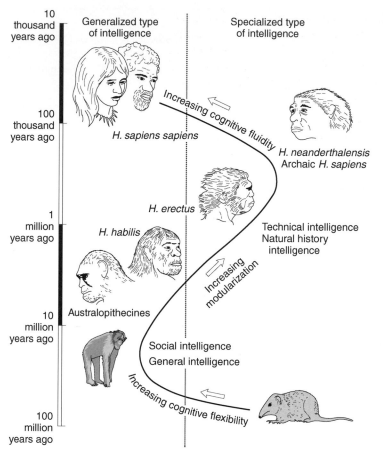

FIGURE 11.4 • Mithen suggests that during the evolution of the mind, selective advantages have oscillated between favoring specialized, hard-wired or modularized intelligence and favoring general intelligence (after Mithen, 1996).

We have now lost our strictly Swiss army knife mind and are conscious of much more than the social world that gave rise to awareness in the first place.

We may now ask how these theories fit into the scheme outlined at the end of the last chapter. First, you might be tempted to raise the zombie objection and argue like this: "I can see why humans evolved introspection, but why couldn't they be zombies that could introspect about their behavior without being *conscious*" (Option 1 in the Concept box in Chapter 10). This, as we have seen, leads to an impasse and Humphrey himself does not reason this way.

That leaves two other possibilities. Do Humphrey and Mithen see consciousness as *itself* having a function that is acted on by natural selection, or do they try to explain (as in Option 3) why any creature capable of introspection or self-reflective insight must inevitably be conscious?

The answer appears to be the former. Both Humphrey and Mithen describe consciousness as an emergent property with specific functions on which natural selection can act, such as "giving the subject a picture of his own brain activity" (Humphrey, 2002: 76).

This may leave us with a fundamental doubt. Is consciousness really the kind of thing that can *be* a surface feature or an emergent property, like fur or wetness or intelligence? As ever, we must remember that consciousness means subjective experience, or "what it is like to be." So the question is, "Does natural selection act on how it *feels* to introspect, or on the behavioral consequences of introspection?" If you decide the latter, then the subjective experience itself has no evolutionary function and remains quite unexplained.

NO FUNCTION FOR CONSCIOUSNESS

A completely different approach is to reject the idea that consciousness has any function and concentrate instead on how conscious creatures like us came to be the way they are.

The most extreme version of this approach is taken by eliminative materialists, such as the Churchlands. They argue that once we understand the evolution of human behavior, skills and abilities, we will have understood everything that we need to understand. The whole idea of consciousness will just slip away, as did the idea of the "life force" or phlogiston. In other words there really is no such thing as consciousness at all.

Less extreme, and much more common, are various forms of functionalism. As we have seen (Chapter 3), many philosophers believe that functionalism cannot account for subjectivity at all, in which case it cannot help with the evolution of consciousness. But others equate subjectivity with functions such as social interaction, language or problem solving. For them, consciousness *itself* has no causal properties or function (one of the reasons why the term "functionalism" can be confusing). Rather, consciousness is equated with those functions, or necessarily accompanies them. In this view consciousness *does* exist, but it is not something separate from those skills. For example, it might be an interesting kind of illusion (Chapter 6) or something more like health or fitness or being alive (Chapter 10).

We have already met one version of this in Dennett's zimbo (Chapter 2). The zimbo is a self-monitoring zombie, and because it can monitor its own internal states, it ends up speaking like we do about, for example, its thoughts, imaginings and intentions. In this theory consciousness is not something extra that has functions of its own. It is not a new, emergent phenomenon on which natural selection can act. Natural selection acts on the ability to think, talk and monitor internal states, and the result is what we call a conscious creature.

Many scientists who work on human evolution implicitly take one or the other of these views but, realizing that consciousness is a tricky problem, tend to avoid saying too much about it. Instead they concentrate on the evolution of our upright gait, our extraordinarily big brains, our unique capacity for language or other special features of human evolution, assuming that the nature of consciousness will become clearer along the way.

Examples include Terrence Deacon's (1997) theory of how the co-evolution of the brain and language gave rise to the "symbolic species" and Merlin Donald's (1991) theory of the co-evolution of human brains, culture and cognition. Both of these assume that human consciousness is tied to the use of symbolic representations, and seek to understand how the capacity for symbolic thought comes about. This association of human consciousness with symbolic thought appears in other theories, such as the "symbolic interactionism" of the American philosopher and social psychologist George Herbert Mead (1863–1931). Mead argued that while other animals may be conscious, only humans become self-conscious, and this self-consciousness is built up first from gestures and other non-symbolic interactions and finally from the symbolic interactions made possible by language. For Mead, consciousness is fundamentally a social, not an individual, construction.

A different evolutionary picture is provided by Claxton, who argues that consciousness started out as a rare phenomenon associated with the sudden super-alertness required in reacting to sudden emergencies.

> It did not emerge "for a purpose." It came along with the developing ability of the brain to create these transient states of "super-activation" as a useless by-product, of no more functional interest than the colour of the liver, or the fact that the sea, under certain conditions, bunches up, rolls over and turns white.
>
> (Claxton, 1994: 133)

The sad thing, says Claxton, is that while consciousness began as a rarity, like a violent sneeze, or even an orgasm, we now live in an almost perpetual state of low-grade emergency. "Originally associated with a marvellous mechanism for spotting and responding to basic emergencies, it has become . . . a mechanism for constructing dubious stories whose purpose is to defend a superfluous and inaccurate sense of self" (1994: 150). In this view, the consciousness that we prize so highly is a kind of modern sickness.

The most recent origin for consciousness was suggested by American psychologist Julian Jaynes, in his controversial book *The Origin of Consciousness in the Breakdown of the Bicameral Mind* (1976). Going back 3000 years to the earliest written records he searched for clues to the presence or absence of a subjective conscious mind. The first text that allowed him accurate enough translation was the *Iliad*, an epic story of revenge, blood and tears, which describes events that probably occurred around 1230 BC, and were written down around 900 or 850 BC. "What is mind in the Iliad?" asks Jaynes. "The answer is disturbingly interesting. There is in general no consciousness in the Iliad" (Jaynes, 1976: 69).

What he means is that there are no words for consciousness, nor for mental acts. Words that later come to mean "mind" or "soul" mean much more concrete things like blood or breath. And there is no word for will and no concept of free will. When the warriors act, they do so not from conscious plans, reasons or motives, but because the gods speak to them. In fact the gods take the place of consciousness. This is why Jaynes describes these people's minds as "bicameral" (meaning two-chambered). They were split. Actions were organized without consciousness and the result was heard as inner voices. We would now call these voices hallucinations, but they called them gods. So "Iliadic man did not have subjectivity as do we; he had no awareness of his awareness of the world, no internal mind-space to introspect upon" (Jaynes, 1976: 75). On Jaynes' view, our modern conception of consciousness as subjectivity describes something that is itself a recent invention.

We can now see that there is no consensus over when consciousness evolved. Proposals range from billions of years ago to only a few thousand.

UNIVERSAL DARWINISM

All the theories considered so far are based on evolution by natural selection acting on *genes*, but this is not the only way in which evolutionary theory can

> *"It is an empty and misleading metaphor to call religion, science or any other human activity a 'virus' or 'parasite'.*" *Memes are a "useless and essentially superstitious notion."*
>
> **Midgley**, 1994

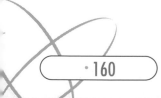

●   CONSCIOUSNESS

be applied to understanding the mind. As we saw in Chapter 10, the process of natural selection can be thought of as an algorithm. At its simplest: if you have variation and selection and heredity, then you must get evolution. The value of seeing evolution as a general process or algorithm is to realize that it can work on anything, just so long as there is something that varies, and is selectively copied. In other words you can have other replicators and other evolutionary systems. This principle is what Dawkins (1976) calls "Universal Darwinism."

So are there any other evolutionary processes? The answer is yes. In fact it turns out that many processes once thought to work by instruction or teaching, in fact work by selection from pre-existing variation. This is true of the immune system and of many aspects of development and learning (Gazzaniga, 1992). For example, the development of young brains entails the selective death of many neurons and connections; learning to speak entails generating all kinds of strange noises and then selecting from those. Dennett (1995a) provides an evolutionary framework for understanding the various design options available for brains, in which each level empowers the organisms to find better and better design moves. He calls it the "Tower of Generate-and-Test." At each level, new variants are generated and then tested. By using the same Darwinian process in new ways, new kinds of minds are created.

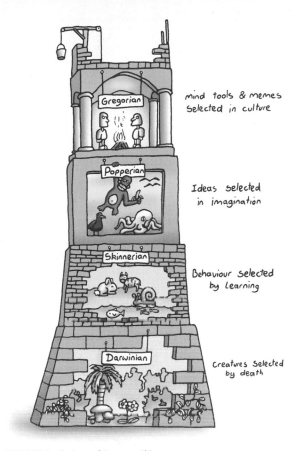

FIGURE 11.5 ● The Tower of Generate-and-Test

mind tools & memes selected in culture

Ideas selected in imagination

Behaviour selected by Learning

Creatures Selected by death

Of most interest here are Darwinian theories of brain function that might throw light on consciousness. One example was proposed by Nobel Laureate Gerald Edelman (1989; Edelman and Tononi, 2000a). The theory of "Neural Darwinism" or "neuronal group selection" depends on three main tenets. First, "developmental selection" occurs during the early development of the brain. Neurons send out myriad branches in many directions, providing enormous variability in connection patterns. Then according to which connections are used and which not, the connections are pruned to leave long-lasting functional groups. Second, a similar process of "experiential selection" goes on throughout life, in which certain synapses within and between groups of locally coupled neurons are strengthened and others are weakened, without changes in the anatomy.

Third, there is the novel process of "reentry," a dynamic process in which selective events across the various maps of the brain can be correlated. Reentrant circuits entail massively parallel reciprocal connections between different brain areas, allowing diverse sensory and motor events to be synchronized. The activity of groups of neurons can contribute to consciousness if it forms part of what they call the "dynamic core." This is an ever-changing, yet highly integrated functional group, involving large numbers of widely distributed thalamocortical

MEMES

Origins

Dawkins (1976) coined the term to provide an example of a replicator other than the gene; a cultural replicator.

Definitions

Meme (mi:m), *n. Biol.* (shortened from *mimeme* . . . that which is imitated, after GENE *n.*). "An element of a culture that may be considered to be passed on by non-genetic means, esp. imitation" (*Oxford English Dictionary*, 1998). A meme is any information that is copied from person to person or between books, computers or other storage devices. Many mental contents are not memes because they are not acquired by imitation or copying, including perceptions, visual memories and emotional feelings. Skills or knowledge acquired by ordinary learning are not memes. For example, your skateboard is a meme (it has been copied), but your skill in riding it is not (you had to learn by trial and error and so does your friend who watches you enviously).

Memeplex

Abbreviated from "co-adapted meme complex," a memeplex is a group of memes that are passed on together. Memeplexes form whenever a meme can replicate better as part of a group than it can on its own. Memeplexes range from small groups of words, such as sentences and stories, to religions, sciences and works or art, or financial and political institutions.

Selfplex

A memeplex formed when people use language that includes references to self. Sentences such as "I believe x," "I think y," "I hate z" give an advantage to x, y and z over simply stating them. In the process they give rise to the false belief that there is an "I" who has the beliefs, thoughts and desires. The function of this false belief is to spread the memes.

FIGURE 11.6 ● St. Paul's Cathedral is a meme-spreading monument. The beautiful vistas, awesome dome, inspiring paintings and delightful music all make people want to worship there, and in the process they spread the memes of Christianity.

neurons with strong mutual interactions. According to Edelman and Tononi, these principles provide the basis for understanding both the ongoing unity and endless variety of human consciousness.

This theory is certainly based on selectionist principles. It is not so clear, however, that it includes any principle of heredity. Recall that the evolutionary algorithm requires three processes: variation, selection and heredity. In Edelman's theory variant patterns are generated and selected, but there seems to be no mechanism for copying variants to make new ones. Put another way, there is no replicator.

William Calvin (1996) is an American neuroscientist whose theory does include such copying. He describes the brain as a Darwin machine and sets even higher standards, listing six requirements for a truly Darwinian creative process. According to his theory all are satisfied in the brain. Most important is his understanding of copying. Throughout the cerebral cortex, he argues, are spatiotemporal firing patterns that represent concepts, words or images. These patterns depend on the way cortical cells are wired up in columns, and with both lateral inhibition and lateral excitation at different distances. The result is hexagonal structures about half a millimeter across that can be copied or cloned, and that compete for survival in a truly Darwinian process. Imagine a vast, ever-shifting quilt of hexagons, all jostling to survive and get copied, some cloning whole areas like themselves while others die out. Consciousness is the currently dominant patch of the hexagonal patterned quilt.

Note that these two theories deal with Darwinian processes within one brain. Our last theory deals with copying between one brain and another, achieved at the top level of Dennett's tower.

MEMES AND MINDS

Memes are ideas, skills, habits, stories or any kind of information that is copied from person to person. They include written and spoken words, rules like driving on the left (or the right) and habits like eating with chopsticks (or a knife and fork), as well as songs, dances, clothes fashions and technologies. The theory of memes is highly controversial and has been criticized by biologists, sociologists, anthropologists and philosophers (see Aunger, 2000). Nevertheless it potentially provides a completely new way of understanding the evolution of consciousness.

The term "meme" was originally coined by Dawkins (1976) to illustrate the principle of Universal Darwinism and to provide an example of a replicator other than the gene.

Memes count as replicators because they are information that is copied with variation and selection. Take the example of a joke. In your lifetime you have probably heard thousands of jokes, but you probably remember very few of them, and pass on even fewer. So every joke has to compete to get copied. Or think about books: for every best seller there are millions of copies of unpopular books sitting unread on the shelves. If you think about how many memes bombard you every day, it is obvious that there is enormous selection pressure. There is also copying with variation. Memes are copied by imitation, teaching and reading, and by photocopying and all the computer processes of the modern information age. Sometimes they are copied perfectly, but variation is introduced either when the copying is imperfect, as in misremembering and forgetting, or when old memes are combined in new ways to produce new memes. This means that the whole of human culture can be seen as a vast new evolutionary process based on memes, and human creativity can be seen as analogous to biological creativity. In this view, biological creatures and human inventions are both designed by the evolutionary algorithm. Human beings are the meme machines that store, copy and recombine the memes (Blackmore, 1999).

Viral memes

Some memes succeed because they are true or useful or beautiful, while others succeed by using various tricks to persuade people to copy them. Viral memes include chain letters, e-mail viruses and ineffective therapies. Dawkins refers to religions as "viruses of the mind" because they infect people by using threats and promises, as well as self-protective tricks, such as rewarding faith and discouraging doubt.

PRACTICE
IS THIS A MEME?

As many times as you can, every day, ask yourself, "Am I conscious now?" Then consider whatever you were conscious of when you asked the question. For example, you might have been conscious of having a conversation, or watching TV or looking out of the window. Now ask, **"Are these memes?"**

The theory of memetics is not built on an *analogy* with genes, although it is often described that way (Searle, 1997). Rather, memes are one kind of replicator and genes are another, and they both work on the same evolutionary principles. Analogies can be drawn between them, but often these are not close because the two replicators work in quite different ways.

SELF-ASSESSMENT QUESTIONS

○ Suggest some turning points in evolution that might have marked the appearance of consciousness.

○ Describe Humphrey's "Just-So Story" in your own words.

○ According to Humphrey, what is the biological function of consciousness?

○ On what grounds does Barlow criticize Humphrey's theory? What other criticisms can you think of?

○ Describe two or three theories in which consciousness has no biological function.

○ Think of as many ways as possible in which Darwinian processes may be involved in the evolution of mind.

○ What are memes? Compare two theories that make use of memes in understanding consciousness.

Among the differences are that genes are based on information stored in molecules of DNA, and copied with extremely high fidelity, while memes depend on the variable fidelity copying of human interactions.

Among the similarities are that both genes and memes compete selfishly to be copied, their only interest being self-replication. Some memes succeed because they are useful to us, such as the vast memeplexes of technology, political and financial institutions, and all of the arts and sciences. At the other end of the spectrum are viral memes—those that use tricks to get themselves copied. Many of these are essentially "copy me" instructions backed up with threats and promises, such as e-mail viruses, chain letters and religions (Dawkins, 1976). Based on these principles, memetics has been used to explain many aspects of human behavior and human evolution, including the origins of our big brains and our capacity for language (Blackmore, 1999).

Dennett has used the concept of memes as a central part of his theory of consciousness. He describes a person as "the radically new kind of entity created when a particular sort of animal is properly furnished by—or infested with—memes" (1995a: 341) and a human mind as "an artifact created when memes restructure a human brain in order to make it a better habitat for memes" (ibid.: 365). In his view the human brain is a massively parallel structure that is transformed by its infection with memes into one that *seems* to work as a serial machine. Just as you can simulate a parallel computer on a serial one, so the human brain simulates a serial machine on parallel machinery. He calls this the "Joycean machine," so called after James Joyce's stream-of-consciousness novels. So, with this virtual machine installed, we come to think about one thing after another, and to use sentences and other mental tools, in a way that suits the memes.

This is how the self, the "center of narrative gravity" (see Chapter 3) comes to be constructed; "our *selves* have been created out of the interplay of memes exploiting and redirecting the machinery Mother Nature has given us" (Dennett, 1995a: 367). The self is a "benign user illusion of its own virtual machine!" (Dennett, 1991: 311).

But perhaps the illusion is not so benign after all. Another possibility is that this illusion of self is actually harmful to *us*, although it benefits the *memes*. In this view the self is a powerful memeplex (the selfplex) that propagates and protects the memes, but in the process gives rise to the illusion of free will, and to selfishness, fear, disappointment, greed and many other human failings. Perhaps without it we might be happier and kinder people, although it is hard to imagine being conscious without a self (Chapter 27).

In Dennett's view "Human consciousness is *itself* a huge complex of memes (or more exactly, meme-effects in brains)" (ibid.: 210), but this presents two problems. First, memes, by definition, can be copied. Yet our own ineffable, private, conscious experiences cannot be passed on to someone else; that is the whole problem and fascination of consciousness. Second, the memes can, arguably, be dropped without consciousness disappearing. For example, at moments of shock, or when silenced by the beauty of nature, the mind sometimes seems to stop.

The same effect can be cultivated through meditation and other practices (Chapter 26). Far from losing consciousness, as Dennett's theory would imply, people say that they become *more* conscious at such moments. This suggests that perhaps human consciousness is distorted into its familiar self-centered form by the memes, rather than that it *is* a complex of memes (Blackmore, 1999). If so, what is left when the memes go away?

Dawkins believes that "We, alone on earth, can rebel against the tyranny of the selfish replicators" (Dawkins, 1976: 201) and Csikszentmihalyi urges us to "achieve control over your mind, your desires, and your actions . . . If you let them be controlled by genes and memes, you are missing the opportunity to be yourself" (Csikszentmihalyi, 1993: 290), but who is this self who is going to rebel?

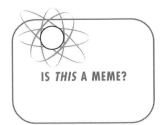

IS *THIS* A MEME?

" We, alone on earth, can rebel against the tyranny of the selfish replicators. "

Dawkins, 1976: 201

" there is no one to rebel "

Blackmore, 1999: 246

READING

Blakemore, C. and Greenfield, S. (1987) *Mindwaves*. Oxford, Blackwell. Chapters by Barlow (pages 361–74) and Humphrey (pages 377–81). Or see the following text.

Humphrey, N. (2002) The uses of consciousness. In *The Mind Made Flesh: Frontiers of Psychology and Evolution*. Oxford, Oxford University Press. See pages 65–85.

Pickering, J. and Skinner, M. (eds) (1990) *From Sentience to Symbols*. Chapters by Huxley (pages 80–9), Humphrey (pages 101–8), Mead (pages 192–7) or Jaynes (pages 223–7).

The function of consciousness

CHAPTER ELEVEN

Animal minds

TWELVE

⑫

What is it like to be a snake? Can you imagine how it feels to slither along through wet grass in search of prey? Maybe you can. But, as Nagel pointed out in "What is it like to be a bat?" (1974), you are probably imagining what it would be like for *you* to be the snake, and that is not the point. The point is what it is like for the snake—that is, if it is like anything at all for the snake.

How can we ever know? We cannot ask the snake to tell us. And even if we could we might not believe, or understand, what it said. This is essentially the problem of other minds again. Just as you can never know whether your best friend is really conscious, so you can never know whether your cat, or the birds in your garden, or the ant you just stood on are (or were) conscious. Humans and other animals show similar expressions of emotions and similar reactions to pleasure, pain and fear, as Darwin (1872) long ago showed. Even so, we must avoid assuming that just because another animal appears to be in pain or to be feeling guilty, or happy or sad, it really has the feelings we attribute to it. As we shall see, our impressions can sometimes be completely wrong.

There are two extreme positions to consider. One is that only humans are conscious. For example, Descartes believed that because they do not have language, all other animals are unfeeling automata, without souls or consciousness. A modern version of this viewpoint is given by Macphail, who argues that "animals are indeed Cartesian machines, and it is the availability

FIGURE 12.1 • Are chimpanzees unfeeling machines? They are highly intelligent and sociable, and can use tools such as twigs, which they use to fish for ants and termites.

"animals are indeed Cartesian machines"

Macphail, 1998: 233

"Humans and higher animals are obviously conscious."

Searle, 1997: 5

of language that confers on us, first, the ability to be self-conscious and, second, the ability to feel" (1998: 233). In his view there is no convincing evidence for consciousness in other species. They are not just devoid of speech and self awareness, but devoid of feeling too.

At the other extreme lies the view that because so many species are physically similar, they must all be conscious. For example, Baars (2001) points out that the known correlates of consciousness are phylogenetically ancient, going back at least to the early mammals. He argues that there are no fundamental biological differences that could justify denying subjectivity to other species when we so readily attribute it to other people. Between these extremes lie theories that, for various reasons, attribute different kinds of consciousness to different species.

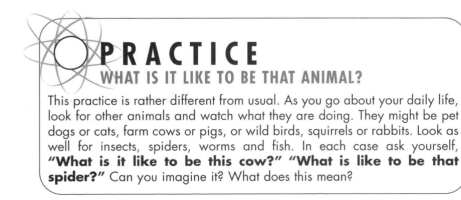

PRACTICE
WHAT IS IT LIKE TO BE THAT ANIMAL?

This practice is rather different from usual. As you go about your daily life, look for other animals and watch what they are doing. They might be pet dogs or cats, farm cows or pigs, or wild birds, squirrels or rabbits. Look as well for insects, spiders, worms and fish. In each case ask yourself, **"What is it like to be this cow?" "What is like to be that spider?"** Can you imagine it? What does this mean?

DIFFERENT WORLDS

Every species has evolved sensory systems to suit its way of life. This simple fact leads to the odd realization that when you have several different species in the same place, they may all be inhabiting essentially different worlds. Let's take the example of an ordinary garden pond with fish, frogs, newts, snails, insect larvae, flies and a human child with a fishing net. We can easily imagine (or think we can) how the pond looks to the child, but the others must experience it in completely different ways. The fish have sense organs for detecting vibrations in the water from which they know what to avoid, what to seek out and when to dive for safety. We have nothing comparable to help us imagine it. The insects have compound eyes quite unlike our image-forming eyes, and many of the animals have chemical senses far more sensitive than our feeble senses of smell and taste.

The frog is particularly interesting. Frogs have eyes with lenses and retinae somewhat like ours, sending signals along the optic nerve to the optic tectum in the brain. It is tempting to imagine that a picture of the frog's world is somehow constructed in its brain to enable it to see, but this is not so. The frog's eye tells the frog's brain just what it needs to know. It tells it about stationary and moving edges, changes in overall illumination, and bugs. The "bug detectors" respond specifically to small moving objects, not to large moving objects or stationary small objects, and direct the frog's tongue to catch flies. An extraordinary consequence of the way this system works is that a frog can literally starve to death surrounded by freshly killed flies. If the fly does not move, the frog does not see it.

We can learn much from thinking about this frog. We might be tempted to think that the child gazing into the pond really does have a picture of the world in her head—a full, rich and detailed picture of the scene—and that by comparison the frog's vision is simply stupid. But think again. The work on change blindness and inattentional blindness (see Chapter 6) shows that we do not hold a detailed picture in our heads either. In fact we may be much more like the frog than we care to admit. Evolution has only designed us to detect selected aspects of the world around us. Just like the frog, we are quite unaware of everything else—yet we feel no gaps.

We may think that the child must be more conscious than the frog, and the frog more conscious than the fly, but why? While many authors make bold assertions about animal consciousness, it is not clear how these can be tested or what they mean. Greenfield proposes that "consciousness increases with brain size across the animal kingdom" (2000: 180). But if she is right, then sperm whales, African elephants and dusky dolphins are all more conscious than you are, and Great Danes and Labradors are more conscious than Jack Russells and Pekinese. Searle claims that "Humans and higher animals are obviously conscious, but we do not know how far down the phylogenetic scale consciousness extends" (1997: 5). But this is not "obvious" and also there is no single phylogenetic scale, or linear sequence, along which animals can be graded from "higher" to "lower." As we have seen, evolution has not produced a line but a very bushy bush.

> " *current thinking about animal consciousness is a mess* "
>
> **Dennett**, 1998a: 337

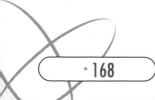

CONSCIOUSNESS

We might try to grade animals by intelligence, but one danger is that we base our idea of intelligence on our own species–specific abilities and fail to appreciate other kinds of intelligence, like that of bees or octopuses or elephants. Even in more familiar creatures comparisons are difficult. On some scales chimpanzees are put near the very top and birds, with their "bird-brains," much lower. Yet chimpanzees can work out how to pile up boxes to reach a suspended banana, and crows can work out how to pull up a string between a beak and foot to reach a suspended nut. Is one more intelligent than the other, or more conscious?

Does one animal suffer more than another? We have empathy for other people when we see them crying or in distress, which may be reasonable on the assumption that they are similar to us. We may also feel empathy for the dog who squeals when hurt, the tiger pacing up and down in a tiny cage or the lobster screaming in boiling water. But could any, or all, of them be Cartesian automata that feel nothing? This is not an empty question because we can build a simple toy dog, wired up so that if you stand on its foot it whines, but few would believe it was capable of suffering. A few switches are not sufficient. But what is sufficient for the capacity to suffer?

FIGURE 12.2 • Crows are capable of highly intelligent behavior and in the wild make tools out of twigs and leaves. In recent studies at Oxford University, Alex Kacelnik and his colleagues (Weir, Chappell and Kacelnik, 2002) have shown that they can also solve demanding and novel problems. This New Caledonian crow, Betty, faced with food inside a deep container, spontaneously bent a piece of wire into a hook to retrieve it. Although chimpanzees have much larger brains, they may not be capable of this kind of inferential reasoning. Is one more intelligent than the other? Is one more conscious?

Marian Stamp Dawkins (1987; see Profile) suggests three sources of evidence for deciding whether an animal is suffering: its general state of health, its physiology and its behavior. She argues that the best measure of how much an animal suffers is how hard it will work to avoid the cause of that suffering. In experiments to try to find out whether battery hens were suffering because they had no litter to scratch in, she was surprised to find that although they preferred cages with litter, they would not push through a heavy curtain or jump a barrier to get to one. She suggests that we should not rely on empathy to decide whether an animal is suffering but should allow it to tell us by observing its behavior; the more complex are the ways it can use to escape from unpleasant things, the more it is capable of suffering.

Do other species experience pain as we do (Chapter 16)? Does it really *hurt*? The question may seem impossible to answer but we need not despair. In studying human consciousness we have made progress by learning about perception, memory, attention and other relevant abilities. We can do the same by looking at some of the abilities most likely to give us insight into animal consciousness.

Marian Stamp Dawkins (b. 1945)

Marian Stamp Dawkins is Professor of Animal Behaviour in the Department of Zoology at Oxford University and Fellow of Somerville College. Her life-long interest in whether other animals are conscious has led her to studies of the evolution of animal signals, why fish on coral reefs are so brightly colored, and how animals recognize each other. Above all she is concerned with the assessment of animal welfare, especially that of broiler chickens and laying hens. She has developed methods for finding out how much other species are capable of suffering and how we humans can tell when they are. She has published widely on animal consciousness, including her book *Through Our Eyes Only? The Search for Animal Consciousness*.

SELF-RECOGNITION

You are not only aware of the world around you but of yourself as an observer. You have self-consciousness. Although we cannot know when young children first become self-conscious, they start referring to "me" and then "you" between 18 months and two years of age. But what about other animals? Are cats, or dogs, or dolphins aware of themselves? Do they have a sense of "I" as a conscious being observing the world? Although they cannot tell us directly, there are other ways of trying to find out. The best known is to see whether they can recognize themselves in a mirror.

Dogs and cats obviously cannot. As any pet owner will attest, kittens will rush up to a mirror, look for the other kitten inside it, and then quickly get bored. Many birds continue to treat their own image as a rival indefinitely, as do some fish. They clearly have no concept that the mirror reflects their own body. But what about our nearest relatives, the great apes?

Charles Darwin (1872) was the first to report the experiment. He put a mirror in front of two young orangutans at the zoo who, as far as he knew, had never seen one before. He reported that they gazed at their own images in surprise, often moving and changing their point of view. They then approached close and protruded their lips toward the image, as if to kiss it. Then they made all sorts of faces, pressed and rubbed the mirror, looked behind it, and finally became cross and refused to look any longer.

Sadly, we cannot tell whether these orangutans recognized themselves or not: whether they were looking at their own lips or trying to kiss another orangutan, for example. An attempt to find out more was not made until a hundred years later, when the comparative psychologist Gordon Gallup (1970) gave a mirror to a group of pre-adolescent chimpanzees. Initially they reacted as though they were seeing other chimpanzees, but after a few days they were using the mirror to look inside their mouths or to inspect other normally invisible parts of their bodies. Watching chimpanzees do this is certainly impressive. It seems obvious from the way they pick their teeth and make funny faces that they recognize themselves, but can we be sure?

To find out, Gallup anesthetized these same animals and placed on them two red marks, one on an eyebrow ridge and one above the opposite ear. When they came round from the anesthetic and looked in the mirror, they saw the marks and tried to touch them or rub them off, just as you or I would probably do. By counting the number of times the chimpanzees touched the marks compared with how many times they touched the same place on the unmarked

side, Gallup could be fairly sure that they did indeed see the reflection in the mirror as that of their own body.

Subsequently many other species have been tested. Human children fail the test until they are somewhere between 18 months and two years old. Chimpanzees vary a great deal, but generally do touch the spots. Of the three other species of great ape, orangutans and bonobos have been found to behave like the chimpanzees, but gorillas do not. The only gorilla to succeed has been Koko, a highly trained gorilla who has learned to communicate with humans using American Sign Language (ASL). When asked what she saw in the mirror, she signed "Me, Koko." That Koko behaved so differently from other gorillas may seem surprising, but in fact it is well known that enculturated apes acquire many skills that their wild, or captive, conspecifics do not. Just what the relevant skills are in this case, though, we simply do not know.

FIGURE 12.3 • When we look in a mirror we recognize ourselves in the reflection, but which other animals can do this? Cats, dogs, and many other species treat their reflections as though they are another animal, but some apes and dolphins may be able to recognize themselves. Does mirror self-recognition imply self-consciousness?

In many similar tests monkeys have shown no self-recognition, even though they use mirrors in other ways. For example, they can learn to reach things seen only in reflection, and will turn around toward someone they have seen in a mirror. Yet they do not pass the spot test. From this it has been widely assumed that only great apes are self-conscious, that there is a great divide in consciousness between us and the rest. But there are several problems with this conclusion.

First, the test is not fair for many species. For example, dolphins and whales are extremely intelligent and communicative creatures, and some of them enjoy playing with mirrors, but they have no hands to touch a spot even if they wanted to. Even for creatures that do, the test requires an animal that grooms itself and would want to remove a mark if it knew it was there. Trying to give gorillas the benefit of the doubt, Gallup (1998) put marks on their wrists. They did indeed try to remove these marks but not the marks seen only in the mirror.

Another problem is that while apes sometimes interpret staring as friendly, as humans do, most monkeys find staring threatening, so the test may fail simply because the monkey will not look at itself carefully enough. American psychologist Marc Hauser (2000) got around this problem using cotton-top tamarins, small tree-living monkeys with a spectacular tuft of white hair on their heads. Once they were used to the mirror he anesthetized them and applied bright pink, blue or green hair dye to their tufts. The monkeys stared at the tuft, and most of them touched it at least once. Some moved their hands in front of the mirror as if testing the effect, and some seemed to be trying to look at their backsides using the mirror. Hauser concluded that these monkeys did have self-recognition after all, although this conclusion remains tentative.

We still do not know for sure which species can and cannot recognize themselves in a mirror, but in any case the more serious problem is that we do not know what mirror recognition would tell us about self-awareness even if we did. It does not necessarily follow that because an animal can recognize its own body in a mirror, it has either a concept of self or self-awareness. For example, an ape might work out the contingencies between making movements and seeing effects in the mirror without concluding that the arm in the mirror is its own. Or it might conclude that the mirror shows its own body without having any concept of itself as seen by others, or as an agent or experiencer.

There is lively debate over this issue. Gallup (1998) is convinced that chimpanzees not only recognize themselves in mirrors but have a concept of self and self-awareness. He even suggests that with this self-concept comes the beginnings of autobiographical memory and awareness of a personal past and future. In Damasio's terms (1999), this would mean that chimpanzees might have extended consciousness and autobiographical selves as well as core consciousness.

Primatologist Daniel Povinelli (1998) agrees that they have a concept of self, but not that they are aware of their own internal psychological states. He suggests that "self-recognition in chimpanzees and human toddlers is based on a recognition of the self's behaviour not the self's psychological states." Even more skeptical is British psychologist Cecilia Heyes (1998), who agrees only that they are capable of "mirror-guided body inspection," and argues that chimpanzees have no self-concept and no understanding of mental states.

THEORY OF MIND

One aspect of human consciousness is that we have beliefs, desires, fears and other mental states, and we attribute these same mental states to others. That is, we have a "theory of mind." According to Dennett (1987) we readily adopt what he calls "the intentional stance," understanding other people's behavior by treating them *as if* they have hopes, fears, desires and intentions. The intentional stance is a very powerful tool for understanding, controlling and predicting the world around us. It makes deception possible as well as empathy.

Babies are not born with these abilities. Sometime during their second year they begin to follow another person's gaze to see what they are looking at and to look at what is pointed at, rather than at the pointing finger. By the age of three they can talk about their own and others' desires and preferences. But at this age they cannot understand that someone else may not be able to see what they can see or may have a false belief. This is the age at which a child playing hide-and-seek may hide her head under a pillow and shout "come and find me." Numerous experiments have shown that between the ages of three and five the various aspects of having a theory of mind develop.

CONSCIOUSNESS

In 1978 two psychologists, David Premack and Guy Woodruff, asked, "Does the chimpanzee have a theory of mind?" The relevance of this question to us here is that if other animals do not have a theory of mind, and they cannot attribute mental states to others or to themselves, it seems impossible that they could be conscious in the human sense. Mirror self-recognition is one aspect of this. Other relevant skills include the ability to deceive others, to understand what others can see or know and the capacity for imitation.

DECEPTION

To deceive someone means to manipulate what they believe. A butterfly with a brilliant eye pattern on its wing is deceiving predators, as is a camouflaged stick insect, or a plover that feigns a broken wing to distract a predator away from its nest. In these cases the camouflage or the behavior is genetically encoded, but human deception is rather different. You might deliberately try to convince someone that you didn't steal their chocolates or lose their book, or that you really do love them. You can only do this if you know that someone else can have a false belief.

This kind of social intelligence was largely underestimated until the 1980s when Humphrey argued that social, rather than technical or practical, intelligence was what drove the increase in brain size among primates. With its emphasis on social manipulation, deceit and cunning, this became known as the "Machiavellian Hypothesis" after Niccolò Machiavelli, the devious political adviser of sixteenth-century Italian princes (Whiten and Byrne, 1997).

Clearly humans are adept at deceit, but what about other primates? Many researchers working in the wild have reported fascinating stories of primates apparently deceiving each other (Byrne and Whiten, 1988). Monkeys and baboons will distract the attention of others in order to snatch food, or watch until others are fighting to grab an opportunity to mate with a receptive female. Rhesus monkeys may withhold their normal food calls so as to eat without sharing what they find, especially if they are very hungry or have found highly prized food. Swiss ethologist Hans Kummer watched for some 20 minutes while a female hamadryas baboon gradually moved herself about two meters, while still sitting, until she was behind a rock where she began grooming a young male, behavior that would not be tolerated by the leading male. Had she worked out what the other baboon could and could not see?

KNOWING WHAT OTHERS CAN SEE OR KNOW

Some monkeys give alarm calls to warn others of approaching danger. Calling is risky and so it would be safest to call only when it could be useful. Yet many monkeys apparently call regardless of whether others have already seen the threat, or even whether there are others around. The primatologists Dorothy Cheney and Robert Seyfarth carried out an experiment with a Japanese macaque mother. When put on the opposite side of a barrier from her infant, the mother gave the same number of alarm calls to denote an approaching predator whether or not her infant could see it. From this, and many other studies, Cheney and Seyfarth (1990) concluded that monkeys do not have a theory of mind.

What about chimpanzees? A chimpanzee will follow another's gaze, as though trying to see what the other is looking at. But this need not imply that chimpanzees have a concept of seeing. They might have an evolved tendency to look where someone else is looking. To determine whether they have a concept of what another chimpanzee can see, careful experiments are needed.

Chimpanzees beg for food from humans and from each other. In an ingenious series of experiments Povinelli and his colleagues (1998) used this behavior to find out whether chimpanzees know what someone else can see. First they tested the chimpanzees to make sure that they begged for food from an experimenter out of their reach, and did not beg for inedible items. Then two experimenters offered them food; one experimenter had a blindfold over her mouth and the other had one over her eyes. The chimpanzees came into the lab, paused, and then begged for the food. But they were just as likely to gesture to the person who could not see them as the one who could. This was true even when one experimenter had a bucket over her head. Sometimes, when their begging failed to elicit any food, they begged again, as though puzzled at getting no response.

One test seemed to work. When one person turned her back, the chimpanzees were less likely to gesture to her. However, when both experimenters sat with their backs to the apes and one looked back over her shoulder, the chimpanzees gestured randomly to both. They seemed oblivious to the fact that there is no point begging to someone who cannot see you. This is dramatically different from the behavior of human children who can understand this before they are three years old.

IMITATION

Humans are the consummate imitative generalists, says psychologist Andrew Meltzoff. We imitate each other spontaneously and easily, and even infants can imitate sounds, body postures and actions on objects performed by adults. By 14 months of age toddlers can delay imitation for a week or more, and they seem to know when they are being imitated by adults and take pleasure in it (Meltzoff, 1996). As adults we imitate far more than we may realize. We copy the body language of people we like and mirror their facial expression when engrossed in conversation. In this way imitation underlies the capacity for empathy.

FIGURE 12.4 • Do chimpanzees have a theory of mind? Can they understand what another person can and cannot see? In Povinelli's experiments, chimpanzees were just as likely to beg for food from an experimenter who had a bucket over her head as from one who could see.

CONSCIOUSNESS

It is perhaps because imitation seems so easy that we tend to think of it as a trivial skill and assume that other animals can do it as easily as we can. They cannot.

Nineteenth-century scientists like George Romanes (1848–94) and Charles Darwin assumed that dogs and cats learned by imitation, and that apes could "ape," and they told many stories of actions that looked like imitation. In 1898 the psychologist Edward Lee Thorndike (1874–1949) defined imitation as "learning to do an act from seeing it done," which captures the notion that to imitate means to learn something new by copying someone else. A century later it is clear that this ability is far from trivial. The observing animal must not only watch the model but must remember what it has seen and then convert that into actions of its own—even though these actions may look totally different from its own perspective. Computationally this is a very complex task.

It is now clear that, with the exception of some birds and cetaceans imitating songs, there are very few species that can imitate. Even some of the classic cases turn out to be explicable in other ways. For example, in the 1920s in England, small birds, blue tits and coal tits, were found to be pecking the foil tops of milk bottles left on doorsteps. Ethologists studied the way the habit started in a few places and then spread contagiously across the country. But this turned out not to require imitation at all. It seems more likely that once one bird discovered the trick by trial and error, the jagged pecked tops attracted the attention of more birds who then learned, by individual learning, that the bottles contained cream.

Even the famous Japanese macaques who learned to wash sweet potatoes may not, in fact, have learned by imitation. Young macaques follow their mothers about, and it may be that once one family learned the new skill, others followed her into the water and then, by accident, dropped their sweet potatoes and learned the trick of getting clean and salty sweet potatoes for themselves. This would fit with the fact that the whole troop only learned very slowly. Young children, with their avid delight in imitation, would learn such a skill in a few minutes rather than years.

There is clear evidence of culture in chimpanzees, in that different groups of chimpanzees use different ways of processing food, fishing for termites with sticks, or using leaves to soak up water, but there is ongoing controversy over how much these cultural skills are learned by true imitation rather than by other kinds of social learning (Heyes and Galef, 1996; Tomasello, 1999).

Some whales and dolphins have local dialects in their songs, or signatures by which they recognize other individuals, and they copy songs back after hearing them (Reiss, 1998). There is also evidence that captive dolphins can imitate the actions of their human keepers, which is particularly interesting since their bodies are so very different. If imitation implies the capacity for empathy, then it is perhaps to these cetaceans that we should look for clues. Although we do not yet know how widespread imitation is, we must conclude that it is much rarer than most people realize, and is probably confined to only a few species.

This may be important for understanding human evolution because memes are defined as "that which is imitated." This means that only a species capable of copying another's behavior can have memes and sustain a culture based on memetic evolution. One theory is that imitation—not introspection, Machiavellian intelligence or the capacity for symbolic thought—set humans on a different evolutionary path from other great apes; it was memetic evolution that gave us big brains and language (Blackmore, 1999).

Imitation may be relevant to consciousness for another reason. If the concept of self is a memeplex (see Chapter 11), then it is the ability to imitate that gives humans a sense of self and hence self-consciousness.

LANGUAGE

The greatest divide of all is that we have language and other species do not. As Dennett suggests, "Perhaps the kind of mind you get when you add language to it is so different from the kind of mind you can have without language that calling them both minds is a mistake" (Dennett, 1996b: 17).

If there is no self-concept without language, then other animals are not self-conscious. If language makes human consciousness the way it is, then the con-

FIGURE 12.5 ● Chantek was brought up like a human child and taught American Sign Language from an early age. He was also trained to play "Simon says," but although he can laboriously imitate some human actions, he does not take delight in imitation as human children do.

sciousness of other creatures must be quite different from ours. If human consciousness is an illusion created by language, then other creatures might be free of that illusion. Alternatively you might argue that language makes little difference, that the heart of consciousness is about visual awareness, hearing, thinking, feeling emotions, and suffering. In that case the divide between us and other creatures would not be so wide.

Using true language means being able to put arbitrary symbols together in an unlimited number of ways using grammatical rules to convey different meanings. Children in every culture pick up the language around them with extraordinary speed and agility without being specifically taught and without being corrected for their mistakes. They have what is sometimes called a "language instinct" (Pinker, 1994).

Other animals certainly have complex methods of communication. For example, bees can communicate detailed information about the direction and distance of a food source by dancing. Peacocks communicate how strong and beautiful they are by flashing their enormous tails. Vervet monkeys make several different alarm calls for different kinds of predators. But in all these cases the meaning of the signals is fixed and new meanings cannot be made by combining them.

Many attempts have been made to teach language to other animals, in particular the other great apes. Early attempts failed because other apes do

not have the vocal apparatus needed to make the right sounds. Realizing this, in the 1960s, Allen and Beatrix Gardner tried teaching American Sign Language (ASL) to a young chimpanzee, Washoe, who lived with them and was treated like a human child. Washoe certainly learned many signs, but critics argued that she did not understand what the signs meant, that the experimenters were erroneously interpreting natural chimpanzee gestures as signs and that she was not really acquiring true language (Terrace, 1987; Pinker, 1994).

Subsequently other chimpanzees also learned ASL, as did gorillas and an orangutan, Chantek. Like Washoe, Chantek was fostered by humans from a young age and learned hundreds of signs, but he did not learn them as a child would, just by watching. His hands had to be molded into the right shapes. Now nearly 30 years old he understands much spoken English and seems to understand the crucial difference between such commands as "put the stick on

ACTIVITY
Zoo choice

In a "balloon debate" every participant has to convince the others that they should not be thrown out of the balloon for ballast. In this debate the same horrible choice is made between species.

Imagine that just one animal is going to be released from its cage in the zoo, or from cruel conditions in a pharmaceutical laboratory, and returned to the wild. Which species should it be?

Choose several different species and someone to defend each one, or let students pick their own favored species. Each person is given a set length of time (e.g., two or five minutes) to make their case. Afterward the audience votes on which animal is to be released. If the choice proves easy, vote on which should go second and third.

This debate can be held without prior planning. Alternatively, ask students to prepare their case in advance. They might bring photographs, videos or other kinds of evidence. They might learn about the social and communication skills of their chosen species, or about its intelligence, capacity for insight, memory, sensory systems or pain behavior. The aim is to explore the nature of animal suffering.

the blanket" or "put the blanket on the stick," suggesting some understanding of grammar. Even so his own sentences tend to be short, repetitive and are mostly demands for food. Other apes have learned to communicate using magnetized plastic chips on a board or modified computer keyboards.

Despite the real achievements of these apes, there remain glaring differences between their use of language and that of human children. While children show a great delight in naming things and telling other people about them, the apes seem mostly to use signs as a way of getting what they want (Terrace, 1987). As Pinker puts it, "fundamentally, deep down, chimps just don't 'get it'" (Pinker, 1994: 340).

Apes are not the only animals to be taught human language. Alex, an African gray parrot, has learned to answer questions about the shape, color, number and material of objects shown to him, and unlike the apes, he can speak English words easily. Bottlenosed dolphins have been given interactive underwater keyboards with which they can ask for playthings and answer questions (Reiss, 1998). They can also imitate artificial sounds made by the keyboard and then use the sounds spontaneously. It seems possible that dolphins will prove better language learners than many apes have been, and even that they have their own underwater language. This speculation aside it seems that we humans are alone in our use of language.

THE SNAKE

So what is it like to be a snake? Imagine a snake feeding on mice (Sjölander, 1995). First it has to find a mouse and strike accurately, which it does by vision (some snakes use temperature sensors rather than sight). Once the mouse is dead the snake locates it by smell, not seeming to be able to see it anymore. Once it has found the mouse it has to locate the head in order to swallow it the right way. This it does by touch only, even though, in principle, it ought to be able to see or smell the head. In this way, in catching its prey, the snake's senses seem quite unconnected with each other. The snake can have no notion of object constancy and no concept that there is one thing, a mouse, that it is catching and eating. There are just sights, and smells, and feels, and then nice food.

Is the snake conscious? You might answer "Yes," that any creature with senses lives in its own world of experiences, however simple or primitive those might be. You might say "No," the snake lacks some critical ability without which there is

SELF-ASSESSMENT QUESTIONS

○ What does a frog see?

○ How might you tell whether an animal is suffering? Can you be sure?

○ Which animals can recognize themselves in a mirror? What does this tell us about self-consciousness?

○ List three or more skills which suggest that an animal has a theory of mind.

○ Describe two experiments designed to find out whether an animal knows what another animal can see.

○ Which species are capable of imitation? What implications does this have for consciousness?

○ Do other species have language? Why is this relevant to consciousness?

FIGURE 12.6 • Green tree pythons have heat-sensing pits along their lips to detect warm-blooded prey but use other senses once the mouse or rabbit is caught. When resting, they loop their coils over the branches of trees and in that position may sometimes search stochastically, for minutes at a time, for the prey they are already holding in the coils of their own body.

no consciousness, such as sensory integration greater intelligence, a self-concept, a theory of mind, memes or language.

If you wanted to be really skeptical, you might say that human consciousness is a grand illusion and there is nothing it is like to be us. In that case there would be no sense in asking, "What is it like to be a snake?"

Gallup, G.G. (1998) Can animals empathize? Yes. *Scientific American*, 9(4), 67–76. Also at http://www.zoosemiotics.helsinki.fi/Can%20Animals%20EmpathizeYES.doc

Pinker, S. (1994) *The Language Instinct*. New York, Morrow. See pages 332–49.

Povinelli, D.J. (1998) Can animals empathize? Maybe not. *Scientific American*, 9(4), 67–76. Also at http://www.zoosemiotics.helsinki.fi/Can%20Animals%20EmpathizeMAYBE%20NOT.doc

Animal minds
CHAPTER TWELVE

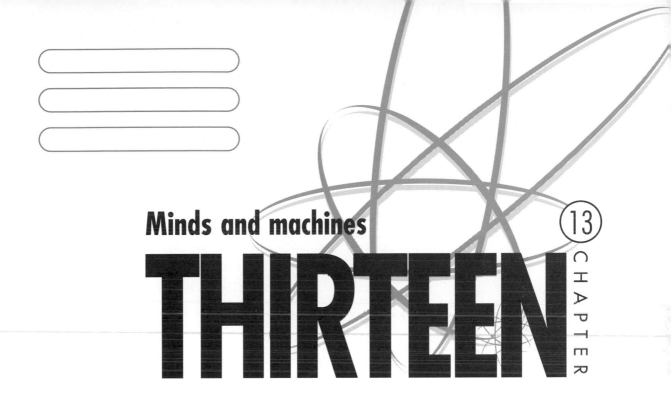

Minds and machines

THIRTEEN

(13)

C H A P T E R

Is there something special about human beings that enables us to think, and see, and hear, and feel, and fall in love, that gives us a desire to be good, a love of beauty, and a longing for something beyond? Or are all these capacities just the products of a complicated mechanism? In other words am I just a machine?

This age-old question can be tackled from either direction. Either we can start with the biology and try to understand the mechanics of how natural systems work, or we can build artificial systems and see how far they can match a human being.

In consciousness studies the two endeavors are converging. From the natural direction, science has successively explained more and more of the mechanisms of perception, learning, memory and thinking until there remains an open question about consciousness. That is, when all these abilities have been fully explained, will consciousness be accounted for too, or will something still be left out?

From the artificial direction, better and better machines have been developed until the obvious question becomes whether they are conscious. If machines could do all the things we do, just as well as we do them, would they be conscious like us? How could we tell? Would they *really* be conscious, or just simulating consciousness? Would they *really* understand what they said and read and did, or would they just be acting *as if* they understood. We arrive at the same question: "Is there something extra that is left out?"

These are some of the central questions that we will explore in this section. While the main objective is to think about artificial consciousness (which we may call AC), this is so closely bound up with the topic of artificial intelligence (AI) that we need to begin there and with the long history of attempts to build mind-like machines.

MIND-LIKE MACHINES

From the fourth century BC the Greeks made elaborate marionettes, and later complete automatic theaters, with moving birds, insects and people, all worked by strings and falling-weight motors. Hero of Alexandria reputedly made temple doors that opened automatically and statues with hidden speaking tubes. These machines mimicked living things in the sense that they moved like them, but it was not until much later that the idea of thinking machines became possible.

In the seventeenth century, Descartes argued that the human body was a mechanism but that no mechanism alone was capable of speech and rational thought; *res cogitans*, or thinking-stuff, was needed for these uniquely human abilities. It is important to realize that rationality was often prized above all other qualities of the human mind, and was assumed to be a product of consciousness. As we shall see, it has turned out that rational, logical thinking is far easier for artificial machines to do than are some of the things that animals do easily, like seeing, finding food or mates and showing emotions. So nowadays we no longer assume that rationality is the sign of a conscious mind at work, and we may be less impressed by mathematical machines. But to begin with the greatest challenge in making mind-like machines seemed to be to make a machine that could calculate.

In 1642, the French philosopher and mathematician Blaise Pascal (1623–62) built the first ever digital calculating machine, which was refined by Gottfried von Leibniz (1646–1716) to add, multiply and divide using interconnected rotating cylinders. Leibniz is best known as the discoverer, independently of Newton, of calculus, and for his philosophy that matter consists of little minds, or monads. He argued against Descartes' idea that the mind could affect the brain, and speculated about the possibility of a thinking, perceiving machine. Suppose there were such a machine, he said, and that we could conceive of it getting larger and larger so that we could go inside it, like entering a mill. Inside we would find only pieces working upon one another and never anything to explain the perception. Leibniz's thought experiment applies equally well to the human brain. Imagine making the neurons bigger and bigger so that we could go inside. What would we see but synapses and chemicals working upon one another?

During the eighteenth century, automata became immensely popular, with the most famous including a flute-playing boy, a duck with a digestive system and the earliest chess-playing machine. This was made by Wolfgang von Kempelen and displayed in 1770 before the Viennese court. It consisted of a wooden cabinet, behind which was seated an impressive life-size wooden figure of a man wearing an ermine-trimmed robe, loose trousers and a turban. Doors could be opened to show the elaborate system of cogs and wheels inside. When wound up, the "Turk" as he rapidly became known, played chess. He lifted and moved the pieces with his mechanical hands and was said to be able to beat most challengers within half an hour. The Turk toured the great cities of Europe for decades without its trick being exposed. But a trick it certainly was (Standage, 2002).

FIGURE 13.1 • The mechanical Turk was the first ever chess-playing machine. His hands were moved by intricate machinery under the table, but the real player was hidden inside.

Automata continued to fascinate people, and to frighten them. In 1818 Mary Shelley captured this fear in her novel about Frankenstein and his gruesome monster. But soon the technology began to be used for more scientific purposes.

In the 1830s the British mathematician Charles Babbage (1792–1871) was infuriated by having to use mathematical tables full of human errors, and so conceived the idea of a "difference engine" that could compute the tables accurately and even print them. This machine was never completed, and the even more ambitious "analytical engine" was never even started. The analytical

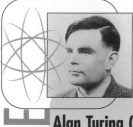
Alan Turing (1912–1954)

Born in London and educated at Cambridge, Alan Turing was an extraordinarily brilliant mathematician. He is often called the father of both computer science and artificial intelligence, partly because of his famous work on computable numbers, which led to the idea of the Universal Turing Machine. He also created the Turing test, which pits a machine against a person as a way of finding out whether the machine can think. Some 30 years after the Second World War, Turing was revealed as the master code-breaker who had broken the famous Enigma cipher. He also created the first functioning programmed computer, the Colossus, to read the highest-level German secret codes. He was a homosexual and was eventually arrested and tried for what was then illegal behavior. He died in June 1954 of cyanide poisoning, probably by suicide.

engine was to have had a processing unit of cogs and wheels controlled by punched cards, like those used in looms for weaving cloth, which would have allowed it to carry out many different functions. This was probably not technically feasible at the time, yet it has taken its place in history as the first general-purpose, programmable calculating machine.

Among the ideas that were fundamental to such machines was Boolean algebra, invented by the British mathematician George Boole (1815–64). As a young man, working as an assistant teacher in Doncaster in 1833, Boole went walking one day on the Town Fields. There he had a sudden insight, one of the famous "Eureka!" moments of science. He saw that just as mathematical principles could explain the function of cogs in machines, so they might be able to explain what he called "the laws of thought," and in this way he believed that mathematics might explain the human mind. He showed how logical problems could be expressed as algebraic equations and therefore be solved by mechanical manipulation of symbols according to formal rules. This required only two values, 0 and 1, or false and true, and the rules for combining them. Boole did not succeed in solving the mystery of mind, as he had hoped, but Boolean algebra was fundamental to the computer revolution.

In the 1930s, the American mathematician and founder of information theory, Claude Shannon (b. 1916), realized that Boolean algebra could be used to describe the behavior of arrays of switches, each of which has only two states, on or off. He used a binary code and called each unit of information a "binary digit" or "bit." All this made possible the idea that logical operations could be embodied in the workings of a machine.

As so often happens, it was the pressures of war that drove on the invention of computing machinery. The first general-purpose computers were built in the Second World War, to decode German ciphers and to calculate the tables needed to guide bombs. The master code-breaker, though this was only revealed 30 years after the war ended, was the brilliant English mathematician Alan Turing (1912–54; see Profile).

Turing worked on algorithms—that is, entirely mechanical mathematical procedures that are completely well defined in operation. Problems are said to be computable if they can be solved by using an appropriate algorithm. Turing proposed the idea of a simple machine that could move an indefinitely long tape backward and forward one square and print or erase numbers on it. He showed that this simple machine could specify the steps needed to solve *any* computable problem.

CONSCIOUSNESS

The principle underlying this is an abstract machine, now known as a Turing machine. An important aspect of this idea is that the abstract machine is "substrate neutral" or "multiply realisable." That is, it can use tapes or chips, or be made of brain cells, beer cans, water pipes or anything else at all, as long as it carries out the same operations. This gives rise to the idea of the Universal Turing Machine—a machine that can, in principle, imitate any other Turing machine. The "in principle" is needed because the machine theoretically needs an unlimited memory store and unlimited time in which to do its calculations. Even so, modern computers can be thought of as Universal Turing Machines, since many different "virtual machines," such as word-processing packages or spreadsheets, can be run on the same actual machine.

The first computers, using electromechanical relays and then valves, were very slow and cumbersome. Even so, they inspired comparisons with the human mind. During the Second World War, the Cambridge psychologist, Kenneth Craik (1914–45) began to develop such comparisons, arguing that the human mind translates aspects of the external world into internal representations. When he died at the age of 31 in a car crash, he was already exploring what became one of the dominant paradigms in psychology for the rest of the century. He argued that perception and thinking, and other mental processes, consist of building internal representations and manipulating them according to definite rules, as a machine might do. This in turn gave rise to the idea that what we are conscious of is these internal representations, or mental models; in other words, the contents of consciousness are mental representations.

As computers rapidly became faster, smaller and more flexible, it became easier to refer to them as "thinking" or "intelligent," and so "artificial intelligence" seemed possible. For the first 30 years or so, all attempts to create AI depended on a human programmer writing programs that told the machine what to do. These programs implemented algorithms and thus processed information according to explicitly encoded rules. This is now referred to as GOFAI, or "Good Old-Fashioned AI."

One problem for GOFAI is that the information the computers process is treated as symbolizing things in the world, but these symbols are not grounded in the real world except by the human programmer. So, for example, a computer might calculate the stresses and strains on a bridge, but it would not know or care anything about bridges; it might just as well be computing stock market fluctuations or the spread of a deadly virus. Similarly the computer might print out written replies to typed questions and give a plausible show of making sense, but the computer itself would not know what it was doing. Such machines could be seen as merely manipulating symbols according to formal rules. For this reason this traditional approach is also called "rule-and-symbol AI."

From this emerged the "computational theory of mind." As Searle later described it,

> Many people still think that the brain is a digital computer and that the conscious mind is a computer program, though mercifully this

BRAINS AND COMPUTERS COMPARED

Digital vs analog

The vast majority of computers are digital in their operation, even though they may simulate analog processes. A digital system works on discrete states, whereas an analog system works on continuous variables. In music, for example, digital CDs code the frequency and intensity of sound by discrete digits, whereas analog vinyl records represent them by contours in the groove. Digital coding makes higher-fidelity copying possible because slight variations are automatically eliminated as long as they are not large enough to switch a 0 to a 1, or vice versa.

Is the human brain digital or analog? The answer is both. A neuron either fires or not, and to this extent is digital, yet the rate of firing is a continuous variable. Then there are other analog processes. Imagine the axon of one brain cell leading to a synapse on the dendrite of a second brain cell (see Fig. 13.2). When the first cell fires, neurotransmitters

view is much less wide-spread than it was a decade ago. Construed in this way, the mind is to the brain as software is to hardware.

(Searle, 1997: 9)

Searle distinguished two main versions of this theory: "Strong AI" and "Weak AI." According to Strong AI, a computer running the right program would be intelligent and have a mind just as we do. There is nothing more to having a mind than running the right program. Searle claimed to refute this with his famous Chinese Room thought experiment (which we consider in Chapter 14). According to Weak AI, computers can *simulate* the mind. They may usefully simulate many mental processes of thinking, deciding and so on, but however good they are they can never create *real* mind, *real* intentionality, *real* intelligence or *real* consciousness, but only *as if* consciousness. Similarly, a meteorologist's computer may simulate storms and blizzards but will not start blowing out heaps of wet, cold snow.

To understand these arguments, and the developments in computer science that followed, it may be

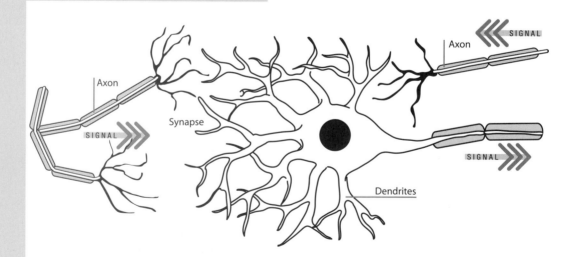

FIGURE 13.2 • The state of polarization of any part of the post-synaptic membrane varies continuously (analog) depending on the effects of many synapses at different distances. When the polarization at the cell body reaches a critical threshold, the second cell fires (digital).

helpful to be clear about some differences between human brains and good old-fashioned digital computers (see Concept).

DEVELOPMENTS IN COMPUTING

From the big, slow computers of the 1950s progress was dramatic and, some say, exponential. According to Moore's Law on Integrated Circuits, the number of transistors on a chip doubles every two years. Remarkably this observation (not really a true law), first made in 1965, seems to have held ever since. But this remarkable expansion describes just brute computing power. Meanwhile there have been some more fundamental changes in AI, which may be relevant to understanding consciousness.

CONNECTIONISM

The 1980s saw the flowering of "connectionism," a new approach based on artificial neural networks (ANNs) and parallel distributed processing. Part of the motivation behind neural nets was to try to model the human brain more closely, although even now ANNs are extremely simple compared with human brain cells. The big difference from traditional AI is that ANNs are not programmed; they are trained. To take a simple example, imagine the task of looking at photographs of people and deciding whether they are male or female. Humans can do this easily (though not with 100 percent accuracy), but no one can explain how. We cannot articulate the rules so as to tell a machine how to do it. With an ANN we don't need to. The system is shown a series of photographs and for each one it produces an output. If this is wrong the network is adjusted and it is shown the next, and so on. Although it begins by making random responses, the trained network can correctly discriminate new faces, as well as the ones it has seen before.

How does it do this? The network is made up of many units, each of which resembles a neuron in the sense that it is a simple processor that sums the inputs it receives according to a mathematical

are released across the synapse, changing the state of polarization of the membrane of the second cell briefly and for a short distance around the synapse. Now imagine lots of other synapses having similar effects, but at slightly different times and different distances from the cell body. All these many effects on the membrane summate over the complex surface. Then, if the polarization at the cell body reaches a critical threshold, the second cell fires. The process of summing is analog, but the final output—to fire or not to fire—is digital. It is not possible to characterize the brain simply as either digital or analog.

Serial vs parallel

Many digital computers, and certainly all the early ones, process information very fast, but serially, i.e., one thing after another. They have a single central processing unit and can only work simultaneously on different tasks by dividing the tasks up and switching between them. By doing this, a serial machine can simulate a parallel machine.

By comparison neurons operate very slowly, but the brain is a massively parallel device. There is no central processor but millions of simultaneously operating cells. Not only are there different areas for vision, hearing, planning and so on, all operating in parallel all the time, but within small areas of the brain, patterns of information move about in complex networks that have no serial organization. The brain does seem to have bottlenecks though, such as limited attention and short-term memory (Chapter 4). Also many outputs, including spoken and written language, are serial. In this sense the brain is a parallel machine simulating a serial machine; this is Dennett's Joycean machine (Chapter 11).

Computable vs non-computable

A computable procedure is one that can be described explicitly, and any such procedure can be carried out by a computer program (this is known as the Church–Turing thesis). Turing himself showed that there are also noncomputable functions that cannot be handled by a machine. Computational functionalism is the doctrine that the brain is essentially a Turing machine and its operations are computations. If this is true then it should be possible to reproduce all human abilities by carrying out the right computations. Those who reject computational functionalism (and Strong AI) argue that such computations would only *simulate* human functions, that there is more to the mind and consciousness than running the right program. Some people argue that consciousness is not computable (see Chapter 14).

Deterministic vs non-deterministic

A machine that always produces the same output from the same input and the same internal state is deterministic; one that can produce different outcomes is non-deterministic. Digital computers are deterministic machines. Note that this does not mean that their outcome must be predictable. For example, chaos theory shows that for some deterministic processes the outcome can be vastly different if the starting conditions vary only very slightly. Nor does it mean that computers cannot be creative. The evolutionary algorithm (Chapter 10) is *par excellence* a deterministic procedure that yields creativity. Computers can simulate non-deterministic systems by adding pseudo-randomness.

Brains, at least at one level, are non-deterministic. They are warm, wet and noisy, and therefore cannot always produce the same output to the same input. Neurons are living, growing entities, whose electrical properties change as their dendrites grow or move. Synapses form and decay, and their strength changes in response to use. So the machine itself is never the same from one moment to the next. At a smaller scale, though, the underlying molecular processes are usually assumed to be deterministic. This is one reason why there appears to be no room for free will, and adding randomness, as one can do with a computer, does not help with this problem (Chapter 9). Going smaller still, one reaches the level of quantum effects and quantum indeterminacy. Some have argued that this is the ultimate source of human creativity, free will and consciousness.

function, and produces an output. The units are connected in a network of parallel connections, each connection having a weight, or strength, that can be varied. A simple network might consist of three layers of units: an input layer, a hidden layer, and an output layer. For the example above, the input layer would need enough units to encode an array corresponding to the input photographs, and the output layer would need two units corresponding to "male" and "female." For a more complex task, such as identifying actual faces, it would need as many output units as the number of faces it had to recognize. During training, a program compares the net's actual output with the correct output and makes adjustments to the weights accordingly. The best known of these programs uses the back-propagation algorithm (meaning that the error is propagated backwards into the network to update the weights). As training proceeds the errors get gradually smaller until the network is able to respond more or less correctly. If the training set of photographs is appropriately chosen, the network should now perform well on a completely new photograph.

Note that the process of adjusting the weights is algorithmic, or rule-based, and the whole system may be run on a digital computer. However, the output can be analog and the system contains nothing like a computer program that tells it how to recognize men and women. The ANN works this out for itself, and even its creators cannot know exactly how it did it or what the weights mean. Unlike traditional machines, connectionist networks do not just do what their programmers tell them to do. This is a long way from good old-fashioned rule-and-symbol AI.

EMBODIED COGNITION

The machines described so far are all disembodied. They sit in boxes or on benches, and their interactions with the world are through humans. When computers were first put to work controlling robots, the results were less than impressive. Most could only carry out a few simple, well-specified tasks within highly controlled environments. For example, special block worlds were made, in which the robots had to avoid or move the blocks. The task of designing a robot seemed to mean getting it to build ever-better representations of the world and of the tasks it was supposed to perform. It therefore seemed sensible to start with simplified actions in simplified worlds.

The implicit model of mind underlying this approach was similarly disembodied. It was assumed that the essence of thinking is abstract and rule-based, and can be done away from the messiness of arms, legs and real physical problems. We might contrast this with a child learning to walk. She is not taught the rules of walking; she just gets up, falls over, tries again and eventually walks. The connectionist approach is far more realistic than GOFAI, but perhaps it matters that the child has actual wobbly legs, that the ground is not flat and that there are real obstacles in the way.

Embodied or enactive cognition are names for the general idea that mind can be created only by interacting in real time with a real environment, the idea "that cognition is not the representation of a pregiven world by a

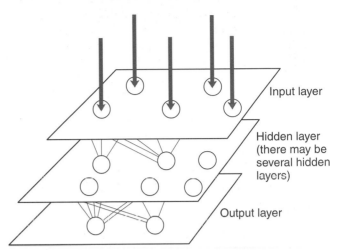

FIGURE 13.3 • This artificial neural network (ANN) has just three layers of units: the input layer, the output layer and a hidden layer in between. During training, the weights on the connections between the units are adjusted until the network provides the correct output. Such a network can learn to recognize faces, to produce sounds in response to written text, and many other tasks, depending on what is connected to the input and output units.

pregiven mind but is rather the enactment of a world and a mind" (Varela et al., 1991: 9). British philosopher Andy Clark talks about "putting brain, body, and world together again" (1997). In this view the real world is far from being a messy complication we can do without; rather it provides the very constraints, information storage and feedback that make perception, learning and intelligence possible. Creating artificially intelligent machines this way means constructing real, physical, autonomous agents that move about in the real world. It means working from the bottom up rather than the top down. This approach is sometimes called situated robotics, or behavior-based (as opposed to knowledge-based) robotics.

One consequence of working this way is that intelligent behaviors can emerge from simple systems. There are many examples of such emergence in biology, especially among the social insects. For example, termites build extraordinary structures that look as though they must be built to a plan, when in fact they emerge from simple rules about when to add mud and when to remove it, embodied in the individual termites.

A simple example in robots is following walls. Imagine you watch a small wheeled robot moving along next to a wall. It does not bump the wall or wander far away from it, but just wiggles along, reliably following the bends and turning the corners. How? It might have been cleverly programmed with the goal of following the wall, with an internal representation of the wall, and with ways of coping with each eventuality, but in fact it need not be. All it needs is a tendency to veer to the right and a sensor on the right side that detects close objects and causes it to turn slightly to the left whenever it does

FIGURE 13.4 • Termites rebuilding their mound after damage. Each individual termite follows simple rules about when to add mud and when to remove it. None has a plan of the overall mound, yet the complex system of tunnels and walls emerges. Is consciousness an emergent phenomenon like this?

FIGURE 13.5 • In Bristol in 1948–9, Grey Walter built Elmer and Elsie, two prototype "tortoises." Later six more were built and displayed at the Festival of Britain in 1951. They had a phototube eye, two vacuum tube amplifiers that drove relays to control steering and drive motors, and a Perspex shell. They moved about in a lively manner until their batteries ran low, when they crawled back into their hutch, exhibiting not only autonomous and self-preserving behavior but the beginnings of artificial intelligence. In 1995 what is thought to be the last remaining Grey Walter tortoise was rescued.

so. By correct balancing of the two tendencies, wall-following behavior emerges.

Here we have a concrete example of that slippery concept, an emergent property. A useful and apparently intelligent behavior has emerged from an extremely simple system. This might help us to think about the idea that consciousness is an emergent property as Humphrey (1987) and Searle (1997) claim it is.

INTELLIGENCE WITHOUT REPRESENTATION

A remarkable feature of the wall-following robot is that it has no internal representation of the wall it is following, nor of the rest of its environment, nor of its goal. It does not need them. Although traditional AI is based on the assumption that intelligence is all about manipulating representations, Rodney Brooks (see Profile, Chapter 15) and his colleagues at MIT have long been building robots that have no internal representations at all (Brooks, 1991: 2002).

Brooks' "creatures" can wander about in complex environments such as offices or labs full of people and carry out tasks such as collecting up rubbish. They have several control layers, each of which carries out a simple task in response to the environment. These are built on top of each other as needed and have limited connections enabling one layer to suppress or inhibit another. This is referred to as "subsumption architecture" because one layer can subsume the activity of another. The creature's overall behavior looks intelligent to an observer but, says Brooks, "It is only the observer of the Creature who imputes a central representation or central control. The Creature itself has none; it is a collection of competing behaviors" (1991: 406).

This is related to Marvin Minsky's (1986) idea of "the society of mind," that intelligence emerges from many separate modules doing many simple things all at once, to Ornstein's description of the mind as a "squadron of simpletons," and to Dennett's (1991) idea that we can trade in the audience in the Cartesian theater and the "Central Meaner" for a pandemonium of stupid homunculi that carry out simple tasks that can easily be done by machines. By building robots this way, Brooks discovered that "When we examine very simple level intelligence we find that explicit representations and models of the world simply get in the way. It turns out to be better to let the world itself serve as its own model" (Brooks, 1991: 396). Although Brooks makes no claims to biological significance, this is exactly the same conclusion that O'Regan, Noë and others have come to from the research on change blindness in humans (see Chapter 6). It seems that representations may not be necessary for building effective robots, and evolution may not have used them when building our vision system either.

> *"It turns out to be better to use the world as its own model."*
>
> **Brooks**, 1991

All this is highly relevant to understanding consciousness. Along with GOFAI goes the idea that conscious experiences are inner representations of the world, or that the contents of consciousness are the current mental model. This idea may seem intuitively plausible, but it suffers from certain difficulties. For example, it is not clear exactly how a mental model can *be* an experience, nor why some mental models in the brain are conscious while most are not. These are the familiar problems of subjectivity and of the magic difference between information processing that is conscious and that which is not.

Doing away with representations may solve some problems, but it raises others. In particular the non-representational approach has difficulties dealing with experiences that are not driven by continuous interaction with the outside world, such as imagining, reasoning and dreams. In representational theories it is easy to think that when I dream of flying across Bristol to the castle in the clouds, my brain is constructing representations of castles and clouds, but if there are no representations, what could it be doing? This is a challenge for embodied cognition and for enactive and sensorimotor theories.

PRACTICE
AM I A MACHINE?

As many times as you can, every day, ask yourself, **"Am I a machine?"**

The idea of this exercise is to watch your own actions and consider them in light of the ideas presented here. Are you like a simple autonomous robot? Could an artificial machine ever do what you are doing now? If so, would the machine feel like you do? You may discover that asking these questions while going about your ordinary life makes you feel more machine-like. What is going on here?

If you find an inner voice protesting "But I am not a machine!" investigate who or what is rebelling against the idea.

There have been many other important developments in AI, but the few covered here at least provide a sketchy outline, and this should help us in the next chapter when we ask whether a machine can be conscious. But before that, let's consider a question with a long and controversial history: the question of whether a machine can think.

THE TURING TEST

Turing's classic paper of 1950 begins, "I propose to consider the question 'Can machines think?'" He dismissed the idea of answering the question by analyzing the terms "machine" and "think" as like collecting a Gallup poll of opinions, and proposed instead a test based on what machines can do.

What, then, is a good test of what a machine can do? Among all the possible tests one can think of, two come up again and again. The first is playing chess. Surely, people have thought, if a machine can play chess then it must be intelligent and it must be able to think. Descartes would presumably have been impressed by such a machine since, like his contemporaries, he prized rationality above all other human qualities. Indeed, the kind of rational thinking required to play chess has long been valued above things that "lower" animals can do easily, such as walk about and see where they're going. So it is perhaps not surprising that in the early days of computing it seemed a great challenge to build a computer that could play chess.

After the trick games played by the Turk, the first serious game took place in Manchester in 1952, with Turing playing the part of a machine against a human opponent. He had written a program on numerous sheets of paper and consulted them at every move, but was easily defeated. In 1958 the first game was played with an IBM computer and from then on computer chess improved rapidly. Most chess programs relied on analyzing several moves ahead. This quickly produces a combinatorial explosion, because for every possible next move there are even more possible next moves after that. Programmers invented many ways to get around this, but to some extent computer chess got better just by brute force computing power. In 1989 the computer Deep Thought took on the world chess champion Garry Kasparov, who told reporters that he was defending the human race against the machine. This time the machine lost, but eventually, in 1997, its successor, Deep Blue, beat Kasparov in a standard tournament match.

Deep Blue consisted of 32 IBM supercomputers connected together. It contained 220 special chess chips and could evaluate 100 million positions per second. No human being plays chess like this. So, is Deep Blue intelligent? Can it think? Searle (1999) says not, arguing that Deep Blue, like the Turk, relied on an illusion. The real competition, he says, was between Kasparov and the team of

(Activity continued)

One problem is that the organizer may unwittingly give away clues about which person is which. Even so, this version works well, even if done with only a screen in the corner of the room. However, if you want a tighter method and are willing to prepare the set-up in advance, try the high-tech version.

High-tech version

Provide each contestant with a computer and a data projector that makes their typed answers visible to the class. The contestants can be hidden, either in another room or behind a screen. It is important that however the answers are projected, they are clearly labeled X and Y. The organizer collects the written questions as before, and the contestants type their answers on their computer. In a pinch, one computer can be used and the contestants can take turns, but this is slower and can lead to confusion if not well organized. The game can also be played on-line.

This game provides an ideal introduction to discussing the most important aspect of the Turing test: what questions should you ask the machine, and why.

FIGURE 13.6 • Progress in artificial intelligence has been dramatic, from Pascal's earliest calculating machine to Deep Blue, shown here playing Garry Kasparov. Does this explosion of computing power create artificial consciousness?

engineers and programmers, not the machine. The team said that they never thought their machine was truly intelligent. It was an excellent problem solver in one domain but could not teach itself to play or learn from its own games. So can Deep Blue think? The answer is it depends what you mean by "think," and investigating that, as Turing pointed out, is not a useful way to proceed.

Instead Turing chose something altogether different for his test: whether a computer could hold a conversation with a human. Descartes had long since claimed this to be impossible and, interestingly, this was one of the skills attempted by the Turk. In its earliest version, having finished the chess, the Turk would invite people to ask questions and reply to them by pointing at letters on a board. But this was soon dropped from the show. Although audiences were often skeptical, they could just about believe in a chess-playing automaton, but once it claimed to be able to answer questions, they assumed it was a trick and the fascination was lost (Standage, 2002). Perhaps, even then, holding a conversation was implicitly perceived as being harder than playing chess.

The Turk looked like a human, but Turing did not want this to confuse his test for a thinking machine, so he cleverly avoided this problem. First he described "the imitation game." The object of this game is for an interrogator, or judge (C), to decide which of two people is a woman. The man (A) and the woman (B) are in another room so that C cannot see them or hear their voices. C can only communicate with them by asking questions and receiving typed replies. A and B both try to reply as a woman would, so C's skill lies in asking the right questions.

Turing goes on,

We now ask the question, "What will happen when a machine takes the part of A in this game?" Will the interrogator decide wrongly as often when the game is played like this as he does when the game is played between a man and a woman? These questions replace our original, "Can machines think?"

(Turing, 1950)

Turing provides a critique of his own test. He points out that it neatly separates the intellectual and physical capacities of a person and prevents beauty or strength from winning the day. On the other hand it may be too heavily weighted against the machine because a man pretending to be a machine would always fail if tested on arithmetic. He wonders whether the test is unfair because machines might be able to do something that ought to be described as thinking but that is very

SELF-ASSESSMENT QUESTIONS

O List some landmarks in the history of intelligent machines.

O Describe Turing's original machine. What is a universal Turing machine?

O What is GOFAI and what principles is it based on?

O What is the difference between Strong and Weak AI?

O Describe how a simple ANN works. How does this differ from traditional computing?

O Give an example of emergent intelligent action in a simple animal and a simple machine.

O Describe the Turing test. If a machine passed the unrestricted Turing test, what would you conclude about the machine?

FIGURE 13.7 • The trick, whether you are putting a computer to the Turing test, or playing the imitation game, is to know which questions to ask.

"at the end of the century the use of words and general educated opinion will have altered so much that one will be able to speak of machines thinking without expecting to be contradicted"

Turing, 1950

different from what a man does; but he concludes that if any machine could play the game satisfactorily, we need not be troubled by this objection. He gives sample questions and answers that, interestingly, include a chess question, showing how broad and flexible his test is.

Finally he considers many possible objections to the idea that a machine could ever truly be said to think and states his own opinion on the matter:

> I believe that in about fifty years' time it will be possible to program computers, with a storage capacity of about 10^9, to make them play the imitation game so well that an average interrogator will not have more than 70 percent chance of making the right identification after five minutes of questioning . . . at the end of the century the use of words and general educated opinion will have altered so much that one will be able to speak of machines thinking without expecting to be contradicted.

This was a remarkably prescient and carefully worded prediction. Turing was absolutely right about the change in the use of words. I do not expect to be contradicted if I say that my computer is "thinking about it" when it reacts slowly, or if I say "it thinks it's Thursday" when the date is set wrong. On the other hand, even my lowly desktop has a storage capacity far larger than he guessed, and yet no one has any idea how to make it pass the test—nor even how to make the biggest supercomputer in the world do so.

When the 50 years were up, many programs could pass limited versions of the Turing test. For example, people are often fooled in Internet chat rooms and sometimes in the limited scope of psychiatric interviews. In 1990 the first annual Loebner Prize competition was held, for a program that could pass the Turing test. But by 2000 no computer had come close to winning it, in spite

AM I A MACHINE?

of various restrictions imposed to make the test easier. Dennett concluded that "The Turing test is too difficult for the real world" (1998a: 29).

Suppose that some day a machine passes the test. What should we conclude about that machine? The main distinction here is between those people who conclude that the machine must truly be able to think and those who say that it is only *pretending* to think, or that it is *as if* it were thinking. For example, if the winner were a traditional AI program, the computational functionalist would conclude that Strong AI had been vindicated, and the program was truly thinking by virtue of running the right program. Some functionalists would argue that such a traditional program never could pass the test, but that other kinds of machine might, and if that happened they would again conclude that this was real thinking. The alternative is to insist that whatever the machine is doing, and however well it does it, it is still not really thinking; it is not doing the same kind of thing a person does. In other words, there is still something missing from the machine.

All these arguments concern the ability to think, but they are paralleled by similar arguments about consciousness. With these in mind we are ready to ask the trickier question. Could a machine be conscious?

Brooks, R.A. (1991) Intelligence without representation. *Artificial Intelligence 47*, 139–59. Also reprinted, with extra material, in Haugeland (ed.) (1997), 395–420 and at http://www.ai.mit.edu/people/brooks/papers/representation.pdf.

Turing, A. (1950) Computing machinery and intelligence. *Mind 59*, 433–60. Also reprinted in Haugeland (ed.) (1997), and part-reprinted, with commentary, in Hofstadter and Dennett (1981); also at http://www.abelard.org/turpap/turpap.htm.

READING

CONSCIOUSNESS

Could a machine be conscious?

FOURTEEN

Could a machine be conscious? Could a machine have states of mind, inner experiences, subjectivity or qualia? In other words, is there (or could there ever be) "something it is like to be" a machine. Could there be a world of experience *for* the machine?

"We have known the answer to this question for a century," says Searle,

> The brain is a machine. *It is a conscious machine*. The brain is a biological machine just as much as the heart and the liver. So of course some machines can think and be conscious. Your brain and mine, for example.
>
> (Searle, 1997: 202)

This sharpens up the question because what we really mean to ask is, could an *artificial* machine be conscious, or could we *make* a conscious machine.

This question is much more difficult than the already difficult question posed by Turing. When we ask, "Can a machine think?" there are two obvious paths to take. First, you could say that it depends what is meant by "think," with the implication that this is somewhat arbitrary and that there are different answers according to different, equally valid definitions. Second, we may do as Turing did and cut through the arguments by setting an objective test for thinking.

> "*The brain is a machine.* It is a conscious machine."
>
> **Searle**, 1997: 202

Neither of these strategies works for consciousness. First, it does not help to say, "it depends what you mean by consciousness." You may have noticed by now that there is no generally agreed definition of consciousness. Indeed, very few authors even attempt to define consciousness. This is why the closest I have come to defining consciousness in this book is to point out that it has something to do with subjectivity, or "what it is like to be," as in the first paragraph of this chapter. Yet many people are convinced that they know what *they* mean by consciousness. They have a strong intuition that there is nothing arbitrary about it. Either the machine really does feel, really does have experiences, and really does suffer joy and pain, or it does not. The light inside is either on (however dimly) or it is not. This intuition may, of course, be quite wrong, but it stands in the way of dismissing the question "Can machines be conscious?" as merely a matter of definition.

Second, and more troublesome, is that there is no obvious equivalent of the Turing test for consciousness. If we agree that consciousness is *subjective*, then the only one who can know whether a given machine is conscious is the machine itself, and so there is no point in looking for an *objective* test.

The problem becomes clearer if you try to invent a test. An enthusiastic robot builder might, for example, suggest that her machine would count as conscious if it cried when pricked, or replied "Yes" when asked whether it was conscious, or pleaded with people not to turn it off. But the skeptic would say, "It's only got to have a tape player and a few simple sensors inside it. It's only *pretending* to be conscious. It's only behaving *as if* it's conscious."

So suppose she agreed that to pass the test her machine had to be able to laugh at jokes, understand the plot of *Hamlet*, and look deep into your eyes and make you feel loved, and she actually made such a machine. The skeptic might say, "It's still only *pretending* to be conscious. It's just programmed to answer questions about jokes and Shakespeare's plays. It doesn't *really* love you." Then the robot builder might respond, "But I know it's conscious because if it has a sense of humor, understands human tragedy, and can manipulate human emotions, it *must* be."

You may have noticed two very familiar arguments here. The robot builder is a kind of functionalist. She believes not only that thoughts and beliefs are functional states, but that subjective states are too. This means that if her robot carries out certain functions, then it must be conscious—not because it has some extra mysterious stuff called consciousness that *causes* those things to happen, but because doing those kinds of things is what is meant by being conscious. In other words, any machine that could understand *Hamlet*, or look at you in that special way, would also claim to have subjective experiences and think that it was conscious.

The skeptic, meanwhile, is a conscious inessentialist. He believes in zombies. He thinks that however impressive the actions of the machine were, this would not prove it was conscious. His answer would always be, "It's only pretending. Even if it could do everything you and I do, there would still be nothing it was like to *be* that machine. There would be no light of consciousness on inside."

If both of these positions are assumed to be legitimate (and they may not be), then there can be no simple test for machine consciousness. Even if functionalists agreed on precisely which functions were the essential ones (which they have not yet done), and designed a test accordingly, the believer in zombies would reject it. Once again, believing in zombies seems to lead to an impasse. It is a difficult one to escape from.

FIGURE 14.1 • If a robot told you its life story, looked hurt when you offended it and laughed at your funny stories, would you think it was conscious? How could you tell?

Given these difficulties it might seem impossible to make any progress with the question of machine consciousness, but we should not give up so easily. We may be sure that better and cleverer machines will continue to be built, and people will keep arguing about whether they are conscious. Given the circumstances it may be best to ignore these difficulties for the moment and press on as best we can. In this chapter we will consider the argument that machine consciousness is impossible. In the next chapter we will explore ways of making a conscious machine.

CONSCIOUS MACHINES ARE IMPOSSIBLE

There are several plausible—and not so plausible—ways of arguing that a machine could never be conscious. Some of these arguments draw on our intuitions about living things and the nature of awareness, and those intuitions can be both powerful and wrong. It is therefore worth exploring your own intuitions. You may find that some of them are valuable tools for thinking with, while some of them, once exposed, look daft. You may decide that you want to keep some of them in spite of the arguments against them, and that with others you want to go through the painful process of rooting them out. Either way the first step is to recognize your own intuitions. The story of "The Seventh Sally" may help (Lem, 1981; see Activity). Has Trurl just made an amusing model world or has he committed a terrible crime?

The Seventh Sally *or* How Trurl's perfection led to no good

"The Seventh Sally" is a story from *The Cyberiad* by the Polish writer and philosopher Stanislaw Lem, and is reprinted with a commentary in Hofstadter and Dennett (1981). Here is a brief outline.

Trurl, who was well known for his good deeds, wanted to prevent a wicked king from oppressing his poor subjects. So he built an entirely new kingdom for him. It was full of towns, rivers, mountains and forests. It had armies, citadels, marketplaces, winter palaces, summer villas and magnificent steeds, and he "threw in the necessary handful of traitors, another of heroes, added a pinch of prophets and seers, and one messiah and one great poet each, after which he bent over and set the works in motion." There were star-gazing astronomers and noisy children, "And all of this, connected, mounted and ground to precision, fit into a box, and not a very large box, but just the size that could be carried about with ease." Trurl presented this box to the king, explaining how to work the controls to make proclamations, program wars or quell rebellions. The king immediately declared a state of emergency, martial law, a curfew and a special levy.

After a year had passed (which was hardly a minute for Trurl and the king) the king magnanimously abolished one death penalty, lightened the levy and annulled the state of emergency "whereupon a tumultuous cry of gratitude, like the squeaking of tiny mice lifted by their tails, rose up from the box." Trurl returned home, proud of having made the king happy while saving his real subjects from appalling tyranny.

To his surprise Trurl's friend was not pleased, but was horrified that Trurl could have given the brutal despot a whole civilization to rule over. But it's only a model, protested Trur, "all these processes only

(Activity continues on next page.)

Turing (1950) lists nine opinions opposed to his own view that machines *can* think, and some of these are equally applicable to consciousness. Chalmers (1996) and Dennett (1995c) each list four arguments for the impossibility of a conscious robot, and there are many other such lists. Here are some of the main objections to the possibility of conscious machines.

SOULS, SPIRITS AND SEPARATE MINDS

Consciousness is the unique capacity of the human soul that is given by God to us alone. God would not give a soul to a human-made machine, so machines can never be conscious.

If you prefer a non-religious kind of dualism, it might be stated like this:

Consciousness is the property of the non-physical mind, which is separate from the physical brain. No machine could be conscious unless it were given a separate non-physical mind and this is impossible, so machines can never be conscious.

Turing tries to give the best chance to the theological argument (with which he strongly disagrees) by suggesting that the builders of thinking machines, just like people who have children, might be "instruments of His will providing mansions for the souls that He creates" (Turing, 1950, quoted in Hofstadter and Dennett, 1981: 58). The non-religious equivalent would be that if you built the right machine, it would automatically attract or create a non-physical conscious mind to go with it.

If you are inclined toward the theological argument in spite of all its difficulties, then you might like to ask yourself the following question. Suppose that one day you meet a truly remarkable machine. It chats to you happily about the weather and your job. It is wonderfully sympathetic when you find yourself pouring out all your emotional troubles. It explains to you, as well as it can, what it feels like to be a machine, and makes you laugh with funny stories about humans. Now what do you conclude?

1 The machine is a zombie (with all the familiar problems that entails).

2 God saw fit to give this wonderful machine a soul or, if you prefer, that the machine had attracted or created a separate mind.

3 You were wrong, and a machine can be conscious.

This is a good question for winkling out implicit assumptions and strongly held intuitions. Turing suggests that fear and a desire for human superiority motivate the theological objection and also what he calls the "Heads in the Sand" objection: "The consequences of machines thinking would be too dreadful. Let us hope and believe that they cannot do so." Some people may similarly fear the possibility of a machine being conscious.

THE IMPORTANCE OF BIOLOGY

Only living, biological creatures can be conscious; therefore a machine, which is manufactured and non-biological, cannot be.

At its simplest, this argument is mere dogmatic assertion, or an appeal to vitalism. Yet it might be valid if there were shown to be relevant differences between living and non-living things. One possibility is that the functions of neurons can never be replicated by artificial means. For example, it might turn out that only protein membranes just like those in real neurons can integrate enough information, quickly enough and in a small enough space, to make a conscious machine possible, or that only the chemical neurotransmitters dopamine and serotonin can give rise to the subtlety of emotional response needed for consciousness. In this case robot builders would probably make use of these chemicals, raising the question of whether their machines were biological or not and blurring the concept of an artificial machine. But all this will become clearer as technology advances.

A second argument is that biological creatures need to grow up and learn over a long period before they become conscious; machines have no history and so cannot be conscious. This has some force if you think only of machines that are constructed in factories and pumped out ready to go, but it may well turn out that the best (or the only) way to make effective robots is to give them an extended period of learning in a real environment, and this would surely not

(Activity continued)

take place because I programmed them, and so they aren't genuine . . . these births, loves, acts of heroism, and denunciations are nothing but the minuscule capering of electrons in space, precisely arranged by the skill of my nonlinear craft, which —." His friend would have none of it. The size of the tiny people is immaterial, he said, "don't they suffer, don't they know the burden of labor, don't they die? . . . And if I were to look inside your head, I would also see nothing but electrons." Trurl, he says, has committed a terrible crime. He has not just imitated suffering, as he intended, but has created it.

What do you think? Has Trurl committed a terrible crime?

FOR A GROUP DISCUSSION

This story can provoke the most heated, and insightful, disagreements. Ask everyone to read the story in advance and to write down their answer to the question, "Has Trurl committed a terrible crime?": "Yes" or "No." Check that they have done so, or ask for a vote.

Ask for two volunteers who have strong opinions on the question, one to defend Trurl, the other to accuse him. This works best if the participants really believe in their respective roles. Trurl's defender first presents his case that the tiny people are only an imitation. His accuser then argues for the reality of their pain and suffering. Others can ask questions and then vote. Has anyone changed their mind? If so, why? Is there any way of finding out who is right?

COG – THE HUMANOID ROBOT

Cog is an upper-torso humanoid robot, designed as much to learn about human intelligence as to construct an intelligent machine. It (Cog is deliberately sexless) is just a body with arms and a head, and with dozens of motors to move its arms, neck, waist and eyes, in roughly human ways. Altogether it has 21 mechanical degrees of freedom.

Conceived in 1993 by Brooks and his colleagues at MIT (Brooks et al., 1998), Cog is the embodiment of their unconventional approach to robotics. Instead of using monolithic control, elaborate internal models and general-purpose processing, Cog is built on the principles of embodied cognition. Cog has no detailed knowledge of the world fed into it, but learns as a child would by developing its skills gradually through practice. Direct physical coupling between its actions and its perception allows Cog to function without complex internal representations, and sensory integration improves its performance. For example, Cog can turn its eyes toward a source of noise and use vestibular feedback to stabilize images from its moving cameras. Social interaction is critical for human learning, and for Cog too. Cog can find faces and eyes, share attention with a human caregiver, follow pointing gestures and imitate head nods. All these social skills, basic as they are, improve its capacity to learn more from the humans around it.

Cog's brain is not one single control system but a changing network of heterogeneous processors, including microcontrollers for controlling its joints, video and audio pre-processors, and a core of hundreds of PC computers connected by ethernet. Cog's visual system mimics some, but not all, of the capabilities of the human visual system. For example, each moveable eye has a wide-angle camera and a narrow-angle camera to capture a foveal view. For a vestibular system Cog has three rate gyroscopes and two linear accelerometers mounted in its head, and for hearing it has two microphones, which send analog auditory signals to the digital processor network. An elaborate kinesthetic system provides feedback on the

disqualify them from counting as machines. We have already seen in the discussions of connectionism, embodied cognition and situated robotics that such periods of learning may indeed be necessary.

Searle is well known for arguing that there is something special about the biology, as in his theory of "biological naturalism" (1992). His main claim is that "brains cause minds." This seems to imply that brains and minds must be distinct from each other, but he denies being a property dualist or indeed any kind of dualist (2002). He stresses that although consciousness is nothing over and above its neurological base, it is ontologically distinct in the sense that it must be experienced (see Chapter 25). He explains that "biological brains have a remarkable biological capacity to produce experiences, and these experiences only exist when they are felt by some human or animal agent" (1997: 212). Even so, Searle does not claim that brain tissue is necessary for consciousness. He argues that other systems could be conscious too, but only if they had equivalent causal powers to those of the brain. However, he does not say just what those causal powers are.

MACHINES WILL NEVER DO X

There are some things that no machine can possibly do because those things require the power of consciousness.

Turing (1950: 61) offers a selection of things said to be impossible for a machine:

> Be kind, resourceful, beautiful, friendly . . .
> have initiative, have a sense of humor, tell
> right from wrong, make mistakes . . . fall
> in love, enjoy strawberries and cream . . .
> make someone fall in love with it, learn
> from experience . . . use words properly,
> be the subject of its own thought . . . do
> something really new.

It is a good list; 50 years later machines still cannot do most of them. Yet, as Turing points out, the claim is based on people's extrapolation from machines they have actually seen, rather than any principled reason why machines could not do such things.

The last is particularly interesting and relates to what is often called "Lady Lovelace's objection." Ada Lovelace, Lord Byron's daughter, studied mathematics, became fascinated by Babbage's ideas, and wrote the only full account we have of his analytical engine. She famously said that "The Analytical Engine has no pretensions to *originate* anything. It can do *whatever we know how to order it* to perform." This suggests that the machine could not be creative, and the same argument has often been applied to modern computers. But it seems less and less applicable as time goes by. Computers can already write poems, make pictures and compose music. Some do this by simple algorithms combining ready-made segments, some use neural networks and parallel processing, and some use genetic or evolutionary algorithms.

state of all the joints and motor drivers, and Cog has the beginnings of a simple tactile system.

Cog has no integrated memory, certainly no episodic memory, and no sense of time. It cannot understand language and cannot speak. But Cog is developing all the time, and may eventually acquire these abilities. Already some of Cog's caregivers are wondering about their obligations to Cog. They treat Cog as if it *matters* what they do to it. But could things *really* matter to Cog, when it has only the simplest of preferences and goals? This depends what you think about *real* mattering and *real* suffering; are they special biological or human attributes forever denied to machines, or are they just more of the kind of thing Cog has (Dennett, 1998b)?

Is Cog gradually becoming conscious or is that impossible? Perhaps Cog will soon try to tell us.

These are computer versions of the familiar evolutionary algorithm (Chapter 10); they (1) take a segment of computer code or program, (2) copy it with variations, (3) select from the variants according to some specified outcome, and (4) take the selected variant and repeat the process. Is this *real* creativity or only *as-if* creativity? That rather depends on what you think *real* creativity is. If you think that real creativity is done in some special way by the power of consciousness, then perhaps machines are not really creative. But the alternative is that human creativity depends on processes just like those described above. It may depend on complex neural networks adjusting their connections in novel ways, or it might arise from the copying, selection and recombination of old memes to make new ones. In that case biological creativity, human creativity and machine creativity would all be examples of the same evolutionary process in operation and none would be more *real* than the others.

PRACTICE
ARE *YOU* CONSCIOUS?

As many times as you can, every day, ask, **"Are you conscious?"**

This exercise is a little different from previous ones because it is directed outward not inward. Watch other people, machines or animals as you come across them and ask, "Are *you* conscious?" As with other exercises, the idea is not to intellectualize about it, nor to argue with yourself in words, but just to *look*. So walk around for an hour or two (or a day or two), looking at things around you and asking, "Are *you* conscious?"

Could a machine be conscious?
CHAPTER FOURTEEN

If there are some things that machines can never do, we are far from knowing what they are and why.

None of the general arguments considered so far has demonstrated that a machine cannot be conscious. There are two further arguments that are much more specific and much more contentious.

THE CHINESE ROOM

Among Turing's list of arguments against machine thinking is what he calls "the argument from consciousness." This argument, he says, might be used to invalidate his test on the grounds that "the only way by which one could be sure that a machine thinks is to *be* the machine and to feel oneself thinking." The machine might then describe its feelings, but no one would be justified in taking any notice. He rejects this argument on the grounds that it leads only to solipsism—the view that we can never know anything about other minds than our own—and in this way defends his test. Yet this argument is not to be so easily defeated. Some 30 years later it gained its most powerful advocate in the philosopher John Searle, with his famous Chinese Room thought experiment.

Searle proposed the Chinese Room as a refutation of Strong AI, that is, the claim that implementing the right program is all that is needed for understanding. It is most often used to discuss problems in AI and the understanding of language, but many people, including Searle himself, believe that the Chinese Room has important implications for consciousness.

Searle took, as his starting point, Roger Schank's programs, which used scripts to answer questions about ordinary human situations, such as having a meal in a restaurant. Such programs were firmly in the GOFAI tradition. They manipulated symbols according to formal rules and incorporated representations of knowledge about the relevant topic. Supporters of Strong AI claimed that these programs really understood the stories that they answered questions about. This is what Searle attacked.

"Suppose that I'm locked in a room and given a large batch of Chinese writing. Suppose furthermore (as is indeed the case) that I know no Chinese, either written or spoken," begins Searle (1980: 417–18). Inside his room Searle has lots of Chinese squiggles and squoggles, together with a rule book in English. People outside the room pass in two batches of Chinese writing which are, unbeknown to Searle, a story, in Chinese of course, and some questions about the story. The rule book tells Searle which squiggles and which squoggles to send back in response to which "questions." After a while he gets so good at following the instructions that from the point of view of someone outside the room, his "answers" are as good as those of a native Chinese speaker.

He next supposes that the outsiders give him another story, this time in English, and ask him questions about it, also in English. He answers these just as a native English speaker would—because he *is* a native English speaker. So his answers in both cases are indistinguishable. But there is a crucial difference. In the case of the English stories he *really* understands them. In the case of the Chinese stories he understands nothing.

CONSCIOUSNESS

So here we have John Searle, locked in his room, acting just like a computer running its program. He has inputs and outputs, and the rule book to manipulate the symbols, but he does not understand the Chinese stories. The moral of the tale is this: a computer running a program about Chinese stories (or indeed anything else) understands nothing of those stories, whether in English or Chinese or any other language, because Searle has everything a computer has and he does not understand Chinese.

FIGURE 14.2 • Searle asks us to imagine that he is locked in a room. People pass squiggles and squoggles in. He looks up what to do in his rule book and passes out more squiggles and squoggles. Unbeknown to him the symbols being passed in are Chinese stories and questions, and the symbols he passes out are answers. To the people outside he seems to understand Chinese, but he is like a computer, manipulating symbols according to rules and he does not understand a word.

Searle concludes that whatever purely formal principles you put into a computer, they will not be sufficient for *real* understanding. Another way of putting it is that you cannot get semantics (meaning) from syntax (rules for symbol manipulation). Any meaning or reference that the computer program has is in the eye of the user, not in the computer or its program. So Strong AI is false.

The Turing test is also challenged because in both languages Searle claims he passes the test perfectly, but in English he *really* understands, while in Chinese he doesn't understand at all. Note that, for Searle, this shows that there is something extra that he has and the computer does not. This something is *real* (as opposed to *as-if*) intentionality. He concludes that "Whatever it is that the brain does to produce intentionality, it cannot consist in instantiating a program since no program, by itself, is sufficient for intentionality" (Searle, 1980: 424). The something is also, he claims, *subjective*, and this is where the argument becomes directly relevant to consciousness.

Reaction to the Chinese Room has been ferocious for decades. Searle (1980) himself listed six replies and rebutted them in turn, and many more followed. Among them, the "systems reply" argues that while Searle himself might not understand Chinese, the whole system consisting of him and the room does. Searle responds that he could internalize all the rules and do the manipulations in his head and he still wouldn't understand Chinese. The "robot reply" suggests putting a computer into a robot and letting that interact with the outsiders, but Searle responds that adding a set of causal relations with the outside world makes no difference because you could put *him* inside the robot and he would still just be manipulating symbols and would still not understand Chinese. The "brain simulator reply" proposes a program that simulates the actual sequence of neuron firings in a real Chinese brain. Searle responds that as long as this program only simulates the formal properties of the brain, it misses the crucial causal properties that allow brains to cause minds, the properties that cause consciousness and intentional states.

The argument started as a refutation of Strong AI. Have things changed with the advent of connectionism and behavior-based robotics? The robot reply was a step in this direction because it suggested that interaction with the real world was essential for understanding or intentionality. As McGinn puts it, "Internal manipulations don't determine reference, but causal relations to the environment might" (1987: 286). Another way of saying this is that the symbols must be grounded in the real world, because it is only through symbol grounding that we humans come to understand and have intentional states (Harnad, 1990; Velmans, 2000). Similarly, Chalmers (1996) points out that a computer program is a purely abstract object, while human beings are physically embodied and interact causally with other physical objects. The bridge between the abstract and the concrete, he says, lies in *implementation*. Having the right program is not sufficient for consciousness but implementing it is.

Dennett presses a version of the systems reply. The problem with this thought experiment, he suggests, is that Searle misdirects our imagination by luring us into imagining that a very simple table-lookup program could do the job when really "no such program could produce the sorts of results that would pass the Turing test, as advertised" (Dennett, 1991: 439). Complexity does matter; so even if a hand calculator does not understand what it is doing, a more complex system, like one that passes the Turing test, could. He suggests that we should think of understanding as a property that emerges from lots of distributed quasi-understanding in a large system (ibid.).

We might go even further and reject Searle's thought experiment on the grounds that it instructs us to imagine something impossible. He claims that with only the Chinese symbols and his rule book (or even with the rules memorized and inside his head), he really could pass the Turing test without understanding a word of Chinese. But what if he couldn't? It might turn out that symbol grounding, or learning by interactions with the real world, or something else again, is necessary for passing the test as well as for understanding a language. In this case there are only two options. Either he does not have these necessities and his symbol manipulations fail to convince the Chinese people outside, or he does and that means he comes to understand the Chinese in the process. Either way, the scenario Searle described in the original thought experiment might be impossible.

There is no final consensus on what, if anything, the Chinese Room shows. Some people think it shows nothing. Some people think it demonstrates that you cannot get semantics from syntax alone, and a machine could not be conscious simply by virtue of running the right program. Some (perhaps a minority) agree with Searle that it demonstrates a fundamental difference between the *real, conscious* intentionality that we humans have and merely *as-if* intentionality. In this case machines could only be conscious if they had the same causal properties as living human brains, whatever those properties are.

FROM NON-COMPUTABILITY TO QUANTUM CONSCIOUSNESS

There are some things that machines cannot do, so if we humans can do even one of these things then that proves we cannot be mere machines, and we must have something extra—consciousness.

ARE *YOU* CONSCIOUS?

CONSCIOUSNESS

That is the essence of our last argument against the possibility of machine consciousness. Turing calls it the "mathematical objection."

The first step is true. As we have seen (see Concept, Chapter 13), there are some functions that are non-computable, that is, some things that a Turing machine cannot do. So, for example, if a machine takes part in the Turing test, there are some questions to which it will either give a wrong answer or fail to answer at all, however much time is allowed for a reply (Turing, 1950). A similar conclusion comes from Gödel's Theorem, which states that for any sufficiently powerful logical system, statements can be formulated that can neither be proved nor disproved within that system. This is known as the Incompleteness Theorem because it shows that all sufficiently powerful axiomatic systems are necessarily incomplete.

Can we conscious humans transcend such limitations? Many people say "No." Turing pointed out that we humans are notoriously error-prone and should not feel superior just because machines are fallible. We might even revel in our limitations, as does mathematician and computer scientist Douglas Hofstadter in his deeply playful exploration of mathematics, music and mind (Hofstadter, 1979). He likens Gödel's Theorem to the impossibility of understanding ourselves and to the Zen paradox inherent in wondering whether I exist or not.

But some say "Yes," including British mathematician Roger Penrose. In two books and many articles, Penrose (1989; 1994a) claims that mathematical *understanding* is something that goes beyond mere computation, and that mathematicians can intuitively see non-computable truths. This *real* understanding requires conscious awareness, he says, and since at least one aspect of understanding is beyond computation, then consciousness itself must be beyond computation.

His argument goes much further than any we have considered so far. For example, Searle and others argue that consciousness can only be simulated, and not actually created by doing the right computations, but Penrose argues that it cannot even be simulated. In his view, conscious understanding is something completely different from computation. He is not a dualist and believes that "our brains are completely controlled by physics of some kind" (Penrose, 1994b: 243) but it needs to be an entirely new kind of physics, one that can deal with the non-computable.

His proposed new principle is based on quantum theory. Penrose explains that there are two levels of explanation in physics: the familiar classical level used to describe large-scale objects, and the quantum level used to describe very small things and governed by the Schrödinger equation. Both these levels are completely deterministic and computable. The trouble starts when you move from one to the other. At the quantum level superposed states are possible. That is, two possibilities can exist at the same time, but at the classical level either one or the other must be the case. When we make an observation (i.e., working at the classical level) the superposed states have to collapse into one or other possibility, a process known as the collapse of the wave function.

Some physicists, notably Eugene Wigner, have claimed that consciousness causes the collapse of the wave function, and this idea has inspired many popular and spiritual theories about quantum consciousness (Zohar and Marshall, 2002). This is not what Penrose means. Penrose argues that all conventional interpretations of the collapse of the wave function are only approximations, and instead proposes his own theory of "Objective Reduction." This new process is gravitational but non-local in nature, and hence can link things in widely separated areas, making large-scale "quantum coherence" possible. This can only happen when the system is isolated from the rest of the environment, but Penrose suggests that it might allow for hidden non-computational action that the brain might somehow exploit.

Where in the brain could such a process be going on? Penrose builds on the suggestion first made by Stuart Hameroff that consciousness emerges from quantum coherence in the microtubules. Microtubules are, as their name suggests, tiny tube-like proteins found in almost all cells of the body. They are involved in supporting the cell's structure, in cell division and in transporting organelles within the cell. Hameroff and Penrose propose them as the site of non-algorithmic quantum computing because of their shape, the spiral structure of their walls and because any quantum-coherent effect within them could be kept reasonably isolated from the outside.

SELF-ASSESSMENT QUESTIONS

⊙ List the main arguments against the possibility of conscious machines.

⊙ What problems would you face in designing a test for whether a machine is conscious?

⊙ In what ways is biology thought to be important for consciousness?

⊙ What things can machines never do? And what things do people claim machines can never do?

⊙ Describe the Chinese Room thought experiment. What is it supposed to show?

⊙ Summarize Penrose and Hameroff's theory. Does it help to explain consciousness?

Why is this relevant to consciousness? Hameroff argues that the real problems for understanding consciousness include the unitary sense of self, free will and the effects of anesthesia, as well as non-algorithmic, intuitive processing. All these, he claims, can be explained by quantum coherence in the microtubules. Non-locality can bring about the unity of consciousness, quantum indeterminacy accounts for free will, and non-algorithmic processing, or quantum computing, is done by quantum superposition. Penrose adds that his new theory of objective reduction might help to explain the odd timing effects found by Libet (Chapter 9). "There is a kind of 'backward effect,'" he says, "so that it looks as though you can almost influence the past within time scales of about half a second" (1994b: 249) He suggests that when "classical reasoning about the temporal ordering of events leads us to a contradictory conclusion, then this is a strong indication that quantum actions are indeed at work!" (1994a: 388).

Does this theory really solve the problems of consciousness? Almost certainly not. Computer engineer and futurist Ray Kurzweil (1999) rejects

Penrose's theory at the outset. "It is true that machines can't solve Gödelian impossible problems. But humans can't solve them either." Humans can only estimate them, and so can computers, including quantum computers that exploit superposition and quantum decoherence. He adds that quantum computing cannot be restricted to humans. Any mechanisms in human neurons capable of quantum computing should be replicable in a machine, and there is already evidence that quantum computing is a real possibility for the near future.

Grush and Churchland (1995) take Penrose's argument step by step and reject it at every one. Microtubules occur throughout the body, and not just in the brain. Drugs are known that damage the structure of microtubules but appear to have no effect on consciousness. Some anesthetics affect microtubules, but many others do not, even though they obliterate consciousness. There is no evidence that microtubules are implicated in other major changes in consciousness, such as sleep–wake cycles. Concerning the physics, microtubules cannot provide the conditions of purity and isolation required by Penrose's theory, nor could effects be transmitted from one microtubule to another as is required for explaining the unity of consciousness. In addition the theory provides no explanation of how the quantum effects could interact with effects at the level of neurons, neurotransmitters and neuromodulators, when the microtubules are supposed to be isolated from their environment.

More generally we might question whether the theory is relevant to consciousness at all. Doesn't it just replace one mystery (subjective experience)

> *"Pixie dust in the synapses is about as explanatorily powerful as quantum coherence in the microtubules."*
>
> **Churchland**, 1998: 121

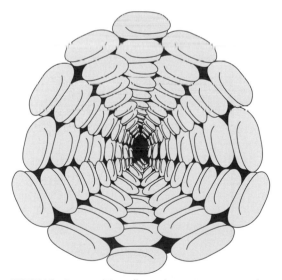

FIGURE 14.3 ● Penrose and Hameroff argue that consciousness emerges from quantum coherence in the microtubules. Microtubules are structural proteins in cell walls. They are shaped like a hollow tube with a spiral structure in their walls (after Penrose, 1994b).

with another (quantum coherence in the microtubules)? If quantum computing does occur in the brain, this is very important, but it only adds another layer of complexity to the way the brain works. If there is a "hard problem," it might be rephrased here as, "How does subjective experience arise from objective reduction in the microtubules?" The strange effects entailed in quantum processes do not, of themselves, have anything to say about the experience of light or space or pain or color. Nor does invoking the peculiar time-related effects of quantum theory explain the peculiarities of conscious judgments about time. One of the strengths of the theory is supposed to be that it accounts for the unitary sense of self but, as we have seen, this sense may itself be an illusion that requires no such explanation in terms of non-locality and quantum coherence.

Grush and Churchland (1995) ask why such a flimsy theory has proved so popular. Perhaps, they suggest, because some people find the idea of explaining consciousness by neuronal activity somehow degrading or scary, whereas "explaining" it by quantum effects retains some of the mystery. They conclude that "the argument consists of merest possibility piled upon merest possibility teetering upon a tippy foundation of 'might-be-for-all-we-know's . . . we judge it to be completely unconvincing and probably false" (ibid.: 12).

It seems that none of these arguments proves the impossibility of a conscious machine.

READING

Grush, R. and Churchland, P.S. (1995) Gaps in Penrose's toilings. *Journal of Consciousness Studies* 2, 10–29.

Lem, S. (1981) The Seventh Sally *or* How Trurl's own perfection led to no good. In D.R. Hofstadter and D.C. Dennett (eds) (1981) *The Mind's I*. New York, Basic Books. With commentary, pages 287–95.

Penrose, R. (1994b) Mechanisms, microtubules and the mind. *Journal of Consciousness Studies* 1, 241–9.

Searle, J. (1980) Minds, brains, and programs. *Behavioral and Brain Sciences* 3, 417–57. Also reprinted in Hofstadter and Dennett (1981) with commentary by Hofstadter, pages 353–82.

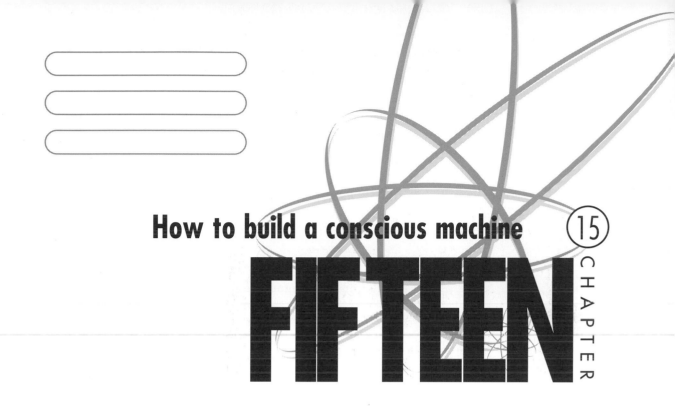

How to build a conscious machine

FIFTEEN

"Nobody today knows how to design a machine that is conscious" (McGinn, 1987: 280). Even so, many materialists and functionalists assume that conscious machines are possible, and many robotics and computer engineers are trying to build them. In this chapter we will ignore the arguments that machine consciousness is impossible, as well as the two major problems discussed in Chapter 14: that consciousness is undefined, and that we do not know how to recognize it. Rather than let these huge problems prevent progress, we will do as most roboticists do and press on regardless to see how far we can get. It may even turn out that looking for a conscious machine will shed light on the nature of consciousness itself.

There are two main ways of setting about the task. The first asks how to build a machine that *seems* to be conscious; the second asks how to build a machine that really *is* conscious (whatever that means).

I'M SURE IT LIKES ME

When Tamagotchis hit the playgrounds, children all over the world started caring for mindless little virtual animals, portrayed on tiny, low-resolution screens in little hand-held plastic boxes. These young caregivers took time to "wash" and "feed" their virtual pets, and cried when they "died." Soon the craze was over. The Tamagotchi meme had thrived on children's caring natures,

Rodney Brooks (b. 1954)

Growing up in Adelaide, South Australia, Rodney Brooks was "a nerd in a place that did not know what a nerd was." At 10 he was already trying to build computers on 10 cents' pocket money a week, and as a teenager made robots inspired by Grey Walter's tortoises. In 1977 he left Australia, giving up a PhD in mathematics, to become a research assistant at the Stanford Artificial Intelligence Laboratory, where he worked on robot vision and did a PhD in computer science. Since 1984 Brooks has been at MIT, where he is Professor of Computer Science and Director of the Artificial Intelligence Laboratory. His work on behavior-based robotics was inspired by several weeks spent as a guest in a house over a river in Thailand, where he watched insects walk, fly and land effortlessly, with only tiny nervous systems. He is responsible for the idea of intelligence without representation, for the Cog project and for the phrase "fast, cheap and out of control."

"there can be conscious machines —us"

Dennett, 1991: 432

but then fizzled out, perhaps because the target hosts quickly became immune to such a simple trick.

We humans seem to adopt the intentional stance toward other people, animals, toys and machines on the flimsiest of pretexts. Often this tactic of attributing mental states to other systems is the best way to understand them or to interact appropriately with them, but it is not an accurate guide to how those other systems really work. For example, consider the wall-following robots (see Chapter 13), whose useful behavior emerged from a couple of sensors and some inherent bias. Or consider the equally simple robots that can gather pucks into heaps. They roam around with a simple shovel-like collector on the front which either scoops up any pucks they bump into or drops them when it has too many. As a consequence, after some time, the pucks are all collected into piles. Observers readily assume that the robots are "trying" to gather up the pucks. In reality the robots have no goals, no plans, no knowledge of when they have succeeded, and no internal representations of anything at all.

This should remind us that our attributions of intentionality are not to be trusted. A strong impression that a given machine is trying to achieve a goal is no guarantee that it is. And perhaps the same logic should apply when thinking about people as about other machines. As Brooks puts it, "we, all of us, overanthropomorphize humans, who are after all mere machines" (2002: 175).

We may be less willing to adopt the "phenomenal stance," in which we attribute subjectivity to others (Metzinger, 1995a). Yet we may feel sorry for cartoon characters, love and cherish our dolls and teddies and cringe when we accidentally step on an insect. If asked whether we truly believe that Mickey Mouse, our favorite dolls, or ants and wood lice have subjective experiences, we may emphatically say "no" and yet still behave toward them as though they do. In this way our natural tendencies to treat others as intentional, sociable and feeling creatures all confuse the question of artificial consciousness.

This confusion is likely to get deeper as more and more interesting machines are constructed. Among the interesting machines already with us are some specifically designed to elicit social behavior from the people they meet.

One of the dangers faced by Cog's designers (see Concept, Chapter 14) was that when Cog began looking around and interacting with objects in its environment, it might have hurt either itself or others in the process. In an attempt to show that Cog was safe, one of its designers, Cynthea Breazeal, was videotaped playing with Cog, shaking a whiteboard eraser in front of it. Cog reached out and touched the eraser and Cynthia shook it again. It looked to observers as though Cynthia and Cog were taking turns in a game.

In fact Cog was not capable of taking turns, a skill that was scheduled for years further on in its developmental chart. It seemed that Breazeal's own behavior was coaxing more abilities out of Cog than had been put in. This set her thinking about how humans interact socially with machines, and to find out more, she built Kismet (Breazeal, 2001), a human-like head with some simple abilities built in. She then brought people to meet Kismet and asked them to "speak to the robot." Remarkably they did just that. Although some people found it very difficult, many began chatting happily, moving their bodies in synchrony with Kismet's, reflecting its emotional state in their own facial expressions, pointing out things to Kismet, and apparently becoming concerned if Kismet seemed to be offended or upset. They behaved as though Kismet were alive. They behaved as though Kismet were conscious.

You might want to jump to the obvious conclusion that the human provides all the real meaning in these interactions and that only the human is conscious. You might be sure that Kismet can't be conscious because it's just a pile of metal and a set of simple routines. But it is worth pausing first to note some similarities between us and it.

Brooks says of Kismet, "There was no place that everything came together and no place from which everything was disseminated for action" (Brooks, 2002: 92). In other words Kismet has no Cartesian theater—but we don't either. As Dennett (1991) says of us conscious humans, there is no theater where "it all comes together" and no center from which the orders are issued by a Central Meaner. There are similarities in our structure too. Like Kismet, we humans have been built with something like a subsumption architecture. That is, evolution kept whatever worked, dropped what did not, and piled new routines on top of old ones in haphazard interacting layers without an overall plan.

CONCEPT

KISMET, THE SOCIABLE ROBOT

Kismet was just a head on a moving neck. It had large eyes, eyebrows, ears with microphones inside them that moved like a dog's, and movable red lips. The eyes, like Cog's eyes, could saccade so that observers could tell where it was looking. Foveal cameras were positioned behind the eyes, and wide-angle cameras, for peripheral vision, were hidden where its nose should have been. It was controlled by a set of 15 computers all doing different things. They used different operating systems and different ways of communicating with each other, with no single computer in overall control.

Kismet was provided with a whole set of routines, each designed to be cheap, fast and just adequate. First, it had to control its vision and attention. To see objects clearly, they had to be the right distance from the cameras, so Kismet drew back if something was too close and craned its neck forward if something was too distant. This made identification easier, but as a consequence it also made Kismet appear to be interested in things. If people came too close, it pulled back, giving them a natural social cue to do the same.

Kismet paid attention to three things: movement, saturated colors and skin color. It weighed these three features across its field of view and then looked in the direction with the highest weight, the weighting depending on its current mood. Kismet's mood, or emotional state, was a combination of three variables: valence (or happiness), arousal (level of stimulation) and stance (openness to new stimuli). Different cues could move its state about within this three-dimensional emotional space. If Kismet was lonely, it would look for skin color and human interaction. If it was overstimulated, it would reject excitement.

Kismet could also hear and make sounds, although it had no understanding of words. Instead, it used human prosody in its interactions, that is, the pitch patterns that humans use in speech. For example, all over the world mothers use exaggerated prosody when speaking to their infants, and their infants can detect approval, prohibition, attention-getting and soothing. Kismet, too, could detect these four prosodic patterns, and they affected its mood accordingly.

Finally Kismet could convey its emotional state in two ways. First, it could produce prosodic (though meaningless) sounds, according to its mood. Second, it had facial expressions, and could move its eyebrows, lips and ears to express its current position in the three-dimensional emotional space.

People responded to Kismet as though to a child, talking, coaxing, pointing things out and mirroring Kismet's facial expressions. They behaved as though Kismet was alive.

FIGURE 15.1 • Cynthia Breazeal with Kismet, the sociable robot. Kismet has a vision system with four-color CCD cameras, an auditory system, an expressive motor system with 15 degrees of freedom in face movements and a vocalization system able to communicate personality and emotional quality.

Kismet is, of course, much simpler than us, but let us imagine some fanciful future descendants of Kismet who are even better at social interactions. Imagine Whizmet who is still just a head and neck but has real human-like skin that can convey even more facial expressions, eyes that cry real tears accompanied by convincing sobs, and activated by systems that respond to the person who is in front of it. Imagine that Whizmet can respond appropriately to emotions displayed by a human: laughing when the human laughs or sympathizing and comforting someone who is upset. Imagine a Whizmet that is even more sensitive to other people's emotions than any human being could be. What would you say now? Would you still be sure that Whizmet is just a pile of bits, or would you think that maybe it was conscious?

An obvious response is this. We know that simple systems can mislead us into thinking they have plans, goals and beliefs when they haven't, and more complex ones can mislead us even more. So we should not be fooled. We should only conclude that Whizmet acts *as if* it is conscious, when it is not *really* conscious.

An alternative response is this. There is no dividing line between *as if* and *real* consciousness. Being able to sympathize with others and respond to their emotions is one part of what we mean by consciousness. Kismet has a little bit of it and Whizmet has a lot. Whizmet is not conscious in the way that we are because it is only a social machine without all the other abilities we have, but within its limited domain its consciousness is as real as any that there is.

Which is right? And how can we find out?

THEY'RE ALREADY CONSCIOUS

In 1979, John McCarthy, one of the founders of AI, claimed that machines as simple as thermostats can be said to have beliefs. John Searle was quick to challenge him, asking, "John, what beliefs does your thermostat have?" Searle admired his courageous answer, for McCarthy replied, "My thermostat has three beliefs. My thermostat believes it's too hot in here, it's too cold in here, and it's just right in here" (Searle, 1987: 211).

The thermostat was a good choice. Although extremely simple, it has two of the crucial features required of an autonomous agent: it perceives its environment, and it responds to changes by acting on that environment. A thermostat is not an abstraction or a disembodied computation: it is grounded in the real world through its actions—simple as they are.

You might think that McCarthy was joking, or that he didn't mean that thermostats have *real* beliefs like ours. But this implies that you think there is a difference between *real* intentionality and only *as if* intentionality. It is important to consider here whether you think such a distinction is valid or not. Searle, as we saw in the previous chapter, argues that only biological human beings have the real thing, whereas computers and robots behave *as if* they understand languages, believe things and have experiences. If you agree with Searle, then you have to decide what the difference is between the real thing and the simulation.

Alternatively you might reject the distinction. You might say that the beliefs of thermostats are just as real as human beliefs, although far simpler, or you might say that the whole idea of *real* beliefs is misguided and that all human intentionality is *as if* intentionality. Either way, humans and machines have the same kind of beliefs, and there is no gulf between the real thing and the simulation. In this case we humans are already surrounded by believing machines.

Are any of today's machines conscious? To some people intentionality implies consciousness. As we saw in Chapter 14, the Chinese Room argument was designed to deal with intentionality but was used by both Searle and some of his critics to have implications for consciousness, in the sense that only a conscious being could *really* understand Chinese. According to this interpretation, if any machine has beliefs, it must therefore be conscious.

Others draw a firm distinction between intentionality and consciousness, but then the same dichotomy between the *real* and the *as if* arises for consciousness too. If you believe that there is a sharp divide between *real* consciousness and *as if* consciousness, then robot builders need to find out what *real* consciousness is and whether it can be put into a machine. Alternatively, if there is no difference between *real* consciousness and *as if* consciousness, we humans are already sharing our world with the beginnings of AC.

FIND X AND PUT IT IN A MACHINE

Suppose that humans have some magic "X," by virtue of which they are *really* conscious. If we wanted to make a conscious machine, we might then proceed by finding out what X is and putting it into a machine, or we might build a machine in such a way that X would naturally emerge. The machine would then, theoretically at least, be conscious.

McGinn (1999) calls the property that would explain consciousness C* and asks whether C* is possible in inorganic materials or not. He concludes that we cannot possibly know. According to his mysterian theory the human intellect is incapable of understanding how organic brains become conscious, so

"we, all of us, overanthropomorphize humans, who are after all mere machines"

Brooks, 2002: 175

"My thermostat has three beliefs. . . . it's too hot in here, it's too cold in here, and it's just right in here."

McCarthy, in Searle, 1987: 211

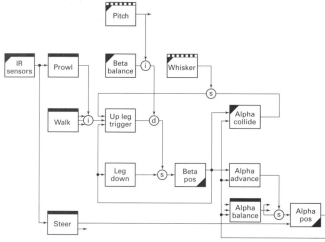

FIGURE 15.2 ● The robot Genghis, which has six legs, making it look very insect-like. The six pyroelectric sensors arrayed at the front of the robot allow it to sense the presence of heat-emitting mammals. The diagram above shows the fifty-one augmented finite-state machines (AFSMs) that transform Genghis from a pile of metal, plastic and silicon into an artificial creature. Those with a uniform outline are replicated six times, once for each leg; those with a striped top are replicated twice. AFSMs with a triangle in their upper left corner receive inputs from one or more sensors. Those with a triangle in their lower right corner have outputs that command a motor. (Brooks 2002)

there is no hope of us ever finding C* or knowing whether a machine could have it.

Others are less pessimistic. One of the strongest proponents of AC is Chalmers, who rejects the Chinese Room and other arguments against computationalism. Even though he is a dualist, he claims that any system with the right sort of functional organization would be conscious. He argues "not just that implementing the right computation suffices for consciousness, but that implementing the right computation suffices for rich conscious experience like our own" (Chalmers, 1996: 315). He does not go on to say what the "right computation" is. Nevertheless he suggests trying to find X as a way forward.

How might we do this? One way is to build on existing theories of consciousness. For example, according to Global Workspace Theories (GWTs) the contents of consciousness are representations being processed in the GW. The GW is itself a large network of interconnected neurons, and its contents are conscious by virtue of the fact that they are made globally available to the rest of the system, which is unconscious. In these theories X is global availability. So presumably a machine should be conscious if it is designed with a GW whose contents are made available to the rest of its system.

American mathematician Stan Franklin has built a software agent called IDA. This Intelligent Distribution Agent was developed for the US Navy to help solve the problem of assigning thousands of sailors to different jobs. To do this she has to communicate with the sailors by e-mail in natural language, as well as adhere to numerous Navy policies and job requirements. IDA is built on the basis of a Global Workspace architecture, with coalitions of unconscious processes finding their way into a Global Workspace from where messages are broadcast to recruit other processors to help solve the current problem. Franklin describes IDA as being functionally conscious in the sense that she implements GWT, but she is not self-conscious, and of most relevance here, he sees no convincing evidence that she is phenomenally conscious. Franklin concludes that IDA is not *really* a conscious artifact. Note also that IDA is a software agent and so is not permanently tied to any particular physical machine, raising the question of just what it is that we refer to as conscious.

As another example, one might build on evolutionary theories of the brain (see Chapter 11). For example, according to Edelman and Tononi's (2000) theory, consciousness depends on the existence of a large dynamic core of widely distributed thalamocortical neurons with reentrant connections. It might be possible to build a machine with a similar functional organization and therefore conclude that it must be conscious. Note that the dynamic core is, like the GW, a large group of neurons working together, but the mechanisms underlying the two are different, and consciousness is not equated with global availability in Edelman and Tononi's theory.

According to quantum theories none of this would produce *real* consciousness because that can only be achieved with quantum mechanical effects. For example, in Penrose and Hameroff's version, consciousness emerges from quantum coherence in the microtubules. On this basis one might try to build a quantum computer that achieved this kind of integration across large parts of its system. One might then conclude that it was *really* conscious.

FIGURE 15.3

None of this avoids the two big problems mentioned at the start. First, we do not know what consciousness is. Each of these theories (and many others) says something about what consciousness is or from what it emerges, but if the appropriate machine were built, critics could still argue that this particular theory was wrong and therefore the machine was not conscious after all. Second, we have no test for whether a machine is conscious or not, so even if one of these machines claimed to be conscious, stayed awake all night worrying about consciousness and passed the Turing test, we would still not know for sure that it was *really* conscious, even though we might have learned a lot from the machine.

DELUDED MACHINES

There is a completely different way of thinking about X. Perhaps consciousness is not what it seems to be, but is a grand illusion (see Chapter 6). According to this view, we may believe that we are conscious observers, experiencing a continuous stream of contents passing through our conscious minds, but we are wrong because there is no Cartesian theater, no audience, no "actual phenomenology" and no continuous stream of conscious experiences (Dennett, 1991; Blackmore, 2002). In this view *as if* consciousness is the only kind there is. We humans certainly *seem* to be conscious, and that requires explaining, but the right kind of explanation is one that accounts for why we have this particular illusion. This means that a machine would only be conscious in the way we are if it were subject to the same kind of illusion. The task is, then, to understand how the illusion comes about and then design a similarly deluded machine.

The most obvious contributor to the illusion is language. For example, the self has been described as a construct of language, a "center of narrative gravity," a "benign user illusion" that emerges in creatures who use language or a "self-plex" constructed by and for the replication of memes (see Chapters 8 and 11). The implication here is that if any machine were capable of using language, and capable of talking about "I," "me" and "mine," it would also fall for the illusion that it was an experiencing self, and would then be conscious like us.

SPEAKING MACHINES

There is a long history of attempts to create speaking machines. Charles Darwin's grandfather, Erasmus Darwin, built one around 1770. It could (just about) say "Mama" and "Papa." An entrepreneur offered him £1000 if he could get it to recite the Lord's Prayer and the Ten Commandments, but his money was perfectly safe. Since then the most exquisite speaking machines have been built, from the humble tape recorder to hi-fi quadraphonic sound systems. These machines merely transmit broadcast speech, or replay recorded speech, but others can read aloud from printed text or turn spoken language into print, although they usually operate only in limited domains. Then there are computers that will tell you, in a comprehensible, if annoying, voice, that they think you have made a mistake and would like to "help" you. None of these, however, can be said to understand what they say.

Early attempts to teach machines language used the GOFAI approach, trying to program computers with the right rules. But natural languages are notoriously resistant to being captured by rules of any kind. Such rules as there are always have exceptions, words have numerous different meanings, and many sentences are ambiguous. A machine programmed to parse a sentence, construct a tree of possible meanings and choose the most likely may completely fail on sentences that you and I have no trouble understanding. Pinker (1994: 209) gives some examples.

- Ingres enjoyed painting his models in the nude.

- My son has grown another foot.

- Visiting relatives can be boring.

- I saw the man with the binoculars.

The most famous example was encountered by an early computer-parser in the 1960s. The computer came up with no less than five possible meanings for the well-known saying "Time flies like an arrow," giving rise to the aphorism "Time flies like an arrow; fruit flies like a banana."

Machines analyzing language this way could not be said to understand the languages they were taught. They remained like Searle inside his Chinese Room, shuffling symbols back and forth. The advent of neural nets and connectionism improved the prospects. For example, early neural nets learned relatively easily how to pronounce written sentences correctly without being programmed to do so, even though the correct pronunciation of a word often depends on the context. Even so, these machines could not be said to speak or understand true language.

A real shift occurred with an approach that comes out of evolutionary theory or memetics. One of the fundamental principles in memetics is that when organisms can imitate each other, a new evolutionary process begins. Memes are transmitted by imitation, compete to be copied, and thereby evolve. This approach gives rise to the perhaps surprising implication that once imitation occurs, language may spontaneously appear (Blackmore, 1999). For example, if a group of organisms is capable of copying sounds, then those sounds will compete to be copied. The most useful sounds, and those with the highest copying fidelity, will do best. Digitization into words increases fidelity, and the use of different word orders increases the niches available. The result is language, an evolving system in its own right.

This theory implies that the same should happen among machines capable of imitation. There is evidence from both computer simulations and studies of robots to confirm this. For example, Luc Steels (2000), a computer scientist at the Free University of Brussels, has built robots that can make sounds, detect each other's sounds, and imitate them. They have simple vision and categorization systems, and can track each other's gaze while looking at a board with colored shapes on it. Through imitating each other when looking at the same thing, the robots come to agree on sounds that refer to the shapes they are looking at, although a listening human may have no idea what they are referring to. Other experiments have investigated the spontaneous emergence of

FIGURE 15.4 ● The "talking heads" are robots that imitate each other's sounds while looking at the same object. From this interaction words and meanings spontaneously emerge. Could human language have emerged the same way? Does the robots' use of meaningful sounds imply consciousness? (Steels, 2000)

vowel sounds and of syntactic structures and grammar. The general conclusion from this, and related work, is that language can be treated as an evolving system in which both syntax and semantics emerge spontaneously.

This has implications for machine consciousness. First, it implies that machines might learn human language rather like human children do, if they were capable of imitation and shared gaze, and if they spent time with groups of humans. Second, it implies that groups of imitating machines would spontaneously invent their own language, a language that would not necessarily be comprehensible to humans. Would they then invent self-reference, with words for "I," "me" and "mine"? If so, according to Dennett's (1991) theory, a center of narrative gravity would form. The machines would then become deluded into thinking they were an experiencing self.

Similarly, the memes they copied might gain a replication advantage by being associated with the words "I," "me" and "mine," and so a selfplex would form, with beliefs, opinions, desires and possessions, all attributed to a non-existent inner self.

Third, the memetics approach implies that machines capable of imitation would be qualitatively different from all other machines, in the same way that humans differ from most other species. Not only would they be capable of language, but their ability to imitate would set off a new evolutionary process: a new machine culture. If we and the machines communicated freely, then we would all partake in the same expanded culture, but if the machines only imitated each other (perhaps because we humans were not capable of copying them), their culture would evolve separately from ours. Either way, these machines would be conscious in just the way that we humans are and for the same reason, because they were meme machines that constructed a false sense of an experiencing self (Blackmore, 2002). We may encounter many such deluded machines in the not-too-distant future.

CONSCIOUS FUTURES

. . . initial downloads will be somewhat imprecise. . . . As our understanding of the mechanisms of the brain improves and our ability to accurately and noninvasively scan these features improves, reinstantiating (reinstalling) a person's brain should alter a person's mind no more than it changes from day to day.

(Kurzweil, 1999: 125)

For Kurzweil, and some other futurists, human immortality will be assured by technological progress. All we need to do is to increase the speed and accuracy of the scanning processes already available, copy the relevant aspects of a brain's organization into a computer, and—hey presto!—we live on. As Kurzweil notes, we all change from day to day anyway, so a small change as we shift from bio- to silicon body should hardly be noticed.

Although such prospects have long been confined to thought experiments (Chapter 8), some people now think that it might really happen, and perhaps we should prepare ourselves. We may ask two questions. First, will the resulting creature be conscious? And second, will it be the same conscious person as before? As we have already seen, answers to the first question depend on whether you think there is anything special about the biology, or whether the organization alone is sufficient for consciousness (as in functionalism). Answers to the second question depend on whether you are an ego or bundle theorist. If the opportunity ever comes, you may need to decide whether the operation really will make you immortal or not, but perhaps by then enough people will already have been copied and will be telling you that it's fine and that they still feel just the same, for you not to worry.

Kurzweil is, according to Brooks, one of those "who have succumbed to the temptation of immortality in exchange for their intellectual souls" (Brooks, 2002: 205). According to Brooks, "We will not download ourselves into machines; rather, those of us alive today, over the course of our lifetimes, will morph ourselves into machines" (ibid.: 212). To some extent this is already happening with hip replacements, artificial skin, heart pacemakers and especially with cochlear implants. These electronic devices have nothing like the sensitivity of a real human cochlea, and nothing like the number of connections to the brain, but they already enable profoundly deaf people to hear a good range of sounds, and are being improved rapidly to make enjoying music a real possibility. Retinal implants will be much more difficult because of the far greater number of neurons that join real retinae to their brains. Nevertheless, the basic principles are well known and these devices will surely come.

Replacements, or enhancements, for other body parts may be all metal and plastic, but they may alternatively be made from organic tissue, grown specially outside the body. On the output side, some severely disabled people can already control external devices by thinking. This is made possible by implanted electrodes that detect brain activity in motor cortex and use the signals to control wheelchairs, robots or a computer mouse. "The distinction between us and robots is going to disappear," says Brooks (2002: 236).

Imagine now a much more exciting possibility; rather than a cochlear or retinal implant you can have an extra memory chip, an implanted mobile phone or a direct brain link to the Internet. Fanciful as these ideas may seem at the moment, they are clearly not impossible and would have implications for consciousness if they came about. So some speculation may be interesting.

Let's consider first the memory chip. Suppose that you have tiny devices implanted in your brain and can buy vast quantities of information to load

"The distinction between us and robots is going to disappear."

Brooks, 2002: 236

How to build a conscious machine
CHAPTER FIFTEEN

into them. Since they have direct neural connections, the result is that your memory is vastly expanded. What would this feel like? It might, oddly enough, not feel odd at all.

Let me ask you a question. What is the capital of France? I presume that the answer just "popped into your mind" (whatever that means) and that you have no idea where it came from or how your brain found it. The situation with the memory chip would be just the same, only the world available to you would be greatly expanded.

Now add the implanted mobile phone, so that you can contact anyone at any time. With electrodes to detect your motor intentions you could phone a friend any time by just thinking about them. And, finally, add permanent access to the web. What would it be like to be such an enhanced person?

Do you think of your own hard disc as part of yourself? Many people do. From kids who have constructed entire virtual game worlds in their computers to academics whose life's work is a series of Word documents, there are many people alive today who would be utterly distraught if their hard disc were destroyed—they would have lost a part of themselves. Now suppose that you also have permanent, very fast access to the Internet, with efficient search facilities and the skill to use them. Now it may seem as though the whole of the net is as good as part of your hard drive—it is part of you and you would feel bereft without it. Now interface all that directly to your brain. With implanted electrodes detecting your intentions you only have to think clearly enough about what you want to search for, and it pops into your mind just as the word "Paris" did. It's all there. The whole of the web is part of you, and it is part of every other fully wired person as well.

Much of what you find on the web is junk and lies, but then ordinary memory is like that too. The skill of navigating through the vastness of cyberspace would only be an extension of the skills of using ordinary, fallible, memory now. The odd thing is that everyone would have access to the same material.

An interesting question then arises. Who, or what, is conscious? Is it you, the web as a whole, the group of people using it, or what? According to GWTs, information becomes conscious when it is made globally available to the rest of the brain. In this speculative future the whole of the web is globally available to everyone. Does that mean it would all be conscious? And if so, to whom or what? The notion of "consciousness as global

SELF-ASSESSMENT QUESTIONS

O People are generally bad at judging whether machines or other creatures have goals, desires or intentions. Give two or three examples that illustrate this.

O Describe Kismet. What has been learned about machine consciousness from Kismet's behavior?

O Do thermostats have beliefs?

O Choose any theory of consciousness. How would you set about creating a conscious machine on the basis of that theory?

O Why is it so difficult to give true language to machines?

O What are the implications of machine imitation?

O Compare Kurzweil's and Brooks' visions for the future of conscious machines.

availability" seems to provide a curious conclusion here.

If consciousness is unified by a (real or illusory) self, then nothing much changes by adding more memory, but once people are so intimately linked with each other, the whole concept of self seems under threat. What would make an item of information "my" memory rather than yours? Perhaps having a physical body is still the anchor to which a sense of self adheres, but that too may be threatened.

CONSCIOUSNESS IN CYBERSPACE

A teenage girl, pretending to be a boy, flirts in an Internet chat room. Most of the other people she meets there are just that—people—but some are bots: programs designed to generate text and appear to be people (Turkle, 1995). Virtual warriors inhabit millions of home computers, winning and losing battles in countless games, and acquiring personalities that are known the world over. Virtual actors live and die in films. A virtual television presenter

FIGURE 15.5

stands in the studio, enthusiastically introducing a real, live human. Crawlers amble around the World Wide Web collecting information on behalf of search engines or communications companies. They are autonomous and go where they like. All of these entities depend on physical substrates for their existence, but none has a permanent physical home. Could they be conscious?

These few examples raise the important question of what kind of thing can be said to be conscious. We often say that a person is conscious, or wonder whether our dog is. Nagel asked, "What is it like to be a bat?" not "What is it like to be a computation?" or "What is it like to be a bat's idea of a bat?" or "What is it like to be a virtual self?" Several authors have argued that consciousness can only arise in physical objects that have boundaries and interests of their own, such as organisms and robots (Cotterill, 1998; Humphrey, 1992). Perhaps this is not true.

I do not mean to imply something like free-floating psychic entities or astral bodies, but the possibility of conscious software agents that exist without being tied to one particular physical body. For example, they might be distributed across many machines. What, then, would give such entities any coherence, such that they could reasonably be said to be conscious?

According to meme theory, memes tend to clump together into memeplexes regardless of the substrate supporting them. So we should expect increasingly well-structured memeplexes to form in cyberspace and compete with each other for survival. They would be purely informational entities with increasingly sophisticated barriers letting some kinds of information in and rejecting

"WHAT IS IT THAT IS
CONSCIOUS?"

other kinds. If they began using self-reference, then other memes could take advantage of this, elaborating their concepts of self. They would be much like selfplexes. Would they think they were conscious?

We should expect a future in which increasing numbers of artificial personalities communicate routinely with us, answering the phone, dealing with our banking and shopping, and helping us find the information we want. They will probably be increasingly difficult to distinguish from what we now call real people, and we will respond to them as though they are. When they claim to be as conscious as you are, will you believe them?

READING

Brooks, R.A. (2002) *Flesh and Machines.* New York, Pantheon. Chapters 8 and 9, pages 172–212.

Chalmers, D. (1996) *The Conscious Mind.* New York, Oxford University Press. See Chapter 9, "Strong artificial intelligence," pages 313–22.

Dennett, D.C. (1998) The practical requirements for making a conscious robot. In Dennett, D.C. (1998b) *Brainchildren: Essays on Designing Minds.* Cambridge, MA, MIT Press, pages 151–70.

Kurzweil, R. (1999) *The Age of Spiritual Machines.* New York and London, Texere. See Chapter 6, "Building new brains."

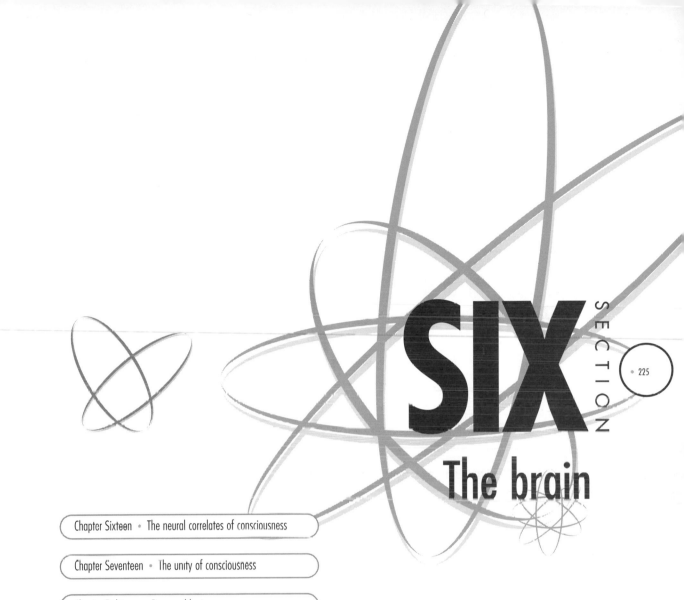

SIX

• 225

The brain

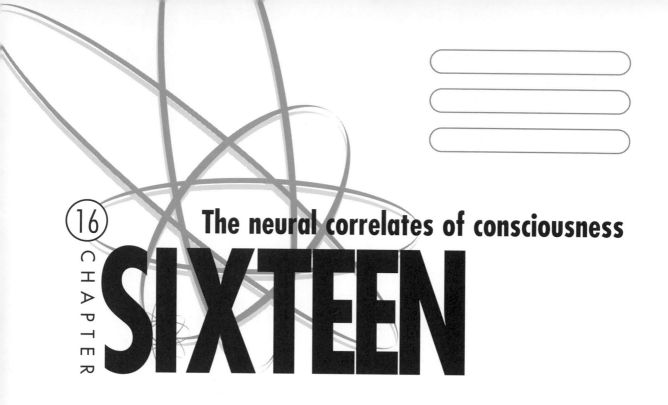

16 The neural correlates of consciousness

SIXTEEN

If you could look right inside a brain and see everything that was happening there, would you then understand consciousness?

Identity theorists and eliminative materialists say yes. If we could observe brain activity in sufficient detail and at many different levels of organization, then we would understand everything that the brain was doing, and since consciousness *is* the activity of brains, it follows that we would understand consciousness. Mysterians say no. They claim that we can never understand consciousness, even with the most detailed and subtle understanding of brain function possible.

Between these simple extremes are many other, less straightforward, answers. The issue at stake is the relationship between brain activity and conscious experience. In other words, by looking into the brain we directly confront the explanatory gap, the hard problem, and the whole mystery of the relationship between mind and brain. This mystery is obvious whichever method you use for looking into the brain. If you dissect a human brain with a scalpel and look with the naked eye, you see a few pounds of soft grayish tissue with a wrinkly surface and not much inner detail. If you attach electrodes to the scalp, you can get a readout of activity on the surface. If you use some of the modern methods of scanning, then you get multi-colored representations of what is happening inside. But in every case the mystery is obvious—how can this

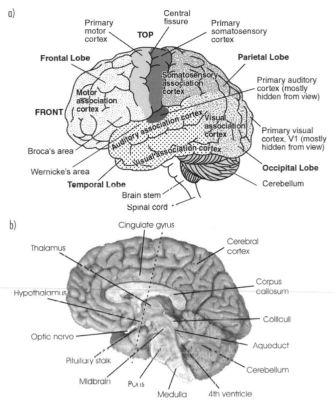

a)

FIGURE 16.1 • a) Schematic drawing of the surface of the human brain, left side, showing the four major lobes; frontal, parietal, occipital and temporal. b) Section through a human brain.

physical lump of stuff, with its electrical and chemical activity, be the seat of consciousness?

A powerful method of evading the mystery and getting on with theoretically neutral research is to look for the neural correlates of consciousness (NCC), that is, to study some aspect of neural functioning and correlate it with reports of conscious experience (Metzinger, 2000). But which aspect of neural functioning is appropriate? Measurements have been made, and theories proposed, at every scale from single molecules to large-scale assemblies of neurons, for it is not yet obvious just what we should be looking for.

When thinking about NCCs, it is important to remember all the usual warnings about the meaning of "correlation," in particular, that a correlation is not the same as a cause. This familiar trap is easy to fall into when dealing with something as slippery as consciousness, so we need to be especially careful. When any correlation is observed between two events, A and B, there are three possible causal explanations: A might have caused B; B might have caused A, or some other event or process; C, might have caused them both. Alternatively, A and B might actually be the same thing even though they do not appear to be.

MAPPING THE BRAIN

Single cell recording

Fine electrodes are inserted into living cells to record their electrical activity. Although widely used in animal studies, this technique is, for obvious reasons, rarely used in humans.

Electroencephalogram (EEG)

The EEG measures changes in electrical potential using electrodes on the scalp. The potentials measured arise from the combined activity of many cells in the underlying area of the brain. Electrical brain activity was first measured in 1875, and the human EEG first described in 1929 by the German psychiatrist Hans Berger who showed that the resting alpha rhythm (8-1-2 cycles per second) is blocked by opening the eyes or doing mental arithmetic. By the 1930s the EEG was routinely used in neurology. In the 1960s computer averaging improved the study of event-related potentials (ERPs), including evoked potentials in response to specific stimuli, readiness potentials that build up gradually before a response is made and potentials associated with unexpected events. Although the EEG has poor spatial resolution, it is still a valuable research tool because of its good temporal resolution.

X-ray computed tomography (CT)

Developed in the early 1970s, CT scans are computer-generated images of tissue density, produced by passing X-rays through the body at many different angles and measuring their attenuation by different tissues. The same mathematical techniques for constructing the images are used in newer forms of scanning.

Positron emission tomography (PET)

Emission tomography is a technique for imaging the distribution of radioactivity following administration of a radioactive substance. In PET, atoms that emit positrons are incorporated into glucose or oxygen molecules, allowing brain metabolism and blood flow to be measured directly. Radiation detectors are arrayed on the head in several rings, allowing several slices of brain to be studied

In some cases the right explanation is obvious. To give a simple example, imagine that you watch at a railway station and every so often you see hundreds of people gathering on the platform, always followed by a train arriving. If correlation implied cause, you would have to conclude that the people on the platform caused the train to appear. Obviously you won't because you know that both events were caused by something else: a railway timetable. When it comes to consciousness, however, things are not always that obvious, and we can easily jump to false conclusions. For example, you may recall that according to Wegner's theory of conscious will (Chapter 9), it is precisely this kind of confusion between correlation and cause that leads us to the illusion that our thoughts cause our actions.

So when correlations are found between neural events and conscious experiences, we must consider all the possibilities. Perhaps neural events cause conscious experiences. Perhaps conscious experiences cause neural events. Perhaps something else causes both of them. Perhaps neural events *are* conscious experiences. Perhaps we have so misconstrued one or other that none of these is true.

UNCONSCIOUSNESS

People often refer to someone as "unconscious" when they are alive but unresponsive. What is the difference between being conscious and unconscious in this sense? If we could study the brains of a conscious and an unconscious person, we might learn a good deal about the necessary and sufficient conditions for being conscious. Sleep is sometimes thought of as a form of unconsciousness, but it is in fact a rather complex mixture of different states and will be considered later (Chapter 23).

Coma and persistent vegetative state are forms of unconsciousness and can be induced by damage to the reticular formation in the brain stem. It has long been known that the ascending reticular activating system, running from the brain stem up through the thalamus, activates widespread regions of the cortex and its functioning is necessary for consciousness, and for the normal cycle of waking and sleeping states. However, it is not sufficient for consciousness, for there is more to consciousness than just being awake. Indeed it was shown during the nineteenth century that animals with the whole of the cortex removed can still show an alternation of sleeping and waking states, even though they are obviously incapable of any normal behavior or perception.

Perhaps a more interesting state to consider here is anesthesia. Anesthetics are mostly rather non-specific in their effects, and even after nearly two centuries of use, their mechanisms of action are not well understood. Gases like chloroform and nitrous oxide produce a general effect, rendering the person who inhales them immobile, insensitive to pain and unable to communicate or to remember what happened during the anesthesia. By contrast, modern anesthetics usually consist of at least three different drugs designed to have three different effects; one abolishes responsiveness, one produces amnesia and one is a muscle relaxant. It is likely that the many drugs capable of producing unconsciousness do so in several different ways, and no drug can be said specifically to abolish consciousness without any other effects.

Is there a specific part of the brain on which all unconsciousness-inducing drugs act? Studies of the brain activity associated with different types and depths of anesthesia suggest not. For example, in experiments with the anesthetics propofol and isoflurane, PET scans showed a global reduction in neuronal functioning with increasing doses, but no evidence of any specific "consciousness circuits" that were affected when the person became unconscious (Alkire et al., 1998).

Anesthetics differ widely in their chemical structure, but all of them are relatively small molecules and are hydrophobic. That is, they are soluble in fats but not in water. This means that they bind to the lipid layers in cell membranes, suggesting that this might be their site of action. Beyond that, theories about their mechanism differ widely. Some concentrate on which areas of the brain are primarily affected, such as the reticular activating system, or the thalamus through which sensory information passes on its way to sensory cortex. Others deal with effects on specific neurotransmitters, or on receptors in cell membranes. Obvious problems are that different theories

simultaneously. PET has good spatial resolution but the disadvantage of having to use radiation.

Nuclear magnetic resonance (MRI)

MRI measures the radio signals emitted by some atomic nuclei (e.g., ^{1}H, ^{13}C and ^{31}P) when they are placed in a magnetic field and excited by radio frequency energy. The radiation emitted provides information about the chemical environment of the nuclei. In the 1970s the idea of using hydrogen atoms in the body for imaging was introduced. This led to methods for mapping human brain function known as fMRI (functional MRI), which can provide extremely detailed images of the living brain. Early methods required injections of a paramagnetic substance, but in the 1990s totally non-invasive methods followed, including the use of BOLD (blood oxygen level-dependent) contrast, which allows measurement of local brain metabolism. fMRI measures neuronal activity only indirectly, depending on metabolic and hemodynamic responses to neural activity, and this limits its temporal resolution. Spatial resolution is very good and improving. For brain scanning, the head has to be placed inside the scanner and kept very still. The results are displayed using false color to produce the familiar colored images of the brain in action.

Transcranial magnetic stimulation (TMS)

In TMS, or repetitive TMS (rTMS), a coil held over the brain generates a pulsed magnetic field that stimulates neurons in a focused area by inducing small local currents. When motor areas are stimulated, involuntary movements occur. If the precise area stimulated is located by scanning, this allows motor cortex to be accurately mapped. Similarly, visual or speech areas can be mapped because TMS suppresses function in the area stimulated. TMS can also be used to induce particular experiences or altered states of consciousness (Chapter 24).

may be true for different anesthetics, single anesthetics may have multiple effects and consciousness may be affected by different means in different cases.

Among all these many theories, two have been used to seek the NCC. The first is Penrose and Hameroff's theory of quantum coherence in microtubules. Hameroff, who is an anesthesiologist himself, originally developed his theory because of evidence that some anesthetics affect the cellular microtubules. However, this has not been widely accepted as an explanation of anesthesia, and we have already considered other problems with this theory (see Chapter 14).

The second is proposed by German neuroscientist Hans Flohr. He argues, first, that the final common pathway for all causes of unconsciousness is the inhibition of processes dependent on N-methyl-D-aspartate (NMDA) receptors and, second, that the necessary and sufficient conditions for consciousness are the occurrence of higher-order self-reflexive representations. What does this mean?

At low doses, the dissociative anesthetic, ketamine, induces changes in body image, distortions of self, and feelings of dissociation from the surroundings, and it is used as a recreational drug for these reasons. At higher doses it abolishes consciousness. Ketamine acts as an antagonist of the NMDA receptor, blocking the normal excitatory effect of glutamate on the post-synaptic membrane containing the receptors. These receptors are part of a complex that modifies the strength of the synapse, and other anesthetics act on other parts of this complex, including nitrous oxide, or laughing gas, which is a completely different kind of molecule but has somewhat similar effects to ketamine. From this Flohr concludes that the normal functioning of the NMDA synapse is necessary for consciousness.

Of course, the normal functioning of all sorts of things is *necessary* for consciousness, but Flohr argues that the proper functioning of this system is also *sufficient*. The reason is, he suggests, that NMDA synapses act as Hebbian coincidence-detectors. In the 1940s, long before the operation of synapses was even partly understood, Hebb proposed a simple rule: cells that fire together once are more likely to fire together in the future, and vice versa. He showed that if this is the case, then groups of cells will form that all tend to fire together when any one of them fires. He called these "cell assemblies," and suggested that they are the physical building blocks of mental representations (Hebb, 1949). Hebb's ideas have been widely used in theories of learning and memory, in the development of artificial neural networks and in theories of consciousness.

Flohr builds on the idea of Hebbian cell assemblies to develop a representational theory of consciousness similar to HOT theories (see Chapter 3).

> Roughly speaking, to be conscious, in this view, is to be in a specific cognitive state, that of having a mental representation by which the system represents its own actual state as its own state. Being conscious of something means that a mental representation is

accompanied by, or embedded in, a second, higher-order representation to the effect that the system itself is in a certain state.

(Flohr, 2000: 252–3)

In this scheme, the connection of first-order representations to a self representation produces the subjective character of conscious states. All this requires large-scale neuronal assemblies and a binding mechanism that makes them possible, that is, the NMDA synapses. Anesthetics abolish consciousness because they interfere with the functioning of NMDA synapses. The NCC is the functioning NMDA synapses and the cell assemblies they support.

One problem for Flohr's hypothesis is that properly functioning NMDA synapses are as necessary for unconscious and non-reflexive cell assemblies as they are for conscious ones (Hardcastle, 2000). Another is that other anesthetics work quite differently from ketamine. For example, etomidate is known to act specifically by potentiating the GABA receptor (Franks and Lieb, 2000). To sustain Flohr's hypothesis, one must argue that etomidate indirectly inhibits NMDA receptor activity. In this case the two drugs should induce the same unconscious state, but they do not. For example, etomidate does not have the same analgesic or psychoactive effects as ketamine. This is part of the wider problem that countless chemicals ultimately induce unconsciousness, but they do so in different ways, and the unconscious state they induce is not simply a lack of something called consciousness.

Although in principle we should be able to understand consciousness by studying its absence, neither the logic nor the science is straightforward. Abolishing consciousness is not like pulling out a single component or switching off a light.

CONSCIOUS VISION

Crick asks, "What is the 'neural correlate' of visual awareness?" (Crick, 1994: 204). He explains that he is looking for the correlates of the "vivid representation in our brains of the scene directly before us" (ibid.: 207). Similarly, Damasio describes the main task facing the neurobiology of consciousness as "the problem of how the movie-in-the-brain is generated" (1999: 11). So, rather than looking for the NCs of consciousness in general, they are looking for NCs of particular kinds of experiences, in this case visual experiences.

Crick admits that "so far we can locate no single region in which the neural activity corresponds exactly to the vivid picture of the world we see in front of our eyes" (1994: 159) but suggests that "at any moment in time, consciousness will correspond to a particular type of activity in a transient set of neurons that are a fraction of a much larger set of potential candidates" (ibid.: 207). He then goes on to ask where these neurons are in the brain, whether they are of any particular type and what is special about either the way they fire or their connections.

"so far we can locate no single region in which the neural activity corresponds exactly to the vivid picture of the world we see in front of our eyes"

Crick, 1994: 159

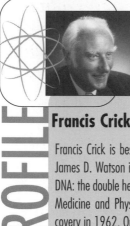

Francis Crick (b. 1916)

Francis Crick is best known for his collaboration with James D. Watson in their discovery of the structure of DNA: the double helix. They received the Nobel Prize in Medicine and Physiology for this world-changing discovery in 1962. Originally studying physics in London, Crick spent the war years working for the Admiralty. He left in 1947, wanting to pursue the mystery of life and the boundary between living and non-living things, and so trained in biology, getting a PhD in X-ray diffraction at the University of Cambridge in 1954. Years later he changed tack again and began theoretical work on vision, the function of dreams and the nature of consciousness. He is a professor at the Salk Institute in La Jolla, California, where he collaborates closely with Christof Koch. He describes his main interest as discovering whether "there are particular neurons in the brain whose firing corresponds to what we see . . . In other words, to discover the neural correlates of (visual) consciousness."

So is there some special place in the brain where consciousness is generated, or where conscious experiences happen? In answer to the "where" question, Crick says that "Consciousness depends crucially on thalamic connections with the cortex," and especially on reverberatory circuits between the thalamus and cortical layers 4 and 6 (ibid.: 252). MacKay suggests that "the physical correlate of our conscious experience is likely to be the cooperative to-and-fro traffic between cortical and deeper levels of neural activity" (ibid.: 15). In contrast, Cotterill (1995) suggests that the "site" for consciousness is likely to be the anterior cingulate, and Ramachandran claims that "the circuitry that embodies the vivid subjective quality of consciousness resides mainly in parts of the temporal lobes (such as the amygdala, septum, hypothalamus and insular cortex) and a single projection zone in the frontal lobes—the cingulate gyrus" (Ramachandran and Blakeslee, 1998: 228).

There are dangers in trying to locate consciousness in this way. They are seen in extreme form in Descartes' idea that the pineal gland might be the seat of the soul, and in the view that William James pilloried of there being a single "pontifical neuron" to which "our" consciousness is attached. Also damage to almost any area of the brain has some effect on consciousness, and so in some sense the whole brain is involved. This was certainly James's own view. He said that "The consciousness, which is itself an integral thing not made of parts, 'corresponds' to the entire activity of the brain, whatever that may be, at the moment." He favored this view "because it expresses the bare phenomenal fact with no hypothesis," but he was under no illusion that this solved the problems. "The ultimate of ultimate problems, of course, in the study of the relations of thought and brain, is to understand why and how such disparate things are connected at all" (James, 1890, Vol. 1: 177). This problem remains, whichever areas are favored.

Note that Crick is looking for a "special" place, or a special way of firing, because of a familiar problem; that is, that most of what goes on in the nervous system is unconscious. This is especially obvious in the visual system, in which an enormous amount of processing goes on in parallel all the time, and yet we seem only to be aware of a tiny fraction of it. This problem lies right at the heart of the mystery of consciousness. If some processing is conscious and some is not, what is the magic difference? Do some cells have a special ingredient that makes their activities conscious? Are some kinds of firing able to create subjective experiences while others cannot? Does connecting cells up in a special way, or in certain-sized groups, make consciousness happen in those cells but not in others? Put like this none of the options sound very plausible. But if we accept that only a tiny fraction of visual processing is conscious, then there has to be some answer.

A good way to tackle the problem, without getting too tangled up in these difficulties, is to look for the neural correlates of conscious visual experiences and compare them with unconscious vision.

COMPETING FOR CONSCIOUSNESS

Look at the Neckar cube in Figure 16.2. Keep your eyes fixated on the central dot and watch what happens. The Neckar cube is a simple example of an ambiguous figure. That is, it can be seen in two mutually incompatible ways. Even though you are keeping your eyes still, you should find that the cube flips back and forth between the two different interpretations. It is impossible to see both at once, or to combine the views into one, so you experience alternation or rivalry.

Another form of rivalry, called binocular rivalry, is found when different images are presented to the two eyes. For example, a picture of the seaside might be shown to the right eye and a face to the left, or a vertical grating to the left eye and a horizontal grating to the right. In such cases the face and ocean are not combined into one picture, nor do the gratings fuse into a plaid. Instead perception seems to flip between the two.

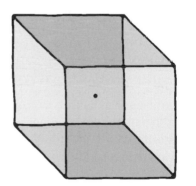

FIGURE 16.2 • The Neckar cube; a simple example of rivalry. Keep your gaze on the central spot while looking at the cube. There are two equally likely interpretations that tend to alternate: one with the front face up and to the left, the other with the front face down and to the right. You may be able to flip views deliberately and vary the speed of alternation.

What is going on here? Early theories suggested that the flipping was due to eye movements or other peripheral effects, but keeping the eyes still does not stop the alternation, and peripheral theories have not generally fared well. It seems more likely that the flipping occurs somewhere further up the visual system. But how does this relate to the subjective experience? It feels as though the two views are competing for consciousness. It seems as though first one, and then the other, gains access to consciousness and thus you become aware of it. This simple phenomenon provides an ideal situation for investigating the relationship between the objective facts (input to the eye, events in the visual system and so on) and the

"We know two things concerning what we call our psyche or mental life: firstly, its bodily organ ... and secondly, our acts of consciousness ... and, so far as we are aware, there is no direct relation between them."

Freud, 1949: 1

subjective facts (being conscious of first one of the pictures and then the other).

The first experiments of this kind were done with macaque monkeys (Logothetis and Schall, 1989; Sheinberg and Logothetis, 1997). Macaques can be trained to report which of two pictures they are seeing by pressing a lever. Their responses under conditions of binocular rivalry are much like ours. For example, when shown a vertical grating to one eye and a horizontal grating to the other, or gratings moving in different directions, their lever presses indicate that what they see flips from one to the other. Logothetis and his colleagues trained monkeys in this way and then recorded from various areas of their brains using electrodes in single cells. They were looking for those areas where the activity corresponded not to the unchanging visual input, but to the changing perceptions reported by the monkey's behavior.

Cells in early visual cortex, such as area V1, responded to the unchanging input. For example, some cells responded to vertical stripes, some to motion in different directions, and some to particular stimuli, but their behavior did not change when the monkey's perception changed. Further along the visual pathway (for example, in MT and V4) some of the cells responded to what the monkey reported seeing. Finally, in the inferior temporal cortex (IT) almost all the cells changed their response according to what the monkey reported seeing. So if the monkey pressed the lever to indicate a flip, most of the cells that were firing stopped firing and a different set started. It looked as though activity in this area corresponded to what the monkey was consciously seeing, not to what was in front of its eyes.

FIGURE 16.3 • The principle behind Logothetis's experiments. When monkeys are shown a different display to each eye, they report binocular rivalry just as humans do. They cannot speak, but they can indicate which display they are currently seeing by pressing a lever.

Does this mean that the NCC lies in IT? One problem here is that the connection with consciousness depends on assuming that monkey perceptions are conscious in the same way as ours. This seems reasonable given the way they respond, but of course we cannot know for sure, and those who believe that language is necessary for consciousness might argue that the monkey's responses tell us nothing about consciousness (see Chapter 12). The experiments were carried out with monkeys because you cannot readily insert electrodes into living human brains, but recent developments in imaging techniques have made it possible to do an equivalent study in humans.

Lumer, Friston and Rees (1998) used fMRI to detect changes during binocular rivalry. Subjects wore stereoscopic glasses and were presented with a red drifting grating to one eye, and a green face to the other. They pressed keys to indicate which they were consciously seeing. These very different stimuli allowed the experimenters to investigate activity in brain areas specialized for

CONSCIOUSNESS

the analysis of faces, as well as for color and form. They were especially interested in finding areas where activity was significantly higher during periods when the face was seen compared with when the grating was seen. They found it bilaterally (on both sides of the brain) in occipito-temporal areas of the ventral pathway, including some parts of the fusiform gyrus that are known to be involved in the processing of faces. In addition they found many prefrontal areas where activity correlated with the image seen.

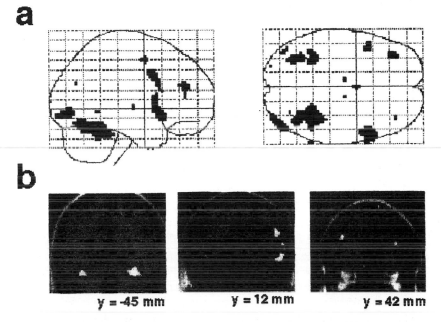

FIGURE 16.4 • Neural correlates of perceptual state during rivalry. (a) Brain areas showing greater fMRI activity during perceptual dominance of the face compared with periods during which the face was unseen are shown as see-through projections onto lateral (left) and horizontal (right) representations of standard stereotactic space. (b) Activation maps during face perception in selected coronal sections, overlaid onto normalized anatomical MRIs. Activity is shown in the fusiform gyri (left), middle and inferior frontal gyri (center), and dorsolateral prefrontal cortex (right). Distance from the anterior commissure is indicated below each coronal section (Lumer, 2000, p. 234).

They also investigated the flipping process itself. To do this, they recorded a subject's series of key presses and then played back the same sequence of images to the subject. They could then compare brain activity for exactly the same sequence of images, but with the important difference that in one case the flipping occurred spontaneously, while in the other it was predetermined. Any differences in activity between the two should then reveal which areas of the brain are involved in causing the flip to occur. Such differences were found in many areas, including parts of the parietal and frontal cortex that have previously been implicated in selective attention (Lumer, 2000). These results add to a body of work suggesting that conscious visual experiences are correlated not with activity in V1 and other early parts of the sensory pathways but with more central areas.

What can we conclude? Some researchers describe these areas as visual consciousness areas (ffytche, 2000) or as sites where consciousness is generated (Chalmers, 2000). Ramachandran suggests that the studies may help to narrow down "those brain processes that are qualia laden as opposed to those that are not" (Ramachandran and Hubbard, 2001: 24). Crick and Koch (1995) suggest that we are not conscious of the processing in early sensory areas but only of the later results of that processing: "it is the transient results of the computations which correlate with qualia; most of the computations leading up to those results are likely to be *un*conscious" (Crick and Koch, 2000: 104). More specifically they follow the philosopher Ray Jackendoff (1987) in arguing that it is intermediate levels of computation that are associated with qualia rather than either the lowest or highest levels.

Serious problems remain. First, most of these results provide only correlations, although Nancy Kanwisher (2001) has explored the ways in which research like this may be used to tease apart the necessary and sufficient conditions for consciousness, and so to get closer to causal explanations. Second, none of these interpretations touches the central mystery. They provide no explanation of how computations could "correlate with qualia," how consciousness could be "generated" in one brain area rather than another or what it means for some processes to be "qualia laden" while others are not.

A possibility worth considering is that the whole enterprise is misconceived. For example, if vision is a grand illusion (see Chapter 6), then there is no "vivid representation in our brains of the scene directly before us" and no "movie-in-the-brain." So looking for their neural correlates is doomed to failure (Blackmore, 2002); so too is the search for the neural correlates of the contents of consciousness, because consciousness is not a container, and there are no contents of consciousness.

PAIN

Pain hurts. But what does that mean? The all-too-familiar experience of pain raises, in stark form, all the fundamental questions about NCCs. On the one hand, pain is subjective. The International Association for the Study of Pain defines it as "an unpleasant sensory and emotional experience associated with actual or potential damage, or described in terms of such damage," and adds "Pain is always subjective."

Perhaps you suspect that your friend who complains at the slightest hint of pain is just a wimp, but how can you know? Just as we cannot know whether your red qualia are just like mine, so we cannot know just how bad someone else's pain really feels. They might either be being terribly brave in the face of agonizing pain, or faking it.

On the other hand, pain correlates with neural events. When someone is injured, numerous chemical changes take place, and signals pass along specialized thin, unmyelinated, neurons called C-fibers to the spinal cord, thence to the brain stem, thalamus, and to various parts of the cortex including somatosensory cortex (the precise location depending on where the injury was) and cingulate cortex (Chapman and Nakamura, 1999). Interestingly the correlation between the amount of pain experienced and the amount of activity in these areas turns out to be rather close, with fMRI and PET studies showing larger areas of cortical activation when pain is rated as more intense. This suggests that there are reliable neural correlates of the amount of pain someone is experiencing.

But what does this correlation mean? Does the neural activity *cause* the subjective experience of hurting? Does the pain *cause* the neural activity? Are the neural activity and the subjective pain both caused by something else? Is the pain in fact nothing other than the neural activity? Or have we perhaps so misconstrued the situation that we are led to ask impossible questions?

Hold out your bare arm and give it a really good pinch. Now consider this unpleasant feeling. What is it like? While you can still feel it, ask the questions above. Do any of these possibilities really seem right?

PRACTICE
WHERE IS THIS PAIN?

Look out for any pain you may experience this week, whether a pounding headache or a stubbed toe. Now look straight into the pain. Experience it as fully as you can. Ask, **"Where is this pain?"**

Odd things can happen when you stare into the face of pain. Make a note of what happens for you.

It might help to explore another question: "Where is this pain?" Common sense says it is in your arm, which is certainly where it *seems* to be. Identity theorists would locate it in the brain, or perhaps also in all the C-fibers and other activated parts of the nervous system. Dualists would say that it is in the mind and therefore strictly has no location. There are other possibilities too. For example, Velmans uses this question to help explain his "reflexive model of consciousness": that "all experiences result from a reflexive interaction of an observer with an observed" (2000: 113). He rejects both dualism and reductionism, and claims that the experienced world and the physical world are the same thing. Using this model the pain really is in the arm.

But what if you have no arm? Amputees who experience phantom limbs sometimes suffer excruciating pain in a knee, elbow or finger that doesn't

PHANTOM PHENOMENA

After losing an arm or leg, more than 90 percent of people experience a vivid "phantom limb" that can last for years or even decades. There are also reports of phantom breasts, phantom jaws and even phantom penises that have phantom erections. Phantom legs can be cramped into uncomfortable positions and hands clenched so hard that the fingers seem to be cutting into the hand. The pain can be excruciating and terribly hard to treat (Melzack, 1992; Ramachandran and Blakeslee, 1998).

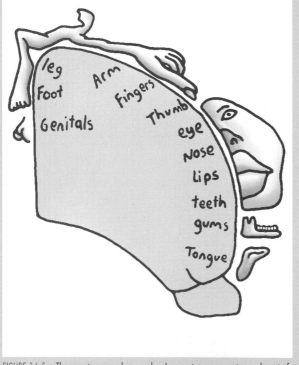

FIGURE 16.5 • The somatosensory homunculus. In somatosensory cortex each part of the body is represented in a different area. When input from one part is missing, the input from other parts can invade that area. According to Ramachandran, this can explain why amputees sometimes feel real cold on their face as cold in their phantom fingers or sexual stimulation as a touch on their phantom foot.

physically exist. Their pain feels as clearly physically located as yours does.

WHOSE PAIN?

We began with "pain hurts" but perhaps we should say "pain hurts me." What makes pain painful is the fact that *I* don't like it, that it's *my* pain and I wish I didn't have it. Can there then be pains without selves who feel them? And if a self is needed, just how much of a self, and what could the neural correlates of that be?

Consider the case of animals whose spinal cords have been severed. If a stimulus that would normally be painful is applied to the leg of a spinal dog, the dog shows no signs of distress, but its leg automatically withdraws. Occasionally the same thing happens in humans if they have broken their neck or spine. If prodded in the leg, they will deny feeling anything, although the leg pulls back. The isolated spinal cord can even be taught to make responses by training it with stimuli that would be painful for a whole person but that are not felt at all by the paralyzed person.

So does the spinal cord feel the pain? This is not a daft question. The idea of conscious spinal cords may seem daft, but if you reject this idea, then you must also reject the idea that simple animals who only have the equivalent of spinal cords can feel pain. There are also problems with the role of pain in learning. Is the actual feeling of pain, or pain-qualia, necessary for avoidance learning? If you say "No," you are led to epiphenomenalism, or to conscious inessentialism and the possibility of pain-free zombies who just learn without *experiencing* the pain. If you say "Yes," then surely the isolated spinal cord does feel pain.

Macphail (1998) is among those who deny that other animals can feel pleasure and pain, even though they can learn. Damasio argues that a self is needed for feeling pain. He argues that neural patterns are not enough—for pain to be painful, and to have the emotional qualities it does, you have to know you are having the pain as well.

Knowing that you have pain requires something else that occurs *after* the neural patterns that correspond to the substrate of pain—the nociceptive signals—are displayed in the appropriate areas of the brain stem, thalamus, and cerebral cortex and generate an image of pain, a feeling of pain.

(Damasio, 1999)

Damasio is no dualist and so this next stage is also in the brain. It is "the neural pattern of you knowing, which is just another name for consciousness" (1999: 73). So with this view the necessary neural correlates for pain are to have both the activity in the pain system, and the neural pattern of self.

This allows Damasio to distinguish between self-willed actions and automatic reactions, such as removing your hand from the hotplate before *you*

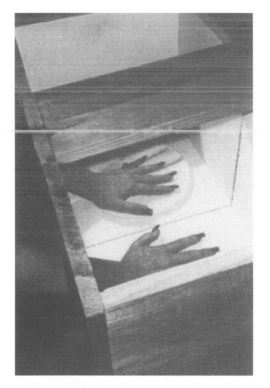

FIGURE 16.6 ● Ramachandran's mirror box has two holes in it, one for the real hand (in this case the right hand) and one for the phantom. When patients look in they can see two normal hands. When asked to make symmetric movements they seem to see, and feel, their phantom moving. In some cases this has freed them from years of pain.

The thought of a pain in a non-existent limb is so odd that when Silas Weir-Mitchell coined the term "phantom limb" in 1872, at a time when thousands of soldiers had limbs removed from injury or gangrene, he wrote anonymously for fear of ridicule. So where is the pain and what causes it? Perhaps the most obvious theory is that the pain is caused by damage in the stump or severed nerves, and that the nerves then pass signals to the brain, which, wrongly, assumes that the familiar limb is still there. Accordingly, many surgeons have operated on the stump, performed another amputation, cut the sensory nerves, and even operated on the spinal cord to stop the pain, often without success.

A completely different theory starts from the observation that heat, cold or a touch on the *face* can sometimes be felt as heat, cold or touch on the phantom hand. A touch on the genitals can be felt on a phantom foot. The reason appears to be that the somatosensory cortex contains a complete, though highly distorted, map of the body in which the face is represented next to the hand. In the absence of sensory input from the hand, that from the face starts to invade the hand area, with the result that the person feels a touch as being in both places.

Ramachandran (Ramachandran and Blakeslee, 1998) has developed a novel way of treating phantom pains, especially for those whose phantom hands are rigidly fixed in a painful position, or whose fingers are digging into their phantom palm. He argued that when we clench our fist, feedback from the hand tells us when to stop clenching, but for people with no hand the motor signals to clench just keep on going, causing the pain. He positioned a mirror vertically in front of a patient so that he could see the reflection of his normal hand in the mirror, just where his phantom should be. When the patient moved his normal hand, he saw what appeared to be the phantom moving, thus providing the necessary feedback. In about half the cases tested by Ramachandran the effect was dramatic. The phantom seemed to move and the pain was eased. In one case, after some practice with the mirror, a painful phantom arm that had lasted ten years completely disappeared. Ramachandran claims to have been the first to "amputate" a phantom limb.

SELF-ASSESSMENT QUESTIONS

- What is an NCC?

- What does it mean to say that a correlation is not a cause? Think up some examples in which people have wrongly assumed cause from correlation (they are widespread in media science reporting).

- Describe two theories that relate the effects of anesthetics to consciousness.

- Why does perceptual rivalry provide a useful paradigm for studying the NCC? Describe two experiments using this technique.

- What are the neural correlates of pain? Describe two theories that try to explain why pain hurts.

even felt the pain. But notice that the patterns are "displayed," a notion that implies someone who is watching the display and hence raises all the problems of the Cartesian theater. As in Global Workspace Theories, where the contents of consciousness are displayed to the unconscious audience in the rest of the brain, this display is not a magic screening for a psychic homunculus, but is neural activity being made available to other patterns of neural activity. Even so, the problem remains. What is special about this interaction between two neural patterns? What transforms it into a self experiencing pain?

The notion of display is avoided by treating sensation as a kind of action. In explaining "How to solve the mind–body problem," Humphrey says that "sensory awareness is an *activity*. We do not *have* pains, we *get to be* pained" (2000: 13). So when I feel a pain in my hand, I am not sitting there passively absorbing the sensations coming in; "I am in fact the active agent" reaching out with an evaluative response and experiencing this efferent activity. In this way he redescribes the "mind" side of the mystery. "Thus the phantasm of pain becomes the sensation of pain, the sensation of pain becomes the experience of actively paining, the activity of paining becomes the activity of reaching out to the body surface in a painy way" (ibid.: 15). The "hard problem" is, he claims, transformed into a relatively easy problem, although others disagree (see the commentaries following Humphrey, 2000).

Note that Humphrey's theory, although similar, differs from O'Regan and Noë's sensorimotor theory (see Chapter 6). They tried to escape from both dualism and the Cartesian theater by doing away with the idea that perception consists in *representing* the world or the perceiving self. But for Humphrey the organism "needs the capacity to form *mental representations* of the sensory stimulation at the surface of its body and how it feels about it" (ibid.: 109).

We do not know what are the necessary and sufficient conditions for consciousness in general or for particular conscious experiences. We do, however, know a little about the correlations between brain events and reports of experience. We know, for example, that more activity in the pain system means more intense pain. We might then wonder—will we one day be able to look into someone's brain and thereby know exactly what they are experiencing?

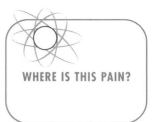

WHERE IS THIS PAIN?

Crick, F. (1994) *The Astonishing Hypothesis.* New York, Scribner. See pages 203–8.

Kanwisher, N. (2001) Neural events and perceptual awareness. *Cognition 79, 89–113.* Also reprinted in S. Dehaene (ed.) *The Cognitive Neuroscience of Consciousness.* Cambridge, MA, MIT Press, 89–113.

Ramachandran, V.S. and Blakeslee, S. (1998) *Phantoms in the Brain.* New York, Humphrey. See pages 39–62.

A good resource for a seminar is **Humphrey, N.** (2000) How to solve the mind–body problem. *Journal of Consciousness Studies 7, 5–20,* with commentaries (pages 21–97) and reply (pages 98–112). The target article is also reprinted in Humphrey (2002) *The Mind Made Flesh: Frontiers of Psychology and Evolution.* Oxford, Oxford University Press, pages 90–114. Each student can read one or two of the ten commentaries, for presentations or a group discussion.

The neural correlates of consciousness

CHAPTER SIXTEEN

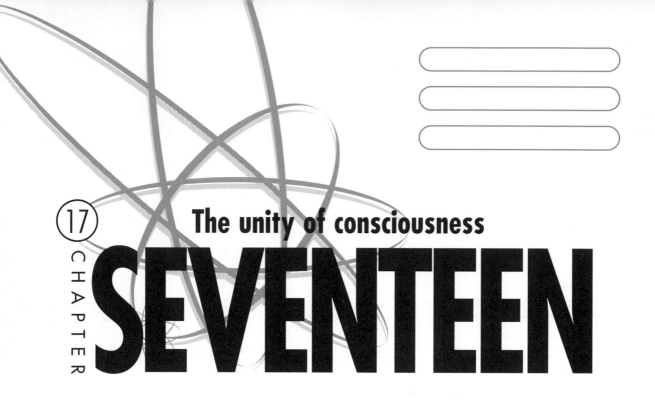

The unity of consciousness

SEVENTEEN

*Consciousness is
an integral thing
not made of parts.*

James, 1890

*" The unity of
consciousness is
illusory. "*

Hilgard, 1986: 1

Why do we seem to have only *one* consciousness? Why is consciousness, as James puts it, "an integral thing not made of parts," when the brain is such a massively parallel and complicated multi-tasking organ? Why do we feel as though there is just one conscious mind in here that is experiencing a unified world? This classic problem from philosophy takes on a new significance in the context of modern neuroscience (Cleeremans, 2003).

The problem is quite simple to state. When we look at the brain side of the great divide, we see nothing but complexity and diversity. At any given time, countless different processes are all going on at once, and in different areas. For example, right now your visual system is probably processing multiple inputs and dealing with color, motion and other features in different visual areas. At the same time, processing is going on in other sensory areas, in memory systems and in emotional systems. Thoughts are bubbling along, movements are being planned and coordinated and sentences are being constructed. All these diverse processes are linked up through multiple routes and connections, but as we have already seen (see Chapter 5), there is no single place in the brain where everything is brought together. All the parts just keep doing their different things all at once.

However, when we look at the mind side of the divide, things seem to be unified. It seems as though, right now, there is one "me" and one more or less continuous stream of experiences happening to me now. The German philosopher Thomas Metzinger claims that "One thing cannot be doubted from the first-person perspective: I always experience the wholeness of reality *now*" (Metzinger, 1995b: 429). He calls this living reality a "'phenomenal Holon,' an experientially present whole" (Metzinger, 1995b: 429). The question is, how can such unity arise from such diversity?

There are several aspects to the question of unity. One concerns the self. We might rephrase the question as "Why do I seem to be a single subject of experience, when there is no single self inside the brain?" This unity of the self applies both synchronically—I seem to be a unified self at any given moment—and diachronically—I seem to be the same self now as I was a few moments ago, and even a few years ago. We have already considered the nature of the experiencing self in Section 3. Here we will consider other aspects of the problem of unity. For example, how are the different features of objects brought together to make a single object (the binding problem)? How are the different senses brought together to make a unified experienced world (multi-sensory integration)? What happens when consciousness is more or less unified than normal (unusual experiences)?

Among the many theories about unity, a tempting, but ultimately unworkable, option is dualism. Dualists believe that consciousness is intrinsically unitary, each person having their own single consciousness that is quite different from their physical brain. Indeed it was partly the argument from unity that led Descartes to his dualism. The best (almost the only) modern example is that of Eccles, whose work on consciousness was largely motivated by the problem of the unity of experience (Eccles, 1965). His preferred solution was that "*the unity of conscious experience is provided by the self-conscious mind and not by the neural machinery of the liaison areas of the cerebral hemisphere*" (Popper and Eccles, 1977: 362). He argued that the mind plays an active role

> "*I cannot distinguish in myself any parts, but apprehend myself to be clearly one and entire.*"
>
> **Descartes**, 1641

PRACTICE
IS THIS EXPERIENCE UNIFIED?

As many times as you can every day, ask yourself, **"Is this experience a unity?"**

You might like to begin, as usual, by asking "Am I conscious now?" and then explore what you are conscious of, all the time attending to whether the experience is unified. You might try this: pay attention to your visual experience for a few seconds. Now switch attention to sounds. You will probably be aware of sounds that have been going on for some time. Have the sight and sound just become unified? What was going on before? What role does attention play in this? You can do the same with verbal thoughts and sensory experiences. Is your consciousness always unified? Is it now?

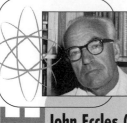

in selecting, reading out and integrating neural activity, molding it into a unified whole according to its desire or interest. The problem for Eccles, as with all dualist theories, is how this mind–brain interaction takes place. The theory provides no explanation of *how* the separate mind carries out its selecting and unifying tasks, and for this reason very few people accept this theory.

A far more constructive approach is to try to find out how the brain carries out the integrating and unifying functions, and the majority of the examples considered here are of this type. A third, and final, approach is to reject the idea that consciousness really is unified at all. Perhaps, on closer inspection, we might find that the apparent unity is illusory. In this case the task is to explain how we can possibly be so deluded.

THE BINDING PROBLEM

Take a coin, toss it and catch it again in your hand. How does this object, the coin, appear to you as it flies? You might like to toss it a few times and watch carefully. What do you see?

I assume that you see a single object fly up in the air, twist over and over and land in one piece on your hand. Bits don't fly off. The silver color doesn't depart from the shape, and the shape doesn't lag behind the motion. But why not?

Think now of what is happening in the visual system. Information extracted from a rich and rapidly changing image on the retina takes one route through the superior colliculus to the eye movement system and thereby controls your visual tracking of the moving coin. It also takes another route through the lateral geniculate to visual cortex. In V1 there are many retinotopic maps (that is, the organization of cells reflects the layout on the retina), and here the processing of edges, lines and other basic features of the image takes place. Other visual cortical areas are devoted to handling other aspects of the information, including color, movement and the form of objects. In these areas the original mapping is lost and features are dealt with regardless of where on the retina the image fell. In addition, different processes take different lengths of time. For example, auditory processing is faster than visual processing, and color is processed faster than form. Then there are the two major visual streams to consider, the dorsal stream controlling the fast action you needed to catch the coin deftly (if you did) and the ventral stream leading to perception. There is no single place and time at which everything comes together for the falling coin to be consciously perceived as one thing.

The problem described here needs to be distinguished from other aspects of the binding problem that are not related to consciousness (Revonsuo, 1999). The more general binding problem in cognitive science concerns how conjunctions of properties are represented, ranging from the binding of shape and color in detecting blue triangles or red squares, to the binding of words and phrases to their roles in sentences. Static binding, in which associations are learned over time, and which can be modeled in neural nets, does not concern us here. The problem for consciousness has more to do with dynamic binding occurring in real time. As the coin flips, what keeps the color, form, movements and other attributes of the coin together?

This problem is intimately bound up with both memory and attention. For example, try remembering entering your own front door. To do this successfully, lots of features have to be imagined at once: the color of the door, the flowers growing round it, the pile of rubbish in the corner, the key on its ring and the way you have to turn it. The result is a more or less unified memory of something you do every day, and all that information can be held

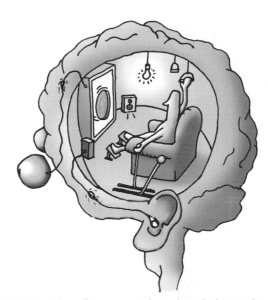

FIGURE 17.1 • Is there a flipping coin somewhere in the mind or brain? We know that the color, motion and shape of the coin are processed in different brain areas, but how are these features bound together to produce the single experience of a flipping coin? The binding problem cannot be solved by imagining that they are all brought together for display to an observer inside the brain.

briefly in working memory. As we have seen, some theories of consciousness, such as Global Workspace Theory, relate consciousness to working memory.

Some people argue that the binding problem is precisely the same problem as understanding how attention works. In this view, as long as you attend to the flipping coin or the image of the door, then their various attributes are bound together. When you think about something else, the diverse attributes fall apart, and the coin and the memory no longer exist as unified wholes in your consciousness.

There is evidence that attention is required for binding. For example, when people's attention is overloaded or diverted, they sometimes see illusory conjunctions—in other words, the wrong features are bound together. Bilateral damage to parietal cortex, which affects attention, can cause binding deficits, and in visual search tasks focused attention is necessary for finding unknown conjunctions. Anne Treisman, a British psychologist working at Princeton, interprets the relationship in terms of "feature integration theory" (Treisman and Gelade, 1980). When we attend to objects, temporary object files bind groups of features together on the basis of their spatial locations. For Treisman (2003) binding is central to conscious experience, and conscious access in perception is always to bound objects and events, not to free-floating features of those objects or events.

Other factors suggest that, closely related as they are, binding and attention cannot be the same thing. For example, binding is also required for tasks that are carried out unconsciously. Think of how you catch the coin. The fast visuo-motor control system in the dorsal stream has a complex computational task to carry out in real time. It must track the current speed and trajectory of the coin and direct your hand to the right place, with the right fingers in position, to catch the coin as it drops. For this task, at least the form and movement of the coin must be bound together with each other, not with the movement of some other object in the vicinity. If you swat away a fly, return a fast serve or avoid a puddle as you run down the road, the features of these objects must be well enough bound together to be treated as wholes. Yet you do all these things very fast and can do them quite unconsciously and without paying attention to them. There are obviously close relationships between attention, consciousness and binding, but just what sort of relationships is not yet clear.

BINDING BY SYNCHRONY

The best-known theory relating binding and consciousness is that proposed by Francis Crick and Christof Koch (1990). In the 1980s studies of the cat's visual cortex had revealed oscillations in the range of 35 to 75 hertz (i.e., 35–75 cycles per second), in which large numbers of neurons all fired in synchrony with one another. These are often referred to as "gamma oscillations" or (rather inaccurately) as 40-hertz oscillations. Christof von der Malsburg was the first to suggest that this coordinated firing might be the basis of visual binding, that is, that all the neurons dealing with attributes of a single object would bind these attributes together by firing in synchrony. Crick and Koch took the idea a stage further by suggesting that "this synchronized firing on, or near, the beat of a gamma oscillation (in the 35- to 75-Hertz range) *might be the neural correlate of visual awareness*" (Crick, 1994: 245).

They argued that "consciousness depends crucially on some form of rather short-term memory and also on some form of serial attentional mechanism" (Crick and Koch, 1990: 263). Building on this, they argued that the thalamus controls attention by selecting the features to be bound together by synchronization of firing. Crick concludes that "Consciousness . . . exists only if certain cortical areas have reverberatory circuits (involving cortical layers 4 and 6) that project strongly enough to produce significant reverberations" (Crick, 1994: 252).

For Crick this theory has implications for the evolution and function of consciousness. He

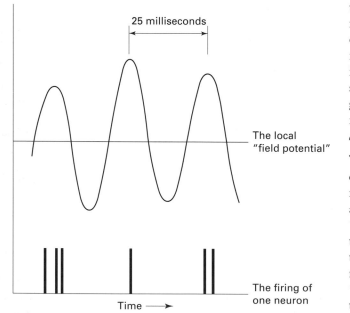

25 milliseconds

The local "field potential"

The firing of one neuron

Time →

FIGURE 17.2 • A simple figure to illustrate how some neurons fire in a 40-hertz rhythm. (A 40-hertz oscillation repeats every 25 milliseconds.) The smooth curve represents the local field potential. This is a measure of the average "activity" of many of the neurons in that neighborhood. The short vertical lines show the firing of just one neuron. Notice how, when this neuron fires, it fires "on the beat" of some of its neighbors, represented by the local field potential. (The usual sign convention for plotting the field potentials has been reversed.) (Caption from and figure after Crick, 1994) suggests that it may be more efficient for the brain to have "one single explicit representation," once and for all, rather than sending information, in tacit form, to many different parts of the brain. In other words, he makes a distinction between explicit and tacit (conscious and unconscious) information, and he thinks that the unity of consciousness is real and not illusory.

Subsequent research in animals has demonstrated that neuronal synchrony is related to perceptual integration, the construction of coherent representations, attentional selection and awareness. There is also evidence from humans. Using human scalp EEG, Catherine Tallon-Baudry and her colleagues in Lyon, France, showed that gamma oscillations were much stronger during feature binding tasks and in tasks in which subjects had to hold the representation of an object in short-term memory while searching a display than during control tasks (Tallon-Baudry and Bertrand, 1999). They also studied two patients who had electrodes implanted in extrastriate visual areas during their treatment for epilepsy. When these patients were asked to hold a visual image in mind while performing a matching task, visual areas separated by several centimeters became synchronized, with oscillations in the β range (15–25 Hz). They take these results to confirm Hebb's (1949) 50-year-old suggestion that short-term memory is sustained by reverberating activity in neuronal loops.

Dynamic binding by neural synchrony does not necessarily involve oscillations. Andreas Engel, Wolf Singer and their colleagues in Frankfurt, Germany, have been pursuing a somewhat different line (Engel et al., 1999a; Singer, 2000). In their model, objects are represented in the visual cortex by assemblies of synchronously firing neurons, although the synchronization may not be based on oscillations. For example, in Figure 17.3 the lady and her cat are each represented by one such assembly of cells. Each assembly consists of neurons that detect specific features of the objects, such as color, movement or orientation. The relationship between the many different features is then encoded by temporal correlation among the neurons. This means that neurons forming part of one represented object fire together, and they fire out of synchrony with neurons representing other objects at the same time. This allows for figure-ground segregation as well as for the rich representation of individual objects without confusion between them.

Note that this kind of synchrony may or may not use oscillations, whether at 40 hertz, or any other frequency. This proposal is not incompatible with Crick and Koch's theory, but it allows for many kinds of synchronized neural activity apart from that based on oscillations.

In support of this hypothesis, Engel and his colleagues review many studies showing that synchronization between cells occurs widely in both perceptual and motor systems, and report their own studies designed to find out whether this synchronization is functionally important. As one example, they used implanted electrodes to record from single cells in cats with strabismic amblyopia. These cats have a squint, which means that one eye is impaired in fixation, acuity and feature binding. Cells driven by the normal eye showed much stronger correlations than those driven by the amblyopic eye. They conclude

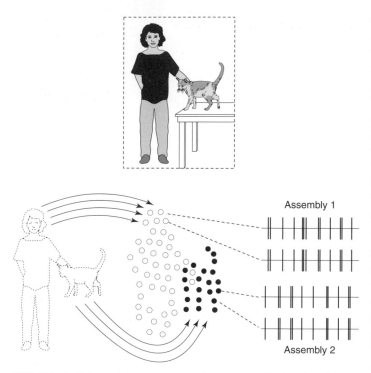

FIGURE 17.3 ● Establishment of coherent representational states by temporal binding. The model assumes that objects are represented in the visual cortex by assemblies of synchronously firing neurons. In this example, the lady and her cat would each be represented by one such assembly (indicated by open and filled symbols, respectively). These assemblies comprise neurons which detect specific features of visual objects (such as, for instance, the orientation of contour segments) within their receptive fields (lower left). The relationship between the features can then be encoded by the temporal correlation among these neurons (lower right). The model assumes that neurons which are part of the same assembly fire in synchrony, whereas no consistent temporal relation is found between cells belonging to different object representations (caption from and figure after Engel et al., 1999a, p. 131).

Assembly 1

Assembly 2

that arousal and selective attention are characterized by enhanced synchrony in the relevant populations of neurons, and that "temporal binding may indeed be a prerequisite for the access of information to phenomenal consciousness" (Engel et al., 1999a: 133). In their view, synchronization is necessary, but not sufficient, for consciousness. For consciousness, information must also enter short-term memory, a suggestion that brings the theory closer to Global Workspace Theories.

These theories all attempt to solve the binding problem in ways that are relevant to the unity of consciousness. But although they explain how selected information is held together to provide unified percepts, we may still wonder whether this accounts for subjectivity. Some of the phrases used imply Cartesian materialism: "the view that nobody espouses but almost everybody tends to think in terms of" (Dennett, 1991: 144). For example, Revonsuo talks about the "direct neural correlate of the content of phenomenal visual awareness" (1999: 183), Crick mentions a "single explicit representation," Engel et al. use the phrase "access to phenomenal consciousness" and Singer tries to account for the "inner-eye function" and how particular contents "reach the level of awareness" (2000: 134). Although they are all trying to explain phenomenal awareness (subjectivity, or "what it's like") in neural terms and without magic, the implication is that when unconscious information becomes unified it magically "enters consciousness." What this means remains unexplained.

MULTIPLE CONSCIOUSNESSES

All the theories of neural binding considered so far assume that the final result is not only unified conscious percepts but some kind of overall integration, or even a unified field of experience such as Metzinger's Holon. The very concept of the unity of consciousness is questioned by British neurobiologist Semir Zeki, who proposes instead that there are as many microconsciousnesses as there are processing nodes in a system, a view encountered with skepticism by Engel et al. (1999b). We have already met the idea that one brain might sustain more than one consciousness, such as in cases of multiple personality or split brains (see Chapter 7), but for Zeki a multiplicity of consciousnesses is the norm; the unification that comes with self-consciousness is an exception that is only possible through language.

Zeki (2001) describes the primate visual system as consisting of many separate, specialized systems, working in parallel, each of which is autonomous and reaches a perceptual end point at a different time. For example, the different attributes of an object, such as orientation, depth, facial expressions or shapes, are processed in different regions and at different speeds. Color (processed in V4 and V4∝) may be processed as much as 80 ms ahead of motion (processed in V5) (Zeki and Bartels, 1999). Thus some attributes must be perceived before others, even though we are not aware of this perceptual asynchrony. In Zeki's view, each of these separate cortical systems has its own conscious correlate.

These systems consist of many hierarchically organized nodes, and each node has multiple inputs and outputs, both cortical and subcortical. This multiplicity of connections, and the fact that no node is a recipient only, implies that "there is no terminal station in the cortex" (Zeki, 2001: 60–1), "no final integrator station in the brain" (Zeki and Bartels, 1999: 225), no "pontifical neuron" (James, 1890). Zeki explains that there is no need for microconsciousnesses to "be reported to a 'center' for consciousness, or a 'Cartesian Theater'" (Zeki, 2001: 69). "Visual consciousness is therefore distributed in space and time" (ibid.: 57).

Zeki's suggestion is not a form of panpsychism (the view that everything is conscious), and he does not claim that *all* neural processing is conscious. This means that he must still distinguish between the conscious and the unconscious processes. He speculates that neural activity remains implicit as long as it requires further processing; when processing is complete, it becomes explicit or conscious. He discusses people with blindsight (see Chapter 18) who report being conscious of aspects of early motion processing that would be implicit in normal people, and there are other similar effects with other kinds of brain damage. This leads Zeki to propose that "cells whose activity is only implicit can, in the right circumstances, become explicit. Put more boldly, cells can have double duties, rendering the incoming signals explicit or not, depending on the activity at the next node" (ibid.: 66).

So although Zeki firmly rejects any central terminus, or Cartesian theater, his theory is still a form of Cartesian materialism. Dennett describes Cartesian materialism as "the view that there is a crucial finish line or boundary somewhere in the brain, marking a place where the order of arrival equals the order of 'presentation' in experience because *what happens there* is what you are conscious of" (Dennett, 1991: 107). Zeki's finishing line is the point at which information that was previously "implicit" is "rendered explicit" or conscious. This process of "rendering" remains unexplained and essentially mysterious.

MULTISENSORY INTEGRATION

All the theories considered so far have concentrated on vision, perhaps because the visual system is much better understood than many other parts of

IS THIS EXPERIENCE UNIFIED?

"I am one *person living in* one *world."*

Metzinger, 1995a: 127

SYNESTHESIA

"What a crumbly, yellow voice you have," said S. "To this day I can't escape from seeing colors when I hear sounds. What first strikes me is the color of someone's voice."

S. was the famous "mnemonist," or memory man, described by the great Russian psychologist Aleksandr Romanovich Luria. S. could remember vast tables of numbers, or learn poems in languages he did not understand, and repeat them without error many years later, yet his life was very difficult. He could not hold down a job, found communication difficult and could not forget the pains of his childhood. Every sight, sound or touch set off experiences in every other sense too, "for S. there was no distinct line, as there is for others of us, separating vision from hearing, or hearing from a sense of touch or taste" (Luria, 1968: 27). S. was a synesthete, perhaps one of the most complex synesthetes ever described.

In synesthesia, events in one sensory modality induce vivid experiences in another. In the most common form, written

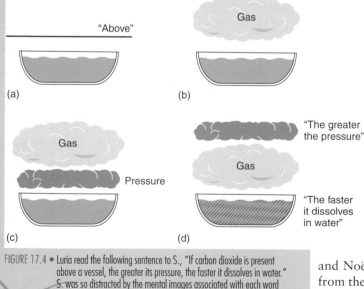

FIGURE 17.4 • Luria read the following sentence to S., "If carbon dioxide is present above a vessel, the greater its pressure, the faster it dissolves in water." S. was so distracted by the mental images associated with each word that he could not understand this simple rule (after Luria, 1968).

the brain. However, we must not forget that binding has to occur between the senses as well as within them. This is not a trivial matter, not least because the senses are so different. For example, while vision depends largely on spatial analysis, hearing uses temporal analysis. How are these two very different processes integrated?

Think of the way you turn your head and eyes to look straight at someone who calls your name, or the way that the smell and touch and sight of the sandwich in your hand all seem to belong to the same object. Or think of a cat out hunting. It listens to the rustling in the undergrowth, creeps carefully between the leaves, feeling its way with its whiskers, spies the poor vole and pounces. As we saw in Chapter 12, snakes need surprisingly little multisensory integration, but cats and rats construct a spatial map around themselves in which information from their eyes, ears, whiskers and paws is all integrated. When information from both sight and sound comes from the same position, then responses are enhanced, and information from one sense can affect responses to another sense in many ways (Stein et al., 2001).

Multisensory integration depends on neurons responding to input from more than one sense. Although such multisensory neurons are found in many areas of the brain, the most important area is the superior colliculus in the midbrain. Cells here may respond to more than one sense even at birth, but their multisensory capacity increases with experience and with increasing connections into the cortex. We should also note the odd fact that, for most of us, the senses remain easily distinguishable. That is, we are not confused as to whether we heard, saw or touched something. This ability is not as obvious as it may seem because all the senses work by using the same kinds of neural impulses. So some explanation is needed for why they are experienced as so distinct (O'Regan and Noë, 2001). Perhaps we can learn something from the phenomenon of synesthesia, in which the senses are not so distinct. Many people can remember that as children they sometimes heard smells or tasted sounds, and in some people this mixing of the senses remains part of their lifelong experience.

Multisensory integration makes possible a world in which objects can be recognized as the same thing, whether they are touched, seen, tasted or heard. But just how this kind of integration gives rise to the subjective sense of existing in one world, or to Metzinger's "phenomenal Holon," remains to be seen.

REENTRY AND THE DYNAMIC CORE

The unity of consciousness is the starting point for Edelman and Tononi's theory (2000a; 2000b). They set out to explain two key features of consciousness, "that each conscious state is an indivisible whole and, at the same time, that each person can choose among an immense number of different conscious states" (Edelman and Tononi, 2000b: 139). That is, they want to explain both the integration or unity of consciousness, and its differentiation or complexity.

"Consciousness abhors holes or discontinuities" they say (Edelman and Tononi, 2000b: 141). It remains inherently unified and coherent, even in brain-damaged patients who deny their own paralysis or blindness (see Chapter 18) and in split-brain patients who report no halving of their vision or splitting of their awareness (see Chapter 7). Yet at the same time consciousness is extraordinarily informative. What makes a conscious state informative is not how many chunks of information it appears to contain but the fact that it is just one of potentially billions of other possible states. Think of how many people you have seen in your lifetime, or how many paintings or how many frames from movies, and you will begin to appreciate how many different conscious states are possible. This is a vast amount of information, for you can discriminate between all these states and each state has different behavioral consequences.

According to their theory of reentry by neuronal group selection (see Chapter 11), consciousness depends upon ongoing, recursive, highly parallel signaling

letters or numbers are seen as colored, but people can hear shapes, see touches or even have colored orgasms. In "The man who tasted shapes," American neurologist Richard Cytowic (1993) describes how a chicken sauce set off his research on synesthesia. One day, while cooking, his friend Michael blurted out "there aren't enough points on the chicken," and then, hoping that no one else had heard, had to explain what he meant.

Many synesthetes hide their special abilities, and it is difficult to know how common synesthesia is. In the 1880s Galton estimated it at 1 in 20, whereas modern estimates range from 1 in 200 to 1 in 100,000 (Baron-Cohen and Harrison, 1997). Synesthesia runs in families, is more common in left-handers, is six times more common in females than males and is associated with improved memory but poorer math and spatial ability. It is especially prevalent among poets, writers and artists. The experiences cannot be consciously suppressed, and when tested after many years most synesthetes report that exactly the same shapes or forms or colors are induced by the same stimuli.

Synesthesia has often been dismissed as fantasy, overly concrete use of metaphor or as exaggerated childhood memory, but none of these ideas can explain the phenomena. In several experiments Ramachandran and Hubbard (2001) aimed to show that synesthesia is a true perceptual rather than cognitive phenomenon. They showed that the induced colors can lead to pop-out in complex displays, allowing synesthetes to detect concealed shapes, such as triangles or squares, more easily than controls. This showed that the synesthetes were not confabulating and that the phenomenon is more than mere memory for associations.

Among more recent theories, Cytowic emphasizes the connection with emotions and the limbic system, while Ramachandran suggests that shape—color synesthesia is caused by a mutation that causes cross-activation between visual areas (especially V4 and V8) and the number area, which lie close together in the fusiform gyrus.

within and between areas of the thalamus and cortex. This makes sense of Libet's findings that although a behavioral response to thalamic stimulation can occur very quickly, it takes about half a second of activity to produce a conscious experience. According to Edelman and Tononi, this time is required for the functional closure of long reentrant loops and reentrant interactions between distant regions of the brain. Activity in such long loops is necessary for consciousness but not sufficient. For example, consciousness does not occur in states of global synchrony, such as deep sleep or epileptic seizures, but requires the potential for a rich and diverse repertoire of different neural patterns. Consciousness requires complexity as well as integration.

They distinguish two types of consciousness. First, there is primary consciousness, which many animals have and which allows for the construction of a scene, the maintenance of short-term memory and hence a "remembered present." This entails the construction of functional clusters, defined by the fact that connections within the cluster are stronger than those outside it. These clusters can depend on interactions between widely separated areas and make possible the integration of different features of the same object that are processed in different parts of the brain. Based on this theory, they have built

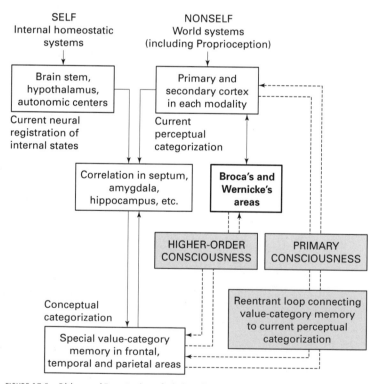

FIGURE 17.5 • Edelman and Tononi's scheme for higher-order consciousness. A new reentrant loop appears during the evolution of hominids and the emergence of language. The acquisition of a new kind of memory via semantic capabilities and ultimately language leads to a conceptual explosion. As a result, concepts of the self, the past and the future can be connected to primary consciousness. Consciousness of consciousness becomes possible (after Edelman and Tononi, 2000a, p. 194).

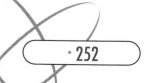

large-scale computer models of cortical integration which can be trained to solve conjunction problems such as discriminating a red cross from a green cross and a red square. They conclude that "These simulations revealed how reentry can solve the binding problem by coupling neuronal responses of distributed cortical areas to achieve synchronization and global coherence" (Edelman and Tononi, 2000a: 119).

Then there is higher-order consciousness, which emerged later in evolution, and depends on re-entrant connections between language and conceptual systems. This allows for the construction of a "dynamic core" and a coherent self operating with a system of values. The dynamic core is a large functional cluster that is always changing, but maintains continuity and integration through its many reentrant loops. The vital connections are within the core, and a boundary is maintained by the relative lack of connections to the rest of the system.

At different times the dynamic core can involve completely different brain areas, leaving others still active but not part of the core. Some support for this hypothesis is provided by studies of binocular rivalry in which Edelman and Tononi looked for coherence between brain areas. They measured coherence between distant brain regions that responded to a stimulus and found higher coherence when the subject was aware of the stimulus than when he was not.

The dynamic core hypothesis avoids the need for any particular area, or type of neuron, or special firing rate mysteriously to be conscious while others are not. Instead, if we ask what the difference is between neural activity that contributes to consciousness and that which does not, the answer is that it depends whether that activity is or is not part of the dynamic core at that time. Consciousness is not a property of brain cells as such, but of the dynamic interactions of the continually changing core, although how this accounts for subjectivity is not clear. Note that this hypothesis has much in common with Global Workspace Theories, for example, both involve short-term memory and depend on a distributed

(Activity continues on page 255)

ACTIVITY
Are you a synesthete?

If you have a large class, or other group of people that you can easily test, you can ask people whether they ever experience one sense in response to another, or whether they used to do so as a child. Some people can describe vivid memories of seeing colored music, or experiencing tastes and smells as having a particular shape, even though they can no longer do so. You may find people who claim all sorts of extravagant associations and florid experiences. Here are two simple tests that might help detect whether they are making it up or not

1. RETESTING ASSOCIATIONS

This test needs to be done over two separate sessions, without telling participants that they will be retested. In the first session read out, slowly, a list of numbers in random order (e.g., 9, 5, 7, 2, 8, 1, 0, 3, 4, 6) and a list of letters (e.g., T, H, D, U, C, P, W, A, G, L). Ask your group to visualize each letter or number and write down what color they associate with it. Some will immediately know what color each number is, while others may say they are just making up arbitrary associations. Either way they must write down a color.

Collect their answers and keep them. In a second session (say a week or several weeks later), read out the same letters and numbers but in a different order (e.g., 6, 3, 8, 1, 0, 9, 2, 4, 5, 7 and P, C, A, L, T, W, U, H, D, G) and again ask them to write down an associated color. Give them back their previous answers and ask them to check (or to check a neighbor's) and count how many answers are the same. True synesthetes will answer almost identically every time they are tested.

2. POP-OUT SHAPES

Tell the group that you will show them a pattern in which a simple shape is hidden. When they see the shape, they are to shout out "Now." Emphasize that they must *not* say the name of the shape and give the game away, but must just shout "Now." As soon dynamic process. However, there is an important difference. In GWTs the contents of the workspace are conscious because they are displayed or made available to the rest of the system. In the dynamic core hypothesis there is no equivalent of this theater-like display or global availability.

UNITY AS ILLUSION

Escaping completely from Cartesian materialism is very difficult. This is why there is a hard problem. One potential way forward is to drop the idea that the unity of consciousness is about unifying representations or experiences, and think instead in terms of unity of action. British biophysicist Rodney Cotterill says

I believe that the problem confronted during evolution of complex organisms like ourselves was not to unify conscious experience but rather to avoid destroying the unity that Nature provided. . . .
singleness of action is a vital requirement; if motor responses were not unified, an animal could quite literally tear itself apart!

(Cotterill, 1995: 301)

He concludes that consciousness arises through an interaction between brain, body and environment.

In a similar vein, Humphrey asks what makes the parts of a person belong together—if and when they do. Although Humphrey himself may be made up of many different selves, he concludes that

these selves have come to belong together as the one Self that I am because they are engaged in one and the same enterprise: the enterprise of steering me—body and soul—through the physical and social world. . . . my selves have become co-conscious through collaboration.

(Humphrey, 2002: 12)

British philosopher Susan Hurley (1998) rejects the conventional idea of consciousness as a filling in the "Classical Sandwich" between input and output or perception and action. Instead she emphasizes that perception, action and environment are intimately intertwined. The unity of consciousness arises from a dynamic stream of low-level causal processes and multiple feedback loops linking input and output in an organism she describes as a loosely centered "dynamical singularity" with no clear external boundaries.

These views are all versions of enactive, or action, theories of consciousness. They treat consciousness

SELF-ASSESSMENT QUESTIONS

◉ What is meant by "the unity of consciousness"? Why is it a problem?

◉ Describe the binding problem(s).

◉ What is the relationship between binding and attention?

◉ Describe two theories of binding by neural synchrony.

◉ Explain Zeki's theory of microconsciousnesses.

◉ How does Edelman and Tononi's theory account for unity and diversity?

◉ What is synesthesia, and how can it be tested?

as a kind of acting or doing, rather than a kind of perceiving or receiving of information. In such theories, being conscious means interacting with the world, or reaching out to the world. This shifts the burden of explanation away from trying to explain how the contents of consciousness are unified, for it is obvious that a single organism, whether an amoeba or a man, has to have unified action. The tricky part is now to understand how action can *feel* like something. This is tackled most directly by sensorimotor theory (O'Regan and Noë, 2001: Chapter 6) in which the *feeling* of sensations comes about when we are in the process of acting; being conscious is manipulating the contingencies between the external world and what we can do with it.

Finally, some people reject the notion that consciousness is unified at all. James asked of consciousness "does it only seem continuous to itself by an illusion?" (1890, i: 200). We have already considered theories that treat the stream of conscious vision as an illusion. Could the apparent unity of consciousness be an illusion too? This question is complicated by the fact that whenever we ask ourselves, "Am I conscious now?" the answer always seems to be "Yes." We cannot catch ourselves *not* being conscious, and when we do find ourselves being conscious, there seems to be one me, and one unified experience. But what is it like the rest of the time?

One possibility is that there is nothing it is like most of the time (Blackmore, 2002). Rather, there are multiple parallel streams of processing going on, as in Dennett's theory of multiple drafts. None of these is "in" consciousness or "out" of consciousness; none has a magic extra something that the others lack; none has been rendered explicit or brought into consciousness. Then, every so often, we ask, "Am I conscious now?" or "What am I conscious of?" or in some other way we inquire into what is going on. Then, and only then, is a temporary stream of consciousness concocted, making it seem as though we have been conscious all along. At these times, recent events from memory are brought together by paying attention to them, and the appearance of a unified self having unified experiences is created. As soon as attention lapses, the unity falls apart and things carry on as normal. Just as the fridge door is usually closed, so we are

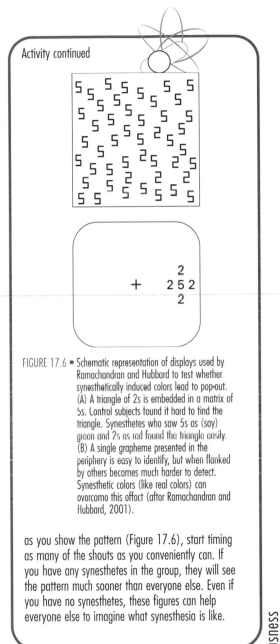

Activity continued

FIGURE 17.6 ● Schematic representation of displays used by Ramachandran and Hubbard to test whether synesthetically induced colors lead to pop-out. (A) A triangle of 2s is embedded in a matrix of 5s. Control subjects found it hard to find the triangle. Synesthetes who saw 5s as (say) green and 2s as red found the triangle easily. (B) A single grapheme presented in the periphery is easy to identify, but when flanked by others becomes much harder to detect. Synesthetic colors (like real colors) can overcome this effect (after Ramachandran and Hubbard, 2001).

as you show the pattern (Figure 17.6), start timing as many of the shouts as you conveniently can. If you have any synesthetes in the group, they will see the pattern much sooner than everyone else. Even if you have no synesthetes, these figures can help everyone else to imagine what synesthesia is like.

usually in a state of parallel multiple drafts. Only when we briefly open the door is the illusion created that the light is always on.

SUPERUNITY AND DISUNITY

Perhaps we may learn something about the unity of consciousness by studying unusual cases such as the superunity of synesthesia, in which people hear sounds in color, see shapes in tastes, or listen to touches on their skin. Then there are situations in which the unity of consciousness is lost. We have already considered some of the more dramatic instances, such as multiple personality and fugues, and the effects of splitting the brain by cutting the corpus callosum (see Chapter 7). Other examples include out-of-body and near-death experiences, in which consciousness seems to be separated from the physical body, and mediumship, trances and hypnosis in which consciousness can seem to be divided (see Chapters 23, 24). Examples like these led Hilgard (1986) to his neo-dissociation theory according to which consciousness is frequently divided. Although many people assume that consciousness is necessarily unified, there are plenty of reasons for doubt.

READING

Edelman, G.M. and Tononi, G. (2000b) Reentry and the dynamic core: neural correlates of conscious experience. In T. Metzinger (ed.) *Neural Correlates of Consciousness.* Cambridge, Mass., MIT Press, 139–51.

Engel, A.K., Fries, P., König, P., Brecht, M. and Singer, W. (1999) Temporal binding, binocular rivalry, and consciousness. *Consciousness and Cognition* 8, 128–51.

Ramachandran, V.S. and Hubbard, E.M. (2001) Synesthesia—a window into perception, thought and language. *Journal of Consciousness Studies* 8, 3–34.

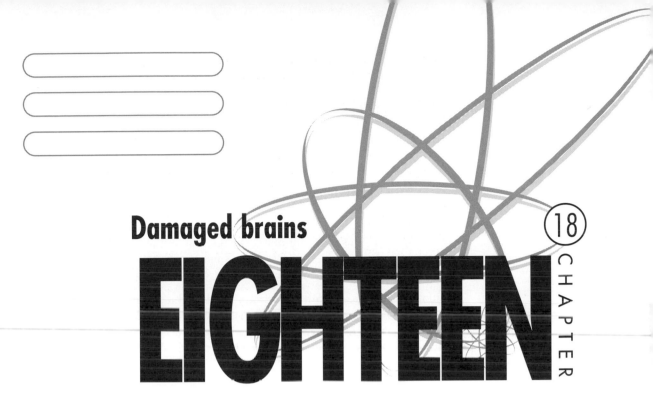

Damaged brains

EIGHTEEN

What is it like not to notice that you don't notice half the world? What is it like to be blind but believe that you can see, or to be paralyzed but convinced that you can move? What is it like to be suspended in the present moment with no memory? These, and many other questions, are prompted by the neuropsychological changes caused by brain damage. Here we will consider just three examples that have particular relevance to consciousness.

PRACTICE
IS THIS EXPERIENCE PERCEPTION OR MEMORY?

As many times as you can, every day, ask yourself, **"Is this perception or memory?"**

Starting with immediate sensory experience, you can investigate how much of what you are experiencing now would change if you had no memory, no words or labels to attach to things and no learned associations. Is consciousness possible at all without memory? Look! Write down your answer—"Yes" or "No."

AMNESIA

"What year is this, Mr. G.?" asked the neurologist Oliver Sacks (1985).

"Forty-five, man. What do you mean?" he went on, "We've won the war . . . There are great times ahead."

"And you, Jimmie, how old would you be?"

"Why, I guess I'm nineteen, Doc."

Sacks then had an impulse for which he never forgave himself. He took a mirror and showed the 49-year-old gray-haired man his own face. Jimmie G. became frantic, gripping the sides of his chair and demanding to know what was going on. Sacks led him quietly to the window where he saw some kids playing baseball outside. He started to smile and Sacks stole away. When he returned a few minutes later, Jimmie G. greeted him as a complete stranger.

Jimmie G. had Korsakoff's syndrome, and nothing can be done to restore memory in such cases. Jimmie's amnesia was "a pit into which everything, every experience, every event, would fathomlessly drop, a bottomless memory-hole that would engulf the whole world" (Sacks, 1985: 34).

Korsakoff's is the most common form of amnesic syndrome, and is caused by the toxic effects of alcohol, as well as thiamine deficiency caused by malnutrition in heavy drinkers. It typically involves specific destruction of the mamillary bodies and the dorso-medial nucleus of the thalamus, as well as other more diffuse damage to frontal lobes. As is typical in these cases, Jimmie G. suffered from two kinds of amnesia. First, there is anterograde amnesia, which is the inability to form new long-term memories. Short-term memory remains intact, with patients gaining normal scores on tests. This means it is possible to talk, play games, do calculations (as long as they can be done relatively quickly), remember a phone number long enough to dial it and even do certain kinds of work, but as soon as thoughts or perceptions leave working memory, they are gone. The patient is isolated in a very brief present.

Second, there is retrograde amnesia, which is a loss of long-term memory that stretches back into the past. This also occurs after accidents, concussion or trauma, in which case there is usually a period of blank memory for the accident itself, and for a variable time before. This blank period sometimes shrinks with recovery. In Jimmie G.'s case his retrograde amnesia stretched back to the end of the war, even though he had remained in the Navy until 1965, and was only hospitalized with alcoholic delirium in 1970. In Korsakoff's syndrome, episodic memory (that is, memory for the events of one's life) remains perfectly good for the far past, before the blank period, but no new episodic memories are laid down.

Although this may sound like a complete loss of all memory, it is not. Classical conditioning remains unimpaired so that patients easily learn to blink to a sound if it is paired with a puff to the eye, to associate certain smells with lunchtime, or to respond to a given visitor with pleasure, even if they claim never to have seen that person before. Procedural learning also remains intact. Not only do amnesics frequently retain such skills as driving a car or typing, but they can learn new ones as well. They might, for example, learn to control a computer mouse, improving at every session while denying they have ever encountered such a gadget before.

This was true of H.M., the most famous case of amnesic syndrome. H.M. was a young engineer who suffered from intractable temporal lobe epilepsy. In 1956, when all other treatments had failed, he had parts of both temporal lobes including both hippocampi removed, leaving him with devastating and permanent memory loss. In the 1960s he was trained to follow a moving target with a pointer and to do mirror writing, skills at which he rapidly improved while denying that he had ever done them before. He also showed evidence of priming: getting quicker at recognizing fragmented pictures and completing words if they had been shown before, even though he could not consciously remember having seen them. For this reason, amnesic syndrome is sometimes described as a dissociation between performance and consciousness (Farthing, 1992; Young, 1996).

Are amnesics conscious? Surely the answer is yes. They are awake, responsive, able to converse, laugh and show emotion. But who is conscious? Without the capacity to lay down new memories, their self is a person trapped in the past, unrelated to the events and people of the present. They have lost the interaction between current and stored information that, according to Weiskrantz (1997), makes possible the "commentary" that underlies conscious experience. Some amnesics repeatedly exclaim, "I have just woken up!" or "I have just become conscious for the first time!" C.W. was a professional musician struck with dense amnesia by herpes simplex encephalitis (Wilson and Wearing, 1995). Although he could still sight-read music, extemporize, and even conduct his choir, his episodic memory was almost completely destroyed. He kept a diary of what was happening to him and there he recorded, hundreds of times, over a period of nine years, that he was now fully conscious, as if he had just woken from a long illness. He was conscious all right, but trapped in an ephemeral present, unconnected with the past.

Asking amnesics about such matters is difficult. As Sacks puts it

> If a man has lost a leg or an eye, he knows he has lost a leg or an eye; but if he has lost a self—himself—he cannot know it, because he is no longer there to know it.
>
> (Sacks, 1985: 34)

Amnesics create no memory of a continuous self who lives their life, or, as some would say, no illusion of a continuous self who lives their life.

Amnesia will come to many of us, and to our parents and loved ones, in the form of Alzheimer's or senile dementia. In this form it is less specific and comes on gradually. For some time the person may have enough memory to realize their predicament, which makes it all the harder. Yet, as the Russian psychologist Luria pointed out to Sacks, "a man does not consist of memory

Antonio Damasio (b. 1944)

Until confronted by patients with frontal lobe damage, Antonio Damasio accepted the traditional view that "sound decisions came from a cool head" and that reason and emotion are separate. Since then much of his work has suggested the opposite. According to his "somatic marker" hypothesis, the ability to feel emotions is intrinsic to rationality and decision making, and is closely bound up with dynamic, on-line representations of what is happening in the body. In *Descartes' Error* (1994) he explains that the mistake was to tear body and mind apart. In *The Feeling of What Happens* (1999) he distinguishes between core consciousness and extended consciousness, and between the proto-self, core self and autobiographical self. He claims that the conscious mind and its private, subjective experiences are not illusions but real entities that must be investigated as such. Born in Portugal, Damasio is Van Allen Professor and Head of Neurology at the University of Iowa College of Medicine, and Adjunct Professor at the Salk Institute.

alone. He has feeling, will, sensibilities, moral being—matters of which neuropsychology cannot speak" (Sacks, 1985: 32).

NEGLECT

How would you react if you had a stroke that left you paralyzed on one side of your body? Perhaps you would feel frustrated, frightened or depressed, or perhaps you would try to be brave and immediately start finding ways to cope. It is much harder to imagine that you might not think there was anything wrong, yet this is what happens in anosagnosia (Damasio, 1999; Weiskrantz, 1997).

A patient who is completely paralyzed down his left side may say that he can move perfectly well if he wants to, while making excuses for not trying to get out of bed. Another may readily explain that she is paralyzed on one side yet still ask for her knitting needles to give her something to do. Part of their mind seems to know the facts, while another part does not. Psychoanalytic theories interpret the denial as psychologically motivated or as a coping strategy based on childhood experiences, but this does not fit the facts. For example, anosagnosia only occurs with damage to particular parts of the right parietal lobe and not with damage to the left. Damasio (1999) describes it as leaving "core consciousness" intact while damaging the "extended consciousness" that goes beyond the here and now, and at its height is uniquely human. The connections between autobiographical memory and the body representation based in the right parietal lobe are destroyed, and this affects the core self as well.

Perhaps the most extreme example of such denial is Anton's syndrome, first described in 1899. Patients with Anton's syndrome are blind and yet insist that they can see. When they bump into things, as they frequently must, they confabulate, inventing an ingenious range of excuses rather than concluding that they are blind. Sacks describes one completely blind man who acknowledged that his eyes were not all that good but said that he enjoyed watching television. Watching television, for him, meant listening attentively and inventing scenes to go along with the soundtrack. "He seemed to think, indeed, that this was what 'seeing' meant, that this was what was meant by 'watching TV,' and that this is what all of us did" (Sacks, 1992: 188).

You might be wondering what such people are experiencing. Surely, you might think, they must either be seeing a blank darkness in front of them (like a seeing person does with their eyes closed), or they must be hallucinating and seeing things that are not there. If you think this way, you may be imagining that there must always be *something* on the screen in the Cartesian theater. If so, it is worth remembering James's unnoticed "gaps" and the troublesome case of filling in the blind spot (see Chapter 6). As we saw, there may be no need for the blind spot to be filled in. As Dennett put it, there is a lack of "epistemic hunger" in that part of the visual field. There are no neurons corresponding to that spot saying "tell me what's there." Perhaps Anton's syndrome is more like this than like ordinary blindness. When I shut my eyes, the expected information is missing so I see a blank darkness, but if I had no neurons to expect the information, then there would be no sign that anything was missing (there would be an absence of information rather than information about an absence). Perhaps this is what Sacks meant when he said of his blind patient, "Thus he had apparently lost the very idea of seeing."

Some people do not lose their sight, but instead lose half their world. In the phenomenon of hemifield neglect, or unilateral neglect, patients seem not to realize that the left-hand side of the world even exists (Bisiach, 1992). Like anosagnosia, hemifield neglect occurs only with right-brain damage. After a stroke to the right hemisphere, one woman applies make-up only to the right side of her face, and eats only from the right side of her plate. A man shaves only the right side of his beard, and sees only the right side of a photograph.

Many tests reveal the peculiarities of this condition. When asked to copy a drawing of a flower, some patients accurately copy the right half, while others squash all the petals onto the right side. When asked to draw a clock face, some just leave out the left half, while others squash all the numbers onto the right; either way they do not draw a complete face. When asked to draw maps, they may distort them so as to squeeze important cities or landmarks into just one side. And when asked to bisect a horizontal line, they typically mark it far to the right of the mid-point, suggesting that they do not see the left-hand part of the line. However, it is not as though they have lost half their vision, which would be simple enough, but that they have lost something much more fundamental.

In Milan, Italian neurologist Edoardo Bisiach asked his neglect patients to imagine that they

"*without direct experience we will never know what is it like to be a patient affected by unilateral neglect*"

Bisiach, 1988: 117

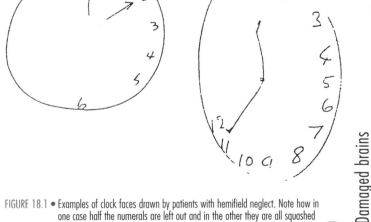

FIGURE 18.1 • Examples of clock faces drawn by patients with hemifield neglect. Note how in one case half the numerals are left out and in the other they are all squashed around onto one side of the clock face. (Marshall and Halligan, 1993)

Damaged brains **CHAPTER EIGHTEEN**

were standing in the beautiful cathedral square. First, he asked them to imagine standing at one side, facing the fantastic Duomo with its pinnacles and magnificent façade, and to describe what they saw. They knew the piazza well and described the buildings that would lie to their right if they were standing in that position, leaving out all those on the left. But they had not forgotten the very existence of those on the left. When asked to imagine standing on the other side, facing the other way, they described all the buildings they had previously left out (Bisiach and Luzzatti, 1978).

Hemifield neglect can partly be explained as a deficit of attention, in that patients simply do not attend to, or have their attention drawn to, the left-hand side of their world, and to some extent they can be helped by training them to keep turning from side to side, like a lighthouse. Yet clearly the unattended side is not completely blanked out. Emotional stimuli shown in the neglected field can influence attention, and stimuli that are not consciously seen can prime later responses. In one experiment patients were shown two pictures of a house, identical except that one had flames pouring from a window on the left-hand side. While insisting that the houses were identical, patients still said they would prefer to live in the one that was not on fire (Marshall and Halligan, 1988). Although subsequent studies have shown rather different results for the house test, the conclusion remains that stimuli that are not consciously seen can still affect behavior.

FIGURE 18.2 ● The figure used to test covert processing in a patient with neglect of the left half of visual space (Marshall and Halligan, 1988). The patient claimed that the figures looked identical. Yet when asked which house she would prefer to live in she chose the bottom one, although she said she was just guessing. In the original, the fire in the top figure was colored red.

Weiskrantz describes it this way: "The subject may not 'know' it, but some part of the brain does" (Weiskrantz, 1997: 26), but perhaps this implies a unitary, superordinate "subject" who watches the workings of the lower mechanisms. According to Bisiach (1988) there is no such entity, for the task of monitoring inner activity is distributed throughout the brain. When lower-level processors are damaged, higher ones may notice, but when the higher ones are gone, there is nothing to notice the lack.

Bisiach (1988) claims that we can never know what it is like to suffer neglect, but perhaps we already do. Remembering the snakes, and the fish in the garden pond (see Chapter 12), it is easy to accept that we neither see in the infra-red nor notice its absence. In this sense we all live our lives in a profound state of neglect.

BLINDSIGHT

Imagine the following experiment. The subject is D.B., a patient who has had a small non-malignant brain tumor removed. The tumor had encroached into area V1 and, since input from the right visual field goes to the left visual brain and vice versa, removal of V1 on one side left him blind on the other (a condition called hemianopia). If he looks straight ahead and an object is placed on his blind side, he cannot see it.

In the experiment D.B. is shown a circle filled with black and white stripes in his normal field. Naturally enough he says he can easily tell whether the stripes are vertical or horizontal. Now he is shown the same thing in his blind field. He says he can see neither the circle nor the stripes, for he is blind there. Even so, the experimenters encourage him to guess which way the stripes go. He protests that this is pointless, because he cannot see anything, but nevertheless he guesses. He is right 90 or 95 percent of the time.

"Blindsight" is the oxymoronic term invented for this strange phenomenon by Oxford neuropsychologist Lawrence Weiskrantz. Together with neuropsychologist Elizabeth Warrington, he tested D.B. from the early 1970s for 10 years or more (Weiskrantz, 1986; 1997). Since then many other blindsight patients have been tested, the most famous of whom is G.Y., who suffered traumatic head injury in a car accident when he was eight years old. Most "blindseers" (as we may call them) have extensive damage to visual striate cortex on one side, which causes degeneration of cells

> **ACTIVITY**
> **Blind for an hour**
>
> This is a simple exercise designed to give a hint of what it is like to be blind. You need to work in pairs and can take turns to be blindfolded or to be the guide. You need a good blindfold that does not allow you to peek. It is possible just to wear dark glasses and to keep your eyes closed, but the temptation to open them is too great for most people, so a blindfold is easier.
>
> Take an hour for the exercise and plan what you will do. For example, you might go shopping, or take a walk, or go to a party or visit friends. Try to do as much as you can without help, but be careful to avoid dangerous activities such as cooking. Your guide must take responsibility for crossing roads and other obvious dangers, and should stay close to you all the time.
>
> Afterward, think about what surprised you. Which things were easier or more difficult than you had expected? What happened in social situations?
>
> If you are blind, this exercise is no use to you, but you can be of great help to others. You might teach them to use a long cane, or discuss the ways in which you cope without vision.
>
> For a devastating and insightful description of what it is like to go blind, see Hull (1990).

FIGURE 18.3 • Which way do the stripes go? When such a display was shown to the blind field of a subject with hemianopia (blind on one side), he said he could see nothing at all. Yet when pressed to guess, he was able to discriminate vertical from horizontal stripes with over 90% accuracy. This is how the term "blindsight" originated (after Weiskrantz, 1997).

down through the lateral geniculate and even to the retina, while other, non-cortical visual pathways are left intact. Other similar phenomena such as "deaf hearing," "blindsmell" and "numbsense" have added to the cases in which people deny having conscious sensory experiences and yet behave as though they can see, hear, smell or feel (Weiskrantz, 1997).

Blindsight seems to be tailor-made for resolving philosophical arguments about consciousness. Yet it has not done so. Blindsight has been used to support qualia and to reject them, to bolster zombies and to undermine them, and to support controversial distinctions between different kinds of consciousness (Block, 1995; Dennett, 1991; Holt, 1999). The arguments have been so long and fierce that it is worth considering blindsight in some detail.

What is going on? Superficially, the most obvious interpretation goes something like this. The blindseer has vision without consciousness. He is an automaton or a partial zombie who can "see" functionally but has none of the visual qualia that go with normal seeing. This proves that consciousness is something separate from the ordinary processes of vision. It proves that qualia exist and functionalism is wrong.

FIGURE 18.4 • The blindsight subject has to be pressed to guess the orientation of a line he cannot see. Yet his guesses can be very accurate. Is he a partial zombie who has vision without conscious vision?

If it were valid, this line of reasoning would have many other implications. For example, it would hold out the hope of finding the place in the brain where "consciousness happens," the place where visual qualia are produced or where representations "enter consciousness." We would know, for example, that qualia happen in V1 while all the rest of vision goes on elsewhere. This would encourage speculations about the evolution of consciousness, for if we have qualia *as well as* vision, then there must be some extra function for consciousness.

But this apparently natural way of thinking about blindsight walks straight into all the usual troubles we have met before: the Cartesian theater where consciousness happens, the Cartesian materialist idea of a "finishing line" marking entry into consciousness, the "hard problem" of how subjective qualia can be produced by objective brain processes and a magic, unexplained, difference between those areas that are conscious and those that are not. This explains why blindsight has become such a *cause célèbre*. Either it really has all these dramatic and mysterious consequences and they need explaining, or there is something wrong with the "obvious" interpretation.

What could be wrong? The first possibility is that blindsight does not really exist. This possibility has been pushed to the limit. Skeptics have raised three main objections (Kentridge and Heywood, 1999; Weiskrantz, 1986). First they suggested that light might have strayed from the blind field into the seeing field. This was dealt with by flooding the seeing field with bright light

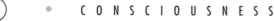

CONSCIOUSNESS

so that if there were any stray light from the other side, it would not be detectable, and this made no difference to the phenomenon. In other experiments, the stray light function was measured and found not to account for the effects. Finally, the blind spot was used as a control, on the grounds that stray light should have the same effects there if it were responsible for blindsight. In this experiment, the subject guessed whether or not there was a light, while it was shone either on his blind spot or on some other part of his blind field. In all cases he said he saw nothing, but when the light was on his blind spot, he guessed at chance, while on neighboring areas of his blind field he guessed significantly above chance. Stray light cannot account for blindsight.

The second objection was that blindsight is nothing more than degraded normal vision—in other words, blindseers have severely restricted visual function and severely degraded qualia to match. One way of testing this is to ask subjects to give confidence ratings for their guesses. In normal subjects, confidence correlates closely with the accuracy of detection, but in blindsight this is not so. Another way is to use the "commentary-key paradigm," developed by Weiskrantz, in which subjects not only press keys to say where, when or whether a stimulus is there but also have two commentary keys to press. One indicates that "yes," they had some experience of the stimulus (a feeling, knowing, tingle or whatever), and the other "no," they had no experience at all. Using this paradigm, blindseers have been shown to respond very accurately while claiming no awareness at all (Weiskrantz, 1997).

A related argument is that blindseers are just overly cautious about saying they can see something. In the terminology of signal detection theory (see Chapter 19), it is not their sensitivity that is affected but their response criterion that is raised. This, and other objections, have been countered by German physiologist Petra Stoerig (Stoerig and Cowey, 1995). For example, the response criterion can be altered by varying the proportion of stimuli to blank trials, but this does not affect blindsight.

Another possibility was that blindsight might depend on residual islands of cortical tissue. Although some patients do have such residual visual cortex, there are many who do not. PET and fMRI scans of G.Y. show no activity at all in V1, suggesting that his blindsight depends on other structures. There are something like 10 separate, parallel pathways from the eye to different parts of the brain. About 85 percent of cells take the major route through the lateral geniculate to primary visual cortex, but the rest go via the superior colliculus to various other cortical and subcortical areas. These are not affected by destruction of V1. The evidence suggests that true blindsight occurs when V1 is destroyed and these other pathways remain intact.

Blindsight can be detected in many ways. For example, while denying consciously seeing anything, subjects can make saccades to stimuli, point to the location of objects, mimic the movement of lights or objects in the blind field, and show pupillary and other emotional responses to stimuli they cannot see. G.Y., for example, can discriminate different facial expressions presented in

SENSORY SUBSTITUTION

Can the blind learn to see? Retinal implants, or completely artificial eyes, may one day be possible, but for the moment the task of wiring them into the brain is too difficult. Fortunately there is another way of solving the problem: by substituting one sense for another.

The first attempts at sensory substitution were made by Paul Bach-y-Rita in the late 1960s (Bach-y-Rita, 1995). Signals from low-resolution cameras on special glasses went to an array of just 16 x 16 vibrators fixed to a subject's back. Even with this crude device people could walk about, read signs and even identify faces. Much higher-resolution devices followed (called Tactile Vision Substitution Systems —TVSS), with tactile arrays on the back, abdomen, thigh and fingertips. After sufficient training with TVSS, blind people experienced the images as being out in space rather than as vibrations on their skin, and they learned to make judgments using parallax, depth, looming and other visual cues.

The tongue is far more sensitive than the back, and is highly conductive, so more recent brain–machine interfaces have used 144 gold-plated electrodes on the tongue. By moving the video camera around, either by hand or on the head, the subject can explore the environment in the way that sighted people do by moving their eyes. The effects are dramatic. Within a few hours, one congenitally blind woman was able to move about, grasp objects and even catch and toss a ball rolled toward her. She especially asked to see a flickering candle — something she had never been able to experience through any other sense (Bach-y-Rita and González, 2002).

A similar array on the tongue was used to replace vestibular feedback in a woman who had lost her vestibular system and therefore could not walk, or even stand upright, on her own. She could stand almost immediately using the new system, and without any training.

his blind field. This ability was shown to depend on information in the minor pathway running through the superior colliculus and amygdala (Morris et al., 2001). Stimuli in the blind field can prime or bias detection of stimuli in the seeing field, and there are other odd effects. For example, if a half circle is shown in the seeing field, a half circle is reported, and if shown in the blind field, nothing is reported. But if both halves are shown together, a complete circle is seen (Weiskrantz, 1997).

Several blindseers can correctly guess the color of stimuli they cannot see. As Weiskrantz points out, "The subjects seemed to be able to respond to the stimuli that would normally generate the philosophers' favourite species of 'qualia,' namely colours, but in the absence of the very qualia themselves!" (Weiskrantz, 1997: 23).

The phenomenon of blindsight is therefore real enough, but what does it tell us about consciousness? "Does it provide a disproof (or at any rate a serious embarrassment) to functionalist theories of the mind by exhibiting a case where all the *functions* of vision are still present, but all the good juice of *consciousness* has drained out?" asks Dennett. Not surprisingly he replies "It provides no such thing" (Dennett, 1991: 325).

To explain why not, Dennett notes that in most experiments blindseers have to be prompted to guess and are given no immediate feedback on their success. Dennett now imagines training a blindsight patient by giving him feedback on his guesses until he comes to realize that he has a useful ability. Next he is trained, again by giving feedback, to guess on his own, without being prompted. After this training he should spontaneously be able to talk about, act upon and use the information from his blind field just as well as from his seeing field. Others have dubbed this "super blindsight" (Block, 1995; Holt, 1999), and it has been much disputed.

The argument really hinges on this question—if the superblindseer could really use the information about a stimulus in his blind field in this way, would that mean he was necessarily conscious of it? It is worth trying to imagine this in some detail to decide your own answer. Functionalists would say yes (because being conscious *is* performing these functions), while those who believe in the existence of qualia, conscious inessentialism and the possibility of zombies would say no (because the functions and the qualia are separate things and the superblindseer has one but not the other).

FIGURE 18.5 • Superblindsight. Imagine that a patient with blindsight is trained to make spontaneous guesses about things he cannot see.

There is some evidence that bears on this. First, it is important to realize just how impoverished blindsight is. In spite of their remarkable ability to detect stimuli and simple features without awareness, blindseers generally cannot recognize forms or identify familiar objects. They cannot (or at least do not) use their blindsight in ordinary life (in this sense they really are blind). When thirsty, they would not pick up and drink from a glass of water that lay in their blind field (Marcel, 1986). They have to be prompted, and even pushed, to make their accurate guesses in the laboratory. Indeed some have, understandably, refused to cooperate, and only a few are willing to spend days, weeks or even years guessing at things they

FIGURE 18.6 • Pat Fletcher with Peter Meijer, the inventor of soundscapes (left), and David Chalmers (right). She is wearing headphones and has tiny video cameras concealed in her glasses. A notebook computer in her backpack carries out the video-to-audio transformations that enable her to see well enough to walk about, pick up objects and even recognize people. But is it seeing? She says it is.

In a completely different approach, sound is used to replace vision. In Peter Meijer's (2002) method a video image is converted into "soundscapes": swooping noises that might be thought of as sound-saccades, in which pitch and time are used to code for left–right and up–down in the image. He put the necessary software on the web, and among those who tried it was Pat Fletcher (2002), who was blinded in an industrial accident in 1999. The system took her many months to master, unlike the tactile systems, but eventually she began to see depth and detail in the world.

But is it really vision? Fletcher says it is, and that she does not confuse the soundscapes with other sounds. She can have a conversation with people while using the soundscapes to look at them, and she even dreams in soundscapes.

All this has profound implications for the nature of sensory awareness. The ease with which one sense can stand in for another suggests that there is nothing intrinsically visual about information that goes in through the eyes, or intrinsically auditory about information that comes in through the ears. Rather, the nature of the information and the way it changes with a person's actions are what determine how it is experienced. This fits well with sensorimotor theory, which treats vision and hearing as different ways of interacting with the world. The same conclusion is reached from experiments in which the sensory systems of ferrets are rewired soon after birth. If visual information is routed to auditory cortex, that cortex develops orientation-selective responses, maps of visual space and control of visual behavior as visual cortex normally would (Sur and Leamey, 2001). In other words, it seems as though the nature of the input determines the way sensory cortex is organized.

This kind of research might help solve a classic mystery: how the firing of some neurons leads to visual experiences while identical kinds of firing in different neurons leads to auditory experiences. Perhaps more important for the blind, it suggests that seeing does not necessarily need eyes.

SELF-ASSESSMENT QUESTIONS

○ What is amnesic syndrome? Which kinds of memory are lost and which are retained?

○ Describe two or more amnesic patients. What do their cases tell us about consciousness?

○ What is Anton's syndrome and how might it be explained?

○ Describe some experiments that reveal the nature of the deficits in hemifield neglect.

○ What is blindsight? How is it caused, and how can it be detected?

○ Compare the arguments that have used blindsight to support the possibility of zombies with those that use blindsight to undermine it.

○ What is sensory substitution and why might it be relevant to consciousness?

cannot see. So the hypothetical superblindseer has abilities way beyond those of actual blindsight.

Second, blindseers are sometimes aware of certain kinds of stimuli in their blind field, especially fast-moving, high-contrast ones. This is known as the "Riddoch phenomenon" since its discovery in 1917 by the Scottish neurologist George Riddoch (1888–1947), who worked with injured soldiers in the First World War. This residual ability makes sense in terms of the anatomy because the minor visual pathway has projections to V5, which is motion-sensitive. Indeed activity in V5 has been shown in G.Y. by PET scan (Barbur et al., 1993).

Using the commentary-key paradigm, Weiskrantz showed that G.Y. could accurately detect both slow- and fast-moving stimuli, but was only aware of the fast ones. Morland (1999) explored this awareness further by getting G.Y. to match the speed of moving stimuli shown in his blind field to those in his seeing field. The results showed that the two were perceived as equivalent. In other words, as far as motion is concerned G.Y.'s perception in the blind field is the same as that in his seeing field. Yet G.Y. does not identify the experience as really "seeing"; he explained that "the difficulty is the same that one would have in trying to tell a blind man what it is like to see" (Weiskrantz, 1997: 66). This makes sense because it is very difficult to imagine what it is like to see movement without seeing the thing that is moving, yet that is the ability that G.Y. has. Morland concludes that primary visual cortex is not needed for consciousness, but it is needed for binding the features of objects. So the experience of movement in blindsight is just that—seeing movement that is not bound to a moving object.

Some patients show appropriate eye movements to track displays they cannot see, or can mimic the path of an invisible stimulus with their hands. Some can make reasonably accurate movements to grasp invisible objects, and even to post invisible cards through slots with the correct orientation. This may seem very odd, but it makes sense in terms of the distinction between the dorsal and ventral streams. Milner and Goodale (1995) suggest that "blindsight is a set of visual capacities mediated by the dorsal stream and associated subcortical structures" (Milner and Goodale, 1995: 85). This fits with the finding that the accuracy of some responses in blindsight (such as limb movements) is higher than others (such as eye movements), as well as with Weiskrantz's observation that "the intact field seems to be biased towards object identification, and the blindsight field towards stimulus detection" (Weiskrantz, 1997: 40). If this is correct, it means that the detection of stimuli in blindsight is based on visuomotor responses.

Milner and Goodale also note that G.Y. reports a different non-visual experience when asked to use different visuomotor responses. They do not conclude that consciousness is obliterated along with the ventral stream, but rather that there may be "a distinct non-visual experiential state associated with each different visuomotor system activated" (Milner and Goodale, 1995: 79). In their view blindsight should not be seen as perception without consciousness, but as action without perception.

A third kind of evidence comes from studies of sensory substitution, in which people are given information in one sense to replace another—for example, touch or sound to replace vision. They, too, have trouble describing what the experience is like, but with practice it comes to seem more and more like seeing. If this is correct, it suggests that consciousness comes along with increasing function, rather than being something separate from it.

What can we now conclude about the status of blindsight? Is it really a mysterious phenomenon that proves the existence of qualia and the possibility of zombies?

Among those who think so, Marzi (1999) argues that the residual functions in blindsight are "banned from consciousness" because the neural activity does not reach the "consciousness centers." Holt (1999) argues that blindsight and superblindsight are both evidence for the reality of qualia, although he leaves open the question of whether qualia are epiphenomenal or identical to neural states or processes. Stoerig and Cowey (1995) refer to blindsight as visual processing in the absence of phenomenal vision. They suggest that conscious access to processed information requires higher cortical structures, and its function is to enable conscious retrieval, thinking and planning.

In his paper "On a confusion about a function of consciousness," Block (1995) rejects this kind of argument. In his view, it reveals a confusion between two kinds of consciousness (see Chapter 2). Access consciousness is the availability of information for use in reasoning, speech and action. Phenomenal consciousness is experience, or "what it is like" to be in a given state. He argues that stimuli in blindsight are both access-unconscious (because the patient cannot use the information) and phenomenally unconscious (because the patient denies experiencing them), but that people confuse the two, wrongly giving a function to P-consciousness that really belongs to A-consciousness. Note, however, that according to the way we are using the term "consciousness" in this book, only P-consciousness counts as "consciousness," which is why I have not used Block's distinction here. For Block, the superblindsight case is indeed a partial zombie who has A-consciousness (because he can talk

"the difficulty is the same that one would have in trying to tell a blind man what it is like to see"

G.Y., patient with blindsight

about stimuli in his blind field) but no P-consciousness (because he still has no visual qualia). In this view the mystery of P-consciousness remains.

For others the mystery is disappearing as we learn more about the phenomena. As far as Dennett is concerned all the kinds of evidence discussed here weigh against both zombies and qualia. The superblindseer would not go on denying having qualia, but would acquire experiences to match the quality of the abilities he came to have. If he could be trained to act on, and talk about —in other words, to have access to—stimuli in his blind field, then he would also become conscious of them.

Weiskrantz suggests that blindseers lack what he calls the "commentary stage" in which information becomes available for comment, either verbally or in other ways. So, again, the superblindseer who could comment on his own abilities would therefore become conscious of them. This is similar to the HOT theory in which information is conscious only if there is a higher-order thought to the effect that the person is experiencing it.

Finally, Milner and Goodale suggest that "Blindsight is paradoxical only if one regards vision as a unitary process" (Milner and Goodale, 1995: 86). In their view of the visual system, there is no single visual representation that is used for all purposes, but lots of semi-independent subsystems: those in the ventral stream leading to perception and those in the dorsal stream to fast visuomotor control. Any or all of these can give rise to different kinds of experience. Once again, the mystery looks quite different to those who are prepared to abandon the idea of unified consciousness, or a show in the Cartesian theater.

"blindsight does not support the concept of a zombie; it undermines it"

Dennett, 1991: 323

READING

Block, N. (1995) On a confusion about a function of consciousness. *Behavioral and Brain Sciences* 18, 227–87.

Kentridge, R.W. and Heywood, C.A. The status of blindsight. *Journal of Consciousness Studies* 6, 3–11.

Sacks, O. Read any chapter from *The Man who Mistook his Wife for a Hat* (1985) or *An Anthropologist on Mars* (1995).

SEVEN

• 271

Borderlands

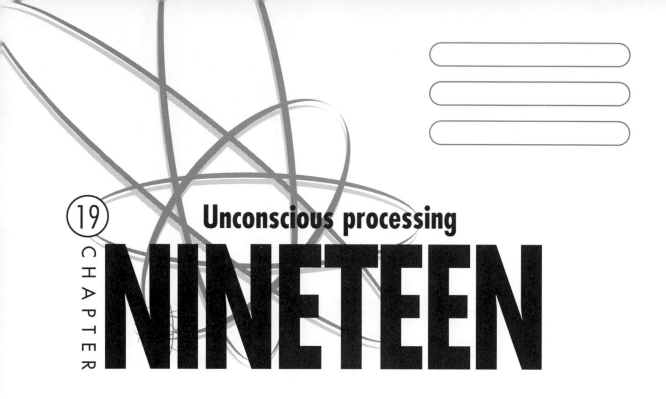

19

Unconscious processing

NINETEEN

"As the light changed to green and I crossed the street," recalls physicist Leo Szilard, "it . . . suddenly occurred to me that if we could find an element which is split by neutrons and which would emit *two* neutrons when it absorbs *one* neutron, such an element, if assembled in sufficiently large mass, could sustain a nuclear reaction." Before he reached the other side of the street, the basic ideas for nuclear energy and the atom bomb were all in place (Rhodes, 1986: 28).

Similar stories of "Eureka moments" are dotted throughout the literature of science. One Sunday afternoon, in the spring of 1765, James Watt went walking on the green in Glasgow, worrying about the loss of heat in the Newcomen steam engine. As he walked, the idea of the separate condenser came to him, an idea that was to transform steam power and kick-start the industrial revolution. "I had not walked further than the Golf-house when the whole thing was arranged in my mind."

Creative work sometimes seems to happen by itself. Coleridge claimed to have fallen into an opium-induced sleep and awoken three hours later with hundreds of lines of his famous epic poem "Kubla Khan" ready composed, and Paul McCartney is said to have woken one morning humming the tune to the song "Yesterday," and thinking he must have heard it somewhere. This world-famous song had, as it were, written itself.

Some of these stories are doubtless exaggerated, and some were invented long after the fact. For example, there is evidence that earlier versions of "Kubla Khan" were written before the famous dream, and doubt has been cast on Newton's claim that in 1666, his laws of motion were "occasioned by the fall of an apple" in quite the way he described (Kollerstrom, 1999). Nevertheless, there is no doubt that complicated and novel ideas can sometimes seem to spring to mind, fully formed, as though with no conscious effort.

Such leaps of creative genius do not come out of nowhere, and we must not underestimate the amount of training and deliberate effort that these creative people had undertaken *before* their inspiration struck. The interesting point is that when all that work is done, creative thinking seems to happen on its own.

If this seems peculiar, we must remember that highly complex perceptual and learning processes go on all the time without awareness. For example, you have no conscious knowledge of how you judge distances, recognize objects from unfamiliar angles or make aesthetic judgments. You once learned the quickest route to the shops, the name of the highest mountain in the world and the dates of the Second World War, but if I asked you now you would not be able to tell me when you learned them, a phenomenon called "source amnesia." You once learned your native language, and how to ride a bike, but you can probably remember little of the learning process.

Some of these skills have become less conscious, or "automatized," with time. For example, when you first learned to read, every word was difficult and you were probably conscious of each letter, but now you read quickly and with no awareness of individual letters. Baars (1997a) suggests, as an example of his method of contrastive analysis, that you turn the book upside down and try reading it like that, forcing yourself to go back to a slower and more deliberate kind of reading. He predicts that a brain scan would show much more activity in the difficult, and more conscious, case, than in the routine, or automated case. With automatization, skills that were once difficult soon become unconscious.

So what is unconscious processing? Is it the work of a separate mind with its own intelligence, emotions and powers, as seems to be implied in the popular idea of "unleashing the power of the unconscious" or in fears that advertisers can use "subliminal messages" to force us to buy their products against our own conscious wills? Is there a kind of unintelligent under-mind that plods along doing boring useful jobs for the truly intelligent conscious mind, or is the whole idea that we can separate conscious processes from unconscious processes ultimately misguided?

The whole issue of the unconscious has been deeply controversial throughout the history of psychology (see Chapter 1), and still is so today. Here we shall consider the evidence that perception, learning, memory, problem solving and insight can all occur unconsciously.

> *"Even today, when the reality of unconscious perception has been confirmed beyond reasonable doubt . . . there remains almost unshakeable resistance."*
>
> **Dixon**, 1981: 181

UNCONSCIOUS PERCEPTION

Suppose you are sitting at dinner, chatting with your friends, oblivious to the hum of the microwave in the corner—until it stops. Suddenly you realize that it was humming along all the time. Only in its silence are you conscious of the noise.

This simple, everyday phenomenon seems odd because it suggests perception without consciousness. It suggests that all along, in some unconscious way, you must have been hearing the noise. It challenges the simplistic notion that perception implies consciousness and that "I" must know what my own brain is perceiving (Merikle et al., 2001).

The phenomena of unconscious (or implicit, or subliminal) perception have been known about since the very early days of psychology. For example, in the 1880s, Charles Peirce and Joseph Jastrow (1885) studied how well they could discriminate between stimuli of different weights and brightnesses. When the brightnesses or weights were so closely matched that the researchers had no confidence in their ability to tell them apart, they made themselves guess, and to their surprise they did better than chance. This was one of the earliest demonstrations of perception without consciousness. At about the same time, another American psychologist, and friend of William James, Boris Sidis (1898) displayed letters or digits on cards so far away that the subjects could barely see them, let alone say which they were. Yet when he got the subjects to guess, they also did better than chance. Both these effects have something in common with demonstrations of blindsight (see Chapter 18), except that the effects occur in everyone. The crucial finding is that people deny consciously detecting something while their behavior shows that they *have* detected it.

CONSCIOUSNESS

Sidis concluded that his results showed "the presence within us of a secondary subwaking self that perceives things which the primary waking self is unable to get at" (1898: 171). Even if we reject his notion of the two selves, the conclusion that his results demonstrate unconscious perception seems reasonable. However, resistance to the possibility of subliminal perception was extraordinarily strong right from the start (Dixon, 1971).

In the early experiments, conscious perception was defined in terms of what people said. This fits with the common intuition that each of us is the final arbiter of what is in our own consciousness; if we say we are conscious or unconscious of something then (unless we are deliberately lying) we are. Yet this intuition is problematic for several reasons.

One problem is that whether people say they have consciously seen (or heard or felt) something depends on how cautious they are being. This became clearer in the mid-twentieth century with the development of signal detection theory. This mathematical theory requires two variables to explain how people detect things like sounds, flashes of light or touches on the skin. One variable is the person's sensitivity (how good their eyes are, how acute their hearing is, and so on). The other is their response criterion (how willing they are to say "yes, I see it" when they are unsure). These two can vary independently of each other. Of most relevance here is that at different times someone may have exactly the same sensitivity but, without necessarily realizing it, apply a different criterion. For example, if there is a financial incentive to detect a light when it comes on and no penalty for a false positive, then most people will set a very lax criterion and claim to see it when they are not sure. But if saying "I see it" when it's not there makes them look stupid or lose money, then they will set their criterion much higher.

This means that there is no fixed threshold (or limen) that separates the things that are "really seen" or "really experienced" from those that are not. It implies, once again, a difficulty with the idea that things are unequivocally either "in" consciousness or "out" of consciousness. If there is no fixed limen, then the concepts of subliminal and supraliminal perception become much more complicated.

Another problem stems from the behaviorist suspicion of verbal reports. Some behaviorist researchers did not want to believe what people said about their own subjective experiences but wanted more reliable "objective" measures of consciousness. But this is a rather curious idea. On the one hand, making a verbal report by speaking or writing is just as much an objective action as is pressing a button or pointing. For this reason I shall not refer to verbal reports as "subjective measures" as some writers do. But on the other hand, if *all* objective measures of discrimination are taken as evidence of *conscious* perception, then evidence for *unconscious* perception seems to be ruled out by definition (Kihlstrom, 1996). In other words, this move would define away the whole idea that people might be able to demonstrate, by their behavior, detection of stimuli that they personally knew they were not conscious of.

In spite of the confusion, in the 1970s and 1980s, these objections prompted progress in both research methods and theory. The basic requirement was to demonstrate a dissociation between two measures, one taken to indicate conscious perception and the other to indicate unconscious perception. Marcel (1983) adapted the method of semantic priming in which one word (the prime) influences the response to a second word (the target). For example, if the prime and the target word are semantically related (e.g., doctor and nurse), recognition of the target is faster. Marcel made such primes undetectable by flashing a visual mask immediately after them, yet semantic priming still occurred. This seemed to mean that people's word recognition was affected by primes they did not see. Other kinds of masked priming were also used, but controversy ensued because while some people successfully replicated the effects, many others failed.

The controversy was resolved when Canadian psychologists James Cheesman and Philip Merikle (1984; 1986; see Profile) proposed a distinction between what they called the "objective threshold" and the "subjective threshold." The objective threshold is defined as "the detection level at which perceptual information is actually discriminated at a chance level" whereas the subjective threshold is "the detection level at which subjects claim not to be able to discriminate perceptual information at better than a chance level" (Cheesman and Merikle, 1984: 391). The latter is, naturally, higher than the former.

Cheesman and Merikle used a Stroop-priming task in which subjects had to name a color after being primed with a color word. Congruent color words reduce reaction time, but incongruent words increase it (this is the Stroop effect). The question was whether undetectable primes would affect reaction times. Cheesman and Merikle measured subjects' objective threshold using a reliable four-alternative forced-choice procedure, and their subjective threshold by asking them to judge their own ability to discriminate the words. They found a priming effect (i.e., evidence for unconscious perception) with primes below the subjective threshold but none at all when they were below the objective threshold.

Their conclusion was that unconscious perception occurs primarily when information is presented below the subjective threshold but above the objective threshold. They were then able to show that previous experiments had confused these two different kinds of threshold, with some measuring one and some the other. From this we can conclude that the objective threshold really is the level below which stimuli have no effect of any kind, but there is a level above that at which a stimulus can have an effect even though the person denies being conscious of it.

Many of these experiments used words as stimuli and implied the possibility of unconscious semantic analysis. This possibility has been argued over for a hundred years or more, with many arguments about just how much meaning can be extracted from a stimulus that a person denies seeing. Kihlstrom concludes that "With respect to subliminal stimulation, the general rule seems to be that the further the stimulus moves from the subjective threshold, the less likely it is to be subject to semantic analysis" (Kihlstrom, 1996: 38–9). This is just one example showing that the effects of stimuli can differ when they are above or below different thresholds.

Some of the most striking experiments on unconscious perception concern the emotional effects. Threatening pictures that people deny seeing can produce emotional reactions and can alter perceptual thresholds, suggesting the odd conclusion that you may be less likely to consciously perceive a threatening stimulus than a neutral one, even if they are otherwise equally visible. Claims have been made that the emotional effects can be exploited for subliminal advertising, making people buy more cola or eat more potato chips, but there is no evidence to support them. There is also no evidence that the many available self-help subliminal tapes are actually of any use (Merikle, 2000).

A longer-lasting, and somewhat unnerving, effect was found in a controversial study of people undergoing general anesthesia (Levinson, 1965). A mock crisis was staged during a real operation, by the experimenter reading out a statement to the effect that the patient was going blue and needed more oxygen. A month later the ten patients were hypnotized and asked whether they remembered anything that had occurred during their operation. Four of the ten remembered the statement almost verbatim, and a further four remembered something of what was said. This conjures up visions of people being unconsciously affected by horrific scenes from operating theaters, but generally the unconscious effects under anesthesia, although they can be detected, are found to be small (Kihlstrom, 1996; Merikle and Daneman, 1996). Exceptions can occur in those one to two in a thousand patients whose anesthetic is wrongly administered or monitored. In the worst cases they experience severe pain and fear but can do nothing to make their state known.

Preferences can also be affected by unconsciously perceived stimuli. In a famous study (Kunst-Wilson and Zajonc, 1980) subjects were shown meaningless shapes so briefly that none reported seeing them. Responses were measured in two ways. In a recognition task subjects had to choose which of two shapes had been presented before. They could not do this, as shown by their chance results (50 percent). In a preference task they were simply asked which of the two they preferred. In this test they chose the one that had been shown before 60 percent of the time. This is a good example of how two dif-

> *"There is simply no evidence that regular listening to subliminal audio self-help tapes or regular viewing of subliminal video self-help tapes is an effective method for overcoming problems or improving skills."*
> **Merikle**, 2000

ferent objective measures of awareness, neither of which is a verbal report, can lead to different answers.

But which measure tells us what the subjects were *really* conscious of? This question is a natural one for the Cartesian materialist, who believes that there must be an answer, that things must be either in or out of consciousness. An alternative is to reject this distinction and say that there is no ultimately "correct" measure of whether someone is conscious of something or not. There are just different processes and responses, and different ways of measuring them.

In a later development of this line of research, subjects had to rate a series of Chinese ideographs according to whether they thought each represented a "good" or a "bad" concept (Murphy and Zajonc, 1993). One group of subjects saw either a smiling face or a scowling face for one second before each one. They were told to ignore these faces and concentrate only on rating the ideographs. The second group were shown the faces for only 4 ms, which is not long enough to see them. The fascinating result was that the first group managed to ignore the faces, but the second group were influenced by the faces they claimed not to see. If the invisible face was smiling, they were more likely to rate the ideograph as "good."

This is another example that shows how information can have different effects when it is above or below a threshold. Merikle and Daneman (1998: 12) conclude that "unconsciously perceived information leads to automatic reactions, whereas consciously perceived information leads to much more flexible reactions." This may be so, but we should be careful not to jump to the unwarranted conclusion that consciousness *causes* the flexible reactions. It is equally possible that more flexible reactions cause consciousness, that flexible reactions and conscious processes are the same thing or that both are caused by something else.

Brain scans have also been used to investigate unconscious perception. For example, an fMRI study showed that unconsciously perceived fearful faces led to greater activity in the amygdala than did happy faces (Whalen et al., 1998), and a PET study showed that angry faces activated the right but not the left amygdala (Morris et al., 1998). This confirms that even when information is not consciously perceived, it can have effects in the same parts of the brain that would be activated by consciously seen stimuli of the same kind.

Dehaene and his colleagues used ERPs (event related potentials) and fMRI to investigate activation by unconscious primes. They found activity not only in sensory areas but also in motor areas, suggesting covert responses to the unseen masked stimuli. They concluded that "A stream of perceptual, semantic, and motor processes can therefore occur without awareness" (Dehaene et al., 1998: 597). This is reminiscent of William James's contention that "Every impression which impinges on the incoming nerves produces some discharge down the outgoing ones, whether we be aware of it or not" (James, 1890, ii: 372).

CONSCIOUSNESS

This brings us back to that troublesome "magic difference." If every impression produces discharges, what is the difference between the ones we are aware of and those we are not?

THE IMPLICATIONS OF UNCONSCIOUS PERCEPTION

The evidence for unconscious perception shows that some popular ideas about consciousness have to be wrong. To make this clear, let's consider three ways of thinking about consciousness.

The first is the traditional (and ever tempting) theory of the Cartesian theater. In this view consciousness is like a multi-sensory cinema. Information comes into consciousness, whereupon "I" can experience and act on it. In its most extreme view this theory assumes that perception is always conscious, and that sensory information can only lead to action once it has passed through the theater of consciousness. We have already found lots of reasons for rejecting this view, and subliminal perception provides one more.

The second view accepts this step but still fails to throw out the theater metaphor. So the idea is something like this: sensory information enters the system whereupon two distinct things can happen to it. Some goes into consciousness and is acted on consciously, while some bypasses consciousness and is acted on unconsciously, perhaps by using routes through the brain that lead to motor output without actually reaching consciousness.

This second theory, a form of Cartesian materialism, is probably the most common in consciousness studies today. While rejecting the notions of a homunculus watching events on a mental screen, it retains the essential idea that things are either "in" or "out" of consciousness. Phrases such as "enters consciousness," "available to consciousness" or "reaching consciousness" often (though not invariably) imply such a theory. The tricky issues surrounding the border between "in" and "out" of consciousness are sometimes dealt with by proposing a "fringe" consciousness, or by concentrating solely on the clear cases, not the "fuzzy" ones such as blindsight or subliminal perception as, for example, does Baars (1988).

Yet the findings discussed above might suggest a more radical third theory. To recap: perceptual thresholds are not fixed but depend on variable response criteria; there is no undisputed measure for deciding whether something has been consciously perceived or not; and there are many stimuli that are deemed to be consciously perceived by some measures and not by others. All this threatens the idea that any stimulus is unequivocally either "in" or "out" of consciousness. It suggests instead that sensory information is processed in a wide variety of ways, with different consequences for different kinds of behavior. Some of these behaviors are usually taken as indications of consciousness,

"The results of all the studies . . . are unequivocal in showing that stimulus information is perceived when either subjective or objective measures indicate that the observers were unaware of the critical stimuli."

Merikle et al., 2001: 118

ACTIVITY
Incubation

Incubation is the process of putting a problem "on the back burner" or just allowing a solution to come by itself—if it will. Three steps are required. First, you have to do the hard work of struggling with the problem or acquiring the necessary skills. Second, you have to drop the struggle and leave the problem to itself, perhaps by engaging in some other activity or just sleeping on it. In this second stage, any conscious effort is likely to be counterproductive. Third, you have to recognize the solution when it appears.

Here are three simple brainteasers that you can use to practice incubation. If you are working on your

FIGURE 19.1 • Move three coins to turn the triangle upside down.

FIGURE 19.2 • Draw just two squares to provide each pig with its own enclosure.

(Activity continues on next page)

such as verbal reports or choices between clearly perceptible stimuli, while others are usually considered to be unconscious, such as fast reflexes, guesses or certain measures of brain activity. In between lie many behaviors that are sometimes taken to indicate consciousness and sometimes not. *But there is no right answer.*

In this third theory nothing is ever "in" or "out" of consciousness, and phrases such as "reaching consciousness" or "available to consciousness" are either meaningless or are shorthand for "leading to verbal report" or "available to influence behaviors taken to indicate consciousness."

The major problem for this third theory is what people say about their own experience. Many people say that they know for sure what is in their consciousness and what is not, even if they cannot always explain what they mean. Any theory of this kind must therefore deal with this intuition. One approach is to try to explain how the illusion comes about (Dennett, 1991). Another is to show how these misguided intuitions disappear with practiced introspection (Chapter 27).

Unless some such way out is found, we are left at an impasse. The evidence on unconscious processing suggests that we should reject any firm distinction between what is conscious and what is not; ordinary intuitions about consciousness depend utterly on such a distinction. This is a familiar situation and just one more reason why the problem of consciousness is so perplexing.

SOLVING PROBLEMS

We can now return to the cases outlined at the start, in which people apparently solve difficult problems unconsciously. Since there is no doubt that unconscious learning and perception occur, there is no reason, in principle, why unconscious problem solving should be impossible. But does it really happen? And if it does, just how clever can we expect it to be? This is the basis for the disagreement between those who claim that "intelligence increases when you think less" (Claxton, 1997) and those who claim that "your unconscious is stupider than you are" (Kihlstrom, 1996).

In one experiment, Dianne Berry and Donald Broadbent at Oxford University (1984) set up a computer game that simulated production in a sugar factory. The subjects' task was to stabilize the output of sugar by controlling input variables such as the size of the workforce or the financial incentives, but they were not told the fairly complex equations that determined the effects of their moves. Over several days, their performance improved significantly, and they became remarkably good at controlling sugar production, but when asked explicitly what they were doing, they could not say. Further experiments showed that the subjects' confidence in their ability was more closely related to their explicit knowledge than to their actual ability to do the task. In some studies explicit knowledge was negatively correlated with actual ability, suggesting that for some tasks, the people who are best at performing them are worst at explaining how they do it. If the ability to verbalize what has been learned is taken as a measure of conscious learning, then in these examples, unconscious learning is more effective than conscious learning.

Another example comes from a series of hundreds of experiments by Pavel Lewicki and his colleagues at the University of Tulsa (Lewicki et al., 1992) on the nonconscious acquisition of information. In this experiment, subjects see a computer screen divided into quarters. Arrays of apparently random digits then appear in all four quadrants and the subjects' task is to search for a particular digit—say 5—and press one of four buttons according to which quadrant the 5 appears in. They must do this many times in blocks of seven trials.

Unbeknown to the subjects the position of the 5 is determined by a fairly complex algorithm such that, by knowing its position in the first, third, fourth and sixth trials (and you must know all of these, not just some), you can work out where it will be on the last, seventh, trial. The interesting ques-

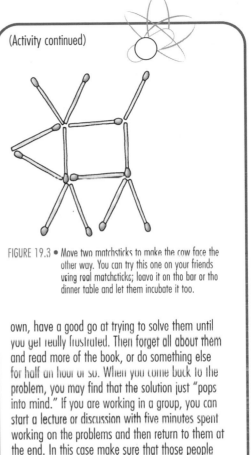

(Activity continued)

FIGURE 19.3 ● Move two matchsticks to make the cow face the other way. You can try this one on your friends using real matchsticks; leave it on the bar or the dinner table and let them incubate it too.

own, have a good go at trying to solve them until you get really frustrated. Then forget all about them and read more of the book, or do something else for half an hour or so. When you come back to the problem, you may find that the solution just "pops into mind." If you are working in a group, you can start a lecture or discussion with five minutes spent working on the problems and then return to them at the end. In this case make sure that those people who solve the problems quickly, or who have seen them before, do not give the answers away and spoil the experience for everyone else. The solutions are given on page 285.

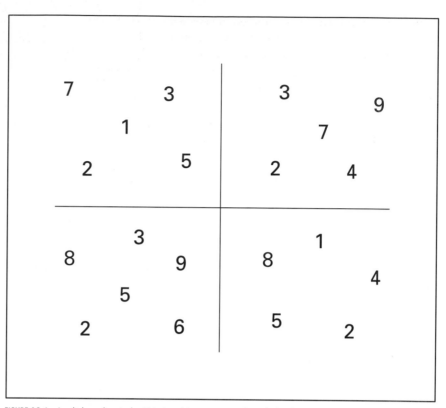

FIGURE 19.4 ● In which quadrant is the 6? In Lewicki's experiments subjects had to detect a target digit in a grid of numbers for blocks of seven trials. The position of the target digit followed a pattern such that its position on the first, third, fourth and sixth trials predicted its position on the seventh. Subjects became quicker at finding it on the crucial seventh trial, even though they had no idea that they were doing so, and were unable to say anything about the pattern.

> "it is sometimes a good idea to pull off the Information Super-Highway into the Information Super Lay-By"
>
> **Claxton**, 1997: 14

tion is whether the subjects can, either consciously or unconsciously, make use of this information. If they can, then they will get quicker at responding on the crucial seventh trial. The results showed that they could. Responses on the seventh trial became progressively faster than responses on the other six.

Lewicki then showed his subjects the results and asked them whether they had been aware of their improved performance. They said they had not. Furthermore they had no idea what kind of information they might have been using. He then gave them six more trials and asked them *consciously* to predict the position for the seventh trial. They did no better than chance (i.e., 25 percent correct).

In another experiment (Lewicki et al., 1987) subjects whose results showed they had performed well at the task were given unlimited time in which to

● CONSCIOUSNESS

study the arrays and even offered financial rewards for explaining how it was done ($100, which was a large sum at that time). Some of them spent many hours trying to find the "hidden" pattern. They still failed.

Lewicki even tried the experiment with professors from his own university who knew what his research was about (Lewicki et al., 1988). The professors improved on the seventh trial as before, but then the crucial co-variation in the sequence was changed. They noticed the change, but none of them could work out what had happened. Some, being psychology professors, suspected other explanations, such as threatening subliminal stimuli being presented. None of them came close to discovering what was really going on.

Preschool children (age four to five) also learned the task easily, and this is at an age when they are incapable of understanding conditional relations. Although this may seem odd, it fits with the fact that children of that age have usually mastered very complex rules of language that they cannot articulate, or even understand if they are explained. Lewicki concludes that "as compared with consciously controlled cognition, the nonconscious information-acquisition processes are not only much faster but are also structurally more sophisticated" (Lewicki et al., 1992).

Not surprisingly, there have been disagreements about just how clever unconscious cognition really is, with some stressing its limitations (Greenwald, 1992) and others stressing its potential. Claxton (1997) suggests that many tasks are best done without the interference of consciousness, or "deliberation-mode." He compares a child inattentively fiddling with a Rubik's cube while chatting, and successfully solving it, with an adult struggling to work it out consciously and giving up in despair. For some purposes, the slow "tortoise mind" is more effective than the fast "hare brain" even if, for most purposes, it is not.

FLOW

When athletes, musicians, scientists or chess masters are deeply engrossed in their favorite activity, they sometimes enter an "optimal state of experience" in which time and self disappear and everything seems to flow. This special state was studied by Chicago psychologist Mihaly Csikszentmihalyi after he had worked extensively with a group of artists. Sometimes they worked for hours on end, deep in concentration, as though their painting was the most important thing in the world, but when it was finished, they would put it away and not even look at it again. For these people, painting was *intrinsically* rewarding, unlike the *extrinsic* rewards of fame, riches or even the completed work. The reward of all this hard work was the activity itself.

Csikszentmihalyi (1975) discovered that finding flow depends on getting the right balance between the challenge a person faces and the skills they bring to tackling it. When a challenge is too great, anxiety results; when too slight, boredom sets in. But when challenges and skills are perfectly matched, flow can take over. The challenge can be any opportunity that a person is capable of responding to, from the vastness of the sea in sailors, to math homework in school children, from concluding a successful business deal, to enjoying a happy relationship.

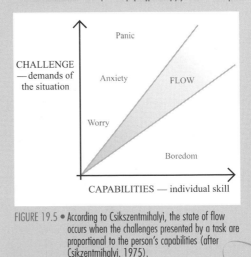

FIGURE 19.5 • According to Csikszentmihalyi, the state of flow occurs when the challenges presented by a task are proportional to the person's capabilities (after Csikszentmihalyi, 1975).

As a person improves in skill, the challenge has to increase, so to find that flow again, the player has to find a better opponent, and the mountaineer a more difficult climb. When we are tired or ill or aging, we must find challenges that match our lesser skills. But having once experienced flow, people are keen to find it again. Flow forces people both to stretch themselves and to know themselves.

Flow has been studied in Japanese motorcycle gangs, surgeons, prisoners in solitary confinement and women at work (Csikszentmihalyi and Csikszentmihalyi, 1988). In all cases people describe similar experiences. They are so deeply engrossed that action and awareness seem to merge into one. Time loses its meaning as hours seem to slip by in moments, or moments seem to last forever. It is an experience in which "all the contents of consciousness are in harmony with each other, and with the goals that define the person's self" (Csikszentmihalyi and Csikszentmihalyi, 1988: 24). "In flow the self is fully functioning, but not aware of itself doing it . . . At the most challenging levels, people actually report experiencing a *transcendence* of self" (1988: 33). The skier feels at one with the slope, the turns, the snow and the fear of falling. "The mountaineer does not climb in order to reach the top of the mountain, but tries to reach the summit in order to climb" (1988: 33).

Although flow is usually described as a state of consciousness, it might better be described as a state in which the distinctions between conscious and unconscious processing disappear. All a person's skills are called upon, and there is no longer any self to say just what "I" am conscious of.

INCUBATION AND CREATIVITY

This slow mind can be seen at work in the process of incubation. Sometimes people may work deliberately and analytically on a problem and fail to solve it. Then, if they take a rest or do something else, the solution just "pops into mind." Many scientists, artists and writers have described this process, often stressing that the hard work has to be done first, but is not, on its own, enough. Other unconscious processes have to take place as well, and these need time, and leaving alone. Although it is difficult, if not impossible, to study incubation in the real world of science and art, the same kind of sudden insight can sometimes be revealed by trying to solve tricky puzzles and devious brain-teasers.

These phenomena can help us better understand the nature of intuition and creativity. While some people seem to think of intuition as inexplicable or even paranormal, it may be better thought of as the ability to make decisions or draw conclusions without explicit processing or reasoned thinking.

There are at least three major components to intuition. First, there are all the cognitive processes discussed above, in which the brain extracts information from complex patterns to guide behavior. This probably contributes to many everyday skills, from playing computer games or finding your way around the web, to guessing when the line will be shortest in the supermarket.

Then there are all the social skills we cannot articulate, from getting the "feeling" that someone is untrustworthy, to judging when is the best time to break bad news to your best friend. Social skills, like linguistic skills, are easy for children to pick up but extremely hard to formalize. For this reason they are sometimes thought inferior or are undervalued in comparison with explicit, intellectual skills. But we should appreciate the complexity of what is involved. Take the example of judging someone untrustworthy. Among other things, this may depend on long years of meeting people who look, stand, move their eyes and twitch in different ways, and then noting (quite unconsciously) whether they kept their word or not. No one can explain how to do this, but most of us do it all the time.

The notion of "women's intuition" is sometimes laughed at, but women may be more intuitive, in this sense, because they generally have better verbal skills, are more interested in relationships, and gossip more about social matters than men do. In this way, if they spend a lot of time soaking up the covariations in the vastly complex social world, they may more often be right when they say "I don't trust that man" or "I think those two are falling in love."

The third strand is the emotions, though these cannot be separated from the rest. Intuitive knowledge often comes in emotional form, as when people say "I just felt it was right" or "I knew I had to act just then." Although emotion and reason have traditionally been separated, research reveals that reason cannot operate without the capacity to feel emotions. Damasio (1994) has studied many patients with frontal lobe damage who have lost normal emotional responses and become emotionally flat. Far from turning into super-rational decision makers, they become almost paralyzed with indecision. For some, every little choice becomes a nerve-racking dilemma to be resolved only by long and careful thought. They retain the ability to weigh alternatives rationally, but lack the feelings that make decisions "seem right." *Star Trek*'s Mr. Data is implausible. If he truly had no feelings, he would not be able to decide whether to get

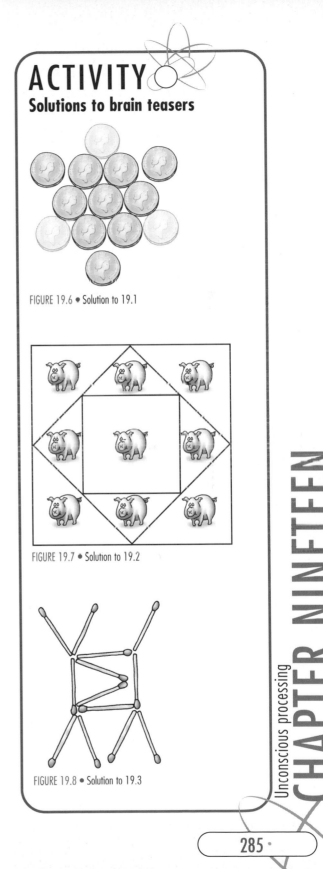

ACTIVITY
Solutions to brain teasers

FIGURE 19.6 • Solution to 19.1

FIGURE 19.7 • Solution to 19.2

FIGURE 19.8 • Solution to 19.3

up in the morning, when to speak to Captain Picard or whether the Klingons were bluffing or not.

Creativity can partly be understood in the way all these explicit and intuitive skills come together in one person. Yet there remains something of a paradox about the source of creativity. Many creative writers, thinkers, scientists and artists claim that their best work just "comes" to them. They have no idea how they do it, and indeed often feel that "they" did not really do it at all. It is as though the poem, the solution to the scientific problem, or the painting just shaped itself without any conscious effort, or even any awareness on the part of the creator. Creative people tend to score high on measures of imagery, fantasy-proneness, hypnotizability, and "absorption"; that is, they can easily become so absorbed in a book, film or their work that they are oblivious to everything else. Some describe this feeling of total immersion as a state of "flow" (Csikszentmihalyi, 1975).

This kind of selfless creativity sometimes leads to claims that there is a cosmic creative force, or a power of consciousness beyond the mind. Such powers are usually thought of as deeply mysterious or even beyond the reach of science. However, as we have already seen (in Chapter 10), there is a very real and scientifically studied cosmic force that was responsible for all of biological design: the evolutionary algorithm. Perhaps this same process is at work in human creativity.

To think about creativity in this way, we must see individual creators in their social and intellectual context. When James Watt was worrying about heat loss, it was because he had seen steam engines and knew about the manufacturing processes of his time. When inspiration came to Szilard, he was deeply immersed in the atomic science of his day; when Coleridge fell into his sleep, he had just been reading a book about the palace built by the Khan Kubla. In other words they had been soaking up the memes around them.

In this view, what makes creative people unique is the special ways in which they bring those memes together to make new ones. To do this recombination effectively, they need the motivation to learn the necessary technical knowledge and skills, the ability to process masses of information non-consciously and the intuition to feel which of the billions of possible combinations is worth pursuing. In this way the individual meme

SELF-ASSESSMENT QUESTIONS

○ Give some examples of "Eureka moments." Why are they relevant to non-conscious processing?

○ What do subliminal perception and blindsight have in common?

○ Describe at least two experiments in which a dissociation was found between conscious and unconscious perception.

○ In which ways have emotional responses to unconscious stimuli been demonstrated?

○ Describe Lewicki's experimental method.

○ What is intuition?

○ Describe some of the processes involved in creativity.

•   C O N S C I O U S N E S S

machine is an indispensable part of the creative act, but the real driving force comes not from the individuals, nor from the power of consciousness, nor even from the power of the unconscious, but from the creative force of that familiar mindless process, the evolutionary algorithm.

WAS THIS DECISION CONSCIOUS?

READING

Kihlstrom, J.F. (1996) Perception without awareness of what is perceived, learning without awareness of what is learned. In M. Velmans (ed.) *The Science of Consciousness*. Philadelphia, Routledge, 23 46.

Merikle, P.M. and Daneman, M. (1998) Psychological investigations of unconscious perception. *Journal of Consciousness Studies* 5, 5–18.

Unconscious processing
CHAPTER NINETEEN

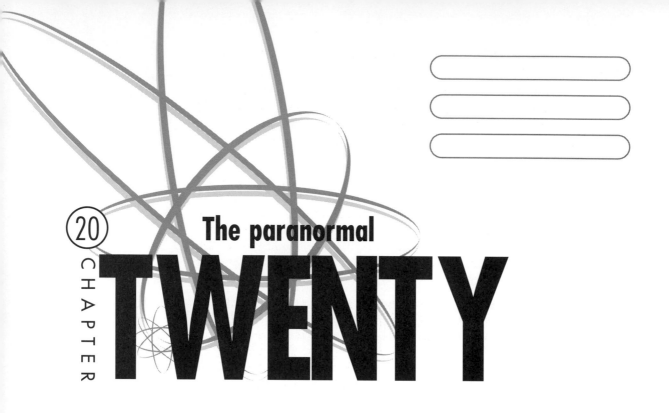

I woke up with an overpowering sense of dread. It was a terrible dream and the feeling wouldn't leave me. I was in the hospital . . . running . . . endless corridors . . . openings left and right . . . greenish light all around . . . I knew I must keep running. Then I was right by a hospital bed and there was my best friend, Shelley, lying there covered in blood and bandages. Dead. Three hours later I got the phone call. Shelley was killed instantly in a car crash the night before.

There are at least two good reasons for studying claims of paranormal phenomena. One is that the experiences are very common, and levels of belief are high. In a Gallup poll of over 1000 Americans, a quarter claimed to have communicated with someone else by ESP, and half believed in ESP (Gallup and Newport, 1991). In a British survey of over 6000 people, 59 percent believed in ESP with higher belief among women than men (Blackmore, 1997).

The other is that paranormal phenomena, if they occur, would have wide-reaching implications for science. For example, if telepathy occurs, double-blind experiments would be unreliable, as would any psychology experiment that involves keeping information from the participants. Telepathic experimenter effects could potentially ruin the results of experiments in every field of science. And if precognition occurs, then fundamental assumptions about time and space have to be revised. There might also be implications for a science of consciousness.

The popular view seems to be that psychic phenomena are evidence for the "power of consciousness." Proof of their existence is sought in the hope of overthrowing materialist theories of the mind, and experiences like the one above are cited as evidence that consciousness is independent of time and space.

Within parapsychology, terms involving "consciousness" are common, including "anomalous effects of conscious intention," "consciousness interactions" or "consciousness related anomalies." One book that reviews parapsychology is called *The Conscious Universe: The Scientific Truth of Psychic Phenomena*, and its author, American parapsychologist Dean Radin, is director of the Consciousness Research Laboratory. He argues that "Understanding such experiences requires an expanded view of human consciousness" (Radin, 1997).

For all these reasons, claims of the paranormal deserve scrutiny. If they are false, then the widespread beliefs and frequent reports of psychic experiences cannot be explained in terms of genuine paranormal occurrences and must be explained some other way. If they are true, then we must work out the implications for a science of consciousness. In this chapter we will explore some paranormal claims and consider what they tell us about consciousness.

FROM SPIRITUALISM TO PSYCHICAL RESEARCH

In 1848, in Hydesville, New York, two young girls called Kate and Margaretta Fox heard raps and bangings at the end of their bed. Inventing a code of the "two taps for yes" kind, they claimed to be communicating with the spirit of a man buried beneath their wooden house. Neighbors and visitors wanted to communicate with the spirits too, and soon the Fox sisters began giving public demonstrations. This story is usually credited as the start of spiritualism and the inspiration for the field of psychical research.

From the start there was controversy, with some investigators claiming that the girls had cheated, although they could not say how. Then, in a dramatic public confession in 1888, the Fox sisters demonstrated how they had clicked their toe joints against the bed to produce the sounds, a confession they later retracted. Critics accepted the confessions as the end of the matter, while supporters argued that the sisters were by then penniless and alcoholic and had been bribed into confessing (Brandon, 1983; Podmore, 1902).

By the end of the nineteenth century, "spirit mediums" were practicing across Europe and the USA. At some séances, the "sitters" sat in a circle around a table, with their hands placed gently on top. The medium then summoned the spirits, and the table began to move, with the spirits answering questions by tipping the table or banging its legs on the floor. The more dramatic séances took place in complete darkness, with spirit voices emanating from luminous floating trumpets, music mysteriously playing, and touches and cold breezes being felt. Sometimes a translucent, grayish substance called ectoplasm was exuded from the bodies of certain mediums and even "materialized" into the bodily form of spirits.

Among many famous mediums was Eusapia Palladino, an orphan from Naples who apparently levitated herself and other objects, materialized extra limbs, caused inexplicable noises and made furniture glide about. In 1895 she was caught cheating, but some researchers remained convinced that she had produced genuine phenomena under controlled conditions (Gauld, 1968). The only medium said never to have been caught cheating was Daniel Dunglas Home (pronounced Hume). He worked in reasonably well-lit rooms, handled live coals without getting burnt, materialized glowing hands, levitated heavy tables and even floated bodily out of one window and into the next (Gauld, 1968).

FIGURE 20.1 • In the heyday of spiritualism mediums were tied up inside a "cabinet" while the ladies and gentlemen watched. In a deep trance, they claimed to exude ectoplasm from various orifices of the body and so create fully formed spirits that could move around the room, touching the astounded sitters and even answering their questions.

Unfortunately, mediums wanting to enhance their act could readily purchase equipment such as muslin drapes, trumpets, luminous paint, spirit-writing slates and special chairs from which they could easily escape, even if skeptical observers tied them to the chairs with ropes. Whether any mediums operated entirely without such aids has never been resolved. Some argue that any medium who is caught cheating once must always be presumed to cheat, while others argue that the pressures on even the best of mediums can force them to resort to fraud in exceptional circumstances. The same arguments were played out a century later when Uri Geller traveled the world bending spoons, starting watches, and claiming to be able to read minds (Marks, 2000; Randi, 1975), and again when "channeling" appeared as the latest incarnation of mediumship.

While most Victorian scientists ignored the antics of spiritualism, some took them seriously, realizing the implications for science if the claims were true. As we have seen, Faraday convinced himself that they were false (see Chapter 9), but others came to the opposite conclusion. The famous British chemist Sir William Crookes took photographs of supposedly materialized spirits and was convinced that Home's powers implied a new form of energy (Gauld, 1968).

The main motivation for some of these investigators was their antagonism to materialism. Victorian physics was enormously successful, and the radical, new ideas of Darwinism seemed to undermine the special status of humanity and to threaten moral values. Some people saw spiritualism as providing the evidence that was needed to refute materialism and prove the reality of life after death. If the spirits of the dead could appear and speak, then materialism must be false.

It was in this context that, in 1882 in London, the Society for Psychical Research (SPR) was founded by a small group of highly respected scientists and scholars. Their objectives were "to examine without prejudice or pre-possession and in a scientific spirit those faculties of man, real or supposed, which appear to be inexplicable on any generally recognized hypothesis," a statement that still appears on every issue of the SPR journal. As a starting point, they established committees to study the main mysteries of the day: thought transference, mesmerism, apparitions and haunted houses, and the physical phenomena of mediumship.

One of their first major achievements was the "Census of Hallucinations," in which 17,000 people were asked whether they had ever seen or felt something, or heard a voice, that was not due to any physical cause (Sidgwick et al., 1894). Among the hallucinations of named people, far more than could be expected by chance occurred within 12 hours either way of that person's death. It seemed to be evidence "that the mind of one human being has affected the mind of another, without speech uttered, or word written, or sign made;—has affected it, that is to say, by other means than through the recog-nised channels of sense" (Gurney et al., 1886: xxxv). Thousands of accounts of spontaneous experiences were collected and published, including telepathy, psychic dreams, apparitions and collective hallucinations

Of course most of these accounts were collected long after the event and could not be directly verified. Recognizing this, the investigators began carrying out experiments, including experiments with mediums, studies of hypnosis, and tests for thought transference or telepathy. They had some successes, but generally they failed to convince the scientific community of the reality of psychic phenomena. The whole subject remained bogged down in claims of fraud and was associated with the increasingly dubious practices of spiritualism. It was to escape this reputation, and to develop new methods and terminology that, in the 1930s, the new field of parapsychology was born.

PARAPSYCHOLOGY

Parapsychology was the brainchild of J.B. Rhine (see Profile, p. 292) and Louisa Rhine, two biologists at Duke University in North Carolina (Mauskopf and McVaugh, 1980). Like the psychical researchers before them, they had far-reaching ambitions. They wanted to find evidence against a purely materialist view of human nature and fight against the powerful behaviorism of their time. They thought that their new science was the way to demonstrate the inde-pendent agency of the mind, and even to solve the mind–body problem.

They began by defining, and operationalizing, their terms. J.B. Rhine's first book, in 1934, launched the term "extrasensory perception" (ESP). This was

"*Of fundamental importance, indeed, is this doctrine of telepathy . . . Among those implications none can be more momentous than the light thrown by this discovery upon man's intimate nature and possible survival of death.*"

Myers, 1903, Vol. 1: 8

J.B. Rhine (1895–1980)

Joseph Banks Rhine, known as "the father of modern parapsychology," was trained as a botanist, and inspired to study the paranormal when attending a lecture on spiritualism by Arthur Conan Doyle. He and his wife, Louisa, coined the name "parapsychology" to distinguish the new field they created from both mainstream psychology and from psychical research. They invented the term extrasensory perception (ESP), and defined the four varieties of psi. They began their experiments in 1927 in the psychology department at Duke University in North Carolina, where they established the first parapsychology laboratory in 1935. While J.B. (as he was always known) concentrated on laboratory studies, Louisa collected accounts of spontaneous psychic experiences. In 1962 they founded the independent Foundation for Research on the Nature of Man (FRNM), and in 1995, on the 100th anniversary of J.B.'s birth, it was renamed the Rhine Research Center. The Rhines are widely remembered for their pioneering work, even though their early claims to have proved the existence of ESP did not stand the test of time.

> *"remote viewing must signify the existence of an astonishing hidden human potential"*
>
> **Targ and Puthoff**, 1977: 9

designed as a general term used to cover three types of communication that occur without the use of the senses: telepathy in which the information comes from another person; clairvoyance in which it comes from distant objects or events; and precognition in which it comes from the future. These terms are still defined this way in parapsychology, although their popular meanings are rather different.

For each of these terms the Rhines described an experimental paradigm for testing it. When testing telepathy, a receiver, or percipient, had to guess the identity of a target being looked at by a sender, or agent. To make the task as easy as possible, a set of simple symbols was developed and made into cards called ESP cards, or Zener cards (after their designer Dr. Karl Zener). The symbols were a circle, square, cross, star and wavy lines; there were five of each in a pack of 25 cards. For testing clairvoyance, a similar method was used except that the pack was randomized out of sight of anyone. In precognition experiments its order was determined *after* the guesses had been made. The Rhines believed that everyone has some paranormal ability even if it is very weak. So they tested ordinary people, rather than only those who claimed special psychic powers.

With five possibilities to choose from, mean chance expectation is one hit in five guesses. In fact their subjects rarely scored much more than five, but by amassing huge numbers of guesses, and applying the appropriate statistical tests, the Rhines obtained significant, above-chance, results. They started a controversy that has never really disappeared.

A few years later they took another controversial step. One day a gambler came to their laboratory claiming that he could affect the roll of dice by the power of his mind. Rhine turned this into an experimental method, first using hand-thrown dice and then a dice-throwing machine. The results were not as impressive as the ESP results but nevertheless seemed to suggest some paranormal ability. Instead of the older term "telekinesis" the Rhines called this "psychokinesis," or PK (Rhine, 1947). They also coined the term "psi" to cover any paranormal phenomena or the hypothesized mechanism underlying them. Thus psi includes both ESP and PK.

These terms have been useful for parapsychology, but their negative definition has caused serious problems. All forms of psi are defined as communication *without* the use of the normal senses or forces. This means that psi researchers have to go to ever-greater lengths to rule out all "normal" interactions, and critics can always think of new reasons why the phenomena might be normal after all. Another consequence of the definitions is that parapsychology keeps shrinking because when phenomena such as hypnosis, hallucinations or lucid dreams are explained by psychology, they cease to count as paranormal.

The controversy provoked by the Rhines spread around the world and prompted numerous methodological criticisms. In the first experiments the cards were held up in front of receivers, and the patterns could be faintly detected through the back. Dice had to be checked for bias, the subjects separated more carefully and the possibility of recording errors dealt with. The most important problem, however, was the randomization. In the early psychical research experiments, senders had been allowed to choose what to send; for example, they were asked to draw the first thing that came to mind. This meant that receivers could appear to be telepathic if they knew the sender well, or could guess what the sender might choose. Using ESP cards ruled out this problem, but shuffling them proved to be an inadequate method of randomization.

For this reason, mechanical shuffling devices were invented, or log tables were used to decide the order of the cards. Nowadays parapsychologists use random number tables, or random number generators (RNGs) based either on computer pseudo-random algorithms or on truly random processes such as radioactive decay. All this is necessary to rule out any systematic biases that might produce spurious correlations between the target sequences and the order of guesses. Finally the Rhines' statistical methods were criticized until in 1937 the President of the American Institute of Mathematical Statistics declared that if the experiments were performed as stated, the statistical analysis was essentially valid (Rhine, 1947).

Soon others, appreciating the importance of these findings if they were true, tried to replicate them. The story of one man's attempts illustrates all the trials and tribulations of research in parapsychology then, and since.

Samuel G. Soal was a mathematician at Queen Mary College, London. Inspired by the Rhines' results, he spent five years accumulating thousands of guesses with several subjects, and yet was completely unsuccessful. He would probably have given up except that another British researcher, Whateley Carington, claimed that in his experiments the subjects sometimes picked the target one before or one after the intended target, a phenomenon that later became known as the "displacement effect." So, following Carington's suggestions, Soal laboriously checked all his guesses against the symbols before and after the original target. To his surprise, the results of one subject, Basil Shackleton, showed highly significant scores for the card ahead.

Retrospective "fishing" in data cannot prove anything, but it can provide predictions for future experiments. So Soal invited Shackleton back for more

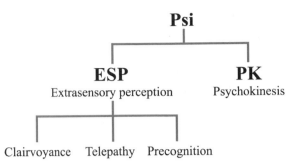

FIGURE 20.2 • Terms used in parapsychology. "Psi" is a general term that refers to all kinds of paranormal phenomena or the supposed mechanism underlying them. There are four forms of psi.

"Remote viewing is nothing more than a self-fulfilling subjective delusion."

Marks, 2000: 92

ACTIVITY
Telepathy tests

1. AN IMPRESSIVE DEMONSTRATION

Stand in front of the group (or ask someone who is good at acting the part to do so) and say something like this: "I have the special power of being able to transmit my thoughts to others. I am now going to draw two simple shapes, one inside the other and I want you to pick up my thoughts." Out of sight of the audience, draw a triangle inside a circle, fold the paper carefully and hide it away in a pocket. "I am sending my thoughts into your mind. Please try to feel my thoughts and draw what you see." When everyone has done their drawing, show them the original.

Typically, about 25 percent of the audience will have a direct hit, and others will have come close. Ask them how they think it worked.

The answer is population stereotypes. There are, in fact, rather few simple shapes to choose from; triangles and circles are most popular. If you want to rule out the possibility that telepathy was involved as well, you could think about a hexagon inside a square while the audience are drawing. Other examples to use can be found in Marks (2000: 311–17).

2. A POOR EXPERIMENT

Ask for a volunteer to act as sender, ideally someone who claims telepathic ability. Give them a pen and paper and ask them to leave the room and draw "at random" whatever comes to mind. Agree on a time limit, say two minutes, for the drawing. Everyone else must relax quietly and think about the sender. After two minutes they all try to draw what the sender drew. When they have finished, ask the sender to return and reveal the drawing.

This is the basic method that was used in "thought transference" experiments in the 1890s. You can use it to explore all the methodological issues that modern parapsychology has grappled with.

Sender choice

If the sender chooses the target, hits can occur because the people know each other or because

(Activity continues on next page)

tests, predicting that the same pattern would be found. To ensure that Shackleton could not cheat, rigid controls were employed, and respected scientists were invited to observe all the experiments. This time Soal was successful. Indeed, the odds against these new results occurring by chance were $10^{37}:1$ (that is, 10 followed by 37 zeros) (Soal and Bateman, 1954). These experiments became the mainstay of the evidence for ESP and, because of the apparently impeccable controls and powerful results, many scientists and philosophers took them seriously (West, 1954). Even Turing was concerned at the havoc ESP would play with his proposed test for an intelligent machine (see Chapter 13). "These disturbing phenomena seem to deny all our usual scientific ideas. How we should like to discredit them! Unfortunately the statistical evidence, at least for telepathy, is overwhelming" (1950: 66).

But this was not the end of the story. Other researchers failed to replicate the Rhine–Soal results and some began making accusations of fraud. Then one of Soal's senders claimed that she had seen Soal changing figures in the target list. This provoked a flurry of reanalyses and investigations of Soal's work, none of which either conclusively incriminated nor exonerated him.

In the 1970s, Betty Markwick, a member of the Society for Psychical Research, joined those determined to clear Soal's name. She had access to a computer (rare in those days) and began to search through the log tables for the sequences Soal had used for his randomization. She knew that if she could match up the log tables to the actual target sequences, she could prove that he had not changed them. She failed. But she did not give up. Instead she began a long and tedious search through his target sequences by hand. To her surprise, she came across some repeated sequences which would be very unlikely to occur in the log tables. Then, even more surprising, she found sequences that appeared to be repeated except that they had a few extra numbers added in. She returned to the computer and searched again for just such sequences.

When she did so, she found that all of the extras corresponded to ESP hits, and when these extras were removed, the results fell to chance (Markwick, 1978). It had taken a quarter of a century of hard work to solve the mystery, and in that time thousands of people had been taken in.

Parapsychologists generally accepted Markwick's conclusions, but many still believed that other results were genuine. They found "signs of psi" such as "psi missing" (scoring consistently *below* chance), the "decline effect" (a decline in scores through the course of an experiment or session) and the "sheep-goat" effect (believers in psi score higher than disbelievers) (Schmeidler and McConnell, 1958).

The sheep-goat effect suggested that belief and motivation might be important, and if experimenters needed these qualities too, the many failures to replicate might be explained in terms of a "psi-mediated experimenter effect." The way to test this is to run exactly the same experiment with two different experimenters, and indeed a few such experiments have provided successful results for the believing experimenter but not for the psi-inhibitory experimenter (West, 1954; Wiseman and Schlitz, 1998). But this effect is also hard to replicate, and critics argue that the differences in results depend on how carefully the experiments are controlled, not on their experimenters' beliefs.

This brief history of the first century of research shows how difficult parapsychology is. The results never seem to be good enough to convince the skeptics, and yet the skeptics cannot prove the negative—that paranormal phenomena do not exist.

ESP—EXTRASENSORY PERCEPTION

Traditional card guessing experiments are exceedingly boring. The subjects get tired, and the significance of the results can only be demonstrated statistically. By contrast, reports of psychic dreams, premonitions and real-life ESP are exciting. The challenge for modern parapsychology was to capture this in the lab.

One of the best-known attempts was the ESP-dream research at the Maimonides Medical

---

(Activity continued)

they both pick up cues from the environment or from the experimenter. Targets must be randomly chosen.

Judging the result

When two drawings look similar, it is impossible to judge chance expectation (you can try using drawings you have collected). Solutions include forced-choice methods using cards or preselected sets of objects, and the more complex free-response methods used for ganzfeld and remote viewing.

Sensory leakage

Could anyone have heard or seen the drawing being made? Could they have changed their own drawing after the target was revealed?

Fraud

Could the sender have told friends in advance, or arranged a code for tapping the answer on the floor? Could the experimenter have set the whole thing up?

FIGURE 20.3 • Suppose that in a telepathy experiment the sender draws the picture on the left and the receiver that on the right. How does the experimenter decide whether this is evidence for telepathy or not? The target was a boat and the response was a house—so it must be a miss. But the shapes are remarkably similar—so perhaps it is a hit after all. Problems like this forced the development of better methods, including forced-choice and free-response methods.

3. A (REASONABLY) CONTROLLED EXPERIMENT

Advance preparation: remove the court cards from a pack of playing cards, leaving 40 cards of four suits. Use a computer pseudo-RNG, or random number tables, to decide the target order. If you use tables (log tables will do), stick a pin into the page without looking and begin from there. Assign 1 — hearts, 2 — spades, 3 — clubs, 4 — diamonds, and ignore all

(Activity continues on next page)

(Activity continued)

other numbers in the table. Make a record of the target order. Arrange the cards in that order with the first card on the top when the pack is face down. Place an unused card on the bottom to conceal the last card. Seal the pack in an opaque envelope. Seal the list in another envelope. Find a suitable room where the sender can work alone. Get two stopwatches. Prepare answer sheets as in Figure 20.4.

Trial	Target suit	Guessed suit	Tick if correct
1			
2			
3			
4			
5			
...			
40			
		Total correct:	

FIGURE 20.4 • Answer sheet for experiment 3. Receivers record all their guesses in column 3. The experimenter then reads out the target list so that they can fill in column 2. Finally they check for hits and complete the last box. This is the number to go into the class histogram.

The experiment

Choose a sender as before. Give her a stopwatch and the sealed pack, and arrange the exact time at which she will turn over the first card. The sender then goes to the appointed room, opens the envelope and places the pack face down on the table. At the prearranged time she turns over the first card and concentrates on it, turning the rest of the cards at 15 second intervals. The whole test will take 10 minutes. Meanwhile, you call out the numbers 1–40 at the correct times, and the receivers write down which suit they think the sender is looking at.

When the test is complete, ask the sender to return. Call out the target sequence and ask each person to check their neighbor's scores. If you have a large enough group (say 20 or more), the best way to

(Activity continues on next page)

Center in New York (Ullman et al., 1973). This pioneered "free-response" methods instead of "forced-choice." Sleeping subjects were monitored in the lab and then freely reported their dreams (rather than having to say "square, circle, circle" and so on). Meanwhile an agent looked at a randomly chosen target such as a colorful picture or a sequence of slides. Dramatic correspondences were found between the dreams and targets but, as in the early thought transference experiments, this presented the problem of estimating how frequently such coincidences would be expected by chance. The solution was to provide a small set of possible targets (usually just four or six). Using this method, either the subject or an independent judge matches the dream imagery against each of the set in turn and tries to pick the true target. In this way, simple statistics can be applied to an interesting free-response experiment. The results for the early dream studies were well above chance, but other laboratories failed to replicate these positive results, and the dream studies were dropped. However, the basic method was later applied in other ways.

In "remote viewing" a target person goes to a randomly selected remote location and looks around for a specified length of time. Meanwhile the subject sits and relaxes, reporting any impressions or images that arise. Afterward either the subject, or an independent judge, tries to match up the impressions with a set of possible target locations and to pick the right one. This method became famous when physicists Russell Targ and Harold Puthoff (1977), at the Stanford Research Institute in California, obtained highly significant results. Then two psychologists, David Marks and Richard Kammann, argued that there were clues in the transcripts that might have been used to obtain spurious results. This led to a controversy in the prestigious journal *Nature* and attempts by others to determine the relevance of these clues (Marks, 2000).

In 1995, the American Institutes for Research reported on "Stargate," a 24-year, $22-million, government-funded research project on the feasibility of using remote viewing for intelligence gathering. Arguments about the adequacy of the methods used and the significance of the results followed (Hyman, 1995; Utts, 1995; Wiseman and Milton, 1998). American statistician Jessica Utts described Stargate as providing some of the most solid evidence of psi to date, whereas Marks described it as "a series of closed-off, flawed, non-validated, and nonreplicated studies," concluding that "Remote viewing is nothing more than a self-fulfilling subjective delusion" (Marks, 2000: 92). Regardless of who is right, the US government decided that remote viewing could not be used for gathering intelligence. There is also no evidence that any other country has successfully employed ESP for spying.

Finally, by far the greatest controversy of all has surrounded ESP in the ganzfeld. Subjects in a ganzfeld experiment lie comfortably, listening to white noise or sea-shore sounds through headphones, and wear half ping-pong balls over their eyes to produce a uniform white or pink field (the ganzfeld): a technique designed to produce a psi-conducive state of consciousness. While in the ganzfeld, they report everything they experience and this is recorded for judging afterward. Meanwhile a sender in a distant room views a picture or video clip. After half an hour or so, subjects are shown four such pictures or videos, and are asked to decide which one was the target. Alternatively, independent judges make the decision by comparing the transcripts of the session with the possible targets. Many researchers have reported success with this method, and even claimed that the ganzfeld provides a replicable method for inducing psi, but critics disagree.

Let us suppose that experiments like these one day produce reliable evidence for ESP. What would the implications be for understanding consciousness? Interestingly, although many researchers claim that this would prove the power of consciousness, or the independence of mind, there is little in the experiments to support this claim. Even in the most successful ESP experiments, subjects are not consciously aware of which guesses are hits and which are misses (if they were, these guesses could be separated out

(Activity continued)

show the results is to build up a histogram on a board or computer. Ask each person in turn to call out how many hits they got, and add their result to the growing picture. At first the results may seem impressive, or strange, but they will tend ever closer to a normal distribution with a mean at 10. If the results deviate from 10 and you wish to test them statistically, use a normal approximation to binomial, or a one-sample t-test using 10 as the expected value (but see below).

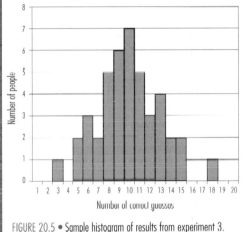

FIGURE 20.5 • Sample histogram of results from experiment 3. Unless psi is operating in your experiment, you are likely to get a normal distribution with a mean of 10.

This method solved most of the problems of Test 2, but others remain. Because many receivers guessed at the same target sequence, their scores are not independent and most statistical tests are invalid. This is called the stacking effect and can be avoided by using individual target sequences or by taking only the majority vote from the whole group. Sensory leakage or fraud might still have taken place, and you may discuss whether they could ever be completely ruled out. Also note that the test is not a pure test of telepathy because clairvoyance could be used directly on the cards. This makes it a GESP (general ESP) test.

Other psi experiments, with more detailed instructions, can be found in Blackmore and Hart-Davis (1995).

THE GANZFELD CONTROVERSY

The first ganzfeld experiment was published in 1974 by the American parapsychologist Charles Honorton. Attempts at replication produced varying results, steadily improving techniques and many years of argument, all culminating in the 1985 "Great Ganzfeld Debate" between Honorton and American psychologist Ray Hyman (1985). Both carried out meta-analyses of all the available published results, but they came to opposite conclusions. Hyman argued that the positive results could all be explained by methodological errors and multiple analyses. Honorton argued that the overall effect size was large and did not depend on the number of flaws in the experiments, and that the results were consistent, not dependent on any one experimenter, and revealed regular features of ESP. In a "joint communiqué" (Hyman and Honorton, 1986) they detailed their agreements and disagreements, and made recommendations for the conduct of future ganzfeld experiments.

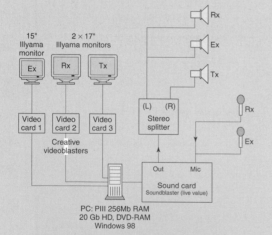

FIGURE 20.6 • Following the success with the Princeton autoganzfeld, a similar system was set up at Edinburgh University. The sender, receiver and experimenter are all in separate rooms. The experimenter's room contains the control system shown here. The computer is a Pentium III 500 MHz with three video cards (primary display to experimenter's room, isolated secondary and tertiary displays to the sender's and receiver's rooms, respectively.) and a DVD drive (containing digitized video and audio). There is a two-way audio link between Experimenter and Receiver, and a one-way audio link from Experimenter to Sender (after Honorton et al., 1990).

and the scoring rate dramatically improved). So ESP is not a skill that can be exercised voluntarily.

Some methods, such as the ganzfeld, do involve a mild altered state of consciousness, but it has never been shown that subjects who enter a deeper state do better, or that an altered state is necessary for success in the ganzfeld. There is also no consensus over what it is about the ganzfeld that makes it psi-conducive, if indeed it is. Hypnosis has also been used as an induction technique, but again there has been no clear demonstration that an altered state of consciousness helps. In the absence of experiments of this kind we have no idea which of a potentially unlimited number of untested variables are relevant. The connection with consciousness seems to come entirely from theoretical suppositions about how ESP might work. There is no direct evidence that consciousness is involved in any way.

PK — PSYCHOKINESIS

Psychokinesis, or PK, is the ability to affect objects or events without touching them or using any ordinary force. Research into PK includes studies of table tipping and levitation, the early experiments with dice, studies of metal bending with Uri Geller and the many children who emulated him (Marks, 2000; Randi, 1975), and studies of distant mental influence on living systems (DMILS) (Braud and Schlitz, 1989). However, the majority of modern PK research is on micro-PK, the supposed effect of the human mind on microscopic, quantum mechanical or probabilistic systems.

Micro-PK research began in the 1970s with experiments in which subjects willed a light to move either clockwise or counter-clockwise around a circle. The direction was controlled by a truly random process: particles emitted from a strontium-90 radioactive source. Since then many other kinds of PK machines have been used, not just to demonstrate PK but to test competing theories.

The "observational theories," which are derived from quantum physics, describe psi not as a force operating in real time, but as a shift in probabilities caused by conscious observation of the results. So according to these theories, PK occurs at the moment when feedback is given, not when the particles are emitted. This extraordinary effect was apparently confirmed in an experiment using pre-recorded targets (Schmidt, 1976). A radioactive source generated random numbers and these were converted into clicks on the left and right channels of an audio tape. The tape was later played to subjects whose task was to influence the clicks to one side or the other. The tapes were then stored for hours, days or even weeks before playing to the subjects. When they were played, an excess of clicks in the chosen direction was found. To rule out the possibility that subjects were physically affecting their tape by ordinary PK, copies of the original output were kept, unseen by anyone, and compared with the tape after the experiment was completed. In some experiments subjects were given the same targets four times over. In this case the retro-PK effect was stronger.

If time-displaced PK effects like this seem impossible or nonsensical, it may be worth bearing in mind that all forms of psi are, from some perspectives, impossible, and perhaps probabilistic quantum effects are no more impossible than "ordinary" psi.

Sadly, these dramatic effects did not prove replicable by other researchers, but many new methods were subsequently developed. For example, at the Princeton Engineering Anomalies Research Lab, or PEAR, American engineer Robert Jahn and his colleagues collected enormous amounts of data using quantum mechanical random number generators (RNGs). All data were automatically recorded, direction of aim was counterbalanced, and baseline conditions were recorded for control. Other researchers have used similar methods and, as in the case of the ganzfeld, meta-analysis has been used to try to determine whether there is an overall effect in the entire database.

The first major meta-analysis included nearly 600 RNG-PK studies (Radin and Nelson, 1989). It found chance results in control conditions but significant deviations from chance in experimental conditions. This effect, though exceedingly small in size, was consistent throughout the data base, not related to methodological quality and not dependent on the work of just a few investigators. The authors interpreted this as "evidence for consciousness-related anomalies in random physical systems" (Radin and Nelson, 1989: 1499).

In 1994 the original meta-analysis was republished in *Psychological Bulletin* (Bem and Honorton, 1994), along with impressive new results obtained with a fully automated ganzfeld procedure carried out at Honorton's laboratory in Princeton. This "autoganzfeld" was hailed as a fraud-proof technique that would finally provide a repeatable experiment for parapsychology, but criticisms began again with the suggestion that acoustic leakage might have occurred (Wiseman et al., 1996).

Another problem concerned nine studies carried out by British psychologist Carl Sargent at Cambridge University. The original meta-analyses included 28 studies, and these nine comprised nearly a third of them. The Sargent studies also had the second highest effect size after Honorton's. Having failed to obtain significant results myself, I visited Sargent's laboratory in 1979 and found that the experiments, which looked so well controlled in print, were far from fraud-proof and suffered from many errors and failures to follow the protocol. I concluded that the results could not be relied upon as evidence for psi (Blackmore, 1987; Sargent, 1987). This experience contributed to my transformation from belief in ESP to skepticism (Blackmore, 1996).

Following the apparent success of the autoganzfeld, more replications followed, but few were successful. Then another meta-analysis of 30 new studies found no evidence for ESP (Milton and Wiseman, 1999), while another, including 10 new studies, did (Bem et al., 2001). The arguments look set to continue (Milton, 1999).

From this, and two further meta-analyses, they concluded that consciousness has a direct effect on matter. However, there followed debates about which experiments should have been included, the heterogeneity of the studies, the importance or otherwise of various potential flaws in the methods and so on. A subsequent meta-analysis by different authors revealed a very much smaller effect size, and one that could be reduced to chance levels by the addition of just a few more non-significant studies (Steinkamp et al., 2002). Thus the whole question of the existence of micro-PK remains in doubt, and similar doubts apply to the dice experiments, with a meta-analysis of the "effects of consciousness on the fall of dice" showing barely significant overall effects (Radin and Ferrari, 1991).

Those parapsychologists who are convinced of the evidence for PK frequently make explicit claims that consciousness is involved. This makes sense in terms of their underlying theories. For example, some are dualists and believe that non-physical mind, or consciousness, acts as a force on the physical universe. Others favor theories based on quantum physics, suggesting that consciousness directly affects the collapse of the wave function, or that consciousness is independent of time and space. However, there is nothing in the experiments themselves that directly tests this connection with consciousness.

In a typical PK experiment the subject tries to influence a visual or auditory display controlled by an RNG. A bias in the intended direction is then taken as evidence for PK. But there is a big leap from this correlation to a causal explanation involving "the effect of consciousness." The controls done do not show that the intention has to be a conscious one, and indeed comments in the published papers suggest that some subjects actually do better when not thinking about the task or when doing something completely different like reading a magazine. This suggests that conscious intent might even be counterproductive. Controls do show that the subject is necessary, but they do not identify what it is about the subject's presence that creates the effect. It might be their unconscious intentions or expectations, it might be some change in behavior elicited by the instructions given, or it might be a mysterious resonance between the RNG and some unidentified neural process or brain function. To find out whether the effect is due to consciousness, relevant experiments would have to be done and so far have not been.

THE POWER OF COINCIDENCES

We may now return to the kinds of spontaneous experience outlined at the start and ask how they are to be explained. In later chapters we will consider dreams (Chapter 23), as well as out-of-body, near-death and mystical experiences (Chapter 24), but what makes the experience described at the start of this chapter so interesting is that it apparently involved telepathy or precognition. Like many of the most common psychic experiences, this comes down to a matter of probabilities.

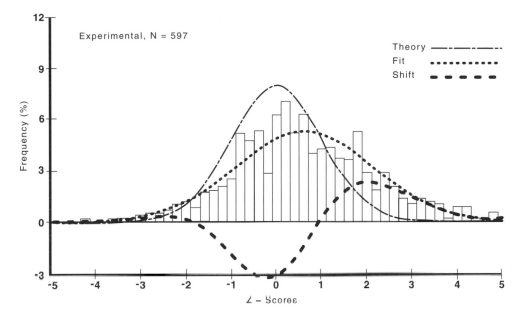

FIGURE 20.7 • The results of Radin and Nelson's meta-analysis of 597 published RNG-PK studies. The bars show the distribution of Z-scores, a measure of the deviation from the expected mean. If chance alone were operating, the distribution should have a mean of 0, shown here as "theory." The dotted line shows the best fit to the data and the "shift" shows that there was an excess of studies with positive Z-scores (after Radin and Nelson, 1989).

It is notoriously hard to judge how likely any given coincidence is, so it is possible that people misinterpret chance coincidences as far more unlikely than they really are, and then look for explanations. If no good explanation is available, they assume the event was paranormal. Consistent with this hypothesis, people who are better at making probability judgments are less likely to report psychic experiences or to believe in the paranormal (Blackmore and Troscianko, 1985; French, 1992).

People also remember the details that come true and forget the rest. In the example at the start of this chapter, the dreamer saw Shelley in a hospital bed, but since she died at the scene, she was probably never bandaged and not in the hospital, but such details are easily overlooked.

One British statistician used some simple assumptions to calculate the odds of anyone dreaming that a named person died when that person actually did die within 12 hours of the dream. Given the number of people who die every day, and assuming that each person only has one dream in their entire lifetime in which someone they know dies, he calculated that one such coincidence will happen to someone in Britain every two weeks. If you were that person, wouldn't you be convinced it was paranormal?

PRACTICE
LIVING WITHOUT PSI

The possibility of ESP is comforting. We might sense when a loved one is in danger, share our deepest feelings with others or find ourselves guided by a supernatural power. For this exercise, try living without such comfort.

If you believe in psi, or angels, or life after death, or spirits, take this opportunity to live without them. You need not abandon your beliefs forever. Just set them aside for a few days and see how the world looks when you know you are completely on your own.

Skeptics should do this too. You may be surprised to find yourself *willing* something to happen even though you know you cannot affect it, or hoping someone will just know when you need them. Ask yourself this. Do we live better or worse for a belief in the paranormal? Don't give a glib, intellectual answer. Look and see what happens when you try to give it up completely.

SELF-ASSESSMENT QUESTIONS

○ If paranormal phenomena exist, what are the implications for science?

○ Why was psychical research founded, and what were its main aims?

○ Define all the main terms used in parapsychology.

○ Why is the randomization of targets so important in psi experiments? What are the best methods?

○ Describe two or more experiments that use free-response methods for testing ESP.

○ Outline the ganzfeld controversy. What conclusion do *you* draw?

○ How is micro-PK tested? What are the implications for consciousness?

IMPLICATIONS

There probably are no paranormal phenomena. In spite of a century and a half of increasingly sophisticated research we still cannot be sure. However, we may safely conclude this much: if psi exists it is an extremely weak effect. No progress has been made at all in identifying how it works or in developing theories to explain its peculiarities, and there is no direct evidence that ESP and PK are effects of consciousness.

Some people seem to think that rejecting the paranormal also means rejecting spirituality. As we shall see (in Chapter 27), this is not necessary at all. Although some spiritual traditions claim miracles and supernatural powers, many decry chasing after the paranormal, and there is nothing intrinsically spiritual about the ability to bend spoons at a distance, levitate one's body or pick up thoughts from someone else's mind.

And there is one last curious fact to note. Most of what we have learned so far in this book seems to point away from the idea of consciousness as a separate entity or as having any powers of its own to affect the world. Yet this "power of consciousness" is what many parapsychologists explicitly seek. In this way, parapsychology seems to be growing ever further away from the progress and excitement of the rest of consciousness studies.

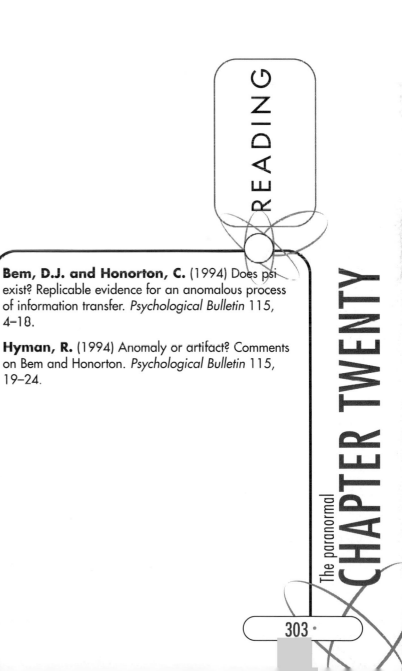

READING

Bem, D.J. and Honorton, C. (1994) Does psi exist? Replicable evidence for an anomalous process of information transfer. *Psychological Bulletin* 115, 4–18.

Hyman, R. (1994) Anomaly or artifact? Comments on Bem and Honorton. *Psychological Bulletin* 115, 19–24.

The paranormal
CHAPTER TWENTY

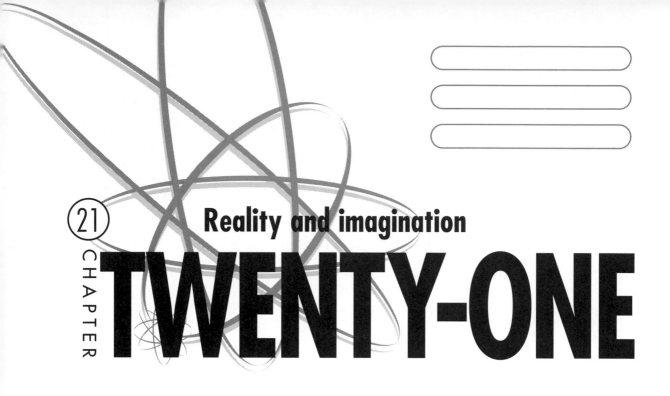

I was lying on my back in bed and drifting off to sleep, when I suddenly realized I couldn't move. I could hear this horrible buzzing, vibrating noise, and I could feel something—or someone—in the room with me. I tried to see who it was but I couldn't move anything but my eyes. Then I saw this dark shape looming up over the end of the bed. I tried to scream, but I couldn't breathe, and nothing came out but a strangled cry. A heavy weight started pressing down on my chest and I could feel, and smell, the dark shape coming closer and closer. I heard or felt it say something to me, but I couldn't make out the words. It touched my arms and legs and began pulling me out of bed.

Imagine that this experience happened to you. What would you think?—that is, once your heart stopped pounding and the smell of the creature left your nostrils? Would you comfort yourself with the thought that the menacing black figure wasn't *real* at all and was only *imagined*? Or might you decide that it was an alien come to abduct you, or perhaps the ghost of someone who had died? Either way you face a problem. If the creature was *real*, why did the door remained closed and the bed covers undisturbed? Why did no one else see the creature coming through the house? Obviously it wasn't real in that public sense. On the other hand if it was only *imagined*, how could it have such a powerful effect on you, and make your heart pound and your hands sweat? Obviously *something* happened to you, and the experience itself was real enough, wasn't it? Thinking this way can make us deeply confused about the difference between reality and imagination.

Perhaps we should be confused. Let's take a more ordinary example. Suppose you walk into your kitchen and see your black cat on the chair. You look again and realize that it's actually a friend's pullover, left in a heap, with one arm dangling. The strange thing is that if you had not looked again, and someone had asked you to, you could have described how the cat was sitting, which way its ears were pointing and how its tail hung down off the seat.

FIGURE 21.1

You may say that the pullover was real and the cat was imagined, but now consider the same thing happening when the cat is actually there. In a brief glimpse you could not have taken in all those details, and yet they were mostly correct. Were they real or imagined?

These questions bring us straight back to all the familiar philosophical problems of perception, and to the central problem of consciousness: the difference between the objective and subjective worlds. Perhaps it may help to learn about the strange experiences that hover between reality and imagination.

REALITY DISCRIMINATION

In everyday life we discriminate "real" from "imagined" all the time without noticing the skill involved. That is, we distinguish our own internally generated thoughts from external, public, reality: a skill called reality monitoring (Johnson and Raye, 1981) or reality discrimination. Experiments in which people are asked to see or hear some stimuli, and to imagine others, show that many different features can be used, including how stable, detailed or vivid the experiences are, and whether they can be voluntarily controlled. By and large mental images are less vivid, less stable and more easily manipulated than perceptions. So we don't usually confuse the two.

We can, however, be tricked. In her classic experiment, Cheves Perky (1910) asked subjects to look at a blank screen and to imagine an object on it, such as a tomato. Unbeknown to the subjects, she back-projected a picture of a tomato onto the screen and gradually increased the brightness. Even when the picture was bright enough to be easily seen, the subjects still believed that they were imagining it. Similar effects have been found since, and show that reality discrimination is affected by whether we expect something to be real or imagined.

Distinguishing memories of events that really happened from events we have only imagined is particularly difficult, and its failure results in false memories —that is, convincing "memories" of events that never actually happened. By

Ronald K. Siegel (b. 1943)

Ronald Siegel is a pioneer of drug studies and explorer of altered states of consciousness. In the 1970s he and his colleagues trained people to become "psychonauts," that is, to go into altered states and report what they experienced as it happened. He has researched the effects of LSD, THC, marijuana, MDMA, mescaline, psilocybin and ketamine, among other drugs, and has acted as consultant on several investigations of drug use. He is not just an experimenter and theoretician, but has trained in martial arts, experienced sleep paralysis, taken part in shamanic rituals and was once locked in a cage for more than three days without food or water, all in the interests of investigating consciousness. He has a PhD in psychology from Dalhousie University and is Associate Research Professor at the University of California in Los Angeles.

and large real memories are more easily brought to mind, and are more vivid and detailed than false memories. Sometimes real memories can be identified because we can put them in context with other events or remember when and how they happened, a skill called source monitoring. This is not important for learning skills and facts. For example, you may reliably and correctly remember the speed of light, the capital of Germany and the name of the man next door, without needing to remember when or where you learned them, but for autobiographical memory the context is important. If the memory of an event in your life is vivid, detailed and plausible, and fits with other events in time and place, then you are more likely to judge that it really happened.

Mistakes are inevitable. Often this does not matter, as when we have a vivid "memory" of running away from home at age four because the story has become part of family history, or when we "remember" that day on the beach because we've seen the photo so many times. False memories are more problematic when people "remember" sexual abuse that never happened, or identify suspects they never saw (Loftus and Ketcham, 1994). In these cases it is important to find out the truth of what happened by some kind of independent verification. However, this does not mean that there is a sharp dividing line between "real" memories and "false" memories. All memories are reconstructions of the past and in that sense are imagined, even when they are correct.

This dividing line is particularly interesting when it concerns experiences for which there can be no public corroboration, like dreams, fantasies and hallucinations. Did I *really* experience that horrible dark creature in my room that night? What does this question mean?

HALLUCINATIONS

The term "hallucination" is not easy to define, although some rough distinctions can be helpful if not applied too rigidly. Hallucinations were distinguished from illusions early in the nineteenth century, on the basis that hallucinations are entirely internal whereas illusions are misperceptions of external things. So "illusions" include all the familiar visual illusions such as the Muller–Lyer illusion or Ponzo illusion, as well as misperceptions such as seeing a pullover as a cat. By contrast, hallucinations are perceptual experiences in the absence of an appropriate external stimulus. This distinction is still used, but we should note that there is no clean dividing line. For example, imagine that someone sees the ghost of a headless monk float across the altar in church. We might say that there was nothing there and that the monk was a hallucination, or alternatively that a faint swirl of candle smoke or incense was misperceived and that the monk was an illusion.

True hallucinations are sometimes distinguished from pseudo-hallucinations, in which the person knows that what is seen or heard is not real. So, for example, if you heard a voice telling you that the thought-police were coming to get you, and you believed they were, you would be suffering a true hallucination, but if you heard the same voice as you were nodding off over your computer, and realized you were working too late, that would be a pseudo-hallucination. One problem with this distinction is that, if taken too literally, there are probably very few true hallucinations. Even with a double dose of LSD most people still know that the enormous monster towering above them is really a tree, and when a young naval officer climbs from the cabin and takes the wheel in the midst of a storm hundreds of miles from shore, the exhausted lone sailor knows that no one else can really be aboard the ship.

FIGURE 21.2 ● On LSD trips the floor can turn into a carpet of snakes, cars into space ships, and trees into monsters. But typically the tripper still knows that the monster is really a tree and is therefore technically having a pseudo-hallucination, not a true hallucination.

A final distinction is between hallucinations and mental imagery. Hallucinations are sometimes distinguished from imagery by their resemblance to publicly shared perceptions rather than private thoughts, or by their uncontrollability. If we voluntarily imagine a tropical beach with the sound of waves lapping on the sand, this is usually called imagery, but if the vision forces itself on our mind and won't go away, it would be called a hallucination. But even this distinction is far from clear. For example, the images that come on the borders of sleep (see below) are often called "hypnagogic imagery" rather than "hypnagogic hallucinations" although they are not voluntary or easily controllable. Rather than try too hard to delimit these categories, some prefer to think of a continuum with true hallucinations at one end and imagery at the other, but even this may not help if there are multiple dimensions involved.

These distinctions are discussed by British psychologists Peter Slade and Richard Bentall (1988) who propose the following working definition of a hallucination:

> Any percept-like experience which (a) occurs in the absence of an appropriate stimulus, (b) has the full force or impact of the corresponding actual (real) perception, and (c) is not amenable to direct and voluntary control by the experiencer.

Hallucinations are frequently associated with madness, and in particular with schizophrenia. Schizophrenia is probably the most common single cause of psychiatric disability throughout the world, affecting something like 1 percent of the population. It is difficult to define, difficult to understand and tends to be diagnosed differently at different times and in different countries. Although the symptoms are highly variable, the core is a loss of the sense of personal control. Schizophrenics may be convinced that people with psychic powers are forcing them to act the way they do or that an evil entity is controlling them. The most common kind of hallucination is hearing voices, such as aliens plotting evil deeds or fairies chattering in the walls. Some schizophrenics feel that other people are inserting thoughts into their mind; some hear their own thoughts being spoken out loud as though by someone else. At their worst, these hallucinations are vivid and compelling, uncontrollable and experienced as completely real (Frith, 1995).

Although hallucinations are often thought of as purely pathological, or as primarily a symptom of mental illness, there are many reasons for rejecting this view. First, as we have seen, there is no clear dividing line between them and other experiences; second, hallucinations are widespread in the normal population; third, there are wide cultural variations in attitudes toward hallucinations with some, like contemporary Western culture, relegating them largely to pathology, while other cultures value them highly.

One of the first attempts to study hallucinations in the general population was the Society for Psychical Research's "Census of Hallucinations" (Gurney et al., 1886; Sidgwick et al., 1894); 17,000 people were asked, "Have you ever, when believing yourself to be completely awake, had a vivid impression of seeing or being touched by a living being or inanimate object, or of hearing a voice; which impression, so far as you could discover, was not due to any external physical cause?" When obvious cases of illness and dreaming were ruled out, 1684 people (almost 10 percent) said they had. Visual hallucinations were more common than auditory, females reported more hallucinations than males, and the most common type was a vision of a living person. Some 50 years later West (1948) found similar results but, unlike the original SPR survey, he found no convincing evidence for telepathy.

In the 1980s, the Launay–Slade Hallucination Scale was developed, and several surveys showed that large numbers of healthy people reported experiences usually associated with pathology, such as hearing a voice speaking one's thoughts aloud. Scores on the scale were approximately normally distributed. This suggests that the tendency to hallucinate varies along a continuum, so that pathological cases are at one extreme rather than constituting something completely different (Slade and Bentall, 1988). This scale has subsequently been used to explore the rather complex relationships between the tendency to hallucinate and other variables such as reality monitoring, vividness of imagery, schizotypal personality and susceptibility to hypnosis.

CONTEXTS AND CONTENTS OF HALLUCINATIONS

While some hallucinations occur spontaneously, others are caused by drugs, illness, starvation and sleep deprivation, or by the use of ritual practices such as rhythmic drumming, whirling, dancing, chanting, flagellation or control of the breath. Sensory deprivation is a powerful way to induce hallucinations. It is as though, when deprived of input, the sensory systems find patterns in what little information they have, lower their criterion for what to accept as real or turn to internally generated stimulation instead. In the 1930s, British neurologist Hughlings Jackson suggested the "perceptual release" theory of hallucinations: that memories and internally generated images are normally inhibited by a flow of information from the senses, and so they are released when input is disrupted or absent. American psychologist Ronald Siegel (see Profile, p. 306) likens this to a man looking out of the window near sunset. At first, all he sees is the world outside. Then, as darkness falls, the reflection of the fire inside and the room it illuminates take over and now he sees them as though they lie outside. In this way inner images come to seem real (Siegel, 1977).

This happens to people who immerse themselves in sensory deprivation tanks, to lone explorers and climbers and to people who become blind through either retinal or brain damage. The latter is called Charles Bonnet syndrome and is very common in older people who have cataracts, macular degeneration or retinal damage through diabetes. Sometimes sufferers don't tell anyone about their experiences for fear that they are going mad, and they can be much reassured by knowing that their situation is common. Fortunately the visions are rarely threatening or scary (Ramachandran and Blakeslee, 1998). Sometimes

FIGURE 21.3 • The four form constants are found in decorations and works of art all over the world. Here spirals and lattices form part of a Peruvian textile design. The anthropomorphized plants in the lower corners are a cactus that produces hallucinogenic sap used for a "vision quest."

FIGURE 21.4 • Hallucinated tunnels can be simple dark spaces leading to a bright light, schematic tunnel patterns, or realistic tunnels like sewers, subways or caverns. In his experiments with THC, psilocybin, LSD and mescaline, Siegel found that after 90 to 120 minutes colors shifted to red, orange and yellow, pulsating movements became explosive and rotational, and most forms were lattice-tunnels, such as this one which has complex memory images at the periphery (Siegel, 1977).

the deaf hear hallucinated sounds, such as choirs singing, hymns and ballads or even whole orchestras playing. Others hear meaningless melodies, rumbling noises or isolated words and phrases. Occasionally the sounds can be so realistic that the deaf person tries to find the source and stop them.

Although there is no limit to the variety of hallucinations, there are some remarkable common features, suggesting a consistency that reflects underlying sensory processes. Persistent forms include spirals, concentric patterns, wavy lines and bright colors. Mandalas based on circular forms are common, especially in meditation traditions, and the Swiss psychoanalyst Carl Jung (1875–1961) included the mandala as one of the archetypal forms of the collective unconscious, describing it as the symbol of a harmonious self. These persistent patterns can be seen on shamans' drums, cave paintings, ritual designs, and clothing and artifacts from many cultures.

The reason for these similarities was first investigated in 1926 by Heinrich Klüver at the University of Chicago. Klüver studied the effects of the hallucinogenic drug mescaline, extracted from the peyote cactus, and found that the brightly colored images persisted with eyes open or closed, and tended to take on four repeated forms. These "form constants" were (1) gratings and lattices, (2) tunnels, funnels and cones, (3) spirals, and (4) cobwebs. All are found in the hallucinations caused by drugs, fever, migraine, epilepsy, near-death experiences, hypnagogic imagery and in the imagery of synesthetes.

The reason may lie in the way the visual system is organized, and in particular in the mapping between patterns on the retina and the columnar organization of primary visual cortex (Cowan, 1982; Bressloff et al., 2002). This mapping is well known from both monkey and human studies, and is such that concentric circles on the retina are mapped into parallel lines in visual cortex. Spirals, tunnels, lattices and cobwebs map onto lines in different directions. This means that if activity spreads in straight lines within visual cortex, the experience is equivalent to looking at actual rings or circles. One possible cause of lines of activation in visual cortex is disinhibition. Hallucinogenic drugs, lack of oxygen and certain disease states can all affect inhibitory cells more than excitatory ones, causing an excess of activity that can spread linearly. The result is hallucinations of the familiar four form constants.

There are also similarities in the movement and colors of hallucinations. Siegel and Jarvik (1975) trained volunteers to report on their hallucinations when taking a variety of drugs, including LSD, psilocybin, THC (one of the active ingredients of cannabis) and various control drugs and placebos. When the trained "psychonauts" were given amphetamines and barbiturates, they reported only black and white forms moving about randomly, but the hallucinogenic drugs produced tunnels, lattices and webs, explosive and rotating patterns, and bright colors, especially reds, oranges and yellows.

As for more complex hallucinations, although they vary much more widely than the simple forms, there are common themes, including cartoon-like characters, scenes from childhood memory, animals and mythical creatures, fantastic cities and buildings, and beautiful scenery. In Siegel and Jarvik's drug studies, simple hallucinations came first, then a shift to tunnels and lattices, and then more complex hallucinations. During the peak hallucinatory periods the subjects often described

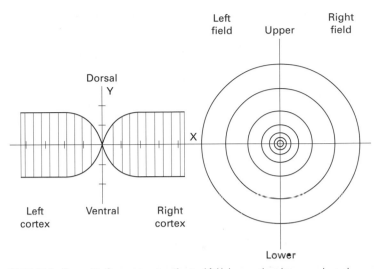

FIGURE 21.5 • The mapping from eye to cortex. The visual field shown on the right is mapped onto the corresponding cortical pattern on the left. Stripes of activity in cortex are therefore experienced as though due to concentric rings in the visual field. Stripes at other angles produce spirals. According to Cowan this can explain the origin of the four form constants (after Cowan, 1982).

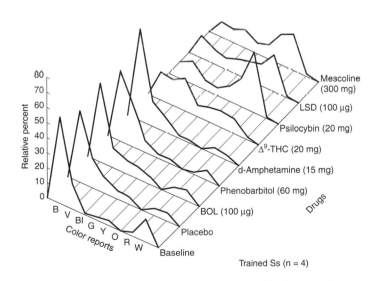

FIGURE 21.6 • Siegel and Jarvik trained psychonauts to report on their experiences while taking various drugs. Mean percentage distributions for color are shown here. B black, V violet, Bl blue, G green, Y yellow, O orange, R red, W white (after Siegel and Jarvik, 1975).

themselves as becoming one with the images. They stopped using similes and described their images as real. In other words, they were no longer having pseudo-hallucinations.

Visual hallucinations in the blind not only include the form constants and vivid colors but also visions of children, animals, buildings or landscapes, distorted faces with prominent eyes and teeth and even copies of the same object arranged in rows or columns (Ffytche and Howard, 1999). In an fMRI study, several such patients were asked to report the beginning and end of hallucinations while their brain activity was recorded. Hallucinations of faces were associated with activity in the face area, objects with activity in the object area, color in color areas, and so on. For complex visions the features simply added up: activity in both object and color areas was associated with a colored object, while activity in a texture area without activity in a color area was associated with a colorless texture (Ffytche, 2000).

These few simple examples confront us again with the hard problem, and with some tricky questions about reality. First, we know (at least roughly) what

PRACTICE
STAYING AWAKE WHILE FALLING ASLEEP

The easiest way to explore the borderland between reality and imagination is to hover on the edge of sleep. Do this exercise for a week and you may be rewarded with fascinating hallucinations and insights. The visions and sounds may be frightening for some people, and you should not pursue it if you find it too unpleasant.

Go to bed as usual, lie in your normal position, but then try to keep your body absolutely still and your mind clear and empty. When any thoughts arise, gently let them go, as you might when practicing meditation. Look into the darkness in front of you and watch for patterns. Listen attentively for sounds. When you see or hear things, or feel odd twitches in your muscles, do not let them startle you, but try to stay relaxed and keep watching.

There are two difficulties. First, the exercise may keep you awake when you want to sleep, or force you to have a clear mind when you would rather indulge in fantasy or worry. I can only suggest that the visions may be worth the loss of sleep, and that in fact you will not take much longer to go to sleep than normal, however it feels.

Second, you may find that you drop off to sleep too fast. One suggestion from the western occult tradition is to lie on your back, holding one lower arm vertical. As you fall asleep, the arm drops and wakes you. This way you can oscillate between sleep and waking. In any case, lying on your back makes hypnagogic imagery and sleep paralysis more likely. Like many of these exercises, this one rapidly gets easier with practice.

sort of cortical activity causes someone to have a vivid hallucination of a bright yellow tunnel. But how can the conscious experience of a yellow tunnel (that throbbing, pulsating, vivid, realistic tunnel sucking me now into its golden light) be *caused* by, or simply *be* that neural activity? Second, is the tunnel "real"? In one sense it is not real because there is no physically detectable tunnel present, but in another it is real because there is physically measurable activity in the person's brain. Also, tunnels are common in hallucinatory experiences and to that extent can be shared and publicly verified. But what sort of reality is this?

THE BORDERS OF SLEEP

We can now return to the experience described at the start, which occurred on the edge of sleep, when sensory input is reduced. Hallucinations are very common in this state and were first described in 1848 by the French physician Alfred Maury, who called them hypnagogic images or hypnagogic hallucinations. Those that occur on waking are called hypnopompic images (Mavromatis, 1987).

ACTIVITY
Discussing hypnagogia

The exercise in the Practice section lends itself well to group work. Ask everyone to practice "staying awake while falling asleep" for several days, to keep a pencil and paper by the bed and to write down anything they experience.

It may be impossible to record the experiences immediately as they happen because the most interesting ones happen right on the edge of sleep, but they can be written down, or drawn, in the morning. Ask participants to bring any notes and drawings to the discussion.

Were there common themes? Are the form constants discernible in the descriptions? Is there any pattern to who did and did not have hallucinations? Did anyone experience sleep paralysis or body distortions? Was the experience pleasurable?

Again, the form constants are common, and many people describe flying or falling through tunnels, tubes or cones, or through black spaces lit by stars. They see whirling circles or suns, luminous points or streaks and vibrating colored threads. More rarely people see animals, people, mythical creatures or complex landscapes, or they hear chattering and muttering voices. Sometimes people who have been doing something for many hours in the day, see perseverative images of those things as they fall asleep, such as weeds if they have been gardening or endless shoals of fish if they have been snorkeling. Others hear their own name being called distinctly as they fall asleep, and this can be so realistic that they get up to see who is there. A few people learn to control their hypnagogic images, but they say it is more like "wishing" than "willing" because you don't always get what you wanted (Mavromatis, 1987). Mostly the experiences are vivid and uncontrollable, but they are not mistaken for reality.

One of the oddest phenomena that occurs in this borderland is sleep paralysis. Everyone is paralyzed during REM sleep, so that their dreams are not acted out, but normally they are unaware of this. Awareness during sleep paralysis occurs either when the normal paralysis of REM sleep begins too early, when the person is just falling asleep, or when it persists too long as they are waking up. The experiencer feels completely paralyzed, apart from their eyes, and may see visions, hear noises and feel as though a great weight is

SLEEP PARALYSIS

The experience described at the start of this chapter is a typical account of sleep paralysis (SP) or awareness during sleep paralysis (ASP). It was derived from hundreds of cases collected by placing advertisements in magazines (Parker and Blackmore, 2002). SP is one of the symptoms of the serious sleep disorder narcolepsy, and for that reason is often treated as pathological. People who experience it are sometimes assumed to be mentally or physically ill and even given inappropriate treatment. In fact SP is very common in normal and healthy people, although it occurs more often when people are under stress or have disturbed or unpredictable sleep patterns. Shift workers, doctors and nurses often experience SP, and one of its many names is "night nurses' paralysis." Surveys in Canada, China, England, Japan and Nigeria show that between 20 and 60 percent of people have experienced it at least once (Parker and Blackmore, 2002; Spanos et al., 1995).

SP most commonly occurs during sleep-onset REM, although it can also occur on waking. Either way, the person feels awake, but the voluntary muscles are paralyzed, as they are during REM. Not surprisingly, this combination can be extremely unpleasant, especially when it is unexpected. SP can be induced in the laboratory by waking subjects up, keeping them awake for an hour and then letting them sleep again.

The most common features of SP are fear and the sense of presence, usually an evil or frightening presence, but occasionally a friendly one. Other common features include feeling pressure on the chest, hearing humming, buzzing or grinding noises, feeling vibrations through the body, touches on the limbs and sensations of floating or flying or out-of-body experiences (Cheyne et al., 1999). Many people are terrified because they believe that the presence is a real ghost, or alien, or because they think they must be going mad. Knowing something about SP makes it much less frightening. Most of the features of SP, especially the sense of presence, have been induced by

sitting on their chest and suffocating them. Here, then, is the explanation for the experience at the start of this chapter and for the long history of fairy abductions, ghost visitations, incubi and succubi.

These visitors are not real in the sense of being physically present in the room, but neither can they be dismissed as having no reality at all. First they depend on physical events in the body and brain, and second they play a role in human history and culture. Perhaps this is how we should understand the notion of the collective unconscious. Because we all share the same kind of brain, we are all prone to experiencing the same kinds of visitations by recognizably similar creatures. Like other archetypal phenomena, these creatures have a kind of shared reality. If we treat them as real in the ordinary sense, we are simply wrong. But if we dismiss them as unreal, we may fail to do them justice.

CONJURING OTHER WORLDS

All of us conjured other worlds when playing as children—inventing food and drinks for dollies' teatime, imagining illnesses to be cured by "doctors and nurses" and creating invisible cargoes to be carried by toy trucks on imaginary roads. Many children, especially only children, have imaginary playmates. Some children play and talk with the same friend for many years, though not often past the age of 10. In the early years the playmates are described as solid and real, but older children rarely see them that way. Most imaginary companions are people, usually of the same sex as the child, but they can be animals, invisible toys, storybook characters and even things like clouds or doorknobs (Siegel, 1992). These friends take part in conversations, games and all sorts of creative activities.

This capacity for creating other people and other worlds leads through into adulthood in the form of creative writing, poetry, art and the fantasies of daydreams and visions. There is wide variation in what is known as fantasy proneness, with about 5 percent of people being classified as having a

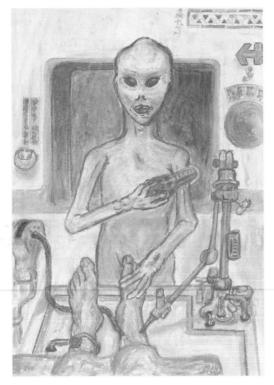

FIGURE 21.7 • David Howard suffers from narcolepsy, a sleep disorder characterized by periods of sleepiness or sudden sleep during the day, as well as abnormalities of dreaming sleep and hallucinations. During narcoleptic episodes he claims to have been frequently abducted by aliens, operated on by them and taken to their ships and planets. His paintings show the rich details of his memory of these experiences.

transcranial magnetic stimulation, in particular by stimulation of the temporal lobes (Persinger, 1999).

Some regular experiencers learn to prevent awareness during sleep paralysis by avoiding sleeping on their back and getting regular sleep. When it occurs, the best way to cope is just to relax and wait for it to stop, which it usually does within a few seconds, although it is difficult to follow this advice if you are terrified. The best method of breaking out of the paralysis is to concentrate on moving just a little finger or toe, or to blink rapidly. However, some people enjoy the experience and learn to induce it at will.

Many cultures have sleep paralysis myths, such as the incubus and succubus of medieval lore, and the seductive Babylonian Lilitu or demoness of the wind. The "Old Hag" of Newfoundland is "The terror that comes in the night" (Hufford, 1982), sitting on victims' chests and trying to suffocate them. Folklore has it that she can be deliberately sent to "hag" people. The same experience is called Kanashibari in Japan, Ha-wi-nulita or being squeezed by scissors in Korea, Kokma attacks by the spirits of unbaptized babies in St. Lucia, and Phi um, or the feeling of being enveloped by a ghost, in Thailand.

The latest SP myth may be alien abductions. These normally occur at night and, in addition to the pale gray alien with large almond-shaped eyes, include all the usual features of paralysis: suffocation, floating sensations, sense of presence, touches on the body and vibrating or humming noises. It seems that peoples in many times and places have invented myths and entities to account for this common physiological occurrence.

"fantasy prone personality" (Wilson and Barber, 1983). These people are far more likely to have had imaginary playmates as children. They are more susceptible to hypnosis, more creative, have a richer and more diverse fantasy life, and more often report unusual experiences and belief in the paranormal.

In contemporary western culture, other worlds are usually confined to fiction or to private fantasy, but in many other cultures they are deliberately cultivated and shared. In many cultures certain people train to become shamans. This word came originally from the Siberian Chuckchee tribe but is now widely used to describe men and women who can enter spirit worlds, cure sickness through magic or contact spirits and other invisible beings. Usually shamans follow elaborate rituals, often but not always involving hallucinogenic drugs, to reach these other worlds (Krippner, 2000).

One such culture is that of the Yąnomamö, a fierce group of Native Americans living deep in the forest between Venezuela and Brazil (Chagnon, 1992). Their world of myths and invisible entities consists of four parallel layers, one above

> **"There are no hallucinations with peyote. There are only truths."**
>
> Huichol shaman

> **"there are no more gods or Demons than there are images of those things in the brain"**
>
> Siegel, 1992: 31

the other, including the third layer of forests, rivers and gardens in which they live. Accomplished shamans can call the beautiful *hekura* spirits from the sky, hills, trees or even from the edge of the universe to enter their bodies through the chest and there to find another world of forests and rivers within.

To call *hekura*, the shamans prepare a complex hallucinogenic green powder called *ebene*, paint themselves elaborately with red pigment, put on their feathers and blow the powder into each other's nostrils through a long hollow tube. Coughing, gasping, groaning and dribbling green mucous from the nose, they then call the *hekura*, who soon come glowing out of the sky along their special trails into the shaman's chest, from where they can be sent to devour the souls of enemies or to cure sickness in the village.

Sometimes researchers have been invited to join such ceremonies and take the drugs themselves. Siegel describes a long night spent with a Huichol Indian shaman in Mexico, matching him gulp for gulp in drinking a potent alcoholic liquor made from the agave plant and a gruel made from the peyote cactus, which contains the hallucinogen mescaline. When the first waves of nausea had passed, Siegel opened his eyes and "the stars came down." They darted about, leaving tracer patterns in the air. When he tried to grab one, a rainbow of afterimages followed his moving hand. Then there were patterns, all the familiar form constants and much more. A lizard crawled out of his vomit, followed by thousands of army ants in party hats. "*Stop it! I want answers, not cartoons!*" he pleaded, and he asked the shaman about hallucinations. The answer came clear "There are no hallucinations with peyote. There are only truths" (Siegel, 1992: 28–9).

Back home in his California laboratory, Siegel knew that what he had seen was all in his own mind.

> How do you tell this holy man who believes he has the power to see the gods that there are no more gods or Demons than there are images of those things in the brain? How do you tell a poor naked farmer who has only his peyote dreams that the world of our dreams is all inside our minds?
>
> (Siegel, 1992: 31)

But we may wonder whether this distinction between "real" and "in the mind" is all that clear. The *hekura* dancing down their shimmering trails and the stars coming down from the sky are not physical, publicly measurable objects. Yet they have been seen again and again by countless peoples separated in time and space in their different cultures across the world. To this extent, they are publicly available. If you took the right mixture of drugs, in the right setting, you would see them too. What sort of reality does that give them?

One controversial player on this edge of reality is anthropologist Carlos Castaneda, famous for his many books about his teacher, the Yaqui Indian Juan Matus (Castaneda, 1968). As the story goes, Castaneda first met the old *brujo*, or medicine man, in the summer of 1960 at a bus depot in a border town in Arizona. While Castaneda prattled on about how much he knew about peyote, and what he wanted to learn, don Juan peered at him patiently with shining eyes, knowing that Castaneda was talking nonsense. But they met again and Castaneda became don Juan's apprentice for four years. This "man of knowledge" taught his disciples by explanations of sorcery, by taking them through strange rituals and journeys, and by using three types of hallucinogen: peyote, which contains mescaline; jimson weed, or datura, which contains tropane alkaloids including atropine; and various mushrooms containing psilocybin (Chapter 22). According to don Juan, peyote is a teacher who teaches the right way to live, while the other drugs are powerful allies that can be manipulated by the sorcerer. Castaneda passed through ordeals of sickness, pain and confusion, and whole worlds of visions that were, according to don Juan, not hallucinations but concrete aspects of reality. They were not "as if" but were real. Castaneda dubbed them "a separate reality" (1971).

After many years of training, Castaneda began learning to "see": a non-ordinary way of looking, in which people appear as fibers of light, as luminous eggs in touch with everything else and in need of nothing. His head once turned into a crow and flew away, he heard a lizard speak and became a brother to the coyote. On one occasion he used jimson weed to fly, as medieval witches were once supposed to do by using the chemically related

Psychic

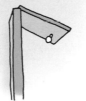

FIGURE 21.8 • The doorway test for auras. The psychic claimant stands facing the edge of an open doorway. A target person, whose aura the psychic says he can see clearly, takes up one of two possible positions, perhaps five times in each, in random order. At position (A) neither she nor her aura should be visible; at position (B) her body is not visible but her aura should easily be seen, sticking out past the side of the doorframe. At each trial the psychic must say whether he sees the aura sticking out or not. There is no published evidence that anyone has ever been able to pass this test, suggesting that whatever auras are, they are not physically present in the space around the body.

WHAT'S REAL ANYWAY?

FIGURE 21.9

SELF-ASSESSMENT QUESTIONS

○ What factors are involved in reality monitoring?

○ What are the differences between perceptions, imagery, hallucinations and pseudo-hallucinations?

○ Describe some of the ways in which hallucinations can be induced.

○ What are the form constants and how can they be explained?

○ What is sleep paralysis, and what are its most common features?

○ Describe some of the drugs used by shamans, and the worlds they claim to see.

deadly nightshade, *Atropa belladonna*. He argued with himself and with don Juan that his actual physical body could not have flown, yet it apparently ended up half a mile from don Juan's house. Finally he learned to keep death ever-present and not to be so concerned with his ordinary self—indeed to stop the internal dialogue and erase his personal history.

Similar experiences are reported with ayahuasca, a common hallucinogenic drink made in many parts of South America, and said to be "one of the most sophisticated and complex drug delivery systems in existence" (Callaway, 1999: 256; Metzner, 1999). Like many other sacred drug mixtures, ayahuasca contains DMT, *dimethoxytryptamine*, along with β-carbolines. When smoked or injected, DMT is a terrifyingly powerful fast-acting hallucinogen, which tends especially to evoke colorful visions of snakes and serpents, and "seems to have all the cognitive contents of a firework display" (Callaway, 1999: 263). When eaten it is normally inactivated by the enzyme monoamine oxidase (MAO), but ayahuasca contains MAO inhibitors, the β-carbolines harmine, tetrahydroharmine and harmaline. This creates a long-lasting hallucinogenic mixture whose exact effects can be controlled for different purposes by fine variations in the method of preparation.

Experienced ayahuasca users travel in this world or other worlds, according to their traditions, and describe non-ordinary ways of seeing. They claim that the gods, demons, heavens and hells they visit are as real, or even more real, than the ordinary world of normal vision. They describe gaining spiritual insights and a deeper understanding of reality and of themselves.

BUT IS IT REAL?

What are we to make of this? Like Castaneda in his skeptical anthropologist mode, we may claim that all the experiences are "in the mind," that they are imaginary and not real. It turns out that his books themselves were more works of fiction than accurate ethnographic records of research. Writer Richard de Mille made a thorough study of

Castaneda's works and concluded that "Marked anachronisms or logical conflicts in Castaneda's work must argue that his text is an imaginative fabrication rather than a factual report" (de Mille, 1978: 197). He describes the results as a mess: "The wisdom of the ages folded into an omelet with the neurosis of the century" (de Mille, 1978: 18). Yet at the very least Castaneda forces us to wonder about the nature of hallucinations.

Take those luminous eggs and radiating fibers, reminiscent of the haloes of Christian saints, and the auras of the Theosophical tradition. Auras are a good example of something that is commonly reported, has consistent features and yet is not physically present. Kirlian photography, which is sometimes claimed to record auras, actually measures the corona discharge from charged surfaces, and Kirlian photographs do not resemble seers' descriptions of auras. More relevant here is that no one has ever passed the "doorway test" designed to find out whether psychic claimants can see an aura sticking out from behind a wall (see Figure 21.8).

Seeing auras may seem trivial, but the lessons learned from other-world experiences cannot be so lightly dismissed. Those who are trained in the use of hallucinogenic drugs learn things that no novice has any inkling of. Experienced travelers learn to look calmly into their very worst fears, face up to death, confront or lose themselves, and many other lessons. Special skills are needed for exploring the worlds revealed this way, and those who acquire this kind of wisdom recognize it in others. Understanding all these phenomena is not helped by drawing a sharp line between reality and imagination.

READING

Metzner, R. (ed.) (1999) *Ayahuasca: Human Consciousness and the Spirits of Nature.* New York, Thunder's Mouth Press. Read any of the brief accounts of experiences with ayahuasca in Chapter 1, and Chapter 4 by **J.C. Callaway** on the neuropharmacology of ayahuasca.

Siegel, R.K. (1992) *Fire in the Brain.* New York, Penguin. Read Chapter 1, The psychonaut and the shaman, and Chapter 5, The succubus.

EIGHT

Altered states of consciousness

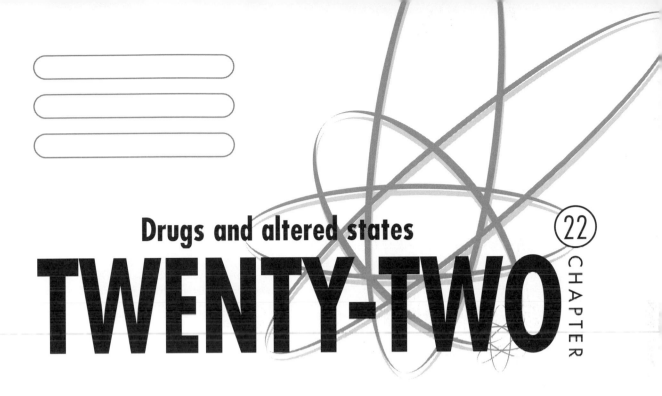

Drugs and altered states

TWENTY-TWO

One conclusion was forced upon my mind at that time, and my
impression of its truth has ever since remained unshaken. It is that
our normal waking consciousness, rational consciousness as we call it,
is but one special type of consciousness, whilst all about it, parted
from it by the filmiest of screens, there lie potential forms of
consciousness entirely different. We may go through life without
suspecting their existence; but apply the requisite stimulus, and at a
touch they are there in all their completeness, definite types of
mentality which probably somewhere have their field of application
and adaptation. No account of the universe in its totality can be final
which leaves these other forms of consciousness quite disregarded.
How to regard them is the question.

James, 1902: 388

This is, indeed, the question, and in this chapter we will consider the nature
of altered states in general, and drug-induced states in particular.

DEFINING ASCS

James's "other forms of consciousness" would now be called "altered states
of consciousness," or ASCs, a concept that seems simple but is notoriously difficult to define. We get drunk and so feel and act differently; we let ourselves be

Charles T. Tart (b. 1937)

Charley Tart not only carried out the first survey into what it's like to be stoned, but is responsible for the idea of "state-specific sciences" and for popularizing the concept of "altered state of consciousness." As a teenager in New Jersey he worked as a radio engineer, studied electrical engineering at MIT and only then switched to psychology for his doctorate. He worked on hypnosis with Ernest Hilgard at Stanford University, and then spent 28 years as Professor of Psychology at the University of California at Davis. His beliefs in the paranormal and life after death were always controversial, and when he became the first holder of the Bigelow Chair of Consciousness Studies at the University of Nevada in Las Vegas, other professors claimed the university had marred its reputation by hiring someone whose writing was clear, readable and found in new-age bookstores. Having worked on out-of-body experiences, lucid dreams and many areas of parapsychology, transpersonal psychology and consciousness studies, Tart's work on consciousness is first-personal as well as academic. He holds a black belt in aikido, teaches meditation and mindfulness and tries to be both a scientist and a spiritual seeker.

hypnotized and cannot remember what we did; we sleep and dream and wake up to say "that was only a dream." In all these cases something has obviously changed, but what? As soon as we start to think more deeply about altered states of consciousness, the problems begin.

The first difficulty concerns whether to define ASCs objectively or subjectively. Taking objective definitions first, we might define ASCs in terms of how they were induced—for example, by mind-altering drugs or by procedures such as hypnosis or progressive relaxation. Then we might label different drug-induced states according to which drug the person took, saying that someone was drunk on alcohol, stoned on cannabis, tripping on LSD or spacey from ecstasy. But numerous problems make this unsatisfactory. How do we know that your state of tripping is anything like mine? How do we know whether two slightly different drugs produce the same, or different, ASCs? And how can we measure the similarity so as to make such decisions? Then there is the issue of dosage. How much cannabis does someone need to take to say that they have reached the stoned ASC? Even if two people do experience similar states, the dose required may be quite different for each person. Similarly we might say that someone is in a hypnotic state when they have undergone a particular hypnotic procedure, but that same procedure might have no effect on someone else (see Chapter 23). Defining and categorizing ASCs by the way they are induced is not satisfactory.

Perhaps a better solution is to define ASCs on the basis of physiological and behavioral measurements, such as heart rate, cortical oxygen consumption, ability to walk in a straight line or expressions of emotion. One problem here is that very few ASCs are associated with unique physiological patterns (a partial exception is sleep, see Chapter 23) or with physiological or behavioral changes that map directly onto changes in experience. As brain scans and other measures improve, we may find such consistent patterns, in which case we could safely define the states in terms of those measures. But it may turn out that very small changes in physiology can be associated with large changes in subjective state, and vice versa, so that no direct mapping is possible. For the moment we should be careful about defining a state of consciousness (SoC) in terms of physiological variables. There is a danger of losing the very essence of ASCs, which is how they feel for the person concerned.

The alternative is to define ASCs subjectively, and this is the most common strategy. A popular textbook says that "an *altered state of consciousness* exists whenever there is a change from an ordinary pattern of mental functioning to a state that *seems* different to the person experiencing the change" (Atkinson et al., 2001: 191). For Charles Tart (see Profile), who originally coined the term, an ASC is "a qualitative alteration in the overall pattern of mental functioning, such that the experiencer feels his consciousness is radically different from the way it functions ordinarily" (Tart, 1972: 1203). In a textbook on consciousness, American psychologist William Farthing defines an ASC as "a temporary change in the overall pattern of subjective experience, such that the individual believes that his or her mental functioning is distinctly different from certain general norms for his or her normal waking state of consciousness" (Farthing, 1992: 205).

Such definitions seem to capture the basic idea of ASCs but raise problems of their own. First, they compare ASCs with a normal SoC, but what is normal? Normality for one person might range through bleary-eyed breakfast eating to concentrated hard work, and from relaxing alone with music to excited conversation with friends. Arguably the "breakfast-eating state of consciousness" differs as much from the "excited conversation" as being stoned differs from being straight, and yet most people would unhesitatingly say which were "normal" states. So the subjective definition of ASCs depends on comparing them with normal states, but we cannot pin those down either.

> *"our normal waking consciousness . . . is but one special type of consciousness, whilst all about it, parted from it by the filmiest of screens, there lie potential forms of consciousness entirely different"*
>
> **James**, 1902: 388

PRACTICE
IS THIS MY NORMAL STATE OF CONSCIOUSNESS?

As many times as you can, every day, ask yourself, **"Is this my normal state of consciousness?"**

When you have decided, you might like to ask some other questions. How did you decide? What is normal about it? Is it always obvious what state you are in, and if so why? If not, what does this tell you about ASCs?

Another problem is inherent in the whole idea of a subjective definition. Although defining ASCs subjectively may help us to decide for *ourselves* whether we are in an ASC, as soon as we try to tell other people about it our words become just another objective behavior from their point of view. Also, think of the drunk who staggers about claiming that he feels perfectly normal, or the first-time marijuana smoker who giggles at his own hand for 10 minutes while claiming there is no effect. In these cases we may think that physiological measures would be more appropriate than words. In other cases we may be sure that the person's own words are the best measure of their state, but there are still problems because ASCs are so hard to describe, and different people have different prior experience, different expectations and different ways of describing things. Training may help, but this raises other problems such as how to compare the experiences of trained explorers with those of novices.

FIGURE 22.1

You may have noticed that lurking among these problems is an old familiar one. Is there really such a thing as a conscious experience that exists apart from the things people do and the descriptions they provide of it? Or is consciousness itself just those behaviors and descriptions, as claimed, for example, by eliminative materialism and some functionalists? If such theories are correct, then we should be able to understand ASCs fully by studying physiological effects and what people do and say, and there should be no mystery left over. Yet for many people this does not do justice to what they feel. They enter a deep ASC and everything seems different. They struggle to describe it but somehow the words are not enough. They *know* what they are experiencing but cannot convey it to anyone else. They *know* that their conscious experience is something more than any changes in their behavior or words they can say. Are they right?

WHAT IS ALTERED IN AN ASC?

"What is altered in an altered state of consciousness?" is a strange but interesting question. Optimistically, we might say that "consciousness" has changed. If this is so, studying what is altered in ASCs should reveal what consciousness itself really is. Sadly, everything we have learned about consciousness so far shows that this is impossible. We cannot measure changes in something called consciousness in isolation from changes in perception, memory and other cognitive and emotional functions, so to study ASCs we must study how these functions have changed.

All the definitions given above, as well as comparing ASCs with a normal state, mention "mental functioning," and Tart defines a state of consciousness, or SoC, as "a qualitatively distinct organization of the patterning of mental functioning" (Tart, 1972: 1203). So which kinds of functioning are involved?

Farthing (1992) provides a list:

1 attention

2 perception

3 imagery and fantasy

4 inner speech

5 memory

6 higher-level thought processes

7 meaning and significance

8 time perception

9 emotional feeling and expression

10 arousal

11 self-control

12 suggestibility

13 body image, and

14 sense of personal identity.

In one way or another, this list probably covers all the mental functions that there are, suggesting that ASCs cannot be fully understood without understanding changes to the whole system. Some ASCs involve changes to all these functions, while others primarily involve just one or two, and we shall meet many examples of these in the rest of this section. For now, we might pick out just three major variables that often change during ASCs.

Attention can change along two main dimensions. First, attention may be directed outward or inward. For example, in dreams sensory input is cut off and attention is entirely inward. Good hypnotic subjects may also ignore the world around them and concentrate entirely on the hypnotist's suggested fantasies. Many methods for inducing ASCs manipulate this dimension either by reducing sensory input, as in meditation or deep relaxation, or overloading it as in some ritual practices. Second, attention may be broadly or narrowly focused. Someone high on marijuana may attend finely to the leaf pattern on the carpet for many minutes at a time. Such a change in attention can profoundly affect subjective state, but the effects cannot be cleanly separated from the associated changes in perception, memory and emotion. For example, the leaf pattern might look quite different from normal, become of overwhelming significance, bring up long-lost childhood memories and raise deep emotions—or gales of laughter.

Memory changes in many ASCs, and this is linked with effects on thinking and emotion. For example, many mind-altering drugs reduce short-term memory span. This has a debilitating effect on conversation if you cannot remember what it was you meant to say before you get to the end of the sentence, but it can also create more focused attention on the here-and-now and even a sense of liberation. Time can also seem to speed up, slow down or change completely, an effect that has long been linked with changes in memory. For example, a doctor experimenting with cannabis more than a century ago noted dry mouth, aimless wandering, slurred speech, freedom from worry and an irresistible tendency to laugh.

> The most peculiar effect was a complete loss of time-relation; time seemed to have no existence. I was continually taking out my watch, thinking that hours must have passed, whereas only a few minutes had elapsed. This, I believe, was due to a complete loss of memory for recent events.
>
> (Dunbar, 1905: 68)

MAPPING STATES OF CONSCIOUSNESS

If SoCs could be accurately mapped, we might understand how each relates to the others, how each can be induced and how to move from one state to another, but the task is not easy. Imagine a vast multi-dimensional space in which a person's current state is defined by hundreds of variables, each representing the activity in one of numerous mental functions. This is just too confusing to work with. To make the task more manageable, we need to answer two main questions: first, can we simplify the space and use just a few dimensions and, second, how discrete are the SoCs? Are they possible anywhere in the multi-dimensional space, or are they neatly delimited and confined to certain parts of it?

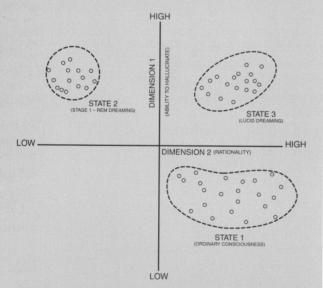

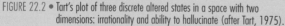

FIGURE 22.2 • Tart's plot of three discrete altered states in a space with two dimensions: irrationality and ability to hallucinate (after Tart, 1975).

The early psychophysiologists tried to map visual and auditory sensations in multi-dimensional spaces, but the first attempt at systematic mapping of states of consciousness was made by Tart (1975). He described a

Arousal is a third general variable that changes in ASCs. Some deep states of meditation are characterized by very low arousal and deep relaxation, and more drastic practices can reduce the metabolic rate so far that little food and oxygen are required. In such a state trained yogins may keep immobile for long periods and may even be buried alive for days at a time, even though most of us would die in the same circumstances. At the other extreme are ASCs of the highest arousal, such as religious and ritual frenzies or speeding on amphetamines. Changes in arousal can affect every aspect of mental functioning.

Thinking about these three variables we might imagine some kind of three-dimensional space in which different ASCs can be positioned or, more realistically, a very complex multi-dimensional space within which all possible ASCs might be found. This way of thinking leads to the idea of mapping SoCs, and indeed many attempts to do this have been made, including simple three-dimensional maps (see Chapter 23), more complex maps, and schemes based on ascending levels of consciousness (Hobson, 1999; Metzner, 1971; Tart, 1975).

DRUG-INDUCED STATES

Psychoactive drugs are all those that have effects on mental functioning or consciousness. In some form or other they are found in every society, and human beings seem to have a natural appetite for taking them (Weil, 1999). They can be broadly classified into several major groups, most of which are mentioned only briefly here, with the emphasis being on the last group, the psychedelics.

STIMULANTS

Central nervous system (CNS) stimulants include nicotine, caffeine, cocaine and the large group of drugs based on amphetamine. Cocaine is an alkaloid derived from the South American shrub *Erythroxylon coca*, whose leaves have long been chewed by laborers and farmers to help cope with exhaustion and hunger. It induces a mental state of intense pleasure, great energy and increased confidence. Freud described it as a magical drug before he discovered some of its drawbacks. Cocaine is now a common street drug, either inhaled into the nose as a powder or converted to freebase form and smoked as crack cocaine—a form in which it is particularly fast-acting and extremely addictive. Cocaine works by inhibiting the reuptake of dopamine. It induces tolerance—that is, increasing doses are required for the same effect—and it has unpleasant withdrawal symptoms. Heavy users sometimes experience hallucinations, including formication, the very odd and highly specific hallucination of bugs crawling under the skin.

Amphetamine, also known as speed, is another dopamine reuptake inhibitor, and has similar energizing effects to cocaine. Tolerance develops with repeated use, and withdrawal causes depression and lethargy. Long-term heavy use can lead to paranoid delusions and hallucinations.

simple space with two dimensions: irrationality and ability to hallucinate. By plotting a person's position in this space he imagined just three major clusters corresponding to the states of dreaming, lucid dreaming (Chapter 23) and ordinary consciousness. All other positions in the space cannot be occupied, or are unstable. So you may briefly hover between waking and dreaming, but this state is unstable and rapidly gives way to one of the others. For this reason Tart refers to the occupied areas as "discrete states of consciousness." To move out of such a region, you have to cross a "forbidden zone" where you cannot function or cannot have experiences until you reach a discretely different experiential space. In other words, you can be here or there, but not in between. Just how many states are discrete like this we do not know.

Although the basic principles of spaces, maps and discrete states are clear, many questions remain, and there are still no generally accepted maps for most SoCs.

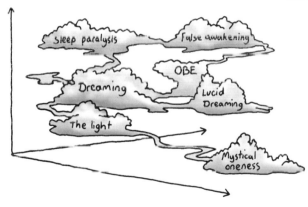

FIGURE 22.3 • It is easy to imagine altered states connected in a vast space, but difficult to turn this idea into a realistic working map. How discrete are the different states? Where do the paths between them go? And which are the most important dimensions to use?

There are many other drugs derived from amphetamine, including many of the recent designer drugs. Perhaps the best known of these is 3,4-methylene-dioxy methamphetamine, MDMA, or ecstasy. MDMA has both amphetamine-like effects and hallucinogen-like effects so it is also sometimes classified as a psychedelic or hallucinogen (see below). MDMA has three main effects in the brain: inhibiting serotonin reuptake, inducing release of serotonin and inducing release of dopamine. Subjectively it has a curious mixture of effects,

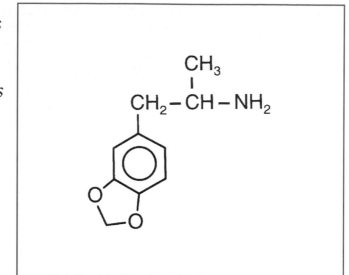

FIGURE 22.4 • "Ecstasy," "E" or "X-TC" are street names for MDMA (3-4-methylenedioxy-methamphetamine), a synthetic, psychoactive drug with hallucinogenic and amphetamine-like properties. Its structure is similar to two other synthetic drugs, MDA and methamphetamine, which are known to cause brain damage.

including increased energy, enhancement of tactile and other sensations, and feelings of love and empathy, for which it is sometimes referred to as an "empathogen" (Holland, 2001; Saunders, 1993). The effects, as with so many other psychoactive drugs, are highly dependent on the setting in which it is taken. The most common use is at parties and raves, when the increased energy makes dancing all night easy, and bombardment with music and light adds to the effects, but MDMA can also be used to enhance intimacy and sex, for solving personal problems and for healing and psychotherapy (Metzner and Adamson, 2001). When taken alone, especially when in beautiful surroundings such as mountains or the ocean, MDMA can lead to a profound sense of union with the universe and love for all creation, and some raves are regarded as spiritual events by those involved (Saunders et al., 2000).

Like many amphetamine derivatives MDMA produces tolerance and is addictive. It is neurotoxic and there is evidence of damage to the serotonergic system from even moderate use, although the long-term effects in humans are not yet fully known (Holland, 2001). People who use MDMA to explore ASCs or for spiritual purposes tend not to take it frequently or mix it with other drugs, and may therefore be less likely to suffer the damage associated with overuse and abuse.

CNS DEPRESSANTS

These include alcohol (which also has some stimulating effects), some inhalants of abuse, barbiturates and minor tranquilizers.

NARCOTICS

These include heroin, morphine, codeine and methadone. Although these drugs have powerful effects on mood and are highly addictive, they do not generally induce the kinds of ASC that might help us understand consciousness. An exception is opium, described in the autobiography of the English essayist and critic Thomas De Quincey (1821) as inducing visions of the utmost beauty and as the key to paradise, until he met the horrors and terrifying nightmares of addiction.

ANTIPSYCHOTICS

Major tranquilizers include lithium carbonate and chlorpromazine and are used primarily in the treatment of schizophrenia.

ANTIDEPRESSANTS

The three major types are tricyclic antidepressants (TCAs), selective serotonin reuptake inhibitors (SSRIs), which increase the availability of serotonin by slowing its removal from the synapse, and monoamine oxidase inhibitors (MAOIs), which slow the breakdown of noradrenaline, dopamine and serotonin.

ANESTHETICS

Most anesthetics do not produce interesting ASCs, and, indeed, they have been designed not to do so. However, some of the anesthetic gases and solvents, such as ether, chloroform and nitrous oxide, can induce quite profound ASCs.

When William James penetrated that filmy screen into another form of consciousness, he had inhaled nitrous oxide mixed with air, a gas first discovered by Sir Humphrey Davy. From the mid-nineteenth century, it was extensively used in dentistry and surgery, but it is now most familiar as the "gas and air" used for pain relief in childbirth. Davy bravely experimented with many gases by taking them himself, and he breathed his first dose of nitrous oxide on 11 April 1799. He described an immediate thrilling, a pleasure in every limb and an intensification of both vision and hearing. He lost concern with external things and entered a

STATE SPECIFIC SCIENCES

Tart (1972) proposed the creation of "state-specific sciences" (SSSs), likening SoCs to paradigms in science. Paradigms are general scientific frameworks within which normal science operates and whose assumptions usually remain unquestioned until there are so many anomalies that a scientific revolution or paradigm shift has to occur, leading to a new paradigm (Kuhn, 1962). Within a paradigm a certain self-consistent logic applies, certain rules are taken for granted, and all data are interpreted within that framework. Within a different paradigm, other rules apply. The same is true, says Tart, of SoCs. They too involve rules and ways of seeing things that are self-consistent but different from those used in other SoCs.

If this is so, then different states may need different kinds of science. The research would have to be carried out in the relevant SoC and the results communicated between people who were also in that state. This would necessitate trained and highly skilled practitioners able to achieve given states, to agree that they had achieved those states and to work within them. They might then investigate any natural phenomena, but the ways they did so, and their findings, would only make sense to people also working within that state.

There are no published SSSs, although it is possible that some scientists are doing SSS and communicating with each other in ASCs, without revealing their results in public. There is no doubt that many scientific breakthroughs have been made by people who saw their problems differently in an ASC and then brought that insight back to the normal SoC, but this is not the same thing. In any case, this proposal is interesting because it questions the usual assumption that the "normal" state is the only, or best, state in which science can be done.

new world of ideas, theories and imagined discoveries. Remarkably, on returning to normality, he claimed that "Nothing exists but thoughts."

This sounds just like what Tart had in mind when he described different SoCs as having different logics, or different ways of seeing the world. It sounds as though Davy had been made into an idealist, that his philosophical beliefs were different in the ASC. A century later another explorer of anesthetics said just the same after inhaling ether mixed with air.

> Then it dawned upon me that the only logical position was subjective idealism, and, therefore, *my* experience must be reality. Then by degrees I began to realise that I was the One, and the universe of which I was the principle was balancing itself into completeness.
>
> (Dunbar, 1905: 73–4)

James described the drug as stimulating an artificial mystical consciousness, in which it reveals "depth beyond depth of truth," which fades out when the drug wears off, often leaving only nonsense words behind. Yet the sense of meaning and insight remain, insights that have been compared with those of Zen (Austin, 1998). There is an experience of reconciliation, said James, a monist rather than dualist insight, "as if the opposites of the world, whose contradictoriness and conflict make all our difficulties and troubles, were melted into unity" (James, 1902: 388). As James himself said, the question is how to regard these insights (Chapter 24).

Ketamine is a dissociative anesthetic and NMDA antagonist, which also produces interesting effects in sub-anesthetic doses. It disrupts working memory, episodic memory and semantic memory, with measurable effects lasting for several days. It is rarely used as an anesthetic for humans because it can induce schizotypal symptoms, feelings of unreality and dissociation, and terrifying nightmares. Nevertheless, it is quite commonly taken orally as a recreational drug.

FIGURE 22.5 • Can taking a drug really change your philosophy?

On the theory that you can often learn about something by switching it on and off, Richard Gregory (1986) chose an intravenous infusion of ketamine as a way to explore consciousness. Under controlled conditions in the laboratory he was shown ambiguous figures and random dot stereograms, and given words to read and many other tests. The walls began to move and he heard a loud buzzing noise. He felt unreal and floating, as though he were in another world like a bubble full of bright colors and shapes. He even experienced synesthesia for the only time in his life when the bristles of a brush were felt as orange, green and red. Interesting as this was, the whole experience was deeply unpleasant for Gregory. He concluded that he had learned little about consciousness and had no enthusiasm for repeating the experience.

My own attempts to induce an out-of-body experience with ketamine were far more pleasant. "I am lying back in some yielding, flowing softness . . . I seem to be disintegrating, falling apart into separate pieces and then into nothing at all. Then back together and flying" (Blackmore, 1992: 274).

Ketamine has been used in different settings as a sacred or therapeutic drug. It is then as much a psychedelic as an anesthetic. The floating sensations can turn into out-of-body experiences or full-blown near-death experiences (see Chapter 24), and it can be used to explore the issues of birth, life and death (Jansen, 2001). Gregory's unpleasant experience in the laboratory illustrates how important set and setting are in determining the effects of psychoactive drugs.

PSYCHEDELICS

The effects of drugs in this group are so strange and varied that there is no firm agreement over their name. I have called them "psychedelics," meaning

FIGURE 22.6 • *Cannabis sativa* is a beautiful fast-growing annual that thrives in a wide variety of climates, shown here ready for harvest in a greenhouse in Britain. The leaves and flowering heads are smoked as grass, and hash can be made from the resin and pollen.

mind-manifesting, but other names are often used, including "psycholytic," meaning loosening the psyche or mind, "psychotomimetic," meaning madness-mimicking, "hallucinogenic," meaning hallucination-inducing, and "entheogen," meaning releasing the god within. Some of these names are not very helpful. For example, few features of psychosis are mimicked by these drugs although existing psychosis can be aggravated, and true hallucinations are actually rather rare (Julien, 2001; Shulgin and Shulgin, 1991).

The major psychedelics include DMT (dimethyltryptamine, an ingredient of ayahuasca), psilocybin (found in "magic mushrooms"), mescaline (derived from the peyote cactus) and many synthetic drugs including LSD (lysergic acid diethylamide), numerous phenethylamines (Shulgin and Shulgin, 1991) and many drugs in the tryptamine series with varying effects and time courses (Shulgin and Shulgin, 1997). Most of them structurally resemble one of the four neurotransmitters: acetylcholine, noradrenaline (norepinephrine), dopamine and serotonin (Julien, 2001). They can all be toxic at high doses but are not generally addictive. Standing out all on its own, and rather lamely classified as the only minor psychedelic, is the best known and most widely used of all—cannabis.

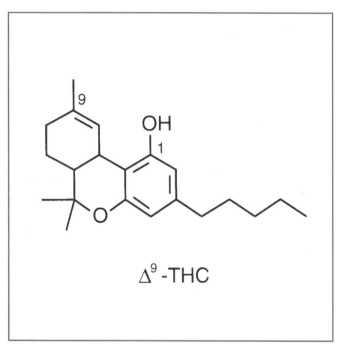

FIGURE 22.7 ● The structure of THC

CANNABIS

The familiar and beautiful plant *Cannabis sativa* has been used medically for nearly 5000 years, and as a source of tough fiber for clothes and ropes for even longer (Earleywine, 2002). In the nineteenth century it was widely used as medicine, but since then medical use and knowledge have been restricted by over half a century of prohibition (Grinspoon and Bakalar, 1993). Nineteenth-century scientific explorers of cannabis and the artist members of the Club des Haschischins, such as Balzac and Baudelaire, ate hashish. This is a dark brown or reddish solid derived from the resin scraped from the leaves and stems, the pollen, oil and sometimes powdered flowers and leaves as well. Cannabis can also be made into a tincture with alcohol, a drink mixed with milk, sugar and spices, or cooked with butter. As a recreational drug in the twenty-first century it is most often smoked, either in the form of hash mixed with tobacco or burnt in special pipes, or as grass—the dried leaves and flowering heads—smoked on its own. As with any drug, smoking makes for rapid absorption into the bloodstream, avoiding enzymes in the digestive system that can break down some constituents, and allows for easy control over the dose.

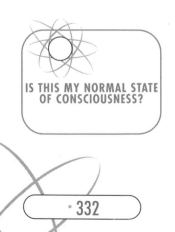

IS THIS MY NORMAL STATE OF CONSCIOUSNESS?

● CONSCIOUSNESS

The main active ingredient is delta-9-tetrahydrocannabinol, and this, together with cannabinol and cannabidiol, produce the main psychoactive effects, by acting on the cannabinoid receptor. However, there are over 60 other cannabinoids unique to the plant, all of which have slightly different effects on the brain and the immune system, and hundreds more chemical constituents that may all affect each other and change the effect of the final mixture (Earleywine, 2002; Farthing, 1992; Julien, 2001). The main active ingredients are all fat soluble and can remain dissolved in body fat for some time after smoking. With its complex and varying mixture of psychoactives, cannabis nicely illustrates the difference between natural psychoactive mixtures, which include ayahuasca and drugs derived from mushrooms and cacti, and the simpler or starker effects of synthetic psychedelics.

Describing the subjective effects of cannabis is not easy, partly because "Most people cannot find the words to explain their sensations" (Earleywine, 2002, 98) and partly because the effects differ so widely from person to person. Some people become self-conscious, disorientated and paranoid and rarely repeat their experience, while others experience delight, novelty, insight or just relaxation and go on to strike up a positive, sometimes life-long, relationship with the drug. Nevertheless, research has revealed some typical effects. In the first major survey of cannabis use, Tart (1971) asked over 200 questions of 150 people, mostly Californian students, who had used the drug at least a dozen times. Other studies have subsequently administered cannabis, or just THC, in the laboratory and recorded the effects.

Users report many emotional effects, including euphoria and relaxation at lower doses, and fear and paranoia at higher doses. Sensory effects include enhancement of all the senses, enhanced depth perception, improved sexual responsiveness and enjoyment, slowing of time, widening of space and a focus on the present. Synesthesia is sometimes reported at high doses. Openness to experience increases and some people find a sense of the sacred or divine. Memory, especially short-term memory, is often felt to be impaired. Creative thought and personal insight are often reported, but so are mental fogginess, slowed thinking and inability to read.

ACTIVITY
Discussing ASCs

People who have had experience of ASCs often enjoy talking about them, whether to share their insights, laugh about their exploits or explore their fears. This needs a supportive and safe environment and you, as leader of any discussion, must decide whether you can provide it or not. In Europe cannabis has been decriminalized in many countries, and many other recreational drugs are tolerated, but in North America anti-drug laws are stringent. If you cannot talk freely, restrict the discussion to alcohol, sleep and spontaneous ASCs. You might ask the following questions.

- Why do you induce ASCs? What do you gain from them?

- How can you tell when you have entered an ASC?

- Is one person's ASC (such as being drunk or stoned) the same as someone else's?

Another exercise requires advance preparation but avoids problems of prohibition. Ask participants to bring along a short description of an ASC. This can either be someone else's — for example, from a book or website — or their own. They read this out loud and ask everyone else to guess which ASC is referred to. Discussing how they decided leads naturally to all the other interesting questions about ASCs.

Laboratory studies show that the perceived effects on memory are roughly accurate, with short-term memory severely disrupted while episodic and semantic memory remain generally good. On the other hand, the enjoyable experience of enhancement of the senses is not verified by objective tests, "people think marijuana can enhance some visual processes, and laboratory research suggests it actually impairs some of them" (Earleywine, 2002: 105).

What can we learn about ASCs from this extraordinary mixture of complex effects? Here we have a range of states, sought out by millions of people worldwide, which we seem able to describe only as a mish-mash of effects on cognitive and emotional functions. As for mapping them, the task seems daunting. Not only is it difficult to position being stoned in relation to other ASCs, but being stoned itself varies widely. Experienced users can discriminate between cannabis that induces heady or intellectual experiences, mellow or relaxing ones or "laughing grass" that makes everything funny. We are very far from a science of ASCs that can make sense of all this.

MAJOR PSYCHEDELICS

> I was . . . back in a world where everything shone with the Inner Light, and was infinite in its significance. The legs, for example, of that chair—how miraculous their tubularity, how supernatural their polished smoothness! I spent several minutes—or was it several centuries?—not merely gazing at those bamboo legs, but actually *being* them—or rather being myself in them; or, to be still more accurate . . . being my Not-self in the Not-self which was the chair . . . four bamboo chair legs in the middle of a room. Like Wordsworth's daffodils, they brought all manner of wealth—the gift, beyond price, of a new direct insight into the very Nature of Things.
>
> (Huxley, 1954: 20–1; 25)

This is how Aldous Huxley, novelist and author of *Brave New World*, described some of what happened when "one bright May morning, I swallowed four-tenths of a gramme of mescaline dissolved in half a glass of water and sat down to wait for the results" (Huxley, 1954: 13). In *The Doors of Perception*, he describes how a vase of three ill-assorted flowers became the miracle of creation; how time and space became insignificant; his own body seemed perfectly capable of acting without him; and how everything simply was, in its own isness or suchness.

Mescaline, or trimethoxyphenylethylamine, is the main active ingredient in the San Pedro cactus *Trichocereus pachanoi* and in peyote, a small, spineless desert cactus, *Lophophora williamsii*, which has apparently been used for ritual purposes for 7000 years (Devereux, 1997). Traditionally the top of the peyote is dried to make mescal buttons, which are then chewed to invoke deities and open up other worlds. Mescaline is also produced synthetically and is then used on its own without the complexity of the 30 or so other alkaloids that are found in peyote. Mescaline makes the world seem fantastic and colorful, which is reflected in the art it has inspired, and gives "the conviction

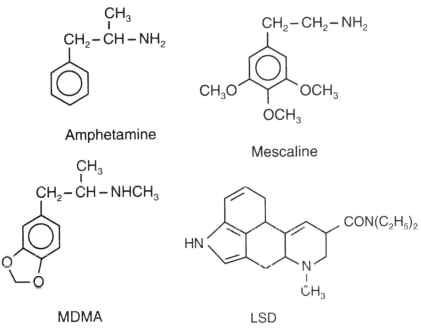

FIGURE 22.8 • The structure of some major psychedelics: amphetamine, mescaline, LSD and MDMA

that this is a view of the essential nature of the universe" (Perry, 2002: 212), and this is probably its most characteristic effect. Some users describe it as more hallucinogenic and less self-revealing, or self-destroying, than some of the other psychedelics, especially LSD.

The structure of mescaline resembles noradrenaline (norepinephrine). Several of the other major hallucinogens resemble serotonin and work by increasing or mimicking its effects. This is true of the active constituents of morning glory seeds, and many mushrooms of the *Psilocybe* genus, which contain psilocybin and psilocine. Synthetic psilocybin is also made. When it was readily available and legal in the 1960s, Timothy Leary and other members of the "Harvard psilocybin project" used psilocybin to encourage people to "turn on, tune in, drop out" (Stevens, 1987).

The final drug in this category is often considered to be the ultimate mind-revealing psychedelic: LSD, or d-lysergic acid diethylamide.

LSD has a famous history (Stevens, 1987). In 1943, Albert Hoffman, a chemist at the Sandoz laboratories in Basel, Switzerland, was working with ergot, a deadly fungus that grows on rye. For eight years he had been synthesizing a long series of ergotamine molecules in the hope of finding a useful medicine. Then on Friday 16 April he synthesized a batch of LSD-25. He began to feel unwell, went home to bed, and experienced a stream of fantastic hallucinations.

Hoffman suspected that, although he hadn't deliberately taken any, the LSD might somehow have caused the hallucinations. Like any chemist wanting to test psychoactive drugs on himself (Shulgin and Shulgin, 1991), he decided to begin with what he thought was a tiny dose. On Monday the 19th, at 4:20 in the afternoon, with his assistants present, he started his tests with 250 micrograms. At 4:50 he noted no effect, at 5:00 some dizziness, visual disturbance and a marked desire to laugh. Then he stopped writing, asked for a doctor to be called and, with one of his assistants, set off for home on his bicycle.

Although he cycled at a good pace, he seemed to be getting nowhere. The familiar road looked like a Dali painting and the buildings yawned and rippled. By the time the doctor arrived, Hoffman was hovering near his bedroom ceiling, watching what he thought was his dead body. Instead of the fascinating hallucinations he had had before, this time he was in a nightmare and assumed that he would either die or go mad. Of course he did neither, and this first acid trip is now regularly celebrated with re-enactments of his famous bicycle ride (Stevens, 1987).

LSD turned out to be active in tiny doses, and in fact Hoffman had taken the equivalent of two or three tabs of acid. Like many people since, he had discovered that acid produces the sense of going on a journey, or trip, that can include joy, elation, wondrous hallucinations, deep insights and spiritual experiences, as well as terrifying horror and despair, and the disintegration of self. To many users it seems that it opens up all the contents of their mind, revealing memories, hopes, fears and fantasies—both good and bad. This is why there can be bad trips as well as good, and why the term psychedelic is appropriate.

LSD was central to the spirit of the 1960s and the hippie movement, and had deep effects on many people. Among them was Richard Alpert, a young, rich and highly successful Harvard psychologist. Along with Timothy Leary, Ralph Metzner and others, he had first turned on with psilocybin. He then began to find psychology unrewarding and his life empty. Chasing the insights of the drug he and five others once locked themselves in a building for three weeks and took 400 micrograms of LSD every four hours. It was "as if you came into the kingdom of heaven and you saw how it all was and . . . then you got cast out again" (Alpert, 1971; Stevens, 1987). He realized that he did not know enough, went to India to study eastern religions and became Baba Ram Dass.

Psychedelics have changed many people's lives, encouraged them to value kindness and love above all and given them the conviction that, for

SELF-ASSESSMENT QUESTIONS

○ What is an ASC? Should ASCs be defined objectively or subjectively?

○ What is altered in an ASC?

○ Explain the idea of state-specific sciences.

○ List the main categories of psychoactive drugs.

○ Describe the mode of action and psychological effects of MDMA.

○ List as many psychedelic drugs as you can. In what ways are their effects similar and different from each other?

○ What is a bad trip?

once, they saw things as they really are. But are they right? Are any of these drug-induced ASCs valid, truth-giving, truly spiritual experiences, or are they just the ramblings of poisoned minds? We shall return to James's question of how to regard them when we have looked at a range of ASCs, from sleep and dreams to mystical experiences.

Earleywine, M. (2002) *Understanding Marijuana.* New York, Oxford University Press. See Chapter 5, pages 97–119, on the subjective effects of cannabis.

Jay, M. (ed.) (1999) *Artificial Paradises: A Drugs Reader.* New York, Penguin. Contains brief extracts from De Quincey, Huxley, Freud, Davy, Hoffman, Shulgin, James, Siegel, Leary, Tart, Grof and many others.

Tart, C.T. (1972) States of consciousness and state-specific sciences. *Science* 176, 1203–10. Also available at: http://www.paradigm-sys.com/display/ch_articles2.cfm?ID=53

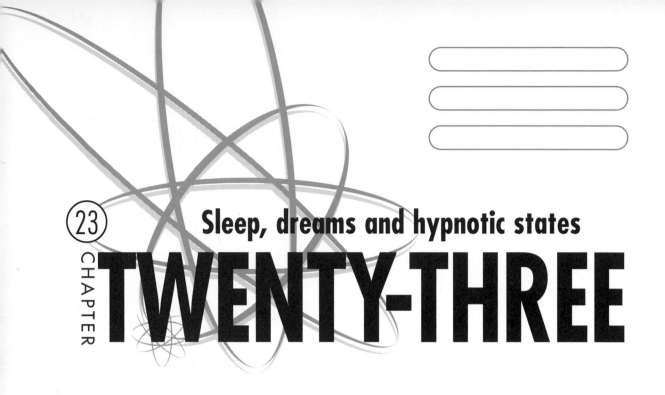

(23)

Sleep, dreams and hypnotic states

TWENTY-THREE

I was on a ski lift, a double-seater chair, moving slowly up into the high snowy peaks. It was cold and dark—nearly dawn, and the deep blue sky was lightening where the sun was about to break through. "But this lift isn't supposed to open until 8:30 am," I thought. "How did I get here? Lifts don't run in the dark. What's going on?" I began to panic. I looked down and realized that I had no skis on, and you need skis to get safely off the lift. I would have to run and hope I didn't fall. As my boots were about to hit the ground I suddenly knew the answer. I was dreaming, and with that realization it was as though I had woken up. Of course lifts don't run in the dark. I looked around, conscious in my own dream, gazing at the beauty of the morning mountains as the sun streamed over the peaks.

This is an example of a lucid dream, a dream in which you know, at the time, that you are dreaming. This ability to, as it were, wake up inside a dream, prompts all sorts of interesting questions about sleep, dreams and ASCs. What does it mean to say that "I become conscious" in a lucid dream? Aren't you conscious in ordinary dreams? What are dreams anyway? Are they experiences or only stories constructed on waking up? And who is the dreamer? In this chapter we will skim over the basics of sleep and dream research, for they are well covered in many texts (e.g., Empson, 2001; Hobson, 2002; Horne,

1988), and concentrate instead on what ordinary dreams, as well as some more exotic kinds of dreams, can tell us about consciousness.

WAKING AND SLEEPING

Every day we all go through a cycle of states that are usually divided for convenience into three: waking, REM sleep (rapid eye movement sleep) and non-REM sleep, with a typical night's sleep consisting of four or five cycles. These states are defined by physiological and behavioral measures including how easily the person can be awakened, their muscle tone, eye movements and brain activity as measured by either EEG or scans. In REM sleep the brain is highly active and the EEG resembles that of waking, although, paradoxically, the sleeper is harder to waken than during non-REM sleep. Even in non-REM sleep the overall firing rate of neurons is as high as in waking states, but the pattern is quite different, with the EEG dominated by long slow waves rather than complex fast ones.

The neurochemistry and physiology of these states are well researched. For example, the inhibitory neuromodulator, adenosine, is thought to be the main sleep inducer. During sleep, the REM cycle is controlled by the reticular formation in the pons in the brainstem, and not by higher brain areas, which are unnecessary for normal sleep cycling. Within the brainstem are cholinergic

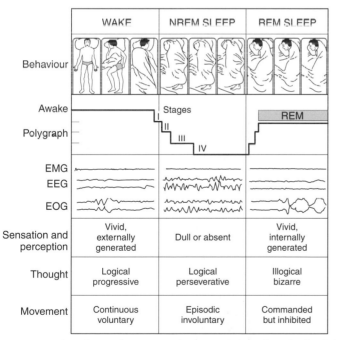

	WAKE	NREM SLEEP	REM SLEEP
Behaviour			
Awake / Polygraph		Stages	REM
EMG			
EEG			
EOG			
Sensation and perception	Vivid, externally generated	Dull or absent	Vivid, internally generated
Thought	Logical progressive	Logical perseverative	Illogical bizarre
Movement	Continuous voluntary	Episodic involuntary	Commanded but inhibited

FIGURE 23.1 • Behavioral states in humans. States of waking, NREM sleep and REM sleep have behavioral, polygraphic and psychological manifestations. The sequence of these stages is represented in the polygraph channel. Sample tracings of three variables used to distinguish state are also shown: electromyogram (EMG), which is highest in waking, intermediate in NREM sleep and lowest in REM sleep; the electroencephalogram (EEG) and electro-oculogram (EOG), which are both activated in waking and REM sleep and inactivated in NREM sleep. Each sample is approximately 20 seconds (after Hobson 2002).

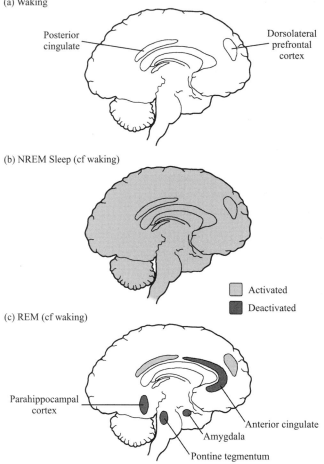

(a) Waking

Posterior cingulate

Dorsolateral prefrontal cortex

(b) NREM Sleep (cf waking)

☐ Activated
■ Deactivated

(c) REM (cf waking)

Parahippocampal cortex

Anterior cingulate

Amygdala

Pontine tegmentum

FIGURE 23.2 • Summary of PET study evidence of brain region activation in NREM and REM sleep. Compared to the blood flow distribution in waking (a), the global decreases observed in NREM sleep (b) suggest widespread deactivation consistent with the greatly diminished capacity of conscious experience early in the night. In REM sleep (c), many regions are activated about their levels in waking (solid black) while others are deactivated (shaded) (Hobson 2002).

REM-on nuclei and aminergic (both noradrenaline and serotonin) REM-off nuclei, which reciprocally activate and inhibit each other and control the switching of states. Sensory input is blocked at the thalamo-cortical level in non-REM sleep and at the periphery in REM sleep. In REM sleep the brainstem also blocks motor commands at the level of spinal motor neurons so that whatever is going on in motor cortex does not result in physical activity.

In these and other ways the physiological states can be recognized, but what about the experience? As is now well known, when people are woken from REM sleep, they typically report that they were having complex and often bizarre dreams, sometimes very bizarre, as in the following excerpt.

I was at a conference and trying to get breakfast but the food and the people in line kept changing. My legs didn't work properly and I found it a great effort to hold my tray up. Then I realised why. My body was rotting away, and liquid was oozing from it. I thought I might be completely rotted before the end of the day, but I thought I should still get some coffee if I had the strength.

I cannot say that this is a typical dream, for there is probably no such thing, but it has familiar elements that most people will recognize. The contents of dreams have been thoroughly studied using questionnaires, interviews and by analyzing reports using a scoring system originally developed in the 1960s by Hall and van de Castle (Domhoff, 1996). This counts such elements as settings, characters, emotions, social interactions and misfortunes, all of which show remarkable consistency across times and cultures, with reliable sex differences, and reliable differences between the dreams of adults and children. For example, men dream more about other men than women do and have more aggressive interactions. Children, by contrast, dream more often about animals, suffer more dream misfortunes and are more often the victim of aggression than its initiator. Dream logic is wonderfully unlike waking logic, with people being composites, objects transforming into other objects and people doing things for the strangest reasons. All this is accepted by the dreamer who neither notices how peculiar it all is nor realizes that it is a

CONSCIOUSNESS

dream. Most dreams are forgotten unless the sleeper is woken during the dream or wakes naturally from it, and even then most are soon forgotten if they are not mentally rehearsed or written down.

By contrast, when sleepers are woken from non-REM sleep, they less often report vivid, complex and dynamic dreams, and more often say either that nothing was going on in their mind or that they were thinking. As a simple example: "I was thinking about my nephew. It's his birthday soon and I must send him a card." Or "I was asleep. I wasn't thinking about anything or dreaming about anything."

This correlation between physiological states and subjective reports has supported decades of productive research into sleep and dreaming and made it possible to map the three major states in terms of their physiology. A good example is the AIM model, developed by American psychiatrist and sleep researcher Allan Hobson, and named after its three dimensions: Activation energy (for example, as measured by the EEG), Input source (either external or internal), and Mode (the ratio of amines to cholines) (Hobson, 1999). Mode requires a little more explanation. During waking the amine neurotransmitters and neuromodulators, including noradrenaline and serotonin, predominate and are essential for rational thought, volition and directing attention. During REM sleep acetylcholine takes over and thinking becomes delusional, irrational and unreflective. The ratio of these two is Hobson's Mode.

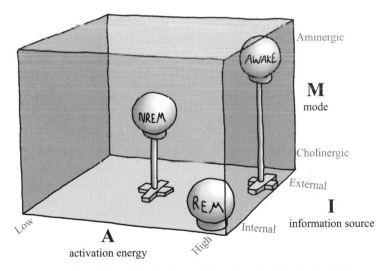

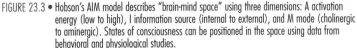

FIGURE 23.3 • Hobson's AIM model describes "brain-mind space" using three dimensions: A activation energy (low to high), I information source (internal to external), and M mode (cholinergic to aminergic). States of consciousness can be positioned in the space using data from behavioral and physiological studies.

States can now be positioned in what Hobson calls "brain-mind space" by measuring them along these three dimensions. He stresses that it is an entirely artificial model, yet it is based on specific data, it recognizes the continuously changing nature of brain-mind states, and it allows for any state of the brain-mind to be positioned within it. Adding time as a fourth dimension, falling

THE EVOLUTION OF DREAMS

Why did dreaming evolve? The question here is not why *sleep* evolved. There are many competing theories about the evolutionary functions of REM and non-REM sleep in different species (Horne, 1988), but the trickier question concerns dreams. Do they have a function of their own or are they an inevitable concomitant of certain states of sleep? As with the question of the evolution of consciousness itself (see Concept, Chapter 10), we can find examples of the three main approaches.

Flanagan argues that "dreams are evolutionary epiphenomena" and they have no adaptive function whatsoever. "Dreaming came along as a free ride on a system designed to think and to sleep" (Flanagan, 2000: 100, 24). Note that, unlike traditional epiphenomenalism, he does allow that dreams, while having no function, can have effects. Hobson (2002) also considers dreams to be epiphenomena, but on different grounds: that the content of dreams has no significant influence on waking behavior, and many people function perfectly well without recalling their dreams.

By contrast, dreaming has a crucial biological function according to the Threat Simulation Theory proposed by Finnish psychologist Antti Revonsuo. During most of human evolution physical and interpersonal threats were serious, giving a reproductive advantage to those who survived them. So dreaming evolved to simulate these threats and repeatedly practice dealing with them. In support of the theory, Revonsuo (2000) shows that modern dreams include far more threatening events than people meet in waking life, and the dreamer usually engages appropriately with them. A broader view of "dreaming as play" is proposed by Humphrey (1983; 1986). We dream not just to gain practice with threats, but to practice all sorts of physical, intellectual and social skills. "Dreaming represents the most audacious and ingenious of nature's tricks for educating her psychologists" (Humphrey, 1983: 85).

The main contenders against this kind of theory treat dreaming as a necessary by-product of random cortical asleep and cycling through the normal sleep stages can be represented as moving from one region of the space to another, while large areas remain unoccupied. As in Tart's original conception, these occupied areas are discrete SoCs. Obviously the map is crude, and the reality is much more complicated (Solms, 2000), but it still provides a scheme for relating sleep states to other conditions, such as delirium or unconsciousness, and places them in the context of the various neurotransmitter systems that control the overall state of the brain.

A different way of looking at consciousness during sleep is provided by Edelman and Tononi (2000), who argue that complex and unified conscious experience depends on a constantly changing dynamic core of activity supported by reentrant connections between the cortex and thalamus. In this theory the overall amount of neural activity is not important: what matters is that it is distributed and integrated, but continuously changing. In non-REM sleep, with its long slow waves, this differentiation is lost and consciousness with it.

FROM PHYSIOLOGY TO EXPERIENCE

Dream research seems to provide a classic, and well-studied, example of the NCCs (neural correlates of consciousness). That is, various physiological, neurochemical and behavioral variables can be correlated with subjective descriptions of a dream. This suggests the possibility of either reducing the SoCs entirely to physical states or equating the experiential with the physical, as Hobson implies with his "brain-mind space." There would then be just one space and one concept of dreaming sleep, not two. But things may not be that simple.

First, the correlation, while real enough, is not perfect. In the early days of sleep research, REM sleep and dreaming were often treated as equivalent, but subsequently people became more careful in referring either to the physical state or to the reported experiences. Vivid dreaming is reported in about 70–95 percent of awakenings from REM sleep and roughly 5–10 percent of non-REM sleep, while mentation of some sort is reported from about 50 percent of non-REM awakenings, although none of these figures can be precise because they vary with the criteria used (Empson, 2001; Nielsen, 2000). This suggests that being physiologically in REM sleep does not guarantee dreaming, and dreaming can occur without the physiological state of REM (Solms, 2000). In other words, REM is neither a necessary nor a sufficient condition for dreaming.

Second, REM can occur when dreaming seems unlikely or even impossible. For example, human fetuses spend about 15 hours a day in REM sleep, babies spend less as they grow older, and children and adults less still. Yet fetuses cannot have anything like adult dreams because dreaming depends on prior experiences and on highly developed cognitive abilities, which babies lack. For example, adults' dreams frequently include events of the previous day, but a fetus has few interesting events to dream about. People with no visual experience, such as those born blind, do not dream in pictures but in words, ideas, and auditory and tactile images. They have plenty of experiences and a rich sense of self. But the new-born baby has neither well-developed senses nor the capacity for imagery, self-awareness and language.

As children grow older, their dreams closely reflect their developing cognitive abilities. Their dreams turn from rather static, single dream images reported at age five or six, to more lively and moving imagery at age six or seven, with a dreamed self appearing only after the age of about seven years (Foulkes, 1993). We can therefore be sure that, whatever is going on in a fetus during REM sleep, it is not anything like an adult's dream.

The same argument applies to sleep in other species (Empson, 2001; Horne, 1988). Reptiles do not have REM sleep but many birds and mammals do. Dolphins, although extremely intelligent, have very little, and only one half of their brain sleeps at a time. Mice and rats, dogs and cats, monkeys and apes all have REM sleep, and when we see their eyelids flickering or their whiskers twitching, we can easily imagine that they are dreaming. But are we right to do so? Once again we hit that curious property of consciousness that we can never know. We can guess, and based on what we know of their cognitive abilities, some of them might be enjoying complex visual and auditory images, but we know they cannot construct narrative structures or describe their dreams in words. From all this we must conclude that in terms of our current understanding, dreaming and REM sleep are not the same thing.

Where can we go from here? One possibility is that the physiology and the phenomenology can never be reduced to, or equated with, each other, that the

activation, which occurs for other reasons. For example, Crick and Mitchison (1983) proposed that cortical neural networks become overloaded during learning and that the function of REM sleep is to remove superfluous connections by randomly flooding them. According to this theory we dream so that we can forget. There are several other theories relating dreaming to memory consolidation (Hobson, 2002), but in spite of a great deal of research the relationship between dreaming and memory is still not clear (Vertes and Eastman, 2000).

Whether dreams have an evolutionary function or not, we can still use them in our own lives. Theories of dream interpretation, especially those based on Freud's psychoanalysis, have not generally stood the test of time (Hobson, 2002; Webster, 1995) but studying our own dreams can be valuable in all sorts of ways. They can reveal our inner motivations and hopes, help us face our fears, encourage growing awareness and even be a source of creativity and insight.

CONCEPT

IS HYPNOSIS AN ASC?

The term "hypnosis" comes from the Greek *hypnos* for sleep, and nineteenth-century researchers, such as the British surgeon James Braid and the French neurologist Jean Charcot, believed that subjects fell into a sleep-like state and became somnambulists, or sleepwalkers. Others argued that there was no special hypnotic state and that all the effects were due to suggestion and imagination, an argument that turned into the twentieth-century battle between "state theorists" and "non-state theorists."

Applying Tart's definition we should easily accept that hypnosis is an ASC because some subjects do feel that their mental functioning is radically different from normal. However, the traditional view of the hypnotic state carries far more contentious implications than this. The traditional view—held, for example, by Morton Prince and Pierre Janet—was that hypnosis is a dissociated state in which part of the mind is cut off from the rest. The hypnotist takes control over the somnambulist, who behaves and thinks differently, and is capable of feats that are impossible in the normal waking state. This was updated in the 1970s into Hilgard's neo-dissociationist theory. Hilgard (1986) argued that in the normal state there are multiple

FIGURE 23.4 • The hidden observer. Although a hypnotic subject with his hand in freezing water may claim to feel no pain, Hilgard discovered that by giving an appropriate signal, he could talk to a hidden part of the person who *was* in pain. This forms part of the evidence for neo-dissociationist theories.

fathomless abyss can never be crossed. Another possibility is that with further research, and more complex and realistic modeling of brain states and neurochemistry, we will learn exactly how to reduce one to the other (Churchland, 1988). If this happened we would no longer need to speak separately about dreaming and sleep states, and we really would have "brain-mind states." At the moment this is not the case and we must be satisfied with correlations.

Although frustrating, this problem is relatively easy to understand, but there are some much trickier issues confronting the whole idea of dreams as ASCs. Some philosophers have gone so far as to question whether dreams are experiences at all (Dennett, 1976; Malcolm, 1959).

ARE DREAMS EXPERIENCES?

Of course dreams are experiences, you might say, and many would agree with you. The *Oxford English Dictionary* defines a dream as "A train of thoughts, images, or fancies passing through the mind during sleep." This sounds very much like a stream of consciousness happening during sleep or a show in the night-time Cartesian theater. Psychology textbooks usually include sections on "states of consciousness during sleep" and many of them *define* dreaming as a state of consciousness (e.g., Atkinson et al., 2000; Carlson, 1999). Searle agrees, "Dreams are a form of consciousness, though of course quite different from full waking states" (1997: 5) and Hobson defends the common-sense view like this: "Our dreams are not mysterious phenomena, they are conscious events. Here's the simplest test: Are we aware of what happens in our dreams? Of course. Therefore, dreaming is a conscious experience" (1999: 209).

But are we really aware in our dreams? Suppose that I wake from a dream and think, "Wow, that was a weird dream. I remember I was trying to get some coffee . . ." At the time of waking I seem to *have been having* the dream. Indeed I am completely convinced that a moment ago I was dreaming of being in the cafeteria, even if the details slip quickly away and I cannot hang onto them, let alone report them all. But there are some serious problems here.

Some of these problems concern the self. Although I am sure that "I" was dreaming, the self in the dream was not like my normal waking self. This strange dream-self never realized, during the dream, that it was a dream; she accepted that the people and the food kept changing in impossible ways, showed little disgust or surprise at the state of her body, and in general treated everything as though it was real. Was it really me who dreamt it?

This lack of insight is more than an odd quirk because it casts doubt on the usual assumption that dreams are ASCs. You will recall that Tart defined an ASC as "a qualitative alteration in the overall pattern of mental functioning, such that the experiencer feels his consciousness is radically different from the way it functions ordinarily." Clearly there is "a qualitative alteration in the overall pattern of mental functioning," but the odd thing is that the experiencer does *not* realize this. So by this definition we are forced to the curious conclusion that the ordinary dream, that most classic of all ASCs, is not really an ASC at all. Oddly enough, by the same definition, a lucid dream *is* an ASC because now the experiencer *does* realize it is a dream.

Other peculiarities concern the status of the dream: if I start to doubt whether I really did have that dream, the only evidence to call on is my own memories, and those are vague and fast fading. One response to such doubts goes back to 1861, when Maury described a long and complicated dream about the French Revolution, which culminated in his being taken to the guillotine. Just as his head came off, he woke to find that the headboard of his bed had fallen on his real neck just where the blade had sliced through his dream neck. He proposed that dreams do not happen in real time but are entirely concocted in the moment of waking up. This theory is psychologically plausible in the sense that humans are very good at constructing stories and quick at confabulating. But it is not true.

In the 1950s, when subjects in the sleep lab were asked to describe their dreams, the descriptions

control systems under the direction of an executive ego, but in hypnosis the hypnotist takes over some of the control and monitoring, making the subject feel as though his actions are involuntary and that suggested hallucinations are real. This fits with recent theories of how the sense of conscious will is constructed (Wegner, 2002). Against this, non-state theorists argue that hypnotic subjects are playing a social role to please the experimenter, are using imaginative and other strategies to comply with what they believe they are supposed to do, or are simply faking it (Spanos, 1991; Wagstaff, 1994).

In support of dissociation, Hilgard discovered the phenomenon of the hidden observer. When a hypnotized subject claimed not to feel the pain of having his hand in a bath of freezing water, Hilgard said, "When I place my hand on your shoulder, I shall be able to talk to a hidden part of you . . ."; this hidden part then described the pain it felt, and could remember and do things that the hypnotized subject previously could not. Critics responded by demonstrating that the hidden observer could be made, by appropriate suggestions, to feel less pain instead or to behave in other ways to match the expectations given (Spanos, 1991).

The crucial experiments compare "real" hypnotized subjects with control subjects who are asked to fake being hypnotized or to imagine and experience the hypnotic suggestions without any induction procedure. The argument is that if controls show the same phenomena as "really hypnotized" subjects, the idea of a special hypnotic state is redundant. Many experiments have shown no differences between the groups, so supporting the non-state view, but there are interesting anomalies. One example is "trance logic" in which hypnotized subjects seem able to accept illogicalities in a way that controls cannot. For example, when asked to hallucinate a person who is actually present, they may see two people while simulators tend to see only one. When regressed to childhood, they may describe feeling simultaneously grown up and like a child, while simulators claim only to feel like a child. This trance logic is reminiscent of the changed logic found in some drug states (Chapter 22) and in mystical experiences (Chapter 24).

British psychologist Graham Wagstaff concludes that "in over one hundred years we seem to be no further forward in deciding whether there is an altered state of consciousness that we can call 'hypnosis'" (Wagstaff, 1994: 1003).

Ernest Ropiequet Hilgard (1904–2001)

Hypnosis was once considered the preserve of tricksters, cranks and charlatans, until Ernest Hilgard, risking his reputation as a Professor of Psychology at Stanford, set up the Stanford Laboratory of Hypnosis Research with his wife Josephine, in 1957. Born the son of a doctor in 1904 in Belleville, Illinois, he first studied chemical engineering and then switched to psychology for his doctorate at Yale in 1930, moving to Stanford in 1933 where he stayed the rest of his life. Hilgard won numerous awards for scientific contributions to nearly every field of psychology, especially learning and states of consciousness, but he is best known to students of psychology for his undergraduate textbook.

Hilgard pioneered research into the use of hypnosis for giving up smoking and for pain relief. When a subject whose left hand was in freezing water claimed to feel no pain, Hilgard asked the right hand to do some automatic writing. "It's freezing. It hurts" wrote the hand and so was discovered the "hidden observer." Hilgard studied possession, fugues and multiple personality, and considered dreams and hallucinations to be dissociative states. His neo-dissociation theory remains one of the foremost theories of hypnosis.

" Are we aware of what happens in our dreams? Of course. Therefore, dreaming is a conscious experience. "

Hobson, 1999: 209

they gave were longer the longer they had been in REM sleep, and when woken after either 5 or 15 minutes of REM, they did far better than chance at guessing which it was. Other experiments used the incorporation of external stimuli into dreams. Many people have the experience of dreaming about a church bell ringing or a wolf howling, only to wake to the sound of their alarm clock. Sounds, taps on the skin, flashes of light, and drips and sprays of water have all been used in experiments, and when they don't wake the sleeper, can sometimes influence dream content, allowing dream events to be timed. The results show that dreams take about the same time as it takes to visualize the events when awake. All this suggests that dreams are not concocted in a flash on waking up, but really do take time.

Other responses to these doubts are more subtle. Dennett (1976) provides a selection of fanciful theories that play with the relationship between experience and memory. One is the "cassette theory of dreams." In this theory the brain holds a store of potential dreams recorded and ready for use. On waking from REM sleep a "cassette" is pulled out of store, to match the sound of the alarm clock if necessary, and—hey presto!—we seem to have been dreaming. On this theory there really are no dreams. There are no events or images presented in consciousness but only recollections of dreams that were never actually experienced. "On the cassette theory it is not like anything to dream, although it is like something *to have dreamed*. On the cassette theory, dreams are not experiences we have during sleep" (Dennett, 1976: 138).

Now the point of this theory is not that it might be literally true, but that it helps us to think about another possibility. Dennett goes on to suppose that the equivalent of cassette dreams might be composed unconsciously during the prior REM sleep. We now have two theories: the normal theory that dreams are experiences happening in consciousness or presented to consciousness during sleep, and the new theory that dreams are composed unconsciously during sleep and then "remembered" on waking up. The question is this. Could we ever tell which was right?

The answer seems to be no. This is another of those differences that makes no difference. It is no good asking dreamers whether the events really occurred in consciousness because all they have is their memories and they will always say "Yes." And it is no good looking inside their brain to find out whether the events really did happen "in consciousness" or not. With sophisticated methods we might see the neural events that correlate with imagining cups of coffee or trying to walk, but we can never find out whether those neural events were "in consciousness" because there is no special place in the brain where consciousness happens and no magic difference between conscious neural firings and unconscious ones. To put it in terms of Dennett's later theory (1991), there is no Cartesian theater in which the dreams either were, or were not, shown. We are left with two empirically indistinguishable theories, one of which requires events to be "presented" or "displayed" in consciousness, while the other does not.

You will probably have recognized these ideas from previous chapters, and be able to pursue them to what might be called a retro-selective or backward-weaving theory of dreams. We might describe it as follows.

During REM sleep numerous brain processes are going on at once, none of which is either in or out of consciousness. On waking up a story is concocted by selecting one out of a vast number of possible threads through the multiple and confusing scraps of memory that remain. The chosen story fits the timing, but it is only one of many such stories that might have been selected and there is no right one, no version that actually happened "in consciousness," for there is no such thing as being "in consciousness." In this extreme theory dreams are not conscious experiences. They do not happen "in consciousness." But then nor does anything else.

"it is not like anything to dream, although it is like something to have dreamed"

Dennett, 1976: 138

FIGURE 23.5 • According to the retro-selective theory, dreams are not ongoing conscious experiences at all. They are concocted retrospectively on waking by selecting from the myriad trains of thoughts and images that were going on in parallel in the dreaming brain. So on waking, this dreamer might recall that he had ripped some flowers from their pot, rushed off on skis to escape retribution, arrived in a forest and had a picnic and a bottle of wine under a pine tree. With many more parallel processes going on than are shown here, a very large number of potential dreams are possible, and alarm clocks ringing or other sounds on waking might easily influence which was selected.

STRANGE DREAMS

When I realized that the ski lift and the mountains and the rising sun were all a dream, I wanted to fly, soaring up into the cold morning air over the mountain peaks. Flying dreams are reported by about half the population, and are usually pleasant or even joyful. Falling dreams are also common and sometimes end with a myoclonic jerk, an involuntary muscle spasm that occurs on the borders of sleep. Most such dreams are not lucid dreams—that is, the dreamer rarely thinks "Hey, I can't fly in normal life—this must be a dream."

Another odd kind of dream is the "false awakening" in which the person dreams of having woken up. Everything can look quite normal and so the dreamer gets on with dressing and eating breakfast until he really wakes up and has to start all over again. At this point he may be sure he really is awake, but again may not be. A famous example was described by the French biologist Yves Delage in 1919. Delage was asleep when he heard a knock at the door. He got up to find a visitor asking him to come quickly and attend to a friend who was ill. He got up, dressed and started to wash, whereupon the cold water on his face woke him up and he realized it was only a dream. Back in bed he heard the same voices again and, fearing he must have fallen asleep, leapt out of bed and repeated the dressing and washing four times before he really woke up (Green, 1968a).

In some false awakenings people report greenish glows, light emanating from objects, eerie feelings, and humming or buzzing sounds. These are all reminiscent of hypnagogic hallucinations (see Chapter 21) and prompt the odd thought that it may sometimes be impossible to know whether one is awake and hallucinating, or only dreaming one is awake. In the first case the bedroom is real even if the hallucinations are not, but in the second, the whole room and everything in it are dreamed. Experiences like this, in which the whole environment is replaced by hallucinations, are sometimes called 'metachoric experiences' (Green and McCreery, 1975). This doubt extends over crisis apparitions, fairy abductions, alien visitations and even some drug experiences. Without physiological monitoring we cannot know whether the person had their eyes open, as they often claim, or was fast asleep.

Why don't we realize we are dreaming at the time? This is the oddest and most frustrating thing about ordinary dreams—that we can fly, drive a Porsche across the sea, or survive the devastation of an atom bomb with no insight at all. Sometimes, however, critical doubt creeps in, prompted by strong emotions, by incongruities in the dream, or by recognizing recurring themes from previous dreams (Green, 1968a; Gackenbach and LaBerge, 1986). If we ask the question, "Am I dreaming?" we are having what the English psychologist, and pioneer of lucid dream research, Celia Green, calls a "prelucid dream." Even then, it is common for dreamers to give the wrong answer. There are accounts of people asking dream characters whether they are dreaming, splitting into two and arguing over whether they are dreaming, or trying to pinch themselves to find out. Of course the pinching test fails for those who dream a dream pinch and feel a realistic dream hurt.

FIGURE 23.6 • How can you test whether you are dreaming? In 1920s London, Oliver Fox made many tests of astral projection and lucid dreaming. "I dreamed that my wife and I awoke, got up, and dressed. On pulling up the blind, we made the amazing discovery that the row of houses opposite had vanished and in their place were bare fields. I said to my wife, 'This means I am dreaming, though everything seems so real and I feel perfectly awake. Those houses could not disappear in the night, and look at all that grass!' But though my wife was greatly puzzled, I could not convince her it was a dream. 'Well,' I continued, 'I am prepared to stand by my reason and put it to the test. I will jump out of the window, and I shall take no harm.' Ruthlessly ignoring her pleading and objecting, I opened the window and climbed onto the sill. I then jumped, and floated gently down into the street. When my feet touched the pavement, I awoke. My wife had no memory of dreaming" (Fox, 1962).

LUCID DREAMS

When the correct conclusion is reached, the dream becomes lucid. As Hobson puts it, "part of my brain-mind wakes up and . . . then I can have a lot of fun. I can watch the dreams . . . I can influence the dream content" (Hobson, 2002: 142). Lucid dreams certainly feel that way, but what could "part of a brain-mind" mean, and who is controlling what? The phenomenon of lucid dreaming presents some challenging questions about consciousness.

The term "lucid dream" was coined by the Dutch psychiatrist Frederik van Eeden in 1913, and although the name does not describe this kind of dream at all well, it has stuck. A lucid dream is defined as a dream in which you know *during the dream* that you are dreaming.

PRACTICE
BECOMING LUCID

If you are taking part in the class activity, try whichever induction technique is assigned to you. Otherwise, practice this one.

Take a pen and write a large "D" on one hand, for Dreaming, and a large "A" on the other, for Awake. As many times as you can, every day, look at these two letters and ask, **"Am I awake or am I dreaming?"** If you get thoroughly into the habit of doing this during the day, the habit should carry over into sleep. You may then find yourself looking at your hands in a dream and asking, "Am I awake or am I dreaming?" This is a prelucid dream. All you have to do is answer correctly and you're lucid.

Did it work? What happened in the dream? What happened to your awareness during the day?

This realization can have extraordinary concomitants. Not only do people describe lucidity as like "waking up in the dream" or "becoming conscious while dreaming," but many claim that once lucid they can fly or float, take charge of the course of their dream, or change the objects and scenery at will. Note the temptation here to say that consciousness causes these changes, or enables the dreamer to control the dream, but this causal conclusion is not warranted by the correlation. All we know is that in lucid dreams critical thinking, dream control, flying, and the sense of being more awake, or more conscious, or more "myself," all occur together. To understand why, we need to know more about lucid dreams.

Surveys show that about 50 percent of people claim to have had at least one lucid dream in their lives, and about 20 percent have one a month or more. This figure may be unreliable because it is difficult to explain what the question means. Although anyone who has had a lucid dream will recognize the description, others may misunderstand. With this proviso, surveys show no correlations with age, sex, personality measures or basic demographic variables, but the same people tend to report lucid dreaming, flying and falling dreams, and out-of-body experiences (Blackmore, 1982; Gackenbach and LaBerge, 1988; Green, 1968a).

Lucid dreams were long considered beyond the pale of serious sleep research and were studied by psychical researchers and parapsychologists. Even in the mid-twentieth century many psychologists rejected claims of lucidity, arguing that self-reflection and conscious choice are impossible in dreams, so lucid dreams must really occur before or after sleep or during "micro-awakenings."

They were proved wrong. The breakthrough was made simultaneously and independently by two young psychologists, Keith Hearne at the University of Hull in England and Stephen LaBerge at Stanford University in California. The problem they faced was simple. In REM sleep the voluntary muscles are paralyzed, so a dreamer who becomes lucid cannot shout out "Hey, listen to me, I'm dreaming" or even press a button to indicate lucidity. What Hearne and LaBerge both realized was that dreamers could still move their eyes. In Hearne's laboratory, Alan Worsley was the first to signal from a lucid dream. He decided in advance to move his eyes left and right eight times in succession whenever he became lucid. Using a polygraph, Hearne picked up the signals. He found them in the midst of REM sleep (1978), a finding that has been confirmed many times since (LaBerge, 1990).

Further research has shown that lucid dreams last an average of two minutes, although they can last as long as 50 minutes. They usually occur in the early hours of the morning, nearly half an hour into a REM period and toward the end of a burst of rapid eye movements. Onset tends to coincide with times of particularly high arousal during REM sleep and is associated with pauses in breathing, brief changes in heart rate, and skin response changes, but there is no unique combination that allows the lucid state to be identified by an observer without the dreamer signaling.

The method of signaling from lucid dreams allows some of the classic questions about dreams to be finally answered because correlations between dream content and physiology can be timed accurately, and lucid dreamers can be given pre-sleep instructions to carry out particular activities during their dream and then signal as they do so. One example is the classic question of how long dreams last. When lucid dreamers counted to ten during lucid dreams and again during waking, they took about the same length of time to do so, and they were able accurately to estimate the time taken by events during their dreams.

Another question concerns whether the eye movements seen during REM sleep actually correspond to dream events. By luck sleep researchers have occasionally noticed left to right movements just before a person woke up and reported watching a tennis game, but no luck is needed if lucid dreamers can

(Activity continued)

A more arduous version of this is LaBerge's MILD (Mnemonic Induction of Lucid Dreaming) technique (for more details see LaBerge, 1985; LaBerge and Rheingold, 1990). Wake yourself with an alarm in the early hours of the morning. If you have been dreaming, mentally rehearse the dream or, better still, get up and write it down. As you go to sleep again, visualize yourself back in the dream but this time you realize it is a dream. Keep rehearsing the dream until you fall asleep.

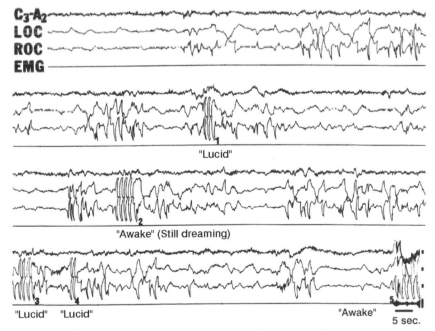

FIGURE 23.7 • A typical signal-verified lucid dream. Four channels of physiological data (central EEG [C3-A2], left and right eye movements [LOC and ROC], and chin muscle tone [EMG]) from the last 8 min of a 30 min REM period are shown. On awakening the subject reported having made five eye movement signals (labeled 1–5 in figure). The first signal (1, LRLR) marked the onset of lucidity (LaBerge, 2000).

deliberately create a game to watch and then signal when they are doing so. Several experiments show that eye movements do indeed reflect dream events. Furthermore, experiments tracking moving objects during the dream revealed that lucid dream eye movements resemble the smooth pursuit of waking vision rather than the saccadic eye movements associated with imagination (LaBerge, 1985; 1990).

Another question concerns how much of the nervous system is involved when physical actions are dreamed. In other experiments, lucid dreamers signaled as they performed different actions. The muscles that would be used for those actions in waking life twitched slightly during the dreams. Voluntary breathing during dreams coincides with actual breathing, and in one study a woman's erotic, lucid dream coincided with actual sexual arousal and a measurable orgasm (see LaBerge, 1990, for review).

Few people have frequent lucid dreams, and even fewer are able to induce them at will as Alan Worsley and the other special subjects can. There are, however, techniques that can help. Some involve specially designed machines. These work on the twin principles of first detecting REM sleep and then delivering a stimulus that is strong enough to increase arousal slightly, but not strong enough to wake the sleeper. Hearne's (1990) *Dream Machine* detects changes in breathing and gives a weak electric shock to the wrist. LaBerge's DreamLight detects eye movements and then uses lights and sounds as stimuli. Of 44 subjects who used the DreamLight in the laboratory, 55 percent had at least one lucid dream and two had their first-ever lucid dream this way (LaBerge, 1985). The later NovaDreamer packs all the hardware into goggles that can be worn at home.

Other methods include maintaining awareness while falling asleep (see Chapter 21), LaBerge's MILD technique (see Activity) and other methods that increase awareness during the day rather than just at night. These are based on the idea that we spend much of our time in a waking daze and if we could only be more lucid in waking life, it might carry over into dreaming. These methods are similar to the age-old techniques of meditation and mindfulness (see Chapter 26). Indeed advanced practitioners of meditation claim to maintain awareness through a large proportion of their sleep, and research has found associations between practicing meditation and increased lucidity (Gackenbach and Bosveld, 1989).

AM I AWAKE OR
AM I DREAMING?

SELF-ASSESSMENT QUESTIONS

○ What are REM and non-REM sleep and how are they identified?

○ Describe Hobson's AIM model.

○ Are ordinary dreams experiences? Are they ASCs? Provide arguments for and against.

○ Explain the retro-selective theory of dreams.

○ Define the following: flying dream, false awakening, metachoric experience, lucid dream.

○ Describe the method of signaling from lucid dreams. Give three or more examples of experiments made possible by this technique.

○ Do dreams have an evolutionary function? List three types of answers.

○ What is the difference between the state and non-state theories of hypnosis?

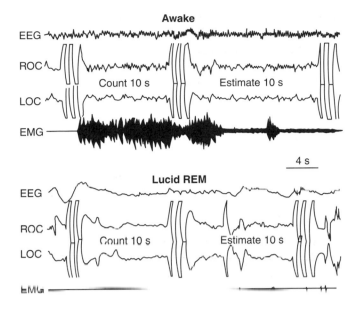

Awake

EEG

ROC

Count 10 s   Estimate 10 s

LOC

EMG

4 s

Lucid REM

EEG

ROC

Count 10 s   Estimate 10 s

LOC

EMG

FIGURE 23.8 • Dream time estimations. LaBerge asked subjects to estimate ten second intervals by counting, "one thousand and one, one thousand and two, etc." during their lucid dreams. Signals marking the beginning and end of the subjective intervals allowed comparison with objective time. In all cases, time estimates during the lucid dreams were very close to the actual time between signals (after LaBerge, 2000).

Becoming lucid feels like waking up or becoming more conscious. Can we now understand what that means? We have a few clues, such as the increased arousal that accompanies lucidity, and the changed sense of self and volition, but we still have no coherent theory to make sense of this dramatic change in consciousness. Perhaps lucid dreaming serves above all to show how limited is our understanding of consciousness.

Dennett, D.C. (1976) Are dreams experiences? Reprinted in D.C. Dennett (1978) *Brainstorms: Philosophical Essays on Mind and Psychology*. Montgomery, Vt., Bradford Books.

Hobson, J.A. (2002) *Dreaming*. New York, Oxford University Press. A useful introduction for students who have not studied the basics of sleep and dreaming.

LaBerge, S. (1990) Lucid dreaming: psychophysiological studies of consciousness during REM sleep, at http://www.lucidity.com/SleepAndCognition.html.

24

Exceptional human experience

TWENTY-FOUR

> I remember the night, and almost the very spot on the hill-top, where
> my soul opened out, as it were, into the Infinite, and there was a
> rushing together of the two worlds, the inner and the outer. It was
> deep calling unto deep—the deep that my own struggle had opened
> up within being answered by the unfathomable deep without,
> reaching beyond the stars. I stood alone with Him who had made me,
> and all the beauty of the world, and love, and sorrow, and even
> temptation . . . nothing but an ineffable joy and exaltation remained.
>
> James, 1902: 66

This religious experience, recounted by a clergyman and included in William
James's classic *The Varieties of Religious Experience* (1902), was not merely
a temporary ASC, but one that profoundly affected the man's life. Like many
others who have experiences of this kind, he described it as ineffable—or
impossible to put into words—"I feel that in writing of it I have overlaid it
with words rather than put it clearly."

Today this might be labeled an "exceptional human experience" (EHE)—a
broad category encompassing psychic visions, hypnotic regression, lucid
dreams, peak experiences and religious and mystical experiences. The term
was coined by American parapsychologist Rhea White (1990) to describe
experiences that entail a shift away from the usual feeling of self as something

inside the skin and toward a greater sense of self. Thus EHEs are not merely odd or inexplicable experiences, but self-transformative ones.

Some of these experiences prompt paranormal or supernatural claims. Others are taken as evidence for God, souls or spirits, or life after death. So they raise many questions. Are any of these claims valid? Is there a common theme running through the experiences, or are they just a loose collection of unrelated oddities? And what can they tell us about the nature of self and consciousness? Responses to these questions may be divided for convenience into three rough groups.

First, the dismissive response treats all EHEs as inventions or lies, as uninteresting by-products of brain states or as pathological states that need treatment.

Second, the supernatural response uses EHEs as evidence that materialist science is wrong and must be expanded to include the paranormal, the existence of the soul, the power of consciousness to reach beyond the body or the existence of God. Paranormal events are often seized upon to justify the importance and validity of the experiences. This may be an understandable reaction against the dismissers but, as we shall see, it may detract from understanding the deeper core of some experiences.

Third, the naturalistic response treats the experiences as normal rather than paranormal and seeks to understand them without recourse to gods, spirits or psychic powers and without any need to overthrow fundamental scientific principles.

We have already considered some EHEs, such as putatively telepathic and precognitive experiences (see Chapter 20), dissociative states (see Chapters 7 and 8) and other-world experiences (see Chapter 21). Here we concentrate on those that disrupt the ordinary sense of being a conscious self looking out from inside the skin, in the spirit of White's original notion. These include out-of-body, near-death and mystical experiences.

OUT-OF-BODY EXPERIENCES (OBEs)

I was lost in the music, Grateful Dead or Pink Floyd probably, and rushing down a dark tunnel of leaves toward the light, when my friend asked "Where are you?" I struggled to answer, trying to bring myself back to the room where I knew my body was sitting. Suddenly everything became crystal clear. I could see the three of us sitting there. I watched, amazed, as the mouth below said, "I'm on the ceiling." Later I went traveling, flying above the roofs and out across the sea. Eventually things changed and I became first very small and then very big. I became as big as the whole universe, indeed I *was* the whole universe. There seemed no time, and all space was one. Yet, even then, I was left with the knowledge that "However far you go, there's always something further." The whole experience lasted about two hours. It changed my life.

FIGURE 24.1 • Rushing down a tunnel of leaves to an out-of-body experience (Blackmore, 1982).

An OBE is an experience in which a person seems to perceive the world from a location outside their physical body. In other words it feels as though "you" have left your body, and can move and see without it. The precise definition is important. OBEs are defined as an *experience*. So if you feel as though you have left your body, you have, by definition, had an OBE. This leaves open for investigation the question of whether anything actually leaves the body during an OBE.

OBEs can occur at almost any time. People have had them when walking down the street, sitting quietly, or even driving a car, and apparently carried on with what they were doing. But most OBEs share the common precipitating factors of relaxation, disruption of the body image, and reduced sensory input. OBEs usually last only a few seconds or minutes, but in rare cases can last for many hours (Blackmore, 1982; Green, 1968b). In "parasomatic" OBEs there seems to be a second duplicate body outside the physical; in "asomatic" OBEs the person seems to be just disembodied awareness or a point of consciousness (Green, 1968b).

OBErs (people who have OBEs) say that the world looks as real as normal, or even "more real," and that OBEs are nothing like dreams. Vision and hearing seem to be clearer and reach further than normal, and some claim to see paranormally at a distance. In rare cases, time and space seem to disappear as in mystical experiences. After an OBE people's attitudes and beliefs are often changed, usually in positive ways, and their fear of death is reduced (Gabbard and Twemlow, 1984).

Although this is an odd experience, it is relatively common, with somewhere between 15 and 20 percent of people claiming at least one during their life. Some people have frequent OBEs, especially during childhood, and a few learn to control them at will. There appears to be no correlation with age, sex, educational level or religion, but OBErs do score higher on measures of hypnotizability, capacity for absorption, and belief in the paranormal (Irwin, 1985). They also have better dream recall and more frequent lucid dreams (Gackenbach and LaBerge, 1988). There is no evidence for any association with psychopathology, and although OBEs can sometimes be frightening, they are not a symptom of mental illness (Blackmore, 1996b).

OBEs are not easy to induce, although there are lots of popular books describing how to do it. In the early days of psychical research, hypnosis was used to induce "traveling clairvoyance" or "astral projection," while modern experiments tend to use relaxation and imagery exercises instead. Some drugs can induce OBEs, especially the psychedelics LSD, psilocybin, DMT and mescaline, and the dissociative anaesthetic ketamine, which often induces feelings of body separation and floating.

What do OBEs tell us about consciousness? While some people take them as proof that consciousness is independent of the body, there are many other possible explanations.

THEORIES OF THE OBE

OBEs are often so compelling that they leave people convinced that their consciousness left their body and that it can survive death, even though neither of these conclusions follows logically from the *experience*. Nineteenth-century psychical researchers thought that consciousness could be "exteriorized" during "traveling clairvoyance," and talked of the soul or spirit separating from the physical temporarily during life, in preparation for permanent separation at

FIGURE 24.2 ● In the nineteenth century, psychical researchers hypnotized mediums to test for "traveling clairvoyance." The medium's spirit was supposedly able to travel great distances and report on what it saw there.

death. At the same time the new religion of Theosophy taught that we each have several bodies—physical, etheric, astral—and several higher bodies, all of which can separate. When consciousness leaves the physical in the form of the astral body, sometimes remaining connected by a silver cord, the experience is known as "astral projection," a term that is still widely used today.

Such theories are a form of dualism and face the same insuperable problems (Chapter 1). For example, if the astral body really sees the physical world

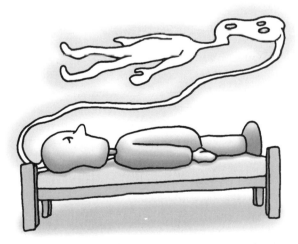

FIGURE 24.3 ● The most obvious theory of OBEs is that a spirit, soul, or astral body leaves the physical and can travel without it. This faces serious problems. What is the phantom made of? How does it communicate with the physical body? Does it travel in the physical world or a replica world of thoughts? How can it gain information from the world without eyes and ears, and without being detected?

during astral projection, then it must be interacting with it and hence it must be a detectable physical entity, yet it is supposed to be non-physical, and all attempts to detect it have failed. On the other hand, if the astral body is non-physical, then it cannot interact with the physical world so as to see it. There are other problems too. If we can see and hear and remember so clearly with our conscious astral body, why should we need physical eyes, ears and a brain at all?

To avoid these difficulties, some parapsychologists have described OBEs as imagination plus ESP, with nothing actually leaving the body (Alvarado, 1992). This avoids the problems of dualism, but at the cost of having to invoke the paranormal. Even so, if people really can see and hear at a distance during OBEs, then either we must surmount the problems of dualism, or we must accept ESP. So can they?

There are two kinds of paranormal phenomenon we might look for in OBEs: detection of the astral double (a kind of PK), and OB vision by the double (ESP). From the 1880s onward many attempts were made to photograph the astral body, with less than convincing results. Most ambitious were 1930s experiments with cloud chambers in which small animals, such as mice or frogs, were killed and then photographed as they died, revealing clouds apparently hovering around them. Another method was to weigh the soul of patients dying of tuberculosis or other wasting diseases. Apparently about an ounce was lost at the moment of death, but loss of water vapor and bodily fluids was not controlled for, the moment of death was often indeterminate, and none of these results was successfully replicated (Alvarado, 1982; Blackmore, 1982).

In the 1970s, a variety of detectors were tried including people, animals, strain gauges, thermistors, and detectors of electrical conductivity, infrared and ultraviolet radiation. The experiments were far better controlled than previous ones, but the results were disappointing. "Overall, no detectors were able to maintain a consistent responsiveness of the sort that would indicate any true detection of an extended aspect of the self" (Morris et al., 1978).

Much more common are claims that people can see at a distance during OBEs. Among the classic cases, the most frequently cited is the Wilmot case, reported in 1903. Mr. Wilmot was on a steam ship, traveling from Liverpool to New York when, during a violent storm, both he and his cabin-mate saw an apparition of Wilmot's wife. Apparently she had set out to seek her husband, fearing for his safety, and had seemed to cross the

FIGURE 24.4 • Cloud chambers are normally used to detect subatomic particles, which leave a trail of water droplets as they pass through super-cooled water vapor. In the 1920s psychical researchers adapted the technique to detect the astral double. A small animal, such as a frog, mouse or grasshopper, was placed in the inner chamber. A poison was then introduced to kill the animal whose soul would then pass out through the cloud chamber and so be detected. Photographs of phantom frogs, grasshoppers and mice were obtained, but were barely distinguishable and never replicated.

ocean and make her way to his cabin. According to Wilmot the description she gave of the ship was correct in all particulars even though she had never seen it. Sadly, the only account of these events is given by Mr. Wilmot himself, and this lack of independent verification seems to be true of all the classic cases (Blackmore, 1982).

In the 1960s and 1970s many experiments were carried out but with disappointing results. There was one famous success when a subject, Miss Z, slept in the laboratory and correctly reported a five-digit number placed on a shelf above the bed (Tart, 1968), but lack of controls and signs of a disrupted EEG record at the very time she claimed to see the number make it possible that she climbed up to look. Had the number been in the next room, the evidence would have been far more convincing. The experiment was never successfully repeated. Later experiments with other special subjects achieved some success but barely above chance levels, and in a test of 100 unselected subjects, most thought they could see the targets, but in fact got them wrong. Overall, the evidence for ESP during OBEs is not compelling (Alvarado, 1982; Blackmore, 1982; 1996b).

FIGURE 24.5 • An alternative to laboratory tests. For several years, during the 1980s, I displayed targets in my kitchen, out of view of the window, so that anyone who claimed to have OBEs could try to see them. These were a five-digit number, one of twenty common words, and one of twenty small objects. They were selected using random number tables, and changed regularly. OBErs could try to visit from their own home, or anywhere else, during spontaneous OBEs.

The alternative is that, in spite of how it feels, nothing leaves the body in an OBE. This means that the experience must be explained in terms of psychology or neuroscience, and this has met with much more success.

First, are they ASCs? In Tart's definition they are, because the person feels that their mental functioning and consciousness are radically different from normal. Second, are they a kind of dream? OBEs are certainly not ordinary dreams. They feel like lucid dreams in that one feels fully conscious and able to fly around and control things in another world, but they do not feel like ordinary dreams. Many OBEs take place when the person is wide awake, and physiological studies show that experimental OBEs are associated with a relaxed waking state similar to drowsiness, but not deep sleep and certainly not REM sleep.

Psychoanalytic theories describe the OBE as a dramatization of the fear of death, as regression of the ego or as reliving of the trauma of birth, and Jung himself saw it as part of the process of individuation (Alvarado, 1992), but such theories are frustratingly untestable.

Psychological theories generally start from the finding that OBEs occur when sensory input and the body image are disrupted. In response to this disruption, the cognitive system tries to cope by constructing a new (if inaccurate) body image, and a plausible world derived from memory and imagination, using the kinds of bird's eye views that are common in memory and dreams. This new world seems real as long as normal input is not restored. These theories

FEATURES OF THE NDE

A man is dying and, as he reaches the point of greatest physical distress, he hears himself pronounced dead by his doctor. He begins to hear an uncomfortable noise, a loud ringing or buzzing, and at the same time feels himself moving very rapidly through a long dark tunnel. After this, he suddenly finds himself outside of his own physical body . . . Soon other things begin to happen. Others come to meet and to help him. He glimpses the spirits of relatives and friends who have already died, and a loving, warm spirit of a kind he has never encountered before—a being of light—appears before him. This being asks him a question, nonverbally, to make him evaluate his life and helps him along by showing him a panoramic, instantaneous playback of the major events of his life. At some point he finds himself approaching some sort of barrier or border, apparently representing the limit between earthly life and the next life. Yet, he finds that he must go back to the earth, that the time for his death has not yet come . . . He is overwhelmed by intense feelings of joy, love, and peace . . . Later he tries to tell others, but he has trouble doing so. In the first place, he can find no human words adequate to describe these unearthly episodes. He also finds that others scoff, so he stops telling other people. Still, the experience affects his life profoundly, especially his views about death and its relationship to life.

(Moody, 1975: 21–3)

Moody provided this account of a prototypical NDE and divided it into 15 main features. American psychologist Kenneth Ring then stripped the NDE down to the "Core Experience" consisting of five features: feelings of peace, body separation (OBE), entering the darkness (Moody's dark tunnel), seeing the light, and entering the light. He developed a "Weighted Core Experience Index" (WCEI),

account for the conditions under which OBEs occur and explain why the OB world is rather like the world of imagination. Research confirms that people who have OBEs are better at spatial imagery, and better at switching viewpoints in imagery. OBErs also have superior dream control skills and more often dream of seeing themselves from above, as in a bird's eye view (Blackmore, 1996b; Irwin, 1985).

Perhaps most important here is the connection between OBEs and the body image. Two studies using direct brain stimulation suggest a close link. In the 1930s the pioneer of electrical brain stimulation was American neurosurgeon Wilder Penfield. He operated on epileptics when there was no other treatment available and electrically stimulated the surface of the brain to locate the epileptic focus. On one occasion, when stimulating the temporal lobe, his patient cried out "Oh God! I am leaving my body" (Penfield, 1955: 458). Over half a century later, with much finer electrodes and greater precision, a team of neurosurgeons in Geneva, Switzerland, achieved the same result with another epileptic patient. When a weak current was passed through a subdural electrode on the right angular gyrus, she reported sinking into the bed or falling from a height. With increased current she said, "I see myself lying in bed, from above, but I only see my legs and lower trunk." This was induced twice more, as were various body image distortions. The researchers attributed her OBE to a failure to integrate somatosensory and vestibular information caused by the stimulation (Blanke et al., 2002).

The temporal lobe has long been implicated in OBEs, and the Canadian neuroscientist Michael Persinger (1983; 1999) has proposed that all religious and mystical experiences are artifacts of temporal lobe function. Temporal lobe epileptics report more such experiences, and Persinger has induced OBEs, body distortions, the sense of presence and many other experiences using TMS.

Knowing which parts of the brain are involved in OBEs helps us to understand them, but does not, on its own, settle the major debate. At one extreme, some skeptics take this evidence to mean they can reject the experiences as "most probably the result of temporal lobe seizures or some other aberration in brain physiology" (Shermer, 2000: 97). At the other extreme, pediatrician and NDE researcher Melvyn Morse believes that the experiences are "generated by neuron activity within the Sylvian fissure," and that this area is therefore "the seat of the soul," "the place where the material and the spiritual worlds meet" (Morse, 1990: 109, 110).

NEAR-DEATH EXPERIENCES (NDEs)

It is quite remarkable that right across ages and cultures, people coming close to death report a consistent set of experiences. There are "returned from the dead" writings in Tibetan Buddhism, a description in Plato's *Republic* and myths from as far apart as Ancient Greece, nineteenth-century Native Americans and contemporary European folklore. Nineteenth century psychical researchers collected accounts of "death-bed visions" reported from the bedsides of those who died, and as medical expertise grew in the twentieth century, "near-death experiences" were reported by survivors.

The term "near-death experience" (NDE) was coined in 1975 by an American physician, Raymond Moody. He interviewed about 50 survivors of close brushes with death and produced a composite account. Subsequent studies broadly confirmed the main components: a tunnel, an OBE, a brilliant white or golden light, positive and loving emotions, visions of another world, meetings with other beings, a life review and the decision to return (Blackmore, 1993; Ring, 1980). NDEs cannot be attributed to medication given near death because they tend to be less complex, not more so, with medication. They can also occur in those who just think they are going to die, such as mountaineers who escape unhurt from terrifying falls.

Most NDEs are pleasant and even blissful, but several studies have collected accounts of hellish experiences. These include cold grayness, nothingness and

CONCEPT CONTINUED

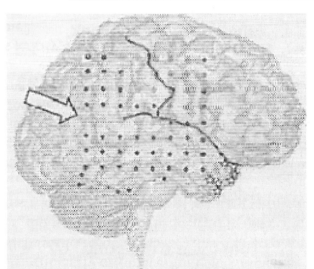

FIGURE 24.6 • Three-dimensional surface reconstruction of the right hemisphere of the brain from magnetic-resonance imaging. Subdural electrodes were implanted in the brain of an epileptic patient undergoing presurgical evaluation: the locations at which focal electrical stimulation (ES) evoked behavioral responses are shown. Out-of-body experiences (OBEs), body-part illusions and vestibular responses were induced at the site marked with the arrow (Blanke et al., 2002: 269).

Exceptional human experience

CHAPTER TWENTY-FOUR

PRACTICE
WHAT SURVIVES?

As many times as you can, every day, take a look at your own body and ask yourself, **"When this body is gone, what will remain?"**

> *"An individual who should survive his physical death is also beyond my understanding, nor do I wish it otherwise; such notions are for the fears or absurd egoism of feeble souls."*
>
> **Albert Einstein**, 1945

> *"I do believe ... that we continue to have a conscious existence after our physical death and that the core experience does represent its beginning, a glimpse of things to come."*
>
> **Ring**, 1980: 254

frightful vacuums, as well as chattering demons, black pits, naked zombie-like creatures, people chained and tormented and other symbols of traditional hell. According to some estimates as many as 15 percent of NDEs are hellish, but it is difficult to be accurate because people may be keen to forget them and unwilling to talk about them. Interestingly, suicide attempters generally report positive NDEs and are less likely to try to kill themselves again. Most NDErs report highly positive after-effects including a new interest in spirituality and in caring for others, although some are left depressed and a few find themselves estranged from family and friends by the changes that take place.

The early studies collected accounts retrospectively, making it impossible to know how common NDEs are, but later prospective studies found out. In Britain, medical researcher Sam Parnia and his colleagues interviewed all survivors of cardiac arrest in a Southampton hospital during one year. Seven out of 63 (11 percent) reported memories, of which four counted as NDEs on the Greyson NDE scale. None had an OBE. There were almost no differences on physiological measures between the NDErs and others (Parnia et al., 2001).

In the Netherlands, cardiologist Pim van Lommel studied 344 consecutive patients successfully resuscitated after cardiac arrest. A total of 62 (18 percent) reported an NDE, of whom 41 (12 percent) described a core experience. NDEs were not associated with the duration of cardiac arrest or medication received. When 37 of the NDErs were interviewed two years later, almost all retold their experiences exactly. When compared with those who had not had NDEs, they reported increased belief in an afterlife, reduced fear of death, a greater interest in spirituality and increased love and acceptance for others. Eight years after the events all the patients showed positive changes, but those without NDEs were less interested in spirituality and did not believe in life after death (van Lommel et al., 2001).

INTERPRETING NDEs

Dismissing NDEs as fabrications or wish-fulfilment is unreasonable. The similarities across ages and cultures, and the reliability of the findings, suggest that NDEs have something interesting to teach us about death and consciousness. The question is, what?

A common reaction, as to OBEs, is that NDEs are proof of the existence of a soul or spirit that can leave the body and survive death. The majority of NDE researchers probably subscribe to this "afterlife hypothesis." For Ring (1980) the experiences "point to a higher spiritual world" and provide access to a "holographic reality." Others say that NDErs glimpse their essential self, transcend their ego, access a separate spiritual reality, or even that their personal electromagnetic force field is changed by seeing the light (Morse, 1993). Van Lommel (van Lommel et al., 2001) claims that NDEs push the limits of our understanding of the mind–brain relation, and Parnia and Fenwick (2002) believe that understanding NDEs requires a new science of consciousness.

Two types of evidence are commonly given for this kind of interpretation. First, NDErs describe clear states of consciousness with lucid reasoning and memory when their brain is severely impaired or even in a state of clinical death. "How could a

FIGURE 24.7 • In Victorian times, most people died at home, surrounded by their families. Reports of death-bed experiences were common, including other worlds, beautiful music and visions of those who had already "passed over" coming to greet the newcomer. Occasionally observers said they saw the dying person's spirit leaving the body and going up into the light.

ACTIVITY
The survival debate

The topic of survival after death is emotionally charged. In this activity students are asked to put the case *against* their own prior beliefs.

Some will find this extremely hard and some may refuse to do it. Some will get embarrassed and some will keep saying things like "I don't really believe this but . . ." There is no need to put pressure on anyone to take part, but you may point out that anyone who really understands a difficult issue should be able to explain the arguments on either side equally well. You need to explain the activity very clearly to everyone at the start. This is a very good exercise in thinking objectively about emotional issues.

The whole procedure should be kept light-hearted if possible. The objective is not to come to an answer about this impossible question, nor even to find out what people think. It is to loosen up everyone's thinking, to get them to face the arguments against their own beliefs, to laugh at their own inconsistencies, and to consider the validity of other people's opinions. It can be done with or without prior preparation.

If you have a manageable-sized group the exercise can be done with the whole class. Otherwise divide the students into small groups (of about 4–10). Ideally, ensure that each group contains some people who believe in life after death and some who do not. In each group choose two people to speak — one a believer and the other not. First the non-believer presents the case *for* believing in life after death (for, say, five minutes maximum). Then the believer presents the case *against*. You can remind them that everyone else knows they think the opposite; their job is to do the best presentation they can. Everyone else then asks them questions that they have to answer within their assigned role.

In discussion afterward, explore why this exercise is so difficult for some people, and ask the presenters what they have learned from their task.

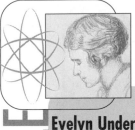

Evelyn Underhill (1875–1941)

Think of mysticism and many people think of Evelyn Underhill, who wrote such classics as *Mysticism* and *The Essentials of Mysticism*. Born in Wolverhampton, England, she studied history and botany at King's College for Women, London. She later became the first woman ever to lecture at Oxford University. She began writing stories and poetry before she was 16, and her books on human spiritual consciousness were not just scholarly tomes; *Practical Mysticism* is subtitled "A little book for normal people." In her thirties she converted to Christianity and during the First World War she became a pacifist. She spent her mornings writing and her afternoons in spiritual direction. In advising people how to live a sane spiritual life, she urged them to make time for quiet meditation or prayer every day and to meet God in "the sacrament of the present moment." For Underhill mysticism was not about complicated religious doctrines but was to be found directly in the midst of ordinary life and work. Those who knew her say that she lived by the principles she taught, with kindness and devotion to others.

clear consciousness outside one's body be experienced at the moment that the brain no longer functions during a period of clinical death with flat EEG?" asks van Lommel (van Lommel et al., 2001: 2044). The problem here is that we do not yet know whether NDEs take place just before the crisis, during it, just after it or even during the process of trying to describe it to someone else. If clear consciousness were really possible with a completely flat EEG, this would indeed change our view of the mind–brain relationship, but so far this has not been conclusively demonstrated.

Second, there are many claims of the paranormal, including compelling accounts of people seeing things at a distance that they could not possibly have known about. Morse (1990) gives many moving accounts of NDEs in young children, some of whom described events happening at the time. Van Lommel reports the case of a 44-year-old man brought into the coronary care unit in a coma, in which he remained for more than one and a half hours while a nurse removed his dentures for intubation, and he received heart massage and defibrillation. He was still comatose when transferred to intensive care. When he saw the same nurse for the first time a week later, he said, "Oh, that nurse knows where my dentures are." (van Lommel et al., 2001) and described where she had put them in a drawer. Among other well-known cases are that of Maria, a patient in Seattle who was dashed to a hospital at night in an ambulance and yet correctly described the tennis shoe she saw on a third-floor window ledge.

These cases are potentially important because if they are true, then there is something seriously wrong with all materialist and functionalist theories of consciousness. Sadly it is impossible to know whether they are true. In no case has even minimal independent corroboration been provided. For example, there is no record of the comatose man having described the nurse's appearance or the location of his dentures before he saw her again, and we have only her story to go on. In the Seattle case, Maria never made a statement herself, and the only account is given by her social worker (Blackmore, 1993).

One way to find out would be to provide randomly selected, concealed targets that NDErs could see during their experience. Several experiments of this kind have been attempted, for example, with boards suspended below the ceiling of cardiac wards, but so far with no success (Parnia et al., 2001).

The alternative, naturalistic approach to understanding NDEs is known as the "dying brain hypothesis" (Blackmore, 1993). Severe stress, extreme fear and cerebral anoxia all cause cortical disinhibition and uncontrolled brain activity, and we already have most of the ideas needed to understand why this should cause NDEs. Tunnels and lights are frequently caused by disinhibition in visual cortex, and similar noises occur during sleep paralysis (see Chapter 21). OBEs and life reviews can be induced by temporal lobe stimulation, and the positive emotions and lack of pain have been attributed to the action of endorphins and encephalins, endogenous opiates that are widely distributed in the limbic system and released under stress. The visions of other worlds and spiritual beings might be real glimpses into another world, but against that hypothesis is evidence that people generally describe other worlds that fit their cultural upbringing. For example, Christians report seeing Jesus, angels and a door or gate into heaven, while Hindus are more likely to meet the king of the dead and his messengers, the Yamdoots.

There is no doubt that some NDErs are changed by their experience. The dying-brain hypothesis rejects the idea of a soul, spirit or astral self that leaves the body, but it does not preclude the possibility that during NDEs people really are transformed, and that the deepest transformation happens in those whose NDE blows apart the illusion of a separate self.

WHEN THIS BODY IS GONE, WHAT WILL BE LEFT?

MYSTICAL EXPERIENCES

> All at once, without warning of any kind, I found myself wrapped in a flame-colored cloud. For an instant I thought of fire, an immense conflagration somewhere close by in that great city; the next, I knew that the fire was within myself. Directly afterwards there came upon me a sense of exultation, of immense joyousness accompanied or immediately followed by an intellectual illumination impossible to describe. Among other things, I did not merely come to believe, but I saw that the universe is not composed of dead matter, but is, on the contrary, a living Presence; I became conscious in myself of eternal life. It was not a conviction that I would have eternal life, but a consciousness that I possessed eternal life then . . . That view, that conviction, I may say that consciousness, has never, even during periods of the deepest depression, been lost.
>
> (James, 1902: 399)

This is how Canadian psychiatrist Richard Maurice Bucke described what happened one night in a hansom cab on his way home from an evening spent with friends reading the poetry of Shelley, Keats and Walt Whitman. He proceeded to study similar experiences in history and literature, and coined the term "cosmic consciousness" to describe them. He described cosmic consciousness as a third form of consciousness: as far above human self-consciousness as that is above the simple consciousness that we share with other animals. Its prime characteristic is "a consciousness of the cosmos, that is, of the life and order of the universe" (Bucke, 1901: 3), along with an intellectual and moral elevation, and a sense of immortality in the present moment.

> *"The most beautiful and profound emotion we can experience is the sensation of the mystical. It is the source of all true science."*
>
> **Albert Einstein**, quoted in Deikman, 2000: 75

Such experiences are usually called "religious experiences" or "God experiences" if they involve religious symbolism or a deity (Persinger, 1999). They are surprisingly common. Thousands of cases, mostly of Christian influence, have been collected by the *Religious Experiences Research Unit*, founded by Oxford biologist Sir Alister Hardy in 1969 (Hardy, 1979). The term "mystical experience" is rather broader and is probably impossible to define in a way that does the experiences justice. Perhaps the best we can do, as many authors have, is to list their common features.

James (1902) proposed four marks that justify calling an experience "mystical."

The first is *ineffability*. That is, the experience somehow defies description in words. People feel that anything they say is misleading and the experience cannot be imparted to others. A mystical experience cannot, therefore, be a meme, unlike the term "mystical experience" which is a meme.

The second is *noetic* quality, a term that James coined to describe the sense that mystical states are states of knowledge, insight or illumination. They carry a curious, and lasting, sense of authority.

Third is *transiency*. They rarely last more than half an hour or an hour before fading to a kind of afterglow. After this they cannot be clearly remembered but are easily recognized when they recur, allowing for continuous inner development.

Fourth is *passivity*. Although circumstances can be arranged, and disciplines can be followed, to make mystical experiences more likely, they cannot be induced to order, and once they begin the mystic feels as though his own will is in abeyance.

Many other writers have made different lists but nearly all include these four qualities. Many, such as the philosopher Walter Stace (1960), stress the sense of unity, or the loss of self in the One. Others add the loss of time and space to the loss of self. D.T. Suzuki, who is credited with bringing Zen to the West, adds a *sense of the beyond*, an *impersonal tone* (which is emphasized more often in Zen satori experiences than in Christian mysticism), a feeling of *exaltation* and *affirmation*, by which he means an accepting attitude toward all things that exist. This is perhaps where mystical experiences touch the rest of life. In James's opinion "At bottom the whole concern of both morality and religion is with the manner of our acceptance of the universe" (1902: 41).

SELF ASSESSMENT QUESTIONS

○ What are EHEs? Make a list of experiences that might be included.

○ How is an OBE defined? Under what conditions do OBEs occur and to whom?

○ What is the evidence that something leaves the body during an OBE?

○ How common are NDEs and what are their main features?

○ What are the two main theories used to account for NDEs?

○ Can you define a mystical experience? Describe two or more schemes that list the components of mystical experiences.

○ What is the evidence that genuine mystical experiences can be induced by drugs?

Walter Pahnke, an American minister and physician, includes nine items in his list: unity, transcendence of time and space, positive mood, sense of sacredness, noetic quality, paradoxicality, ineffability, transiency and persisting positive changes in attitudes and behavior. This list came not from spontaneous mystical experiences but from his work with LSD. Before it was made illegal, he worked with Richard Alpert and Timothy Leary giving LSD to prisoners. He also worked with the terminally ill, giving them just one or a very few trips in carefully and empathically arranged settings. Through these experiences, many at last found peace, love and the acceptance of both life and death (Pahnke, 1971).

The possibility that authentic mystical experiences can occur with drugs offends some religious believers, but many researchers have concluded that they can, including the authors of the largest survey of LSD experiences, *The Varieties of Psychedelic Experience* (Masters and Houston, 1967). Pahnke himself put the question to the test. In the famous "Good Friday Experiment" he gave pills to 20 Boston divinity students before the traditional Good Friday service in 1962, ten receiving psilocybin and ten an active control (nicotinic acid). Whereas the control group experienced only mild religious feelings, eight out of ten of the psilocybin group reported at least seven of his categories of mystical experience (Pahnke, 1963; 1967). Nearly 30 years later most of the psilocybin group remembered their experiences with clarity and described long-lasting positive effects (Doblin, 1991).

Deep mystical experiences seem to go beyond any narrowly religious view. In *The Essentials of Mysticism*, the English Christian mystic Evelyn Underhill (1875–1941; see Profile, p. 364), sought to "disentangle the facts from ancient formulae used to express them" (Underhill, 1920: 1) and came to the essence of mysticism as the clear conviction of a living God in unity with the personal self. Yet she allowed the widest possible latitude in what she meant by "God," agreeing with the fourteenth-century work *The Cloud of Unknowing* that God may be loved but not thought. So whatever it is that is seen, or understood, or united with, it cannot be described—or even thought about.

HOW TO REGARD THEM

We can now return to James's question: how to regard those other forms of consciousness beyond "the filmiest of screens."

Paranormal and supernatural explanations fare badly. They gain little support from the evidence and face apparently insuperable theoretical obstacles. Even so, they are enormously popular. Along with these paranormal and supernatural interpretations goes the argument that materialist science falsely ignores our true spiritual nature and that it should embrace the possibilities of other worlds, other dimensions of reality, and conscious selves beyond the physical.

We might usefully ask whether this dualist conception of the universe is really more *spiritual* than the scientific, monist, view. And if so why? Many mystics specifically reject paranormal claims as missing the point. Underhill (1920) calls them "off the track," and James declares they "have no essential mystical significance" (James, 1902: 408 n.). In Zen Buddhism trainees are taught to ignore visions, miracles and faith-healing. "They are no better than dreams which vanish for ever on awakening. To hold on to them is to become a prey to superstition" (Kennett, 1972: 27).

An alternative, though much less popular, view is that the deepest mystical insights are not only monist and non-paranormal, but are perfectly compatible with science. They might be summarized as "the universe is one, the separate self is an illusion, immortality is not in the future but now, everything is as it is and there is nothing to be done." If these insights are valid, what needs overthrowing is not monist science but the vestiges of dualist thinking that still lurk within it. In this view, the specific features of OBEs and NDEs depend on our evolved human brains, but if all these contingent details are stripped away, deeper mystical truths are revealed. These may be less comforting for those who hope for personal survival of death, but they are at least compatible with our scientific understanding of the universe.

Finally there remains a last, most skeptical view, that either we biological creatures are incapable of seeing the truth or that there are no deep truths to be seen. This would leave us with nothing but the ultimate mystical experience, that about which nothing can be said.

Blackmore, S.J. (1991) Near-death experiences: in or out of the body? *Skeptical Inquirer* 16, 34–45, and at http://www.susanblackmore.co.uk/articles/si91nde.html.

Doblin, R. (1991) Pahnke's "Good Friday Experiment": a long-term follow-up and methodological critique. *The Journal of Transpersonal Psychology* 23, and at http://www.druglibrary.org/schaffer/lsd/doblin.htm. This forms a good basis for discussion.

Parnia, S. and Fenwick, P. (2002) Near-death experiences in cardiac arrest: visions of a dying brain or visions of a new science of consciousness. *Resuscitation* 52, 5–11.

READING

NINE

First-person approaches

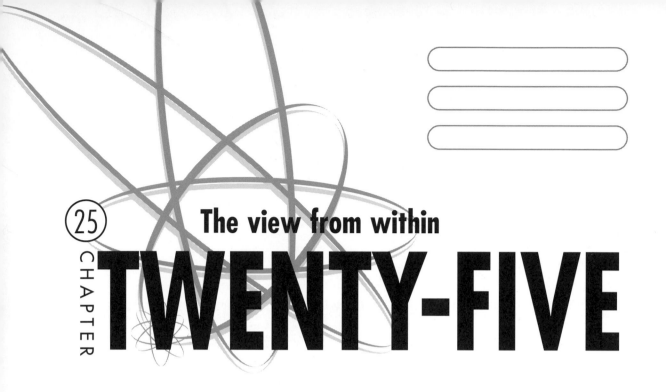

The view from within

TWENTY-FIVE

Introspective Observation is what we have to rely on first and foremost and always. The word introspection need hardly be defined—it means, of course, the looking into our own minds and reporting what we there discover.

(James, 1890, Vol. 1: 185)

What do you discover when you look into your own mind? William James was confident: "*Every one agrees that we there discover states of consciousness*" he said. But a hundred years later we might be inclined to raise a few awkward questions. What does looking mean? Who is looking into what? Does the looking itself change what is seen? Does reporting destroy what we are trying to describe? Can everything be reported when some experiences are supposed to be ineffable? What are states of consciousness anyway?

These are difficult questions. Nevertheless, we might agree that looking into our own minds is an essential part of studying consciousness. After all, it is the private, ineffable, what it's like to be, that is what we are trying to explain. So we cannot run away from the exercise. We have already met many examples of people looking inward and reporting what they see. These include the methods of trained introspection developed by Wundt and Titchener, as well as James's descriptions of the "flights and perchings" in the stream of consciousness, of getting up on a cold morning, and his studies of religious experiences. Then there are various introspections on the experience of self, Csikszentmihalyi's studies of flow, and numerous adventures into altered states. Clearly this personal approach has a role to play in the study of consciousness. But what sort of role?

The study of consciousness is sometimes divided into two fundamentally different approaches: the objective third-person approach and the subjective first-person approach. Between these two there is sometimes added another: the second-person, or inter-subjective, approach (Thompson, 2001). There has been fierce argument over whether studying consciousness is fundamentally different from studying anything else, and whether it therefore requires a completely different approach from the rest of science. At the extremes, some people demand a complete revolution in science to take in the mysteries of consciousness, while others insist that we need no new approaches at all. The argument takes two forms, which are often confused but are worth distinguishing. One concerns first- versus third-person *science*; the other concerns first- versus third-person *methods*.

There are at least three problems with the notion of first-person *science*. First, science is, by its nature, a collective activity in which data are shared, ideas are exchanged, theories are argued over, and tests are devised to find out which works better. The results of all this work are then published for everyone else to see and to demolish or build upon further. Science, in this sense, is not something you can do on your own, suggesting that there can be no private science. Second, objectivity is valued in science because of the dangers of personal bias obscuring the truth. So when one theory is easier or more comforting than another, the scientist is trained to set aside prior beliefs and maintain an open mind in the face of the evidence, suggesting that subjectivity might be damaging to science. Third, as soon as inner explorations are described or spoken about, those descriptions become data for third-person science. In this sense there can be no first-person *data* (Metzinger, 2003).

All these are arguments against a first-person *science* of consciousness, but none of them necessarily rules out a role for subjective experience, inner work, or first-person *methods* in third-person science. For example, even in the strictest falsificationist theory of science, there is a role for inner work and private inspiration in the process of generating hypotheses. As we have seen, such inspiration has often happened in science, and this is entirely valid as long as the fruits of the inner work can be publicly tested. Also, as we have seen, there has been a long history of the public reporting of subjective impressions. None of these count as first-person *science* because their data were publicly shared. But they might be counted as first-person *methods* to the extent that they involve systematic self-observation or self-exploration.

We can now see the difference between arguing for a first-person *science* of consciousness and arguing for first-person *methods* in a science of consciousness. If we argue only for first-person methods, we may then ask whether those methods need to be fundamentally different from the methods used in any other sciences—such as psychology, biology or physics—or whether they are basically the same.

What appears to give the arguments a special twist when it comes to studying consciousness is that the inner life is itself the phenomenon we are trying to explain, so we have to turn our scientific methods inward. Here we meet a familiar argument. If there really are two separate worlds—the inner and outer—then a science of consciousness is different from any other science and needs special methods for examining inner worlds. On the other hand, if dualism is false and the inner and outer worlds are one, then a science of consciousness need be no different from any other science.

If you think that a science of consciousness must be a fundamentally new kind of science, then you probably think that special first-person methods are what is needed. If you think that a science of consciousness must be basically the same as any other science, then you must ask what role, if any, first-person methods can play, and whether they have anything special to contribute.

Either way it is worth exploring these methods. They include private intellectual inquiry, inner creative work, moral and spiritual development, personal exploration of altered states of consciousness and disciplined training of attention and observation. All these are forms of private, inner work that may, or may not, contribute to the public process of coming to understand the nature of consciousness.

In this chapter we shall first consider the furious debates that have raged over the role of first-person methods, and then consider some of those methods themselves.

THE BATTLE OF THE As AND Bs

"I'm captain of the A team," proclaims Dennett, "David Chalmers is captain of the B team," and so begins the battle over what Dennett calls "The fantasy of first-person science" and Chalmers calls "First-person methods in the science of consciousness."

For Chalmers, the science of consciousness is different from all other sciences because it relates third-person data to first-person data. Third-person data include brain processes, behaviours and what people say, while first-person data concern conscious experience itself. He takes it for granted that there are first-person data.

> It's a manifest fact about our minds that there is something it is like to be us—that we have subjective experiences—and that these subjective experiences are quite different at different times. Our direct knowledge of subjective experiences stems from our first-person access to them. And subjective experiences are arguably the central data that we want a science of consciousness to explain.
>
> (Chalmers, 1999)

"the development of more sophisticated methodologies for investigating first-person data . . . is the greatest challenge now facing a science of consciousness."

Chalmers, 2002

At the moment we have excellent methods for collecting third-person data, says Chalmers, but we badly need better methods for collecting first-person data. The science of consciousness must hunt for broad connecting principles between first- and third-person data, such as certain experiences going along with certain brain processes or with certain kinds of information-processing. What he calls a "fundamental theory of consciousness" would formulate simple and universal laws that explain these connections. Yet, argues Chalmers, data about conscious experience cannot be expressed wholly in terms of measures of brain processes and the like. In other words, first-person data are irreducible to third-person data (Varela and Shear, 1999).

Along with Chalmers, the B team includes Searle, Nagel, Levine, Pinker and many others. Searle (1997) agrees with Chalmers about the irreducibility, although they disagree about much else (Chalmers, 1997). He puts it this way: "consciousness has a first-person or subjective ontology and so cannot be reduced to anything that has third-person or objective ontology. If you try to reduce or eliminate one in favor of the other you leave something out" (Searle, 1997: 212).

> *"consciousness has a first-person or subjective ontology and so cannot be reduced to anything that has third-person or objective ontology"*
>
> **Searle**, 1997: 212

Searle asks us to pinch our own forearms. Do it now and see what happens. According to Searle, two totally different kinds of thing happen. First, neuron firings begin at the receptors and end up in the brain and, second, a few hundred milliseconds after the pinch, we experience the *feeling*, or quale, of pain. These are the objective and subjective events, respectively, and one *causes* the other. By "subjective ontology" Searle means that "conscious states only exist when experienced by a subject and they exist only from the first-person point of view of that subject" (ibid.: 120).

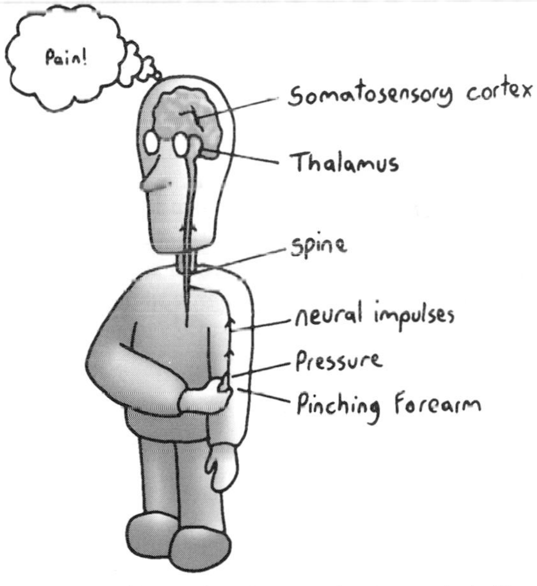

According to Searle the difference is not just epistemic—that you can *know* about your pain in a way that nobody else can—but is ontological—pains and other qualia have a subjective or first-person *mode of existence*, while neuron firings have an objective or third-person mode of existence. This difference is important. Others

FIGURE 25.1 • According to Searle's "subjective ontology," two completely different things happen when you pinch yourself. There are the objective effects on skin and neurons, and the irreducible subjective fact of feeling the pain.

have argued that consciousness is epistemically irreducible. For example, Metzinger explains that our conscious experience "is truly an *individual* first-person perspective. Our phenomenal model of reality is an *individual* picture. Yet all the functional and representational facts constituting this unusual situation can be described objectively, and are open to scientific inquiry" (2003: 589). For Searle there is not just a subjective point of view, but irreducible subjective *facts*, and these are what a science of consciousness has to explain.

"Searle's proposed 'first-person' alternative leads to self-contradiction and paradox at every turning," claims Dennett (1997: 118). On his A team he lists the Churchlands, Andy Clark, Quine, Hofstadter and many others. For them, studying consciousness does not mean studying special inner, private ineffable qualia, but studying what people say and do, for there is no other way of getting at the phenomena, and when we really understand all the third-person facts about brains and behavior there will be nothing else left to explain.

According to Dennett, the B teamers fall for the "Zombic Hunch." He says of Chalmers:

> He insists that he just *knows* that the A team leaves out consciousness. It doesn't address what Chalmers calls the Hard Problem. How does he know? He says he just does. He has a gut intuition, something he has sometimes called "direct experience." I know the intuition well. I can feel it myself. . . . I feel it, but I don't credit it.
>
> (Dennett, 1997)

For Dennett, then, falling for the Zombic Hunch is like going on crediting the intuition that living things have some kind of extra spark to them, or that the sun goes around the earth. So he asks us, "do you want to join me in leaping over the Zombic Hunch, or do you want to stay put, transfixed by this intuition that won't budge?" (Dennett, 2001). What we need to do, he says, is to accept that it *seems* that way even though we know it is not.

Here we meet another classic argument: the incorrigibility of the first-person view. The B team argues that we have privileged access to our own inner states; that is, only we can observe them and we cannot be wrong about them. The A team contends that we only have privileged access to how it *seems* to us. Dennett suspects that "when we claim to be just using our powers of inner *observation*, we are always actually engaging in a sort of impromptu *theoriz-*

PRACTICE
IS THIS REALLY HOW IT IS?

As many times as you can, every day, look into your present experience and ask yourself, **"Is this experience how it *seems* to me, or is this how it really is?"**

This is not an easy one, but if you have been doing the practice all along, you should have no trouble. The trick is to take any aspect of your present experience and then look or listen very hard. If you come up with thoughts like, "Well I know I'm seeing that shape of grayish-white paper," you know that you are theorizing or conceptualizing about how it seems to you, or how you think it must seem. So let go of all those thoughts and try to look into the experience itself. Do you find an experience itself?

ing." In other words, we are always creating fictions about our inner lives, and it is these fictions that a science of consciousness must explain.

In these differences we can hear echoes of familiar arguments" those about qualia, zombies, conscious inessentialism, AI and the function of consciousness, to mention just a few. They all amount to "that schoolyard dialectic: 'You've left something out!' 'No I haven't.' 'Yes you have.' 'No I haven't.' 'Yes you have.' etc., etc." (Raffman, 1995: 294).

FIGURE 25.2 • The ultimate philosophical argument.

We will return to these differences, and to Dennett's proposed alternative of heterophenomenology, but first we need to look at some more traditional first-person methods.

PHENOMENOLOGY

The term "phenomenology" is used in several different ways. Sometimes it refers to a person's inner world (their "phenomenology"), but here we are concerned with phenomenology as a method, and there are two meanings for that. In the broad sense it refers to any methods for the systematic investigation of phenomenal experience (Stevens, 2000). In the narrower sense it refers specifically to the tradition based on Husserl's philosophy, and its later developments by Martin Heidegger, Maurice Merleau-Ponty and others. Here we are concerned not so much with the philosophy, which is often obscure and difficult for outsiders to understand, but with the methods that Husserl advocated for getting to the experience itself.

Husserl argued that there can be no meaningful distinction between the external world and the internal world of experience, and he emphasized the importance of lived experience over scientific abstractions. In order to explore this lived experience he suggested that one should suspend, or bracket, all one's preconceptions, and prior beliefs, especially those about the nature of the external world and its relationship to experience. He called this process the epoché. By this procedure he claimed to be able to study experiences directly, without tracing them back to what they refer to in the world.

As we shall see (in Chapter 26), this method of suspending judgment has much in common with traditional methods of meditation and contemplative training, and also with shifts in awareness that can happen spontaneously. Astrophysicist Piet Hut (1999) likens it to an experience he had with his first

DO WE NEED A NEW KIND OF SCIENCE?

The table below is an attempt to lay out the arguments between those who believe that we need a fundamentally new kind of science and those who do not. Dennett calls them the A team and the B team, but remember that this is only shorthand. No one has signed up for these teams, and in reality there are far more than two positions to consider. So don't take the table too seriously — just use it as a way to remember the main issues at stake. You might like to fill in your own answers too.

	A	B	Your view
We need a new kind of science to study consciousness	No	Yes	
First-person data are irreducible to third-person data	No	Yes	
Third-person research leaves something out	No	Yes	
Introspection observes the experiences themselves	No	Yes	
We must avoid the Zombic Hunch	Yes	No	
The role of first-person methods	Not essential	Essential	

Note that the last row leaves room for uncertainty. Clearly the B team believes that first-person methods are essential, but it is not as clear what the A team thinks or should think. For those who say "No" to all the first four statements, the simplest response is to say that first-person methods are inessential and so to ignore them. But another response is possible. Even if you believe that all data are third-person data and there really are no "experiences themselves," it is still possible to think that private practices such as inner intellectual work, training in attention and concentration, and the practices of meditation and mindfulness may provide especially valuable third-person data for a science of consciousness. Perhaps these should not be called first-person methods, but the name seems appropriate, as long as they are not confused with a "first-person science." These methods are considered in the last two chapters.

camera. After intensively taking photographs in his familiar hometown, he seemed to have landed in a different world and to be seeing things "in a new light." Indeed he seemed to see the world *as light.* Anyone who has learned to paint or draw will recognize this experience. The learning seems to be less about how to use the pen, ink or paint, and more about new ways of seeing, or how to look at things directly without being distracted by how you think they ought to be. In the same way the phenomenological "gesture of awareness" is about seeing the world anew.

Husserl's aim was what he called an eidetic reduction—a way of finding the essential features, or invariants, of people's experience. He wanted to get "back to the things themselves!" and this way hoped to discover the structure of consciousness. But his project ran into many difficulties. His essential method of epoché has not been widely adopted, nor has it led to a true science of experience that can stand on an equal footing with the natural sciences, as he hoped.

This is not to say that phenomenology has disappeared. The method has been used in many different contexts, such as exploring emotional states, or describing what it is like to undergo certain experiences, with the intention of discovering the essence of these experiences (Stevens, 2000). The typical method involves several stages of analyzing interviews or written accounts of experiences. First comes the epoché or setting aside of assumptions about the experience. Then a summary or narrative digest is produced, and then the significant themes are extracted to find the fundamental constituents of that kind of experience in general.

Arguably the result of this use of phenomenology is not a first-person method but a third-person one. Although the original intention was to explore lived experience by seeing through preconceptions, the actual method used depends on analyzing what people say. In this sense it is no different from many other kinds of psychology, which use questionnaires, structured and unstructured interviews, role playing and the analysis of written texts to draw out the constituents of people's experiences. In this sense the original

intention of throwing oneself into a
new way of being in the world has
been lost.

Perhaps this is not surprising, for it is
hardly an easy task to undertake an
inner transformation by throwing off
one's preconceptions and going
beyond conceptualization back to the
things themselves. It is much easier to
talk about it. As Hut notes, "Reading
about the epoché typically leads a
student to contemplate the *concept* of
the epoché, rather than really *performing* the epoché (a danger Husserl
kept warning about)" (Hut, 1999:
242). In other words, the first-person
method slips all too easily away.

A related problem is that much of
phenomenology is incomprehensible
to those not steeped in its language.
For example, this is how the French
philosopher Natalie Depraz explains
her use of the phenomenological
reduction as an embodied practice:

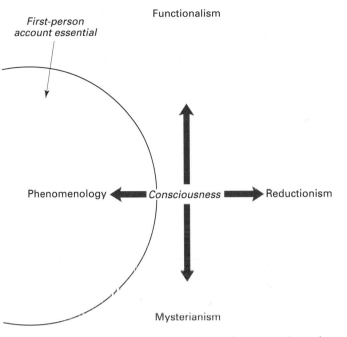

FIGURE 25.3 • Varela (1996) devised this two-dimensional scheme for categorizing theories of
consciousness. Use it to try to position as many theories as you can.

> I am proposing to bring to light a renewed reductive method,
> whereby the spectator is given a specific embodiment, and where the
> operation inherent in the reductive gesture is taken up again through
> the logic of its own reflexivity. By thus aggravating the oxymoron of
> the practical and the theoretical, internal to the reduction in its
> Husserlian heritage, my point is that, in fact, reflection and
> incarnation, contemplation and action are not opposed until each
> begins to fertilize the other, thereby intensifying each other to the
> point of becoming virtually indistinguishable from each other.
>
> (Depraz, 1999: 97)

Perhaps she means that when you look deeply into the distinction between
subject and object, the difference seems to disappear. If so, this is an insight
found in many traditions, and it is not clear how phenomenology helps.

NEUROPHENOMENOLOGY

Neurophenomenology is the name given by Chilean neuroscientist Francisco
Varela (see Profile, p. 378) to a "quest to marry modern cognitive science and
a *disciplined approach* to human experience" (1996: 330). He agrees with Searle
that first-person experience is not reducible to third-person descriptions, but
proposes a new way of dealing with this irreducibility. Chalmers' hard problem

Francisco Varela (1946–2001)

Born in Chile, Francisco Varela studied biology there before moving to the USA to do a PhD on insect vision at Harvard, and then to work in France, Germany, Chile and the United States. He once said that he pursued one question all his life: Why do emergent selves, or virtual identities, pop up all over the place, whether at the mind/body level, the cellular level or the transorganism level? This question motivated the three different kinds of work that he is best known for: the notion of autopoiesis, or self-organization in living things, the enactive view of the nervous system and cognition, and new ideas about the immune system. Critics claim that his ideas, though fluently described, are incomprehensible, and even friends have described him as a revolutionary who threw out too much of the accepted science. He practiced Buddhist meditation for many years as a student of Chögyam Trungpa Rinpoche, and his Buddhist practice informed all his work on embodied cognition and consciousness. He was uniquely both a phenomenologist and a working neuroscientist, and he coined the term neurophenomenology. Until his death he was Director of Research at CNRS (National Institute for Scientific Research) at the laboratory of Cognitive Neurosciences and Brain Imaging in Paris.

cannot be solved, he says, by piecemeal studies of neural correlates of experience but requires a strict method for rediscovering the primacy of lived experience. Anyone following this method must cultivate the skill of stabilizing and deepening their capacity for attentive bracketing and intuition, and for describing what they find.

Varela describes the basic working hypothesis of neurophenomenology as that "Phenomenological accounts of the structure of experience and their counterparts in cognitive science relate to each other through reciprocal constraints" (1996: 343). So the findings of a disciplined first-person approach should be an integral part of the validation of neurobiological proposals.

What does this mean in practice? Varela gives some examples. He suggests that as techniques for brain imaging improve, "we shall need subjects whose competence in making phenomenological discriminations and descriptions is accrued" (ibid.: 341). This makes sense if it means gaining more accurate descriptions of experiences in order to correlate them with brain scans, and in other contexts he explores the value of spiritual disciplines in this endeavour (see Chapters 26 and 27), but he gives no examples of how the phenomenological method helps.

Another example is the exploration of temporality (Varela, 1999). Potentially the sense of time is a rich area for study, because we know that experienced time cannot be the same as neural time, and that all sorts of anomalies arise when we try to pin down the "time at which consciousness happens" (see Chapters 4 and 5). Perhaps disciplined first-person study of experienced time might help.

According to Varela, this means a disciplined exploration of "the structure of nowness as such" or of what James called the "specious present." As James and others have described it, there is a three-fold structure in which the present experience, or "now," is bounded by the immediate past and future. Husserl introduced the idea of *retention*, which intends the just-past, and *protention* of the immediate future. Based on his work in neuroscience and in particular on self-organizing systems, Varela attempts to relate the structure discovered phenomenologically to the underlying self-organizing neural assemblies. He explains that "the fact that an assembly of coupled oscillators attains a transient synchrony and that it takes a certain time for doing so is the explicit correlate of the origin of nowness" (1999: 124). Varela describes this as the major gain of his approach.

To help us understand the place of neurophenomenology in a science of consciousness, Varela provides a simple diagram with four directions in which theories of consciousness can go. He positions the best-known thinkers on it, but restricts himself to "naturalistic approaches," excluding quantum mechanical theories and dualism. In the north are various theories that Varela labels as functionalist, claiming that this is the most popular position in cognitive science. These are all theories that rely entirely on third-person data and validation. Opposite them, in the south, are the mysterians who claim that the "hard problem" is insoluble. On one side are the reductionists, epitomized by the Churchlands, and Crick and Koch, who aim to reduce experience to neuroscience. Opposite them comes phenomenology, with an area cordoned off to include only those who believe that a first-person account is essential, including Varela himself.

This diagram is helpful for thinking about the relationships between different theories, but it also highlights the role of first-person approaches in a science of consciousness. Varela implies that there is a real difference between those theories that take first-person experience seriously and make it essential to their understanding of consciousness, and those that do not. But are they really so different? Baars thinks not: "We already have a systematic study of human conscious experience, and it is called 'psychology'" (1999: 216). He suggests that if we look at what psychologists have been doing for more than a century, we find that they have always studied the things that people say about their experience. Yes we need phenomenology, in the broad sense, but we do not need to start from scratch.

Varela claims that only theories within the cordon make first-person accounts essential, but is this really so? To take examples from each quadrant, Nagel surely takes the first-person view seriously in developing his idea of what it's like to be a bat, even though he says we can never know. Crick, for all his extreme reductionism, talks about such aspects of consciousness as pain and visual awareness and bases his theory on people's descriptions of what they see. And Dennett, even though he is accused of denying consciousness or explaining it away, begins by describing his own experience of sitting in his rocking chair watching leaves rippling in the sunshine and tries to account for "the way the sunset looks to me now." It turns out not to be trivial to divide theories into those that take the first-person view seriously and those that do not.

ACTIVITY
Positioning the theories

Varela has positioned some of the best-known theories of consciousness on a simple two-dimensional diagram. Before looking at where Varela himself places the theories, try to use his diagram to do this task yourself.

For a class exercise give each student a copy of the empty diagram (Figure 25.3) and ask them to place on it every theory of consciousness they can think of, or you can do the exercise together on the board. This is a useful revision exercise and a good way of drawing together ideas from the whole course. Point out that there are no right answers. Although Varela devised the scheme, he is not necessarily right about where each theory should go. When everyone has filled in as many theories as they can, show them Varela's version (Figure 25.4).

How well do they agree? Every discrepancy can be used to discuss the theories and to test students' understanding of them. In addition you might like to criticize the scheme itself. For example, are there really theories of consciousness for which first-person accounts are not essential? Can you come up with a better scheme?

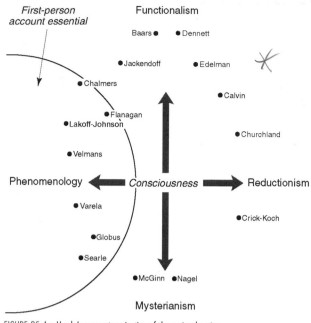

FIGURE 25.4 • Varela's own categorization of the major theories.

First-person account essential

Functionalism

Baars ●   ● Dennett

● Jackendoff   ● Edelman

● Chalmers

● Calvin

● Flanagan
● Lakoff-Johnson

● Churchland

● Velmans

Phenomenology ◄—— *Consciousness* ——► Reductionism

● Varela

● Crick-Koch

● Globus

● Searle

● McGinn ● Nagel

Mysterianism

A REFLEXIVE MODEL

Some people reject the distinction between first- and third-person methods altogether. Velmans (2000a; 2000b) points out that all sciences rely on the observations and experiences of scientists. Scientists can discover objective facts in the sense of inter-subjective knowledge, but there are no observations in science that are truly objective in the sense of being observer-free. He proposes a thought experiment in which the subject and observer in a psychology experiment change places.

Imagine there is a subject who is looking at a light and an experimenter who is studying her responses and her brain activity. The normal way of describing this situation is that the subject is having private first-person experiences of the light, while the experimenter is making third-person observations. Now all they have to do is to move their heads so that the subject observes the experimenter and the experimenter observes the light. In this swap nothing has changed in the *phenomenology* of the light, yet the light has

> " *We already have a systematic study of human conscious experience, and it is called 'psychology'* "
>
> **Baars**, 1999: 216

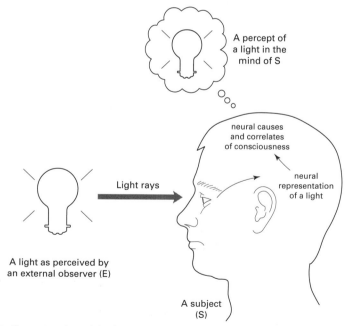

A percept of a light in the mind of S

neural causes and correlates of consciousness

Light rays

neural representation of a light

A light as perceived by an external observer (E)

A subject (S)

FIGURE 25.5 • The conventional way of describing perception. According to Velmans (2000b), this entails two kinds of dualism: a split between the observer and the observed, and a split between the public objective phenomena in the world or brain, and the private subjective experiences in the mind.

● C O N S C I O U S N E S S

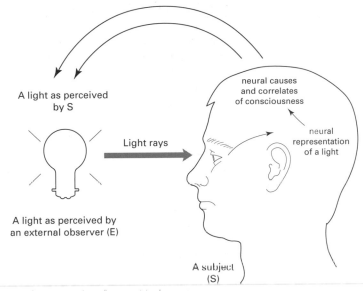

FIGURE 25.6 • Velmans's (2000b) "reflexive model" of perception.

supposedly gone from being a private experience to a public and objective stimulus. This, says Velmans, is absurd, and leaves us asking the fundamental question "Is the phenomenon subjective or objective?"

Velmans thus rejects the dualism between subjective and objective phenomena and proposes instead a "reflexive model of consciousness." He argues that our usual way of describing experiments misdescribes the phenomenology of perception and hence misconstrues the problems facing a science of consciousness.

> This reflexive model accepts conventional wisdom about the physical and neurophysiological causes of perception—for example, that there really is a physical stimulus in the room that our experience of it *represents*. But it gives a different account of the nature of the resulting experience. According to this nondualist view, when S attends to the light in a room she does not have an experience *of* a light "in her head or brain," with its attendant problems for science. She just sees a light in a room.
>
> (Velmans, 1999: 301)

Velmans uses his model to argue that many of the problems traditionally associated with a science of consciousness disappear. He agrees with the usual assumption that each of us lives in our own private phenomenal world and also that there are actual physical objects and events that people can agree about. So what psychologists do in their experiments, whether they are studying mental or physical phenomena, is to establish repeatability and intersubjectivity. This, he claims, does away with the distinction between first-person and third-person methods. In both cases the motto should be "*If you carry out these procedures you will observe or experience these results*" (2000b: 347).

This motto is important. Think of the effects of drugs—"if you take this drug you will experience these results" (see Chapter 22), or of practicing mental disciplines—"if you follow this procedure you will experience an OBE" (see Chapter 24), "if you meditate this way for many years you will gain this insight" (see Chapter 26). Yet Velmans's reflexive model has serious problems. Velmans claims that his theory is nondualist, and yet it rests entirely on the supposition that we have private experiences, and those experiences represent the external "things-themselves." This underlying dualism is intrinsic to Velmans's theory.

HETEROPHENOMENOLOGY

Heterophenomenology (which might be translated as "the study of other people's phenomena") is an awkward name for our final method of studying consciousness. According to Dennett (1991; 2001), it involves taking a giant theoretical leap, avoiding all tempting shortcuts, and following "the *neutral* path leading from objective physical science and its insistence on the third-person point of view, to a method of phenomenological description that can (in principle) do justice to the most private and ineffable subjective experiences" (1991: 72).

Imagine you are an anthropologist, says Dennett, and you are studying a tribe of people who believe in a forest god called Feenoman and can tell you all about his appearance, habits and abilities. You now have a choice. You can become a Feenomanist like them, and believe in their god and his powers, or you can study their religion with an agnostic attitude. If you take the latter path you collect different descriptions, deal with discrepancies and disagreements, and compile as well as you can the definitive description of Feenoman. You can be a Feenomanologist.

This is possible because you are not treating Feenoman as a creature who might jump out from behind a tree and give you the *right* answers. Instead you are treating him as an "intentional object," a kind of fiction like Sherlock Holmes or Dr. Watson. In fiction some things are true or false within the story, but others are neither. So, to use Dennett's example, it is true that Holmes and Watson took the 11:10 to Aldershot one summer's day, but it is neither true nor false that that day was a Wednesday because the author does not tell us. Similarly there is no point in trying to find out whether Feenoman *really* has blue eyes: on this, and all other questions about Feenoman, the beliefs of the Feenomanists are authoritative.

SELF-ASSESSMENT QUESTIONS

○ What are first-person, second-person and third-person approaches to consciousness? Give examples of each.

○ What is the difference between a first-person science and first-person methods?

○ Explain the argument between the A team and the B team.

○ What is the phenomenological reduction?

○ Explain the principles of neurophenomenology. How might it contribute to a science of consciousness?

○ What is the reflexive model of perception?

○ Explain what Dennett means by heterophenomenology. What are the three steps involved, and what is the end product?

This is the attitude that Dennett urges us to adopt in his method of heterophenomenology. It "neither challenges nor accepts as entirely true the assertions of subjects, but rather maintains a constructive and sympathetic neutrality, in the hopes of compiling a *definitive* description of the world according to the subjects" (Dennett, 1991: 83). The subjects may, like the Feenomanists, protest "But Feenoman is *real*," "I really *am* having these qualia," to which you, the heterophenomenologist, can only nod and reassure them that you believe they are sincere. This, says Dennett, is the price we have to pay for the neutrality that a science of consciousness demands. While heterophenomenologists accept people's descriptions of how things *seem* to them, "we have to keep an open mind about whether our apparent subjects are liars, zombies, or parrots dressed up in people suits" (ibid.).

FIGURE 25.7 • The Feenomanologist collects his data from the Feenomanists.

So heterophenomenology studies everything and anything that people do and say, and accepts that they are genuinely trying to describe how things seem to them, and beyond that retains an open mind.

What does this mean in practice? Dennett describes the method in three steps. First, the data are collected. This might include taking brain scans, asking people to press buttons when they see something, or asking them to describe their mental images or emotions. Second, the data are interpreted. This step is unavoidable if we want to use the data, and might include turning the brain scans into colored pictures, relating the button presses to the stimuli presented, and turning the speech sounds into words that we write down and understand as descriptions of mental images. Third, and this is the crucial step, we adopt the intentional stance. That is, we treat the subject as a rational agent who has beliefs, desires and intentionality. We allow that she pressed the button because she wanted to tell us that she saw the green blob, and spoke those words because she was trying to describe her complex mental image or the powerful emotion she felt when you showed her that picture.

There may be inconsistencies that have to be investigated or ironed out, but in spite of these difficulties the method leads easily enough to the creation of a believable fiction: the subjects' heterophenomenological world.

> This fictional world is populated with all the images, events, sounds, smells, hunches, presentiments, and feelings that the subject (apparently) sincerely believes to exist in his or her (or its) stream of consciousness. Maximally extended, it is a neutral portrayal of exactly *what it is like to be* that subject—in the subject's own terms, given the best interpretation we can muster.
>
> (Dennett, 1991: 98)

According to Dennett, this is the basic method that has always been used in the science of psychology, and he has not invented it but merely explained its rationale.

IS THIS EXPERIENCE HOW IT *SEEMS* TO ME, OR IS THIS HOW IT REALLY IS?

But isn't there something left out? Isn't heterophenomenology only studying what people say and leaving out *the experiences themselves*? Isn't it treating their inner world as a fiction when it *really exists*? Isn't it only treating people *as if* they have beliefs, desires, emotions and mental images when they *really do*?

These questions get to the heart of the issue so it is worth trying to be clear about how heterophenomenology responds. Heterophenomenology maintains neutrality on all these points. It leaves open the question whether there is something more to be discovered, pending further investigation. It uses the fiction of the heterophenomenological world much like a physicist might use the fiction of a centre of gravity, or a black hole. It leaves it open whether *as if* intentionality is different from *real intentionality* (see Chapters 12, 13 and 15). Dennett presumably thinks there is no difference, but heterophenomenology, as a method, is not committed either way.

What role remains for 'looking into our own minds'? Dennett has no time for first-person methods. Yet they may still play an important role in third-person science – for example, by providing particularly interesting heterophenomenological worlds. So whether you believe in the possibility of a first-person science of consciousness or not, it is still worth finding out what people who have trained deeply in self-observation have to say about what they find.

READING

Chalmers, D. (1999) First-person methods in the science of consciousness. *Consciousness Bulletin,* University of Arizona, June 1999, http://www.u.arizona.edu/~chalmers/papers/firstperson.html.

Dennett, D.C. (2001) The fantasy of first-person science. Debate with D. Chalmers, Northwestern University, Evanston, Ill., February 2001, http://ase.tufts.edu/cogstud/papers/chalmersdeb3dft.htm.

TWENTY-SIX

The first step is calming the mind. This skill can take many years to master, but then it becomes possible to sit down and let the mind settle. Everything that arises is let go, like writing on water. Nothing is met with judgments, opinions or responses of any kind. Gradually reactions cease and clarity appears. The sounds of birds, the sight of the floor, the itch on the hand, they are just as they are: suchness. In this state insight arises.

Those who practice certain kinds of meditation claim that they awake from illusion and can see directly into the nature of mind. If they are right, their claims are important both for the introspective methods they use, and for what they say about consciousness. But are they right?

Many interesting questions are posed by these practices. Why do people meditate? Is meditation an ASC, and if so what sort? What do experienced meditators claim to see? And how can their claims be validated? We shall first tackle some easier questions. What is meditation? How is it done? Who does it and what are the effects on them? Then we shall be in a position to consider the more difficult questions about the validity, or otherwise, of meditative insights.

METHODS OF MEDITATION

FIGURE 26.1 • Meditation in the full lotus position (Batchelor, 2001).

Most methods of meditation have religious origins. In particular, Buddhism, Hinduism and Sufism have long traditions of disciplined meditation, but comparable methods are found within the mystical traditions of Christianity, Judaism and Islam (Ornstein, 1986; West, 1987). More recently, secular methods have appeared, and many people train in meditation without any religious belief. The most popular of these is transcendental meditation (TM), derived from Hindu techniques and brought to the West by Maharishi Mahesh Yogi. TM is now taught within a large, hierarchical and highly profitable organization, which claims that TM provides deep relaxation, eliminates stress, and promotes health, creativity and inner happiness.

Although there are many methods, the basics of meditation might be summed up in the words "pay attention and don't think." It is hard to believe that such a practice could be of any benefit at all, let alone be capable of the kinds of transformations and insights claimed by some meditators, yet this is essentially the task undertaken. It is surprisingly difficult, as you will know if you have tried, and the many varieties of meditation can be seen as different ways of easing the task. If you have never tried it, just take 10 seconds and see whether you can *not think* for that short length of time.

POSTURE

Meditation usually involves sitting in a special posture. There is nothing mysterious about these postures, and no need to be attached to any particular one. They all serve the same function: to keep the body both alert and relaxed, while keeping still for long periods. It is possible to meditate in any position at all, but the two main dangers are becoming too tense and agitated, or falling asleep. The traditional postures help to avoid both.

"Pay attention and don't think."

Full Lotus   Half Lotus   Burmese   Bench

FIGURE 26.2 • Traditional meditation postures all achieve a stable and comfortable position with a straight back, to encourage a state of alert relaxation. Sitting on a low bench achieves the same objective and is more comfortable for those not used to sitting on the floor.

CONSCIOUSNESS

The best-known posture is the full lotus position. This provides a stable triangle of contact with the floor and a relaxed upright posture with a straight back that takes little physical effort to maintain. It also encourages breathing from the abdomen rather than just the chest. However, it is difficult for people who have sat in chairs all their lives, and not worth struggling with if it is painful. Unnecessary pain, and showing off, are not helpful for meditation. There are many other postures that achieve the desired stability and alertness, including the half lotus and the simpler Burmese position. Many people sit on low benches with their knees on the ground and their back straight. Sitting in a chair is less stable but recommended for people who cannot use other methods. It is best to plant the feet firmly apart on the floor to give stability, and keep the back straight and away from the back of the chair.

During long meditation retreats, sitting is sometimes alternated with very slow walking meditation, or even fast walking or running meditations. In fact meditation can be done in any position at all, and for some traditions the ultimate aim is to integrate meditation into all of life and all activities.

Some traditions advocate particular ways of holding the hands, including resting them gently on the knees either palm up or palm down, resting in the lap, and holding various gestures associated with compassion, openness or other desired qualities. Some use repetitive movements such as repeatedly touching the tips of the four fingers on the thumb. There is no research on the effect of specific hand positions, but it is possible that they make a difference by reminding the meditator of the intended state of mind.

Some positions are tied to ancient theories about chakras, energy lines and other body schemes. Most of these schemes conflict with basic anatomy and have no known physical basis. For example, in traditional Chinese acupuncture a special energy called Qi is said to travel through the body along meridians connecting the acupuncture points. Acupuncture is now known to work by stimulating endorphins and dynorphins, and the effects can be controlled using different frequencies of electrical stimulation, but

ACTIVITY
Meditation

Meditation can be done by yourself or in a group. First sit down comfortably. You should have your back straight but be able to relax. If you know how to sit in a meditation position do so. If you wish to try one, make sure the floor is not too hard, or use a rug or blanket, and choose a firm cushion to sit on. Cross your legs in the way that is easiest for you and make sure that you can keep your back upright and straight without pain. Otherwise, sit upright in a straight chair with your feet flat on the floor and your hands gently resting on your lap. Look at the floor about two feet in front of you, but don't concentrate hard on one spot, just let your gaze rest there gently. If it wanders, bring it back to the same place.

Set a timer to 10 minutes.

Begin by just watching your breath as it flows in and out. When you are ready, begin counting. On each out-breath count "one" silently, and then on the next out-breath "two," and so on. When you get to 10, start again at one, and continue until the timer sounds. That's all.

Your attitude toward everything that arises should be the same: "Let it come, let it be, let it go." When you realize that you have slipped into a train of thought, just let it go and return to watching your breath and counting. Do not fight the thoughts or try to force them to stop. Just let go. Do the same with sounds or sights or bodily sensations; just let them be. This way they won't be distracting at all.

Just one session may show you something about your own mind. If you wish to do more, commit yourself to meditating every single day for a week, perhaps first thing in the morning or twice a day if you think you can manage it. It is better to sit for 10 minutes every day without fail than to try to do more and give up.

the meridians and acupuncture points have been shown to be completely irrelevant, giving no support to the traditional theories (Ulett, 2002). Most other such schemes have not yet been properly tested. They may all prove false, but it is important to remember that the meditation techniques based on visualizing chakras or energy flows may have very powerful effects, even if the chakras and energies themselves do not exist.

BASIC PRINCIPLES

Let it come, let it be, let it go.

Crook, 1990

Common to all forms of meditation are two basic tasks: paying attention and not thinking. Both raise interesting practical and theoretical questions. What do you pay attention to? How do you maintain concentration? How do you stop thoughts? The different methods outlined below give different answers, but almost all techniques share common methods for dealing with unwanted thoughts.

Pushing thoughts away does not work. They may be held at bay temporarily, but then they come back with greater force, or change into other, more persistent, thoughts. Or they may set up emotional states that keep reigniting them. The answer is not to fight against these thoughts but to let them go, and return to the practice. One danger is that you get angry with yourself for being so easily distracted. If that happens, just let the anger go too.

In Buddhism, and especially in Zen Buddhism, letting go is not seen as a way of achieving an ASC or any other goal. It is a way of becoming free from all attachments. So letting go is a task itself (Watts, 1957). As the great teacher Dogen (1200–53) put it, "Enlightenment and practice are one." Dogen is famous for bringing Soto Zen from China to Japan in the thirteenth century. As the story goes, Dogen was sitting one morning in meditation when he heard his master reprimanding another monk who was dozing. The master urged his monks to wake up and work harder, saying, "To realize perfect enlightenment you must let fall body and mind." In that moment Dogen achieved full awakening, or liberation (Kapleau, 1980).

Of all the traditions, Zen is probably clearest about the importance of total attention and clear awareness. In a famous story, a man asked the fourteenth-century Zen master Ikkyu to write for him some maxims of the highest wisdom. Ikkyu wrote "Attention." Dissatisfied with this answer the man asked him to write more. He wrote "Attention. Attention." The man irritably complained that he saw nothing of much depth or subtlety in that. So Ikkyu wrote "Attention. Attention. Attention." Then the angry man demanded to know what attention means and Ikkyu gently answered "Attention means attention."

You may be irritated by such stories. You may think that the only way to really understand attention is to study the brain. In fact there have been many studies of the effects of Zen training on brain function and in particular on changes in the ability to attend (Austin, 1998). But there remains an interesting question about the role of first-person practice. Suppose that a scientist were to practice paying attention mindfully for many years. Would that scientist have something special to contribute to a science of consciousness, or not?

OPEN MEDITATION

Paying attention, fully and single-mindedly, is not easy, and the many meditation methods can be seen as different ways of making it possible. Although there are several schemes, the most common divides them into either open or concentrative methods (Farthing, 1992; Ornstein, 1986; Wallace and Fisher, 1991). Some schemes distinguish active from passive techniques (Newberg and D'Aquili, 2001) but, as we shall see, there are active and passive aspects to them all.

Open, or "opening-up," meditation means being aware of everything that is happening but without responding to it. This is usually done with the eyes open or half-open and in Buddhist meditation, or *zazen*, is often done facing a blank wall. Mindfulness meditation in Buddhism is a form of open meditation, in particular the method of *shikantaza*, which means "just sitting." The basic idea is to be continuously mindful and attentive, and fully present in the moment, paying attention to anything and everything without discrimination.

One of the first effects that meditators notice is how different this is from their normal state of mind. They have "the piercing realization of just how disconnected humans normally are from their very experience" (Varela et al., 1991: 25). Most of the time interesting sights, sounds, events or thoughts drag the attention one way and another, so that the mind is continuously distracted, categorizing and commenting on everything that happens. Paying attention equally and without discrimination means not letting this happen but just sitting with the arising stimuli and treating them all with equal indifference as they arise. This is sometimes called choiceless awareness. With practice, mindfulness meditation leads to a perfectly open state known as bare awareness or bare attention.

This technique is very direct and simple, but difficult to do. When thoughts and distractions arise, the task is to return to the present moment, but this is not easy when the present moment is full of pain in the legs, memories of unhappiness or anticipations of future pleasure. One solution is to meet all distractions with the attitude "Let it come, let it be, let it go" (Crook, 1990). "Let it come" means let the thought, or pain or worry or whatever, arise without trying to prevent it. Once it has come, don't do anything with it. Don't react, don't turn it around in the mind, and above all don't judge it as good or bad. Just let it be. If thoughts are let alone, they will go away on their own. Don't cling onto them. With practice, letting go becomes easier, and thoughts and feelings that would previously have been distracting become just more stuff, appearing and disappearing without response. In mindful, alert awareness the differences between self and other, and the mind and its contents, disappear. This is known as nonduality.

Mindfulness is primarily a meditation technique, and is easier when practiced while sitting quietly. Nevertheless, it can be practiced at all times, and for

Suppose that a scientist were to practice paying attention mindfully for many years. Would that scientist have something special to contribute to a science of consciousness?

FIGURE 26.3

some Buddhists the aim is to remain fully present in every action and every moment of waking life, and even during sleep. This means never giving in to distraction or desire, never dwelling in the past or future, and being open to everything, all the time. This is a radically different way of living.

CONCENTRATIVE MEDITATION

Concentrative meditation means paying focused attention to one thing without distraction, rather than remaining open to the world. In a famous study in the early 1960s, American psychiatrist Arthur Deikman rounded up a group of friends, sat them in front of a blue vase, and asked them to concentrate on it for half an hour, excluding all other thoughts, perceptions and distractions. The effects were very striking, even in the early sessions. The vase seemed more vivid, more rich, or even luminous. It became animated, or alive, and people felt as though they were merging with the vase or that changes in its shape were happening in their own bodies. Deikman argued that as we normally develop through life, we learn to attend increasingly to thoughts and abstractions, and so our perception becomes automatized and dull. The effect of this exercise in concentrated meditative attention was "deautomatization" (Deikman, 1966; 2000).

The most common object for concentration is the breath. Even Zen, with its emphasis on simplicity and directness, uses watching the breath during *zazen*, especially for beginners. One method is to count the out-breaths up to 10 and then start again at one. This is a useful technique for dealing with distraction. One problem with open meditation is that it is possible to get lost in long trains of thought and completely forget the task for minutes at a time. If you are counting the breath, you are much more likely to notice that you have lost count, and even to remember what number you last paid attention to. This

CONSCIOUSNESS

can be quite shocking as well as useful. Another method is just to watch and feel the sensation of air flowing naturally in and out as the chest rises and falls.

Sometimes special techniques are used that alter the breathing rate, the depth, the ratio of in-breath to out-breath, and whether the breathing is predominantly in the chest or abdomen. Different breathing patterns have powerful effects on awareness, and there is evidence that experienced meditators use these effects. For example, during the in-breath, pupils dilate, heart rate increases, and activity in the brain stem increases, as does activity in some higher brain areas. The opposite occurs during the out-breath. Blood gas levels also change. Research shows that experienced meditators spend more time slowly exhaling, and increase abdominal breathing. Overall they may reduce their breathing rate from the normal 12 to 20 or so breaths per minute to as little as four to six breaths per minute, often without ever explicitly being trained to do so, or even realizing that they are doing so. Some meditators stop breathing altogether for periods of many seconds, and one study of TM adepts showed that these stops often coincided with moments of "pure consciousness" or no thought (Austin, 1998).

Some techniques of breath control are associated with theories involving special energies, such as *prana* in yoga and Vedanta. Meditators may be told that they can learn to control this special energy or to direct it through special channels, and some teachers claim to have acquired paranormal and healing abilities this way. A few even abuse the power these claims give them to attract and control disciples. There is as yet no evidence that these special energies exist, even though the techniques themselves can certainly affect the body's natural energy resources.

Mantras are words, phrases or sounds that are repeated either silently or out loud. When thoughts arise the meditator just returns attention to the mantra. Mantras are used in Buddhism, Judaism and Hindu yoga, including the well-known *Om Mani Padme Hum*, which means the jewel in the center of the lotus. In Christianity, the early Desert Fathers used to repeat *kyrie eleison* silently to help them achieve a state of "nowhereness and nomindness" (West, 1987). *The Cloud of Unknowing* recommends clasping a word, such as "God" or "Sin," to your heart so that it never leaves, and beating with it upon the cloud and the darkness, striking down thoughts of every kind, and driving them beneath the cloud of forgetting, so as to find God and achieve "complete self-forgetfulness."

TM is based on mantras, and new students are given a personal mantra. In fact it is assigned on the basis of their age, but probably the words of the mantra do not matter. Although some mantras have great religious significance, their function in meditation is to provide something to focus the wandering attention on, and for this purpose any words will do. Indeed anything will do. Yogins may concentrate on a candle flame, flower, vase, stone or any small object. Some traditions use mental images that range from simple visions of light or God, to the highly elaborate sequences of visualization taught in Tibetan Buddhism.

KOANS

Working with a koan, or *hua tou*, is a method used to induce deep Zen questioning. The method was originally developed in China from the sixth century onward, expounded in the famous Zen text of 100 koans called the *Blue Cliff Record*, and added to by the poet and painter Hakuin (1685–1768) as well as many later commentators. Koans are mainly used in Rinzai Zen, one of the two main sects of Zen, and in Rinzai training monks may be expected to "pass" a series of graded koans, but really koans do not have "right answers." The only right answer is to show that one has "seen the nature" (Kapleau, 1980; Watts, 1957).

Many koans are questions directed at the nature of self, such as "What was your original face before your mother and father were born?" "What is your own mind?" or "Who is it that hears?" It is easy to spend hours, days or even years on any one of these. If you have been doing the practices in each chapter, you will know just what this means. Others may seem completely incomprehensible, such as "The East Mountain strides over the water" or "Stop the moving boat," yet they may have deep effects on the serious questioner. *Hou tous* are slightly different. They are the head, or final words or questions, of a Zen story.

A famous example forms the basis of Korean Zen (Batchelor, 1990; 2001). It comes from the turn of the eighth century when it was common for teachers to point to a house, or the sky, or a leaf, and demand, "What is that?" As the story goes, a young monk walked for many days to find the Zen patriarch Hui Neng at his mountain monastery. When the monk finally arrived, Hui Neng asked him where he had come from and the monk told him about his journey. Hui Neng then asked, "What is this thing that has come and how did it get here?" The monk was speechless and decided to stay and devote himself to pondering this question.

Eight years later he was suddenly awakened and said to Hui Neng, "I have experienced some awakening." "What

Finally, in Zen Buddhism, and in particular in the Rinzai school, practitioners concentrate on a koan, or *hua tou*. These are questions or stories designed to challenge the intellectual mind with paradox or ambiguity and force it into a state of open inquiry. Some meditators use the same koan for a whole lifetime, such as "Who am I?" or the question "What is this?" used in Korean Zen (Batchelor, 2001). Others pass through a series of koans as they develop in understanding. Koans are not designed to be answered but to be used.

How does this bewildering array of methods, all called "meditation," help us to understand consciousness? The answer may be different depending not just on the methods people use but on their reasons for meditating. These fall roughly into three categories.

1 Purely religious or ritual reasons, including gaining merit, going to heaven, or gaining a favorable reincarnation. We shall not consider these further here.

2 Reducing stress, increasing personal skills, and improving life.

3 Seeking insight and awakening, whether in a religious or mystical context or a purely secular one.

RELAXATION AND STRESS REDUCTION

TM is promoted as "the single most effective technique available for gaining deep relaxation, eliminating stress, promoting health, increasing creativity and intelligence, and attaining inner happiness and fulfilment." Because of these claims, doctors and therapists sometimes prescribe meditation as a method of dealing with hypertension and other stress-related diseases. For this reason alone it is important to know whether meditation really does increase relaxation and reduce stress.

What appears be a simple question turns out not to be. In 1983, inspired by the many claims and treatments, American psychologist David Holmes conducted a simple experiment to compare the arousal-reducing effects of meditation with the effect of rest. He tested arousal levels in 10 people who had never meditated before and 10 certified teachers of TM. Each person first sat quietly for 5 minutes. Then the meditators meditated for 20 minutes and the non-meditators just rested. Finally they sat quietly for another 5 minutes. The results were very striking. Both meditation and resting reduced arousal equally. Holmes then tracked down many previous experiments and found that most showed the same results—that is, when the correct controls are employed, the results show that meditation is relaxing but no more so than just resting. He also exposed people to stressful situations and found no evidence that the experienced meditators coped better (Holmes, 1987).

Holmes' research caused a storm of protest from advocates of meditation, and heated debates ensued. These disputes are difficult to resolve because of the many methodological issues involved. One concerns which measures of stress to study, and many have been tried, including heart rate, breathing rate, blood oxygen and carbon dioxide levels, EEG and many more. If one measure shows no effect, people can always claim that a different one would.

Another concerns which kind of meditation to use because different methods may have different effects. By far the majority of studies have used TM, and this is appropriate here because of TM's strong claims to reduce stress. However, this raises special difficulties. Most TM research is done by TM practitioners and teachers, who have been trained over long periods and have committed their lives and a great deal of money to the TM organization. Many of their studies comes from the Maharishi International University in Fairfield, Iowa, or from other TM universities around the world, and many are published in their own journals. Although an increasing number are published in peer review journals and are therefore open to scrutiny, doubts will always be raised when the financial stakes are high.

Returning to more general methodological issues, all research into meditation has to confront several problems, and we can review them here in relation to the research on stress. One decision is whether to make within-subject or between-subject comparisons. In research using within-subject comparisons meditators act as their own controls, perhaps sitting quietly first and then meditating. Using this method, reductions in arousal are usually found, but these must be compared with what would happen if the meditators just rested instead—or perhaps took part in some other relaxing alternative. Only if meditation is more relaxing than, say, listening to music or dozing in a comfy

is it?" asked Hui Neng. The monk replied, "To say it is like something is not to the point." Even so, he agreed that whatever it was it could be cultivated.

Using this koan means that when walking, standing, sitting or lying down, you repeatedly ask the question "What is this?" meaning "What is walking?" "What is it that tastes the tea?" or "What is it before you even taste the tea?" With practice you do not need to repeat the words; it is the doubt or perplexity that matters, not the words. So the question hangs there, always being asked. Your whole body and mind become the question. You don't know.

> *"The key to koan practice is found not in the wording of the koan, but in the quality of perplexity that the koan is able to arouse."*
>
> **Batchelor**, 1994: 208

Experiment	Heart Rate	Electrodermal	Resp.	Blood Pressure	EMG	Other
Bahrke and Morgan	No					O_2, No Temp., No
Boswell and Murray (1979)	No	No				
Cauthen and Prymak (1977)	No	No	No			Temp., No
Credidio (1982)					Yes	Temp., No
Curtis and Wessberg (1975–6)	No	No	No			
Dhanaraj and Singh (1977)	No		No			O_2, Yes Tidal vol., Yes
Elson et al. (1977)	No[1]	Yes[2]	Yes			Temp., No
Goleman and Schwartz (1976)	No[1]	No				
Hafner (1982)				No		
Holmes et al. (1983)	No	No	No[1]	No		
Lintel (1980)		No				
Malec and Sipprelle (1977)	No	No			Yes	
Michaels et al. (1979)	No[1]			No		
Morse et al. (1977)	No	No	No	No	Yes	
Orme-Johnson (1973)		No				
Parker et al. (1978)	No	No		Yes		
Peters et al. (1977b)	No					
Puente (1981)	No[1]	No	Yes		No	
Raskin et al. (1980)					No	
Routt (1977)	No	No	No		No	Blood flow, No
Travis et al. (1976)	No[1]					HR var., No
Walrath and Hamilton (1975)	No	No	No			
Zuroff and Schwarz (1978)	No					

Notes: [1] Reliably *higher* arousal was observed in meditating than in resting subjects.

[2] Meditating subjects were initially more aroused, and hence their greater decrease in arousal may have been due to regression to the mean.

FIGURE 26.4 • Experiments indicating reliably lower somatic arousal among meditating than resting subjects during meditation/rest periods (after Holmes, 1987).

chair, can the claims be supported. A problem for within-subject designs is that it may be impossible to prevent meditators from meditating when they are resting, listening to music or dozing in a comfy chair. One could then argue that the lack of any difference was because they meditated in both conditions. But if you try to avoid this by using novice meditators, you may get no effect because they cannot meditate properly.

A way around this is to use between-subject designs as Holmes did—that is, to compare two different groups of people. This makes sure that the non-meditators are not meditating by mistake, but now there is a different problem. If you use experienced meditators, they are likely to be rather special kinds of people, and they may react differently to stress from a normal control group.

This problem is widespread in meditation research and makes it difficult to choose appropriate control groups. It is known that people who take up meditation are more anxious and neurotic than the average, and more likely to take drugs. In addition, different kinds of people give up after having started —for example, those who give up are more introverted, have a more external locus of control, and start with lower expectations of meditation (Delmonte, 1987).

Nevertheless, it is possible to deal with some of these problems and reach at least tentative conclusions. Farthing concludes that the evidence "shows either no effects of meditation or that the effects of meditation (relaxation, anxiety reduction) can also be achieved by other methods and are not necessarily produced by the meditation technique per se" (Farthing, 1992: 440). Holmes (1987) concluded that the use of meditation for stress reduction was simply not justified by the evidence.

More worrying is that meditation can occasionally have harmful effects, depending on the individual and the stage of meditation (Epstein and Lieff, 1986). Beginning meditators are sometimes overwhelmed, and may suffer depersonalization and derealization bad enough to provoke panic attacks. TM can exacerbate existing depression, increase anxiety and tension, and produce agitation and restlessness. The dangers are particularly severe for people with existing psychological problems, who may develop religious delusions, compelling fantasies and even psychotic episodes through meditation. So claims for meditation as a stress reducer must be tempered by appreciating its potential dangers.

Even harder methodological problems face studies of the long-term effects. Most important is that you cannot rely on people's memories and self-assessments but must study them over long periods. Ideally you would take two similar groups of people and randomly assign them to meditation or

PRACTICE
WHAT IS THIS?

Read the story about Hui Neng and the monk (see Concept and Figure 27.1). Think about the question he asked: **"What is this thing and how did it get here?"**

Think about it as applied to the monk, standing there at the monastery after days of walking in the mountains. Think about it as applied to yourself, sitting here, walking there, realizing you haven't thought about the question for half an hour and now standing here. Think about it whatever you are doing: "What is this thing and how did it get here?" Go on asking the question all the time. The words do not matter. As you carry on practicing they will probably fall away until you begin the question and "Wh....?"

Peter Fenwick (b. 1935)

Peter Fenwick is a neuropsychiatrist who has spent much of his life working with epilepsy, sleep disorders and altered states of consciousness. He was born in Nairobi, Kenya, trained in neurophysiology and then ran the Neuropsychiatry Epilepsy Unit at the Maudsley Hospital in London for 10 years. He worked at Broadmoor Hospital, pursuing his interest in automatic and criminal behavior carried out during unconsciousness, but his particular interest is the problem of mind and consciousness. He has been a meditator himself for nearly 40 years, and his early studies of the EEG during meditation helped to encourage other scientists to study the effects of meditation.

Fenwick has collected over 2000 accounts of NDEs and he designed one of the first experiments to test out-of-body vision in hospital cardiac units, but so far with no success. He does not believe that today's reductionist neuroscience can adequately explain subjective experience, nor the wider transcendent states of consciousness which suggest that the whole universe is a single unity. He says he would like to believe that there is continuation of consciousness (though not personal consciousness) after death, but cannot claim to have found definitive evidence.

non-meditation groups and then a few years later measure any changes. The problems are obvious. If you start with people who were not strongly motivated to meditate, you are bound to get high drop-out rates, and cannot really expect good results, but if you start with highly motivated people, it is not fair to prevent half of them meditating for many years, even if that were possible. Farthing concludes that "Unfortunately, much of the research on long-term effects is flawed, and the better controlled research has often failed to support the claims" (1992: 436). Nevertheless, many meditators claim long-term benefits, including positive changes in personality and mood, reduced anxiety and depression, and enhanced creativity.

SIDDHIS AND PSYCHIC POWERS

Dramatic claims are made for some forms of meditation, such as the acquisition of *siddhis* through practicing yoga. Siddhis are supernatural or paranormal powers such as prophecy, levitation, astral projection and "control over others and the forces of nature." TM makes two claims of this kind. First is levitation or "Vedic flying," and there is a special siddhi program open only to those at the highest level of attainment. There are photographs of people apparently floating above their meditation cushions but these could have been taken at the height of the bounce or hop that meditators use when practicing Vedic flying. No outsiders have ever been shown the flying.

Second is the "Maharishi effect." The claim is that if enough people meditate together in one place, their combined field of consciousness can bring peace to everyone else, and even to the whole planet. According to the Maharishi's "unified field theory of consciousness" the field of pure consciousness underlies the laws of quantum mechanics and is what people tap into when they meditate. This allows them to alter the statistical averaging at quantum mechanical levels, making possible such local effects such as levitation, and global effects such as increasing peace and love in the world. Evidence in support of the Maharishi effect includes falling crime rates, and many improvements in measures of social cohesion, in areas where TMers congregate, such as at TM universities and the TM headquarters in Fairfield, Iowa. Critics argue that appropriate control areas and cities have not been studied, and that some of the effects were only to be expected. For example, when the TM organization buys up a college previously full of young, car-owning, drinking students and fills it with older, committed TMers who stay in and

FIGURE 26.5 • TM practitioners demonstrating Vedic flying. Outsiders have not been allowed to watch the levitation or to take their own photographs.

meditate for several hours a day, obviously crime rates will fall. No research can fairly test TM's claims to have brought down the Berlin Wall, ended the Gulf War, caused stock-market rises, or contributed to the collapse of the Soviet Union.

ALTERED STATES

Meditation is often defined in terms of ASCs, as in these two examples: "*Meditation* is a ritualistic procedure intended to change one's state of consciousness by means of maintained, voluntary shifts in attention" (Farthing, 1992: 421); "meditation can be regarded as a slow, cumulative, long-term procedure for producing an altered state of consciousness" (Wallace and Fisher, 1991: 153). Buddhist teachings include complex schemes for categorizing altered states, such as the various "absorptions," which include states of no-self, no-world, vast spaciousness and the "dropping off of body and mind" (Austin, 1998). In Zen, practitioners may have dramatic kensho experiences, which are glimpses of enlightenment or a "great flash of understanding."

So does meditation really induce ASCs? In Tart's subjective definition it certainly does, because people feel that their mental functioning has been radically altered. As for objective measures, there have been many relevant studies, starting in the 1950s with several that used the EEG. Researchers carried the cumbersome early EEG equipment up to the monasteries and mountain caves of Indian yogis and recorded their brain waves while banging cymbals, flashing lights and plunging their feet in cold water (Bagchi and Wenger, 1957). They found not only that the meditators showed a lot of alpha rhythm, the 8–12-hertz rhythm associated with relaxed waking, but that the alpha rhythm was not blocked by the lights and noise as it would be in non-meditators. This seemed to be evidence of sensory withdrawal.

Then in 1966, 48 Japanese priests and their disciples, with between 1 and 20 years' practice, were studied during *zazen* (Kasamatsu and Hirai, 1966). At the start of the meditation fast alpha appeared, which then slowed and increased in amplitude until runs of theta at 6–7 hertz appeared. This study also looked at habituation. Normally alpha is blocked by a sudden noise and this blocking is diminished if the noise is repeated many times, but these Zen adepts showed no signs of habitation to repeated sounds. All this led to the attractive interpretation that the concentrating yogis studied by Bagchi and Wenger were withdrawn from sensory contact, while the Zen practitioners remained open to all stimuli, treating sounds as essentially new every time. Sadly this simple picture was not confirmed by the mass of somewhat conflicting results that followed in later years (Fenwick, 1987).

One skeptical theory is that meditation is nothing more than sleep or dozing. Here the results are most interesting. Peter Fenwick (1987; see Profile, p. 396) showed that frequency and amplitude profiles of EEG in meditation are not the same as sleep or drowsiness, yet there is evidence that many meditators take microsleeps during meditation, and in one study TMers slept as much as a third of the time while meditating (Austin, 1998). Since naps are known to have beneficial effects on mood and cognitive ability, this might be the explanation of some of the effects of meditation. Yet meditators themselves say they can easily distinguish between the experience of deep meditation and sleep. One interpretation of this is that meditators learn, with inevitable slip-ups, to hold themselves at that interesting transitional level between sleep and wakefulness (see Chapter 21).

Another claim is that meditation produces increased brain coherence, or a closer correlation between the activity of different brain areas, both in the same and the opposite hemisphere. Several EEG studies have demonstrated this, but Fenwick (1987) points out that there is nothing magical about coherence itself. Very high coherence is

SELF-ASSESSMENT QUESTIONS

○ What are the basic principles common to all forms of meditation?

○ Describe the differences between open and concentrative meditation.

○ What is mindfulness? How is it practiced?

○ What is a koan? Give some examples.

○ What are the main methodological problems in research on meditation?

○ Is meditation relaxing? Is it an ASC? Is it a form of sleep? Describe some of the evidence.

○ What is the role of attention in meditation?

found not only during meditation but during epileptic seizures, delta coma and at death.

Further EEG studies have tested Ornstein's (1977) suggestion that meditation shifts the way the brain processes information from a linear left-hemispheric mode to a more holistic and right-hemispheric mode. He points to evidence of right-hemisphere involvement in mystical experiences, and to the dependence of language and concepts about "I, me, and mine" on the left hemisphere. In studies of Buddhist meditators and Franciscan nuns at prayer, medical researchers Andrew Newberg and Eugene D'Aquili used SPECT (single photon emission computed tomography) to show increased activity in a part of the posterior parietal lobe that they call the "orientation association area" because of its involvement in orienting self in the world. There was less activity on the right. Yet overall the evidence from EEG and PET scans "suggests that the brain undergoes no complete right/left split in its functions. Not during meditative states, not during absorptions, not during insights. Instead, the data suggest that far more complex (and interactive) neurophysiological principles are involved" (Austin, 1998: 366).

The lack of consistent evidence may seem disappointing and frustrating, but perhaps it helps to remember that people meditate for many different reasons. For those who are seeking relaxation the answer seems to be that meditation is no better than many other, easier techniques. For those seeking special powers, there is little to encourage them. For those seeking ASCs, there is more positive evidence, and if this is what they seek they may be rewarded. But some people meditate for deeper reasons, and might prefer Fenwick's definition of meditation as "a spiritual discipline leading to a greater understanding of the world" (1987: 116). Such people do not meditate in order to gain something or to achieve a special state of consciousness, but to see through the illusion and wake up.

INSIGHT AND AWAKENING

What happens to those who practice meditation for this last reason? James Austin is an American neurologist who undertook extensive Zen training in Japan and is a long-term Zen practitioner as well as a scientist. On the basis that "Zen training means brain training," he made a thorough study of the relationship between Zen and the brain (Austin, 1998). He described how the Zen trainee finds that thoughts drop out, the bodily self fades, and the perceiving self begins to dissolve. From this perspective, the old assumption that you can't have an experience unless an "I" is there to have it, becomes laughable. Something must be changing in the trainee's brain, but what?

An early clue to long-term changes comes from Kasamatsu and Hirai's (1966) study. They found more theta in the EEG of the most experienced meditators, and a correlation between the length of practice and the changes found. In addition, these changes were related to the Zen master's categorization of his disciples in terms of their advancement on the Zen path, and this method of

WHAT IS THIS?

"*Zen training means brain training.*"

Austin, 1998

classification was better than classifying them by their years of practice. So whatever it was that the master could see, it was reflected in the EEG.

Perhaps one day we will understand exactly what kind of changes accompany Zen insight and awakening. But first we need to ask some searching questions about that "awakening" itself. Is it, or is it not, a way to find out the truth about self, the world and consciousness? After all, the third-person objective methods of science make the same claim. So if they are both right, they should lead to the same place.

READING

Farthing, G.W. (1992) *The Psychology of Consciousness*. Englewood Cliffs, NJ, Prentice Hall. This includes a good review of principles and research on meditation.

West, M.A. (ed.) (1987) *The Psychology of Meditation*. Oxford, Clarendon Press. See especially the chapters by West, Holmes and Fenwick.

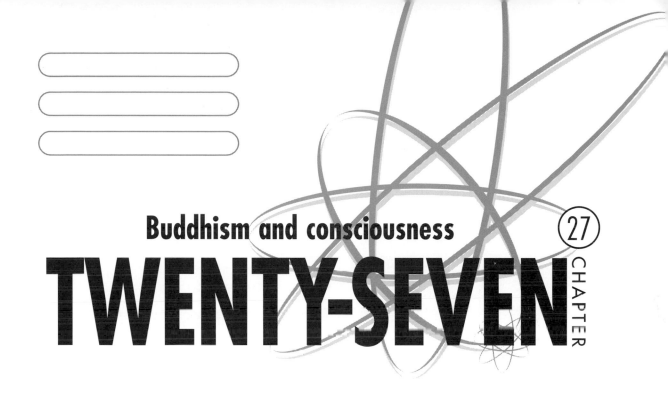

Buddhism and consciousness

TWENTY-SEVEN

Once upon a time, about two and a half thousand years ago, a prince was born in the north of India. His name was Siddhartha Gautama, and he led a happy and indulgent childhood, protected from the harsh realities of life. One day he walked out of his comfortable palace into the streets around and there he saw a sick man, an old man, a beggar and a corpse. Shocked by all the suffering he saw, and by the contrast with his own life, he vowed to search for the meaning of existence. When he was 29 he left behind his wealth, his wife and his young son, and set off to become a wandering ascetic, depriving himself of every comfort and outdoing all the other ascetics of his time by the harsh rigors of his self-imposed discipline. After six years, when almost starving to death, he accepted some milk gruel. He now realized that neither indulgence nor deprivation was the way to truth and chose a middle way. He sat down under a pipal tree and vowed not to get up again until he understood.

On the seventh day, with the morning star shining in the sky, he became enlightened.

Siddhartha knew that what he had realized was there for everyone to see, and yet could not be spoken about. He struggled over whether to try to teach what he had learned, but whether he wanted to or not, people flocked to him for teachings and so he spent the next 45 years of his life traveling widely and teaching the "Four Noble Truths" and a body of other teachings that became

PROFILE

The Buddha

Siddhartha Gautama was born around 563 BCE, in the foothills of the Himalayas, in what is now southern Nepal. His father, Suddhodana, was the ruler of the kingdom of the Shakyas, and his mother was Queen Maya. At the age of 16 he was married to Princess Yasodara, and they lived, by the standards of the time, a luxurious and leisurely life. At the age of 29, soon after the birth of his only child, Rahula, he left home to become a wandering ascetic. For six years he traveled in the Ganges valley, studying with famous religious teachers, and trying to understand suffering. He was said to have practiced all the ascetic and yogic methods then taught, and to have attained mastery of the most elevated states of consciousness, but all this failed to satisfy him. He abandoned all prior teachings and determined to find out for himself. At the age of 35, when sitting under a tree on the bank of the River Neranjara at Buddha-Gaya (in modern Bihar), he became enlightened. Thereafter the tree became known as the Bohdi-tree, or tree of wisdom, and he became known as the Buddha. For a further 45 years he taught all kinds of people, regardless of age, sex, caste or social status, and making no distinction between them. He died at the age of 80 at Kusinara, in modern Uttar Pradesh.

known as the dharma. He urged people not to be satisfied with hearsay or tradition but to look within to see the truth, and it is said that his last words were "Work out your own salvation with diligence."

The Buddha's disciples passed on his great discourses, many of which were recorded, several hundred years later, as the sutras. In spite of his warnings about relying on hearsay and tradition, Buddhism became a great religion, spreading to southern India, Ceylon and Burma as Theravada Buddhism, and elsewhere as Mahayana Buddhism. It spread to Tibet where it took a unique form built on existing folklore, and along the silk route from India to China, where it became Chan Buddhism, to Japan where it became Zen, and eventually to the West (Batchelor, 1994; Humphreys, 1951).

BUDDHISM AND PSYCHOLOGY

It may seem strange to end this book with what looks like a religious doctrine, when ancient dogma or doctrine cannot be what we are after. It is true that, like all religions, Buddhism has accumulated a vast superstructure of memes, including texts, rituals, beliefs, beautiful buildings, sculptures and statues, music and liturgies. Yet what the Buddha saw is not a meme. It cannot be spoken of directly, and can only be transmitted by tricks of pointing or showing, or doing something to provoke another mind into letting go. This is known in Zen as "transmission outside the scriptures."

Buddhism differs from other religions in many ways. It has no god, no supreme creator and no notion of an indestructible human soul. Buddhists are not required to believe anything, but to look for themselves, and have faith that they can wake up. In *Buddhism without Beliefs*, the English scholar and Zen Buddhist Stephen Batchelor (1997) explains that the noble truths are not propositions to be believed, for if they were Buddhism would be just another religion like any other. Instead they are truths to be acted upon. Buddhism is, above all, a method of inquiry into oneself. That inquiry supposedly reveals the emptiness and impermanence of all phenomena, the illusory nature of self, and the origins and ending of suffering.

These may be some of the reasons why many psychologists have turned to Buddhism in their quest to understand the nature of mind and consciousness. Within Buddhism, psychologists have found both methods and theories that touch on the deepest mysteries in the psychology of consciousness. Varela,

Thompson and Rosch (1991) chose Buddhist mindfulness meditation as the most appropriate method to follow and suggested that "the Buddhist doctrines of no-self and of nondualism that grew out of this method have a significant contribution to make in a dialogue with cognitive science" (ibid.: 21). There have also been many books and conferences on East–West psychology from the 1980s onward, and the vast majority of contributions have dealt with Buddhism rather than other traditions (Claxton, 1986b; Crook and Fontana, 1990; Pickering, 1997; Watson et al., 1999; Wilber et al., 1986). Among those a large proportion focus on Zen.

Why Zen? Because, according to Austin, Zen is "the approach most systematic yet most elusive, the clearest yet most paradoxical, the subtlest yet most dramatic" (Austin, 1998: 7), and it is "untainted by belief in the supernatural or the superstitious" (Kapleau, 1980: 64). It is also the form of Buddhism least preoccupied with outward forms. By comparison, Tibetan Buddhists bow before elaborate altars decorated with glorious images of the Buddha, and they learn to visualize numerous deities, each with the appropriate actions, movements, clothes, adornments and colors. There is no doubt that these elaborate techniques can be very powerful for inducing altered states, and for training concentration and attention, but they do not necessarily appeal to those philosophers and scientists who are seeking a deeper understanding of the mind.

Zen has a tradition of throwing all this out and going straight for the point. "Zen is the apotheosis of Buddhism," says Christmas Humphreys, the founder and president of the Buddhist Society in Britain.

> This direct assault upon the citadel of Truth, without reliance upon concepts (of God or soul or salvation), or the use of scripture, ritual or vow, is unique. . . . In Zen the familiar props of religion are cast away. An image may be used for devotional purposes, but if the room is cold it may be flung into the fire.
>
> (Humphreys, 1951: 179–80)

THE FOUR NOBLE TRUTHS

Several weeks after his enlightenment under a tree, the Buddha finally overcame his ambivalence about saying anything at all, and gave a famous discourse to five of his former ascetic friends, in the Deer Park at Sarnath, near Benares. He described how he had found a middle way between indulgence and mortification, a way that leads to complete freedom of heart and mind from the compulsions of craving. He summed it up in the form of the four noble, or ennobling, truths.

Suffering

Often translated as "life is suffering," this does not mean that life is inevitably miserable or full of unhappiness. The word for "suffering" is sometimes translated as "anguish" or "unsatisfactoriness." We suffer when things are not how we want them to be.

The origins of suffering

Suffering arises from craving, desire or clinging. All our suffering is caused by hanging onto the things we like and wanting them to last, and by fearing and rejecting the things we don't like and wanting them to go away. This craving or thirst starts from the false idea of our own existence and traps us in the cycle of "being and becoming," or samsara. By seeing that everything is impermanent and changing, including the self who craves, it is possible to let go.

The cessation of suffering

When we let go of clinging and desire, suffering ends. This realization of the cessation of suffering does not mean that there is no more sorrow or grief, and no more joy, or happiness or fun. It means that we are no longer attached to any of these things, so they just come and go. This extinction of illusion is known as nirvana. When self-centered suffering falls away, truth is obvious and compassion comes naturally.

The way leading to the cessation of suffering

The Buddha recommended an eight-fold path to the cessation of suffering, leading to calm, insight, enlightenment and nirvana. The path consists of right understanding, thought, speech, action, livelihood, effort, mindfulness and concentration. These eight include ethical teachings, mental development and insight, but the emphasis is on developing heart and mind equally. Wisdom and compassion are seen as inseparable.

The four noble truths are not propositions to be believed, but truths to be acted upon.

There is nothing particularly religious or spiritual about this path. It encompasses everything we do. It is an authentic way of being in the world. It begins with how we understand the kind of reality we inhabit and the kind of beings we are.

(Batchelor, 1997: 10)

The path

is a way of life to be followed, practised and developed by each individual. It is self-discipline in body, word and mind, self-development and self-purification. It has nothing to do with belief, prayer, worship or ceremony. In that sense, it has nothing which may popularly be called "religious." It is a Path leading to the realization of Ultimate Reality, to complete freedom, happiness and peace through moral, spiritual and intellectual perfection.

(Rahula, 1959: 49–50)

> "Zen can no more be explained than a joke. You see it or you don't."
>
> **Humphreys**, 1949: 3

The real task in hand is that "the mind may be freed for the light of Enlightenment."

So what is enlightenment? Before the Buddha other people may have become enlightened, and certainly many have done so since. Among them are old and young, men and women, monks and laypeople. They include modern westerners, businessmen, artists, homemakers and psychologists (Kapleau, 1980; Sheng-Yen et al., 2002). Yet it is very hard to say what has happened to them.

The term "enlightenment" is used in at least two main ways (and probably many others too). First, there is the sense in which you can talk about the *process* of enlightenment, which can be fast or slow, sudden and gradual. In this sense there is a path to enlightenment and practices that help people along that path. There can also be enlightenment experiences, called *kensho* in Zen, and these can be deep or shallow—tiny glimpses or deep experiences of opening.

Then there is what is sometimes called ultimate enlightenment, or full awakening. This is not a state of consciousness like a mystical or religious experience, or even a *kensho* experience, which passes away. Indeed it is not a state at all. Everything is just the same, as it always was, because everything is inherently enlightened. There is no path to enlightenment because it is not something that can be gained, and there is no one who gains it, even though there is a path that each of us treads. Those who speak of it at all say that it cannot be explained or described. Anything you say is beside the point. And yet, paradoxically, one person can do things, or say things, to help others become enlightened. So, in some sense, enlightenment can be cultivated. This is the point of the story about Hui Neng and the monk (see Chapter 26). Perhaps the closest we can get to saying anything positive about enlightenment is that it is losing something—dropping the illusions.

All this sounds gloriously paradoxical. It could be glorious nonsense. Or it could be that Zen confronts the same paradoxical problems that the science of consciousness confronts. We have met these many times already. For example, there seems to be both a private inner world and a public outer world. From this duality arises the hard problem and an explanatory gap. Yet as soon as we try to describe our inner world, we find we are providing third-person data for a science of consciousness, and the special inner world is gone.

FIGURE 27.1 • A young monk arrives at Hui Neng's famous mountain monastery. What is it?

We have met illusions too, in perception, and in theories about self and free will. Are these the same illusions that enlightenment sees through? If they are the same, then we might hope to learn something from a tradition that has been struggling with the paradox and penetrating the illusions for two and a half millennia. If not, then this foray into Buddhism may be a waste of time.

One of the big differences we must note before going any further is that science and philosophy have different objectives from those of Buddhism. Science and philosophy are primarily about finding out the truth for its own sake. Buddhism is about finding out the truth in order to transform oneself, to become free from suffering, and even to save all sentient beings from suffering. In this sense Buddhism may be closer to psychotherapy than to science. We must bear these differences in mind when we try to find out whether these very different disciplines lead to any of the same "truths."

TRANSFORMATION AND THERAPY

There is a story from Tibetan Buddhism about a low-caste woodcutter called Shalipa who lived in poverty near the charnel ground where corpses were thrown to rot. All night long wolves howled around the charnel ground and Shalipa was so terrified of what might happen to him that he couldn't eat or sleep or even practice the dharma. One evening a wandering yogin came by asking for food. Shalipa gave him food and then asked him to provide a spell to stop the howling of the wolves. The yogin laughed and said, "What good will it do you to destroy the howling of the wolves when you don't know what hearing or any other sense is. If you will follow my instructions, I will teach you to destroy all fear." So Shalipa moved inside the charnel ground and began to meditate upon all sound as being the same as the howling of wolves. Gradually he came to understand the nature of all sound and of all reality. After nine years he lost all fear and attained great realization, becoming a teacher himself and thereafter always wearing a wolf skin round his shoulders.

We can all recognize Shalipa's initial state, says American psychologist Eleanor Rosch (1997). There he is, shivering in his hut with all his social, psychological, medical and spiritual problems. He is just like us, even though he lived so long ago and so far away. According to Rosch, this is the common state, and that is why our modern psychology is based on such a dualistic and alienated view of human beings. In Buddhism it is called *samsara*, the wheel of existence or the round of birth and death, and enlightenment is freedom from *samsara*. This is why the yogin does not advise Shalipa to sue the owners of the charnel ground, to delve into the meaning of wolf howls in his personal history, or to endure his fate to obtain religious salvation. Instead he teaches him to use his own experience as a means of radical transformation. The new Shalipa has no fear because he has let go of illusion.

In the meeting between Buddhism and psychotherapy, one live question concerns whether, fundamentally, the two endeavors are the same (Claxton, 1986b; Pickering, 1997; Watson et al., 1999). Although both aim to transform the individual, their methods are strikingly different, but so is the kind of transformation they seek. While psychotherapy aims to create a coherent sense of self, Buddhist psychology aims to transcend the sense of self. Types of therapy differ widely, but broadly speaking they all aim to improve people's lives, and to make them happier and less anxious. So a successful outcome for therapy is a person who is happy, relaxed, well adjusted to their society, and able to function well in their relationships and occupation. A successful outcome for a Buddhist might be the same, but it might equally be a hermit who shuns all society and lives in a cave, a teacher who rejects all conventional teachings, or a wild and crazy wise one whose equanimity and compassion shine through their mad behavior.

Claxton suggests that therapy is a special and limited case of the more general spiritual search, but he acknowledges the differences. While therapists and clients may agree to leave certain useful defenses in place, on the spiritual path nothing is left unquestioned. "The quest is for Truth not Happiness, and if happiness or security or social acceptability must be sacrificed in the pursuit of this ruthless enquiry, then so be it" (Claxton, 1986b: 316). For English psychologist and Chan Buddhist John Crook (1980), Zen training can be a "total therapy" in which the cage of identity is broken open.

For some, the spiritual enterprise takes off where therapy ends. There is an old saying, "If you are going to give up your self, you had better make sure it's a good one." This might mean that psychotherapy must come before the greater

FIGURE 27.2 • Tibetan Buddhist thangka with chakras, or circles, containing mantras in Tibetan and Sanskrit, Chinese trigrams and the 12 animals of the Tibetan calendar. Above is Buddha Shakyamuni, and below are war gods and nagas. The lower circle is held by the Demon of Time. In Buddhist tradition sentient beings are trapped in the illusion of samsara, or the wheel of death and rebirth. In its popular form this means the possibility of reincarnation as another person or animal. In its subtler form it means that the three times of past, present and future are all illusory, as is the self who is reborn with every thought. Those who truly realize impermanence, emptiness and no-self are thereby freed from rebirth and illusion.

CONSCIOUSNESS

task of seeing through the self. This was the conclusion reached by American psychologist and Buddhist Jack Engler, for whom the fate of the self became a kind of test case. He studied the effects of Buddhist practice on students with a wide range of different starting points. He found that those who were attracted to Buddhism because of failures in their development of self, or as a way of avoiding dealing with themselves, ran the risk of further fragmenting their already fragile sense of self. He concluded that both a sense of self, and of no-self, are necessary, and in that order. As he put it, "you have to be somebody before you can be nobody" (Engler, 1986: 49).

This view leads to the possibility of a "full spectrum" model of consciousness capable of plotting its development not only from infancy to adulthood, but from immaturity to full enlightenment. There have been several attempts to develop such models, including the complex, multi-level schemes proposed by the Buddhist writer Ken Wilber (Wilber et al., 1986; Wilber, 1997), but theories of psychology and spiritual development are still far from being successfully integrated in this way.

Another question concerns the appropriateness of using Buddhist methods of practice as part of psychotherapy. Some people argue that although psychological and spiritual work address different levels of human existence, spiritual work can have therapeutic value, and therapeutic methods can help in the integration of spiritual insights into ordinary life (Watson et al., 1999). But others emphasize the dangers of mixing spiritual practice with therapy. Meditation, as we have seen, is not a calm and steady process of increasing relaxation, but a deep confrontation with oneself. People who are frail, unhappy, neurotic and deeply afraid may have catastrophic reactions to facing themselves. They want to feel better, and embarking on serious spiritual inquiry is likely to make them feel a great deal worse. And for those who have serious psychopathology to start with, the results can be disastrous (Delmonte, 1987; Epstein and Lieff, 1986).

Despite all these unknowns, many therapists and clinicians do successfully use Buddhist techniques. For example, Jon Kabat-Zinn runs the Center for Mindfulness in Medicine, Health Care and Society, in Massachusetts, and has developed "mindfulness-based stress reduction." His methods emphasize paying attention and developing a non-judging awareness, in order to break through the "unconscious consensus trance that we think of as being awake" (Kabat-Zinn, 1999: 231). Crook is an ethologist and socioecologist as well as a Buddhist teacher, and he integrates therapeutic techniques into his "Western Zen" retreats (Crook and Fontana, 1990). Many others use breathing techniques, mindfulness and meditation in schools, prisons, sports, parenting and many other contexts (Watson et al., 1999).

Those who persevere with spiritual practice say that it naturally gives rise to many positive and therapeutic effects, and in particular that they become more loving and compassionate, and find greater equanimity. This may seem odd, and many have wondered how letting go of desires and goals, giving up your self, and treating everything as impermanent can possibly have such effects. Surely, goes the worry, if you stop controlling yourself terrible things will happen (Levine, 1979; Rosch, 1997). But, says Claxton,

> the dreaded mayhem does not happen. I do not take up wholesale rape and pillage and knocking down old ladies just for fun. The thing that does happen is the reverse . . . shame, embarrassment, self-doubt, self-consciousness, fear of failure and much anxiety ebb away, and as they do so I seem to become, contrary to expectations, a better neighbor.
>
> (Claxton, 1986a: 69)

WAKING UP

Awakening is often described as though it were the endpoint of a long journey along the spiritual path, but some people claim that they just *woke up*, and that their awakening was the beginning, rather than the culmination, of their spiritual life.

The best day of Douglas Harding's life—his rebirthday, as he called it—was when he found he had no head. At the age of 33, during the Second World War, he had long been pondering the question "What am I?" One day, while walking in the Himalayas, he suddenly stopped thinking and forgot everything. Past and future dropped away, and he just looked. "To look was enough. And what I found was khaki trouserlegs terminating downwards in a pair of brown shoes, khaki sleeves terminating sideways in a pair of pink hands, and a khaki shirtfront terminating upwards in—absolutely nothing whatever!" (Harding, 1961: 2).

We can all do what he did next. We can look where the head should be and find a whole world. Far from being nothing, the space where the head should be is filled with everything we can see, including the fuzzy pink end of a nose and the whole world around. For Harding this great world of mountains and trees was completely without "me," and it felt like suddenly waking up from the sleep of ordinary life. It was a revelation of the perfectly obvious. He felt only peace, a quiet joy and the sensation of having dropped an intolerable burden.

> "*It's not a doing but an* un*doing, a giving up, an abandonment of the false belief that there's anyone here to abandon. What else is there to do?*"
>
> **Harding**, 1961: 73

FIGURE 27.3 • The headless view. To others, you are a person in the world. To yourself, you are a space in which the world happens.

• CONSCIOUSNESS

Harding stresses that headlessness is just obvious if only you look clearly. There are not two parallel worlds, an inner and an outer world, because if you really look, you just see the one world, which is always before you. This way of looking explodes the fiction of inside and out, and of the mythical center; it explodes "this terminal spot where 'I' or 'my consciousness' is supposed to be located" (Harding, 1961: 13). He might equally have said that it blows up the Cartesian theater.

Harding soon discovered that others did not share his revelation. Hofstadter calls it "a charmingly childish and solipsistic view of the human condition" (Hofstadter and Dennett, 1981: 30). When Harding tried to explain it to others, they either thought he was mad or said "So what?" but eventually he stumbled upon Zen. There he found others who had seen as he did, such as Hui Neng, who told a fellow monk to see: "See what at this very moment your own face looks like—the face you had before you (and indeed your parents) were born." The saying is one of the most famous of Zen koans and points exactly to this new way of seeing.

John Wren-Lewis was a physics professor with decidedly anti-mystical views when in 1983, at the age of 60, he was poisoned while traveling on a bus in Thailand. A would-be thief gave him some sweets laced with what was probably a mixture of morphine and cocaine, and the next thing he knew was waking up in a dilapidated and dirty hospital.

At first he noticed nothing special, but gradually it dawned on him that it was as if he had emerged freshly made, complete with the memories that made up his personal self, from a radiant vast blackness beyond space or time. There was no sense at all of personal continuity. Moreover, the "dazzling darkness" was still there. It seemed to be behind his head, continually re-creating his entire consciousness afresh, instant by instant, now! and now! and now! He even put his hand up to feel the back of his head only to find it perfectly normal. He felt only gratitude toward everything around him, all of which seemed perfectly right and as it should be.

ACTIVITY
The headless way

Here are two little tricks to do together in class or on your own. Some people can be flipped into an entirely new way of experiencing, but others just say "So what?" So the tricks may, or may not, work for you. Take them slowly and pay attention to your own immediate experience. Don't rush.

POINTING

Point at the window, and look carefully at what you see there. Note both your finger and the place it points at. Point at the floor, and look carefully at where your finger is pointing. Point at your foot and look carefully at what you see. Point at your tummy, and look carefully at what is there. Point at yourself and look carefully at what you see there.

What did you find there?

FIGURE 27.4 ● An exercise in headlessness. How many heads are there? Seeing the world this way, you lose your own head and gain everybody else's.

HEAD TO HEAD

Find a friend to work with. Place your hands on each other's shoulders, and look steadily at your friend's face and head. Now ask yourself, "How many heads are there?" Don't think about what you know, or what must be true, but about your own direct experience now. How many heads can you see? What is, in this present experience, on the top of your shoulders?

Both doctors and patient thought that the effects would soon wear off, but they did not, and years later Wren-Lewis described how his whole consciousness had changed for good.

> I feel as if the back of my head has been sawn off so that it is no longer the 60-year-old John who looks out at the world, but the shining dark infinite void that in some extraordinary way is also "I."
>
> (Wren-Lewis, 1988: 116)

Wren-Lewis found that many aspects of his life had changed. For example, pain is now more of an interesting warning sensation than a form of suffering. His sleep changed completely from his previously rich dream life to a state of "conscious sleep" in which he is fully asleep yet still aware of lying in bed. The 59 years of his former life now seem like a kind of waking dream, living with an illusion of separate selfhood. By contrast to that ordinary consciousness, he describes his experience now as being just the universe "John Wren-Lewising." It might seem that this way of experiencing the world would make ordinary life difficult, but he claims that the practicalities of life are easier, not harder, to deal with because he is not constantly caught up with thoughts about the future.

Wren-Lewis draws some powerful lessons from his sudden transformation. First, his experience could be classed as an NDE, but he comes to the opposite conclusion from that of most NDE researchers (Chapter 24). Rather than showing that personal consciousness can exist apart from the brain, he concludes that his personal consciousness was "snuffed out" and then re-created anew from the radiant dark. As Dennett (1991) suggested, self and consciousness can always be snuffed out like a candle flame, and rekindled later. Wren-Lewis sees that snuffing out and re-creation going on all the time.

As for the spiritual path, Wren-Lewis claims that the very idea is necessarily self-defeating, because it does the one thing that has to be undone if there is to be awakening to eternity: it concentrates attention on the future. The process of seeking itself implies a preoccupation with time, and makes a goal out of what is already here and now. In this he is reflecting the paradox of a path to no-path, found so often in Zen. He particularly rejects those philosophies that are based on schemes of spiritual growth or conscious evolution. Awakening is not the culmination of a journey but the realization that you never left home and never could.

These examples show, unequivocally, that awakening does not have to be the culmination of a long process of training or spiritual development. Harding woke up through lone questioning and happenstance, and Wren-Lewis through a poisoned brain. But this does not mean that training and practice are useless. As one contemporary aphorism has it, enlightenment is an accident, and meditation helps to make you accident-prone.

It is time now to return to our central question. What does all this have to do with a science of consciousness? We saw that both Buddhism and science claim to have ways of finding out the truth. We can now ask whether it is the same truth that they find.

PRACTICE
MINDFULNESS

Your last task is to be mindful for a whole day (or forever if you prefer). If possible, choose a day when you will have time on your own and when you might be walking, doing housework, gardening, driving or taking part in sports, rather than reading, writing and socializing. Decide that you will stay fully present in every moment, and then begin. You must begin with *this* moment and not think about how well you have done so far, or how long you still have to go. Just attend, fully and clearly, to what is going on *now*. You will probably find that it seems easy to begin with, and that everything seems bright and clear when you do, but then you will suddenly realize that you have gone off into some train of thought and lost the mindfulness. Do not get cross with yourself, but just return to the present moment. That's all you have to do.

It is very difficult. Don't get discouraged.

You might like to make notes on how you got on, or discuss the following questions later with friends.

- What made it harder or easier to maintain mindfulness?

- Were you ever frightened?

- Did being mindful interfere with what you were doing?

- How does this task relate to all the previous ones?

- Can you imagine committing yourself to being mindful all your life?

- What is it like being mindful?

ILLUSION, NO-SELF, NO DUALITY

One point that Buddhism and psychology both make is that our experience is, in some sense, illusory. Since an illusion is not something that does not exist but something that is not what it seems, this leaves plenty of room for different interpretations. In science we have already met the idea that the visual world might be a grand illusion, that the stream of consciousness might be illusory, as might both the self and free will. We can now see that there are distinct similarities between the illusions discussed in science and in Buddhism.

In Buddhism all of ordinary experience is said to be illusory. This is said to be because we have wrong, or ignorant, ideas about the nature of the world. The Buddha taught what is called conditioned arising, or co-dependent origination —that all things are relative and interdependent, and that everything arises from something and in turn gives rise to something else. This can be seen as a very early statement of a scientific principle of cause and effect—that there is no magic involved—no skyhooks. Not accepting this is one source of illusion, or ignorance. This principle is applied specifically to consciousness as well as to everything else, and the Buddha denied the possibility of there being consciousness without the matter, sensations, perceptions and actions that condition it (Rahula, 1959).

He also taught that all phenomena are impermanent and empty. This "emptiness," much spoken of, is nothing to do with "nothingness" or "voidness" or any kind of absence. It means that things are inherently empty of self-nature, or empty of inherent existence. Take a car. This collection of bits and pieces comes together, and for a time we call it a car, and then it dissipates into bits again. There is no inherent car-ness there. The illusion is the tendency to treat things as permanent and self-existing. So if someone experiences emptiness during meditation, this does not mean they go into a great void of nothingness, but that they drop the illusion and see all arising experiences as interdependent, impermanent and not inherently divided into separate things.

This is relatively easy to accept for cars, tables, books and houses, but much harder when it comes to one's own self. Central to Buddhism is the doctrine of *anatta*, or no-self. Again this does not mean that the self does not exist, but that it is conditioned and impermanent like everything else. The Buddha urged people to see things as they are, to see that what we call "I," or "being," is only a combination of physical and mental aggregates, which are working together interdependently in a flux of momentary change within the law of cause and effect, and that there is nothing permanent, everlasting, unchanging and eternal in the whole of existence.

(Rahula, 1959: 66)

This is why Parfit (1987) refers to the Buddha as the first bundle theorist.

This theory of no-self went dramatically against the popular beliefs of the Buddha's time, and it goes against the beliefs of all the major religions since. Most religions claim that there is a permanent, everlasting entity called a

SELF-ASSESSMENT QUESTIONS

◉ Describe the life of the Buddha.

◉ Give possible reasons why so many psychologists have chosen to study Buddhism.

◉ What is Zen? And what is meant by awakening?

◉ What are the similarities and differences between psychotherapy and spiritual practice?

◉ Why is the notion of a spiritual path problematic?

◉ Who found that he had no head, and what is meant by the headless way?

◉ Compare and contrast the illusions discussed in consciousness studies with those found in Buddhism.

soul or spirit or *atman*. This may survive death to live eternally in heaven or hell, or may go through a series of many lives until it is finally purified and becomes one with God or a universal soul. The Buddha denied all of this and debated the issue with the best thinkers of his time.

> Buddhism stands unique in the history of human thought in denying the existence of such a Soul, Self, or *Atman*. According to the teaching of the Buddha, the idea of self is an imaginary, false belief which has no corresponding reality, and it produces harmful thoughts of "me" and "mine," selfish desire, craving, attachment . . . It is the source of all the troubles in the world.
>
> (Rahula, 1959: 51)

Even so, it is not easy to give up. A monk once asked the Buddha whether people are ever tormented by finding nothing permanent within themselves. They certainly are, replied the Buddha. A man who hears the teachings thinks, "I will be annihilated, I will be destroyed, I will be no more." So he weeps, mourns, worries himself, and becomes bewildered (Rahula, 1959: 56). This idea of no-self was just as difficult for people to accept then as it is now.

Part of the false conception of self is the idea that it can *do* things. The Buddha was clear on this: "actions do exist, and also their consequences, but the person that acts does not" (Parfit, 1987: 21). The Sri Lankan monk and Buddhist scholar Walpola Rahula explains this in words that could come straight from William James: "there is no thinker behind the thought. Thought itself is the thinker. If you remove the thought, there is no thinker to be found" (Rahula, 1959: 26). Does this mean that free will is an illusion? The question did not arise in Buddhist cultures in the way it has in western philosophy and religion. Even so, if everything is conditioned and relative, and subject to the law of cause and effect, then it is obvious that nothing can be independent and so truly free (Rahula, 1959). Indeed, the fiction of an independent self that could have freedom is part of the problem, and "The aim of dharma practice is to free ourselves from this illusion of freedom" (Batchelor, 1997: 95).

Relevant here is the Buddhist notion of "karma," or volition. Rahula explains that although the term karma means "action" or "doing," in Buddhism it refers only to willed or voluntary actions. These arise from the false idea of a self who thinks and acts, and it is only these kinds of actions that can have good or bad consequences. When the false view is dropped, people continue to act, think and do things, but they no longer accumulate karma because they are free from the false idea that they are a self who acts. Escaping from the wheel of birth and death is, therefore, nothing like the popular idea of being someone who leaves the world of *samsara* and goes to a spiritual realm or another dimension called *nirvana*. Rather, it means being without the illusion of self. This is why Fenwick says that "The characteristic of enlightenment is a permanent freeing of the individual from the illusion that he is 'doing'" (Fenwick, 1987: 117)

How is it possible to live without doing? One answer lies in the simple phrase "as if." You can live *as if* you have free will; *as if* you are a self who acts; *as if*

WHAT IS IT LIKE BEING MINDFUL?

"*The characteristic of enlightenment is a permanent freeing of the individual from the illusion that he is 'doing'.*"

Fenwick, 1987: 117

Buddhism and consciousness

CHAPTER TWENTY-SEVEN

there is a physical world outside yourself. You can treat others *as if* they are sentient beings who have desires, beliefs, hopes and fears—adopting the intentional stance toward others, and toward yourself. This way of living drops any distinction between real and *as if* intentionality, or real and *as if* free will.

Does any of this help us with the "hard problem," and with the dualism that bedevils every attempt to make scientific sense of consciousness? It is said that when people drop all the illusions, nonduality is revealed, and "there is no longer any vestige of a distinction between self and experience" (Claxton, 1986b: 319). In Buddhism this is likened to polishing a mirror. When the mirror is completely spotless, there is no distinction between the world and its reflection.

Have these people really seen nonduality, directly, in their own experience? If they have, could we all see it? Might the psychologists, philosophers and neuroscientists working on the problem of consciousness see nonduality directly for themselves? If so, it seems possible that they might bring together two apparently totally different disciplines: the third-person discipline of science and the first-person discipline of self-transformation. If they did so, might they then understand exactly what had happened in their own brains when all the illusions fell away and the distinction between first and third person was gone? This way the direct experience of nonduality might be integrated into a neuroscience that only knows, intellectually, that dualism must be false.

Would the problem of consciousness then be solved? I do not know. Zen is said to require "great doubt," great determination, and the more perplexity the better. The same might be said of a science of consciousness. I hope that you, like me, are now more perplexed than when you began.

Claxton, G. (1996a) The light's on but there's nobody home: the psychology of no-self. In G. Claxton (ed.) *Beyond Therapy: The Impact of Eastern Religions on Psychological Theory and Practice.* Dorset, Prism Press, 49–70.

Rosch, E. (1997) Transformation of the Wolf Man. In J. Pickering (ed.) *The Authority of Experience: Essays on Buddhism and Psychology.* Richmond, Surrey, Curzon, 6–27. This article is a useful basis for discussing the question "Are psychotherapy and spiritual development the same or different?"

FIGURE 27.5

References

Adams, D. (1979) *The Hitch Hiker's Guide to the Galaxy*. London, Pan.

Aglioti, S., Goodale, M.A. and DeSouza, J.F.X. (1995) Size contrast illusions deceive the eye but not the hand. *Current Biology* 5, 679–85.

Akins, K.A. (1993) What is it like to be boring and myopic? In B. Dahlbom (ed.) *Dennett and His Critics*. Oxford, Blackwell, 124–60.

Alkire, M.T., Haier, R.J. and Fallon, J.H. (1998) Toward the neurobiology of consciousness: using brain imaging and anesthesia to investigate the anatomy of consciousness. In S.R. Hameroff, A.W. Kaszniak and A.C. Scott (eds) *Toward a Science of Consciousness II: The Second Tucson Discussions and Debates*. Cambridge, MA, MIT Press, 255–68.

Alpert, R. (Baba Ram Dass) (1971) *Be Here Now*. San Cristobal, NM, Lama Foundation.

Alvarado, C. (1992) The psychological approach to out-of-body experiences: a review of early and modern developments. *Journal of Psychology* 126, 237–50.

Alvarado, C.S. (1982) ESP during out-of-body experiences: a review of experimental studies. *Journal of Parapsychology* 46, 209–30.

Atkinson, R.L., Atkinson, R.C., Smith, E.E., Bem, D.J. and Nolen-Hoeksema, S. (1999) *Hilgard's Introduction to Psychology*. Fort Worth, TX, Harcourt Brace.

Atkinson, R.L., Atkinson, R.C., Smith, E.E., Bem, D.J. and Nolen-Hoeksema, S. (2000) *Hilgard's Introduction to Psychology* (13th edn). Fort Worth, TX, Harcourt Brace.

Aunger, R.A. (ed.) (2000) *Darwinizing Culture: The Status of Memetics as a Science*. Oxford, Oxford University Press.

Austin, J.H. (1998) *Zen and the Brain: Toward an Understanding of Meditation and Consciousness*. Cambridge, MA, MIT Press.

Baars, B.J. (1988) *A Cognitive Theory of Consciousness*. Cambridge, Cambridge University Press.

Baars, B.J. (1997a) *In the Theater of Consciousness: The Workspace of the Mind*. New York, Oxford University Press.

Baars, B.J. (1997b) In the theatre of consciousness: global workspace theory, a rigorous scientific theory of consciousness. *Journal of Consciousness Studies* 4(4), 292–309; with commentaries and reply, 310–64.

Baars, B.J. (1999) There is already a field of systematic phenomenology, and it's called "psychology," *Journal of Consciousness Studies* 6(2–3), 216–18; also in Varela, F.J. and Shear, J. (eds) (1999) *The View from Within*. Thorverton, Devon, Imprint Academic, 216–18.

Baars, B.J. (2001) There are no known differences in fundamental brain mechanisms of sensory consciousness between humans and other mammals. *Animal Welfare* 10 (supplement), S31–S40.

Bach-y-Rita, P. (1995) *Nonsynaptic Diffusion Neurotransmission and Late Brain Reorganization*. New York, Demos.

Bach-y-Rita, P. and González, J.C. (2002) Tactile sensory substitution in blind subjects. Paper presented at Toward a Science of Consciousness, Tucson, AZ, April 2002. Conference Research Abstracts (provided by *Journal of Consciousness Studies*) abstract number 186.

Baddeley, A.D. (2000) Short-term and working memory. In E. Tulving and F.I.M. Craik (eds) *The Oxford Handbook of Memory*. New York, Oxford University Press, 77–92.

Bagchi, B.K. and Wenger, M. (1957) Electrophysiological correlates of some yogic exercises. *Electroencephalography and Clinical Neurophysiology* 10, 132–49.

Barbur, J.L., Watson, J.D.G., Frackowiak, R.S.J. and Zeki, S. (1993) Conscious visual perception without V1. *Brain* 116, 1293–1302.

Barkow, J.H., Cosmides, L. and Tooby, J. (eds) (1992) *The Adapted Mind: Evolutionary Psychology and the Generation of Culture*. Oxford, Oxford University Press.

Barlow, H. (1987) The biological role of consciousness. In C. Blakemore and S. Greenfield (eds) *Mindwaves*. Oxford, Blackwell, 361–74.

Baron-Cohen, S. and Harrison, J. (eds) (1997) *Synaesthesia: Classic and Contemporary Readings*. Oxford, Blackwell.

Batchelor, M. (2001) *Meditation for Life*. London, Frances Lincoln.

Batchelor, S. (1990) *The Faith to Doubt: Glimpses of Buddhist Uncertainty*. Berkeley, CA, Parallax Press.

Batchelor, S. (1994) *The Awakening of the West: The Encounter of Buddhism and Western Culture*. London, Aquarian.

Batchelor, S. (1997) *Buddhism Without Beliefs: A Contemporary Guide to Awakening*. London, Bloomsbury.

Bem, D.J. and Honorton, C. (1994) Does psi exist? Replicable evidence for an anomalous process of information transfer. *Psychological Bulletin* 115, 4–18.

Bem, D.J., Palmer, J. and Broughton, R.S. (2001) Updating the ganzfeld database: a victim of its own success? *Journal of Parapsychology* 65, 207–18.

Berry, D.C. and Broadbent, D.E. (1984) On the relationship between task performance and associated verbalizable knowledge. *Quarterly Journal of Experimental Psychology: Human Experimental Psychology* 36a, 209–31.

Best, J.B. (1992) *Cognitive Psychology* (3rd edn). St. Paul, MN, West.

Bisiach, E. (1988) The (haunted) brain and consciousness. In A.J. Marcel and E. Bisiach (eds) *Consciousness in Contemporary Science*. Oxford, Oxford University Press, 101–20.

Bisiach, E. (1992) Understanding consciousness: clues from unilateral neglect and related disorders. In A.D. Milner and M.D. Rugg (eds) *The Neuropsychology of Consciousness*. London, Academic Press, 113–37.

Bisiach, E. and Luzzatti, C. (1978) Unilateral neglect of representational space. *Cortex* 14, 129–33.

Blackmore, S.J. (1982) *Beyond the Body: An Investigation of Out-of-the-Body Experiences*. London: Heinemann; reprinted 1992 with new postscript, Chicago, Academy Chicago.

Blackmore, S.J. (1987) A report of a visit to Carl Sargent's laboratory. *Journal of the Society for Psychical Research* 54, 186–98.

Blackmore, S.J. (1993) *Dying to Live: Science and the Near Death Experience*. London, Grafton.

Blackmore, S.J. (1996a) *In Search of the Light: The Adventures of a Parapsychologist*. Amherst, New York, Prometheus.

Blackmore, S.J. (1996b) Out-of-body experiences. In G. Stein (ed.) *Encyclopedia of the Paranormal*. Buffalo, NY, Prometheus, 471–83.

Blackmore, S.J. (1997) Probability misjudgment and belief in the paranormal: a newspaper survey. *British Journal of Psychology* 88, 683–9.

Blackmore, S.J. (1999) *The Meme Machine*. Oxford, Oxford University Press.

Blackmore, S.J. (2002) There is no stream of consciousness. *Journal of Consciousness Studies* 9(5–6), 17–28.

Blackmore, S.J. and Hart-Davis, A.J. (1995) *Test Your Psychic Powers*. London, Thorsons; also published in 1997, New York, Sterling.

Blackmore, S.J. and Troscianko, T.S. (1985) Belief in the paranormal: probability judgements, illusory control and the "chance baseline shift." *British Journal of Psychology* 76, 459–68.

Blackmore, S.J., Frith, C.D. and Wolpert, D.M. (1999) Spatio-temporal prediction modulates the perception of self-produced stimuli. *Journal of Cognitive Neuroscience* 11, 551–9.

Blackmore, S.J., Brelstaff, G., Nelson, K. and Troscianko, T. (1995) Is the richness of our visual world an illusion? Transsaccadic memory for complex scenes. *Perception* 24, 1075–81.

Blakemore, C. and Greenfield, S. (eds) (1987) *Mindwaves*. Oxford, Blackwell.

Blanke, O., Ortigue, S., Landis, T. and Seeck, M. (2002) Stimulating illusory own-body perceptions. *Nature* 419, 269–70.

Block, N. (1995) On a confusion about a function of consciousness. *Behavioral and Brain Sciences* 18, 227–87.

Botvinick, M. and Cohen, J. (1998) Rubber hands "feel" touch that eyes see. *Nature* 391, 756.

Brandon, R. (1983) *The Spiritualists*. London, Weidenfeld and Nicolson.

Braud, W. and Schlitz, M. (1989) A methodology for the objective study of transpersonal imagery. *Journal of Scientific Exploration* 3, 43–63.

Breazeal, C.L. (2001) *Designing Sociable Robots*. Cambridge, MA, MIT Press.

Bressloff, P.C., Cowan, J.D., Golubitsky, M., Thomas, P.J. and Wiener, M.C. (2002) What geometric visual hallucinations tell us about the visual cortex. *Neural Computation* 14, 473–91.

Bridgeman, B., Lewis, S., Heit, G. and Nagle, M. (1979) Relation between cognitive and motor-oriented systems of visual position perception. *Journal of Experimental Psychology: Human Perception and Performance* 5, 692–700.

Broadbent, D.E. (1958) *Perception and Communication*. New York, Pergamon Press.

Brooks, R.A. (1991) Intelligence without representation. *Artificial Intelligence* 47, 139–59; also reprinted, with extra material, in Haugeland (ed.) (1997) *Mind Design II: Philosophy, Psychology, Artificial Intelligence*. Cambridge, MA, MIT Press, 395–420 (page numbers cited are from this version).

Brooks, R.A. (2002) *Robot: The Future of Flesh and Machines*. London, Penguin; and *Flesh and Machines: How Robots Will Change Us*. New York, Pantheon.

Brooks, R.A., Breazeal, C., Marjanović, M., Scassellati, B. and Williamson, M.M. (1998) The Cog Project: Building a Humanoid Robot. In *Computation for Metaphors, Analogy, and Agents*, C. Nehaniv (ed.), Lecture notes in artificial intelligence 1562. New York, Springer, 52–87.

Brown, A. (1999) *The Darwin Wars: How Stupid Genes Became Selfish Gods*. London, Simon & Schuster.

Bucke, R.M. (1901) *Cosmic Consciousness*. Philadelphia, Innes & Sons; also published in 1991, New York, Penguin.

Buss, D.M. (1999) *Evolutionary Psychology: The New Science of the Mind*. Boston, MA, Allyn & Bacon.

Byrne, R.W. and Whiten, A. (eds) (1988) *Machiavellian Intelligence: Social Expertise and the Evolution of Intellect in Monkeys, Apes and Humans*. Oxford, Clarendon Press.

Callaway, J.C. (1999) Phytochemistry and neuropharmacology of ayahuasca. In R. Metzner (ed.) *Ayahuasca*. New York, Thunder's Mouth Press, 250–75.

Calvin, W.H. (1996) *The Cerebral Code: Thinking a Thought in the Mosaics of the Mind*. Cambridge, MA, MIT Press.

Campbell, D.T. (1960) Blind variation and selective retention in creative thought as in other knowledge processes. *Psychological Review* 67, 380–400.

Carlson, N. (1999) *Psychology: The Science of Behavior*. Boston, MA, Allyn & Bacon.

Castaneda, C. (1968) *The Teachings of Don Juan: A Yaqui Way of Knowledge*. University of California Press; also published in 1970, London, Penguin.

CONSCIOUSNESS

Castaneda, C. (1971) *A Separate Reality: Further Conversations with Don Juan*. New York, Simon & Schuster.

Castiello, U., Paulignan, Y. and Jeannerod, M. (1991) Temporal dissociation of motor responses and subjective awareness: a study in normal subjects. *Brain* 114, 2639–55.

Chagnon, N.A. (1992) *Yąnomamö* (4th edn). Orlando, FL, Harcourt Brace, Jovanovich.

Chalmers, D. (1996) *The Conscious Mind*. Oxford, Oxford University Press.

Chalmers, D. (1997) An exchange with David Chalmers. In J. Searle (ed.) *The Mystery of Consciousness*. New York, New York Review of Books, 163–7.

Chalmers, D. (1999) First-person methods in the science of consciousness. *Consciousness Bulletin*. University of Arizona, June 1999, http://www.u.arizona.edu/~chalmers/papers/firstperson.html.

Chalmers, D. (2000) What is a neural correlate of consciousness? In T. Metzinger (ed.) *Neural Correlates of Consciousness*. Cambridge, MA, MIT Press, 17–39.

Chalmers, D.J. (1995a) Facing up to the problem of consciousness. *Journal of Consciousness Studies* 3(1), 200–19.

Chalmers, D.J. (1995b) The puzzle of conscious experience. *Scientific American*, December 1995, 62–8.

Chapman, C.R. and Nakamura, Y. (1999) A passion for the soul: an introduction to pain for consciousness researchers. *Consciousness and Cognition* 8, 391–422.

Cheesman, J. and Merikle, P.M. (1984) Priming with and without awareness. *Perception and Psychophysics* 36, 387–95.

Cheesman, J. and Merikle, P.M. (1986) Distinguishing conscious from unconscious perceptual processes. *Canadian Journal of Psychology* 40, 343–67.

Cheney, D.L. and Seyfarth, R.M. (1990) *How Monkeys See the World, Inside the Mind of Another Species*. Chicago, CV Press.

Cheyne, J.A., Newby-Clark, I.R. and Rueffer, S.D. (1999) Sleep paralysis and associated hypnagogic and hypnopompic experiences. *Journal of Sleep Research* 8, 313–17.

Churchland, P. (1988) Reduction and the neurobiological basis of consciousness. In A.J. Marcel and E. Bisiach (eds) *Consciousness in Contemporary Science*. Oxford, Oxford University Press, 273–304.

Churchland, P.S. (1981) On the alleged backwards referral of experiences and its relevance to the mind–body problem. *Philosophy of Science* 48, 165–81.

Churchland, P.S. (1986) *Neurophilosophy: Toward a Unified Science of the Mind–Brain*. Cambridge, MA, MIT Press.

Churchland, P.S. (1996) The hornswoggle problem. *Journal of Consciousness Studies* 3(5–6), 402–8; also reprinted in J. Shear (ed.) (1997) *Explaining Consciousness – The Hard Problem*. Cambridge, MA, MIT Press, 37–44.

Churchland, P.S. (1998) Brainshy: nonneural theories of conscious experience. In S.R. Hameroff, A.W. Kaszniak and A.C. Scott (eds) *Toward*

a *Science of Consciousness: The Second Tucson Discussions and Debates.*
Cambridge, MA, MIT Press, 109–24.

Clark, A. (1997) *Being There: Putting Brain, Body, and World Together Again.* Cambridge, MA, MIT Press.

Clarke, C.J.S. (1995) The nonlocality of mind. *Journal of Consciousness Studies* 2(3), 231–40; also reprinted in J. Shear (ed.) (1997) *Explaining Consciousness – The Hard Problem.* Cambridge, MA, MIT Press, 165–75.

Claxton, G. (1986a) The light's on but there's nobody home: the psychology of no-self. In G. Claxton (ed.) *Beyond Therapy: The Impact of Eastern Religions on Psychological Theory and Practice.* Dorset, Prism Press, 49–70.

Claxton, G. (ed.) (1986b) *Beyond Therapy: The Impact of Eastern Religions on Psychological Theory and Practice.* London, Wisdom; reprinted 1996, Dorset, Prism Press.

Claxton, G. (1994) *Noises from the Darkroom.* London, Aquarian.

Claxton, G. (1997) *Hare Brain Tortoise Mind: Why Intelligence Increases When You Think Less.* London, Fourth Estate.

Cleeremans, A. (ed.) (2003) *The Unity of Consciousness: Binding, Integration and Dissociation.* New York, Oxford University Press.

Cohen, D. (1987) Behaviourism. In R.L. Gregory (ed.) *The Oxford Companion to the Mind.* Oxford, Oxford University Press, 71–4.

Cotterill, R.M.J. (1995) On the unity of conscious experience. *Journal of Consciousness Studies* 2(4), 290–312.

Cotterill, R.M.J. (1998) *Enchanted Looms: Conscious Networks in Brains and Computers.* Cambridge, Cambridge University Press.

Cowan, J.D. (1982) Spontaneous symmetry breaking in large scale nervous activity. *International Journal of Quantum Chemistry* 22, 1059–82.

Crick, F. (1994) *The Astonishing Hypothesis.* New York, Scribner.

Crick, F. and Koch, C. (1990) Towards a neurobiological theory of consciousness. *Seminars in the Neurosciences* 2, 263–75.

Crick, F. and Koch, C. (1995) Are we aware of neural activity in primary visual cortex? *Nature* 375, 121–3.

Crick, F. and Koch, C. (2000) The unconscious homunculus. In T. Metzinger (ed.) *Neural Correlates of Consciousness.* Cambridge, MA, MIT Press, 103–10.

Crick, F. and Mitchison, G. (1983) The function of dream sleep. *Nature* 304, 111–14.

Crook, J. (1990) Meditation and personal disclosure: the western Zen retreat. In J. Crook and D. Fontana (eds) *Space in Mind: East–West Psychology and Contemporary Buddhism.* London, Element, 156–73.

Crook, J. and Fontana, D. (eds) (1990) *Space in Mind: East–West Psychology and Contemporary Buddhism.* London, Element.

Csikszentmihalyi, M. (1975) *Beyond Boredom and Anxiety.* San Francisco, Jossey-Bass.

Csikszentmihalyi, M. (1993) *The Evolving Self.* New York, HarperCollins.

CONSCIOUSNESS

Csikszentmihalyi, M. and Csikszentmihalyi, I.S. (eds) (1988) *Optimal Experience: Psychological Studies of Flow in Consciousness*. Cambridge, Cambridge University Press.

Cytowic, R.E. (1993) *The Man Who Tasted Shapes*. New York, Putnams.

Damasio, A. (1994) *Descartes' Error: Emotion, Reason and the Human Brain*. New York, Putnams.

Damasio, A. (1999) *The Feeling of What Happens: Body, Emotion and the Making of Consciousness*. London, Heinemann.

Darwin, C. (1859) *On the Origin of Species by Means of Natural Selection*. London, Murray.

Darwin, C. (1871) *The Descent of Man and Selection in Relation to Sex*. London, John Murray.

Darwin, C. (1872) *The Expression of the Emotions in Man and Animals*. London, John Murray; also published 1965, Chicago, University of Chicago Press.

Dawkins, M.S. (1987) Minding and mattering. In C. Blakemore and S. Greenfield (eds) *Mindwaves*. Oxford, Blackwell, 151–60.

Dawkins, R. (1976) *The Selfish Gene*. Oxford, Oxford University Press; a new edition, with additional material, was published in 1989.

Dawkins, R. (1986) *The Blind Watchmaker*. London, Longman.

de Mille, R. (1976) *Castaneda's Journey: The Power and the Allegory*. Santa Barbara, CA, Capra Press.

De Quincey, T. (1821) *Confessions of an English Opium Eater*.

De Weerd, P., Gattas, R., Desimone, R. and Ungerleider, L.G. (1995) Responses of cells in monkey visual cortex during perceptual filling in of an artificial scotoma. *Nature* 377, 731–4.

Deacon, T. (1997) *The Symbolic Species: The Co-evolution of Language and the Human Brain*. London, Penguin.

Dehaene, S. and Naccache, L. (2001) Towards a cognitive neuroscience of consciousness: basic evidence and a workspace framework. *Cognition* 79, 1–37; also reprinted in S. Dehaene (ed.) *The Cognitive Neuroscience of Consciousness*. Cambridge, MA, MIT Press, 1–37.

Dehaene, S., Naccache, L., Le Clec'H, G., Koechlin, E., Mueller, M., Dehaene-Lambertz, G., van de Moortele, P.-F. and Le Bihan, D. (1998) Imaging unconscious semantic priming. *Nature* 395, 597–600.

Deikman, A.J. (1966) Deautomatization and the mystic experience. *Psychiatry* 29, 324–38.

Deikman, A.J. (2000) A functional approach to mysticism. *Journal of Consciousness Studies* 7(11–12), 75–91.

Delmonte, M.M. (1987) Personality and meditation. In M. West (ed.) *The Psychology of Meditation*. Oxford, Clarendon Press, 118–32.

Dennett, D.C. (1976) Are dreams experiences? *Philosophical Review* 73, 151–71; also reprinted in D.C. Dennett (1978) *Brainstorms: Philosophical Essays on Mind and Psychology*. Harmondsworth, Penguin, 129–48.

Dennett, D.C. (1987) *The Intentional Stance*. Cambridge, MA, MIT Press.

Dennett, D.C. (1988) Quining qualia. In A.J. Marcel and E. Bisiach (eds)

Consciousness in Contemporary Science. Oxford, Oxford University Press, 42–77.

Dennett, D.C. (1991) *Consciousness Explained*. Boston, MA, and London, Little, Brown and Co.

Dennett, D.C. (1995a) *Darwin's Dangerous Idea*. London, Penguin.

Dennett, D.C. (1995b) The unimagined preposterousness of zombies. *Journal of Consciousness Studies* 2(4), 322–6.

Dennett, D.C. (1995c) Cog: steps towards consciousness in robots. In T. Metzinger (ed.) *Conscious Experience*. Thorverton, Devon, Imprint Academic, 471–87.

Dennett, D.C. (1995d) The path not taken. *Behavioral and Brain Sciences* 18, 252–3; commentary on N. Block, On a confusion about a function of consciousness. *Behavioral and Brain Sciences* 18, 227.

Dennett, D.C. (1996a) Facing backwards on the problem of consciousness. *Journal of Consciousness Studies* 3(1), 4–6.

Dennett, D.C. (1996b) *Kinds of Minds: Towards an Understanding of Consciousness*. London, Weidenfeld & Nicolson.

Dennett, D.C. (1997) An exchange with Daniel Dennett. In J. Searle (ed.) *The Mystery of Consciousness*. New York, New York Review of Books, 115–19.

Dennett, D.C. (1998) The myth of double transduction. In S.R. Hameroff, A.W. Kaszniak and A.C. Scott (eds) *Toward a Science of Consciousness: The Second Tucson Discussions and Debates*. Cambridge, MA, MIT Press, 97–107.

Dennett, D.C. (1998b) *Brainchildren: Essays on Designing Minds*. Cambridge, MA, MIT Press.

Dennett, D.C. (2001) The fantasy of first person science. Debate with D. Chalmers, Northwestern University, Evanston, IL, February 2001, http://ase.tufts.edu/cogstud/papers/chalmersdeb3dft.htm.

Dennett, D.C. (2003) *Freedom Evolves*. New York, Penguin.

Dennett, D.C. and Kinsbourne, M. (1992) Time and the observer: the where and when of consciousness in the brain. *Behavioral and Brain Sciences* 15, 183–247, including commentaries and authors' responses.

Depraz, N. (1999) The phenomenological reduction as praxis. *Journal of Consciousness Studies* 6(2–3), 95–110; also in Varela, F.J. and Shear, J. (eds) (1999) *The View from Within*. Thorverton, Devon, Imprint Academic, 95–110.

Descartes, R. (1641) *Meditations on First Philosophy*. Paris, trans. 1901 by John Veitch.

Devereux, P. (1997) *The Long Trip: A Prehistory of Psychedelia*. London, Penguin.

Dixon, N.F. (1971) *Subliminal Perception: The Nature of a Controversy*. London, McGraw-Hill.

Doblin, R. (1991) Pahnke's "Good Friday Experiment": a long-term follow-up and methodological critique. *The Journal of Transpersonal Psychology* 23, http://www.druglibrary.org/schaffer/lsd/doblin.htm.

Domhoff, G.W. (1996) *Finding Meaning in Dreams: A Quantitative Approach*. New York, Plenum Press.

Donald, M. (1991) *Origins of the Modern Mind: Three Stages in the Evolution of Culture and Cognition.* Cambridge, MA, Harvard University Press.

Dunbar, E. (1905) The light thrown on psychological processes by the action of drugs. *Proceedings of the Society for Psychical Research* 19, 62–77.

Dunbar, R. (1996) *Grooming, Gossip and the Evolution of Language.* London, Faber & Faber.

Eagleman, D.M. and Holcombe, A.O. (2002) Causality and the perception of time. *Trends in Cognitive Sciences* 6, 323–5.

Earleywine, M. (2002) *Understanding Marijuana: A New Look at the Scientific Evidence.* New York, Oxford University Press.

Eccles, J.C. (1965) *The Brain and the Unity of Conscious Experience.* Cambridge, Cambridge University Press.

Eccles, J.C. (1994) *How the Self Controls its Brain.* Berlin, Springer-Verlag.

Edelman, G.M. (1989) *Neural Darwinism: The Theory of Neuronal Group Selection.* Oxford, Oxford University Press.

Edelman, G.M. and Tononi, G. (2000a) *Consciousness: How Matter Becomes Imagination.* London, Penguin; USA, Basic Books.

Edelman, G.M. and Tononi, G. (2000b) Reentry and the dynamic core: neural correlates of conscious experience. In T. Metzinger (ed.) *Neural Correlates of Consciousness.* Cambridge, MA, MIT Press, 139–51.

Empson, J. (2001) *Sleep and Dreaming* (3rd edn). New York, Palgrave Macmillan.

Engel, A.K., Fries, P., König, P., Brecht, M. and Singer, W. (1999a) Temporal binding, binocular rivalry, and consciousness. *Consciousness and Cognition* 8, 128–51.

Engel, A.K., Fries, P., König, P., Brecht, M. and Singer, W. (1999b) Concluding commentary: does time help to understand consciousness? *Consciousness and Cognition* 8, 260–8.

Engler, J. (1986) Therapeutic aims in psychotherapy and meditation. In K. Wilber, J. Engler and D. Brown (eds) *Transformations of Consciousness: Conventional and Contemplative Perspectives on Development.* Boston, MA, Shambhala, 17–51.

Epstein, M. and Lieff, J. (1986) Psychiatric complications of meditation practice. In K. Wilber, J. Engler and D. Brown (eds) *Transformations of Consciousness: Conventional and Contemplative Perspectives on Development.* Boston, MA, Shambhala, 53–63.

Faraday, M. (1853) Experimental investigations of table moving. *The Athenæum* 1340, 801–3.

Farthing, G.W. (1992) *The Psychology of Consciousness.* Englewood Cliffs, NJ, Prentice Hall.

Fenwick, P. (1987) Meditation and the EEG. In M. West (ed.) *The Psychology of Meditation.* Oxford, Clarendon Press, 104–17.

ffytche, D.H. (2000) Imaging conscious vision. In T. Metzinger (ed.) *Neural Correlates of Consciousness*, Cambridge, MA, MIT Press, 221–30.

ffytche, D.H. and Howard, R.J. (1999) The perceptual consequences of visual loss: "positive" pathologies of vision. *Brain* 122, 1247–60.

Flanagan, O. (1992) *Consciousness Reconsidered*. Cambridge, MA, MIT Press.

Flanagan, O. (2000) *Dreaming Souls: Sleep, Dreams, and the Evolution of the Conscious Mind*. New York, Oxford University Press.

Flanagan, O. and Polger, T. (1995) Zombies and the function of consciousness. *Journal of Consciousness Studies* 2(4), 313–21.

Fletcher, P. (2002) Seeing with sound: a journey into sight. Paper presented at Toward a Science of Consciousness, Tucson, AZ, 8–12 April 2002. Conference Research Abstracts (provided by *Journal of Consciousness Studies*), abstract no. 188.

Flohr, H. (2000) NMDA receptor-mediated computational processes and phenomenal consciousness. In T. Metzinger (ed.) *Neural Correlates of Consciousness*. Cambridge, MA, MIT Press, 245–58.

Foulkes, D. (1993) Children's dreaming. In C. Cavallero and D. Foulkes (eds) *Dreaming as Cognition*. New York, Harvester Wheatsheaf, 114–32.

Franklin, S. (2003) IDA, a conscious artifact. *Journal of Consciousness Studies* 10.

Franks, N.P. and Lieb, W.R. (2000) The role of NMDA receptors in consciousness: what can we learn from the anesthetic mechanisms? In T. Metzinger (ed.) *Neural Correlates of Consciousness*. Cambridge, MA, MIT Press, 265–9.

Franz, V.H., Gegenfurtner, K.R., Bülthoff, H.H. and Fahle, M. (2000) Grasping visual illusions: no evidence for a dissociation between perception and action. *Psychological Science* 11, 20–5.

French, C.C. (1992) Factors underlying belief in the paranormal: do sheep and goats think differently? *The Psychologist* 5, 295–9.

Freud, S. (1949) *An Outline of Psycho-Analysis*. J. Strachey (trans.), London, Hogarth Press.

Frith, C.D. (1995) *The Cognitive Neuropsychology of Schizophrenia* (new edn). London, Psychology Press.

Frith, C.D., Friston, K., Liddle, P.F. and Frakowiak, R.S.J. (1991) Willed action and the prefrontal cortex in man: a study with PET. *Proceedings of the Royal Society, London B* 244, 241–6.

Gabbard, G.O. and Twemlow, S.W. (1984) *With the Eyes of the Mind: An Empirical Analysis of Out-of-body States*. New York, Praeger.

Gackenbach, J. and Bosveld, J. (1989) *Control Your Dreams*. New York, Harper & Row.

Gackenbach, J. and LaBerge, S. (eds) (1988) *Conscious Mind, Sleeping Brain: Perspectives on Lucid Dreaming*. New York, Plenum.

Gallagher, S. and Shear, J. (eds) (1999) *Models of the Self*. Thorverton, Devon, Imprint Academic.

Gallup, G.G. (1970) Chimpanzees: self-recognition. *Science* 167, 86–7.

Gallup, G.G. (1998) Can animals empathize? Yes. *Scientific American* 9(4), 67–76.

Gallup, G.H. and Newport, F. (1991) Belief in paranormal phenomena among adult Americans. *Skeptical Inquirer* 15, 137–46.

Galton, F. (1883) *Inquiries into Human Faculty and its Development*. London, Macmillan.

Gauld, A. (1968) *The Founders of Psychical Research*. London, Routledge & Kegan Paul.

Gazzaniga, M.S. (1992) *Nature's Mind*. London, Basic Books.

Geldard, F.A. and Sherrick, C.E. (1972) The cutaneous "rabbit": a perceptual illusion. *Science* 178, 178–9.

Gibson, J.J. (1979) *The Ecological Approach to Visual Perception*. New York, Houghton Mifflin.

Goodale, M.A., Pelisson, D. and Prablanc, C. (1986) Large adjustments in visually guided reaching do not depend on vision of the hand or perception of target displacement. *Nature* 320, 748–50.

Gould, S.J. and Lewontin, R.C. (1979) The spandrels of San Marco and the panglossian paradigm: a critique of the adaptationist program. *Proceedings of the Royal Society, London B* 205, 581–98.

Green, C.E. (1968a) *Lucid Dreams*. London, Hamish Hamilton.

Green, C.E. (1968b) *Out-of-the-body Experiences*. London, Hamish Hamilton.

Green, C.E. and McCreery, C. (1975) *Apparitions*. London, Hamish Hamilton.

Greenfield, S. (2000) *Brain Story*. London, BBC.

Greenwald, A.G. (1992) New Look 3: unconscious cognition reclaimed. *American Psychologist* 47, 766–90.

Gregory, R.L. (1966) *Eye and Brain: The Psychology of Seeing*. London, Weidenfeld & Nicolson.

Gregory, R.L. (1986) *Odd Perceptions*. London, Routledge.

Gregory, R.L. (1987) *The Oxford Companion to the Mind*. Oxford, Oxford University Press.

Gregory, R.L. (1990) Personal communication.

Grimes, J. (1996) On the failure to detect changes in scenes across saccades. In K. Akins (ed.) *Perception: Vol. 2 Vancouver Studies in Cognitive Science*. New York, Oxford University Press, 89–110.

Grinspoon, L. and Bakalar, J.B. (1993) *Marijuana, the Forbidden Medicine*. New Haven, Yale University Press.

Grush, R. and Churchland, P.S. (1995) Gaps in Penrose's toilings. *Journal of Consciousness Studies* 2(1), 10–29.

Gurney, E., Myers, F.W.H. and Podmore, F. (1886) *Phantasms of the Living*. London, Trubner.

Haggard, P. and Eimer, M. (1999) On the relation between brain potentials and the awareness of voluntary movements. *Experimental Brain Research* 126, 128–33.

Haggard, P., Clark, S. and Kalogeras, J. (2002) Voluntary action and conscious awareness, *Nature Neuroscience* 5, 382–5.

Haggard, P., Newman, C. and Magno, E. (1999) On the perceived time of voluntary actions. *British Journal of Psychology* 90, 291–303.

Hameroff, S.R. and Penrose, R. (1996) Conscious events as orchestrated space–time selections. *Journal of Consciousness Studies* 3(1), 36–53; also reprinted in J. Shear (ed.) (1997) *Explaining Consciousness—The Hard Problem*. Cambridge, MA, MIT Press, 177–95.

Hardcastle, V.G. (2000) How to understand the N in NCC. In T. Metzinger (ed.) *Neural Correlates of Consciousness*. Cambridge, MA, MIT Press, 259–64.

Harding, D.E. (1961) *On Having no Head: Zen and the Re-Discovery of the Obvious*. London, Buddhist Society.

Hardy, A. (1979) *The Spiritual Nature of Man: A Study of Contemporary Religious Experience*. Oxford, Clarendon Press.

Harnad, S. (1990) The symbol grounding problem. *Physica D* 42, 335–46.

Harnad, S. (2001) No easy way out. *The Sciences* 41(2), 36–42.

Harré, R. and Gillett, G. (1994) *The Discursive Mind*. Thousand Oaks, CA, Sage.

Haugeland, J. (ed.) (1997) *Mind Design II: Philosophy, Psychology, Artificial Intelligence*. Cambridge, MA, MIT Press.

Hauser, M.D. (2000) *Wild Minds: What Animals Really Think*. New York, Henry Holt and Co.; London, Penguin.

Hearne, K. (1978) *Lucid Dreams: An Electrophysiological and Psychological Study*. Unpublished PhD thesis, University of Hull.

Hearne, K. (1990) *The Dream Machine*. Northants, Aquarian.

Hebb, D.O. (1949) *The Organization of Behavior*. New York, Wiley.

Helmholtz, H.L.F. von (1856–67) *Treatise on Physiological Optics*.

Heyes, C.M. (1998) Theory of mind in nonhuman primates. *Behavioral and Brain Sciences* 21, 101–48; with commentaries.

Heyes, C.M. and Galef, B.G. (eds) (1996) *Social Learning in Animals: The Roots of Culture*. San Diego, CA, Academic Press.

Hilgard, E.R. (1986) *Divided Consciousness: Multiple Controls in Human Thought and Action*. New York, Wiley.

Hobson, J.A. (1999) *Dreaming as Delirium: How the Brain Goes Out of its Mind*. Cambridge, MA, MIT Press.

Hobson, J.A. (2002) *Dreaming: An Introduction to the Science of Sleep*. New York, Oxford University Press.

Hodgson, R. (1891) A case of double consciousness. *Proceedings of the Society for Psychical Research* 7, 221–58.

Hofstadter, D.R. (1979) *Godel, Escher, Bach: An Eternal Golden Braid*. London, Penguin.

Hofstadter, D.R. and Dennett, D.C. (eds) (1981) *The Mind's I: Fantasies and Reflections on Self and Soul*. London, Penguin.

Holland, J. (ed.) (2001) *Ecstasy: The Complete Guide: A Comprehensive Look at the Risks and Benefits of MDMA*. Rochester, VT, Park Street Press.

Holmes, D.S. (1987) The influence of meditation versus rest on physiological arousal. In M. West (ed.) *The Psychology of Meditation*. Oxford, Clarendon Press, 81–103.

Holt, J. (1999) Blindsight in debates about qualia. *Journal of Consciousness Studies* 6(5), 54–71.

Honorton, H. (1985) A meta-analysis of psi ganzfeld research: a response to Hyman. *Journal of Parapsychology* 49, 51–91.

Horne, J. (1988) *Why We Sleep: The Functions of Sleep in Humans and Other Mammals*. Oxford, Oxford University Press.

Hubbard, B.M. (1997) *Conscious Evolution: Awakening the Power of our Social Potential*. Novato, CA, New World Library.

Hufford, D.J. (1982) *The Terror that Comes in the Night: An Experience Centered Study of Supernatural Assault Traditions*. Philadelphia, University of Pennsylvania Press.

Hull, J.M. (1990) *Touching the Rock: An Experience of Blindness*. London, Arrow Books.

Hume, D. (1739) *A Treatise of Human Nature*.

Humphrey, N. (1983) *Consciousness Regained: Chapters in the Development of Mind*. Oxford, Oxford University Press.

Humphrey, N. (1986) *The Inner Eye*. London, Faber & Faber.

Humphrey, N. (1987) The inner eye of consciousness. In C. Blakemore and S. Greenfield (eds), *Mindwaves*. Oxford, Blackwell, 377–81.

Humphrey, N. (1992) *A History of the Mind*. London, Chatto & Windus.

Humphrey, N. (2000) How to solve the mind–body problem. *Journal of Consciousness Studies* 7(4), 5–20; with commentaries, 21–97, and reply, 98–112; reprinted in Humphrey (2002) *The Mind Made Flesh: Frontiers of Psychology and Evolution*. Oxford, Oxford University Press, 90–114.

Humphrey, N. (2002) *The Mind Made Flesh: Frontiers of Psychology and Evolution*. Oxford, Oxford University Press.

Humphrey, N. and Dennett, D.C. (1989) Speaking for ourselves. *Raritan: A Quarterly Review* 9(1), 68–98; also reprinted, with postscript, in Dennett (1998) *Brainchildren: Essays on Designing Minds*. Cambridge, MA, MIT Press, 31–58.

Humphreys, C. (1949) *Zen Buddhism*. London, Heinemann.

Humphreys, C. (1951) *Buddhism*. Harmondsworth, Penguin.

Hurley, S.L. (1998) *Consciousness in Action*. Cambridge, MA, Harvard University Press.

Hut, P. (1999) Theory and experiment in philosophy. *Journal of Consciousness Studies* 6(2–3), 241–4; also published in F.J. Varela and J. Shear (eds) *The View from Within*. Thorverton, Devon, Imprint Academic, 241–4.

Huxley, A. (1954) *The Doors of Perception*. London, Chatto & Windus.

Hyman, R. (1985) The ganzfeld psi experiment: a critical appraisal. *Journal of Parapsychology* 49, 3–49.

Hyman, R. (1995) Evaluation of the program on anomalous mental phenomena. *Journal of Parapsychology* 59, 321–51.

Hyman, R. and Honorton, C. (1986) A joint communiqué: the psi ganzfeld controversy. *Journal of Parapsychology* 50, 351–64.

Irwin, D.E. (1991) Information integration across saccadic eye movements. *Cognitive Psychology* 23, 420–56.

Irwin, H.J. (1985) *Flight of Mind: A Psychological Study of the Out-of-body Experience*. Metuchen, NJ, Scarecrow Press.

Jackendoff, R. (1987) *Consciousness and the Computational Mind.* Cambridge, MA, MIT Press.

Jackson, F. (1982) Epiphenomenal qualia. *Philosophical Quarterly 32,* 127–36.

James, W. (1890) *The Principles of Psychology* (2 volumes). London, Macmillan.

James, W. (1902) *The Varieties of Religious Experience: A Study in Human Nature.* New York and London, Longmans, Green and Co.

Jansen, K. (2001) *Ketamine: Dreams and Realities.* Sarasota, FL, Multidisciplinary Association for Psychedelic Studies.

Jay, M. (ed.) (1999) *Artificial Paradises: A Drugs Reader.* London, Penguin.

Jaynes, J. (1976) *The Origin of Consciousness in the Breakdown of the Bicameral Mind.* New York, Houghton Mifflin.

Johnson, M.K. and Raye, C.L. (1981) Reality monitoring. *Psychological Review 88,* 67–85.

Julien, R.M. (2001) *A Primer of Drug Action: A Concise, Nontechnical Guide to the Actions, Uses, and Side Effects of Psychoactive Drugs* (revised edn). New York, Henry Holt.

Kabat-Zinn, J. (1999) Indra's net at work: the mainstreaming of dharma practice in society. In G. Watson, S. Batchelor and G. Claxton (eds) *The Psychology of Awakening: Buddhism, Science and Our Day-to-day Lives.* London, Rider, 225–49.

Kanwisher, N. (2001) Neural events and perceptual awareness. *Cognition 79,* 89–113; also reprinted in S. Dehaene (ed.) *The Cognitive Neuroscience of Consciousness.* Cambridge, MA, MIT Press, 89–113.

Kapleau, Roshi P. (1980) *The Three Pillars of Zen: Teaching, Practice, and Enlightenment* (revised edn). New York, Doubleday.

Karn, K. and Hayhoe, M. (2000) Memory representations guide targeting eye movements in a natural task. *Visual Cognition 7,* 673–703.

Kasamatsu, A. and Hirai, T. (1966) An electroencephalographic study on the Zen meditation (*zazen*). *Folia Psychiatrica et Neurologica Japonica 20,* 315–36.

Kennett, J. (1972) *Selling Water by the River.* London, Allen & Unwin; also published by New York, Vintage.

Kentridge, R.W. and Heywood, C.A. (1999) The status of blindsight. *Journal of Consciousness Studies 6*(5), 3–11.

Kihlstrom, J.F. (1996) Perception without awareness of what is perceived, learning without awareness of what is learned. In M. Velmans (ed.) *The Science of Consciousness.* London, Routledge, 23–46.

Klüver, H. (1926) Mescal visions and eidetic vision. *American Journal of Psychology 37,* 502–15.

Kollerstrom, N. (1999) The path of Halley's comet, and Newton's late apprehension of the law of gravity. *Annals of Science 56,* 331–56.

Kosslyn, S.M. (1980) *Image and Mind.* Cambridge, MA, Harvard University Press.

Kosslyn, S.M. (1988) Aspects of a cognitive neuroscience of mental imagery. *Science 240,* 1621–6.

Kosslyn, S.M. (1996) *Image and Brain: The Resolution of the Imagery Debate*. Cambridge, MA, MIT Press.

Krippner, S. (2000) The epistemology and technologies of shamanic states of consciousness. *Journal of Consciousness Studies* 7(11–12), 93–118.

Kuhn, T.S. (1962) *The Structure of Scientific Revolutions*. University of Chicago Press, Chicago.

Kunst-Wilson, W.R. and Zajonc, R.B. (1980) Affective discrimination of stimuli that cannot be recognized. *Science* 207, 557–8.

Kurzweil, R. (1999) *The Age of Spiritual Machines*. New York and London, Texere.

LaBerge, S. (1985) *Lucid Dreaming*. Los Angeles, Tarcher.

LaBerge, S. (1990) Lucid dreaming: psychophysiological studies of consciousness during REM sleep. In R.R. Bootzen, J.F. Kihlstrom and D.L. Schacter (eds) *Sleep and Cognition*. Washington, DC, American Psychological Association, 109–26; and at http://www.lucidity.com/SleepAndCognition.html.

LeBerge, S. (2000). Lucid dreaming: evidence and methodology. *Behavioral and Brain Sciences* 23 (6), 962–3.

LaBerge, S. and Rheingold, H. (1990) *Exploring the World of Lucid Dreaming*. New York, Ballantine Books.

Lanier, J. (1995) You can't argue with a zombie. *Journal of Consciousness Studies* 2(4), 333–45.

Lem, S. (1981) The seventh sally *or* How Trurl's own perfection led to no good. In D.R. Hofstadter and D.C. Dennett (eds) (1981) *The Mind's I*. London, Penguin; with commentary, 287–95.

Levin, D.T. (2002) Change blindness as visual metacognition. *Journal of Consciousness Studies* 9(5–6), 111–30.

Levin, D.T. and Simons, D.J. (1997) Failure to detect changes to attended objects in motion pictures. *Psychonomic Bulletin and Review* 4, 501–6.

Levine, J. (1983) Materialism and qualia: the explanatory gap. *Pacific Philosophical Quarterly* 64, 354–61.

Levine, J. (2001) *Purple Haze: The Puzzle of Consciousness*. New York, Oxford University Press.

Levine, S. (1979) *A Gradual Awakening*. New York, Doubleday.

Levinson, B.W. (1965) States of awareness during general anaesthesia. *British Journal of Anaesthesia* 37, 544–6.

Lewicki, P., Czyzewska, M. and Hoffman, H. (1987) Unconscious acquisition of complex procedural knowledge. *Journal of Experimental Psychology: Learning, Memory and Cognition* 13, 523–30.

Lewicki, P., Hill, T. and Bizot, E. (1988) Acquisition of procedural knowledge about a pattern of stimuli that cannot be articulated. *Cognitive Psychology* 20, 24–37.

Lewicki, P., Hill, T. and Czyzewska, M. (1992) Nonconscious acquisition of information. *American Psychologist* 47, 796–801.

Libet, B. (1982) Brain stimulation in the study of neuronal functions for conscious sensory experiences. *Human Neurobiology* 1, 235–42.

Libet, B. (1985) Unconscious cerebral initiative and the role of conscious will in voluntary action. *The Behavioral and Brain Sciences* 8, 529–39; see also commentaries in the same issue, 539–66, and in Issue 10, 318–21.

REFERENCES

Libet, B. (1991) Scientific correspondence. *Nature* 351, 195.

Libet, B. (1999) Do we have free will? *Journal of Consciousness Studies* 6(8–9), 47–5; also reprinted in B. Libet, A. Freeman and K. Sutherland (eds) *The Volitional Brain: Towards a Neuroscience of Free Will*. Thorverton, Devon, Imprint Academic.

Libet, B., Freeman, A. and Sutherland, K. (1999) *The Volitional Brain: Towards a Neuroscience of Free Will*. Thorverton, Devon, Imprint Academic.

Libet, B., Gleason, C.A., Wright, E.W. and Pearl, D.K. (1983) Time of conscious intention to act in relation to onset of cerebral activity (readiness potential): the unconscious initiation of a freely voluntary act. *Brain* 106, 623–42.

Libet, B., Wright, E.W., Feinstein, B. and Pearl, D.K. (1979) Subjective referral of the timing for a conscious sensory experience: a functional role for the somatosensory specific projection system in man. *Brain* 102, 191–222.

Lindberg, D.C. (1976) *Theories of Vision from Al-Kindi to Kepler*. Chicago, University of Chicago Press.

Lindsay, P.H. and Norman, D.A. (1977) *Human Information Processing: An Introduction to Psychology* (2nd edn). New York, Academic Press.

Loftus, E. and Ketcham, K. (1994) *The Myth of Repressed Memory: False Memories and Allegations of Sexual Abuse*. New York, St. Martin's Press.

Logothetis, N.K. and Schall, J.D. (1989) Neuronal correlates of subjective visual perception. *Science* 245, 761–3.

Lumer, E.D. (2000) Binocular rivalry and human visual awareness. In T. Metzinger (ed.) *Neural Correlates of Consciousness*. Cambridge, MA, MIT Press, 231–40.

Lumer, E.D., Friston, K.J. and Rees, G. (1998) Neural correlates of perceptual rivalry in the human brain. *Science* 280, 1930–4.

Luria, A.R. (1968) *The Mind of a Mnemonist*. L. Solotaroff (trans.), London, Jonathan Cape.

Mack, A. and Rock, I. (1998) *Inattentional Blindness*. Cambridge, MA, MIT Press.

MacKay, D. (1987) Divided brains – divided minds? In C. Blakemore and S. Greenfield (eds) *Mindwaves*. Oxford, Blackwell, 5–16.

Macphail, E.M. (1998) *The Evolution of Consciousness*. Oxford, Oxford University Press.

Malcolm, N. (1959) *Dreaming*. London, Routledge & Kegan Paul.

Marcel, A.J. (1983) Conscious and unconscious perception: experiments on visual masking and word recognition. *Cognitive Psychology* 15, 197–237.

Marcel, A.J. (1986) Consciousness and processing: choosing and testing a null hypothesis. *Behavioral and Brain Sciences* 9, 40–1.

Marks, D. (2000) *The Psychology of the Psychic* (2nd edn). Buffalo, NY, Prometheus.

Markwick, B. (1978) The Soal–Goldney experiments with Basil Shackleton: new evidence of data manipulation. *Proceedings of the Society for Psychical Research* 56, 250–81.

Marshall, J. and Halligan, P. (1988) Blindsight and insight in visuo-spatial neglect. *Nature* 336, 766–77.

Marshall, J. and Halligan, P. (1993) Neuropsychology: imagine only the half of it. *Nature* 364, 193–4.

Marzi, C.A. (1999) Why is blindsight blind? *Journal of Consciousness Studies* 6(5), 12–18.

Masters, R.E.L. and Houston, J. (1967) *The Varieties of Psychedelic Experience*. London, Anthony Blond.

Mauskopf, S.H. and McVaugh, M.R. (1980) *The Elusive Science: Origins of Experimental Psychical Research*. Baltimore: Johns Hopkins University Press.

Mavromatis, A. (1987) *Hypnagogia: The Unique State of Consciousness Between Wakefulness and Sleep*. London, Routledge & Kegan Paul.

McCrone, J. (1999) *Going Inside*. London, Faber & Faber.

McGinn, C. (1987) Could a machine be conscious? In C. Blackmore and S. Greenfield (eds) *Mindwaves*. Oxford, Blackwell, 279–88.

McGinn, C. (1999) *The Mysterious Flame: Conscious Minds in a Material World*. New York, Basic Books.

Meijer, P. (2002) Seeing with sound for the blind: is it vision? Paper presented at Toward a Science of Consciousness, Tucson, AZ, 8–12 April 2002. Conference Research Abstracts (provided by *Journal of Consciousness Studies*) abstract no. 187; soundscapes are described at http://www.seeingwithsound.com/voice.htm.

Meltzoff, A.N. (1996) The human infant as imitative generalist: a 20-year progress report on infant imitation with implications for comparative psychology. In C.M. Heyes and B.G. Galef (eds) *Social Learning in Animals: The Roots of Culture*. San Diego, CA, Academic Press, 347–70.

Melzack, R. (1992) Phantom limbs. *Scientific American* 266, 90–6.

Mercier, C. (1888) *The Nervous System and the Mind*. London, Macmillan.

Merikle, P.M. (2000) Subliminal perception. In A.E. Kazdin (ed.) *Encyclopedia of Psychology*. New York, Oxford University Press, Vol. 7, 497–9.

Merikle, P.M. and Daneman, M. (1996) Memory for unconsciously perceived events: evidence from anesthetized patients. *Consciousness and Cognition* 5, 525–41.

Merikle, P.M. and Daneman, M. (1998) Psychological investigations of unconscious perception. *Journal of Consciousness Studies* 5(1), 5–18.

Merikle, P.M., Smilek, D. and Eastwood, J.D. (2001) Perception without awareness: perspectives from cognitive psychology. *Cognition* 79, 115–34; also reprinted in S. Dehaene (ed.) *The Cognitive Neuroscience of Consciousness*. Cambridge, MA, MIT Press, 115–34.

Metzinger, T. (ed.) (1995) *Conscious Experience*, Thorverton, Devon, Imprint Academic.

Metzinger, T. (ed.) (2000) *Neural Correlates of Consciousness*. Cambridge, MA, MIT Press.

Metzinger, T. (ed.) (2003) *Being No One: The Self-Model Theory of Subjectivity*. Cambridge, MA, MIT Press.

Metzner, R. (1971) *Maps of Consciousness*. New York, Collier Books.

Metzner, R. (ed.) (1999) *Ayahuasca: Human Consciousness and the Spirits of Nature*. New York, Thunder's Mouth Press.

Metzner, R. and Adamson, S. (2001) Using MDMA in healing, psychotherapy, and spiritual practice. In J. Holland (ed.) *Ecstasy: The Complete Guide: A Comprehensive Look at the Risks and Benefits of MDMA*. Rochester, VT, Park Street Press, 182–207.

Midgley, M. (1994) Letter to the editor. *New Scientist*, 12 February, 50.

Miller, G.A. (1962) *Psychology: The Science of Mental Life*. New York, Harper & Row.

Milner, A.D. and Goodale, M.A. (1995) *The Visual Brain in Action*. Oxford, Oxford University Press.

Milton, J. (1999) Should ganzfeld research continue to be crucial in the search for a replicable psi effect? Part 1. Discussion paper and introduction to electronic-mail discussion. *Journal of Parapsychology* 63, 309–33.

Milton, J. and Wiseman, R. (1999) Does psi exist? Lack of replication of an anomalous process of information transfer. *Psychological Bulletin* 125, 387–91.

Minsky, M. (1986) *Society of Mind*. New York, Simon & Schuster.

Mithen, S. (1996) *The Prehistory of the Mind: A Search for the Origins of Art, Religion and Science*. London, Thames & Hudson.

Moody, R.A. (1975) *Life after Life*. Atlanta, GA, Mockingbird.

Moody, T.C. (1994) Conversations with zombies. *Journal of Consciousness Studies* 1(2), 196–200.

Moody, T.C. (1995) Why zombies won't stay dead. *Journal of Consciousness Studies* 2(4), 365–72.

Morland, A.B. (1999) Conscious and veridical motion perception in a human hemianope. *Journal of Consciousness Studies* 6(5), 43–53.

Morris, J.S., DeGelder, B., Weiskrantz, L. and Dolan R.J. (2001) Differential extrageniculostriate and amygdala responses to presentation of emotional faces in a cortically blind field. *Brain* 124, 1241–52.

Morris, J.S., Öhman, A. and Dolan, R.J. (1998) Conscious and unconscious emotional learning in the human amygdala. *Nature* 393, 467–70.

Morris, R.L., Harary, S.B., Janis, J., Hartwell, J. and Roll, W.G. (1978) Studies of communication during out-of-body experiences. *Journal of the American Society for Psychical Research* 72, 1–22.

Morse, M. (1990) *Closer to the Light: Learning from Children's Near-Death Experiences*. New York, Villard Books.

Morse, M. (1993) *Transformed by the Light: The Powerful Effect of Near-Death Experiences on People's Lives*. New York, Villard Books.

Murphy, S.T. and Zajonc, R.B. (1993) Affect, cognition, and awareness: affective priming with optimal and suboptimal stimulus exposures. *Journal of Personality and Social Psychology* 64, 723–39.

Myers, F.W.H. (1903) *Human Personality and its Survival of Bodily Death*. London, Longmans, Green and Co.

Nagel, T. (1974) What is it like to be a bat? *Philosophical Review* 83, 435–50; reprinted with commentary in D.R. Hofstadter and D.C. Dennett

CONSCIOUSNESS

(eds) (1981) *The Mind's I: Fantasies and Reflections on Self and Soul*. London, Penguin, 391–414; and also in Nagel, T. (ed.) (1979) *Mortal Questions*. Cambridge, Cambridge University Press, 165–80.

Nagel, T. (ed.) (1979) *Mortal Questions*. Cambridge, UK, Cambridge University Press.

Nagel, T. (1986) *The View from Nowhere*. New York, Oxford University Press.

Newberg, A. and D'Aquili, E. (2001) *Why God Won't Go Away: Brain Science and the Biology of Belief*. New York, Ballantine.

Nielsen, T.A. (2000) A review of mentation in REM and NREM sleep: "covert" REM sleep as a possible reconciliation of two opposing models. *Behavioral and Brain Sciences* 23, 851–66, 904–1018, 1083–121, with commentaries.

Noë, A. (ed.) (2002) *Is the Visual World a Grand Illusion?* Special issue of the *Journal of Consciousness Studies* 9(5–6), and also published by Thorverton, Devon, Imprint Academic.

Nørretranders, T. (1998) *The User Illusion: Cutting Consciousness Down to Size*. London, Penguin.

O'Hara, K. and Scutt, T. (1996) There is no hard problem of consciousness. *Journal of Consciousness Studies* 3(4), 290–302, reprinted in J. Shear (ed.) (1997) *Explaining Consciousness*. Cambridge, MA, MIT Press, 69–82.

O'Regan, J.K. (1992) Solving the "real" mysteries of visual perception: the world as an outside memory. *Canadian Journal of Psychology* 46, 461–88.

O'Regan, J.K. and Noe, A. (2001) A sensorimotor account of vision and visual consciousness. *Behavioral and Brain Sciences* 24(5), 883–917.

O'Regan, J.K., Rensink, R.A. and Clark, J.J. (1999) Change-blindness as a result of "mudsplashes." *Nature* 398, 34.

Ornstein, R.E. (1977) *The Psychology of Consciousness* (2nd edn). New York, Harcourt.

Ornstein, R.E. (1986) *The Psychology of Consciousness* (3rd edn). New York, Penguin.

Ornstein, R.E. (1992) *The Evolution of Consciousness*. New York, Touchstone.

Pahnke, W. (1963) Drugs and mysticism: an analysis of the relationship between psychedelic drugs and the mystical consciousness. Ph.D. dissertation, Harvard University.

Pahnke, W. (1967) LSD and religious experience. In R. DeBold and R. Leaf (eds) *LSD, Man and Society*. Middletown, CT, Wesleyan University Press, 60–85.

Pahnke, W.N. (1971) The psychedelic mystical experience in the human encounter with death. *Psychedelic Review* 11, http://www.druglibrary.org/schaffer/lsd/pahnke2.htm.

Paley, W. (1802) *Natural Theology; or Evidences of the Existence and Attributes of The Deity, Collected from the Appearances of Nature*. London, Charles Knight (page numbers are from 15th edn, 1815).

Parfit, D. (1984) *Reasons and Persons*. Oxford, Oxford University Press.

Parfit, D. (1987) Divided minds and the nature of persons. In C. Blakemore and S. Greenfield (eds) *Mindwaves*. Oxford, Blackwell, 19–26.

REFERENCES

Parker, J.D. and Blackmore, S.J. (2002) Comparing the content of sleep paralysis and dreams reports. *Dreaming: Journal of the Association for the Study of Dreams* 12, 45–59.

Parnia, S. and Fenwick, P. (2002) Near death experiences in cardiac arrest: visions of a dying brain or visions of a new science of consciousness. *Resuscitation* 52, 5–11.

Parnia, S., Waller, D.G., Yeates, R. and Fenwick, P. (2001) A qualitative and quantitative study of the incidence, features and aetiology of near death experiences in cardiac arrest survivors. *Resuscitation* 48, 149–56.

Pashler, H. (1998) *The Psychology of Attention*. Cambridge, MA, MIT Press.

Paulignan, Y., MacKenzie, C., Marteniuk, R. and Jeannerod, M. (1990) The coupling of arm and finger movements during prehension. *Experimental Brain Research* 79, 431–5.

Peirce, C.S. and Jastrow, J. (1885) On small differences in sensation. *Memoirs of the National Academy of Sciences* 3, 75–83.

Penfield, W. (1955) The role of the temporal cortex in certain psychical phenomena. *The Journal of Mental Science* 101, 451–65.

Penrose, R. (1989) *The Emperor's New Mind*. London, Vintage.

Penrose, R. (1994a) *Shadows of the Mind*. Oxford, Oxford University Press.

Penrose, R. (1994b) Mechanisms, microtubules and the mind. *Journal of Consciousness Studies* 1(2), 241–9.

Perky, C.W. (1910) An experimental study of imagination. *American Journal of Psychology* 21, 422–52.

Perry, E.K. (2002) Plants of the gods: ethnic routes to altered consciousness. In E. Perry, H. Ashton and A. Young (eds) *Neurochemistry of Consciousness: Neurotransmitters in Mind*. Amsterdam, John Benjamins, 205–25.

Persinger, M.A. (1983) Religious and mystical experiences as artifacts of temporal lobe function: a general hypothesis. *Perceptual and Motor Skills* 57, 1255–62.

Persinger, M.A. (1999) *Neuropsychological Bases of God Beliefs*. Westport, CT, Praeger.

Pessoa, L., Thompson, E. and Noë, A. (1998) Finding out about filling-in: a guide to perceptual completion for visual science and the philosophy of perception. *Behavioral and Brain Sciences* 21, 723–802 (including commentaries).

Pickering, J. (ed.) (1997) *The Authority of Experience: Essays on Buddhism and Psychology*. Richmond, Surrey, Curzon.

Pickering, J. and Skinner, M. (eds) (1990) *From Sentience to Symbols: Readings on Consciousness*. London, Harvester Wheatsheaf.

Pinker, S. (1994) *The Language Instinct*. New York, Morrow.

Pinker, S. (1997) *How the Mind Works*. New York, W.W. Norton.

Podmore, F. (1902) *Modern Spiritualism: A History and a Criticism*. London, Methuen.

Popper, K.R. and Eccles, C. (1977) *The Self and its Brain*. New York, Springer.

Povinelli, D.J. (1998) Can animals empathize? Maybe not. *Scientific American* 9(4), 67–76.

Premack, D. and Woodruff, G. (1978) Does the chimpanzee have a theory of mind? *Behavioral and Brain Sciences* 1, 515–26.

Prince, M. (1906) *The Dissociation of a Personality*. New York, Longmans, Green, and Co.

Radin, D. (1997) *The Conscious Universe: The Scientific Truth of Psychic Phenomena*. San Francisco, Harper.

Radin, D.I. and Nelson, R.D. (1989) Evidence for consciousness-related anomalies in random physical systems. *Foundations of Physics* 19, 1499–1514.

Radin, D.I. and Ferrari, D.C. (1991) Effects of consciousness on the fall of dice: a meta-analysis. *Journal of Scientific Exploration* 5(1), 61–83.

Raffman, D. (1995) On the persistence of phenomenology. In T. Metzinger (ed.) *Conscious Experience*. Thorverton, Devon, Imprint Academic, 293–308.

Rahula, W. (1959) *What the Buddha Taught*. London, Gordon Fraser; New York, Grove Press.

Ramachandran, V.S. and Blakeslee, S. (1998) *Phantoms in the Brain*. London, Fourth Estate.

Ramachandran, V.S. and Gregory, R.L. (1991) Perceptual filling in of artificially induced scotomas in human vision. *Nature* 350, 699–702.

Ramachandran, V.S. and Hirstein, W. (1997) Three laws of qualia: what neurology tells us about the biological functions of consciousness. *Journal of Consciousness Studies* 4(5–6), 429–57.

Ramachandran, V.S. and Hubbard, E.M. (2001) Synaesthesia – a window into perception, thought and language. *Journal of Consciousness Studies* 8(12), 3–34.

Randi, J. (1975) *The Truth About Uri Geller*. Buffalo, NY, Prometheus.

Reiss, D. (1998) Cognition and communication in dolphins: a question of consciousness. In S.R. Hameroff, A.W. Kaszniak and A.C. Scott (eds) *Toward a Science of Consciousness II: The Second Tucson Discussions and Debates*. Cambridge, MA, MIT Press, 551–60.

Rensink, R. (2000) The dynamic representation of scenes. *Visual Cognition* 7, 17–42.

Rensink, R.A., O'Regan, J.K. and Clark, J.J. (1997) To see or not to see: the need for attention to perceive changes in scenes. *Psychological Science* 8, 368–73.

Revonsuo, A. (1999) Binding and the phenomenal unity of consciousness. *Consciousness and Cognition* 8, 173–85.

Revonsuo, A. (2000) The reinterpretation of dreams: an evolutionary hypothesis of the function of dreaming. *Behavioral and Brain Sciences* 23, 877–901, 904–1018, 1083–121.

Rhine, J.B. (1934) *Extrasensory Perception*. Boston, MA, Bruce Humphries.

Rhine, J.B. (1947) *The Reach of the Mind*. New York, Sloane.

Rhodes, R. (1986) *The Making of the Atomic Bomb*. New York, Simon & Schuster.

REFERENCES

Ridley, Mark (1996) *Evolution* (2nd edn). Oxford, Blackwell Science.

Ridley, Matt (1996) *The Origins of Virtue*. London, Viking.

Ring, K. (1980) *Life at Death: A Scientific Investigation of the Near-Death Experience*. New York, Coward, McCann and Geoghegan.

Rizzolatti, G., Riggio, L. and Sheliga, B.M. (1994) Space and selective attention. In C. Umiltà and M. Moscovitch (eds) *Attention and Performance XV. Conscious and Nonconscious Information Processing*. Cambridge, MA, MIT Press, 231–65.

Rosch, E. (1997) Transformation of the Wolf Man. In J. Pickering (ed.) *The Authority of Experience: Essays on Buddhism and Psychology*. Richmond, Surrey, Curzon, 6–27.

Rosenthal, D.M. (1995) Multiple drafts and the facts of the matter. In T. Metzinger (ed.) *Conscious Experience*. Thorverton, Devon, Imprint Academic, 359–72.

Ross, D., Brook, A. and Thompson, D. (2000) *Dennett's Philosophy: A Comprehensive Assessment*. Cambridge, MA, MIT Press.

Ryle, G. (1949) *The Concept of Mind*. New York, Barnes & Noble.

Sacks, O. (1985) *The Man who Mistook his Wife for a Hat*. London, Duckworth.

Sacks, O. (1992) The last hippie. *New York Review of Books* 39 (26 March), 51–60.

Sacks, O. (1995) *An Anthropologist on Mars*. New York, Knopf.

Sargent, C. (1987) Sceptical fairytales from Bristol. *Journal of the Society for Psychical Research* 54, 208–18.

Sartre, J.-P. (1948) *The Psychology of Imagination*. New York, Philosophical Library (first published in French, 1940).

Saunders, N. (1993) *E for Ecstasy*. London, Nicholas Saunders.

Saunders, N., Saunders, A. and Pauli, M. (2000) *In Search of the Ultimate High: Spiritual Experiences Through Psychoactives*. London, Rider.

Schmeidler, G.R. and McConnell, R.A. (1958) *ESP and Personality Patterns*. New Haven, CT, Yale University Press.

Schmidt, H. (1976) PK effect on pre-recorded targets. *Journal of the American Society for Psychical Research* 70, 267–92.

Schreiber, F.R. (1973) *Sybil: The True Story of a Woman Possessed by Sixteen Separate Personalities*. Chicago, IL, Henry Regnery.

Schultz, W. (1999) The primate basal ganglia and the voluntary control of behaviour. *Journal of Consciousness Studies* 6(8–9), 31–45; also reprinted in B. Libet, A. Freeman and K. Sutherland (eds) *The Volitional Brain: Towards a Neuroscience of Free Will*. Thorverton, Devon, Imprint Academic, 31–45.

Seager, W. (1999) *Theories of Consciousness: An Introduction and Assessment*. London, Routledge.

Searle, J. (1980) Minds, brains, and programs. *Behavioral and Brain Sciences* 3, 417–57.

Searle, J. (1987) Minds and brains without programs. In C. Blakemore and S. Greenfield (eds) *Mindwaves*. Oxford, Blackwell, 209–33.

Searle, J. (1992) *The Rediscovery of the Mind*. Cambridge, MA, MIT Press.

CONSCIOUSNESS

Searle, J. (ed.) (1997) *The Mystery of Consciousness*. New York, New York Review of Books.

Searle, J. (1999) I married a computer. *New York Review of Books*, 8 April.

Searle, J. (2002) Why I am not a property dualist. *Journal of Consciousness Studies* 9(12), 57–64.

Shear, J. (ed.) (1997) *Explaining Consciousness – The Hard Problem*. Cambridge, MA, MIT Press.

Sheinberg, D.L. and Logothetis, N.K. (1997) The role of temporal cortical areas in perceptual organization. *Proceedings of the National Academy of Sciences USA* 94, 3408–13.

Sheng-Yen, Crook, J., Child, S., Kalin, M. and Andricevic, Z. (2002) *Chan Comes West*. Elmhurst, New York, Dharma Drum.

Shepard, R.N. and Metzler, J. (1971) Mental rotation of three-dimensional objects. *Science* 171, 701–3.

Shermer, M. (2000) *How We Believe: The Search for God in an Age of Science*. New York, Freeman.

Showalter, E. (1997) *Hystories: Hysterical Epidemics and Modern Culture*. New York, Columbia University Press.

Shulgin, A. and Shulgin, A. (1991) *Pihkal (Phenethylamines I Have Known and Loved)*. Berkeley, CA, Transform Press.

Shulgin, A. and Shulgin, A. (1997) *Tihkal (Tryptamines I Have Known and Loved)*. Berkeley, CA, Transform Press.

Sidgwick, H., Sidgwick, E.M. and Johnson, A. (1894) Report on the census of hallucinations. *Proceedings of the Society for Psychical Research* 10, 25–422.

Sidis, B. (1898) *The Psychology of Suggestion*. New York, Appleton.

Siegel, R.K. (1977) Hallucinations. *Scientific American* 237, 132–40.

Siegel, R.K. (1992) *Fire in the Brain: Clinical Tales of Hallucination*. New York, Penguin.

Siegel, R.K. and Jarvik, M.E. (1975) Drug-induced hallucinations in animals and man. In R.K. Siegel and L.J. West (eds) *Hallucinations: Behaviour, Experience and Theory*. New York, Wiley, 81–161.

Simons, D.J. (2000) Current approaches to change blindness. *Visual Cognition* 7, 1–15.

Simons, D.J. and Chabris, C.F. (1999) Gorillas in our midst: sustained inattentional blindness for dynamic events. *Perception* 28, 1059–74.

Simons, D.J. and Levin, D.T. (1997) Change blindness. *Trends in Cognitive Sciences* 1, 261–7.

Simons, D.J. and Levin, D.T. (1998) Failure to detect changes to people during a real-world interaction. *Psychonomic Bulletin and Review* 5, 644–9.

Singer, W. (2000) Phenomenal awareness and consciousness from a neurobiological perspective. In T. Metzinger (ed.) *Neural Correlates of Consciousness*. Cambridge, MA, MIT Press, 121–37.

Sjölander, S. (1995) Some cognitive breakthroughs in the evolution of cognition and consciousness, and their impact on the biology of language. *Evolution and Cognition* 1, 3–11.

Skinner, B.F. (1948) *Walden Two*. New York, Macmillan.

Slade, P.D. and Bentall, R.P. (1988) *Sensory Deception: A Scientific Analysis of Hallucination*. Baltimore and London, Johns Hopkins University Press.

Smiles, S. (1904) *Lives of the Engineers: Boulton and Watt*. London, Murray.

Soal, S.G. and Bateman, F. (1954) *Modern Experiments in Telepathy*. London: Faber & Faber.

Solms, M. (2000) Dreaming and REM sleep are controlled by different brain mechanisms. *Behavioral and Brain Sciences* 23, 843–50, 904–1018, 1083–121.

Spanos, N.P. (1991) A sociocognitive approach to hypnosis. In S.J. Lynn and J.W. Rhue (eds) *Theories of Hypnosis: Current Models and Perspectives*. New York, Guilford Press, 324–62.

Spanos, N.P., McNulty, S.A., DuBreuil, S.C. and Pires, M. (1995) The frequency and correlates of sleep paralysis in a university sample. *Journal of Research in Personality* 29(3): 285–305.

Spence, S.A. and Frith, C.D. (1999) Towards a functional anatomy of volition. *Journal of Consciousness Studies* 6(8–9), 11–29; reprinted in B. Libet, A. Freeman and K. Sutherland (eds) *The Volitional Brain: Towards a Neuroscience of Free Will*. Thorverton, Devon, Imprint Academic, 11–29.

Sperry, R.W. (1968) Hemisphere deconnection and unity in conscious awareness. *American Psychologist* 23, 723–33.

Sperry, R.W. (1980) Mind–brain interaction: mentalism, yes; dualism, no. *Neuroscience* 5, 195–206.

Stace, W.T. (1960) *The Teachings of the Mystics*. New York, New American Library.

Standage, T. (2002) *The Mechanical Turk: The True Story of the Chess-Playing Machine that Fooled the World*. London, Penguin.

Steels, L. (2000) Language as a complex adaptive system. Lecture Notes in Computer Science. Parallel Problem Solving from Nature—PPSN-VI. Volume Editor(s): Schoenauer et al, Springer-Verlag, Berlin.

Stein, B.E., Wallace, M.T. and Stanford, T.R. (2001) Brain mechanisms for synthesizing information from different sensory modalities. In E.B. Goldstein and M.A. Malden (eds) *Blackwell Handbook of Perception*. Oxford, Blackwell, 709–36.

Steinkamp, F., Boller, E. and Bösch, H. (2002) Experiments examining the possibility of human intention interacting with random number generators: a preliminary meta-analysis. Proceedings of the 45th Convention of the Parapsychological Association, Paris, August 2002.

Sterelny, K. (2001) *Dawkins vs. Gould: Survival of the Fittest*. Cambridge, Icon.

Stevens, J. (1987) *Storming Heaven: LSD and the American Dream*. New York, Atlantic Monthly Press.

Stevens, R. (2000) Phenomenological approaches to the study of conscious awareness. In M. Velmans (ed.) *Investigating Phenomenal Consciousness*. Amsterdam, John Benjamins, 99–120.

CONSCIOUSNESS

Stoerig, P. and Cowey, A. (1995) Visual perception and phenomenal consciousness. *Behavioural Brain Research* 71, 147–56.

Strawson, G. (1997) The self. *Journal of Consciousness Studies* 4(5–6), 405–28; also reprinted in Gallagher and Shear (1999) *Models of the Self*. Thorverton, Devon, Imprint Academic, 1–24.

Strawson, G. (1999) The self and the SESMET. *Journal of Consciousness Studies* 6(4), 99–135.

Sully, J. (1892) *The Human Mind: A Text-Book of Psychology*. London, Longmans, Green and Co.

Sur, M. and Leamey, C. (2001) Development and plasticity of cortical areas and networks. *Nature Reviews Neuroscience* 2, 251–62.

Sutherland, K. (ed.) (1995) Zombie earth: a symposium on Todd Moody's "conversations with zombies." *Journal of Consciousness Studies* 2(4), 312–72.

Tallon-Baudry, C. and Bertrand, O. (1999) Oscillatory gamma activity in humans and its role in object representation. *Trends in Cognitive Science* 3(4), 151–62.

Tallon-Baudry, C., Bertrand, O. and Fischer, C. (2001) Oscillatory synchrony between human extrastriate areas during visual short-term memory maintenance. *Journal of Neuroscience* 21(20), RC177 1–5.

Targ, R. and Puthoff, H. (1977) *Mind-Reach*. New York, Delacorte.

Tart, C.T. (1968) A psychophysiological study of out-of-body experiences in a selected subject. *Journal of the American Society for Psychical Research* 62, 3–27.

Tart, C.T. (1971) *On Being Stoned: A Psychological Study of Marijuana Intoxication*. Palo Alto, CA, Science and Behavior Books.

Tart, C.T. (1972) States of consciousness and state-specific sciences. *Science* 176, 1203–10.

Tart, C.T. (1975) *States of Consciousness*. New York, Dutton & Co.

Taylor, J.L. and McCloskey, D.I. (1990) Triggering of preprogrammed movements as reactions to masked stimuli. *Journal of Neurophysiology* 63, 439–46.

Teilhard de Chardin, P. (1959) *The Phenomenon of Man*. London, Collins; New York, Harper.

Terrace, H. (1987) Thoughts without words. In C. Blakemore and S. Greenfield (eds) *Mindwaves*. Oxford, Blackwell, 123–37.

Thigpen, C.H. and Cleckley, H. (1954) A case of multiple personality. *Journal of Abnormal and Social Psychology* 49, 135–51.

Thompson, E. (ed.) (2001) *Between Ourselves: Second-Person Issues in the Study of Consciousness*. A special issue of the *Journal of Consciousness Studies*; also published by Thorverton, Devon, Imprint Academic.

Thompson, E., Pessoa, L. and Noë, A. (2000) Beyond the grand illusion: what change blindness really teaches us about vision. *Visual Cognition* 7, 93–106.

Tomasello, M. (1999) *The Cultural Origins of Human Cognition*. Cambridge, MA, Harvard University Press.

Treisman, A. (2003) Consciousness and perceptual binding. In A. Cleeremans (ed.) *The Unity of Consciousness: Binding, Integration and Dissociation*. Oxford University Press, 95–113.

Treisman, A. and Gelade, G. (1980) A feature integration theory of attention. *Cognitive Psychology* 12, 97–136.

Turing, A. (1950) Computing machinery and intelligence. *Mind* 59, 433–60; also reprinted in J. Haugeland (ed.) (1997) *Mind Design II: Philosophy, Psychology, Artificial Intelligence*. Cambridge, MA, MIT Press, and in D.R. Hofstadter and D.C. Dennett (ed.) (1981) *The Mind's I: Fantasies and Reflections on Self and Soul*. London, Penguin, 53–67 (page numbers cited are from Hofstadter and Dennett).

Turkle, S. (1995) *Life on the Screen: Identity in the Age of the Internet*. New York, Simon & Schuster.

Tye, M. (1991) *The Imagery Debate (Representation and Mind)*. Cambridge, MA, MIT Press.

Ulett, G.A. (2002) Acupuncture. In M. Shermer (ed.) *The Skeptic Encyclopedia of Pseudoscience*. Santa Barbara, CA, ABC-CLIO, 283–91.

Ullman, M., Krippner, S. and Vaughan, A. (1973) *Dream Telepathy*. London, Turnstone.

Underhill, E. (1920) *The Essentials of Mysticism*. London, Dent & Sons.

Ungerleider, L.G. and Mishkin, M. (1982) Two cortical visual systems. In D.J. Ingle, M.A. Goodale and R.J.W. Mansfield (eds) *Analysis of Visual Behavior*. Cambridge, MA, MIT Press, 549–86.

Utts, J. (1995) An assessment of the evidence for psychic functioning. *Journal of Parapsychology* 59, 289–320.

van Lommel, P., van Wees, R., Meyers, V. and Elfferich, I. (2001) Near-death experience in survivors of cardiac arrest: a prospective study in the Netherlands. *The Lancet* 358, 2039–45.

Varela, F.J. (1996) Neurophenomenology: a methodological remedy for the hard problem. *Journal of Consciousness Studies* 3(4), 330–49; also in J. Shear (ed.) (1997) *Explaining Consciousness*. Cambridge, MA, MIT Press, 337–57.

Varela, F.J. (1999) Present-time consciousness. *Journal of Consciousness Studies* 6(2–3), 111–40; also in F.J. Varela and J. Shear (eds) (1999) *The View from Within*. Thorverton, Devon, Imprint Academic, 111–40.

Varela, F.J. and Shear, J. (eds) (1999) *The View from Within: First-Person Approaches to the Study of Consciousness*. A special issue of the *Journal of Consciousness Studies*; also published in book form, Thorverton, Devon, Imprint Academic.

Varela, F.J., Thompson, E. and Rosch, E. (1991) *The Embodied Mind*. London, MIT Press.

Velmans, M. (1999) Intersubjective science. *Journal of Consciousness Studies* 6(2–3), 299–306; also in F.J. Varela and J. Shear (eds) (1999) *The View from Within*. Thorverton, Devon, Imprint Academic, 299–306.

Velmans, M. (2000a) *Understanding Consciousness*. London and Philadelphia, Routledge.

Velmans, M. (2000b) *Investigating Phenomenal Consciousness: New Methodologies and Maps*. Amsterdam, John Benjamins.

Vertes, R.P. and Eastman, K.E. (2002) The case against memory consolidation in REM sleep. *Behavioral and Brain Sciences* 23, 867–76, 904–1018, 1083–121.

Wagstaff, G. (1994) Hypnosis. In A.M. Colman (ed.) *Companion Encyclopedia of Psychology*, Vol. 2. London, Routledge, 991–1006.

Wallace, B. and Fisher, L.E. (1991) *Consciousness and Behavior* (3rd edn). Boston, MA, Allyn & Bacon.

Watson, G., Batchelor, S. and Claxton, G. (eds) (1999) *The Psychology of Awakening: Buddhism, Science and Our Day-to-day Lives*. London, Rider.

Watson, J.B. (1913) Psychology as the behaviorist views it. *Psychological Review* 20, 158–77.

Watts, A.W. (1957) *The Way of Zen*. New York, Pantheon Books.

Webster, R. (1995) *Why Freud Was Wrong: Sin, Science and Psychoanalysis*. London, HarperCollins.

Wegner, D.M. (2002) *The Illusion of Conscious Will*. Cambridge, MA, MIT Press.

Wegner, D.M. and Wheatley, T. (1999) Apparent mental causation: sources of the experience of will. *American Psychologist* 54, 480–92.

Weil, A. (1998) *The Natural Mind: An Investigation of Drugs and the Higher Consciousness*. New York, Houghton Mifflin.

Weiskrantz, L. (1986) *Blindsight: A Case Study and Implications*. Oxford, Oxford University Press.

Weiskrantz, L. (1997) *Consciousness Lost and Found*. Oxford, Oxford University Press.

West, D.J. (1948) A mass observation questionnaire on hallucinations. *Journal of the Society for Psychical Research* 34, 187–96.

West, D.J. (1954) *Psychical Research Today*. London, Duckworth.

West, M.A. (ed.) (1987) *The Psychology of Meditation*. Oxford, Clarendon Press.

Whalen, P.J., Rauch, S.L., Etcoff, N.L., McInerney, S.C., Lee, M.B. and Jenike, M.A. (1998) Masked presentations of emotional facial expressions modulate amygdala activity without explicit knowledge. *Journal of Neuroscience* 18, 411–18.

White, R.A. (1990) An experience-centered approach to parapsychology. *Exceptional Human Experience* 8, 7–36.

Whiten, A. and Byrne, R.W. (1997) *Machiavellian Intelligence II: Extensions and Evaluations*. Cambridge, UK, Cambridge University Press.

Wilber, K. (1997) An integral theory of consciousness. *Journal of Consciousness Studies* 4(1), 71–92.

Wilber, K., Engler, J. and Brown, D. (eds) (1986) *Transformations of Consciousness: Conventional and Contemplative Perspectives on Development*. Boston, MA, Shambhala.

Wilkes, K.V. (1998) [ΓΝΩΘΙ ΣΑΥΤΟΝ] (Know Thyself). *Journal of Consciousness Studies* 5(2), 153–65; also reprinted in S. Gallagher and J. Shear (eds) (1999) *Models of the Self*. Thorverton, Devon, Imprint Academic, 25–38.

Williams, G.C. (1966) *Adaptation and Natural Selection*. Princeton, Princeton University Press.

Wilson, B.A. and Wearing, D. (1995) Prisoner of consciousness: a state of just awakening following herpes simplex encephalitis. In R. Campbell and M. Conway (eds) *Broken Memories*. Oxford, Blackwell.

Wilson, E.O. (1975) *Sociobiology: The New Synthesis*. Cambridge, MA, Harvard University Press.

Wilson, S. and Barber, T.X. (1983) The fantasy-prone personality: implications for understanding imagery, hypnosis and parapsychological phenomena. In A. Shiekh (ed.) *Imagery: Current Theory, Research, and Application*. New York, John Wiley, 340–87.

Wiseman, R. and Milton, J. (1998) Experiment one of the SAIC remote viewing program: a critical re-evaluation. *Journal of Parapsychology* 62, 297–308.

Wiseman, R. and Schlitz, M. (1998) Experimenter effects and the remote detection of staring. *Journal of Parapsychology* 61(3), 197–208.

Wiseman, R., Smith, M. and Kornbrot, D. (1996) Exploring possible sender-to-experimenter acoustic leakage in the PRL autoganzfeld experiments. *Journal of Parapsychology* 60, 97–128.

Wren-Lewis, J. (1988) The darkness of God: a personal report on consciousness transformation through an encounter with death. *Journal of Humanistic Psychology* 28, 105–22.

Wright, R. (1994) *The Moral Animal*. New York, Pantheon Books.

Wundt, W.M. (1874) *Principles of Physiological Psychology*, translated from the German by E.B. Titchener, 1904.

Young, A.W. (1996) Dissociable aspects of consciousness. In M. Velmans (ed.) *The Science of Consciousness*. London, Routledge, 118–39.

Zeki, S. (2001) Localization and globalization in conscious vision. *Annual Review of Neuroscience* 24, 57–86.

Zeki, S. and Bartels, A. (1999) Toward a theory of visual consciousness. *Consciousness and Cognition* 8, 225–59.

Zeman, A. (2001) Consciousness. *Brain* 124, 1263–89.

Zohar, D. and Marshall, I. (2002) *The Quantum Soul*. London, HarperCollins.

Index

INDEX

INDEX

INDEX

449 ·

great chain of being 142–43
Greeks 182
Green, C.E. 348
Greenfield, S. 153, 168
Gregory, R.L. 15, 85–130, 330
Grey Walter, W. 134, 190, 212
Greyson, B. 361, 362

H
Haggard, p130–1
Hakuin 392
Hall, J.A. 340
hallucination 160, 293, 306–19,
    332, 345
  collective 291
  definition of 306–8
  drug induced 327, 335–36
  hypnagogic 307, 310, 313, 348
  hypnopompic 313
  perceptual release theory of 309
  pseudo v true 307, 312
Hameroff, S.R. 33, 208–10, 214,
    230
hand
  alien
  anarchic
  phantom 238–39
  rubber 240
hard problem 3, 18–21, 28, 63, 69,
    210, 226–27, 240, 254, 264,
    312, 374, 377, 404, 414
  origin of term 19, 20
  responses to 31–35
Harding, D.E. 408, 410
Hardy, A. 366
harmaline 318
Harnad, S. 300
Harré, R. 102
hashish 14, 331, 332
haunting 291
Hauser, M. 171
headless way 409
healing 391
Hearne, K. 350, 352
heaven 318, 336, 365, 392
health inessentialism 150–51
Hebb, D.O. 230, 247

Heidegger, M. 375
hell 318
hellish experience 361
Helmholz, H.L.F. von. 15, 52, 56
hemianopia 263
hemifield neglect 260–63
hemisphere 261
  left 103–8, 399
  right 103–8, 399
Hering, K.E.K. 52
Hero of Alexandria 182
heroin 329
heterophenomenology 375, 382–84
Heyes, C.M. 172
higher consciousness 143, 253
higher-order perception theories
    (HOP) 47
higher-order thought theories (HOT)
    47, 230, 270
Hilgard, E.R. (Profile 23, p346),
    101, 256, 322
Hinduism 95, 365, 386, 391
hippocampus 252, 259
Hobbes, T. 155
Hobson, J.A. 341–44, 346, 349
Hodgson, R. 97–98, 102
Hodgson, S. 37
Hoffman, A. 335
Hofstadter, D.R. 28, 207, 374, 409
Holmes, D.S. 392–94, 395
holographic reality 363
Holt, J. 269
homo habilis 157
homunculus 69, 115, 117, 191, 240,
    279
Honorton, C. 298
Hubbard, B.M. 251
Hui Neng 404, 409
Hume, D. (Profile 7, p96) 64, 96, 98,
    109, 114–15, 118, 290
Humphrey, N. (Profile 11, p156)
    148, 151, 153–58, 173, 190,
    240, 254, 342
Humphreys, C. 403, 404
Hurley, S. 254
Husserl, E. 15, 16, 375, 377, 378
Hut, p375, 377

INDEX

INDEX

INDEX

INDEX